T0338282

HEALTHCARE ANALYTICS

Wiley Series in
Operations Research and Management Science

HEALTHCARE ANALYTICS

From Data to Knowledge to Healthcare Improvement

HUI YANG
Florida, USA

EVA K. LEE
Atlanta, USA

Published by John Wiley & Sons, Inc., Hoboken, New Jersey
Published simultaneously in Canada

For general information on our other products and services or for technical support, please contact our Customer Care Department within the United States at (800) 762-2974, outside the United States at (317) 572-3993 or fax (317) 572-4002.

Wiley also publishes its books in a variety of electronic formats. Some content that appears in print may not be available in electronic formats. For more information about Wiley products, visit our web site at www.wiley.com.

Library of Congress Cataloging-in-Publication Data:

Names: Yang, Hui, 1981- author. | Lee, Eva K., author.
Title: Healthcare analytics : from data to knowledge to healthcare
    improvement / Hui Yang, Eva K. Lee.
Description: Hoboken, New Jersey : John Wiley & Sons, 2016. | Includes
    bibliographical references and index.
Identifiers: LCCN 2015047966| ISBN 9781118919392 (cloth) | ISBN 9781118919408
    (online) | ISBN 9781119374664 (ePDF) | ISBN 9781119374640 (ePub)
Subjects: LCSH: Medical care–Data processing. | Medical care–Information
    services.
Classification: LCC R858.A1 Y36 2016 | DDC 362.10285–dc23 LC record available at
http://lccn.loc.gov/2015047966

Typeset in 10/12pt TimesLTStd by SPi Global, Chennai, India

Printed in the United States of America

CONTENTS

4 Statistical Modeling of Electrocardiography Signal for Subject Monitoring and Diagnosis

Lili Chen, Changyue Song, and Xi Zhang

5 Modeling and Simulation of Measurement Uncertainty in Clinical Laboratories

Varun Ramamohan, James T. Abbott, and Yuehwern Yih

**8   Mathematical Modeling of Innate Immunity Responses of Sepsis:
    Modeling and Computational Studies   221**

*Chih-Hang J. Wu, Zhenshen Shi, David Ben-Arieh,
and Steven Q. Simpson*

11   Analysis of Resource Intensive Activity Volumes in US Hospitals   335

Shivon Boodhoo and Sanchoy Das

**12   Discrete-Event Simulation for Primary Care Redesign: Review
     and a Case Study   361**

*Xiang Zhong, Molly Williams, Jingshan Li, Sally A. Kraft,
and Jeffrey S. Sleeth*

LIST OF CONTIBUTORS

James T. Abbott, Roche Diagnostics Corporation, Indianapolis, IN, USA

Hany Y. Atallah, Grady Health System, Atlanta, GA, USA; Department of Emergency Medicine, Emory University School of Medicine, Atlanta, GA, USA

David Ben-Arieh, Department of Industrial and Manufacturing Systems Engineering, Kansas State University, Manhattan, KS, USA

Margrét V. Bjarndóttir, Robert. H. Smith School of Business, Decision, Operations & Information Technologies University of Maryland, College Park, MD, USA

Shivon Boodhoo, Albert Dorman Honors College, Mechanical and Industrial Engineering, New Jersey Institute of Technology, Newark, NJ, USA

Robert E. Brown, Department of Pathology and Laboratory Medicine, University of Texas Medical School at Houston, Houston, TX, USA

Chun-Hung Chen, Department of Operations Research, George Mason University, Fairfax, VA, USA

Lili Chen, Department of Industrial Engineering and Management, Peking University, Beijing, China

Yun Chen, Complex Systems Monitoring, Modeling and Analysis Laboratory, University of South Florida, Tampa, FL, USA

Si-Chi Chin, University of Washington Tacoma, Tacoma, WA, USA

David Czerwinski, Department of Marketing and Decision Sciences, San Jose State University, San Jose, CA, USA

Warren D'Souza, Department of Radiation Oncology, University of Maryland School of Medicine, Baltimore, MD, USA

Sanchoy Das, Healthcare Systems Management Program, Newark College of Engineering, New Jersey Institute of Technology, Newark, NJ, USA

Debasree DasGupta, School of Public Policy, George Mason University, Arlington, VA, USA

Rajesh Ganesan, Department of Operations Research, George Mason University, Fairfax, VA, USA

Monica Gentili, Mathematics Department, University of Salerno, Fisciano, Italy

Yihan Guan, Oracle Corporation, Redwood Shores, CA, USA

Leon L. Haley, Jr, Grady Health System, Atlanta, GA, USA; Department of Emergency Medicine, Emory University School of Medicine, Atlanta, GA, USA

Sung W. Han, Division of Biostatistics, School of Medicine, New York University, New York, NY, USA

Naoru Koizumi, School of Public Policy, George Mason University, Arlington, VA, USA

Nan Kong, Weldon School of Biomedical Engineering, Purdue University, West Lafayette, IN, USA

Sally A. Kraft, University of Wisconsin Medical Foundation, Middleton, WI, USA

Eva K. Lee, Center for Operations Research in Medicine and HealthCare, School of Industrial and Systems Engineering, Georgia Institute of Technology, Atlanta, GA, USA; NSF I/UCRC Center for Health Organization Transformation, Industrial and Systems Engineering, Atlanta, GA, USA; Georgia Institute of Technology, Atlanta, GA, USA

Fabio Leonelli, Cardiac Electrophysiology Laboratory, James A. Haley Veterans' Hospital, Tampa, FL, USA

Jingshan Li, Department of Industrial and Systems Engineering, University of Wisconsin, Madison, WI, USA

Rui Liu, University of Washington Tacoma, Tacoma, WA, USA

Wei Lu, Department of Radiation Oncology, University of Maryland School of Medicine, Baltimore, MD, USA

David S. Matteson, Department of Statistical Science, Cornell University, Ithaca, NY, USA

Mary F. McGuire, Department of Pathology and Laboratory Medicine, University of Texas Medical School at Houston, Houston, TX, USA

Thembi Mdluli, Weldon School of Biomedical Engineering, Purdue University, West Lafayette, IN, USA

Keith Melancon, George Washington University Hospital, Washington, DC, USA

Robert Meyer, Computer Sciences Department, University of Wisconsin, Madison, WI, USA

Sinjini Mitra, Information Systems and Decision Sciences Department, California State University, Fullerton, CA, USA

Rema Padman, The H. John Heinz III College, Carnegie Mellon University, Pittsburgh, PA, USA

Amit Patel, School of Public Policy, George Mason University, Arlington, VA, USA

Eleanor T. Post, Rockdale Medical Center, Conyers, GA, USA

Yunzhe Qiu, Department of Industrial Engineering & Management, College of Engineering, Peking University, Beijing, China

Varun Ramamohan, Purdue University, West Lafayette, IN, USA

Senjuti B. Roy, University of Washington Tacoma, Tacoma, WA, USA

Joyatee Sarker, Weldon School of Biomedical Engineering, Purdue University, West Lafayette, IN, USA

Leyuan Shi, Department of Industrial and Systems Engineering, University of Wisconsin, Madison, WI, USA

Zhenshen Shi, Department of Industrial and Manufacturing Systems Engineering, Kansas State University, Manhattan, KS, USA

Cleveland G. Shields, Department of Human Development and Family Studies, Purdue University, West Lafayette, IN, USA

Steven Q. Simpson, Division of Pulmonary Diseases and Critical Care Medicine, University of Kansas, Kansas City, KS, USA

Jeffrey S. Sleeth, University of Wisconsin Medical Foundation, Middleton, WI, USA

Changyue Song, Department of Industrial Engineering and Management, Peking University, Beijing, China

Jie Song, Department of Industrial Engineering & Management, College of Engineering, Peking University, Beijing, China

Calvin Thomas, IV, Health Ivy Tech Community College, Indianapolis, IN, USA

Carolina Vivas-Valencia, Weldon School of Biomedical Engineering, Purdue University, West Lafayette, IN, USA

Nigel Waters, Department of Geography, George Mason University, Fairfax, VA, USA

Molly Williams, University of Wisconsin Medical Foundation, Middleton, WI, USA

Michael D. Wright, Grady Health System, Atlanta, GA, USA

Chih-Hang J. Wu, Department of Industrial and Manufacturing Systems Engineering, Kansas State University, Manhattan, KS, USA

Daniel T. Wu, Grady Health System, Atlanta, GA, USA; Department of Emergency Medicine, Emory University School of Medicine, Atlanta, GA, USA

Hui Yang, Department of Industrial and Manufacturing Engineering, The Pennsylvania State University, University Park, PA, USA

Yuehwern Yih, Purdue University, West Lafayette, IN, USA

Hao Zhang, Department of Radiation Oncology, University of Maryland School of Medicine, Baltimore, MD, USA

Xi Zhang, Department of Industrial Engineering and Management, Peking University, Beijing, China

Hua Zhong, Division of Biostatistics, School of Medicine, New York University, New York, NY, USA

Xiang Zhong, Department of Industrial and Systems Engineering, University of Wisconsin, Madison, WI, USA

Zhengyi Zhou, Center for Applied Mathematics, Cornell University, Ithaca, NY, USA

PREFACE

Around the world, people are living longer. Health is rooted in everyday life and is critical to the well-being and economics of society. Delivering personalized, quality healthcare in a timely manner and at affordable costs remain major challenges in the United States and around the world. Fueled by rapid digital media advances, healthcare systems in the 21st century are investing more in advanced sensors and robotics, communication technologies, and sophisticated data centers. This facilitates information and knowledge visibility and delivery standardization and performance efficiency through big data analytics.

Meaningful information and knowledge extraction from diverse and rich healthcare data sets is an emergent critical area of research and development. In the general practice of medicine, healthcare providers must be empowered with effective analytical methods and tools that enable and assist them in (i) handling rich data sets generated from genetic screening to specimen tests to patient monitoring to large-scale hospital operations, (ii) extracting useful and meaningful information at different granularities and across heterogeneous healthcare systems, and (iii) exploiting pertinent knowledge for optimization of processes and performance across healthcare systems and the provision of personalized and effective healthcare services.

This book provides a brief overview of the state of the art in healthcare analytics development. It covers a collection of recent research advances in data-driven healthcare analytics from biomedical and health informatics to healthcare simulation and modeling to healthcare service science and medical decision making. The book intends to serve as a reference for healthcare researchers, practitioners, and students. In addition, through the chapters, those who are new to healthcare analytics can learn and understand how to apply analytical methods and tools to diverse healthcare applications. The intended audience includes researchers, practitioners, and graduate students in the healthcare/engineering fields of statistics, data science, system engineering, operations research, and operations management, as well as in biomedical engineering and computer science.

This book is organized into two parts: Part I covers biomedical and health informatics (Chapters 1–8) and Part II focuses on healthcare delivery systems (Chapters 9–19). Specifically, Chapters 1 and 2 address the analytics of genomic and proteomic data. Chapters 3 and 4 analyze physiological signals from patient monitoring systems. Chapter 5 handles data uncertainty in clinical laboratory tests. Chapter 6 covers predictive modeling and presents its applications to a broad variety of clinical and translational projects, while Chapter 7 focuses on predictive usage within radiation oncology. Chapter 8 discusses disease modeling for sepsis.

Part II begins with discussion of system advances for transforming clinic workflow and patient care (Chapter 9). Chapter 10 covers macroanalysis of patient flow distribution. Chapter 11 covers intensive care units while Chapter 12 covers a case study in primary care. Chapters 13 and 14 detail demand and resource allocation, while Chapters 15 and 16 focus on mathematical models for predicting patient readmission (Chapter 15) and postoperative outcome (Chapter 16). The last three chapters deal with physician–patient interactions (Chapter 17), insurance claims (Chapter 18), and the role of social media in healthcare (Chapter 19).

This book focuses primarily on data analytics from the field of Industrial Engineering and Operations Research methodologies drawing technologies from mathematical modeling, optimization, simulation, and computational methods that advance and improve healthcare. Most of the analytic authors are affiliated with the INFORMS community and are members of the healthcare applications society, data mining, simulation, optimization, computing, quality, statistics, and reliability societies. The chapters herein showcase the successful and close collaboration with the healthcare and clinical experts. A rich source of healthcare analytics can be found in the triannual INFORMS Healthcare Conference http://meetings.informs.org/healthcare2015.

At the time of the writing, big data analytics has attracted increasing attention in a broad spectrum of research domains, including biomedical and healthcare areas, where data arose from "omics"; imaging, laboratory, medical records, and operations offer invaluable opportunities. We also note that a number of large-scale data repositories have been established to accelerate the initiatives of big data to knowledge, for example, the Human Connectome Project (www.neuroscienceblueprint.nih.gov/connectome), the Cancer Genome Atlas (cancergenome.nih.gov), and the Physiome Project (www.physiome.org), to name a few.

Lastly, we would like to thank all the authors for their contribution that result in a high-quality book. We also gratefully acknowledge the support in part by the National Science Foundation under Grants CMMI-1454012, CMMI-1266331, IOS-1146882, and IIP-1447289 to editor H .Yang, and IIP-0832390, CNS-1138733, IIP-1361532, and IIP-1516074 to editor E.K. Lee. Finally, we thank the support and encouragement of Susanne Steitz-Filler, Wiley editor, toward the completion of this book and her staff for editorial and production assistance.

HUI YANG
Tampa, FL, USA
May 2015

EVA K. LEE
Atlanta, GA, USA
May 2015

PART I

ADVANCES IN BIOMEDICAL AND HEALTH INFORMATICS

1

RECENT DEVELOPMENT IN METHODOLOGY FOR GENE NETWORK PROBLEMS AND INFERENCES

SUNG W. HAN AND HUA ZHONG

Division of Biostatistics, School of Medicine, Department of Population Health, New York University, New York, NY, USA

1.1 INTRODUCTION

The cell inside of a human body is similar to a manufacturing system producing an appropriate protein that functions according to the specific organ or the part of the body to which it belongs. The nucleus centered at the cell contains the DNA sequence, which is a designed map for the human body. Each time the cell produces a protein, it duplicates a certain part of the DNA sequence and generates mRNA sequences. This is called a transcription process. After leaving the nucleus, the mRNA is attached to a ribosome, and the ribosome interprets the code in mRNA. This is called a translation process. After interpretation, the ribosome generates a sequence of amino acids; then it is folded into a certain type of protein.

The manufacturing system from DNAs to proteins sometimes malfunctions due to the DNA damage, which is known to be a main cause of cancers, also called malignant neoplasms [1, 2]. The DNA damage can occur naturally, but the damage can also be caused by two groups of agents: (i) exogenous agents such as radiation, smoke [3], ultraviolet light [4], and viruses [5]; and (ii) endogenous agents such as diet [6] and macrophages/neutrophils [5]. Such DNA damage leads to epigenetic alteration

Healthcare Analytics: From Data to Knowledge to Healthcare Improvement, First Edition.
Edited by Hui Yang and Eva K. Lee.
© 2016 John Wiley & Sons, Inc. Published 2016 by John Wiley & Sons, Inc.

for DNA repair genes, which play the key roles in preventing cancer cell growth. Reducing the DNA repair gene expression (DNA repair deficiency; [7]) or switching off the function of the DNA repair gene, called silence, finally leads to the development of cancers. For example, MGMT is the DNA repair gene, and most types of colorectal cancers have reduced MGMT expression ([8–11], and [12]). The following are other examples of proteins corresponding to DNA repair genes [1].

- BRCA1 and BRCA2 (breast cancer genes 1 and 2) for breast and ovarian cancers.
- ATM (ataxia telangiectasia mutated) for leukemia and breast cancers.
- XPC (xeroderma pigmentosum) for skin cancers.
- p53 (Li–Fraumeni syndrome) for sarcoma, leukemia, breast, lung, skin, pancreas, and brain cancers.

In addition, the miRNA (micro RNA) outside of the nucleus is known to have an effect on the DNA repair gene because it can reduce the expression of DNA damage response genes or repair genes [1]. For example, miRNA-155 is overly expressed in colon cancers, and it is known to reduce the expression of MLH1, a DNA repair protein [13].

For finding the mechanism of cancer development, understanding the causal relationship in transcriptional regulatory networks is important, and the related inference is often based on the gene network problem. The examples of the application of the network problem are in gene expression analysis or gene–gene expression networks [14–19], protein–protein interaction analysis [20, 21], phenotype networks utilizing gene expression information [22–24], and causal networks linking gene expression and metabolic change [24].

The probabilistic graphical modeling is a popular approach to find causal relationships between variables in cell signal pathways or gene networks [25]. In this chapter, the graphical models are assumed to be directed acyclic graphs (DAGs), in which all the edges are directed edges and contain no cycles [26]. Since the estimation of DAGs is computationally very challenging, we cannot simply apply approaches that are used to estimate undirected graphs [27–29]. First, DAGs with the same set of conditional independence are not identifiable from observational data alone [26]; this is called observational equivalence. Second, the number of possible DAGs exponentially increases as the number of nodes increases [27]. Third, in gene network problems, the number of genes is much larger than the sample size, which is called high-dimensional data.

The DAGs with conditional probability distribution for each child node given its parents are called Bayesian networks. The comprehensive review about learning Bayesian network is in Buntine [30, 31], Heckerman [32], Neapolitan [33], and Daly et al. [34]. Apart from cancer gene problems, the Bayesian network is used in broad applications such as ecology [35, 36], neuroscience [37, 38], distributed sensor networks for change detection, and diagnosis [39–41].

The main approaches to estimate the Bayesian networks are as follows: (i) a score-and-search approach through the space of Bayesian network structures,

(ii) a constraint-based approach that uses conditional independencies identified in the data, and (iii) a hybrid approach. A score-and-search approach is to find a structure corresponding to a good score function value [42] and use a heuristic algorithm to find the solution. The examples of this approach are in Daly et al. [34]. A constraint-based approach is to use a statistical test of conditional independence on the data. One of the efficient methods is the PC algorithm [43]. In high-dimensional contexts, Kalisch and Buhlmann [44] proposed the PC algorithm with a reasonable computational time [43] and proved consistency for sparse DAGs. Hybrid search strategies including the above-mentioned two criteria have also been proposed such as in Tsamardinos et al. [45], where the method used is a Max–Min Hill-Climbing (MMHC) algorithm. The methods mentioned have been successfully proposed to estimate DAGs with a small to moderate number of nodes.

For the score-and-search approach, a network is identified by maximizing a certain score function [31, 33, 42, 46], and several heuristic search algorithms are then developed to find a high score [27, 34]. To overcome high dimensionality in gene expression data, the L1-penalized method or lasso approach has been recently developed. Meinshausen and Buhlmann [28] theoretically show that the neighborhood of a node corresponding to a conditional dependence set can be obtained by a lasso problem, and it is efficient for high-dimensional DAGs. For DAGs, Shojaie and Michailidis [29] used the L1-penalized likelihood with a structural equation model to estimate directed graphs with a known variable order and found that such a problem was transformed into separable subproblems with lasso penalty. Huang et al. [47] used a penalized linear regression that imposes penalties to the coefficient values as well as to acyclic constraints. Fu and Zhou [48] used an adaptive lasso-based score function when the variable order is unknown. However, their objective function without the acyclic constraint is nonconvex, which makes finding the optimal solution infeasible. Han et al. [49] proposed the adaptive lasso-based score function, and it demonstrated superior performance to other methods when the network has a hub structure. In this chapter, we overview the approach based on the lasso-type score function for gene network problems in high-dimensional data.

1.2 BACKGROUND

We explain the basic theoretical background in probabilistic graphical modeling or Bayesian networks. Let us have p random variables, $Y_1, Y_2, \ldots, Y_p$, and the variables have causal relationships with each other. The variables and relationships in probabilistic distribution need to be mapped to p nodes, V, and edge sets, $E (\subset V \times V)$. In other words, the separation in a graph needs to be mapped to the independence in probability [50].

In probabilistic graphical modeling, the d-separation (directed separation) is an important concept described by Pearl [26]. The definition of d-separation is complicated, but it implies the following argument. Suppose we have three node sets V_1, V_2, and V_3. We define that V_2 is a d-separate between V_1 and V_3 if one of the conditions is satisfied:

- All edges between V_1 and V_2 inflow from V_1 to V_2, and all edges between V_2 and V_3 inflow from V_2 to V_3.
- All edges between V_1 and V_2 inflow from V_2 to V_1, and all edges between V_2 and V_3 inflow from V_3 to V_2.
- All edges between V_1 and V_2 inflow from V_2 to V_1, and all edges between V_2 and V_3 inflow from V_2 to V_3.

For all disjoint subsets of V_1, V_2, and V_3, we state that the probability distribution P is faithful to the graph G if the following condition is satisfied.

V_1 and V_3 *are independent given V_2 if and only if V_1 and V_3 are d-separated given V_2.*

Based on the d-separation, we can express the probability distribution by using the Markov property. The probability distribution $f(Y)$ is represented by

$$f(Y) = \prod_{i=1}^{p} f(Y_i|\mathrm{Pa}(Y_i))$$

where $\mathrm{Pa}(Y_i)$ is a set of parents for Y_i.

Another important issue in probabilistic graphical model is observational equivalence. The example of observational equivalence is in Figure 1.1. The three cases in Figure 1.1a–c are not distinguishable based on observational data. They are said to be in one equivalence class. However, based on the data, the case in Figure 1.1d can be distinguished from the other three cases. We say that this case has a v-structure. Such equivalence class causes multiple solutions with the same score function values if we apply the score-and-search approach to estimate a DAG. To show all equivalence classes, the complete partial DAG (cpDAG) can be used, which can be implemented by the "essentialGraph()" function in R package [51].

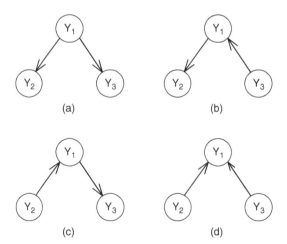

Figure 1.1 Examples of observational equivalence.

1.3 GENETIC DATA AVAILABLE

The technology in recent decades has allowed genome-wide monitoring of DNA and RNA levels on thousands of samples [52]. For example, The Cancer Genome Atlas (TCGA) project seeks to provide a comprehensive landscape of genetic and genomic alternations by profiling DNA copy number, mRNA expression, and miRNA expression for about 20 cancer types. The Genotype-Tissue Expression (GTEx) project studies human gene expression regulation and its relationship to genetic variation. The goal of these projects is to understand global regulation including genetic (from DNA to RNA), transcriptional (among mRNAs), and posttranscriptional processes determining normal cell physiology. Thus, the analysis of these regulatory layers can provide a useful picture of the underlying processes.

Open sources of gene expression data including TCGA and GTEx, or pathway information are in the following link:

- The Cancer Genome Atlas (TCGA) Data (https://tcga-data.nci.nih.gov/tcga/): This data set provides high-level sequence analysis of the tumor genomes and clinical information. The TCGA data consist of several types and levels as follows: Copy Number Variation (Low Pass DNASeq), Copy Number Variation (SNP Array), DNA Methylation, Expression Protein, METADATA, miR-NASeq, RNASeqV2, and Somatic Mutation.
- The GTEx project (http://www.broadinstitute.org/gtex/): The objective of this project is to accumulate the comprehensive data of gene expression across multiple tissues in the human body.
- modENCODE Project (Model Organism ENCyclopedia Of DNA Elements) (http://www.genome.gov/modencode/): This project aims to create the data of a comprehensive encyclopedia of genomic functional elements in the model organisms.
- Pathway Interaction Database (http://pid.nci.nih.gov/index.shtml): This has the maps of biomolecular interactions and cellular processes organized into human signaling pathways. It was a collaborative work between Nature Publishing Group (NPG) and National Cancer Institute (NCI).
- The DREAM5 Network Inference Challenge (http://wiki.c2b2.columbia.edu/dream/index.php/D5c4): This website provides gene expression data, which have been obtained from microorganisms.

1.4 METHODOLOGY

In this section, we explain a recently developed method based on the lasso-type score function. The first two sections describe the model and the score function for the graphical model to estimate the gene network problem, and the next two sections explain technical details.

1.4.1 Structural Equation Model

We express the genes by random variables. Denote by Ψ the $n \times p$ data matrix, where n is the sample size and p is the number of the variables. We assume that an edge is directed, so (j, i) is not in E if (i, j) belongs to E. The causal relationship of random variables in a DAG can be represented by the structural equation model [26, 29, 53]. Let Z_i be a latent variable, which is assumed to follow independent normal distributions. Then, the structural equation model that represents the relationship is

$$Y_i = \sum_{j \in \mathrm{Pa}_i} c_{ij} Y_j + Z_i \tag{1.1}$$

where c_{ij} is a causal effect from a parent j to a child i. Z_i s are latent variables. Denote $Y = [Y_1, Y_2, \dots, Y_p]^T$, and $Z = [Z_1, Z_2, \dots, Z_p]^T$. Here, we assume that the latent vector Z follows the multivariate normal distribution, $MN(0, \Gamma)$, where $\Gamma = \mathrm{diag}[\sigma_1^2, \sigma_2^2, \dots, \sigma_p^2]^T$. Under the unknown variable order, we represent coefficients of Y_j s, c_{ij}, by the coefficient matrix C, where

$$C = \begin{pmatrix} 0 & c_{12} & \cdots & c_{1(p-1)} & c_{1p} \\ c_{21} & 0 & \cdots & c_{2(p-1)} & c_{2p} \\ \vdots & \vdots & \ddots & \vdots & \vdots \\ c_{(p-1)1} & c_{(p-1)2} & \cdots & 0 & c_{(p-1)p} \\ c_{p1} & c_{p2} & \cdots & c_{p(p-1)} & 0 \end{pmatrix}$$

Thus, c_{ij} is the (i, j)th entry of C, and Equation 1.1 can be rewritten by $Y = CY + Z$. In addition, if the variable order is partially known, the blockwise matrix can be used [53], which is represented by

$$C = \begin{pmatrix} \begin{matrix} 0 & 0 & \cdots & 0 & 0 \\ 0 & 0 & \cdots & 0 & 0 \\ \vdots & \vdots & \ddots & \vdots & \vdots \\ 0 & 0 & \cdots & 0 & 0 \\ 0 & 0 & \cdots & 0 & 0 \end{matrix} & \begin{matrix} 0 & 0 & \cdots & 0 & 0 \\ 0 & 0 & \cdots & 0 & 0 \\ \vdots & \vdots & \ddots & \vdots & \vdots \\ 0 & 0 & \cdots & 0 & 0 \\ 0 & 0 & \cdots & 0 & 0 \end{matrix} \\ \begin{matrix} c_{1U_1} & 0 & \cdots & 0 & 0 \\ 0 & c_{2U_1} & \cdots & 0 & 0 \\ \vdots & \vdots & \ddots & \vdots & \vdots \\ 0 & 0 & \cdots & c_{(p-1)U_{p-1}} & 0 \\ 0 & 0 & \cdots & 0 & c_{pU_p} \end{matrix} & \begin{matrix} 0 & c_{12} & \cdots & c_{1(p-1)} & c_{1p} \\ c_{21} & 0 & \cdots & c_{2(p-1)} & c_{2p} \\ \vdots & \vdots & \ddots & \vdots & \vdots \\ c_{(p-1)1} & c_{(p-1)2} & \cdots & 0 & c_{(p-1)p} \\ c_{p1} & c_{p2} & \cdots & c_{p(p-1)} & 0 \end{matrix} \end{pmatrix}$$

Then, the corresponding structural equation model is

$$Y_i = c_{iU_i} U_i + \sum_{j \in \mathrm{Pa}_i} c_{ij} Y_j + Z_i$$

where U_i is an upper-level variable, which regulates the down-level variable Y_i. The example of the upper-level variable is DNA copy number or miRNA, which regulates mRNA.

1.4.2   Score Function Formulation

In the gene network problem, the number of gene expressions is very large, for example, over 10,000, but the sample size is relatively small such as 200–300. Thus, the estimation of gene networks is related to the variable selection problem in high-dimensional data. The well-known method for variable selection uses a discrete manner. One approach is a best subset selection. However, if the number of variables becomes large, the subset selection is computationally infeasible [54]. In addition, due to the discreteness of the approach, the result of the subset selection is unstable [55, 56]. Similarly, most discrete-based approaches may show instability in finding a solution. However, the L1-penalized linear regression leads to a continuous search, and it gives stable and robust estimation [54, 57]. Thus, for high-dimensional data, the lasso approach proposed in Fu and Zhou [48] and [53] is a proper way. In addition, they use adaptive lasso, which can break the equivalence class, and give a high probability of estimating a correct solution among the solutions in the equivalence class. In this section, we discuss a lasso-type approach as a recent development of methodology.

The lasso-type score function can be derived from the L1-penalized log likelihood, which is

$$-\frac{2}{n} \log \prod_{i=1}^{p} f(Y_i | \text{Pa}(Y_i), C) + \text{Pe}(C)$$

where $\text{Pa}(Y_i)$ is the set of parent variables for Y_i, and $\text{Pe}(C)$ is a penalty function for the coefficient matrix C. Based on the L1-penalized log likelihood, Fu and Zhou [48] proposed the score function, which is

$$\min_{C} \sum_{k=1}^{p} \left[\log \left(\frac{1}{n} \| \Psi_k - \Psi C_k \|^2 \right) + \lambda \sum_{j=1}^{p} w_{kj} |c_{kj}| \right] \tag{1.2}$$

subject that the estimated graph is acyclic. In the score function shown as Equation 1.2, Ψ is a $n \times p$ data matrix and Ψ_k is a data vector as the kth variable. C_k is a coefficient vector, $[c_{k1}, c_{k2}, \ldots, c_{k(p-1)}, c_{kp}]^T$, which is a column vector representing the kth row in matrix C. Zou [54] mentioned that the original lasso without the weight term does not provide consistent estimates. Thus, they suggested the adaptive lasso, which used the weights for the coefficient term c_{kj}. Zou [54] suggested $w_{kj} = \left(\frac{1}{|\beta_{kj}|} \right)^{\delta}$, where β_{kj} is the least square estimate from the ordinary least square, while Fu and Zhou [48] suggested $w_{kj} = \min \left(\frac{1}{|\beta_{kj}|}, 10^4 \right)^{\delta}$.

Han et al. [49] proposed another type of score function:

$$\min_{C} \sum_{k=1}^{p} \left[\frac{1}{n} \| \Psi_k - \Psi C_k \|^2 + \lambda \sum_{j=1}^{p} w_{kj} |c_{kj}| \right] \tag{1.3}$$

subject that the estimated graph is acyclic. The notations are the same as in Equation 1.2. The score function in Equation 1.3 is the equivalent form of Shojaie and Michailidis [29], which provides the score function with a known variable order. For the value of the weights, Han et al. [53] used the scaled weight, $w_{kj} = \min\left(\frac{0.0001}{|\beta_{kj}|}, 1\right)^{\delta}$. Han et al. [53] represented the acyclic constraint by the optimization formulation, which is

$$|c_{kj}| \le T_{kj} \qquad (1.4)$$

$$T_{kj} = 0 \text{ or } 1 \qquad (1.5)$$

and

$$T_{i_1 i_2} + T_{i_2 i_1} \le 1 \text{ for all } i_1 \text{ and } i_2$$

$$T_{i_1 i_2} + T_{i_2 i_3} + T_{i_3 i_1} \le 2 \text{ for all } i_1, i_2, \text{ and } i_3$$

$$\vdots$$

$$T_{i_1 i_2} + T_{i_2 i_3} + \cdots + T_{i_p i_1} \le p\text{-}1 \text{ for all } i_1, i_2, \ldots, i_p \qquad (1.6)$$

The score functions proposed by both Fu and Zhou [48] and Han et al. [53] have an advantage. The adaptive lasso score function can break observational equivalence, which expresses the same score function values [51]. If the structure of the graph is a hub network, there exist multiple solutions that give the same objective function value, called score equivalence [51]. Most score-and-search approaches such as penalized likelihood or constraint-based approach such as the PC algorithm cannot distinguish the solutions in the equivalence class since they give the same score function values or the same p-value, respectively. However, the adaptive lasso provides a different score function value to each solution even though they are in the same equivalence class. Furthermore, it gives a high probability of selecting a correct solution among the equivalence class especially in the hub network [53].

However, the score function from Fu and Zhou [48] has several disadvantages in comparison with that from Han et al. [53]. First, the score function from Fu and Zhou [48] in Equation 1.2 used the residual sum of the square from the penalized likelihood to estimate the variance of latent variables, which becomes a log form in the score function. The mean square error from the penalized linear regression is known to be a biased estimate of the variance of the latent variables if the penalty is large. Thus, from the various simulation studies, Han et al. [53] showed that when the penalty is large, the score function from Equation 1.3 gave a higher true positive of edges than the score function from Equation 1.2 given the same false positive, which indicates that the score function from the former gives better performance than the score function from the latter. However, as the penalty becomes small, the performance of the two methods becomes similar. The performance of Equation 1.2 is sensitive to the value of the penalty parameter, but that of Equation 1.3 is robust. Based on the simulation studies with $p = 100$, $n = 500$, and density $= 2$ (average number of parent nodes per child node), the receiver operating characteristic (ROC) curves based on true positive

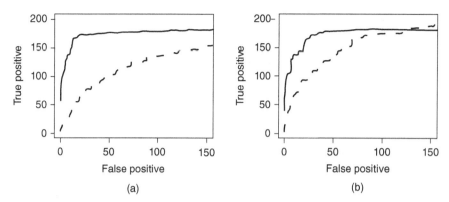

Figure 1.2 Receiver operating characteristic (ROC) curves from the adaptive lasso methods: (a) random network and (b) hub network.

versus false positive is in Figure 1.2a and b. The black solid line indicates the curves from the score function in Equation 1.3, and the gray dash line indicates the curves from the score function in Equation 1.2.

Second, the score function in Equation 1.2 is nonconvex. Thus, Fu and Zhou [48] can find only a local optimal solution at best. Both the nonconvexity of the score function and the acyclic constraints make finding a good solution very hard. In addition, Fu and Zhou [48] proposed a block coordinate descent (BCD) algorithm to obtain a solution from Equation 1.2 to overcome such nonconvexity, but they did not justify the quality of the solution. However, the score function in Equation 1.3 is convex, and it can be transformed into the quadratic programming (QP) problem, which guarantees a global optimal solution. Han et al. [53] implemented the DIST (discrete improving search with TABU list) algorithm to find the solution from Equation 1.3, which is called the cLasso method. They showed that the method based on Equation 1.3 requires smaller computational time than that based on Equation 1.2.

Apart from normal distributions, the lasso framework is easily extended to other distributions. In particular, due to recent technology, some gene expressions such as RNA sequences are recorded in discrete count data, and Poisson log-normal distribution can be used for the RNA sequence measurements. By the assumption of the log-normal data, Han et al. [53] represented the observed compounded Poisson data by

$$Y_k \sim \text{Poisson}(\exp(\sigma_k X_k + \mu_k))$$

where σ_k and μ_k are the standard deviation and average related to the marginal normal variable. In this case, we only observe the count data Y_k, and X_k is treated as unobserved data. Han and Zhong [58] proposed a penalized likelihood score function as follows. Let X be an unobserved normal vector with the X_k in the kth entry. Based on Bayes theorem,

$$P(C|Y) = \int P(C, X|Y)dX \propto \int P(Y|X, C) \times P(X|C)dX$$

The penalized log likelihood can be represented by

$$-\frac{2}{n}\sum_{j=1}^{n}\log\int \exp[h(X|C,y_j)]dX + \mathrm{Pe}(C)$$

where $h(X|C,y_j) = \log P(y|X,C) + \log P(XC)$, and $\mathrm{Pe}(C)$ is a penalty function in terms of the coefficient matrix C. Finding a solution based on the score function is quite complicated. Based on several approximations, they first transformed the score function to the lasso framework, and then searched the solution by using two iterative optimization procedures based on two groups of parameters.

1.4.3 Two-Stage Learning

Since searching for the solution in entire space takes a lot of computational time, much literature uses the two-step learning technique. The first step is to find the potential parents of each child by estimating an undirected graph/skeleton/Markov blanket, and the second step is to identify directionality (or parents). Tsamardinos et al. [45] proposed the MMHC algorithm, which estimates the skeleton by the constraint-based method and identifies the directionality by a score-and-search algorithm. Schmidt et al. [59] used the lasso regression to estimate an undirected graph, and then used a permutation approach based on swapping adjacent variable orders to identify directionality. Neto et al. [22] first estimated an undirected graph, and then estimated a DAG without an acyclic constraint based on the likelihood ratio between one direction and the opposite direction of each edge. Pellet and Elisseeff [60] used feature selection algorithms [61] to estimate a Markov blanket and then identified a directionality based on v-structured patterns. Other examples of the two-stage learning approaches are the Sparse Candidate (SC) algorithm [62] and the Grow-Shrink algorithm [63]. The two-step learning approach is also called a hybrid algorithm in Nagarajan et al. [50].

Huang et al. [47] mentioned that the two-stage procedure has high risk of misidentification of the true parents. If the first stage missed a true parent, the parent is not considered again as a possible parent in the second stage. Thus, they proposed a combined score function, which is

$$\min_{C}\sum_{k=1}^{p}\left[\frac{1}{n}\|\Psi_k - \Psi C_k\|^2 + \lambda_1\sum_{j=1}^{p}|c_{kj}| + \lambda_2\sum_{k\neq j}|c_{kj}\times P_{jk}|\right]$$

where P is a $p\times p$ matrix with 1 in the (i,j) entry if there is a direct path from X_i to X_j, otherwise 0. The acyclic constraint, $\sum_{k\neq j}|c_{kj}\times P_{jk}|$, is plugged into the score function with a second penalty, which is similar to Lagrangian relaxation. They used the BCD algorithm to estimate the network structure.

Han et al. [53] proposed an alternative approach. First, without the acyclic constraints, they minimized the objective function (score function) to find the infeasible solution. They set the infeasible solution as the potential parent set per child. Then, they added the acyclic constraints back to the problem and found the feasible solution. Unlike other hybrid approaches, Han et al. [53] used only one model and score function, but split the solution search algorithm by making it the two-step procedure. Han et al. [53] argued that their approach is more stable that the existing two-stage procedure.

1.4.4 Further Issues

Robustness of the estimation in Bayesian networks for gene network problems is an important issue. The performance of Bayesian networks also depends on the network structure. Han et al. [53] showed that the method with the score function based on Equation 1.3 is robust in terms of the network structure, but the performance of the pc-type algorithm is very sensitive to the network structure. Another issue related to the robustness is that the data are sometimes not complete and have missing parts. Ramoni and Sebastiani [64] discussed robust learning for Bayesian networks with missing data. In addition, most approaches for learning Bayesian networks show point estimator for the causal relations. Thus, several papers have studied how much confidence can be placed in the network estimate [65–67]. Finally, to estimate the correct structure, all variables with causal relationships are assumed to be included before learning.

Another issue in the estimation of the structure of DAGs based on the lasso problems is how to choose the penalty. To minimize average prediction errors, the cross-validation (CV) is suggested since it gives an asymptotic optimal estimate of the penalty. However, the CV does not lead to a consistent model selection for the lasso-type penalty [68]. For the consistency of the model selection, the Bayesian Information Criterion measures are suggested [69, 70]. Tibshirani [57] showed that the lasso gives a stable and correct estimate. Proper tuning parameters need to be selected for a consistent model selection [54, 71, 72]. How to select the best penalty parameter in the network problem is still an open question.

1.5 SEARCH ALGORITHM

In this section, we discuss solution search algorithms to minimize the score function.

1.5.1 Global Optimal Solution Search

The straightforward way to find a global optimal solution is to use total enumeration, which is an exhaustive search in terms of edges by permuting an entire combination of directed edges and selecting the combination that gives the maximum of the score function. For example, suppose that the number of variables is p, then the total number of edges we need to consider is $p(p-1)/2$. Each edge can take three options: one direction, the opposite direction, or an empty edge. Then, the total number of combinations we need to consider is $3^{(p(p-1)/2)}$. However, such approaches are computationally not feasible even when the number of variables is small.

We may use some optimization technique to estimate a DAG based on the traveling salesman problem (TSP) [73, 74]. The straightforward approach [53] to find a global optimal solution is as follows:

- Step 1: Solve the objective function (1.3) without the acyclic constraints.
- Step 2: If cycles exist, add the constraints corresponding to the cycles. Then, solve it again.
- Step 3: If the solution does not have any cycle, it is an optimal solution. Otherwise, go to Step 2.

However, to solve the problem with the above-mentioned approach is also computationally inefficient. For example, the asymmetric TSP [73, 74] presented computational difficulty for long decades [75]. Thus, directly solving the gene network problem requires heavy computational time if p increases.

Another approach described by Han et al. [53] is to find upper and lower bounds of the solution based on the branch-and-bound technique and sub-tour elimination, which are used in the TSP. Since it is almost impractical to include all possible cycles in the formulation in the solution approach, we add acyclic constraints if needed. During the branch-and-bound algorithm, the intermediate solution can be infeasible since it violates the acyclic constraints. For the minimization problem, the solution should be lower bound since it is the optimal solution under the relaxed conditions. Then, we can obtain upper bound of the solution that breaks all cycles. Han et al. [53] implemented the branch-and-bound technique to find the optimal solution, but the computational time is over 2 h even when $p = 20$. Thus, in high-dimensional data, using a heuristic algorithm or meta-heuristic algorithm is preferable.

1.5.2   Heuristic Algorithm for a Local Optimal Solution

To find the solution for the problem with nonconvexity of the acyclic constraints, the ad hoc or rudimentary solution search algorithms have been proposed. Shojaie and Michailidis [29] proposed permutation of variable order since known order indicates directionality between two genes and automatically satisfies acyclic constraints. Such one-time permutation relies on random chance to obtain the corrected order, so it is not a reliable approach. Schmidt et al. [59] swapped adjacent ordered variables and searched the best score function values. Fu and Zhou [48] used BCD algorithm. They started the algorithm from the empty network and added edges or reverse directionality of edges step-by-step while avoiding a cycle. However, they did not consider a leaving edge, which is a necessary step to find a good solution. In the optimization area, a greedy algorithm or Hill-Climbing algorithm is commonly used, which considers adding an edge, reversing an edge, or removing an edge.

Most ad hoc or heuristic algorithms only guarantee a local optimal solution due to acyclic constraints. Han et al. [53] proposed a meta-heuristic algorithm based on a discrete improving search with a TABU list, which is called DIST. In the DIST algorithm, at each iteration, a leaving edge is put in the TABU list and it is not considered as an entering edge in the whole round. Han et al. [53] compared the solution from the DIST algorithm with a global optimal solution when $p = 10$ or 20, and he showed that the solution from the DIST algorithm is close to the global optimal solution. The description of the DIST algorithm is as follows:

- Select an entering edge among all unselected edges, which gives the most improvement in the objective function.
- Select a leaving edge among all selected edges, which breaks the cycle and gives the least harm in the objective function. To find any cycle, use forward and backward Breadth-First Search (BFS) algorithms. Any confirmed leaving edges are put into the TABU list.
- Update the intermediate solution as well as the objective function values.
- Do the above-mentioned three steps repeatedly until all edges are searched. We call it a round. After each round, empty the TABU list and restart the next round.
- If there is no improvement in the objective function value in two consecutive rounds, stop the algorithm. Otherwise, keep running the next round.

1.6 PC ALGORITHM

The well-known alternative method to estimate Bayesian networks is the PC algorithm [43]. Kalisch and Buhlmann [44] applied the PC algorithm to estimate the DAGs with high-dimensional data. It first estimates an undirected graph and removes edges iteratively based on the conditional independence test. This method requires a condition of faithfulness, which is mentioned in Section 1.2. Under the faithfulness condition, the d-separation in a graph is equivalent to the conditional independence relationship. In the multivariate normal distribution, the conditional independence can be derived from partial correlation. Kalisch and Buhlmann [44] used Fisher's Z-transform statistics to test the significance of a partial correlation, which is defined by

$$Z(X, Y|Z) = \frac{\sqrt{n\text{-}\#(Z)\text{-}3}}{2} \log \frac{1 + \rho_{XY|Z}}{1\text{-}\rho_{XY|Z}}$$

If the Z-transform statistics is greater than a certain threshold, it rejects $c_{kj} = 0$, and it adds an edge (i,j) in the graph. After estimating the skeleton, they extended it to a complete partial DAG.

The PC algorithm has been used in high-dimensional data [76–79], and it is known to be computationally feasible to estimate sparse network with the large number of variables. There is an R package in the software, "pcalg()" [44]. Since the performance of those methods is order dependent, which means that they are sensitive to the true variable order, Colombo and Maathuis [80] developed the PC-stable algorithm.

Han et al. [53] compared the method based on the adaptive lasso score function with the PC-stable algorithm by simulation studies. The results showed that the former outperforms the latter in terms of true positive given the same false positive in most scenarios except for the random network with high density. Under the hub network, which is a main structure in gene networks, the adaptive lasso approach performs better than the PC-stable method. Han et al. [53] found that the performance of the PC-stable method is sensitive to the network structure, and as the percentage of isolation of parents increases, the performance of the PC-stable method decreases. Thus, for the gene network problem, which is related mostly to a hub network, the adaptive lasso might be preferable to the PC-stable method.

The computational complexity of the PC algorithm is approximately $O(p^q)$, where q is the maximal size of neighbors and p is the number of variables. On the other hand, the computational complexity of the cLasso method is bounded by $O(\max(nk^2p, np^2))$, where k is the maximum number of parent candidates and n is the sample size. As the complexity shows, if p or k is moderate such as 2, 3, or above, the complexity of the PC algorithm is higher than that of the cLasso method. Han et al. [53] also verified the complexity difference based on the simulation study. Under the random network and $d = 1$, the computational time of the PC algorithm is similar to that of the cLasso method. However, under the hub network or the random network with $d = 2$, the computational time of the PC algorithm is much higher than that of the cLasso method. Especially, under the hub network, from which many possible parents can be derived, with $d = 2$, the computational time of the PC algorithm is much higher than that of the cLasso method.

1.7   APPLICATION/CASE STUDIES

We discuss three examples of the data-driven analytics for gene network problems. In the first example, which is based on open data set of melanoma skin cancers in TCGA Data Portal, we describe how to construct gene networks under partially known variable order and obtain inferences for clinical purposes. In the second example based on Cancer Cell Line Encyclopedia (CCLE) data, we show how to build the network under unknown variable order. In the third example based on flow cytometry data of protein expressions, we describe some tutorials of how to use R softwares to estimate the network.

1.7.1   Skin Cutaneous Melanoma (SKCM) Data from the TCGA Data Portal Website

The incidence rate of melanoma skin cancer increased recently with a lifetime risk of 1 in 50 [81, 82]. The patients with metastatic tumors survive about 7 months on average [83]. Although several therapies such as BRAF mutant kinase inhibitors [84, 85] or CTLA-4 inhibitors [86, 87] have been developed, the results of therapy have not been successful. Fleming et al. [88] found that based on array-based screening, about 18 miRNAs out of 358 miRNAs are potential predictors of recurrence. They revealed that based on statistical analysis of TCGA data, the signature miRNAs regulate functions to melanoma biology such as the immune signaling pathway. In this section, we describe how to construct gene pathways or networks under partially known structure based on Skin Cutaneous Melanoma (SKCM) data from the TCGA Data Portal website (https://tcga-data.nci.nih.gov/tcga/). The TCGA Data Portal provides a platform of data sets containing clinical information as well as genomic data and sequence analysis of various tumors.

The description of the data structure is as follows. The TCGA data consist of several data types (so-called platform types) and levels. The data types are as follows: CNV (Low Pass DNASeq), CNV (SNP Array), DNA Methylation, Expression Protein, METADATA, miRNASeq, RNASeqV2, and Somatic Mutations. Each type has the data in four different levels at most. The data in level 1 are raw data or signals, and the data in level 2 are processed data. The level 3 data are segmented or interpreted with normalization, and the level 4 data are summary or regions of interest data. For our purpose, we use level 3 data.

After downloading the data sets, the file, "file_manifest.txt," showed the main information of data type and sample ID/barcode as well as the corresponding file name containing genomic data. For example, in the file, "file_manifest.txt," there are three columns: "Platform Type," "Sample," and "File Name." It is useful to note that in the sample barcode, the first 10 letters, for example, "TCGA-BF-A1PU," indicate a patient barcode. If we want to find miRNA and mRNA data for a certain sample, say "TCGA-BF-A1PU-01A," we need to search the file name in the "File Name" column, which is matched to a certain platform type and sample barcode. For example, for miRNA data, the file name matching to "miRNASeq" and "TCGA-BF-A1PU-01" is "TCGA-BF-A1PU-01A-11R-A18V-13.mirna.quantification.txt." In the miRNA data file, there are raw count data and normalized count data for each miRNA ID, and we used the normalized count data. The detailed description of the structure of all data sets is in https://tcga-data.nci.nih.gov/tcga/tcgaDataType.jsp.

The clinical information for each sample barcode is in the following folder and file: Clinical>Biotab>biospecimen_sample_skcm.txt. Each tumor sample is matched to a normal sample. The number at the end of the sample barcode is the key to understand the tumor source. For example, the ending number of the sample barcode is 1A for a primary tumor and 06A for a metastatic tumor. The clinical information for each patient is in the folder and file: Clinical>Biotab>clinical_patient_skcm.txt.

We extracted the data of miRNA and mRNA corresponding to primary or metastatic tumors. The number of miRNAs is 1046, and the number of mRNAs is 20,531. The sample size in the miRNA data set is 329, but the sample size in the RNASeqV2 (mRNA) data set is 325. Thus, we removed four samples in the miRNA data that did not match the data set of mRNA. Next, we took a log transformation of each data set and then standardized them by centering and scaling. In the miRNA data, 200 miRNAs have zero values except for at most one value. In the mRNA data, 405 mRNAs have zero values except for at most one value. Thus, after removing unnecessary miRNAs and mRNAs, the total numbers of remaining miRNAs and mRNAs are 846 and 20,126, respectively.

Given the data set, we tried to estimate the gene network with the causal relationship from miRNA to mRNA. We used the lasso-type score function in Equation 1.3. Since we are interested in the causal relationship between the miRNA group and the mRNA group, we use a block matrix for C in Equation 1.3. The penalty parameter is selected based on empirical study in Fleming et al. [88]. The estimated gene network is shown in Figure 1.3, which is drawn by network() and plot() functions

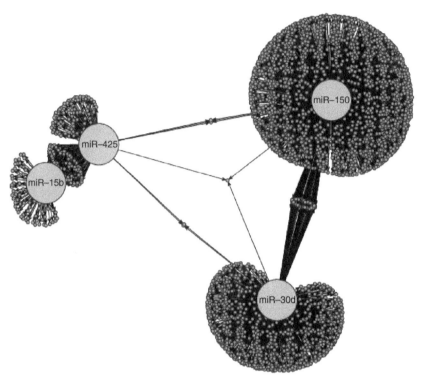

Figure 1.3 Estimated graph: the small dots indicate mRNAs and the large dots indicate miRNAs.

in R software. In this figure, the four large dots indicate miRNA and the small dots indicate mRNAs. Based on the result, the miRNA-150 has a broad effect on many mRNAs, so we included the network related to miRNA-150. We also include the network plot with clinically important miRNA such as miRNA-30d, miRNA-425, and miRNA-15b [88]. After deciding the miRNAs, we selected the mRNAs with significant coefficients to the corresponding miRNAs, the absolute values of which are greater than 0.1. The miRNA-150 was causally related to 1360 mRNAs with high coefficients. A number of selected mRNAs with respect to the other three important miRNAs (miRNA-30d, miRNA-425, and miRNA-15b) are 185, 5, and 15, respectively.

From the result of gene network estimation, we draw inferences for clinical purposes. Since the miRNA-150 gives the main impact for most mRNA, we make a grouping for patients based on mRNAs affected by the miRNA-150. We draw a heat map as shown in Figure 1.4. In the heat map, the rows indicate patient samples and the columns indicate mRNA expression. As shown at the left side in the heat map, the patients can be clustered by two groups such as a low-level group (bottom part) and a high-level group (upper part) based on hierarchical cluster analysis. For each clustered group, we estimate Kaplan–Meier survival curves that are shown in Figure 1.5. The gray dash line indicates the high level group, and the black solid line indicates

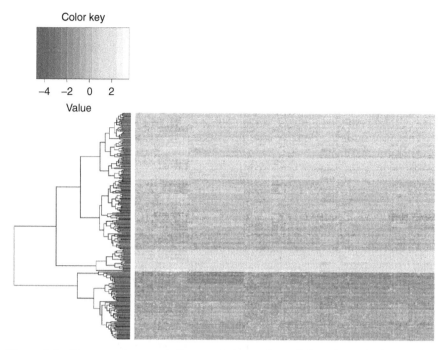

Figure 1.4 Heat map: the rows indicate patient samples and the columns indicate mRNA expression.

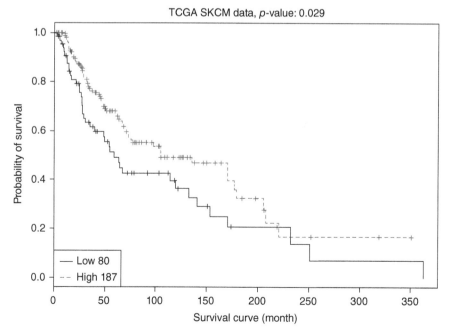

Figure 1.5 Survival curve: the gray dash line indicates the high-level group, and the black solid line indicates the low-level groups.

the low level groups. The *p*-value based on the log-rank test is 0.029, which is less that 0.05 (significance level in biostatistics). This shows that the high-level group has a better survival rate than the low-level group with the statistical significance.

1.7.2   The CCLE (Cancer Cell Line Encyclopedia) Project

It is widely known that p53 is an important gene as a tumor suppressor, which can prevent cancer growth. This p53 controls genes, whose function is DNA repair, cell cycle control, and apoptosis. Under normal conditions, the protein level of p53 drives MDM2 transcription factor, and as a feedback loop, MDM2 regulates the protein levels of p53. MDM2 can block or impair p53 pathway activity. Zhong et al. [89] explained the development of gene expression signature, which is predictive of the response to MDM2 antagonist therapy. Barretina et al. [90] discuss finding a predictive model for anticancer drug sensitivity from CCLE data.

The CCLE contains cancer-related genomic data from 947 human cancer cell lines with 36 tumor types, which are characterized by genomic technology platforms. This data can be downloaded from http://www.broadinstitute.org. To identify mRNAs as the cell line responses to the MDM2, we need to estimate the gene networks. By using a partial model of Equation 1.3, we extracted 16 genes, which have roles in different processes surrounding MDM2. These genes were BRCA1, DDB2, and XPC involved in DNA repair; FDXR in P53-related process; SESN1 and ZMAT3 in cell growth; CCNG1 and CDKN1A in cell cycle arrest; and BAX, EP300, PIDD, RPS27L, and TP53 involved in apoptosis. To estimate the gene network, we applied the method in Equation 1.3 to the data with a penalty parameter as suggested in Han et al. [53]. The estimated network is plotted in Figure 1.6.

1.7.3   Cellular Signaling Network in Flow Cytometry Data

In this section, we provided a tutorial of the usage in R packages to estimate a DAG in a gene network problem. The common example used to explain a network problem is cell signaling in protein expression as in Sachs et al. [91]. Intracellular multicolor flow cytometry can generate observational data of cell signaling molecules [92, 93], and by flow cytometry, we can measure the protein expression and protein modification states such as phosphorylation [93–95]. Based on this finding, Sachs et al. [91] demonstrated that cell signaling data can be used for inferring causal relationships. The multivariate flow cytometry data used in Sachs et al. [91] are collected to identify the effects of different conditions on the intracellular signaling networks of human primary naive CD4+ T cells, which are downstream of CD3, CD28, and LFA-1 activation. Eleven phosphorylated proteins were measured: PKC, PIP2, PLGG, PIP3, AKT, JNK, P38, ERK, MEK, RAF, and PKA.

In this section, we show the examples of R codes for four different estimates for the cellular signaling network and the corresponding network plots, which are shown in Figure 1.7. The following is the R code to show the estimated network plot from Sachs et al. [91].

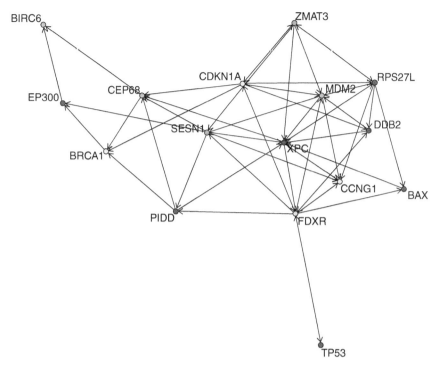

Figure 1.6 Estimate structure in CCLE data with 16 genes, which have roles in different processes surrounding MDM2.

```
> library(network)
> estmated.net <- network(t(estimate_Sachs))
> main.name=paste("(a) Estimate from Sachs et al. [91]",sep="")
> plot(estmated.net,
+ displaylabels=TRUE,
+ boxed.labels=FALSE,
+ mode="circle",
+ vertex.cex=3,
+ arrowhead.cex=2,
+ label.cex=1.0,
+ pad=0.15,
+ label.pos=6,
+ cex.main=1.2,
+ main=main.name)
```

In order to show network plots, "library(network)" needs to be called. "estimate_Sachs" indicates the structure matrix based on the estimated network from Sachs et al. [91]. The estimated network plot is in Figure 1.7a. Next, the R code to show how to obtain the estimated network structure from the cLasso method [53] is as follows:

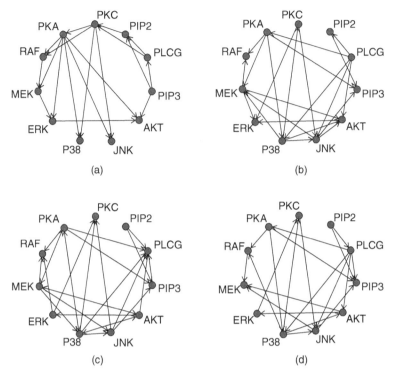

Figure 1.7   Four different estimates for the cellular signaling network. (a) Estimate from Sachs et al. [91]; (b) estimate by cLasso; (c) estimate by PC algorithm; (d) estimate by MMHC algorithm.

```
> delta<-0.15
> cLasso.fit <- cLasso(x.stand=Data.protein.expression,lambda=0.7,
search.index=0,gamma_weight=delta)
> estimate_T_cLasso <- cLasso.fit$est_T
```

The delta in the above-mentioned code is the value of the power for calculating the weight, w_{kj}, in Equation 1.3. The R codes and tutorials will be released as an R package, the name of which is tentatively library(DAGLasso). The estimated network plot is in Figure 1.7b. Then, the next two R codes are the examples of the PC algorithm and the MMHC algorithm. The estimated network plots are in Figure 1.7c and d, respectively. The details of the R codes are in the tutorials provided in the R packages, library(pcalg) and library(bnlearn).

```
> library(pcalg)
> alpha_PC<-0.01
> data_size<-dim(Data.protein.expression)[1]
> data_dim<-dim(Data.protein.expression)[2]
> indepTest <- gaussCItest
> suffStat <- list(C = cor(Data.protein.expression), n = data_size)
```

```
> pc.fit <- pc(suffStat, indepTest, data_dim, alpha_PC)
> g<-pc.fit@graph
> estimate_T_pc_algorithm <-t(as(g,"matrix"))
> library(bnlearn)
> alpha_MMHC<-0.01
> mmhc.fit<-mmhc(Data.protein.expression,alpha=alpha_MMHC)
> g<-mmhc.fit$arcs
> estimate_T_mmhc_algorithm <-matrix(as.numeric(g),ncol=2,
nrow=dim(g)[1])
```

1.8   DISCUSSION

This chapter discusses the recent development of model-based methodologies for estimating cancer gene networks based on the score-and-search approach with the adaptive lasso-based score function, which has been a very important problem in genomic projects for decades. We overviewed the background of Bayesian networks and the available genetic data. We explored structural equation models and the lasso-type score function formulation, which is a recently developed approach in gene network problem. We also discussed an optimization problem to find the solution for the network estimation problem and described the application of the method for data-driven analytics.

1.9   OTHER USEFUL SOFTWARES

There are several software tools visualizing the pathways and networks.

- Pathway Studio (http://www.elsevier.com/online-tools/pathway-studio): Pathway Studio is made from Elsevier Life Science Solutions, and it is a tool for biological decision support. It shows protein–protein interaction and target–drug interaction.
- Ingenuity Pathway Analysis (IPA)(http://www.ingenuity.com/products/ipa): IPA is developed from QIAGEN, and it is a tool to model and analyze the complex biological systems. This tool gives several functions such as causal network analysis, upstream regulator analysis, and downstream effects analysis.

There are also other packages in the R software for estimating DAGs of the Bayesian network under different data types with various techniques. Following are some of the packages that are briefly explained.

- The package, "bnlearn" [96], implements score-based, constraint-based, and hybrid algorithms for learning the structure of Bayesian networks. It supports parameter learning via maximum likelihood and Bayesian estimators and provides inference. This function can be applied to both discrete and continuous data such as Gaussian data.

- The package, "deal" [97] , implements a heuristic search algorithm and defines priors to estimate the Bayesian network in both discrete and continuous data. It can also simulate data sets from a given structure.
- The package, "pcalg" [44], implements the PC algorithm and the extended algorithms for causal structure learning and causal effect estimation.
- The package, "catnet" [98], implements a maximum likelihood-based method to estimate a Bayesian network for categorical data.

ACKNOWLEDGMENTS

Research is supported by NIH-1-R21 GM110450-01.

REFERENCES

[1] Bernstein C, Prasad AR, Nfonsam V, Bernstei H. DNA damage, DNA repair and cancer. In: Clark C, editor. *New Research Directions in DNA Repair*. InTech; 2013. p 413–465.

[2] Bernstein C. 2009. DNA damage and cancer, SciTopics. Available at http://www.scitopics.com/DNA_Damage_and_Cancer.html. Accessed 2014 May 6.

[3] Cunningham FH, Fiebelkorn S, Johnson M, Meredith C. A novel application of the Margin of Exposure approach: Segregation of tobacco smoke toxicants. Food Chem Toxicol 2011;49(11):2921–2933.

[4] Kanavy HE, Gerstenblith MR. Ultraviolet radiation and melanoma. Semin Cutan Med Surg 2011;30(4):222–228.

[5] Handa O, Naito Y, Yoshikawa T. Redox biology and gastric carcinogenesis: The role of *Helicobacter pylori*. Redox Rep 2011;16(1):1–7.

[6] Bernstein C, Holubec H, Bhattacharyya AK, Nguyen H, Payne CM, Zaitlin B, Bernstein H. Carcinogenicity of deoxycholate, a secondary bile acid. Arch Toxicol 2011;85(8):863–871.

[7] Malkin D. Li-Fraumeni syndrome. Genes Cancer 2011;2(4):475–484.

[8] Halford S, Rowan A, Sawyer E, Talbot I, Tomlinson I. O^6-methylguanine-methyltransferase in colorectal cancers: Detection of mutations, loss of expression, and weak association with G:C>A:T transitions. Gut 2005;54(6):797–802.

[9] Shen L, Kondo Y, Rosner GL, Xiao L, Hernandez NS, Vilaythong J, Houlihan PS, Krouse RS, Prasad AR, Einspahr JG, Buckmeier J, Alberts DS, Hamilton SR, Issa JP. MGMT promoter methylation and field defect in sporadic colorectal cancer. J Natl Cancer Inst 2005;97(18):1330–1338.

[10] Psofaki V, Kalogera C, Tzambouras N, Stephanou D, Tsianos E, Seferiadis K, Kolios G. Promoter methylation status of hMLH1, MGMT, and CDKN2A/p16 in colorectal adenomas. World J Gastroenterol 2010;16(28):3553–3560.

[11] Amatu A, Sartore-Bianchi A, Moutinho C, Belotti A, Bencardino K, Chirico G, Cassingena A, Rusconi F, Esposito A, Nichelatti M, Esteller M, Siena S. Promoter CpG island hypermethylation of the DNA repair enzyme MGMT predicts clinical response to dacarbazine in a phase II study for metastatic colorectal cancer. Clin Can Res 2013;19(8):2265–2272.

[12] Mokarram P, Zamani M, Kavousipour S, Naghibalhossaini F, Irajie C, Moradi Sarabi M, Hosseini SV. Different patterns of DNA methylation of the two distinct O6-methylguanine-DNA methyltransferase (O6-MGMT) promoter regions in colorectal cancer. Mol Biol Rep 2013;40(5):3851–3857.

[13] Valeri N, Gasparini P, Fabbri M, Braconi C, Veronese A, Lovat F, Adair B, Vannini I, Fanini F, Bottoni A, Costinean S, Sandhu SK, Nuovo GJ, Alder H, Gafa R, Calore F, Ferracin M, Lanza G, Volinia S, Negrini M, McIlhatton MA, Amadori D, Fishel R, Croce CM. Modulation of mismatch repair and genomic stability by miR-155. Proc Natl Acad Sci USA 2010;107(15):6982–6987.

[14] Friedman N, Linial M, Nachman I, Pe'er D. Using Bayesian networks to analyze expression data. J Comput Biol 2000;7:601–620.

[15] Keller MP, Choi YJ, Wang P, Davis DB, Rabaglia ME, Oler AT, Stapleton DS, Argmann C, Schueler KL, Edwards S, Steinberg HA, Neto EC, Kleinhanz R, Turner S, Hellerstein MK, Schadt EE, Yandell BS, Kendziorski CM, Attie AD. A gene expression network model of type 2 diabetes establishes a relationship between cell cycle regulation in islets and diabetes susceptibility. Genome Res 2008;18:706–716.

[16] Zou M, Conzen SD. A new dynamic bayesian network (dbn) approach for identifying gene regulatory networks from time course microarray data. Bioinformatics 2005;21:71–79.

[17] Imoto S, Kim S, Goto T, Miyano S, Aburatani S, Tashiro K, Kuhara S. Bayesian network and nonparametric heteroscedastic regression for nonlinear modeling of genetic network. J Bioinf Comput Biol 2003;1:231–252.

[18] Beal MJ, Falciani F, Ghahramani Z, Rangel C, Wild DL. A Bayesian approach to reconstructing genetic regulatory networks with hidden factors. Bioinformatics 2005;21:349–356.

[19] Werhli AV, Grzegorczyk M, Husmeier D. Comparative evaluation of reverse engineering gene regulatory networks with relevance networks, graphical Gaussian models and Bayesian networks. Bioinformatics 2006;22:2523–2531.

[20] Jansen R, Yu H, Greenbaum D, Kluger Y, Krogan NJ, Chung S, Emili A, Snyder M, Greenblatt JF, Gerstein M. A Bayesian networks approach for predicting protein–protein interactions from genomic data. Science 2003;302:449–453.

[21] Tu Z, Keller MP, Zhang C, Rabaglia ME, Greenawalt DM, Yang X, Wang IM, Dai H, Bruss MD, Lum PY, Zhou YP, Kemp DM, Kendziorski C, Yandell BS, Attie AD, Schadt EE, Zhu J. Integrative analysis of a cross-loci regulation network identifies app as a gene regulating insulin secretion from pancreatic islets. PLoS Genet 2012;8:e1003107.

[22] Neto EC, Ferrara CT, Attie AD, Yandell BS. Inferring causal phenotype networks from segregating populations. Genetics 2008a;179:1089–1100.

[23] Neto EC, Keller MP, Attie AD, Yandell BS. Causal graphical models in systems genetics: A unified framework for joint inference of causal network and genetic architecture for correlated phenotypes. Ann Appl Stat 2010;4:320–339.

[24] Ferrara CT, Wang P, Neto EC, Stevens RD, Bain JR, Wenner BR, Ilkayeva OR, Keller MP, Blasiole DA, Kendziorski C, Yandell BS, Newgard CB, Attie AD. Genetic networks of liver metabolism revealed by integration of metabolic and transcriptomic profiling. PLoS Genet 2008;4:e1000034.

[25] Markowetz F, Spang R. Inferring cellular networks: A review. BMC Bioinf 2007;8 (Suppl 6):S5.

[26] Pearl J. *Causality: Models, Reasoning, and Inference.* Cambridge: Cambridge University Press; 2009.

[27] Robinson R. Counting unlabeled acyclic digraphs. In: Little CHC, editor. *Combinatorial Mathematics V: Proceedings of the Fifth Australian Conference, Held at the Royal Melbourne Institute of Technology.* Berlin: Springer; 1977. p 28–43.

[28] Meinshausen N, Buhlmann P. High-dimensional graphs and variable selection with the Lasso. Ann Stat 2006;34:1436–1462.

[29] Shojaie A, Michailidis G. Penalized likelihood methods for estimation of sparse high-dimensional directed acyclic graphs. Biometrika 2010;97:519–538.

[30] Buntine WL. Operations for learning with graphical models. J Artif Intell Res 1994;2:159–225.

[31] Buntine WL. A guide to the literature on learning probabilistic networks from data. IEEE Trans Knowl Data Eng 1996;8:195–210.

[32] Heckerman D. A tutorial on learning with Bayesian networks. Technical report MSR-TR-95-06, Microsoft Research; 1995.

[33] Neapolitan RE. *Learning Bayesian Networks.* Series in Artificial Intelligence. Prentice Hall; 2004.

[34] Daly R, Shen Q, Aitken S. Learning Bayesian networks: Approaches and issues. Knowl Eng Rev 2011;26:99–157.

[35] Marcot BG, Holthausen RS, Raphael MG, Rowland M, Wisdom M. Using Bayesian belief networks to evaluate fish and wildlife population viability under land management alternatives from an environmental impact statement. For Ecol Manage 2001;153:29–42.

[36] Borsuk ME, Stow CA, Reckhow KH. A Bayesian network of eutrophication models for synthesis, prediction, and uncertainty analysis. Ecol Model 2004;173:219–239.

[37] Rajapakse JC, Zhou J. Learning effective brain connectivity with dynamic Bayesian networks. Neuroimage 2007;37:749–760.

[38] Li JN, Wang ZJ, Palmer SJ, McKeown MJ. Dynamic Bayesian network modeling of fMRI: A comparison of group-analysis methods. Neuroimage 2008;37:749–760.

[39] Li J, Jin J. Optimal sensor allocation by integrating causal models and set-covering algorithms. IIE Trans 2010;42(8):564–576.

[40] Liu K, Shi J. Objective-oriented optimal sensor allocation strategy for process monitoring and diagnosis by multivariate analysis in a Bayesian network. IIE Trans 2013;45(6):630–643.

[41] Liu K, Zhang X, Shi J. Adaptive sensor allocation strategy for process monitoring and diagnosis in a Bayesian network. IEEE Trans Autom Sci Eng 2014;11(2):452–462.

[42] Broom BM, Subramanian D. Computational methods for learning Bayesian networks from high-throughput biological data in Bayesian inference for gene expression and proteomics marina. In: Do K-A, Muller P, Vannucci M, editors. *Bayesian Inference for Gene Expression and Proteomics.* New York, NY: Cambridge University Press; 2006.

[43] Spirtes P, Glymour C, Scheines R. *Causation, Prediction, and Search.* Cambridge, MA: MIT Press; 2000.

[44] Kalisch M, Buhlmann P. Estimating high-dimensional directed acyclic graphs with the PC-algorithm. J Mac Learn Res 2007;8:613–636.

[45] Tsamardinos I, Brown L, Aliferis C. The max-min hill-climbing Bayesian network structure learning algorithm. Mach Learn 2006;65:31–78.

[46] Heckerman D, Geiger D, Chickering D. Learning Bayesian networks: the combination of knowledge and statistical data. Mach Learn 1995;20:197–243.

[47] Huang S, Li J, Ye J, Fleisher A, Chen K, Wu T, Reiman E, the Alzheimer's Disease Neuroimaging Initiative. A sparse structure learning algorithm for gaussian Bayesian network identification from high-dimensional data. IEEE Trans Pattern Anal Mach Intell 2013;35(6):1328–1342.

[48] Fu F, Zhou Q. Learning sparse causal gaussian networks with experimental intervention: Regularization and coordinate descent. J Am Stat Assoc 2013;108:288–300.

[49] Han SW, Chen G, Belousov A, Essioux L, Zhong H. Estimation of sparse directed acyclic graphs through a penalized likelihood method for gene network inference. Submitted to Journal of the American Statistical Association; 2013.

[50] Nagarajan R, Scutari M, Lebre S. *Bayesian Networks in R: with Applications in Systems Biology*. Springer; 2013.

[51] Chickering DM. Learning equivalence classes of Bayesian-network structures. J Mach Learn Res 2002;2:445–498.

[52] The Cancer Genome Atlas Research Network. Comprehensive genomic characterization defines human glioblastoma genes and core pathways. Nature 2008;455:1061–1068.

[53] Han, SW, Chen, G, Belousov, A, Essioux, L and Zhong, H, Estimation of sparse directed acyclic graphs through a penalized likelihood method for gene network inference, Technical Report; 2014.

[54] Zou H. The adaptive LASSO and its oracle properties. J Am Stat Assoc 2006;101:1418–1429.

[55] Breiman L. Better subset regression using the nonnegative garotte. Technometrics 1995;37:373–384.

[56] Fan J, Li R. Variable selection via nonconcave penalized likelihood and its oracle properties. J Am Stat Assoc 2001;96:1348–1360.

[57] Tibshirani R. Regression shrinkage and selection via the lasso. J R Stat Soc B 1996;58:267–288.

[58] Han SW, Zhong H. Estimation of directed acyclic graphs under Poisson log-normal distribution. Submitted; 2013.

[59] Schmidt M, Niculescu-Mizil A, Murphy K. Learning graphical model structure using l1-regularization paths. AAAI 2007;7:1278–1283.

[60] Pellet J-P, Elisseeff A. Using markov blankets for causal structure learning. J Mach Learn Res 2008;9:1295–1342.

[61] Guyon I, Elisseeff A. An introduction to variable and feature selection. J Mach Learn Res 2003;3:1157–1182.

[62] Friedman N, Nachman I, Péer D. Learning Bayesian network structure from massive datasets: The 'Sparse Candidate' algorithm. Proc. 15th Conf. Uncertainty in Artificial Intelligence; 1999a.

[63] Margaritis D, Thrun S, Bayesian network induction via local neighborhoods. Proc. Conf. Advances in Neural Information Processing Systems; 1999.

[64] Ramoni M, Sebastiani P. The use of exogenous knowledge to learn Bayesian networks from incomplete databases. In Proceedings of the Second International Symposium on Advances in Intelligent Data Analysis, Reasoning about Data (IDA '97), Lecture Notes in Computer Science, 1280, 537–548, Springer; 1997.

[65] Friedman N, Goldszmidt M, Wyner A. Data analysis with Bayesian networks: a bootstrap approach. In Proceedings of the Fifteenth Conference on Uncertainty in Artificial Intelligence (UAI-99), Prade, H., and Laskey, K. (eds), Morgan Kaufmann, 196–205; 1999b.

[66] Peng H, Ding C. Structure search and stability enhancement of Bayesian networks. In Proceedings of the Third IEEE International Conference on Data Mining (ICDM 2003), Wu, X., Tuzhilin, A., and Shavlik, J. (eds), IEEE Computer Society, 621–624; 2003, doi: 10.1109/ICDM.2003.1250992.

[67] Holness GF. A direct measure for the efficacy of Bayesian network structures learned from data. In Proceedings of the Fifth International Conference on Machine Learning and Data Mining in Pattern Recognition (MLDM 2007), Lecture Notes in Artificial Intelligence 4571, 601–615, Springer; 2007.

[68] Wang H, Li B, Leng C. Shrinkage tuning parameter selection with a diverging number of parameters. J R Stat Soc B 2009;71:671–683.

[69] Shao J. An asymptotic theory for linear model selection. Stat Sin 1997;7:221–264.

[70] Shi P, Tsai CL. Regression model selection. a residual likelihood approach. J R Stat Soc B 2002;64:237–252.

[71] Fan J, Peng H. Nonconcave penalized likelihood with a diverging number of parameters. Ann Stat 2004;32:928–961.

[72] Wang H, Li G, Tsai CL. Regression coefficient and autoregressive order shrinkage and selection via the lasso. J R Stat Soc B 2007;69:63–78.

[73] Bellmore M, Nemhauser GL. The traveling salesman problem: A survey. Oper Res 1968;16:538–558.

[74] Burkard RE. Travelling salesman and assignment problems: A survey. Ann Dis Math 1979;4:193–215.

[75] Junger M, Reinelt G, Rinaldi G. The traveling salesman problem. In: Ball M, Magnanti T, Monma CL, Nemhauser G, editors. Handbook on Operations Research and Management Sciences, Networks. Amsterdam: North-Holland; 1995. p 225–330.

[76] Kalisch M, Fellinghauer BAG, Grill E, Maathuis MH, Mansmann U, Buhlmann P, Stucki G. Understanding human functioning using graphical models. BMC Med Res Methodol 2010;10(1):14.

[77] Nagarajan R, Datta S, Scutari M, Beggs M, Nolen G, Peterson C. Functional relationships between genes associated with differentiation potential of aged myogenic progenitors. Front Physiol 2010;1:1–8.

[78] Stekhoven DJ, Moraes I, Sveinbjörnsson G, Hennig L, Maathuis MH, Bühlmann P. Causal stability ranking. Bioinformatics 2012;28(21):2819–2823.

[79] Zhang X, Zhao XM, He K, Lu L, Cao Y, Liu J, Hao JK, Liu ZP, Chen L. Inferring gene regulatory networks from gene expression data by path consistency algorithm based on conditional mutual information. Bioinformatics 2012;28(1):98–104.

[80] Colombo D, Maathuis MH. Order-independent constraint-based causal structure learning. Technical Report, arXiv:1211.3295v2; 2013.

[81] National Cancer Institute. 2013. SEER Stat Fact Sheets: Melanoma of the Skin. Available at http://seer.cancer.gov/statfacts/html/melan.html. Accessed 2013 Jan 29.

[82] Garbe C, McLeod GR, Buettner PG. Time trends of cutaneous melanoma in Queensland, Australia and Central Europe. Cancer 2000;89:1269–1278.

[83] Bedikian AY, Millward M, Pehamberger H, et al. Bcl-2 antisense (oblimersen sodium) plus dacarbazine in patients with advanced melanoma: The Oblimersen Melanoma Study Group. J Clin Oncol 2006;24:4738–4745.

[84] Chapman PB, Hauschild A, Robert C, et al. Improved survival with vemurafenib in melanoma with BRAF V600E mutation. N Engl J Med 2011;364(26):2507–2516.

[85] Solit D, Sawyers CL. Drug discovery: How melanomas bypass new therapy. Nature 2010;468(7326):902–903.

[86] Hodi FS, O'Day SJ, McDermott DF, Weber RW, Sosman JA, Haanen JB, et al. Improved survival with ipilimumab in patients with metastatic melanoma. N Engl J Med 2010;363(8):711–723.

[87] Robert C, Thomas L, Bondarenko I, O'Day S, Weber J, Garbe C, et al. Ipilimumab plus dacarbazine for previously untreated metastatic melanoma. N Engl J Med 2011;364(26):2517–2526.

[88] Fleming NH, Silva I, Miera EV-S, Brady B, Han SW, Hanniford D, Wang J, Shapiro RL, Hernando E, Zhong J, Osman I. Serum-based miRNAs in the prediction and detection of recurrence in melanoma patients, Submitted to Cancer; 2014.

[89] Zhong H, Chen G, Jukofsky L, Geho D, Han SW, Birzele F, Bader S, Himmelein L, Cai J, Alvertyn Z, Rothe M, Essioux L, Burtscher H, Middleton SA, Rueger R, Chen L-C, Dangl M, Nichols G, Pierceall WE. MDM2 antagonist clinical response association with a gene expression signature in acute myeloid leukemia. Br J Haematol 2015;171:432–425.

[90] Barretina J, Caponigro G, Stransky N, Venkatesan K, Margolin AA, Kim S, et al. The cancer cell line encyclopedia enables predictive modelling of anticancer drug sensitivity. Nature 2012;483:603–607.

[91] Sachs K, Perez O, Pe'er D, Lauffenburger DA, Nolan GP. Causal protein-signaling networks derived from multiparameter single-cell data. Science 2005;308:523–529.

[92] Herzenberg LA, Parks D, Sahaf B, Perez O, Roederer M, Herzenberg LA. The history and future of the fluorescence activated cell sorter and flow cytometry. Clin Chem 2002;48(12):1819–1827.

[93] Perez OD, Nolan GP. Simultaneous measurement of multiple active kinase states using polychromatic flow cytometry. Nat Biotechnol 2002;20(2):155–162.

[94] Perez OD, Mitchell D, Jager GC, South S, Murriel C, McBride J, Herzenberg LA, Kinoshita S, Nolan GP. Leukocyte functional antigen 1 lowers T cell activation thresholds and signaling through cytohesin-1 and Jun-activating binding protein 1. Nat Immunol 2003;4(11):1083–1092.

[95] Irish JM, Hovland R, Krutzik PO, Perez OD, Bruserud Ø, Gjertsen BT, Nolan GP. Single cell profiling of potentiated phospho-protein networks in cancer cells. Cell 2004;118(2):217–228.

[96] Scutari M. Learning Bayesian networks with the bnlearn R package. J Stat Softw 2010;35:1–22.

[97] Bottcher SG, Dethlefsen C. Deal: A package for learning Bayesian networks. J Stat Softw 2003;8:1–40.

[98] Balov, N, Salzman, P. 2013. catnet: Categorical Bayesian network inference, http://cran.rproject.org/web/packages/catnet/catnet.pdf. Accessed 2016 Feb 1.

2

BIOMEDICAL ANALYTICS AND MORPHOPROTEOMICS: AN INTEGRATIVE APPROACH FOR MEDICAL DECISION MAKING FOR RECURRENT OR REFRACTORY CANCERS

MARY F. MCGUIRE AND ROBERT E. BROWN

Department of Pathology and Laboratory Medicine, University of Texas Medical School at Houston, Houston, TX, USA

2.1 INTRODUCTION

Despite more than 40 years of cancer research funding in the United States, "outlier" patients with nonstandard cancers or nonstandard disease progression languish at the margins of clinical investigation. Standard-of-care treatment does help many patients overcome the disease, but the benefits are generally limited to those patients whose disease progresses on an "average" trajectory with disease and patient characteristics similar to those upon which the clinical trials for that treatment were carried out. Once it is confirmed that the standard treatment is ineffective and that the cancer is refractory or recurring, oncologists face the daunting task of designing a novel, patient-specific treatment.

With the advent of molecular testing, there is now the opportunity to expand the data available to assist in medical decision making for such outlier patients with complex cancers. In 2007, 3 years after the validation of the human genome,

Healthcare Analytics: From Data to Knowledge to Healthcare Improvement, First Edition.
Edited by Hui Yang and Eva K. Lee.
© 2016 John Wiley & Sons, Inc. Published 2016 by John Wiley & Sons, Inc.

analysis of gene sequence data was discussed as a way to guide treatment decisions and drug development [1]. Although advances in high-throughput, next-generation sequencing (NGS) have made it cheaper and quicker to detect hereditary or acquired gene mutations, there are still challenges in using genomic profiles to guide further treatment in recurrent cancers [2]. For example, tumors are heterogeneous and there may be different gene mutations throughout the tissue; only known cancer-related causative (driver) mutations can be identified; and, finally, there are a limited number of available drugs that target cancer-related mutations [3]. To gain more information, research has turned to the study of the expression levels of a gene's biochemical products, RNAs, or proteins, as indicative of the underlying biological mechanisms amenable to therapy [4]. After the collapse of the drug industry efforts in 2011 to develop gene silencing drugs based on RNA interference (RNAi) [5], preclinical research turned to identifying and interpreting protein signatures that could be targeted for therapy. However, the primary high-throughput technology used for proteomic research, mass spectrometry, has drawbacks for clinical care including a false discovery rate (FDR) of proteins that has to be managed computationally. There was no single methodology that would identify and measure protein signatures accurately, infer their likely molecular interactions, and predict likely drug effects for an individual patient.

Therefore, we developed a novel approach to the personalized identification and interpretation of molecular (protein) signatures in advanced cancers. Overall, morphoproteomics and biomedical analytics combine classical, "gold standard," methods of pathology that identify and characterize protein activity with the latest information on related molecular pathway networks and therapies. One of our goals was to identify drugs that likely will be ineffective against a patient's tumor at a specific time point in treatment, thus reducing treatment costs and lessening toxicity to the patient. The combinations of the pathologist's expertise in morphoproteomics and the scientist's application of analytics give insights into the unique mechanisms that influence disease progression and treatment choices. The methodology is currently used by the clinical Consultative Proteomics Service at the University of Texas Health Science Center in Houston.

2.2   BACKGROUND

In 2014, Robert A. Weinberg, award-winning cancer researcher and author of the key textbook in the field, *The Biology of Cancer* [6], wrote "The coupling between observational data and biological insight is frayed if not broken … we lack the conceptual paradigms and computational strategies for dealing with this complexity" [7]. Genomic (gene) and proteomic (protein) molecular profiles have recently moved from the research laboratory to the clinic, where their interpretation may be limited by the physician's experience and knowledge – two key aspects of medical decision making [8, 9]. Genes and proteins comprise the typical data in a molecular profile (or signature); measuring tools include mass spectrometry and antibody-based approaches. Both tools use algorithms for data preparation, integration, and analysis.

Let us consider the respective roles of data, tools, and algorithms in molecular profiling for clinical decision making.

2.2.1 Data

2.2.1.1 Genes In 2004, the Human Genome Project completed validation and identifications of more than 20,000 genes in human DNA [10]. Today, genotyping is proving to be a useful clinical tool to identify patients with genes that may put them at more risk for certain diseases, such as cancer [11]. Genes produce, or express, molecules such as RNAs and proteins to carry out biological functions; using alternative splicing, a single gene can produce a diversity of proteins [12]. When a gene is mutated or damaged, the gene products may be defective, resulting in altered biological functions and disease, such as cancer [13]. By detecting, quantifying, and localizing the protein activity in tissue or blood, one can gain insights into the underlying biological functions and see how the body has adapted – or not – to defects in gene products.

2.2.1.2 Proteins Proteomics – the study of proteins and their interactions – has emerged as a way to identify the changes over location and time in cellular processes associated with disease progression. In particular, specific cascades of proteins involved in intracellular and extracellular signaling influence treatment decisions. The signaling cascades of molecular interactions are referred to as "pathways" and are visually represented by network graphs with molecules as the nodes (vertices) and molecular interactions as the edges (arcs) that may be directed or undirected. Biological pathway data are available in the literature and in pathway databases, and these data can be used to "connect the dots" between measured and unmeasured proteins to discover new proteins or to expand the molecular data set under analysis. The primary technologies used for proteomics are mass spectrometry or antibody-based methods such as immunoassays and IHC. Mass spectrometry is considered "unbiased" because it is not constrained in advance to examine particular proteins. In contrast, antibody-based approaches require an antibody sensitive and specific to the protein. Although they are considered the "gold standard" for protein identification, antibody-based approaches do not discover new proteins.

2.2.2 Tools

2.2.2.1 Mass Spectrometry (MS) It identifies and quantifies high-throughput proteins by the spectral masses of their associated peptides. Unfortunately, peptides are promiscuous, binding to a variety of proteins [14], and raw MS data require complex postprocessing to limit FDR. Liquid chromatography (LC/MS) and tandem (MS/MS) "shotgun" mass spectrometry lose localization information of the proteins, while matrix-assisted laser desorption/ionization (MALDI-TOF/MS), or "imaging MS" (IMS), can retain broad localization. Currently, IMS technology has issues with spatial resolution [15]. Although mass spectrometry of protein patterns was proposed for clinical diagnosis as early as 2002 [16], the technology still faces challenges; algorithms are still being developed to minimize the FDR incurred by the indirect protein identification [17].

2.2.2.2 Immunoassays These assays measure the presence and concentration of a specific protein in solution using an antibody that detects the protein. Multiplex immunoassays can test multiple biofluid samples for multiple proteins and reverse phase protein microarrays are being used to study leukemia, a cancer suitable for testing via blood or marrow [18].

2.2.2.3 Immunohistochemistry (IHC) IHC visually detects the presence, concentration, location, and distribution of a protein in tissue using an antibody stain. The stained tissue slice is examined under a microscope and scored; there is usually one slide per protein analyzed. IHC is the only proteomic method that can specify the location of a protein within a cell; this is important because some key proteins in cancer have different functions when the majority of them are in the nuclei of the cells in a tumor rather than in the surrounding cytoplasm. Morphoproteomics uses an IHC approach to quantify and assess the activity of key proteins in a patient's tumor.

2.2.3 Algorithms

Algorithms and protocols are used throughout proteomics analyses for molecular data preparation, expansion, and analysis. One important goal is to discover hidden or related molecules that can be added to the measured data; the combined data set of measured and inferred molecules can then be analyzed within the context of the study. There are many molecules that cannot be measured directly by the current tools; yet, those molecules are important for the discovery of new protein interactions and for generating hypotheses about the molecular mechanisms underlying disease. As a result, proteomic algorithms often incorporate methods that link observed protein data to pathway databases and then analyze the combined results. For example, Vaudel proposed a three-step workflow algorithm for MS-based proteomic discovery [19]:

- Step 1. Identify the found proteins. Starting from the raw MS data, generate a list of proteins validated at a specific level of statistical confidence. The proteins are inferred from the peptides and validated using a target/decoy approach. Typically, 1000–2000 proteins are validated at 1% FDR.
- Step 2. Document the biological functions for each protein by first finding the protein's identifier and key information in the UniProtKB, the Universal Protein Resource Knowledge Database (www.uniprot.org). Then, find out which pathways involve the inferred proteins using a pathway database such as Reactome (http://www.reactome.org/).
- Step 3. Add the new MS analysis to the public Proteomics Identification Data repository http://www.ebi.ac.uk/pride/archive/.

Unlike Vaudel's work, our goals went beyond inferring new proteins from MS; we needed to analyze the expanded molecular data sets and their molecular interaction pathway networks within the context of patient care. We were looking for molecular patterns within a single patient. We had tissue data (protein measurements and localization) from tools (morphoproteomics using IHC); we needed algorithms to use that data to find which biological pathways were likely active in the patient and how possible drugs would interact with those pathways. We needed to compare the resulting "molecular signature" of the patient with those of similar patients to explore different therapies. So, we searched the biomedical literature for solutions.

2.2.4 Literature Review

2.2.4.1 Method A search of the PubMed/Medline database was performed for all manuscripts published through June 2014 to identify those with algorithms that used IHC proteomic data to generate and analyze molecular signatures. PubMed, maintained by the United States National Library of Medicine (NLM), contains more than 23 million citations for biomedical literature (http://www.ncbi.nlm.nih .gov/pubmed/). The search was performed using terms from MeSH ("Medical Subject Headings"), a controlled vocabulary hierarchy. The focus MeSH terms were proteomics, human, mass spectrometry, immunoassay, IHC, clinical pathology, pathology/methods, proteomics/methods, and algorithms.

2.2.4.2 Results The first manuscript in the category "proteomics" was published in 1999. Through mid-2014, more than 28,000 articles had been indexed, with just over half including human proteomics. Of the human proteomics, 6601 had mass spectrometry; 2219 had immunoassay, and 969 had IHC. Only 13 were categorized as human proteomics in clinical pathology. In contrast, the more than 3400 manuscripts under pathology/methods dated from 1946, and 3078 were human methods; the 15,591 proteomics/methods dated from 1999, and around half of them were related to human analysis. Table 2.1 summarizes five of the searches – labeled from "A" to "E" in Table 2.1 – related to biomedical analytics and morphoproteomics. In Search A, there were 19 manuscripts under the combined category of pathology/methods, proteomics/methods, and human [20–38]. In the Search B drilldown of Search A, seven included mass spectrometry [26–28, 31, 32, 34, 38]. In the Search C and D drilldowns of Search A, three were categorized as both IHC and immunoassay: Kothmaier et al. compared tissue fixatives used for routine pathology protein analysis [21]; Diaz et al. described a tissue specimen collection procedure for proteomic analysis [26]; and Brown (coauthor of this chapter) described how morphoproteomics can be used by anatomic pathologists for personalized medicine [25].

2.2.4.3 Discussion Recent review studies support the need for molecular technologies and proteomic analysis of clinical samples, but the algorithmic focus is more on improving mass spectrometry and immunoassay tools than on utilizing the more

TABLE 2.1   Literature Search Shows Paucity of Clinical Proteomics Methods

Search Term	# Manuscripts	Oldest Year
proteomics[MeSH Terms]	28,168	1999
proteomics[MeSH Terms] AND human[MeSH Terms]	15,681	1999
(proteomics[MeSH Terms] AND human[MeSH Terms]) AND mass spectrometry[MeSH Terms]	6,601	1999
(proteomics[MeSH Terms] AND human[MeSH Terms]) AND immunoassay[MeSH Terms]	2,219	2002
(proteomics[MeSH Terms] AND human[MeSH Terms]) AND immunohistochemistry[MeSH Terms]	969	2002
(proteomics[MeSH Terms] AND human[MeSH Terms]) AND clinical pathology[MeSH Terms]	13	2003
pathology/methods[MeSH Terms]	3,403	1946
pathology/methods[MeSH Terms] AND human[MeSH Terms]	3,078	1965
proteomics/methods[MeSH Terms]	15,591	1999
proteomics/methods[MeSH Terms] AND human[MeSH Terms]	8,697	1999
A. (pathology/methods[MeSH Terms] AND proteomics/methods[MeSH Terms]) AND humans[MeSH Terms]	19	2003
B. ((pathology/methods[MeSH Terms] AND proteomics/methods[MeSH Terms]) AND humans[MeSH Terms]) AND mass spectrometry[MeSH Terms]	7	2003
C. ((pathology/methods[MeSH Terms] AND proteomics/methods[MeSH Terms]) AND humans[MeSH Terms]) AND immunoassay[MeSH Terms]	3	2008
D. ((pathology/methods[MeSH Terms] AND proteomics/methods[MeSH Terms]) AND humans[MeSH Terms]) AND immunohistochemistry[MeSH Terms]	3	2008
((proteomics/methods[MeSH Terms] AND algorithms[MeSH Terms]) AND human[MeSH Terms]	469	2002
((proteomics/methods[MeSH Terms] AND algorithms[MeSH Terms]) AND human[MeSH Terms]) AND mass spectrometry[MeSH Terms]	267	2002
((proteomics/methods[MeSH Terms] AND algorithms[MeSH Terms]) AND human[MeSH Terms]) AND immunoassay[MeSH Terms]	16	2005
E. ((proteomics/methods[MeSH Terms] AND algorithms[MeSH Terms]) AND human[MeSH Terms]) AND immunohistochemistry[MeSH Terms]	9	2005

Search as of June 11, 2014.
To see manuscripts and updates, enter the search term at http://www.ncbi.nlm.nih.gov/pubmed/.

labor-intensive visual analysis by IHC [39, 40]. Because no MeSH term directly relates to biomedical analytics, the term "algorithm" was used to search PubMed. Looking solely at the 8697 human proteomics/methods, only 469 were categorized as having algorithms; 267 included mass spectrometry, 61 had immunoassay; and 9 included IHC. Of these nine in Search E, six reported on algorithms to improve mass spectrometry (MS), with IHC used to validate the MS finding [41–46]. Two manuscripts focused on imaging as a possible future alternative to proteomic IHC. Balluff et al. reported on a proof-of-principle study that imaging mass spectrometry (IMS) could be used to identify proteomic profiles that correlate with HER2/neu positive breast cancer tissue, stating that IMS would be quicker, cheaper, and more objective than the standard HER2/neu IHC test [47]. Rower et al. investigated a 20-protein signature for invasive ductal breast cancer. The signature was previously developed using principal component analysis and hierarchical clustering on LC-MS data [48]. Using the signature, this study compared tissue analysis by IHC with digital analysis of IHC images from the Human Protein Atlas (www.proteinatlas.org). Both methods differentiated normal tissue from tumor tissue and suggested that IMS would be useful for clinical studies [49]. Finally, Daly et al. presented an algorithm to predict protein concentrations from ELISA immunoassays, using monotonic spline statistical models (MS), penalized constrained least squares (PCLS) fitting, and Monte Carlo (MC) simulation [50]. The authors found that no reports used algorithms or developed models that connect measured proteins with evoked molecular pathways for a specific patient with a disease that had progressed beyond standard treatment.

This literature search demonstrated that there is a lack of clinical laboratory and analytical methods that positively identify, quantify, and localize protein circuitries in human tissue and then use that information for discovery of additional likely protein interactions that influence disease diagnosis, prognosis, and treatment in a single patient. Instead of developing a model that embodied predetermined hypotheses to be perturbed by a variety of data, we chose to use our patient's data to generate hypotheses about their own underlying molecular mechanisms and potential drug interactions. In the following section, we take you through the development of our methodology and show how quantitative algorithms tie together patient data from the pathologist's morphoproteomic analysis with published biological pathways and drug interactions to aid in medical decision making for a single patient.

2.3 METHODOLOGY

Unable to find suitable algorithms, we developed our own methodology. Morphoproteomic analysis was performed to detect and interpret the proteins in the tumor tissue. These data were quantified and input to the pathway generation software to evoke a qualitative "molecular signature" of the patient's likely molecular pathways built from the patient's own tumor data. The molecular signature could be compared quantitatively to those of other patients or to those of the same patient at different times by converting the molecule lists and pathway graphs to matrices. The molecular signature could also be used to evaluate drug resistance and support treatment decisions.

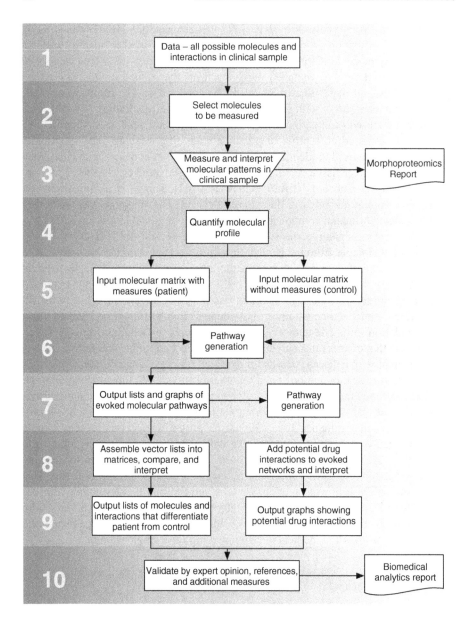

Overview. The methodology is an expanded version of Vaudel's workflow for MS-based proteomic discovery (*vide supra*), adapted for antibody-based approaches rather than mass spectrometry. Following is an overview based on the flowchart depicted in Figure 2.1; details are given in the following sections.

Figure 2.1 Morphoproteomics analysis and biomedical analytics methodology flowchart. (1) The clinical sample from the patient is a tissue sample, such as that taken for a cancer tumor biopsy; it contains a vast amount of data. Here, the focus is on protein data only. (2) Due to the use of antibodies as detectors (one per protein), the set of proteins to be measured is determined in advance. From more than 140,000 human proteins documented in the Universal Protein Resource or "UniProt" (www.uniprot.org), the pathologist selects 10–20 proteins that influence the specific disease and treatment decisions and for which laboratory antibody analysis is available. (3) The protein molecules in the tissue are scored by visual inspection of one protein per antibody stained tissue slide. The pathologist analyzes the set of slides with the patient's clinical tissue samples and writes a Morphoproteomics Report, documenting the proteins found in the tissue samples, their qualitative scores per cellular location (nucleus, cytoplasm, membrane), and interpretation in light of the patient history and potential treatments. (4) The biomedical analyst then converts the morphoproteomic molecular signature, or set of qualitative scores/locations for the patient, into a quantitative molecular signature matrix, consisting of normalized scores and UniProt identifiers. The matrix data are represented in a spreadsheet suitable for input to a biological pathway generation program. (5) The spreadsheet data for the patient(s) and a "control" spreadsheet (with the same proteins as the patient but without scores) are entered into the biological pathway analysis software. (6) The pathway generation software is run. (7) The pathway generation software outputs biological pathway network graphs and molecule lists that incorporate the measured proteins into the most likely pathways. Note that there may be several pathways evoked from a single input data set. The pathways are output as images (jpg, pdf) and the lists of the names of molecules in each pathway as column vectors in a spreadsheet. The pathways may also be interrogated and expanded interactively within the pathway generation software. (8, left) For a single patient sample, the column vectors of the output molecule lists in the patient are compared to the respective column vectors of the output molecule lists in the control. For short-molecule lists, this is done visually. For long-molecule lists, the column vectors are assembled into matrices and the patient's matrix and the control matrix are compared by matrix algebra. For multiple samples, additional column vectors can be added to the matrix. For molecular interaction differences, the pathway images are compared visually for small pathways. For large or complex pathways, the nodes and edges on pathway network graphs are mapped to adjacency or incidence matrices for computational comparison through mathematical software such as MATLAB. (8, right) Within the pathway generation software, drug molecules can be interactively "connected into" the evoked pathway networks to assess their effects. Both the pathologist and the biomedical analyst interpret the results. (9, left) The results of the patient/control comparison are documented. (9, right) Images of the drug interactions with the patient's pathways are output. (10) The output data are assembled and reviewed by the pathologist. Additional literature references are collected, and the pathologist may validate the presence of inferred proteins by IHC. The Biomedical Analytics Report is attached to the Morphoproteomics Report, and the results are discussed with the patient and the oncologist.

2.3.1 Morphoproteomics (Fig. 2.1(1–3))

Morphoproteomics is defined as the identification by IHC of the molecular circuitry of various proteins in a tumor by noting their state of activation (translocation and phosphorylation) and correlative expressions. In morphoproteomic analysis, antibodies recognize sites of activation on the protein analytes that connect them to other molecules in activation cascades. This approach can uncover potential targets, amenable to therapeutic interventions, which are specific for an individual patient's tumor (i.e., customized therapy) [25, 51, 52]. Briefly, formalin-fixed biopsy specimens are sectioned and mounted on glass slides, one slide per protein to be analyzed. These protein "analytes" are selected based on their influence on disease progression and on treatment recommendations; 10–24 or more proteins may be detected. Each slide is incubated with antibody specific for phosphorylated protein followed by binding with a chromogenic probe that enables subsequent visualization via light microscopy. Our laboratory is government certified by CLIA (http://www.cms.gov/Regulations-and-Guidance/Legislation/CLIA/), which allows for these laboratory test results to be used to guide patient care when interpreted by a physician [53]. The processed slides are then sent to the consulting pathologist for morphoproteomics analysis. Each slide is examined individually under the microscope. The protein analyte activity is based on a light microscopic assessment of one or more of the following: the chromogenic signal intensity in cytoplasmic, nuclear, and plasmalemmal (cell) membrane; phosphorylation at putative sites of activation of the molecule using phosphospecific IHC probes, when available; translocation within subcellular compartments; and/or correlative expressions (functional grouping). The percentage of cells expressing specific proteins associated with the speed of tumor development and metastasis (spread) is also determined. This, along with the mitotic index, provides information as to whether the tumor cells are actively dividing – important because some drugs only work when the tumor cells are actively cycling. The consulting pathologist interprets the protein activity pattern, the significance of the molecular profile for treatment options, and makes recommendations to the patient's oncologist based on published literature.

The morphoproteomics approach has been used for more than a decade for insights into rare or recurrent cancers including mesenchymal chondrosarcoma [54], relapsed acute lymphoblastic leukemia [55], head and neck squamous cell carcinoma [53], glioblastoma multiforme (GBM) [56], high-risk neuroblastoma [57], high-grade prostatic intraepithelial neoplasia and prostate cancer [58], cervical squamous carcinoma [59], Ewing family of tumors [60]; anaplastic [61], papillary, and follicular thyroid carcinoma [62]; pediatric brain tumors [63], clear cell sarcoma of the kidney [64], desmoplastic small round cell tumor [65], phyllodes breast tumors [66], sinonasal undifferentiated carcinoma [67], and refractory Hodgkin's lymphoma [68]. Such studies have shown proof-of-concept of the success of this approach for nonstandard cancers, and it is now available as "Consultative Proteomics," a clinical service offered through the Department of Pathology and Laboratory Medicine at the University of Texas Medical School at Houston.

2.3.2 Biomedical Analytics (Fig. 2.1(4–10))

2.3.2.1 Analytics Analytics is a scientific discipline that uses a wide range of quantitative and qualitative approaches to identify meaningful patterns in data in order to make better decisions. The methods fall into three major categories:

descriptive analytics, predictive analytics, and prescriptive analytics. In business analytics, descriptive analytics is used for pattern analysis of historical data; in clinical use, it is used to diagnose, categorize, and describe a disease based on phe notype or typical appearance patterns. In business, predictive analytics is used to find hidden data relationships that may suggest future industry or sales trends; in clinical prognosis, it is used to project the likely disease progression and outcomes over time. Prescriptive analytics integrates information from descriptive and predictive analytics, along with related but heterogeneous data to support decision making. In business, prescriptive analytics is used to suggest new ways to achieve business goals; in clinical practice, it can be used to suggest treatment that will bring a person back to health. Biomedical analytics encompasses the development, extension, and application of theories and methods from analytics to biomedical research and clinical practice.

2.3.2.2 Methods Statistical techniques have been the mainstay of descriptive and predictive analytics; however, they have drawbacks when applied to the practice of medicine. For example, clinical trial studies require more than 300 matched patients to have sufficient predictive power to show treatment safety and benefit [69]. Clinical trials support evidence-based medicine for the average patient who has the average response to the average treatment. Unfortunately, a number of patients fall outside the norm, and physicians have to rely on individual case studies and their own expertise to help the patient.

Pathway analysis through biomedical analytics supports biomedical decision making in small studies or individual cases by using the patient's molecular data to "bootstrap" the production of additional data in the form of biological pathway networks that can be analyzed and compared. Methods used include statistics, matrix algebra, graph theory, and data mining (automatic and manual) to evoke and analyze the molecular pathway data. For example, statistics can be used for dimensionality reduction of input data, as Vaudel did with MS to select the proteins to be evaluated or was done in the shock/trauma study described in the following (see *Input preprocessing in general*, *Fig. 2.1(4)*). Lists of molecule names can be represented as vectors with "0" or "1" per element and embedded as columns or rows in a matrix for algebraic comparisons (Fig. 2.2). Molecular interactions represented visually as directed or undirected graphs can be represented as matrices, thus facilitating comparative analyses using mathematics ranging from simple matrix addition and subtraction to algebraic graph theory. The patterns evoked from the analysis can be used to narrow down or expand the scope of a basic science research study or to suggest approaches for patient care based on pathway dysregulation. Note that biomedical analytics is used to generate hypotheses about biological mechanisms, not confirm them; results must be validated through standard methods such as laboratory tests, imaging, expert opinion, or a patient's response to treatment.

2.3.2.3 Pathway Generation Software (Fig. 2.1(6, 7)) Although the molecular pathways themselves can be generated manually by data mining molecular interaction pathway databases, several online commercial pathway analysis programs are

ID	MOF-Time 1	MOF-Time 2	MOF-Time 3	MOF-Time 4	MOF-Time 5	MOF-Time 6
M1	1	1	0	1	0	1
M2	0	1	0	1	1	0
⋮	⋮	⋮	⋮	⋮	⋮	⋮
M193	1	1	0	0	1	0

ID	NMOF-Time 1	NMOF-Time 2	NMOF-Time 3	NMOF-Time 4	NMOF-Time 5	NMOF-Time 6
M1	0	0	1	0	1	0
M2	0	1	1	1	0	0
...	...	...	...	...	...	...
M193	0	0	1	0	1	0

Figure 2.2 Example of temporal matrices used to compare output molecule lists in the multiple organ failure (MOF) and nonmultiple organ failure (NMOF) study. ID, molecular ID; M column, $N = 1$–193 named molecules evoked by IPA in both outcomes. There was a 1 in the time T column if $M(N)$ was present in that time period and 0 otherwise.

available including MetaCore (http://thomsonreuters.com/site/systems-biology/), Qiagen's Ingenuity Pathway Analysis (IPA) (www.ingenuity.com), and Pathway Studio (http://www.elsevier.com/online-tools/pathway-studio) as well as noncommercial programs such as Reactome (http://www.reactome.org/). These programs output the most likely pathway network graphs derived from manual or automated data mining of biomedical literature and public and proprietary molecular interaction databases. The molecular pathways are represented as network graphs, with the molecules as vertices (nodes) and the molecular interactions as directed arcs (edges) that can be interrogated online for links back to the original information source.

2.3.2.4 Biomedical Analytics Algorithms Pre- and postprocessing algorithms addressed two major challenges of using pathway analysis software for proteomics: first, the pathway programs are primarily designed to take high-throughput input such as DNA/RNA sequencing data or microarray data; second, the programs are limited in export and analysis capabilities. To create algorithms to interface with pathway analysis software, it was necessary to understand how the program generates pathway networks. Therefore, we examined Qiagen's IPA because its pathway generation algorithm was published (http://www.ingenuity.com/wp-content/themes/ingenuity-qiagen/pdf/ipa/IPA-netgen-algorithm-whitepaper.pdf) and so input, processing, and output constraints could be evaluated.

IPA takes as input a list of genes (or proteins) with or without numerical expression data; it grows the likely pathway networks starting with the most interconnected molecules by name in the input list, and then examines the expression or "rank" data to decide the order and placement of additional molecules. Each generated network is limited to 35 molecules, and one input list may generate several networks. By examining the IPA algorithm, the data type "Intensity" was selected because it had a range of 0 to $+\infty$ and would handle a variety of biomedical measures. Other data types such as p-value and fold change were not applicable. For output, IPA supports data export of the lists of the molecules in the networks; however, the networks themselves can only be interrogated online or exported as graphs. This limits comparative analysis of molecular interactions across pathway networks. Both input and output interfaces with IPA were addressed by algorithms specific to the biomedical studies.

2.3.2.5 Input Preprocessing in General (Fig. 2.1(4)) For studies with many patients with many measured molecules, data are selected by dimensionality reduction through nonparametric or parametric statistical methods as appropriate. For example, in a prospective observational study of disease progression in shock trauma, concentrations of 27 blood serum cytokine molecules were measured by immunoassay in 48 patients every 4 h for 24 h [70]. The goal was to find molecular patterns associated with multiple organ failure (MOF) or nonorgan failure (NMOF) in each time period. Nonparametric statistical analysis (Mann–Whitney–Wilcoxon) identified the significant molecules in each of the six time periods for the two outcomes. Their molecular identifiers and median values (converted from pg/ml to pmol/l for consistency with biological signaling processes) were used as input to IPA under the data type "Intensity" that allows values from 0 to $+\infty$ [71].

2.3.2.6 Output Postprocessing in General (Fig. 2.1(7, 8)) Resolution of the second issue, output analysis, can be complex, particularly for studies that generate many networks. Although IPA has added more analysis functionality to its software over the years, only a few networks can be compared at the same time and this must be done online, interactively. As a result, more complex analyses require that the output results be mapped to matrices that can be compared in spreadsheets. Extensive molecule lists or multiple networks require computational support through mathematical software such as MATLAB (http://www.mathworks.com/products/matlab/). IPA outputs lists of the network molecules, which, as vectors, can be assembled into matrices for analysis. However, IPA does not export lists of the molecular interactions (node-directed edge–node) in a network; this must be done by visual inspection of the network graph and an adjacency (node to node) or incidence (edge to node) matrix constructed manually for further computational analysis.

In the shock trauma study (*vide supra*), linear algebra was used to analyze the nodes and edges in the IPA evoked networks. Two matrices were constructed, one for the outcome of MOF and the other for NMOF (see Fig. 2.2 for an example of the temporal matrices constructed). The first matrix column held the molecular IDs of all 193 molecules evoked over all patients over the six time periods. Columns 2–7 represented each time period. In each molecule row, a 1 was placed if the molecule was present in that outcome, and a 0 otherwise; then the matrices were compared and contrasted through logical and arithmetic combinations.

For example, adding the matrices resulted in a 2 if the molecule was present in both outcomes in the same time period, 1 if present in either of the outcomes in the same period, and 0 if absent in that outcome in that time period. The matrix analysis identified seven "neighbor" molecules that differentiated outcomes over time, of which four had never been associated with trauma. The more complex "edge" analysis used graph theory and linear algebra to identify the changing patterns in 4 key functions of molecular interactions (or edges) over time. This analysis also assessed crosstalk, or redundant functional signaling across edges, using the novel metric "XTALK" which was based on the rank of the incidence matrix of the edges [71]. Despite its potential for insights into molecular interactions, edge analysis was not usually carried out for complex networks because it must be done manually due to IPA's lack of edge export capability.

Finally, this method has been confirmed by experimental findings in a mouse model of hemophilia A in a cytokine study of the cellular immune response to clotting factor VIII (FVIII), an essential blood-clotting factor. It was predicted that a newly discovered T-cell-associated cytokine (IL-25) would be associated with development of immune response to FVIII. Follow-up experimental assays confirmed the secretion of this protein by immune cells in mice that generated anti-FVIII response [72].

2.3.3   Integrating Morphoproteomics and Biomedical Analytics

Although morphoproteomics excels at identification and expert interpretation of visible protein circuitries, many proteins present in a tissue or biofluid sample cannot be seen simply because there are no antibodies for them. These unknown proteins affect treatment decisions. Biomedical analytics can be used to infer unknown neighboring molecules based on a list of focus molecules, with or without measures. Generally, morphoproteomics and biomedical analytics produce reports that are not only descriptive but also prescriptive, using validated protein signatures to evoke their likely molecular pathways that influence therapy.

With morphoproteomics reports as the data source (Fig. 2.1(1–3)), biomedical analytics required a different approach than the shock trauma and hemophilia studies. It was not feasible to group and compare patients statistically by outcome because each patient had a unique case of recurrent or refractory (hard-to-treat) cancer that had progressed beyond the standard of care. Comparing a single patient's disease progression over time was hindered by the fact that tumor tissue biopsies were taken over long intervals, unlike the blood draws taken every 4 h in the shock trauma study. Finally, the morphoproteomics raw data scores were calculated in different measures and accompanied by qualitative modifiers. Therefore, new biomedical analytics algorithms were developed for input preprocessing and output postprocessing.

2.3.3.1   Input Preprocessing for Morphoproteomics (Fig. 2.1(4))   Although IPA can take immunoassay cytokine data as input to evoke the likely biological pathway networks as described previously, IPA was not designed to handle heterogeneous IHC data. Morphoproteomics produces semiquantitative data of protein analyte activity in tissue as observed on a slide by a pathologist; measurement units differ depending on the protein. Most protein activity is measured in ranges. There are 15 ranges of histology scores (x to y, $x \leq y$), with x and y values of 0, +/− (meaning 0.5), 1, 2, or 3. The histology score is given for each location (nucleus = N, cytoplasm = C, and plasmalemmal membrane = P) of the protein analyte, as well as the percentage of positive cells in the tumor. A few proteins are measured in percentages or numerically, such as High Powered Fields (HPF). In consultation with the pathologists, each range was normalized to 0–100, with 0 representing no activity, and 100 representing maximum activity and coverage for the range 3 to 3 (3–3+ in pathology

TABLE 2.2   Protein Activity Scores Normalization Worksheet for Pathway Generation (excerpt)

Protein Analyte	UNIPROT_Name	UNIPROT_ID	Path. Score	Norm. Score
c-Myc	MYC_HUMAN	P01106	0–3+, N	45.31
CD8	CD8A_HUMAN	P01732	30/HPF	30.00
IGF-1R(Tyr1165/1166)	IGF1R_HUMAN	P08069	±2+,C–P	32.50
p-c-Met (Tyr1234/1235)	MET_HUMAN	P08581	0–3+. P	45.31
p53	P53_HUMAN	P04637	<1%, N	1.00
ERCC-1	ERCC1_HUMAN	P07992	0–3+, N	45.31

scoring notation). Other non-range scores were also normalized to a 100 scale. In addition, certain proteins, such as mTOR (mammalian target of rapamycin) have different UNIPROT IDs, depending on whether they are localized to the nucleus or the cytoplasm. In that case, two instances of the protein were entered into the worksheet. An excerpt of the normalization worksheet can be seen in Table 2.2.

From this worksheet, a two-column spreadsheet was input online to IPA, with the UNIPROT ID in column 1 and the Normalized Score in column 2, entered as "Intensity." An IPA "Core Analysis" was performed on these data to evoke the most likely pathways.

However, because the IPA algorithm uses only the names of the input molecules at the start of pathway network generation, the effect of the actual scores on "breaking ties" in molecule choice was not seen until later in the network generation process. This means that input lists with the same molecule names will generate the same sets of networks up to a point; after that, the scores influence the network generation. Not only was there a bias from the pathologist's selection of protein analytes, there was also a "search bias" due to IPA's network generation algorithm. The pathologist's biased analyte choice was minimized by expert opinion documented in the morphoproteomics report. To minimize search bias, the biomedical analytics approach generated a second IPA "Core Analysis" based on a "control" single column spreadsheet with only the UNIPROT IDs in column 1. In the previous shock trauma and hemophilia studies, a control list with molecule names only was not required because those studies analyzed multiple rather than single patients (Fig. 2.1(5, 6)).

2.3.3.2   Output Postprocessing for Morphoproteomics (Fig. 2.1(7, 8, left))   Analysis of the resulting pathway networks was done visually for individual cases or by conversion of the output lists or pathway network graphs to matrices when many networks were compared. Evoked pathway networks that were identical in both patient and control were ignored; in matrix form, they would be subtracted out. These common pathways were interpreted as being indicative of similar underlying mechanisms; on the other hand, they could be artifacts of the IPA network generation data mining algorithm.

Once the pathway networks unique to the patient were identified (Fig. 2.1(9)), IPA was used interactively on each network to show the influence of the proposed drug therapy on the likely biological mechanisms (Fig. 2.1(7, right, 8, right)). Supporting literature references were gathered from IPA and augmented by additional manual research for the Biomedical Analytics Report (Fig. 2.1(10)).

2.4 CASE STUDIES

Although the morphoproteomic analysis process remains the same, the choice of the computational and qualitative methods used in biomedical analytics varies depending on the biomedical questions being addressed. Here, we present three applications of our integrative approach. First, biomedical analytics used morphoproteomic data to evaluate the impact of proposed therapy on a patient with advanced pancreatic cancer. In the second example, morphoproteomics and biomedical analytics were used retrospectively to gain insights into why a specific therapy reversed the course of disease in a patient with Hodgkin's lymphoma. Finally, morphoproteomics data from a brain cancer (GBM) were combined with published data defining a molecular hypoxia signature to provide additional evidence of the role of a low oxygen, or hypoxic, microenvironment in cancer that parallels the hypoxic environment in embryonic development.

2.4.1 Clinical: Therapeutic Recommendations for Pancreatic Adenocarcinoma

Pancreatic adenocarcinoma is a cancer that originates in exocrine cells of the pancreas. In this 2013 case study, we were contacted by the patient's oncologists to consult on treatment for a pancreatic adenocarcinoma that, despite over 2 years of neoadjuvant chemotherapy and chemoradiotherapy, had metastasized to the lungs. Immunotherapy was under consideration and a genomic profile report had been prepared.

Morphoproteomic analysis of the tumor tissue (Fig. 2.1(1–3)) scored 34 measured protein analytes by cellular compartment and microanatomical region and made detailed therapeutic recommendations based on the measured molecular signature, the genomic profile, and published research findings. One key morphoproteomic recommendation was a caution as to the efficacy of immunotherapeutic strategies, due to the existing favorable ratio of protein analytes that indicated that the patient's immune system was already quite active. Immunotherapy might not be effective; in fact, it could cause harm or discomfort for the patient and pose the risk of the development of immune dysregulation and of autoimmune-type diseases.

Biomedical analytics was then performed to gain additional insights into the biological pathways that were likely active. The patient's morphoproteomic scores were normalized (Fig. 2.1(4)) and entered into IPA, along with an unscored control list (Fig. 2.1(5)). The patient list and the control list each evoked 8 pathway networks of 35 molecules each (Fig. 2.1(6, 7)). The network molecule lists were exported and combined into matrices to compare which molecules were present in both patient and control, or only in one or the other (Fig. 2.1(8, left)).

Networks #1, #2, #3, #5, #6, and #7 were ignored because they were identical in patient and control; #4 and #8 differed. In Network #4, 11 of the 35 molecules

(a)

(b)

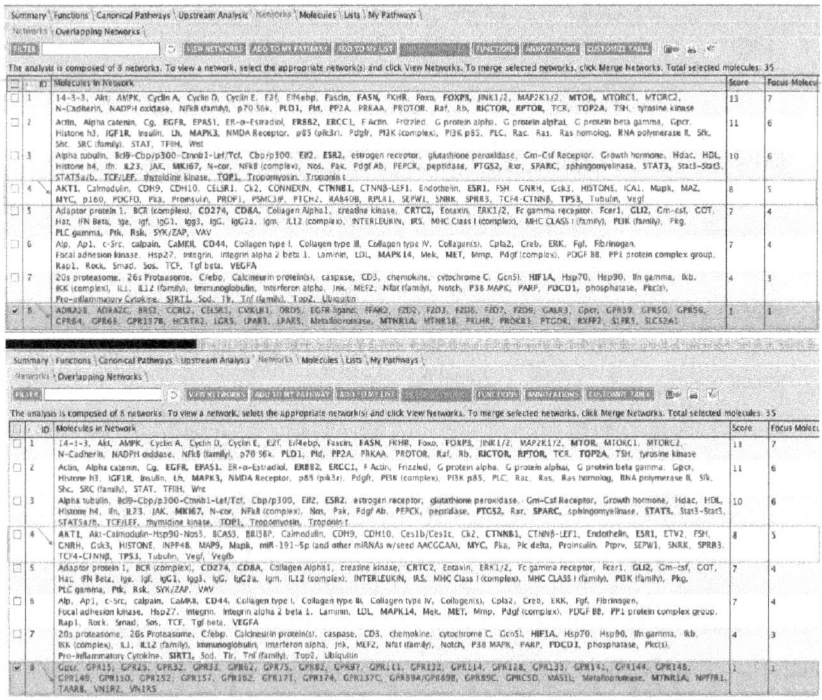

Figure 2.3 Case study. Pancreatic adenocarcinoma. (a) Patient – eight pathway networks evoked from the patient's normalized scores. (b) Control – eight pathway networks evoked from the same protein name list without scores. Only networks #4 and #8 differ.

differentiated the patient from the control. There were major hubs at the molecules MYC and TP53, consistent with the genomic report. In Network #8, 32 of 35 molecules differentiated the patient from the control (see Fig. 2.3 for molecule lists (Fig. 2.1(9, left)); network graphs not shown).

The control evoked 27 general G-protein-coupled receptors around the hub Gpcr, while the patient's network #8 evoked only 6 general G-protein-coupled receptors around the hub Gpcr; the rest were specialized G-protein-coupled receptors associated with carcinogenesis. There was no immune cell trafficking associated with network #4 in either the control or the patient. However, the patient's network #8 had extensive interactions with immune cell trafficking; there was no immune cell trafficking in the control network #8 (Fig. 2.1(10)).

Proposed drugs included celecoxib, metformin, melatonin, trametinib selumetinib, vorinostat, and lovastatin (see Fig. 2.4 for a summary network graph of the proposed drugs and their interactions with molecules associated with immune response in network #8 (Fig. 2.1(8, 9)).

The biomedical analytics supported the morphoproteomic report that the patient's immune system was already very active; drugs that overly increased immune response were to be avoided. The consulting pathologist took this into consideration

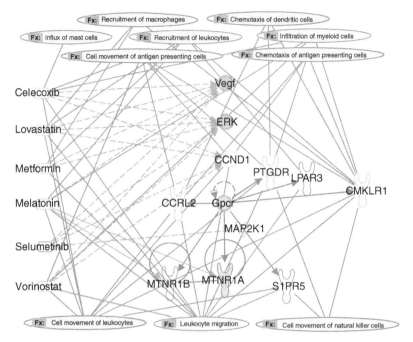

Figure 2.4 Case study: Pancreatic adenocarcinoma, network #8 (edited for clarity) – immunosurveillance and proposed drug therapy. Legend: Proposed drugs: ovals on left. Interactions of drugs with protein analyte molecules (middle): lines (dashed = indirect, solid = direct). Protein analytes: gray = measured by morphoproteomics; white = evoked by IPA. Fx long ovals at top and bottom identify the drugs and protein analyte molecules associated with immune cell trafficking functions. *Source.* Network generated through the use of QIAGEN's Ingenuity® Pathway Analysis (IPA®, QIAGEN Redwood City, www.qiagen.com/ingenuity).

and proposed a combinatorial therapy that included selumetinib, one of the drugs that targeted both networks #4 and #8 (Fig. 2.1(10)).

2.4.2 Clinical: Biology Underlying Exceptional Responder in Refractory Hodgkin's Lymphoma

Hodgkin's lymphoma is a white blood cell cancer characterized by distinctive cell types. Although it may be controlled by standard treatment in patients with early stage disease, some patients continue to relapse. In this 2012 case study, the patient had a history of persistent and extensive Hodgkin's lymphoma and had undergone more than 3 years of standard therapy. The patient researched the disease and came to the oncologist with the request for palliative therapy with an mTOR inhibitor and a histone deacetylase (HDAC) inhibitor before hospice admission. The patient had a dramatic response to the therapy, and the oncologist requested morphoproteomic analysis and biomedical analytics to gain insights into the mechanisms underlying this exceptional remission response.

As in the previous case study, the morphoproteomic report data were quantified, normalized, and entered, along with the control data, into the pathway generation software (Fig. 2.1(1–6)). Molecules unique to the patient were identified (Fig. 2.1(7, left, 9)), and additional pathological findings were added to the pathway network graph (Fig. 2.1(7, right, 8)). The interaction of the proposed drugs, rapamycin and vorinostat, with the evoked pathways was diagrammed (Fig. 2.1(9)) and formatted to show the molecules' cellular locations (see Fig. 2.5).

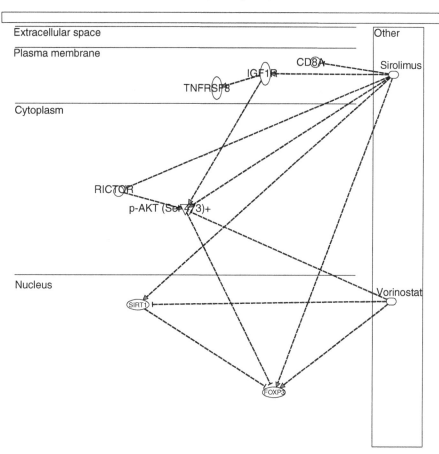

Figure 2.5   Case study: Hodgkin's lymphoma exceptional responder. The combination of the drugs (right), sirolimus and vorinostat, brought key molecules in immune response (left) back into balance. As a result of understanding this control mechanism from morphoproteomics and biomedical analytics, the therapy is now in clinical trials. *Source.* Network generated through the use of QIAGEN's Ingenuity® Pathway Analysis (IPA®, QIAGEN Redwood City, www.qiagen.com/ingenuity).

The integrated biomedical and morphoproteomic analyses (Fig. 2.1(10)) suggested that there was an immune dysregulation of the autoimmune type in Hodgkin's lymphoma that could be managed by rapamycin (sirolimus), generally an mTOR (Raptor) inhibitor, which also expands the T-regulatory cells and vorinostat, an HDAC (SIRT1) inhibitor. This combinatorial therapy used downregulation (t-bar lines) and upregulation (arrow) of key protein expressions in the lymphoma to bring the immune system back into balance. The sirolimus/vorinostat therapy is in an IRB approved phase 1b clinical trial (NCT01266057) and shows promising results, even for patients who have undergone previous therapies [68].

2.4.3 Research: Role of the Hypoxia Pathway in Both Oncogenesis and Embryogenesis

An hypoxic or low-oxygen microenvironment is required for embryonic stem cells to transform into a developing fetus. Similarly, tumor stem cells adapt and proliferate in a hypoxic environment. Cancer therapies targeted to restrict the development of new blood vessels in a tumor may inadvertently make tumor cells more hypoxic, leading to metastatic and recurrent disease.

In this research study, we used morphoproteomics and biomedical analytics to define a conceptual model of an adaptive hypoxia pathway in GBM, an aggressive brain cancer. Archival materials from IRB approved GBM morphoproteomic studies were used. GBM protein analyte scores were normalized and entered into IPA, along with an unscored control (Fig. 2.1(1–5)). Then, 32 unscored molecules from a recognized hypoxia gene signature [73] were also entered into IPA (Fig. 2.1(5)). The control list and the GBM list were differentiated by one unique pathway network of 35 molecules (Fig. 2.1(6, 7, left)). Due to the smaller networks, visual analysis was performed rather than matrix analysis (Fig. 2.1(8)).

The evoked control pathway network showed 11 unique interactions with the hypoxia gene network, while the evoked GBM pathway network showed 17 unique interactions with the hypoxia gene network (Fig. 2.1(9)); see Figure 2.6. Interactions common to both were not counted. The results show the influence of hypoxia in GBM. Both control and GBM networks had a major hub at HTT, a molecule that modulates embryogenesis. GBM had four molecules associated with increased embryogenesis while the control had a molecule that modulates embryogenesis and is implicated in early neuronal development (Fig. 2.1(10)).

The five-drug therapy proposed by morphoproteomics spanned both the GBM pathway network and the hypoxia gene signature network (Fig. 2.1(7, right, 9)). The morphoproteomic results, supported by the biomedical analytics, identified the presence of an adaptive hypoxia pathway in GBM similar to that in embryogenesis, and suggested that cancer treatment should be evaluated to consider if the drugs would increase tumor hypoxia, thus causing the tumor to adapt, proliferate, and resist treatment (Fig. 2.1(10)) [74].

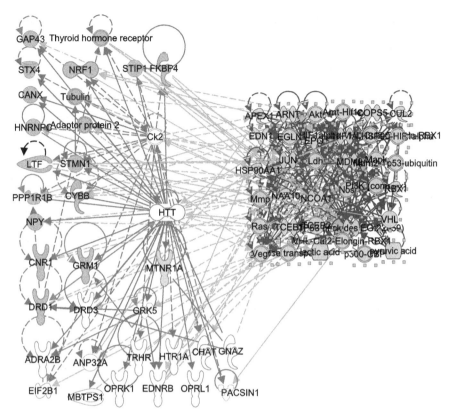

Figure 2.6 Research: Glioblastoma Multiforme (GBM) brain cancer network (left) shows extensive interactions with the hypoxia molecular signature (square formation, right). Legend: Protein analytes (left only): gray = unique to GBM (except MTNR1A); white and MTNR1A = in GBM and control. Interaction lines (dashed = indirect, solid = direct). *Source.* Network generated through the use of QIAGEN's Ingenuity® Pathway Analysis (IPA®, QIAGEN Redwood City, www.qiagen.com/ingenuity).

2.5 DISCUSSION

There is no "standard of care" for recurrent or refractory cancers, and oncologists are faced with making new treatment decisions when previous treatments have failed. Interpretation of molecular signatures and assessment of the current adaptive state of the tumor require specialized expertise, and pathologists are being encouraged to move beyond diagnosis and tumor grading to become involved in patient care [75].

Here, we have shown an integrated method that uses data from the pathologist's morphoproteomic assessment of the protein circuitries in a tumor to evoke biological pathway graphs that can be analyzed visually or computationally through linear algebra and statistical analysis. The combined results of morphoproteomics and biomedical analytics show what key activities are underway in the tumor at the time of biopsy, how those activities are likely influenced by nearby molecular interactions, and what treatments will likely work – or not.

The case studies given as illustrations show proof-of-concept of our integrative approach for medical decision making for recurrent or refractory cancers. As with all analytics methods applied to business or medicine, the results depend on accurate input data, choice of analysis methods, and expert interpretation of results. Here are some of the considerations to be taken into account. Although we are accumulating case studies that may lead to clinical trials, we are currently restricted to working with patients who have failed standard treatment. As a result, findings from an individual case may not be generally applicable. Biological pathway databases are constantly updated; this means that pathway analyses may change over time, with the benefits and drawbacks of revised interpretations. Finally, morphoproteomic analysis, as such, has limited availability: it must be performed by specially trained pathologists with access to certified CLIA laboratories.

Not only does the novel integration of morphoproteomics and biomedical analytics advance the field of clinical proteomics, it is at the forefront of team medicine. The combined methodology bridges the gap between the silos of basic science research and clinical care through context-dependent algorithms. Team approaches, such as this, that include biologists, mathematicians, computer scientists, and clinicians are just beginning to be adopted for preclinical and clinical research; they require key individuals who can translate across the disciplines [76].

2.6 CONCLUSIONS

Much in the same way that business analytics can link an individual company's data to external information such as industry norms, marketing trends, and global economic conditions, so can biomedical analytics link an individual person's data to the vast literature and databases of molecular interactions, genomic, proteomic and metabolic investigations, cellular and organ behavior, and disease case and population studies. The challenge is how to analyze the resulting integrated heterogeneous, multilevel "big data" to gain descriptive, predictive, and prescriptive insights to aid in decision making. The biomedical analytics approach creates new algorithms and computational methods to integrate molecular and clinical data for diagnosis, prognosis, and therapy in disease progression as well as to expand upon deterministic and probabilistic research models [77].

Here, we have shown that pathologists, with their access to multilevel patient data, are at the leading edge of the molecular revolution in clinical medicine. Biomedical analysts can integrate and analyze this data. And, as part of the clinical team, both can improve patient care.

ACKNOWLEDGMENTS

The authors thank Keri Csencsits Smith, Ph.D., for her constructive comments and suggestions.

REFERENCES

[1] Garman KS, Nevins JR, Potti A. Genomic strategies for personalized cancer therapy. Hum Mol Genet 2007;16(2):R226–R232.

[2] Schrijver I, Aziz N, Farkas DH, Furtado M, Gonzalez AF, Greiner TC, et al. Opportunities and challenges associated with clinical diagnostic genome sequencing: A report of the Association for Molecular Pathology. J Mol Diagn 2012;14:525–540.

[3] Sparano J, Ostrer H, Kenny P. Translating genomic research into clinical practice: Promise and pitfalls. Am Soc Clin Oncol Educ Book 2013:15–23.

[4] Roti G, Stegmaier K. Genetic and proteomic approaches to identify cancer drug targets. Br J Can 2012;106:254–261.

[5] Pollack A, Drugmakers' Fever for the Power of RNA Interference Has Cooled. In The New York Times; 2011.

[6] Weinberg RA. *The Biology of Cancer*. 2nd ed. Garland Science; 2013.

[7] Weinberg RA. Coming full circle–from endless complexity to simplicity and back again. Cell 2014;157:267–271.

[8] Elstein AS, Shulman LS, Sprafka SA. *Medical Problem Solving: An Analysis of Clinical Reasoning*. Boston: Harvard University Press; 1978.

[9] Elstein AS. Thinking about diagnostic thinking: A 30-year perspective. Adv Health Sci Educ Theory Pract 2009;14(Suppl 1):7–18.

[10] Schmutz J, Wheeler J, Grimwood J, Dickson M, Yang J, Caoile C, et al. Quality assessment of the human genome sequence. Nature 2004;429:365–368.

[11] Naidoo N, Pawitan Y, Soong R, Cooper DN, Ku CS. Human genetics and genomics a decade after the release of the draft sequence of the human genome. Hum Genomics 2011;5:577–622.

[12] Black DL. Mechanisms of alternative pre-messenger RNA splicing. Annu Rev Biochem 2003;72:291–336.

[13] Skotheim RI, Nees M. Alternative splicing in cancer: Noise, functional, or systematic? Int J Biochem Cell Biol 2007;39:1432–1449.

[14] Olsson N, Wallin S, James P, Borrebaeck CA, Wingren C. Epitope-specificity of recombinant antibodies reveals promiscuous peptide-binding properties. Protein Sci 2012;21:1897–1910.

[15] Sugiura Y, Setou M. Matrix-assisted laser desorption/ionization and nanoparticle-based imaging mass spectrometry for small metabolites: A practical protocol. Methods Mol Biol 2010;656:173–195.

[16] Petricoin EE, Paweletz CP, Liotta LA. Clinical applications of proteomics: Proteomic pattern diagnostics. J Mammary Gland Biol Neoplasia 2002;7:433–440.

[17] Ivanov MV, Levitsky LI, Lobas AA, Panic T, Laskay UA, Mitulovic G, et al. Empirical multidimensional space for scoring peptide spectrum matches in shotgun proteomics. J Proteome Res 2014;13:1911–1920.

[18] Kornblau SM, Coombes KR. Use of reverse phase protein microarrays to study protein expression in leukemia: Technical and methodological lessons learned. Methods Mol Biol 2011;785:141–155.

[19] Vaudel M, Venne AS, Berven FS, Zahedi RP, Martens L, Barsnes H. Shedding light on black boxes in protein identification. Proteomics 2014;14:1001–1005.

[20] LaBaer J. Improving international research with clinical specimens: 5 achievable objectives. J Proteome Res 2012;11:5592–5601.

[21] Kothmaier H, Rohrer D, Stacher E, Quehenberger F, Becker KF, Popper HH. Comparison of formalin-free tissue fixatives: a proteomic study testing their application for routine pathology and research. Arch Pathol Lab Med 2011;135:744–752.

[22] Chen CP, Haas-Kogan D. Neoplasms of the hepatobiliary system: Clinical presentation, molecular pathways and diagnostics. Expert Rev Mol Diagn 2010;10:883–895.

[23] Dadzie OE, Neat M, Emley A, Bhawan J, Mahalingam M. Molecular diagnostics–an emerging frontier in dermatopathology. Am J Dermatopathol 2011;33:1–13; quiz 14–16.

[24] Bohndiek SE, Brindle KM. Imaging and 'omic' methods for the molecular diagnosis of cancer. Expert Rev Mol Diagn 2010;10:417–434.

[25] Brown RE. Morphogenomics and morphoproteomics: A role for anatomic pathology in personalized medicine. Arch Pathol Lab Med 2009;133:568–579.

[26] Diaz JI, Cazares LH, Semmes OJ. Tissue sample collection for proteomics analysis. Methods Mol Biol 2008;428:43–53.

[27] Wisztorski M, Lemaire R, Stauber J, Menguelet SA, Croix D, Mathe OJ, et al. New developments in MALDI imaging for pathology proteomic studies. Curr Pharm Des 2007;13:3317–3324.

[28] Chaerkady R, Pandey A. Applications of proteomics to lab diagnosis. Annu Rev Pathol 2008;3:485–498.

[29] Takikita M, Chung JY, Hewitt SM. Tissue microarrays enabling high-throughput molecular pathology. Curr Opin Biotechnol 2007;18:318–325.

[30] Chen J. Facing difficulties, marching to future. Zhonghua Bing Li Xue Za Zhi 2006;35:642–643.

[31] Schubert W, Bonnekoh B, Pommer AJ, Philipsen L, Bockelmann R, Malykh Y, et al. Analyzing proteome topology and function by automated multidimensional fluorescence microscopy. Nat Biotechnol 2006;24:1270–1278.

[32] Johnson MD, Floyd JL, Caprioli RM. Proteomics in diagnostic neuropathology. J Neuropathol Exp Neurol 2006;65:837–845.

[33] Okuducu AF, Hahne JC, Von Deimling A, Wernert N. Laser-assisted microdissection, techniques and applications in pathology (review). Int J Mol Med 2005;15:763–769.

[34] Chaurand P, Sanders ME, Jensen RA, Caprioli RM. Proteomics in diagnostic pathology: Profiling and imaging proteins directly in tissue sections. Am J Pathol 2004;165:1057–1068.

[35] Bedossa P. Proteomique et pathologie. Ann Pathol 2003;(1):S25–S26.

[36] Waters MD, Olden K, Tennant RW. Toxicogenomic approach for assessing toxicant-related disease. Mutat Res 2003;544:415–424.

[37] Kiechle FL, Holland-Staley CA. Genomics, transcriptomics, proteomics, and numbers. Arch Pathol Lab Med 2003;127:1089–1097.

[38] Angeletti C. Application of proteomic technologies to cytologic specimens. A review. Acta Cytol 2003;47:535–544.

[39] Pierobon M, Wulfkuhle J, Liotta L, Petricoin E. Application of molecular technologies for phosphoproteomic analysis of clinical samples. Oncogene 2014;34:805–814.

[40] Iliuk AB, Arrington JV, Tao WA. Analytical challenges translating mass spectrometry-based phosphoproteomics from discovery to clinical applications. Electrophoresis 2014;35:3430–3440.

[41] Ranganathan S, Williams E, Ganchev P, Gopalakrishnan V, Lacomis D, Urbinelli L, et al. Proteomic profiling of cerebrospinal fluid identifies biomarkers for amyotrophic lateral sclerosis. J Neurochem 2005;95:1461–1471.

[42] Mirabeau O, Perlas E, Severini C, Audero E, Gascuel O, Possenti R, et al. Identification of novel peptide hormones in the human proteome by hidden Markov model screening. Genome Res 2007;17:320–327.

[43] Sanders ME, Dias EC, Xu BJ, Mobley JA, Billheimer D, Roder H, et al. Differentiating proteomic biomarkers in breast cancer by laser capture microdissection and MALDI MS. J Proteome Res 2008;7:1500–1507.

[44] Baek JH, Kim H, Shin B, Yu MH. Multiple products monitoring as a robust approach for peptide quantification. J Proteome Res 2009;8:3625–3632.

[45] McDonnell LA, van Remoortere A, van Zeijl RJ, Dalebout H, Bladergroen MR, Deelder AM. Automated imaging MS: Toward high throughput imaging mass spectrometry. J Proteomics 2010;73:1279–1282.

[46] Vafadar-Isfahani B, Ball G, Coveney C, Lemetre C, Boocock D, Minthon L, et al. Identification of SPARC-like 1 protein as part of a biomarker panel for Alzheimer's disease in cerebrospinal fluid. J Alzheimers Dis 2012;28:625–636.

[47] Balluff B, Elsner M, Kowarsch A, Rauser S, Meding S, Schuhmacher C, et al. Classification of HER2/neu status in gastric cancer using a breast-cancer derived proteome classifier. J Proteome Res 2010;9:6317–6322.

[48] Rower C, Vissers JP, Koy C, Kipping M, Hecker M, Reimer T, et al. Towards a proteome signature for invasive ductal breast carcinoma derived from label-free nanoscale LC-MS protein expression profiling of tumorous and glandular tissue. Anal Bioanal Chem 2009;395:2443–2456.

[49] Rower C, Ziems B, Radtke A, Schmitt O, Reimer T, Koy C, et al. Toponostics of invasive ductal breast carcinoma: combination of spatial protein expression imaging and quantitative proteome signature analysis. Int J Clin Exp Pathol 2011;4:454–467.

[50] Daly DS, Anderson KK, White AM, Gonzalez RM, Varnum SM, Zangar RC. Predicting protein concentrations with ELISA microarray assays, monotonic splines and Monte Carlo simulation. Stat Appl Genet Mol Biol 2008;7:Article21.

[51] Brown RE. Morphoproteomics: Exposing protein circuitries in tumors to identify potential therapeutic targets in cancer patients. Expert Rev Proteomics 2005;2:337–348.

[52] Tan D. Morphoproteomics: A novel approach to identify potential therapeutic targets in cancer patients. Int J Clin Exp Pathol 2008;1:331–332.

[53] Brown RE, Zhang PL, Lun M, Zhu S, Pellitteri PK, Law A, et al. Morphoproteomic and pharmacoproteomic rationale for mTOR effectors as therapeutic targets in head and neck squamous cell carcinoma. Ann Clin Lab Sci 2006;36:273–282.

[54] Brown RE. Morphoproteomic portrait of the mTOR pathway in Mesenchymal chondrosarcoma. Ann Clin Lab Sci 2004;34:397–399.

[55] Brown RE, Bostrom B, Zhang PL. Morphoproteomics and bortezomib/dexamethasone-induced response in relapsed acute lymphoblastic leukemia. Ann Clin Lab Sci 2004;34:203–205.

[56] Brown RE, Law A. Morphoproteomic demonstration of constitutive nuclear factor-kappaB activation in glioblastoma multiforme with genomic correlates and therapeutic implications. Ann Clin Lab Sci 2006;36:421–426.

[57] Brown RE, Tan D, Taylor JS, Miller M, Prichard JW, Kott MM. Morphoproteomic confirmation of constitutively activated mTOR, ERK, and NF-kappaB pathways in high risk neuro-blastoma, with cell cycle and protein analyte correlates. Ann Clin Lab Sci 2007;37:141–147.

[58] Brown RE, Zotalis G, Zhang PL, Zhao B. Morphoproteomic confirmation of a constitutively activated mTOR pathway in high grade prostatic intraepithelial neoplasia and prostate cancer. Int J Clin Exp Pathol 2008;1:333–342.

[59] Feng W, Duan X, Liu J, Xiao J, Brown RE. Morphoproteomic evidence of constitutively activated and overexpressed mTOR pathway in cervical squamous carcinoma and high grade squamous intraepithelial lesions. Int J Clin Exp Pathol 2009;2:249–260.

[60] Zenali MJ, Zhang PL, Bendel AE, Brown RE. Morphoproteomic confirmation of constitutively activated mTOR, ERK, and NF-kappaB pathways in Ewing family of tumors. Ann Clin Lab Sci 2009;39:160–166.

[61] Liu J, Brown RE. Morphoproteomics demonstrates activation of mTOR pathway in anaplastic thyroid carcinoma: A preliminary observation. Ann Clin Lab Sci 2010;40:211–217.

[62] Liu J, Brown RE. Morphoproteomic confirmation of an activated nuclear factor-small ka, CyrillicBp65 pathway in follicular thyroid carcinoma. Int J Clin Exp Pathol 2012;5:216–223.

[63] Wolff JE, Brown RE, Buryanek J, Pfister S, Vats TS, Rytting ME. Preliminary experience with personalized and targeted therapy for pediatric brain tumors. Pediatr Blood Can 2012;59:27–33.

[64] Dhamne S, Brown RE, Covinsky M, Dhamne C, Eldin K, Tatevian N. Clear cell sarcoma of kidney: Morphoproteomic analysis reveals genomic correlates and therapeutic options. Pediatr Dev Pathol 2013;16:20–27.

[65] Subbiah V, Brown RE, Jiang Y, Buryanek J, Hayes-Jordan A, Kurzrock R, et al. Morphoproteomic profiling of the mammalian target of rapamycin (mTOR) signaling pathway in desmoplastic small round cell tumor (EWS/WT1), Ewing's sarcoma (EWS/FLI1) and Wilms' tumor(WT1). PLoS One 2013;8:e68985.

[66] Jardim DL, Conley A, Subbiah V. Comprehensive characterization of malignant phyllodes tumor by whole genomic and proteomic analysis: Biological implications for targeted therapy opportunities. Orphanet J Rare Dis 2013;8:112.

[67] Ansari M, Guo S, Fakhri S, Citardi MJ, Blanco A, Patino M, et al. Sinonasal undifferentiated carcinoma (SNUC): Morphoproteomic-guided treatment paradigm with clinical efficacy. Ann Clin Lab Sci 2013;43:45–53.

[68] Subbiah V, Brown RE, McGuire MF, Buryanek J, Janku F, Younes A, et al. A novel immunomodulatory molecularly targeted strategy for refractory Hodgkin's lymphoma. Oncotarget 2014;5:95–102.

[69] Evans CH Jr, Ildstad ST. *Small Clinical Trials: Issues and Challenges.* Washington, DC: National Academy Press, 978-0309073332; 2001.

[70] Jastrow KM 3rd, Gonzalez EA, McGuire MF, Suliburk JW, Kozar RA, Iyengar S, et al. Early cytokine production risk stratifies trauma patients for multiple organ failure. J Am Coll Surg 2009;209:320–331.

[71] McGuire MF, Iyengar MS, Mercer DW. Data driven linear algebraic methods for analysis of molecular pathways: Application to disease progression in shock/trauma. J Biomed Inf 2012;45:372–387.

[72] McGuire MF. Pathway semantics: An algebraic data driven algorithm to generate hypotheses about molecular patterns underlying disease progression, PhD Dissertation, School of Biomedical Informatics, University of Texas Health Science Center at Houston, Houston; 2011.

[73] Fardin P, Barla A, Mosci S, Rosasco L, Verri A, Versteeg R, et al. A biology-driven approach identifies the hypoxia gene signature as a predictor of the outcome of neuroblastoma patients. Mol Can 2010;9:185.

[74] Brown RE, McGuire MF. Oncogenesis recapitulates embryogenesis via the hypoxia pathway: Morphoproteomics and biomedical analytics provide proof of concept and therapeutic options. Ann Clin Lab Sci 2012;42:243–257.

[75] Al-Zaid T, Somaiah N, Lazar AJ. Targeted therapies for sarcomas: new roles for the pathologist. Histopathology 2014;64:119–133.

[76] McGuire MF, Enderling H, Wallace DI, Batra JS, Jordan M, Kumar S, et al. Formalizing an integrative multidisciplinary cancer therapy discovery workflow. Can Res 2013;73:6111–6117.

[77] McGuire MF, Iyengar MS, Mercer DW. Computational approaches for translational clinical research in disease progression. J Investig Med 2011;59:893–903.

3

CHARACTERIZATION AND MONITORING OF NONLINEAR DYNAMICS AND CHAOS IN COMPLEX PHYSIOLOGICAL SYSTEMS

HUI YANG

Department of Industrial and Manufacturing Engineering, The Pennsylvania State University, University Park, PA, USA

YUN CHEN

Complex Systems Monitoring, Modeling and Analysis Laboratory, Department of Industrial and Management Systems Engineering, University of South Florida, Tampa, FL, USA

FABIO LEONELLI

Cardiac Electrophysiology Laboratory, James A. Haley Veterans' Hospital, Tampa, FL, USA

3.1 INTRODUCTION

Nonlinear dynamics arise whenever multifarious entities of a system cooperate, compete, or interfere. Effective monitoring and control of nonlinear dynamics will increase system quality and integrity, thereby leading to significant economic and societal impacts. For example, heart disease is responsible for one in every four deaths in the United States, amounting to an annual loss of $448.5 billion [1]. Realizing a better quality of cardiac operations will reduce healthcare costs and improve the health of our society. Figure 3.1a shows nonlinear waveforms of 1-lead electrocardiogram (ECG) signals when human heart maintains blood circulation

Healthcare Analytics: From Data to Knowledge to Healthcare Improvement, First Edition.
Edited by Hui Yang and Eva K. Lee.
© 2016 John Wiley & Sons, Inc. Published 2016 by John Wiley & Sons, Inc.

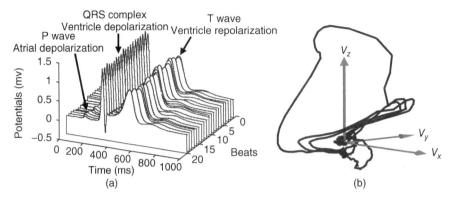

Figure 3.1 Examples of physiological signals: (a) 1-lead ECG in aligned ECG cycles and (b) ECG trajectories in the 3D phase space.

through *orchestrated depolarization and repolarization* of cells. It is common to observe the near-periodic patterns but with hidden temporal variations between heart cycles in these physiological signals. Figure 3.1a shows some of the following common characteristics of ECG signals. (i) Within one cycle, the signal waveforms at different segments change significantly. The reason is that different segments often correspond to different stages of cardiac operations. (ii) Between cycles, the signals are similar to each other but with variations. Near-periodical beatings of human heart provide nourishments to all parts of body and maintain vital living organs.

As complex physiological systems evolve in time, dynamics deal with change. Whether the system settles down to the steady state, undergoes incipient changes, or deviates into more complicated variations, it is dynamics that help analyze system behaviors. Figure 3.1b shows an example of the ECG phase space constructed from multilead ECG signals using the Takens' embedding theorem [2]. As multiple sensors are deployed at various locations, distributed sensing provides multidirectional views of nonlinear dynamics in the underlying processes. Traditional linear methodologies focus on the analysis of *time-domain signals* and attempt to understand a system's behavior by breaking it down into parts and then combining all constituent parts that have been examined separately. This idea underlies such methods as principal component analysis (PCA), Fourier analysis, and factor analysis. These methods encounter difficulties in capturing nonlinear, nonstationary, and high-order variations. The breakthrough in nonlinear theory came with Poincaré's geometric thinking of dynamical systems [3, 4], *which focuses on geometric analysis of nonlinear trajectories in the phase space* (see Fig. 3.1b).

Physiological sensing brings the proliferation of measurements of process dynamics (e.g., action potentials, ECG signals, echocardiogram). The challenge now is to harness and exploit nonlinear complexity underlying sensing signals for quality and integrity improvements in cardiac operations. However, multisensing capabilities are not fully utilized to extract information about nonlinear dynamics in the *phase-space domain*. Particularly, nonlinear dynamical systems defy understanding based on the traditional reductionist's approach, in which one attempts to understand a system's behavior by combining all constituent parts that have been analyzed separately. For example, clinicians had thought that drugs that significantly reduce arrhythmic behaviors in isolated cardiac cells would also do so in the heart until the concept was proven wrong by the failure of two large clinical trials [5]. In order to cope with system complexity and increase information visibility, modern healthcare systems are investing in advanced physiological sensing and patient monitoring, thereby giving rise to big data. Realizing the full potential of big data for healthcare intelligence requires fundamentally new methodologies to harness and exploit complexity. However, available nonlinear dynamics techniques are either not concerned with healthcare objectives or fail to effectively analyze big data to extract useful information for improving healthcare services. There is an urgent need to develop analytical methodologies that fully utilize nonlinear dynamics and chaos principles for advancing healthcare services with exceptional features such as personalization, responsiveness, and superior quality.

Over the past few decades, the theory of nonlinear dynamics has emerged as a powerful technique in the design of superconducting circuits [6], chatter control in mechanical systems [7], laser stabilization [8], precise fabrication of nanomaterials [9], and information security [10]. In addition, several investigations into characterization and modeling of physiological systems, from the cellular level to the system level, have begun to adapt nonlinear dynamics and chaos principles. This chapter reviews some theoretical developments and tools to advance the applications of nonlinear dynamics principles in health care. Specifically, we focus on the authors' recent investigations into sensor-based characterization and modeling of nonlinear dynamics in physiological systems. Case studies and applications in the studies of heart rate variability (HRV) and space–time ECG signals are presented. We hope that our limited and focused review will spur further development of nonlinear dynamics methodologies for improving healthcare services and accelerating the discovery of scientific knowledge in biomedical research.

The remainder of this chapter is organized as follows: Section 3.2 presents a primer on basic concepts of nonlinear dynamics and chaos. Section 3.3 presents two methods (i.e., multifractal analysis and multiscale recurrence quantification) for sensor-based characterization and modeling of nonlinear dynamics. Section 3.4 provides the case studies that adapt principles of nonlinear dynamical systems for healthcare applications. Section 3.5 presents the discussion and conclusions arising out of this study.

3.2 BACKGROUND

Nonlinear dynamics theory has emerged as an important methodology for complex systems modeling and analysis. The basic idea is to model the state evolution of underlying processes by a set of nonlinear differential equations, that is, $\ddot{X} = \frac{dX}{dt} = F(X, \theta), F \in \mathbb{R}^n \to \mathbb{R}^n$, where X is a multidimensional state variable, F is the nonlinear function, and θ is the model parameter. Thus, the solution, that is, $X = f(X(0), t)$, generates a trajectory representing the flow of state evolution

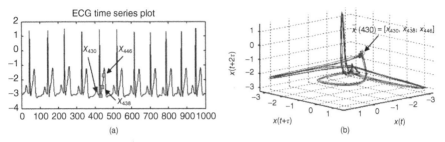

Figure 3.2 An example of time-delay reconstruction: (a) ECG time series and (b) lag-reconstructed ECG attractor.

for a given initial condition $X(0)$. When there is a small perturbation in θ or $X(0)$, the dynamics of a nonlinear process undergo abrupt changes and reveal complex characteristics, including chaos, recurrences, fractals, and bifurcations. Notably, linear systems often attribute irregular behaviors of the system to random external inputs, but nonlinear systems can produce very chaotic data with purely deterministic equations and without stochastic inputs.

Much of the complexity in real-world systems is known to emerge from the underlying nonlinear stochastic dynamics. The exhibited signals from complex systems are often chaotic in nature with irregular behaviors. However, dynamics manifest in the vicinity an attractor **A** (e.g., ECG attractor shown in Fig. 3.2b), an invariant set defined in an m-dimensional state space. Takens' delay embedding theorem [11] shows that system dynamics can be adequately reconstructed by using the time-delay coordinates of the individual measurements because of the high dynamic coupling existing in physical systems. For the time series $X = \{x_1, x_2, \ldots, x_N\}^T$, state vector $\vec{x}$ (Fig. 3.2a) is reconstructed using a delay sequence of $\{x_i\}$ as $\vec{x}(i) = [x_i, x_{i+\tau}, \ldots, x_{i+\tau(m-1)}]$, where m is the embedding dimension and τ is the time delay. Figure 3.2 shows an example of time-delay reconstruction of 3D ECG state attractor from the 1D ECG time series. The optimal embedding dimension m suffice to unfold the attractor is determined by false nearest neighbor (FNN) method [12]. In addition, mutual information [13] is used to minimize both linear and nonlinear correlations for the choice of optimal time delay τ.

If the time delay τ is too small, the attractor will be *restricted to the diagonal* of the reconstructed phase space. However, if the time delay is too large, reconstructed attractor no longer represents the true dynamics. In the literature, there are two traditional approaches for the selection of time delay τ. The first approach is to increase the τ value and then visually inspect that which τ gives the most spread out attractor. The disadvantage of visual inspection is that it only achieves satisfactory results for simple systems. The second approach is autocorrelation function (delay τ):

$$r_\tau = \frac{\sum_{i=1}^{N-\tau}(x_i - \bar{x})(x_{i+\tau} - \bar{x})}{\sum_{i=1}^{N}(x_i - \bar{x})^2}$$

Optimal τ is required to minimize the linear independence, that is, the value when the autocorrelation function first passes through 0. Yet, autocorrelation is a second-order quantity evaluating merely linear dependency among data. Notably, mutual information quantifies both linear and nonlinear dependency between two variables x_i and y_j, which is defined as

$$I(x, y) = \sum_{i,j} p(x_i, y_j) \log \frac{p(x_i, y_j)}{p(x_i) p(y_j)}$$

where $p(x, y)$ is the joint probabilistic distribution, $p(x)$ and $p(y)$ are marginal probabilities. Figure 3.3 shows the practical implementation to compute the mutual information. In the scatter plot of two variables x and y, the histogram is shown for each variable. Marginal probabilities $p(x_i)$ and $p(y_j)$ are computed as the number of points in x_i and y_j divided by the total number of points in the 2D space. The joint probability $p(x_i, y_j)$ is computed as the number of points in box (x_i, y_j) divided by the total number of points in the space. Optimal τ is selected to minimize the general dependency between variables, that is, the first local minimum of Mutual Information function.

The method of FNN was first proposed by Kennel et al. to determine the minimal embedding dimension m suffice to reconstruct system dynamics [12]. In other

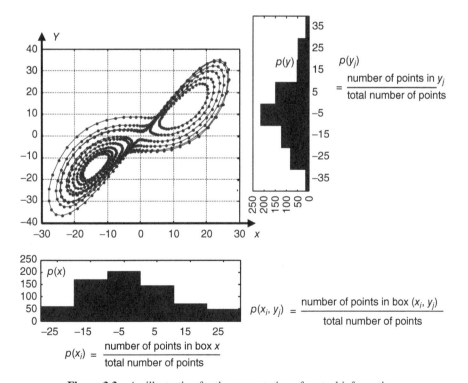

Figure 3.3 An illustration for the computation of mutual information.

words, FNN method is to reconstruct the abstractor in the m-dimensional space that preserves dynamical properties of complex systems in the original phase space. Most importantly, the minimal dimension needs to guarantee the diffeomorphism of reconstruction without any information being lost but without adding unnecessary information. Suppose a m-dimensional attractor is projected to the lower dimensional space (m' dimension and $m' < m$). Due to this projection, the topological structure of the m-dimensional attractor is no longer preserved. Some states are projected into neighborhoods of other states, but they are not true neighbors in the higher dimensional space. These states are called "false neighbors." An optimal dimension for time-delayed embedding is the smallest dimension that minimizes the number of "false neighbors." However, a larger dimension than the optimum leads to excessive computation when investigating the dynamical properties. "Noise" will populate and dominate the extra dimension of the space where no dynamics is operating. The basic idea of FNN is to measure the distances between a state and its nearest neighbors as this dimension increases. This distance should not change if the states are really nearest neighbors.

For a given time series $X = \{x_1, x_2, \ldots, x_N\}^T$, we calculate the change of distances between neighboring states when the embedding dimension is increased from m to $m + 1$. If the embedding dimension is high enough, then the fraction of false neighbors is zero, or at least sufficiently small. The state vector in m-dimensional space is

$$x(i) = (x_i, x_{i+\tau}, \ldots, x_{i+\tau(m-1)})$$

Let us denote the r th nearest neighbor of $x(i)$ by $x^{(r)}(i)$, then the Euclidean distance between $x(i)$ and its neighbor is

$$R_m^2(i, r) = \sum_{k=0}^{m-1} (x_{i+k\tau} - x_{i+k\tau}^{(r)})^2$$

If the embedding dimension is increased from m to $m + 1$, the $(m + 1)$ th coordinate is added to each state vector $x(i)$. Therefore, the distance between $x(i)$ and the rth nearest neighbor that we identified in the mth dimension is

$$R_{m+1}^2(i, r) = R_m^2(i, r) + (x_{i+m\tau} - x_{i+m\tau}^{(r)})^2$$

Then the FNN criterion (i.e., relative change in the distances between neighbors) is

$$\left(\frac{R_{m+1}^2(i, r) - R_m^2(i, r)}{R_m^2(i, r)} \right)^{1/2} = \frac{|x_{i+m\tau} - x_{i+m\tau}^{(r)}|}{R_m(i, r)} > R_{tol}$$

where R_{tol} is the threshold. We now examine the relative change in the distance as a way to see if the states are not really close together when increased to a higher dimensional space.

3.3 SENSOR-BASED CHARACTERIZATION AND MODELING OF NONLINEAR DYNAMICS

Nonlinearity is one of the most ubiquitous properties of physiological systems. Sensor signals capture rich information on the underlying nonlinear dynamics in physiological processes. Linear systems often attribute irregular behaviors of the system to random external inputs, but nonlinear systems can produce chaotic data with purely deterministic equations and without stochastic inputs. Modeling and analysis of nonlinear systems are more challenging than those for a linear system. Effective strategies for modeling and monitoring of physiological systems need to consider enormous amount of sensing data as well as the nonlinear evolution of state variables in the underlying process. In this section, we present a detailed review of two methodologies, namely, multifractal analysis and multiscale recurrence quantification for sensor-based characterization and modeling of nonlinear dynamics.

3.3.1 Multifractal Spectrum Analysis of Nonlinear Time Series

3.3.1.1 Fractal Dimension   The dimension is generally defined as the minimal number of coordinates one has to use to describe a point within the space. For example, a line needs one coordinate to specify a point on it, and therefore its dimension is 1. Similarly, the dimension of a plane is 2 and the dimension of a cube is 3. The *topological dimension* of a set X takes integer values and is defined by induction as 1 + the dimension of its boundary. In other words, the set X has a dimension of d if $\forall x \in X$, there is an arbitrarily small neighborhood of x whose boundary has a dimension of $d - 1$. A set is zero dimensional if there is an arbitrarily small neighborhood of any point x whose boundary is empty. Because the notion of boundary is well defined in mathematics, the inductive dimension effectively describes topological spaces. Indeed, the topological dimension of $\mathbb{R}^d$ is d.

However, fractals are irregular geometric objects that cannot be sufficiently specified using topological dimensions. Fractal objects are self-similar, that is, look similar regardless of the magnification. If one zooms in or out the fractal set, its geometric shape has a similar appearance. Hence, fractal dimension is introduced to describe such "infinitely complex" fractal objects (or shape). Notably, fractal dimension is not topological. Figure 3.4 illustrates the concepts of self-similarity and fractal dimension from the perspectives of scaling and covering. If we reduce the linear size of an object in the Euclidean space $\mathbb{R}^D$ by the scaling factor a in each spatial direction, its measure (length, area, or volume) will increase to $N = a^{-D}$, where N is the number of measure elements to cover the object. As shown in Figure 3.4a, if we reduce the size of a line by $a = 1/2$, then its measure (i.e., length) will increase to $N = (1/2)^{-1} = 2$. In other words, two measure elements are needed to cover the original line. Furthermore, if we reduce the size of a line by 1/3, then its measure will be $N = (1/3)^{-1} = 3$. However, if we reduce the size of a square by 1/2, then its measure (i.e., area) will increase to $N = (1/2)^{-2} = 4$. In addition, nine measure elements ($N = (1/3)^{-2}$) are needed to cover the original square if the line size of the square is reduced by 1/3 in each spatial direction. The scaling rule also holds for the cube. If we reduce the

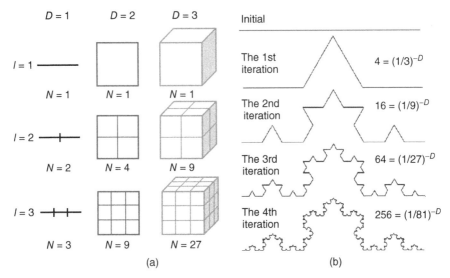

Figure 3.4 Illustration of self-similarity and fractal dimension from the perspectives of scaling and covering for (a) Euclidean geometry, that is, line, square, and cube and (b) Koch curve.

line size of a cube by 1/2 in each spatial direction, then its measure (i.e., volume) will increase to $N = (1/2)^{-3} = 8$. If we reduce the size of a square by 1/3, then its measure will be $N = (1/3)^{-3} = 27$. Figure 3.4a shows how the measure changes with respect to linear scaling. If we take log of both sides of the relationship $N = a^{-D}$, the dimension is $D = -\log N/\log a$.

The dimension D needs not to be an integer, as shown for Euclidean geometry in Figure 3.4a. Figure 3.4b shows an example of the Koch snowflake curve, which has a noninteger dimension. The Koch snowflake curve is generated by starting with a straight line, divide the line into three segments of equal lengths, and then remove the middle third of the line and replace it with two lines that have the same length (1/3) as the remaining lines in both sides. This process recursively iterates to generate the "infinitely complex" Koch curve. Figure 3.4b shows the first four iterations of the process. In each iteration, the length of the curve increases. However, the Koch snowflake curve is self-similar at all scales of magnification. If we follow the scaling and covering rule, the dimension of Koch curve is $D = -\log 4/\log\left(\frac{1}{3}\right) = 1.26$.

Fractal sets have theoretical dimensions that exceed their topological dimensions and can be noninteger values. Self-similarity across scales is a typical characteristic of fractals. Fractal dimension specifies the complexity of a fractal object by measuring the changes of coverings relative to the scaling factor. It also characterizes the space-filling capacity of a fractal object with respect to its scaling properties in the space. Many real-world objects exhibit self-similarity, for example, scribbles, dust, ocean waves, or clouds. In practice, the relationship between scaling and covering is often difficult to be determined. The box-counting method is widely used to estimate the fractal dimension of an irregular object. The basic idea is to cover a fractal set with measure elements (e.g., box) at different scales and examine how the number of boxes changes with respect to the scaling factor [14, 15]. If $N(a)$ is the number of boxes that are needed to cover a fractal object at the scale a, then the fractal dimension D_B specifies how $N(a)$ varies with respect to the scaling factor a as

$$N(a) \propto (1/a)^{D_B}$$

In general, the box-counting dimension is defined as

$$D_B := \lim_{a \to 0} \frac{\ln N(a)}{\ln(1/a)}$$

However, the box-counting dimension D_B may not exist if the limit does not exist. As the upper and lower limits always exist, the upper and lower bounds of box-counting dimension will be

$$\overline{D}_B = \limsup_{a \to 0} \frac{\ln N(a)}{\ln(1/a)}, \ \underline{D}_B = \liminf_{a \to 0} \frac{\ln N(a)}{\ln(1/a)}$$

The box-counting dimension D_B is well defined when the two bounds are sufficiently close to each other.

Figure 3.5 illustrates the use of box-counting method to calculate the fractal dimension of the Koch curve. The number of boxes $N(a)$ required to cover the Koch curve increases when the "box" size decreases, and their relationship follows the power law, that is, $\ln N(a)$ is proportional to $\ln(1/a)$. If $N(a)$ is computed for a range of a, there is a linear relationship between $\ln N(a)$ and $\ln(1/a)$. The slope is an estimate of the fractal dimension. Figure 3.6 shows the plot of $\ln N(a)$ against $\ln(1/a)$ for the Koch curve. It is shown that $\ln N(a)$ linearly increases with respect to $\ln(1/a)$ and the estimated slope is approximately 1.2849, while the theoretical fractal dimension of Koch curve is $\ln 4/\ln 3 = 1.262$.

However, there are several drawbacks in the box-counting method when estimating the dimension of a fractal set. First, if the upper and lower bounds of box-counting dimension are not close to each other, then D_B is not well defined. Second, the upper bound $\overline{D}_B$ may not be countably stable, that is, $\overline{D}_B(\bigcup_{i=1}^{\infty} X_i) \neq \sup_i \{\overline{D}_B(X_i)\}$, where

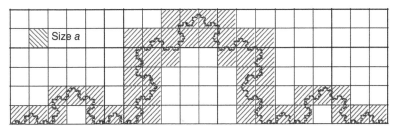

Figure 3.5 An illustration of box-counting method to cover the Koch curve with the box of size a.

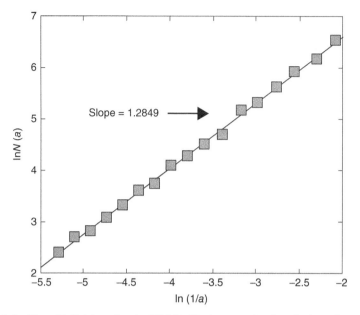

Figure 3.6   Plot of $\ln(1/a)$ against $\ln\ N(a)$ for Koch curve, the slope is the estimated fractal dimension.

X_i is the subset of a fractal set $X = \bigcup_{i=1}^{\infty} X_i$. Third, the lower bound $\underline{D}_B$ may not be finitely stable, that is, $\underline{D}_B(X_i \cup X_j) \neq \max(\underline{D}_B(X_i), \underline{D}_B(X_j))$, where $i \neq j$. Therefore, Hausdorff dimension D_H is further introduced to characterize the fractal set $X \subseteq \mathbb{R}^D$ [14]. For $\varepsilon > 0$, an ε-cover of X is a finite or countable collection of $\{B_i\}_{i=1,2,\dots}$, where the ball $B_i \subseteq \mathbb{R}^D$ and its diameter $|B_i|$ is less than or equal to ε. The δ-total length of $\{B_i\}_{i=1,2,\dots}$ is defined as $\sum_{i=1}^{\infty} |B_i|^{\delta}$. If $\{B_i\}_{i=1,2,\dots}$ is a countable cover of the fractal set X, then the δ-dimenional Hausdorff measure of X is defined to be the limit of the infimum of the δ-total length of $\{B_i\}_{i=1,2,\dots}$.

$$H^{\delta}(\mathrm{X}) = \lim_{\varepsilon \to 0} \inf \left\{ \sum_{i=1}^{\infty} |B_i|^{\delta} \ : \ \{B_i\}_{i=1,2,\dots} \text{ is the } \varepsilon - \text{cover of X} \right\}$$

The Hausdorff dimension D_H of the fractal set X exceeds its topological dimension and is defined as

$$H^{\delta}(\mathrm{X}) = \begin{cases} \infty & \text{if } \delta < D_H \\ 0 & \text{if } \delta > D_H \end{cases}$$

Furthermore, it is worth mentioning that monofractal analysis (i.e., a single fractal dimension) often fails to fully characterize complex scaling behaviors of many irregular objects in the real world [16]. Instead, multifractal analysis utilizes a spectrum of singularity exponents to provide a detailed description of complex scaling behaviors.

Let us denote μ as a measure using the ball $B_i(a)$ centered at x_i of the object. Then the singularity exponent h at location x_i will be

$$h(x_i) = \lim_{a \to 0^+} \frac{\ln \mu(B_i(a))}{\ln(1/a)}$$

The singularity spectrum $D(h)$ is the fractal dimension of the set of all the locations x such that $h(x) = h$:

$$D(h) = D_F(\{x : h(x) = h\})$$

where D_F is the fractal dimension. The singularity spectrum $D(h)$ provides a statistical distribution of singularity exponents $h(x)$. Figure 3.7a shows an example of the multifractal set, namely triadic Cantor set. The Cantor set is constructed as follows:

1. At step $k = 0$, the weight $\mu_0 = 1$ is assigned to the interval $[0, 1]$.
2. At step $k = 1$, the whole interval is divided into three subintervals of equal lengths. The new weights will be $\mu_1 = p_1 \mu_0 = p_1$ for the first subinterval $[0, 1/3]$ and $\mu_2 = p_2 \mu_0 = p_2$ for the third subinterval $[2/3, 1]$, where p_1 and p_2 are two probability values. The second subinterval will have a zero weight.
3. This process is iteratively repeated and then weights are summed over all the steps in the interval $[0, 1]$ to generate the Cantor set.

After k steps, if we consider the first interval $B_1(a = 3^{-k}) = [0, 3^{-k}]$, then the measure $\mu(B_1) = p_1^k \mu_0 = p_1^k$ at the location $x = 0$. Thus, the singularity exponent at $x = 0$ is $h(x = 0) = -\ln p_1 / \ln 3$. Similarly, one can prove that the singularity exponent at $x = 1$ is $h(x = 1) = -\ln p_2 / \ln 3$ for the last interval $B_{2^k}(a = 3^{-k}) = [1 - 3^{-k}, 1]$. If $p_1 = p_2$, then we will have a monofractal Cantor set. If $p_1 \neq p_2$, then there will be a spectrum of singularity exponents, particularly $h(x = 0) \neq h(x = 1)$. Figure 3.7a illustrates a multifractal version of triadic Cantor set with $p_1 = 0.6$ and $p_2 = 0.4$.

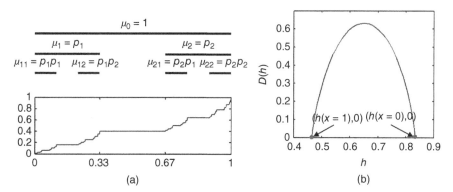

Figure 3.7 (a) Triadic Cantor set with $p_1 = 0.6$ and $p_2 = 0.4$ and (b) $D(h)$ singularity spectrum.

Moreover, the singularity exponents are $h(x = 0) = 0.834$ and $h(x = 1) = 0.465$. As such, we will have $D(h = 0.834) = D_F(\{x = 0\}) = 0$ and $D(h = 0.465) = D_F(\{x = 1\}) = 0$. Figure 3.7b shows the singularity spectrum $D(h)$. Instead of a sole singularity exponent, there is a range of singularity exponents that describes complex scaling behaviors of multifractal Cantor set.

3.3.1.2 *Continuous Wavelet Transformation* Traditionally, box-counting methods leverage the measure elements (e.g., box, square, line) at different spatial scales to cover the fractal set and then examine how the covering changes with respect to the scaling factor. Here, the fractal set refers to an irregular object in the space. The scaling factor refers to the variations of spatial scales of measure elements. However, box-counting methods are not generally applicable to measure fractal dimension of complex time series. First, the scaling factor usually refers to temporal scales instead of spatial ones for a time series. Second, time series involves a range of frequency components that are not specifically considered when dealing with an irregular object in the space. Third, the box-counting technique cannot adequately address the challenge of low-frequency trends (e.g., polynomial) in the time series and thereby fail to measure local scaling properties. New methods and tools to characterize scaling behaviors and quantify fractal dimensions of time series are urgently needed.

Therefore, wavelet functions are widely used as "boxes" in multifractal spectrum analysis of time series. Wavelet functions are building blocks that can be used to simultaneously decompose signal characteristics in both time and frequency domains. Wavelet representations delineate steady and transient components of nonstationary time series into various frequency bands while preserving the time information. In particular, wavelet transform effectively addresses polynomial trends that fail the traditional box-counting techniques. Time–frequency representation (TFR) is particularly useful for revealing the underlying hierarchy that governs the temporal distribution of local singularity exponents.

The continuous wavelet transform (CWT) is an effective TFR that overcomes the resolution problems in the short-time Fourier transform (STFT) [17]. Notably, Fourier analysis interprets the regular structure, for example, dominant frequencies in the signals, but does not provide the temporal localization of frequency components and assumes that spectral components exist at all times (i.e., stationarity). Therefore, STFT employs a local analysis scheme for TFR of nonstationary signals. STFT segments the time series into narrow time windows, narrow enough to be considered stationary, and then takes the Fourier transform of each segment. Furthermore, CWT uses a variable-length wavelet function to address the preset resolution problem of STFT. As shown in Figure 3.8, a narrower wavelet function captures high-frequency transient behaviors in a fine-grained time resolution, and the wider one characterizes low-frequency steady behaviors in a better frequency resolution.

The CWT of signal $x(t)$ using the analyzing wavelet $\psi(\cdot)$ is defined as

$$\mathrm{CWT}_x^\psi(b, a) = \Psi_x^\psi(b, a) = \frac{1}{\sqrt{|a|}} \int_t x(t) \psi^* \left(\frac{t - b}{a} \right) dt$$

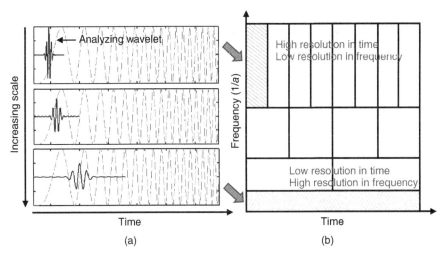

Figure 3.8 (a) Continuous wavelet transform of time series with an analyzing wavelet at different scales and time locations. (b) Time–frequency resolution of wavelet representation.

where CWT_x^ψ represents wavelet coefficients, a is the scale parameter (i.e., measure of frequency), and b is the translation parameter (i.e., measure of time). The mother wavelet $\psi(\cdot)$ is translated and scales to obtain all kernels $\psi\left(\frac{t-b}{a}\right)$. In other words, $CWT_x^\psi(b, a)$ is the cross-correlation of the signal $x(t)$ with the mother wavelet at the scale a and at the time lag of b. If $x(t)$ shares similar patterns to the wavelet function $\psi\left(\frac{t-b}{a}\right)$ at the time location b, then wavelet coefficients $CWT_x^\psi(b, a)$ will be large.

As shown in Figure 3.8a, the mother wavelet is shifted in the time domain with the translation parameter as $\psi(t - b)$ and is expanded or compressed with the scale parameter as $\psi\left(\frac{t}{a}\right)$. Because scale is inversely proportional to frequency, smaller scales correspond to more compact wavelet functions (i.e., high frequency). CWT starts with the small-scale wavelet functions (high frequency) and then proceeds to large-scale wavelet functions (low frequency) where the wavelet function is more expanded. The wavelet function is first set at the beginning of the signal. The inner product of the signal and wavelet function is then computed. The results are normalized by the factor $1/\sqrt{|a|}$, which is ensured that wavelet functions have the same energy. The wavelet function is shifted along the time direction and new coefficients will be calculated. This process is continued until reaching the end of the signal.

The variable-length wavelet function is analogous to flexible windowing in the CWT. Hence, wavelet representation provides a better time–frequency resolution as demonstrated in Figure 3.8b. As aforementioned, small-scale wavelets are more compact (i.e., similar to the use of small window in STFT) and therefore capture the high-frequency components in the time series. Large-scale wavelets are more stretched and have a bigger window size, thereby capturing the low-frequency components. As shown in Figure 3.8b, when the window size is smaller, time resolution is higher but frequency resolution is lower. However, when the window size is bigger, time resolution is lower but frequency resolution is higher. The use of variable-length wavelet functions in CWT provides a trade-off between frequency and time resolutions [17, 18], which is advantageous in multifractal spectrum analysis of complex time series that will be detailed in the next section.

3.3.1.3 *Multifractal Spectrum Analysis*

The wavelet transform modulus maxima (WTMM) method is widely used to quantify multifractal spectrum of a nonlinear time series. This wavelet-based multifractal analysis evaluates the local singularity exponent h through the CWT. Note that the WTMM method uses wavelets in different scales as the box functions to measure the self-similarity in the TFR of time series [19, 20]. Suppose μ is a measure of a fractal set, $\{B_i(a)\}_{i=1,2,\ldots,N(a)}$ is a covering of the support of μ, where $B_i(a)$ is the ith box of size a and $N(a)$ is the number of boxes. For $q \in \mathbb{R}$, the partition function $Z(q, a)$ is defined as

$$Z(q, a) = \sum_{i=1}^{N(a)} \mu_i^q(a), \quad \text{where} \quad \mu_i(a) = \mu(B_i(a)) = \int_{B_i(a)} d\mu$$

Because the rigid box function leads to smooth behaviors that will distort the singularities of time series and impair the estimation of local singularity exponent, wavelet functions are used to substitute traditional box functions. Therefore, the partition function in the new wavelet multifractal formalism is

$$Z(q, a) = \int |\Psi_x^\psi(b, a)|^q db$$

where $\Psi_x^\psi(b, a)$ are wavelet coefficients at location b and scale a. In order to improve the estimability of singularity and avoid the divergence of $Z(q, a)$ for $q < 0$, the integration is further modified to be a discrete summation over the maxima of $\Psi_x^\psi(b, a)$. Hence, the partition function is revised as

$$Z(q, a) = \sum_{l \in \mathcal{L}(a)} |\Psi_x^\psi(b_l(a), a)|^q$$

where $l \in \mathcal{L}(a)$ denotes the maxima line at the scale a, and $b_l(a)$ is the position of the maxima belonging to the line l at the scale a. Figure 3.10b shows an example of CWT, and the black lines are the maxima of wavelet coefficients. More details will be given in the later examples.

Furthermore, because the maxima line is sparse in the wavelet representation and the partition function is unstable for the negative values of q, the WTMM method defines the partition function by replacing the WTMM at the scale a by the supremum values along the maxima line at scales smaller than a:

$$Z(q, a) = \sum_{l \in \mathcal{L}(a)} (\sup_{a' \leq a} |\Psi_x^\psi(b_l(a'), a')|)^q$$

where $\Psi_x^\psi(b_l(a'), a')$ are wavelet transform coefficients at location $b_l(a')$ and scale a', $\sup_{a' \le a} |\cdot|$ is the local maxima of modulus for all scales $a' \le a$, and $l \in \mathcal{L}(a)$ denotes the maxima line at the scale a. Hence, $Z(q, a)$ is the sum of qth powers of the maxima in the wavelet modulus. When $a \to 0^+$, $Z(q, a)$ can be approximated as $Z(q, a) \cong a^{\tau(q)}$, where $\tau(q)$ is the spectrum of singularity exponents that describes the power-law scaling behavior of $Z(q, a)$ with respect to the scale a. As mentioned in Section 3.3.1.1, $\mu_i(a) \propto a^{h(x_i)}$ and $N(a) \propto a^{-D}$. Therefore, the partition function can be approximately expressed as

$$Z(q, a) = \sum_{i=1}^{N(a)} \mu_i^q(a) \cong N(a) \cdot \mu^q(a) \propto \int a^{qh - D(h)} da$$

When $a \to 0^+$, this integration is dominated by the term $a^{qh-D(h)}$. Hence, we have $\tau(q) = qh(q) - D(h)$, where the local singularity exponent $h(q)$ is not constant and is calculated as $h(q) = d\tau(q)/dq$. Furthermore, the multifractal spectrum $D(h)$ can be derived from $\tau(q)$ through a Legendre transform [21]:

$$D(h) = qh - \tau(q)$$

Furthermore, we introduce the generalized devil staircase [22] to demonstrate the differences between monofractal and multifractal sets and the use of WTMM method to derive the multifractal spectrum. The devil staircase is constructed as follows:

1. At the first step, if an interval is divided into four subintervals with equal lengths and different weights p_1, p_2, p_3, and p_4, then we will have the scale $a = 4^{-1}$ and four measures $\mu_i = |p_i|$ ($i = 1, 2, 3, 4$). As such, the partition function is $Z(q, a) = \sum_{i=1}^4 \mu_i^q(a) = |p_1|^q + |p_2|^q + |p_3|^q + |p_4|^q$.
2. If the process is iterated for each subinterval, then there will be 4^K measures (or subintervals) of size $a = 4^{-K}$ to cover the whole interval. Each measure will have the form $\prod_{k=1}^K |\tilde{p}_k|$, where $\tilde{p}_k \in \{p_i, i = 1, 2, 3, 4\}$. The partition function is $Z(q, a) = (|p_1|^q + |p_2|^q + |p_3|^q + |p_4|^q)^K$.
3. Finally, the generalized devil staircase $x_{ds}(t)$ is the cumulative distribution function of all subintervals at the Kth step.

Note that the constraint of weights is $\sum_{i=1}^4 p_i = 1$ and $p_i \in \mathbb{R}$, $i = 1, 2, 3, 4$, which is designed to reach convergence. Base on the definition of $\tau(q)$, one can prove that the singularity spectrum $\tau(q)$ is

$$\tau(q) = \frac{\ln Z(q, a)}{\ln a} = \frac{\ln (|p_1|^q + |p_2|^q + |p_3|^q + |p_4|^q)^K}{\ln \left(\frac{1}{4}^K\right)}$$

$$= -\log_4(|p_1|^q + |p_2|^q + |p_3|^q + |p_4|^q)$$

Figure 3.9a shows the devil staircase with the weights $p_1 = p_2 = -p_3 = p_4 = 0.5$. Here, $x_{ds}(t)$ is generated after six iterations, and hence the fractal set includes $4^6 = 4096$ subintervals. At each iteration of the construction, the order of weights follows exactly p_1, p_2, p_3, and p_4. Note that the devil staircase $x_{ds}(t)$ is everywhere continuous but nowhere differentiable. If we zoom into the first quarter of the devil staircase $x_{ds}(t)$, Figure 3.9b shows distinct self-similar patterns. In addition, we will have the singularity spectrum (see Fig. 3.9c) as

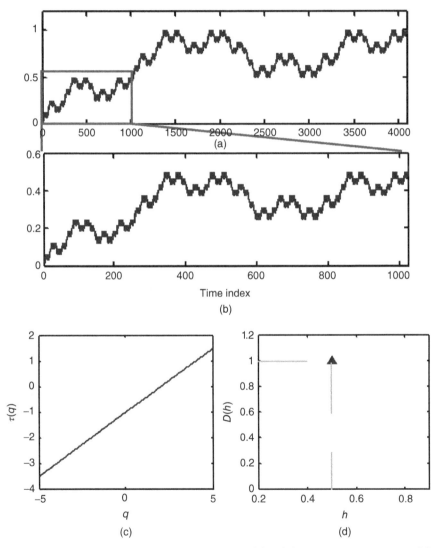

Figure 3.9   (a and b) The generalized devil staircase with weights $p_1 = p_2 = -p_3 = p_4 = 0.5$; (c) singularity spectrum $\tau(q)$ versus q; (d) multifractal spectrum $D(h)$ versus h.

$$\tau(q) = -\ln_4(|p_1|^q + |p_2|^q + |p_3|^q + |p_4|^q) = -\ln_4\left(4\left(\frac{1}{2}\right)^q\right) = \frac{1}{2}q - 1$$

Therefore, the singularity exponent will be $h(q) = d\tau(q)/dq = 1/2$. The fractal dimension is $D(h) = hq(h) - \tau(q(h)) = \frac{1}{2}q - \left(\frac{1}{2}q - 1\right) = 1$ (see Fig. 3.9d). As a result, the devil staircase with weights $p_1 = p_2 = -p_3 = p_4 = 0.5$ is monofractal.

Figure 3.10a shows the random devil staircase with weights as $p_1 = 0.69$, $p_2 = -p_3 = 0.46$, $p_4 = 0.31$, where the relation $p_1 + p_2 + p_3 + p_4 = 1$ still holds. However, at each iteration of construction, the order of weights is chosen randomly from p_1, p_2, p_3, and p_4. Here, $x_{ds}(t)$ is generated after five iterations, and hence the fractal set includes $4^5 = 1024$ subintervals. Due to the randomness in each iteration, the random devil staircase function $x_{ds}(t)$ and the singularity spectrum are difficult to be expressed analytically. Therefore, the WTMM method is used to quantify the multifractal spectrum of the random devil staircase $x_{ds}(t)$.

Figure 3.10b shows the CWT of the random devil staircase $x_{ds}(t)$, where the black lines represent maxima lines. Figure 3.10c shows $\log(Z(q,a))$ versus $\log(a)$ for different q values, which is numerically calculated based on wavelet maxima modulus and the definition of partition function $Z(q,a) = \sum_{l \in \mathcal{L}(a)} (\sup_{a' \le a} |\Psi_x^\psi(b_l(a'), a')|)^q$. Because the singularity spectrum is $\tau(q) = \frac{\ln Z(q,a)}{\ln a}$, the slope of each curve for different $q's$ in Figure 3.10c will be its corresponding $\tau(q)$. As a result, $\tau(q)$ versus q is derived as shown in Figure 3.10d. Note that light gray dots represent the values derived with the use of the WTMM method, and dark gray lines are theoretical curves $\tau(q) = -\log_4(|p_1|^q + |p_2|^q + |p_3|^q + |p_4|^q) = -\log_4(0.69^q + 0.46^q + 0.46^q + 0.31^q)$. Figure 3.10d shows that the spectrum $\tau(q)$ from the WTMM method matches with the theoretical curves. Furthermore, the multifractal spectrum $D(h)$ is derived from $\tau(q)$ through a Legendre transform. Figure 3.10e shows the multifractal spectrum $D(h)$ versus the singularity exponent h. By comparing the WTMM results with the theoretical curves, it is evident that the WTMM method is effective to extract multifractal spectra from a nonlinear time series.

3.3.2 Recurrence Quantification Analysis

Recurrence (i.e., approximate repetitions of a certain event) is one of the most common phenomena in natural and engineering systems. For example, the human heart is near-periodically beating to maintain vital living organs, and manufacturing machines are cyclically forming sheet metals during production. Real-time sensing brings the proliferation of big data (i.e., dynamic, nonlinear, nonstationary, high dimensional) from complex processes. This provides an unprecedented opportunity for data-driven characterization and modeling of nonlinear recurrence behaviors toward system informatics and control. However, most of existing approaches adopt linear methodologies for analyzing dynamic recurrences. Traditional linear methods interpret the regular structure, for example, dominant frequencies in the signals. They have encountered certain difficulties to capture the nonlinearity, nonstationarity, and high-order variations. For example, Fourier analysis does not provide the temporal localization of

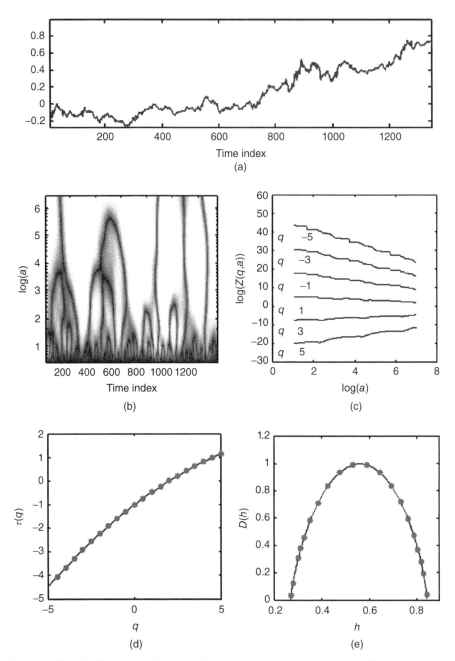

Figure 3.10 (a) The generalized devil staircase with weights $p_1 = 0.69$, $p_2 = -p_3 = 0.46$, $p_4 = 0.31$; (b) continuous wavelet transform; (c) $\log(Z(q, a))$ versus $\log(a)$; (d) $\tau(q)$ versus q; (e) $D(h)$ versus h. Note that light gray dots are calculated from the WIMM method, and the dark gray lines correspond to the theoretical curves.

frequency components and assume that spectral components exist at all times (i.e., stationarity). Instead, system diagnostics and process control are more concerned with aperiodic recurrences and nonlinear recurrence variations.

Therefore, nonlinear recurrence methodologies are urgently needed to handle the underlying complexity in the big data. Poincaré recurrence theorem shows that if a dynamical system has the measure of preserving transformation, its trajectories eventually reappear in the ε-neighborhood of former states [4]. The methodology of nonlinear recurrence analysis is emerged from the theory of nonlinear dynamics and characterizes recurrence behaviors in the high-dimensional state space. The recurrence plot was introduced by Eckmann et al. in the late 1980s [23] to characterize the proximity of states in the phase space. Mathematically, the recurrence plot is defined as $R(i,j) = \Theta(\varepsilon - \|\vec{x}(i) - \vec{x}(j)\|)$, where Θ is the Heaviside function, ε the neighborhood size, and $\| \cdot \|$ is a distance measure. For the lag-reconstructed phase space $\vec{x}(i) = (x_i, x_{i+\tau}, \ldots, x_{i+\tau(M-1)})$, $i = 1, \ldots, N - \tau(M - 1)$, which is lag-reconstructed from a time series, the computation of recurrence plot will be

$$R(i,j) = \Theta\left[\varepsilon - \sqrt{\sum_{m=0}^{M-1} (x_{i+m\tau} - x_{j+m\tau})^2}\right]$$

It is worth mentioning that if the neighborhood size ε is too small, there will be few recurrence points in the plot. Thus, we can hardly learn anything about recurrence structures. However, if ε is too large, almost every point is a neighbor of every other point. In the literature, there are several "rules of thumb" for the selection of ε: (i) a small percentage of the maximum diameter of the state space; (ii) a fixed scale region in the recurrence rate; (iii) fix the number of neighbors for every point; and (iv) take into account the standard deviation of the observational noise. An optimal choice of ε facilitates the characterization of recurrence structures and dynamical properties of complex systems.

As shown in Figure 3.11, recurrence plot captures topological relationships in the state space as a 2D image. If two states are located close to each other in the m-dimensional state space (e.g., 3D space in Fig. 3.11a), the color code is black (Fig. 3.11b). If they are located farther apart, the color is white. The structure of a recurrence plot has distinct topology and texture patterns (Fig. 3.11b). The ridges locate the nonstationarity and/or the switching between local behaviors. The parallel diagonal lines indicate the near-periodicity of system behaviors. Recurrence quantification analysis (RQA) measures intriguing structures and patterns in the recurrence plot, including small structures (e.g., small dots, vertical lines, and diagonal lines), chaos–order transitions, as well as chaos–chaos transitions. A comprehensive review on recurrence quantifiers is reported in Marwan et al., 2007 [24]. Here, we present several examples of recurrence quantifiers as follows: (i) recurrence rate (RR) – a measure of the density of recurrence points in the RP, $\text{RR} = \frac{1}{N^2} \sum_{i,j=1}^{N} R(i,j)$, where N is the number of states in the attractor; (ii) determinism (DET) – the percentage of recurrence points that form the diagonal lines, $\text{DET} = \frac{\sum_{l=l_{\min}}^{N} lP(l)}{\sum_{l=1}^{N} lP(l)}$,

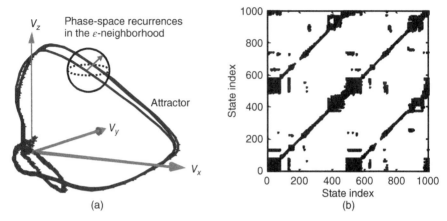

Figure 3.11 (a) An example of ECG trajectories in the 3D phase space; (b) the recurrence plot characterizes the proximity of two states $\vec{x}(i)$ and $\vec{x}(j)$, that is, $R(i,j) := \Theta(\varepsilon - \|\vec{x}(i) - \vec{x}(j)\|)$, where Θ is the Heaviside function and $\|\cdot\|$ is a distance measure.

where $P(l)$ is the histogram of diagonal line length; (iii) entropy (ENT) – Shannon information entropy for the probability distribution of the diagonal line lengths $P(l)$, $\mathrm{ENT} = -\sum_{l=l_{\min}}^{N} p(l) \ln p(l)$; (iv) laminarity (LAM) – the percentage of recurrence points that form vertical lines, $\mathrm{LAM} = \dfrac{\sum_{v=v_{\min}}^{N} vP(v)}{\sum_{v=1}^{N} vP(v)}$, where $P(v)$ is the histogram of vertical line lengths; and (v) trapping time (TT) – the average length of vertical structures, $\mathrm{TT} = \dfrac{\sum_{v=v_{\min}}^{N} vP(v)}{\sum_{v=v_{\min}}^{N} P(v)}$. RQA goes beyond the visual inspection in the RP and provides complexity measures of system dynamics. If we compute the RQA measures in small windows (submatrices) along the line of identity (LOI) of the RP, time-dependent behaviors of system dynamics will be quantified. RQA has successful applications in various disciplines, for example, physiology [25–28], biology [29], economy [30], manufacturing [31], geophysics [32], and neuroscience [28, 33].

3.3.3 Multiscale Recurrence Quantification Analysis

However, complex systems exhibit recurrence characteristics in multiple spatial and temporal scales. Most of existing recurrence methods considered the data in a single scale. In addition, recurrence computation is highly expensive, that is, a squared increase (i.e., $O(n(n-1)/2)$) with the size of data n [3]. This limits the use of recurrence approaches for big data, which are *often collected in real-time monitoring of complex systems*. Multiscale analysis is of fundamental importance to solve engineering and physics problems that have important characteristics in spatial, temporal, and/or frequency scales. For example, multiscale spatial models were developed for the prediction of weather evolution in meteorology [34] and the control of nanomaterial growth in material science [35]. Hilbert–Huang transform empirically decomposes time series into intrinsic mode functions (IMFs) via the sifting process, thereby capturing multiple instantaneous frequencies in the data [36, 37]. In addition, wavelet transform elucidates multiscale information of sensing data in the time–frequency domain [17, 38].

However, very little work has been done to investigate multiscale recurrence dynamics. Our previous research developed a novel multiscale framework to quantify recurrence dynamics in complex systems and resolve computational issues for large-scale data sets [3, 39]. As opposed to traditional single-scale recurrence analysis, we characterize and quantify recurrence dynamics in multiple wavelet scales. As shown in Figure 3.12, wavelet transform decomposes nonstationary VCG signals into various frequency bands for effectively separating the system's transient, intermittent, and steady behaviors. Wavelet packet decomposition (WPD) introduces both the wavelet function and scaling function for an efficient pyramid decomposition of signal space V_j into an approximation space V_{j+1} and a detail space W_{j+1}. The approximation space V_{j+1} and the detail space W_{j+1} are, then, divided iteratively in the next level. This provides a better resolution in both time and frequency scales. As shown in Figure 3.12, the time series $X = \{x_1, x_2, \dots, x_N\}^T$, denoted as $W_{0,0}$, is passed through the low-pass filter $G(\cdot)$ and high-pass filter $H(\cdot)$ and followed by the dyadic subsampling process in each level. This subband coding is repeated to produce the kth level coefficient sets that are denoted as $W_{k,n}$, $n = 0, \dots, 2^k - 1$. The redundancy is removed because each set $W_{k,n}$ is of length $N/2^k$, and the total length in level k is the same as the original time series X. Note that a narrower wavelet function captures high-frequency transient behaviors in a fine-grained time resolution, and the wider wavelet function characterizes

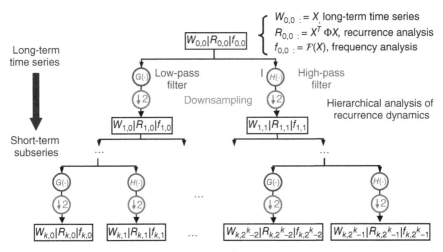

Figure 3.12   Flow diagram illustrating the WPD of a long-term time series X, as well as the hierarchical analysis of recurrence and frequency behaviors. The subband coding (i.e., low-pass filter $G(\cdot)$ and high-pass filter $H(\cdot)$) and dyadic subsampling processes decompose a long-term time series X, defined as $W_{0,0}$, into the kth level subseries that are denoted as $W_{k,n}$, $n = 0, \dots, 2^k - 1$, thereby facilitating the analysis of recurrence dynamics [40].

low-frequency steady behaviors in a better frequency resolution. Thus, a nonstationary time series is resolved into multiple nonoverlapping frequency bands. In addition, the dyadic subsampling in discrete wavelet transforms leads to the reduction of sample size. Notably, wavelet decomposition and subsampling do not lose any information. The original long-term signal can be perfectly reconstructed from wavelet coefficients.

Multiscale recurrence analysis integrates RQA into the framework of wavelet subband coding. In each wavelet scale, recurrence analysis further quantifies nonlinear system dynamics. Our previous research showed that the recurrence plot $R_{0,0}(i,j)|_{i,j=1,...,N}$ of original time series X can be perfectly reconstructed with the kth level of wavelet coefficients $W_{k,n}$ and their recurrence plots $R_{k,n}(i,j)$ [3]. Dynamical properties in the original recurrence plot are preserved after the WPD. Recurrence dynamics pertinent to the original time series are further delineated by computing the recurrence plots from the wavelet subseries $W_{k,0} \cdots W_{k,2^k-1}$. Note that many previous approaches adjusted the threshold ε for an optimal recurrence plot in the presence of noises. Multiscale recurrence analysis is more robust to observational noises because it decomposes the system behaviors into different frequency bands. For example, noises will be separated into the high-frequency band and long-term trend will go into the low-frequency band. When there is a mixture of noise, nonlinear, and nonstationary behaviors, multiscale wavelet decomposition separates the mixture of information into various wavelet scales. This further reduces the complexity of nonlinear dynamics within each scale. These shorter wavelet subseries make expensive recurrence computations not only plausible but also more effective within wavelet scales. Multiscale recurrence analysis facilitates the prominence of hidden recurrence properties that are usually buried in a single scale.

3.4 HEALTHCARE APPLICATIONS

Human heart is essentially an autonomous electromechanical blood pump that operates near-periodically to maintain vital living organs. ECG signals contain a wealth of dynamic information pertinent to cardiac operations, which is indispensable for cardiac care – from monitoring and diagnosis to treatment planning to smart health management. One-lead ECG captures 1D temporal view of space–time cardiac electrical activity. Multilead ECG systems provide multidirectional views of such space–time dynamics [2]. A normal ECG tracing is often segmented into P wave, QRS complex, and T wave (see Fig. 3.1a). Atrial depolarization (and systole) is represented by the P wave, ventricular depolarization (and systole) is represented by the QRS complex, and ventricular repolarization (and diastole) is represented by the T wave [41]. In addition, HRV refers to the fluctuations in the sequential heartbeat intervals, also called RR intervals. Heartbeat dynamics are highly pertinent to the function of autonomic nervous system. Autonomic nervous control brings a greater level of nonlinear dynamics in the presence of nonstationarity and noises. Most existing works focused on the analysis of time-domain ECG signals from a single sensor.

Time-domain algorithms were usually developed to quantify the characteristics of ECG wave deflections (i.e., P, QRS, and T waves) [42–44]. Examples of ECG features include PR interval, RR interval, ST elevation/depression, QT interval, and R amplitude. Also, Fourier analysis was utilized to transform time-domain ECGs to extract hidden features in the frequency domain [45–47]. However, Fourier analysis does not provide temporal location of frequency components and assumes that spectral components exist at all times (i.e., stationarity). Nonstationarity in cardiovascular systems fueled increasing interests in wavelet analysis of ECG signals to delineate local time and frequency information for applications such as adaptive representation [29], PQRST segmentation [48–50], noise cancellation [38], and arrhythmia recognition [51]. Furthermore, nonlinear methods were developed to reconstruct the phase space from 1-lead ECG and then characterize the dynamics of cardiovascular systems [26, 52].

However, many previous works underuse multilead ECG signals and overlook spatiotemporal dynamics in the heart. Multiple sensors at various locations on the human body respond to process changes differently. Time-domain ECG – a projected view of space–time cardiac electrical activity – diminishes important spatial information pertinent to tissue damages in the heart (e.g., myocardial infarction). Most existing methods are influenced by such an information loss, thereby failing to extract effective ECG biomarkers sensitive to cardiac malfunctions. The objective of this study reported in this section is to present two case studies on the characterization and modeling of nonlinear dynamics in cardiovascular systems. First, the approach of wavelet multifractal analysis is developed to quantify nonlinear dynamics in heart rate time series. These fractal features provide useful information about nonlinear scaling behaviors and the complexity of autonomic cardiovascular function. Second, we present a novel multiscale recurrence approach to study disease-altered nonlinear dynamics in the spatiotemporal vectorcardiogram (VCG) signals. As opposed to the traditional single-scale recurrence analysis, we characterize and quantify recurrence behaviors within multiple wavelet scales. Also, wavelet dyadic subsampling makes the expensive recurrence computations not only plausible for the long-term time series but also more effective under the stationary assumptions in multiple wavelet scales.

3.4.1 Nonlinear Characterization of Heart Rate Variability

HRV analysis plays an important role in the detection of disorders in autonomic cardiovascular function. Since the 1980s, linear and frequency-domain approaches are widely used in the HRV analysis but are limited in the ability to capture nonlinear dynamics in the long-term HRV time series. For example, Fourier analysis is efficient to transform data from time domain to frequency domain but does not provide the temporal localization of frequency components. Also, linear statistical methods, for example, analysis of variance (ANOVA), have certain difficulties to capture the nonlinearity, nonstationarity, and high-order variations. Therefore, linear methods tend to bring less realistic characterization and quantification of nonlinear time series. Notably, recent research showed that congestive heart failure (CHF), a major life-threatening cardiac disorder, leads to a loss of multifractality [16]. Heart failure is caused by a loss of cardiac ability to supply sufficient blood flows to the body. As a result, central nervous system controls the heart rate to compensate heart failure by maintaining blood pressure and perfusion, for example, increasing the sympathetic activity. However, autonomic cardiovascular function not only is nonlinear and nonstationary but is also with long-range correlations, at time scales ranging from seconds to minutes to hours. This is significantly different from acute cardiac events pertinent to only a segment of ECG signals. Therefore, long-term time series are necessary to delineate the complex long-range dependence behaviors in multiple scales for the identification of heart failures. Figure 3.13 shows examples of scaling exponents function and multifractal spectrum extracted from HRV time series of healthy control (HC) and heart failure subjects. Scaling exponents $\tau(q)$ of the healthy subject (dark gray dots) are more linear than those of heart failures (light gray crosses). Multifractal spectrum $D(h)$ is obtained through a Legendre transform from the $\tau(q)$ in Figure 3.13a. It is worth mentioning that multifractal spectrum $D(h)$ for the heart failure subject is narrower than healthy control, indicating the loss of multifractality.

This section presents our previous efforts on characterization and modeling of nonlinear dynamics in HRV time series, further evaluating their classification performances. For that purpose, we used three well-known classification algorithms, namely logistic regression (LR), k-nearest neighbor (KNN), and artificial neural network (ANN). We build three classification models for nonlinear features to benchmark the performance in detecting disorders of autonomic cardiovascular function. In this study, we analyzed the 24-h heart rate time series that are gathered from 54 healthy control (HC) subjects and 29 CHF patients, available in the PhysioNet [53]. Heart rate time series is preprocessed to eliminate erroneously large intervals and outliers due to missed beat detections following the same procedure as in [16].

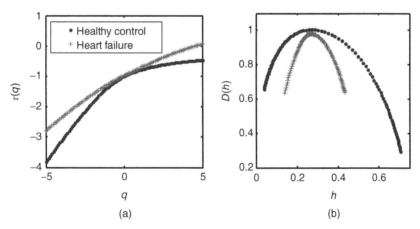

Figure 3.13 (a) Scaling exponents function: $\tau(q)$ versus q and (b) multifractal spectrum: $D(h)$ versus h extracted from heart rate variability time series of healthy control and heart failure subjects.

The preprocessing procedures include (i) a moving-window average filter and (ii) increment smoothing. For the five consecutive points in a moving window, the central point is removed if it is greater than twice the local mean calculated from the other four points. There is no interpolation in this moving-window average filter. The second step calculates differences between adjacent elements in the time series. If the successive increments have opposite sign with amplitudes >3× standard deviation of increment series, both increments will be replaced by the interpolated value in between. The new heart rate time series is, then, reconstructed from the postprocessed series of increments.

3.4.1.1 Feature Extraction We have utilized two alternative approaches, namely wavelet multifractal analysis and multiscale recurrence analysis, to extract nonlinear dynamic features from long-term heart rate time series. Features extracted in the wavelet multifractal analysis include multifractal spectrum $\tau(q)$ and fractal dimension $D(h)$. The fractal features provide useful information about nonlinear scaling behaviors and the complexity of autonomic cardiac function. For multiscale recurrence analysis, six recurrence statistics, namely RR, DET, LMAX, ENT, LAM, and TT, are exacted to quantify the nonlinear recurrence behaviors in wavelet subseries. Therefore, a total of 6×2^k recurrence features are exacted for the kth level WPD. In the case study of HRV, k is chosen from 6 to 9 for all subjects to explore the optimal decomposition level that captures the frequency ranges of disease variations. The neighborhood size ε in recurrence plots was chosen to be 5% of the maximal distance of state space. The total length of each HRV recording is pruned to be 76,000 data points to keep computational consistency for all subjects.

3.4.1.2 Feature Selection The method of sequential feature selection is used to optimally choose a subset of features that are closely correlated with the disease variations [3, 20]. Note that a large amount of features are extracted from three nonlinear approaches. As a result, this may bring the "curse of dimensionality" issues for classification models, for example, increased model parameters and overfitting problems [3, 40, 54]. In addition, such a high-dimensional feature space hinders the development of a deeper understanding of cardiac pathology. Hence, we use the strategy of sequential forward feature selection to optimally choose a subset of features that are strongly correlated with process variations. Starting from an empty feature subset, an additional feature $\jmath^+$ is selected when it maximizes the objective function $\mathcal{J}(S_\ell + \jmath^+)$, which wraps the classification model. This process is repeated until it reaches the desired subset size. Feature selection not only surmounts the model complexity and overfitting problems but also provides faster and more cost-effective models with the optimal feature subset.

3.4.1.3 Feature Analysis As shown in Table 3.1, we evaluated the individual feature separately using two statistical tests, namely unpaired t-test and Kolmogorov–Smirnov (KS) test. There are 10 features for each method that are optimally chosen by the feature selection algorithms. In the unpaired t-test, the smaller p-value indicates more evidence to reject the null hypothesis, that is, the

TABLE 3.1 Unpaired *t*-Test and KS Test for Selected Features

Statistic Tests	Analysis Methods[a]	Test Statistics									
		1st	2nd	3rd	4th	5th	6th	7th	8th	9th	10th
Unpaired *t*-test (*p*-value)	WMA	6.2e–04	3.5e–03	0.012	8.9e–04	3.1e–03	0.030	8.5e–03	0.037	0.020	3.5e–03
	MRA	2.5e–03	4.9e–03	1.8e–03	8.3e–04	0.017	2.5e–05	5.7e–03	0.251	0.153	0.050
Two-sample KS test (KS statistic)	WMA	0.613	0.372	0.324	0.467	0.425	0.343	0.430	0.343	0.375	0.433
	MRA	0.452	0.391	0.340	0.427	0.396	0.429	0.385	0.346	0.335	0.305

[a]WMA, wavelet multifractal analysis; MRA, multiscale recurrence analysis.

feature has the same distribution between HC and CHF groups. In the KS test, a larger KS statistic shows that this feature has more distinct cumulative distribution functions between the HC and CHF groups. Table 3.1 shows that two statistic tests agree on the fact that most of the features are significant, because the majority of p-values are <0.05 and KS statistic >0.3. However, 1D statistical test does not account for the feature dependence in the high-dimensional space.

3.4.1.4 Classification Performance Therefore, we carried out classification experiments with two groups of features to evaluate the combinatorial effects of multidimensional features. Three classification models are KNN, logistic regression (LR), and ANN. As shown in Figure 3.14, the bar plot is used to visualize the statistics of classification performance (i.e., sensitivity, specificity, and accuracy) that are computed from 100 random replications of the fourfold cross-validation.

Figure 3.14a shows the sensitivity, specificity, and accuracy, respectively, for features extracted from wavelet multifractal analysis of heart rate time series. Figure 3.14a demonstrates an average sensitivity of 89.41%, a specificity of 67.72%, and an accuracy of 81.83% for the logistic regression. In addition, KNN and ANN models yielded approximately similar results but with small deviations. Overall, the KNN model was shown to achieve a better accuracy (i.e., 82.44%) than the other two models. Experimental results of three classification models show that the features extracted from wavelet multifractal analysis are significant between CHF and HC subjects.

Figure 3.14b presents the classification results for features extracted from multiscale recurrence analysis of heart rate time series. Notably, multiscale recurrence features lead to generally better results for all three classification models than features extracted from wavelet multifractal analysis. Logistic regression models are shown to further improve the sensitivity to 92.28%, the specificity to 92.65%, and the accuracy to 92.52%. The ANN models are shown to yield approximately the same results (i.e., an accuracy of 92.16%) as logistic regression, but the performance of KNN models is lower than both ANN and logistic regression models. Overall, multiscale recurrence analysis delineates nonlinear and nonstationary behaviors in multiple scales of heart rate time series, and it is shown to yield better results for the classification of healthy control and heart failure subjects.

3.4.2 Multiscale Recurrence Analysis of Space–Time Physiological Signals

The human heart is a 3D object and cardiac electrical activities are near-periodically conducting across space and time. The ECG contains a wealth of dynamic information pertinent to cardiac functioning, but 1-lead ECG only captures one directional view of spatiotemporal heart activities. In contrast, 3-lead VCG monitors the spatiotemporal cardiac electrical activity along three orthogonal X, Y, Z planes of the body, namely, frontal, transverse, and sagittal [39]. However, 3-lead VCG is not as commonly used as 12-lead ECG because medical doctors are accustomed to using the time-domain ECG in clinical applications. Dower et al. [55, 56] and our previous study [57] showed that 3-lead VCG can be linearly transformed to 12-lead

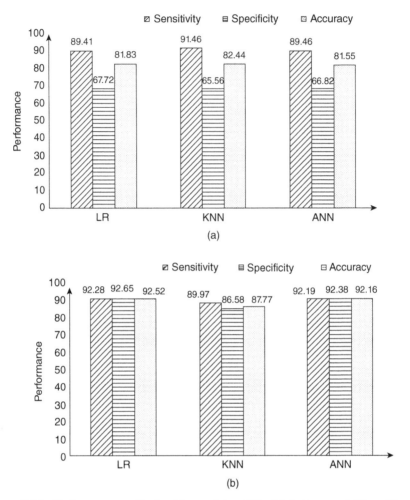

Figure 3.14 Performance results for (a) wavelet multifractal features and (b) multiscale recurrence features using three classification models – logistic regression (LR), k-nearest neighbors (KNN), and artificial neural network (ANN).

ECG without a significant loss of clinically useful information. Thus, 3-lead VCG surmounts not only the information loss in 1-lead ECG but also the redundant information in 12-lead ECG.

However, most of previous nonlinear methods only considered the lag-reconstructed state space from 1-lead ECG signals. Although 3-lead VCG provides a new way to investigate the cardiac dynamical behaviors, few previous approaches have studied the disease-altered recurrence dynamics in the space–time VCG signals. This chapter developed a novel multiscale recurrence approach to not only explore recurrence dynamics but also resolve the computational issues for the large-scale data sets. As shown in Figure 3.15, the long-term VCG signal, followed

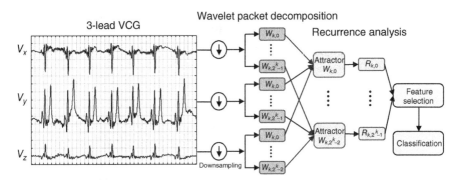

Figure 3.15 Multiscale recurrence analysis of disease-altered VCG signals.

by the dyadic subsampling, is decomposed into wavelet subseries. Each subseries is iteratively decomposed to produce 2^k subsets of wavelet subsignals, denoted as $W_{k,n}$, $n = 0, \ldots, 2^k - 1$, in the kth level. Within each wavelet scale, recurrence analysis is utilized to quantify the underlying dynamics of nonlinear systems. We performed multiscale recurrence analysis of 448 VCG recordings (368 MIs and 80 HCs) available in the PhysioNet PTB Database [53]. Each recording contains 15 simultaneous heart-monitoring signals, that is, the conventional 12-lead ECG and the 3-lead VCG.

Notably, we have previously extracted RQA features from the 3-lead VCG in the original scale for the identification of myocardial infarction subjects [58]. In addition, we utilized the DWT to decompose VCG signals into multiple wavelet scales and compute RQA features from not only the original single scale but also multiple wavelet scales [39]. It is worth mentioning that only 4000 data points in the 3-lead VCG are used for the single-scale and DWT recurrence analysis due to the computational complexity. In the study reported in this section, we further utilized wavelet packet decomposition to not only quantify multiscale recurrence dynamics but also resolve the computational issues for large-scale data sets. It may be noted that the 3-lead VCG of 16,000 data points are utilized for RQA in this present study with the use of WPD dyadic sampling.

As shown in Figure 3.16, multiscale recurrence analyses (i.e., DWT and WPD) show better performances (in terms of correct rates) than the single-scale recurrence analysis. The correct rate using DWT recurrence analysis (93.2% from 10-fold cross-validation) is 2.7% higher than the single-scale recurrence analysis (90.5% from 10-fold cross-validation). Moreover, the proposed WPD recurrence analysis increases the correct rate about 2.9% from the previous DWT recurrence analysis. The correct rate for the identification of MI subjects is 96.1% in the WPD recurrence analysis, which is about 5.6% increase from the single-scale analysis.

In the literature, little has been done to investigate multiscale variations of phase-space recurrences underlying the space–time VCG signals. Previous work focused primarily on the recurrences in time-domain signals from a single sensor. In addition, existing recurrence methods only considered the data in a single scale. Our previous research developed a novel multiscale framework to characterize

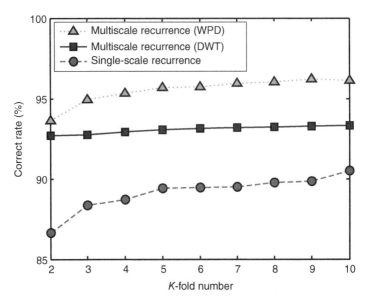

Figure 3.16   The comparison of classification performance between single-scale and multi-scale recurrence analyses.

and quantify the dynamics of transient, intermittent, and steady recurrences within wavelet scales. Multiscale recurrence analysis facilitates the prominence of hidden recurrence properties that are usually buried in a single scale. Our previous research results are summarized as follows: (i) *Single-scale versus multiscale recurrence analysis:* As opposed to the traditional recurrence analysis in a single scale, we delineate the recurrence dynamics into multiple wavelet scales. (ii) *Long-term recurrence analysis:* Few, if any, previous approaches have been capable of quantifying the recurrence dynamics from a long-term time series. Recurrence computation is highly expensive (i.e., $O(n(n-1)/2)$) as the size of time series n increases. The dyadic subsampling in WPD effectively resolves the computational issues for the large-scale recurrence analysis. (iii) *Disease-altered recurrence dynamics*: It is shown that recurrence dynamics are significantly different in wavelet scales between healthy control (HC) and myocardial infarction (MI) subjects. Multiscale recurrence analysis identifies the MI with an average sensitivity of 96.8% and specificity of 92.8%, which is much better (i.e., 5.6% increase) than the single-scale recurrence analysis.

3.5   SUMMARY

Real-world physiological systems show high level of nonlinear and nonstationary behaviors in the presence of extraneous noises. Nonlinear dynamic methods provide significant opportunities to explore the hidden patterns and relationships in complex physiological systems. This chapter presents a review of theoretical developments and tools of nonlinear dynamics principles as well as their applications in healthcare data analytics. Specifically, we showed the methodological details of multifractal spectrum analysis and multiscale recurrence analysis with case studies in modeling and analysis of HRV and space–time ECG signals. From the foregoing, it is evident that healthcare data analytics can be greatly advanced from using sensor-based characterization and modeling of nonlinear dynamics.

We first introduced the methodology of multifractal spectrum analysis and its applications to identify CHF subjects using the 24-h heart rate time series. Experimental results demonstrated the effectiveness to delineate nonlinear and nonstationary behaviors in multiple scales of time series. For the multifractal features, the logistic regression models achieve a sensitivity around 89.41% and an average specificity of 67.72%. KNN and ANN models yielded approximately similar results but with small deviations. The multifractal approach was shown to effectively capture nonlinear dynamic behaviors in the 24-h heart rate time series. In addition, logistic regression models were shown to further improve the sensitivity to 92.28%, the specificity to 92.65%, and the accuracy to 92.52% using features extracted from multiscale recurrence analysis of heart rate time series. In general, overall, multiscale recurrence analysis delineates nonlinear and nonstationary behaviors in multiple scales of heart rate time series, and it is shown to yield better results for the classification of healthy control and heart failure subjects than wavelet multifractal methods.

Furthermore, this chapter presents a novel multiscale recurrence approach to analyze the 3-lead VCG signals for the detection of MIs. Few, if any, previous work studied disease-altered nonlinear dynamics hidden in long-term spatiotemporal VCG signals. Notably, most of existing nonlinear dynamic methods considered the time-delay reconstructed phase space from 1D time series for the investigation of physiological dynamics. Computer experiments demonstrate that the proposed approach yields better performances by characterizing the nonlinear and nonstationary behaviors in multiple wavelet scales. Multiscale recurrence analysis of VCG signals leads to a superior classification model that detects the myocardial infarction with an average sensitivity of 96.8% and specificity of 92.8%, which is much better (i.e., 5.6% increase in terms of correct rates) than the single-scale recurrence analysis.

The theory of nonlinear dynamics has been primarily studied in mathematics and physics. Most of previous works have begun the adaptation of the existing results in nonlinear dynamics body of knowledge into healthcare data analytics. However, realizing the full potential of nonlinear dynamics theory for healthcare analytics calls upon the new advancement of nonlinear dynamics methodologies, as well as integration of existing nonlinear methods with healthcare analysis tools. For example, very little has been done to adapt nonlinear dynamics principles into operational analytics in healthcare systems engineering. Also, nonlinear dynamics researchers have traditionally not addressed the issues of how to construct nonlinear models from the wealth of process data and how to address noises in real-world healthcare processes. These research problems are critically important to improving the performance of healthcare systems and achieving a remarkable reduction of healthcare costs. Future research efforts addressing these problems will advance not only current healthcare practice but also enrich the theory of nonlinear dynamics and further expand its research domain to health care. We hope that our limited and focused review will inform subsequent studies that will focus on the development of novel nonlinear dynamics methodologies for improving healthcare services and optimizing healthcare systems that are so vitally important for smart health.

ACKNOWLEDGMENTS

The authors thank the National Science Foundation (CMMI-1266331, IIP-1447289, and IOS-1146882) for supporting the research presented in this book chapter. In addition, the author (Hui Yang) acknowledges the support of his PhD advisors, Dr Satish T.S. Bukkapatnam and Dr Ranga Komanduri, and his collaborator, Dr Eric S. Bennett, without whose efforts this work would not have been possible.

REFERENCES

[1] American Heart Association Writing Group. Heart disease and stroke statistics – 2014 update: A report from the American Heart Association. Circulation 2014;129:e28–e292.

[2] Yang H, Bukkapatnam STS, Komanduri R. Spatio-temporal representation of cardiac vectorcardiogram signals. BioMed Eng Online 2012;11:16.

[3] Chen Y, Yang H. Multiscale recurrence analysis of long-term nonlinear and nonstationary time series. Chaos, Solitons Fractals 2012;45:978–987.

[4] Katok A, Hasselblatt B. *Introduction to the Modern Theory of Dynamical Systems*. Cambridge University Press; 1995.

[5] Cardiac Arrhythmia Suppression Trial Investigators. Preliminary report: Effect of encainide and flecainide on mortality in a randomized trial of arrhythmia suppression after myocardial infarction. N Engl J Med 1989;321:406–412.

[6] You JQ, Nori F. Atomic physics and quantum optics using superconducting circuits. Nature 2011;474:589–97.

[7] Pratt JR, Nayfeh AH. Design and modeling for chatter control. Nonlinear Dyn 1999;19:49–69.

[8] Roy R, Murphy TW, Maier TD, Gills Z, Hunt ER. Dynamical control of a chaotic laser: Experimental stabilization of a globally coupled system. Phys Rev Lett 1992;68:1259–62.

[9] Ishikawa M. Precise fabrication of nanomaterials: A nonlinear dynamics approach. Chaos 2005;15:047503.

[10] Tenny R, Tsimring LS, Larson L, Abarbanel HDI. Using distributed nonlinear dynamics for public key encryption. Phys Rev Lett 2003;90:047903.

[11] Takens F. Detecting strange attractors in turbulence. In: David R, Lai-Sang Y, editors. *Dynamical Systems and Turbulence, Warwick 1980, Lecture Notes in Mathematics*. Springer-Verlag; 1981.

[12] Kennel MB, Brown R, Abarbanel HDI. Determining embedding dimension for phase-space reconstruction using a geometrical construction. Phys Rev A 1992;45:3403–3411.

[13] Fraser AM, Swinney HL. Independent coordinates for strange attractors from mutual information. Phys Rev A February, 1986;33:1134–1140.

[14] Mandelbrot BB. *The Fractal Geometry of Nature*. New York: Freeman; 1982.

[15] Kenkel NC, Walker DJ. Fractals in the biological sciences. Coenoses 1996;11:77–100.

[16] Ivanov PC, Amaral LAN, Goldberger AL, Havlin S, Rosenblum MG, Struzik ZR, Stanley HE. Multifractality in human heartbeat dynamics. Nature 1999;399:461–465.

[17] Yang H, Bukkapatnam STS, Komanduri R. Nonlinear adaptive wavelet analysis of electrocardiogram signals. Phys Rev E 2007;76:026214.

[18] Leduc J-P. Spatio-temporal wavelet transforms for digital signal analysis. Signal Process 1997;60:23–41.

[19] Muzy JF, Bacry E, Arneodo A. The multifracal formalism revisited with wavelets. Int J Bifurcation Chaos 1994;4:245–302.

[20] Chen Y and Yang H. A comparative analysis of alternative approaches for exploiting nonlinear dynamics in heart rate time series. In Proceedings of 2013 IEEE Engineering in Medicine and Biology Society Conference (EMBC), Osaka, Japan; 2013.

[21] Zia RKP, Redish EF, Mckay SR. Making sense of the Legendre transform. Am J Phys 2009;77:614–22.

[22] Muzy JF, Bacry E, Arneodo A. Wavelets and multifractal formalism for singular signals: Application to turbulence data. Phys Rev Lett 1991;67:3515–3518.

[23] Eckmann J, Kamphorst SO, Ruelle D. Recurrence plots of dynamical systems. Europhys Lett 1987;4:973.

[24] Marwan N, Carmen RM, Thiel M, Kurths J. Recurrence plots for the analysis of complex systems. Phys Rep 2007;438:237–329.

[25] Sun R, Wang Y. Predicting termination of atrial fibrillation based on the structure and quantification of the recurrence plot. Med Eng Phys 2008;30:1105–1111.

[26] Zbilut JP, Thomasson N, Webber CL. Recurrence quantification analysis as a tool for nonlinear exploration of nonstationary cardiac signals. Med Eng Phys 2002;24:53–60.

[27] Marwan N, Kurths J. Nonlinear analysis of bivariate data with cross recurrence plots. Phys Lett A 2002;302:299–307.

[28] Thomasson N, Hoeppner TJ, Webber CL Jr, Zbilut JP. Recurrence quantification in epileptic EEGs. Phys Lett A 2001;279:94–101.

[29] Wu Z. Recurrence plot analysis of DNA sequences. Phys Lett A 2004;332:250–255.

[30] Strozzi F, Zaldivar J, Zbilut JP. Recurrence quantification analysis and state space divergence reconstruction for financial time series analysis. Phy A 2007;376:487–499.

[31] Yang H, Bukkapatnam STS, Barajas LG. Local recurrence based performance prediction and prognostics in the nonlinear and nonstationary systems. Pattern Recognit 2011;44:1834–40.

[32] Siek M, Solomatine DP. Nonlinear chaotic model for predicting storm surges. Nonlin Processes Geophys 2010;17:405–420.

[33] Riley MA, Clark S. Recurrence analysis of human postural sway during the sensory organization test. Neurosci Lett 2003;342:45–48.

[34] Skamarock WC, Klemp JB. A time-split nonhydrostatic atmospheric model for weather research and forecasting applications. J Comput Phys 2008;227:3465–3485.

[35] Huang Q. Physics-driven Bayesian hierarchical modeling of the nanowire growth process at each scale. IIE Trans 2011;43:1–11.

[36] Huang NE, Shen Z, Long SR, Wu MC, Shih HH, Zheng Q, Yen N, Tung CC, Liu HH. The empirical mode decomposition and the Hilbert spectrum for nonlinear and non-stationary time series analysis. Proc R Soc London Ser A 1998;454:903–95.

[37] Wu Z, Huang NE. A study of the characteristics of white noise using the empirical mode decomposition method. Proc R Soc London Ser A 2004;460:1597–1611.

[38] Addison PS. Wavelet transforms and the ECG: A review. Physiol Meas 2005;26:155–199.

[39] Yang H. Multiscale recurrence quantification analysis of spatial cardiac vectorcardiogram (VCG) signals. IEEE Trans Biomed Eng 2011;58:339–347.

[40] Chen Y, Yang H. Self-organized neural network for the quality control of 12-lead ECG signals. Physiol Meas 2012;33:1399.

[41] Yang H, Kan C, Liu G, Chen Y. Spatiotemporal differentiation of myocardial infarctions. Autom Sci Eng 2013;10:938–47.

[42] Malmivuo J, Plonsey R. *Bioelectromagnetism: Principles and Applications of Bioelectric and Biomagnetic Fields*. USA: Oxford University Press; 1995.

[43] Dubin D. *Rapid Interpretation of EKG's: An Interactive Course*. Cover Publishing Company; 2000.

[44] Clifford GD, Azuaje F, McSharry PE. *Advanced Methods and Tools for ECG Data Analysis*. London: Artech House; 2006.

[45] Stridh M, Sormmol L, Meurling C and Olsson B. Frequency trends of atrial fibrillation using the surface ECG. In Engineering in Medicine and Biology Society (EMBC), Proceedings of 1999 Annual International Conference of the IEEE, Atlanta, GA; 1999.

[46] Thakor NV, Zhu Y. Applications of adaptive filtering to ECG analysis: Noise cancellation and arrhythmia detection. Biomed Eng 1991;38:785–94.

[47] Afonso VX, Tompkins WJ, Nguyen TQ, Shen Luo M. ECG beat detection using filter banks. Biomed Eng 1999;46:192–202.

[48] Bukkapatnam STS, Komanduri R, Yang H, Rao P, Lih WC, Malshe M, Raff LM, Benjamin B, Rockley M. Classification of atrial fibrillation episodes from sparse electrocardiogram data. J Electrocardiol 2008;41:292–99.

[49] Li C, Zheng C, Tai C. Detection of ECG characteristic points using wavelet transforms. Biomed Eng 1995;42:21–8.

[50] Saxena SC, Kumar V. QRS detection using new wavelets. J Med Eng Technol 2002;26:7–15.

[51] Lin C, Du Y, Chen Y. Adaptive wavelet network for multiple cardiac arrhythmias recognition. Exp Syst Appl 2008;34:2601–11.

[52] Robert FM, Povinelli RJ. Identification of ECG Arrhythmias Using Phase Space Reconstruction. Lect Notes Comput Sci 2001;2168:411–23.

[53] Goldberger AL, Amaral L, Glass L, Hausdorff J, Ivanov PC, Mark R, Mietus J, Moody G, Peng C-K, Stanley HE. PhysioBank, physiotoolkit, and physionet: Components of a new research resource for complex physiologic signals. Circulation 2000;23:e215–e220.

[54] Shen KQ, Ong CJ, Li XP, Hui Z, Wilder-Smith EPV. A Feature Selection Method for Multilevel Mental Fatigue EEG Classification. Biomed Eng 2007;54:1231–1237.

[55] Dower GE, Yakush A, Nazzal SB, Jutzy RV, Ruiz CE. Deriving the 12-lead electrocardiogram from four (EASI) electrodes. J Electrocardiol 1988;21:S182–7.

[56] Dower GE, Machado HB. XYZ data interpreted by a 12-lead computer program using the derived electrocardiogram. J Electrocardiol 1979;12:249–61.

[57] Dawson D, Yang H, Malshe M, Bukkapatnam STS, Benjamin B, Komanduri R. Linear affine transformations between 3-lead (Frank XYZ leads) vectorcardiogram and 12-lead electrocardiogram signals. J Electrocardiol 2009;42:622–30.

[58] Yang H, Malshe M, Bukkapatnam STS, Komanduri R. Recurrence quantification analysis and principal components in the detection of myocardial infarction from vectorcardiogram signals. In Proceedings of the 3rd INFORMS Workshop on Data Mining and Health Informatics (DM-HI 2008), Washington, DC, USA; 2008.

4

STATISTICAL MODELING OF ELECTROCARDIOGRAPHY SIGNAL FOR SUBJECT MONITORING AND DIAGNOSIS

LILI CHEN, CHANGYUE SONG, AND XI ZHANG

Department of Industrial Engineering and Management, Peking University, Beijing, China

4.1 INTRODUCTION

As a pervasively used physiological signal, electrocardiography (ECG or EKG) is the recording of electrical activities of the heart over a period of time, which aims to measure the electrical impulses generated by cardiac tissue movement [1]. Currently, technologies based on ECG have been widely applied for diagnosis of cardiac diseases due to its clinical significance.

Retrospectively, the development of ECG techniques involves three stages. In the first stage, numerous sensitive galvanometer apparatus such as the capillary electrometer, the string galvanometer, and the Holter Monitor were invented and commenced to record human ECG [2, 3]. A milestone for this stage was the first publication of human ECG in 1887 [4]. The second stage is clinical exploration of the relationship between ECG and several kinds of cardiovascular disorders in terms of the clinical application of ECG [5, 6]. The third stage is the development of computer-aided ECG based on the automatic processing and analysis of the ECG signal from the early 1960s [7].

Currently, modern information technologies become more and more useful in the processing and interpretation of ECG signals automatically with designed algorithms

Healthcare Analytics: From Data to Knowledge to Healthcare Improvement, First Edition.
Edited by Hui Yang and Eva K. Lee.
© 2016 John Wiley & Sons, Inc. Published 2016 by John Wiley & Sons, Inc.

and methods to extract some characteristics. For example, computer-aided ECG can employ more complicated statistical models to explore the relationship between electrocardiographic measurements and physiologic findings [8]. Due to the fastness, low variability, and low cost, computer-aided ECG gains significant attention both in scientific research and healthcare service systems.

In the following section, the basic elements of ECG in terms of the physical mechanism, recording, and waveforms description are briefly introduced. In Section 4.3, several pervasively used automatic techniques for ECG preprocessing, waveform detection, feature extraction, and disease diagnosis are reviewed. A real clinical example in apnea detection is presented in Sections 4.4 and 4.5. Experimental results, discussion and conclusions are summarized in Sections 4.6–4.7.

4.2 BASIC ELEMENTS OF ECG

Most of the disease diagnosis approaches are designed based on extracted characteristics such as waveforms and derived features of ECG signals. Generally, the morphology of ECG signal is formed by iteratively sequential polarization and depolarization of cardiac tissue [8]. Figure 4.1 shows the activation process of a single cardiac fiber to illustrate the generation of ECG signal.

When at rest, the extracellular potentials of a single cardiac fiber are higher than the intracellular potentials, which constitute negative transmembrane potentials. With the stimulus transferring from left to right through the fiber, the left part of the fiber undergoes depolarization when the polarity of the transmembrane potential converts from negative to positive while the right part remains in a resting state. Therefore, the transmembrane potentials are positive on the left and negative on the right, which are associated with inward and outward current flow, respectively. Current flow in each direction is most intense near the site undergoing activation, constituting a source–sink pair represented as a current dipole. As the stimulus transfers through the fiber, the current dipole moves along with the stimulus. After depolarization, the fiber undergoes the recovery process gradually with its transmembrane potentials converting from positive to negative, which results in an

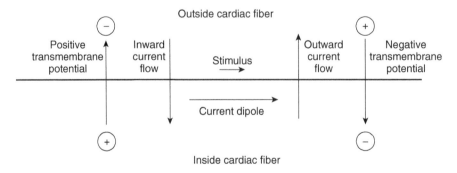

Figure 4.1   Currents and potentials during the activation of a single fiber.

equivalent dipole transferring from less recovered sites to more recovered sites. Changes in potential during recovery require much longer than during activation. In real cases, multiple adjacent fibers are activated in synchrony. Each individual fiber generates a single dipole, respectively, and the combination of the dipoles represents the electrical activity of the entire system.

ECG signals can be recorded by sensing the potentials generated in the activation and recovery process with electrodes placed on the torso. Specifically, an ECG lead is formed by recording the difference in potentials between two electrodes placed at different positions of the human body while one of the electrodes is designated as the positive input and the other as the negative input. In some cases, the negative input of the pair is represented by a combination of several electrically connected electrodes. Since there are multiple positions on the human body for electrodes, various ECG leads can be obtained and the most famous ECG lead system is presented in Table 4.1 [8]. This recording system is the 12-lead ECG composed by three standard limb leads, three augmented limb leads, and six chest leads (precordial leads).

The popularity of 12-lead ECG recording system is partly due to historical reasons. Some other recording systems are also in use aiming at recording more information, which is neglected by 12-lead ECG system with additional leads. In addition, some recording systems are capable to restore and reconstruct a full 12-lead recording at a high accuracy with less number of leads to reduce the complexity of the recording system especially for ambulatory use.

For a typical recorded ECG, the waveforms, segments, and intervals provide a basis for ECG interpretation and analysis. Figure 4.2 depicts the waveforms, segments, and intervals of a typical ECG signal. Five deflections including P, Q, R, S,

TABLE 4.1   Locations of Electrodes and Lead Connections for the Standard 12-Lead ECG

Lead Type	Positive Input	Negative Input
Standard Limb Leads		
Lead I	Left arm	Right arm
Lead II	Left leg	Right arm
Lead III	Left leg	Left arm
Augmented Limb Leads		
aVR	Right arm	Left arm plus left leg
aVL	Left arm	Right arm plus left leg
aVF	Left leg	Left arm plus right arm
Precordial Leads		
V_1	Right sternal margin, fourth intercostal space	Wilson central terminal
V_2	Left sternal margin, fourth intercostal space	Wilson central terminal
V_3	Midway between V_2 and V_4	Wilson central terminal
V_4	Left midclavicular line, 5th intercostal space	Wilson central terminal
V_5	Left anterior axillary line	Wilson central terminal
V_6	Left midaxillary line	Wilson central terminal

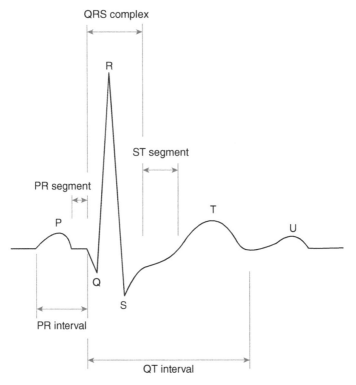

Figure 4.2 Waveforms and intervals for normal ECG.

TABLE 4.2 Origins and Normal Values of Duration for ECG Waveforms

Waveforms	Origin	Normal Duration (ms)
P wave	Atria activation	<120
PR segment	Atrioventricular (AV) conduction	
PR interval	Beginning of P wave to beginning of QRS complex	120–200
QRS complex	Activation of the two ventricles	80–120
ST–T wave	Ventricular recovery	
QT interval	Beginning of QRS complex to end of T wave	250–500

and T can be observed. The T wave may be followed by an additional wave named U wave, which usually has low amplitude [8]. The baseline of ECG is measured as the PR segment as well as the segment from the end of T wave (or sometimes U wave) to the beginning of the next P wave. In normal ECG, the baseline is isoelectric with amplitude of 0 mV.

The origins and normal durations of the waveforms, segments, and intervals are summarized in Table 4.2 [1, 8–10]. The durations and wave amplitudes usually vary between individuals. The normal amplitudes of different waveforms can be found in [11]. Factors such as gender, age, body habitus, and physiology may affect these values. Therefore, physicians would incorporate a number of other factors apart from ECG to implement an accurate diagnosis.

4.3 STATISTICAL MODELING OF ECG FOR DISEASE DIAGNOSIS

ECG signals have been widely applied for disease diagnosis and risk stratification in both clinics and research areas due to intelligible physiological interpretation of related heart activity and convenience to acquire [12, 13]. This chapter will focus on four main aspects of statistical modeling of ECG signals for disease detection:

- *Preprocessing Techniques.* Directly modeling ECG signals is not easy since the collected ECG signals are often contaminated with noise such as baseline drift, electrode motion artifacts, power line interference, and muscle contraction noise [14], and meanwhile the intrinsic properties can be concealed under different clinical conditions. Hence, ECG noise removal is of crucial importance for an accurate clinical diagnosis as noises will deteriorate the quality of ECG signals and lead to misdiagnosis. One of the important objective for ECG study is to separate the valid signal components from undesired noise signals to obtain noise-free ECG.

- *Waveform Detection Methods.* A bunch of clinical information conceals in ECG waveforms (such as P wave, T wave), and derivation of those waveforms will greatly assist real case diagnosis. The objective of the waveform detection techniques is to accurately identify various kinds of waveforms, and the characteristics of detected waveforms can be employed for further analysis.

- *Feature Extraction Approaches.* Another vital aspect of ECG signals is the characterization of ECG signals. The generation of ECG signals could be considered as a nonrenewal random point process with unknown rate [15]. This nonrenewal point process is nonstationary complex for which intrinsic properties can be masked by the complex interaction of different physiological systems. In addition, single derivative usually could not represent the whole underlying physiological mechanism of the signal. Thus, appropriate derivatives should be obtained from original signals to capture the inherent status of subjects.

- *Disease Diagnosis Techniques.* With signal denoising, waveforms detection, and feature extraction, various statistical models can be applied for disease diagnosis and risk stratification according to different types of heart-related diseases.

A typical ECG modeling procedure can be divided into four stages as shown in Figure 4.3. In this section, several conventional signal denoising approaches will be introduced and the strengths and limitations will also be discussed, respectively. Subsequently, waveforms detection techniques and features extracted from different aspects of ECG signals will be summarized. Several disease diagnostic methods based on statistical models and the associated algorithm will be also included in this section.

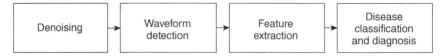

Figure 4.3   Schematic of ECG modeling.

4.3.1 ECG Signal Denoising

ECG signal denoising is of great importance for disease diagnosis since noises may conceal the intrinsic pathological states of subjects, leading to a weak performance of diagnosis methods. Numerous noise removing approaches have been proposed in the literature for ECG signals. Specifically, a few methods are designed to eliminate specific noises existing in ECG signals. These approaches for ECG denoising can be divided into several categories as shown in Figure 4.4.

The denoising approaches can be typically classified into filters/filter banks [16], wavelet-based methods [17–19], empirical mode decomposition (EMD) [20–24] and others such as S-transform [25], and independent component analysis (ICA) [26]. Generally, wavelet and EMD have been extensively studied and gained a great popularity for denoising of ECG signals due to the flexibility and multiresolution. Theoretical details of these two approaches are given in the following sections.

4.3.1.1 Wavelet-Based Methods for ECG Denoising   Wavelet transform (WT) has been recognized as an effective tool for signal processing since it provides information about the frequency characteristics of a signal as well as the time characteristics

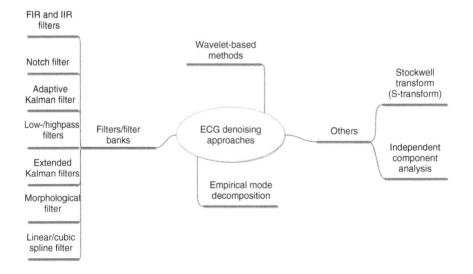

Figure 4.4   Overview of ECG denoising approaches.

of the signal [27]. Both details and approximates can be investigated in the timescale domain, and the multiresolution property allows the noise to be eliminated. Hence, WT has become a viable technique for ECG signal-noise reduction. Theoretically, in wavelet transform, various wavelets are generated from a single basic wavelet $\psi(t)$ known as mother wavelet. Two critical parameters are defined: the scale (or dilation) factors s and the translation (or shift) factor τ. The shifted and dilated versions of the mother wavelet can be expressed as

$$\psi_{s,\tau}(t) = \frac{1}{\sqrt{|s|}} \psi\left(\frac{t-\tau}{s}\right) \tag{4.1}$$

The wavelet transform of a signal $x(t)$ with mother wavelet function $\psi(t)$ can be represented as

$$T(s,\tau) = \int_{-\infty}^{\infty} x(t)\psi * \left(\frac{t-\tau}{s}\right) dt \tag{4.2}$$

The asterisk ($*$) denotes the complex conjugate of the wavelet function. For discrete wavelet transform (DWT), the scale (m) and translation factors (n) are integers for indices that yield the fast computation of wavelet transform coefficients. The family of discrete wavelets can be denoted as

$$\psi_{m,n}(t) = 2^{\frac{-m}{2}} \psi(2^{-m}t - n) \tag{4.3}$$

The DWT [28] of a signal can be regarded that the signal passes through a series of high-pass filters (HPF) and low-pass filters (LPF), which is shown in Figure 4.5.

A number of existing wavelet-based denoising approaches employ various shrinkage techniques based on thresholding of the wavelet coefficients. Denote **x** as the noisy signal vector, T and T^{-1} as the wavelet and inverse wavelet transform, respectively. The wavelet coefficients **w** can be written as

$$\mathbf{w} = T(\mathbf{x}) \tag{4.4}$$

Two different types of thresholding approaches can be found in the literature [29]: hard thresholding (i.e., to delete the wavelet coefficients that are smaller than the threshold and keep all the others unchanged) and soft thresholding (i.e., to delete the

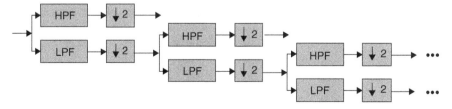

Figure 4.5   Diagram of discrete wavelet transform.

wavelet coefficients that are below the threshold and scale all the other ones based on certain rules). Let λ be the threshold and D be the thresholding operator, then

$$\mathbf{z} = D(\mathbf{w}, \ \lambda) \tag{4.5}$$

where $\mathbf{z}$ is the wavelet coefficient vector after thresholding. The filtered signal with noise free $\mathbf{y}$ can then be reconstructed using inverse wavelet transform

$$\mathbf{y} = T^{-1}(\mathbf{z}) \tag{4.6}$$

In ECG signal analysis, wavelet-based methods have been extensively investigated and most of the developed approaches are effective to eliminate different kinds of noises in ECG signals, such as wavelet neural network method [17] and dyadic stationary wavelet transform (SWT) Wiener filter [19].

Although the multiresolution analysis of WT allows the separation of noise from the signals and wavelet transform-based denoising methods are widely used for ECG signal processing, several limitations of this approach should be addressed. First, practically, the value of threshold for wavelet coefficient shrinkage is usually case-dependent and difficult to determine. Hence, numerous experiments should be conducted to designate thresholds. In addition, the hard thresholding techniques may lead to the oscillation of the reconstructed ECG signals, and some physiological information can be lost during the reconstruction. Comparatively, the soft thresholding methods may reduce the amplitudes of the ECG waveforms and especially reduce the amplitudes of the R waves, which are more critical for the diagnosis of heart-related diseases [25]. Second, the selected wavelet function is used in the whole signal processing procedures, which will generate many false harmonics [21]. Attention should be paid when applying those wavelet-based approaches for ECG signal denoising.

4.3.1.2 Empirical Mode Decomposition for ECG Signal Denoising
Another conventional method for ECG denoising is the EMD, which was developed by Rilling et al. [30] and Huang et al. [31]. EMD decomposes the nonlinear and nonstationary signal into a finite and small number of intrinsic mode functions (IMF), which follows two conditions: (i) the number of local extrema and the zero crossing must be equal or differ by at most one, (ii) at any point, the mean value of the envelope by the local maxima and the envelope defined by the local minima is zero. The IMFs represent the oscillation mode imbedded in the signal and can be searched by iteratively using the envelopes defined by the local maxima and minima. The upper envelope is established by connecting all the local maxima with a cubic spline line. Similarly, the lower envelope is formed by all the local minima. Let $u(t)$ and $l(t)$ be the upper and lower envelopes of signal $x(t)$, respectively. $m(t) = [u(t) + l(t)]/2$ is the mean of these two envelopes and the first component $h_1(t)$ is founded and shown as

$$h_1(t) = x(t) - m(t) \tag{4.7}$$

Then the condition of the IMF is checked for the first component and on satisfying the conditions for IMFs until it becomes the first IMF otherwise, the procedure is repeated till the IMF is found. A criterion that is known as the sum of difference (SD) has been designed to obtain and stop the repeated process:

$$SD = \sum_{t=0}^{T} \frac{|(h_{1(k-1)}(t) - h_{1k}(t))|^2}{h_{1\ (k-1)}^2(t)} \tag{4.8}$$

where $h_{1k}(t)$ represents the kth component and T is the total time length of the signal. A threshold is designated between 0.2 and 0.3, and the first IMF $I_1(t)$ can be obtained until the calculated SD is smaller than the threshold. Then

$$x(t) = I_1(t) + r_1(t) \tag{4.9}$$

where $r_1(t)$ is the residue and contains information of longer period components. The procedure described earlier is applied to all the subsequent $r_i(t)$ and the result is obtained as

$$r_1(t) = I_2(t) + r_2(t)$$

$$\vdots$$

$$r_{N-1}(t) = I_N(t) + r_N(t) \tag{4.10}$$

The process is terminated when the residue $r_N(t)$ becomes a constant and monotonic function. Therefore, the original signal is obtained as

$$x(t) = \sum_{i=1}^{N} I_i(t) + r_N(t) \tag{4.11}$$

where $I_i(t)$ is the ith order IMF, N is the number of IMF, and $r_N(t)$ is the final residue.

Since EMD decomposes a signal into IMFs, most of the denoising methods based on EMD technique follow partial reconstruction of the signal by removing noisy IMFs. Some EMDs and the extended methods are concluded in Table 4.3 [20–24].

An example of applying EMD for ECG signal denoising has been provided in Figure 4.6. The first panel is the original ECG signal, and the remaining panels are the extracted IMFs using the criterion introduced earlier. The noise-free ECG signal can be reconstructed by deleting the undesired IMFs, which contain nonperiodic noise components.

When applied to ECG signal denoising, the EMD-based techniques are remarkably effective to remove the various kinds of noises and serve as a reliable preprocessing step for further analysis. However, the original EMD is likely to remove specific signal information along with the noise while deleting certain noisy IMFs, and this discarded signal information may contain vital pathological state of subjects. Moreover, EMD-based techniques confront with the constraints being

TABLE 4.3   Summary of EMD for ECG Denoising

Author	Method	Target Noise
Manuel Blanco-Velasco et al.	EMD-based denoising method	High-frequency noise and baseline wander
Kang-Ming Chang	Ensemble EMD	Three types: 50 Hz, EMG, baseline wander
J. Lee et al.	EMD and statistical approaches	Motion and noise artifact detection
J. Jenitta et al.	Adaptive filter with EMD and EEMD	White Gaussian noise
Y. Xin	Mean–median filter and empirical mode decomposition	Baseline wander correction

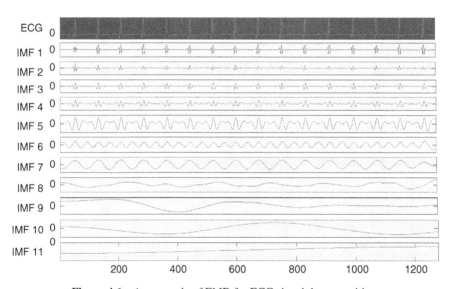

Figure 4.6   An example of EMD for ECG signal decomposition.

essentially defined by an algorithm, and therefore an analytical formulation could not be obtained for theoretical analysis and performance evaluation [30]. Experiments should be performed to validate the effectiveness before further application.

4.3.1.3   Comparison of Different Denoising Methods   Typically, a good denoising approach is supposed to detect different kinds of noises in the ECG signals and filter the signals while ensuring the obtained results are not influenced by undetected artifacts. Most ECG denoising methods are designed to remove specific ECG noises, and care should be taken when applying those methods. For instance, the filters/filter banks are apt to introduce additional artifacts to signals when carrying out denoising and some methods such as Kalman filters tend to remove specific noises, for example,

TABLE 4.4   Summary of Pros and Cons of Different Denoising Techniques

Methods	Pros	Cons
Filters/filter banks	• Easy to be implement • Effective to remove specific kind of noise	• Introduce additional artifacts • Only for specific noise removing • Not consider combined noises • Require prior information of the noise
Wavelet-based methods	• Better performance • Multiresolution analysis • Restore the signal information • Separate the abrupt change in signal	• Gaussian noise • Baseline wander noise • Require numerous experiments for choosing scales and thresholds
EMD	• Adaptive • Various kinds of noises • Data driven • Do not need prior information about noise	• Not for combined noise • Long time for large data set • No analytical form for IMF
S-transform	• Frequency-invariant amplitude response • Time–frequency axis • Better for high-frequency noise	• Gaussian noise
ICA	• Separate the noise components from measured signals	• Linear combinations of independent source signals • Non-Gaussian • Require prior information

white noise. The effect of combined noises is usually not considered and not all artifacts are included. In addition to noise types, prior information is commonly required before implementing the designed denoising methods. To further illustrate this point, summary of advantages and disadvantages for different ECG denoising methods is given in Table 4.4 in terms of those aspects.

4.3.2   Waveform Detection

Waveform detection is a crucial step to evaluate the clinical conditions of subjects. Waveform detection aims to locate and measure various waveforms, segments, and intervals from ECG signals. Due to the striking shape of QRS complex with high amplitude and slope, the detection of QRS complex serves as the basis for detection of other waveforms [32]. However, currently no universal rule has been accepted to define the beginning and end of other waveforms, segments, or intervals [33]. Therefore, we focus on the detection of QRS complex.

4.3.2.1   QRS Detection   A typical QRS detection algorithm constitutes two stages: the preprocessing and the classification [32, 34]. The preprocessing stage includes signal filtering, transforming, or characteristic magnifying; the classification stage

TABLE 4.5   Summary of QRS Detection Methods

Author	Year	Method
Pan et al.	1985	Digital filters
Gritzali et al.	1988	Length and energy transforms
Lin et al.	1989	Adaptive filters
Coast et al.	1990	Hidden Markov models
Trahanias et al.	1990	Syntactic methods
Xue et al.	1992	Neural network
Li et al.	1995	Wavelet-based method
Ruha et al.	1997	Matched filters
Benitez et al.	2001	Hilbert transform-based method
Arzeno et al.	2008	Signal derivatives

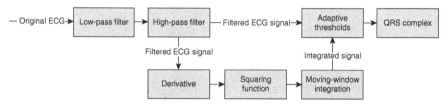

Figure 4.7   Scheme of the QRS detection algorithm.

examines the QRS complex by establishing specific decision-making rules. Most QRS detection algorithms in classification stage are heuristics, which are greatly affected by the preprocessing stage [35]. Therefore, preprocessing stage serves an important role in waveform detection. Table 4.5 summarizes some selected research works, and more details can be referred to the specific literature [36–45]. A systematic review and comparison of QRS detection methods is given in [32].

Among these methods, a pervasively used QRS detection algorithm was widely applied since proposed in [37]. The framework of this algorithm is shown in Figure 4.7. The original ECG signal is initially preprocessed by a LPF and a HPF to attenuate noise. The filtered signal is differentiated followed by point-by-point squaring. After integration with a moving window, an adaptive thresholding method is applied to the integrated signal as well as the filtered ECG signal. To be identified as a QRS complex, a peak must be recognized in both the integrated signal and the filtered signal, which greatly reduces the false-positive rate.

4.3.3   Feature Extraction

Apart from waveforms detected from ECG, critical information can also be extracted from ECG signals. Although the generation of ECGs is a nonrenewal random point process that is difficult to characterize, heart rate variability (HRV) (inverse of heartbeat rate (HR)) derived from ECG signals is an alternative representation of ECG

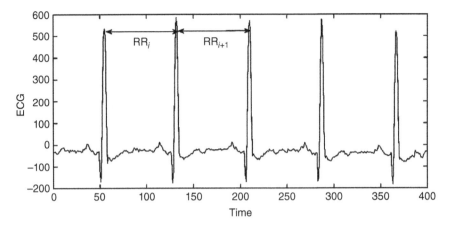

Figure 4.8 An example of RR intervals on ECG signals.

signals and is widely applied for disease diagnosis. An example of RR intervals is shown in Figure 4.8. From a physical perspective, any permutation on ECG can be reflected in RR intervals. Hence, various research works are devoted to analyzing the HRV for status monitoring and diagnosis of subjects. We introduce some commonly used features derived from RR intervals in the following section.

The normal variability in heartbeat rate is due to autonomic neural regulation of the heart and the circulatory system. The balancing action of the sympathetic nervous system (SNS) and parasympathetic nervous system (PNS), which are branches of the ANS, controls the HR. Increased SNS or diminished PNS activity results in cardio-acceleration. Conversely, a low SNS activity or a high PNS activity causes cardio-deceleration [46]. The degree of variability in the HR provides information about the functioning of the nervous control on the HR and the heart's ability to respond. Therefore, HRV provides information about the sympathetic–parasympathetic autonomic balance and has become a hot-spot topic in physiological signal analysis, serving as a vital noninvasive indicator of cardiovascular and autonomic system function, with direct connections to respiratory, central nervous, and metabolic dynamics [47].

A large variety of features including time domain, frequency domain, and non-linear measures are extracted from HRV to characterize the activity of sympathetic activity and parasympathetic activity for subject discrimination [48]. Some features involved in arrhythmia, myocardial infarction (MI) detection, can be summarized in Table 4.6 [49–56]. Moreover, interpretation of time domain and frequency domain features in Table 4.6 can be referred to Table 4.7.

4.3.3.1 Time-Domain Methods From the original RR intervals, a number of parameters can be calculated [46]: SDNN, the standard deviation of the RR intervals; RMSSD, the root-mean-square successive difference of intervals; pNN50%, the number of successive difference of intervals that differ by more than 50 ms

TABLE 4.6 RR-Derived Features in Research

Author	Year	Analysis
Bigger et al.	1993	Frequency domain: ULF, VLF, LF,HF, LF/HF ratio, total power
Vaishnav et al.	1994	SDRR, SDANNi, SD, pNN50, RMSSD
Bigger et al.	1996	Frequency domain: ULF, VLF, LF,HF, LF/HF ratio, total power
Quintana et al.	1997	NN median, variance, SDNN, SDANNi, RMSSD
Tapanainen et al.	2002	Time domain, frequency domain, nonlinear measures
Carpeggiani et al.	2003	SDNN, SDNN index, SDANN, RMSSD, pNN50
Chattipakorn et al.	2007	Time domain, frequency domain, nonlinear measures

TABLE 4.7 Commonly Used Parameters of Time and Frequency Domains of HRV

Parameters	Description	Unit
Time domain		
SDNN	Standard deviation of all NN intervals	ms
SDANN	Standard deviation of 5-min-averaged NN intervals	ms
ASDNN	Average of 5-min standard deviation of NN intervals	ms
RMSSD	Root mean square of successive differences	ms
Frequency domain		
Total power	Power between 0 and 0.4 Hz	ms^2
Low frequency (LF)	Power between 0.04 and 0.15 Hz	ms^2
High frequency (HF)	Power between 0.15 and 0.4 Hz	ms^2
LF/HF ratio	Ratio between LF and HF power	

expressed as a percentage of the total number of ECG cycles analyzed. The statistical parameters SDNN, RMSSD, and pNN50% are found to have larger value for the disease such as periventricular contraction (PVC), sick sinus syndrome (SSS), and atrial fibrillation (AF) due to higher RR variation [57].

4.3.3.2 Frequency-Domain Methods Frequency-domain methods employ the periodogram for power spectral density (PSD) estimation procedure. The methods for the calculation of PSD can be generally classified into nonparametric methods and parametric methods [58]. The comparison of these two methods is summarized in Table 4.8.

4.3.3.3 Nonlinear Methods Although time–frequency domain features are frequently used in analysis, they both suffer from some limitations. The time-domain methods are computationally simple but lack the ability to discriminate between sympathetic and parasympathetic contributions of HRV. On the other hand, the conventional frequency features based on FFT are not very suitable for analyzing nonstationary time series and fail to provide the exact location of an event along the timescale. Moreover, noise in ECG signals will severely degrade the quality of time–frequency domain features. Thus, increasing popularity has gained for

TABLE 4.8   Comparison of Nonparametric Methods and Parametric Methods for PSD Estimation

Methods	Pros	Cons
Nonparametric method	• Simple, for example, FFT • High processing speed	• Less smoother estimate • Rough estimation with small number of samples
Parametric method	• Smoother spectral components • Easy post-processing of the spectrum • Accurate estimation of PSD with small number of samples	• Need more calculation • Require signals to be stationary

nonlinear dynamics in the recent development of physiological data analysis approaches. The nonlinear techniques such as correlation dimension (CD) [59], largest Lyapunov exponent (LLE) [60], SD1/SD2 of Poincare plot [61], approximate entropy (ApEn) [62], and fractal dimension [63] have been widely applied for disease detection, and the results are relatively satisfactory. Statistical details for some nonlinear methods are introduced in the following section.

Approximate Entropy (ApEn)   ApEn is a family of statistics introduced as a quantification of regularity in the data. The statistics were first constructed by Pincus [64]. As an indicator of system regularity and chaos, ApEn facilitates its utility for empirical ECG signal analysis. Compared to time–frequency domain features, ApEn is nearly unaffected by noise below a certain specified filter level r. Additionally, ApEn is scale invariant, model independent, and can be applied to long-time series with good reproducibility. The increasing values of ApEn correspond to more irregularity in the time series. Generally, given N data points from a time series $\{x(n)\} = (x(1), x(2), \dots, x(N))$ and a run length m, ApEn is computed in the following steps [65]:

1. Form $N - m + 1$ vectors $X(1) \dots X(N - m + 1)$ defined by $X(i) = [x(i), x(i + 1), \dots, x(i + m - 1)], i = 1 \dots N - m + 1$. Each i-vector represents m consecutive x values, commencing with the ith data point.

2. Define the distance between $X(i)$ and $X(j)$, $d[X(i), X(j)]$, as the maximum absolute difference between their respective scalar components, that is, the maximum norm

$$d[X(i), X(j)] = \max_{k=1,2,\dots,m} |x(i + k - 1) - x(j + k - 1)| \qquad (4.12)$$

3. For a given $X(i)$, count the number of $j(j = 1 \dots N - m + 1)$ so that $d[X(i), X(j)] \leq r$, denoted as $N^m(i)$. Then, for $i = 1 \dots N - m + 1$

$$C_r^m(i) = \frac{N^m(i)}{(N - m + 1)} \qquad (4.13)$$

$C_r^m(i)$ measures the frequency of patterns similar to a given window length m within a tolerance r.

4. Compute the natural logarithm of each $C_r^m(i)$ and average it over i

$$\phi^m(r) = \frac{1}{N - m + 1} \sum_{i=1}^{N-m+1} \ln C_r^m(i) \qquad (4.14)$$

5. Increase the dimension to $m + 1$. Repeat steps (1)–(4) and find $C_r^{m+1}(i)$ and $\phi^{m+1}(r)$.

6. ApEn is defined as

$$\text{ApEn}(m, r, N) = \phi^m(r) - \phi^{m+1}(r) \qquad (4.15)$$

The accuracy of the estimated approximate entropy can be affected by the value of run length m as can be seen in Figure 4.9 and tolerance r. However, there is a trade-off between probability estimates and information loss when choosing the tolerance r. For small r values, poor conditional probability estimate for ApEn will be obtained. While for large r values, too much detailed system information is lost. To avoid a significant contribution of noise in an ApEn calculation, the value of r should be chosen as a large value. In practice, ApEn have been used for atrial fibrillation (AF) [66], sleep apnea [67], and other diseases.

Detrend Fluctuation Analysis (DFA) Detrend fluctuation analysis was originally proposed as a technique for quantifying the nature of long-range correlations in a time series [68, 69]. DFA aims to detrend variability in a sequence of events and characterizes a time series through a power-law exponent. Let $\mathbf{x}(N) = (x_1, x_2, \ldots, x_N)$

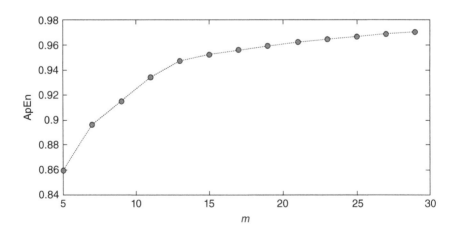

Figure 4.9 Example of ApEn versus parameter m.

be a time series and the computation of DFA involves the calculation of the summed series:

$$y(k) = \sum_{i=1}^{k} \{x(i) - E[x]\} \tag{4.16}$$

where $y(k)$ is the kth value of the summed series and $E[x]$ denotes the average over $\mathbf{x}(N)$. The summed series is then divided into segments of length m and least-squares fit is performed on each of the data segments, providing the trends for the individual segment $y_m(k)$. The root-mean-square fluctuation of the resulting series is then calculated as

$$F(m) = \left\{ \frac{1}{N} \sum_{k=1}^{N} [y(k) - y_m(k)]^2 \right\}^{\frac{1}{2}} \tag{4.17}$$

Since the parameter m is user-specified, the functional dependence of $F(m)$ on m is obtained by evaluations over all segment sizes m.

The power-law exponent α_D that describes the nonlinearity of time series can be obtained by plotting $\log[F(m)]$ against $\log(m)$ and fitting straight lines. The exponent is simply the slope of the linearity fitted segments and has been proposed as a means of differentiating normal from pathological subjects [70].

Although the nonlinear features can characterize the intrinsic properties of signals, those features are sensitive to noise influence. More importantly, the physiological interpretation of nonlinear features can be difficult in some situations. Thus, investigation between physiological mechanism of disease and nonlinear features should be figured out before application.

4.3.4 Disease Classification and Diagnosis

Cardiac disease is a major cause of mortality in the globe. Disease such as cardiac arrhythmias and myocardial infarction (MI) may not be life-threatening. However, those diseases possibly lead to the susceptibility of cardiac arrest, stroke, or sudden cardiac death. Early diagnosis of those cardiac diseases makes it possible to choose appropriate antidrugs and is thus crucial for improving the corresponding therapy.

Numerous cardiac disease detection and classification approaches based on advanced statistical methods as well as machine learning techniques have been proposed in the literature. Specifically, the analysis of ambulatory ECG recordings for cardiac disease detection has received considerable attention. Some advanced classification approaches based on ECG signals are employed to classify the different kinds of cardiac disease according to physiological interpretation. The general principle of these models involves the denoising of ECG signals, feature extraction, and statistical modeling of extracted features. Most previous denoising approaches and features can be applied during statistical modeling for disease diagnosis. The statistical models for disease diagnosis based on ECG signals include time–frequency domain analysis such as Hilbert transform analysis [71], time–frequency analysis

[72], wavelet analysis [73], statistical methods (principal component analysis [74], autocorrelation function [75]), nonlinear analysis (complexity measure [65]), and some advanced statistical learning techniques (neural network [39], support vector machine [76], hidden Markov models [41]). Details of two interesting approaches including artificial neural network (ANN) and support vector machine are provided as follows.

4.3.4.1 *Artificial Neural Network* ANN inspired by animals' central nervous systems have been applied to solve a wide variety of tasks that are hard to solve using ordinary rule-based programming [77]. The utility of ANN includes system identification and control, pattern recognition such as face identification, financial applications, and medical diagnosis [78]. The central idea of ANN is to extract linear combinations of the inputs as derived features, and then model the target as a nonlinear function of these features. A typical form of ANN will be described to illustrate the underlying functioning model.

A neural network is a two-stage classification model, typically represented by a network diagram as in Figure 4.10.

Let $X = (X_1, X_2, \ldots, X_p)$ be the p input variables. $Y = (Y_1, Y_2, \ldots, Y_K)$ is the output variable for K class classification, each output measure $Y_k, k = 1, 2, \ldots, K$ being coded as a $0 - 1$ for the kth class. For a typical feed-forward neural network, the linear combinations of input variables X are transformed into hidden layer $Z = (Z_1, Z_2, \ldots, Z_M)$ through a transform function, where M is the number of hidden units. The transform function known as activation function can be denoted as

$$Z_m = \sigma(\alpha_{0m} + \alpha_m^T X), m = 1, \ldots, M \tag{4.18}$$

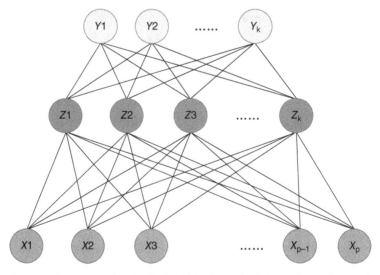

Figure 4.10   Schematic of a single hidden layer, feed-forward neural network.

where $\sigma(v)$ is activation function and α_{0m}, α_m^T are coefficients of the linear combination for the mth hidden unit. Then the output variable Y is modeled as a function of linear combinations of Z, which is denoted as

$$Y_k = f_k(X) = g_k(T), k = 1, \ldots, K \tag{4.19}$$

where $T = (T_1, T_2, \ldots, T_K), T_k = \beta_{0k} + \beta_k^T Z, k = 1, \ldots, K$. The β_{0k}, β_k^T are coefficients of the linear combination for kth class. The output function $g_k(T)$ for kth class transforms the vector of outputs T to make the final decision.

The neural networks can be fitted by minimizing cross-entropy (deviance) with N observations $y_i = (y_{i1}, y_{i2}, \ldots, y_{iK}), x_i = (x_{i1}, x_{i2}, \ldots, x_{ip}), i = 1, 2, \ldots, N$

$$R(\theta) = -\sum_{i=1}^{N} \sum_{k=1}^{K} y_{ik} \log f_k(x_i) \tag{4.20}$$

and the corresponding classifier is $G(x) = \text{argmax}_k f_k(x)$. Different forms of the activation function $\sigma(v)$ and output function $g_k(T)$ with different number of layers are applied according to different problem statements, which lead to various types of neural networks. Neural networks offer a number of advantages, including flexibility and nonlinearity. First, neural networks are capable to automatically learn from data, which acquire knowledge from surroundings by adaptively tuning internal and external parameters. Additionally, neural networks could implicitly detect nonlinear relationships between dependent and independent variables and all possible interactions between predictor variables. Different specialized algorithms such as nonparametric methods and expectation maximization can be used to train neural networks. In practice, physiological data are often correlated and perform with a nonlinear form, and neural networks are well suitable to capture the nonlinear properties among predictors. Therefore, it has been extensively used in heart-related disease diagnosis. As an example for arrhythmia detection, a large variety of extended neural networks have been employed to detect normal beats and abnormal beats and classify different types of arrhythmias. The performances of extensive neural network derivatives for arrhythmias have been summarized in Table 4.9 [79–86].

Table 4.9 shows that neural networks have achieved a good performance when implemented on arrhythmias detection (e.g., fuzzy Kohonen NN and multilayer back-propagation NN). Despite advantages over conventional approaches for modeling nonlinear relationship among predictors, there are some specific issues that need to be addressed. First, many types of networks are, in a sense, the ultimate black boxes. Apart from defining the general architecture of a network, the training and learning progresses could not be observed and the results of trained network could not provide any coefficient to define a relationship. Second, the running time of networks strongly depends on the type of networks applied and will be problematic with a large amount of data. Hence, feature reduction techniques should be designed to reduce the data dimensions to make the networks more efficient.

TABLE 4.9 **Comparison of Performances of Different Extended NNs for Arrhythmia Detection**

NN Derivative	Detection Objective	Feature Set	Performance (%)
ARTMAP NN	Abnormal PVC	Linear predictive coding (LPC) coefficients	99 (spe), 97 (sen)
Fuzzy Kohonen NN	Abnormal beats	Short-time multifractality	97
Fuzzy NN	Types of arrhythmias	RR intervals; average and deviation	>90
KDF-KNN NN	Arrhythmia patient	ECG morphologies; patient information	70.66
Modular NN	Arrhythmia patient	ECG morphologies; patient information	82.22
ELAMN NN	Types of arrhythmias	Morphological features	>95
Multilayer back-propagation NN	Types of arrhythmias	Phase space density values	98.55
Auto-associative NN	Types of arrhythmias	Segmented ECG beats	97

ARTMAP, adaptive resonance theory mapping; spe, specificity; sen, sensitivity; KDF-KNN: kernel difference-weighted k-nearest neighbor.

4.3.4.2 Support Vector Machine The principle of SVM is to simultaneously minimize the structural classification error and maximize the geometric margin between classes, which leads to high performance in practical application. Empirical evidence shows that it performs well in many real learning problems [76]. The theory of SVM can be represented as follows:

Consider a training set $D = \{(x_i, y_i)\}_{i=1}^{N}$, with each input $x_i \in \mathcal{R}^d$ and the associated output $y_i \in \{-1, 1\}$. Define a mapping function $\phi(x)$ that transforms each x_i into a feature space $\mathcal{F}$ with higher dimension where the training samples are linearly separable by a hyperplane. Denote the hyperplane by a vector $\omega \in \mathcal{F}$ and a scalar ω_0 as

$$\omega\phi(x)^T + \omega_0 = 0 \quad \text{s.t} \quad y_i(\omega\phi(x)^T + \omega_0) \geq 1, \forall i \quad (4.21)$$

The optimum separation hyperplane (OSH) is found by maximizing $2/\|\omega\|$, the margin between two classes, or minimizing $\omega\omega^T/2$. By constructing a Lagrangian formulation, the dual problem is to maximize

$$W(\alpha) = \sum_{i=1}^{N} \alpha_i - \frac{1}{2}\sum_{i=1}^{N}\sum_{j=1}^{N} \alpha_i\alpha_j y_i y_j \phi(x_i)\phi(x_j)^T$$

$$\text{s.t.} \sum_{i=1}^{N} y_i\alpha_i = 0 \text{ and } 0 \leq \alpha_i \leq C, \forall i \quad (4.22)$$

where $\alpha = (\alpha_1, \alpha_2, \ldots, \alpha_L)$ is the nonnegative Lagrangian multiplier. C is the regularization parameter as a trade-off between maximizing the margin and minimizing the classification error. The term $\phi(x_i)\phi(x_j)^T$ can be substituted by a kernel function $K(,)$ as

$$\phi(x_i)\phi(x_j)^T = K\ (x_i, x_j) \tag{4.23}$$

After determining the optimum α, the optimum solution for the vector ω is given by

$$\omega = \sum_{i \in SVs} \alpha_i y_i \phi(x_i) \tag{4.24}$$

For any test sample $x \in \mathcal{R}^n$, the output of the SVM model is

$$y = f(x) = \text{sgn}(\omega \cdot \phi(x) + \omega_0) = \text{sgn} \left(\sum_{i \in SVs} \alpha_i y_i K\ (x_i, x) + \omega_0 \right) \tag{4.25}$$

Support vector machine has been widely used in ECG signal classification such as sleep apnea detection [87] and arrhythmia classification [88]. The results of those research works demonstrate its effectiveness in disease diagnosis and classification.

4.4 AN EXAMPLE: DETECTION OF OBSTRUCTIVE SLEEP APNEA FROM A SINGLE ECG LEAD

4.4.1 Introduction to Obstructive Sleep Apnea

Obstructive sleep apnea (OSA) is a clinical disorder characterized by abnormal reduction or complete cease of air flow in sleep for more than 10 s usually caused by partial or complete collapse of the upper airway. OSA will significantly decrease the quality of life, causing daytime fatigue, slow reaction, and heavy snoring and increasing risk for the progression of cardiovascular diseases such as hypertension, coronary arterial disease, and congestive heart failure [89]. In this case study, the ECG signals are divided into minute-by-minute segments, which are labeled as normal or apnea according to clinicians. Features are extracted using various prementioned approaches. Specifically, three signals including RR intervals, R wave amplitudes, and ECG-derived respiration (EDR) signal are derived from the original ECG signal. Features are extracted from each segment of signals with duration of 1 min. Support vector machine is employed for segment classification with the extracted feature set.

4.5 MATERIALS AND METHODS

4.5.1 Database

The example is based on 70 continuous ECG recordings collected from 32 subjects in their sleeping experiments, and the data could be found at PhysioBank. The duration of the ECG recordings ranged from 401 to 578 min (mean: 492 ±32 min) with AHI from 0 to 93.5. The standard modified lead V_2 ECG electrode position was used in these recordings, and the modified V_2 ECG signals were sampled at 100 Hz with 16-bit resolution. These 70 ECG recordings were segmented minute by minute with an annotation normal or apnea assigned to each segment by experts based on the ECG recording as well as other PSG signals.

The 70 recordings were divided into released set with 35 recordings and withheld set with the other 35 recordings by the provider. The recordings in the released set were used to construct the SVM model and estimate unknown parameters, while recordings in the withheld set were used to evaluate the performance of the method.

4.5.2 QRS Detection and RR Correction

QRS detection algorithm was implemented to locate the R waves. In this study, an external package from the BioSig toolbox [90] for QRS detection was employed. RR intervals were then derived by calculating the time span between two adjacent R waves.

The original RR intervals contained physiologically unexplainable points as a result of the poor quality of automatic QRS detection. Therefore, a correction procedure based on a median filter was employed to eliminate unreasonable RR intervals while keeping the duration of the entire RR sequence unchanged. Denote the original RR intervals as $s = (s_1, s_2, \ldots, s_N)$, the width of the median filter as w, the lower bound and upper bound of RR intervals as LB and UB, respectively. The algorithm is described in detail as follows.

Step 1: Select the minimum point in s, denoted as $s_{min} = \min\{s_1, s_2, \ldots, s_N\}$. If $s_{min} \geq LB$, no RR interval is below the lower bound, then go to **Step 3**; otherwise mark s_{min} as a suspect interval, go to **Step 2**.

Step 2: Specify the window $s_w = (s_{min} - w, \ldots, s_{min}, \ldots, s_{min} + w)$, which centers at s_{min} containing $2w + 1$ points. Calculate the median value s_{med} of the windows followed by comparison of the following two absolute distances.

$$d_1 = \left|s_{min} + \min\{s_{min-1}, s_{min+1}\} - s_{med}\right| + \left|\max\{s_{min-1}, s_{min+1}\} - s_{med}\right| \tag{4.26}$$

$$d_2 = 2\left|\frac{1}{2}(s_{min} + \max\{s_{min-1}, s_{min+1}\}) - s_{med}\right| + \left|\min\{s_{min-1}, s_{min+1}\} - s_{med}\right| \tag{4.27}$$

If $d_1 < d_2$, merge s_{min} with its smaller neighbor into one RR interval; otherwise average s_{min} with its larger neighbor. Go back to **Step 1** for the next suspect interval.

Step 3: Select the maximum point of s as $s_{max} = \max\{s_1, s_2, \ldots, s_N\}$. If $s_{max} \leq$ UB, end the algorithm; otherwise mark the RR interval as a suspect and go to **Step 4**.

Step 4: Specify the window centered at s_{max} with $2w + 1$ points and calculate the median s_{med} of the window. Compare the following two absolute distances:

$$d_1 = k \left| s_{max} / k - s_{med} \right| + \left| \min \{ s_{max-1}, s_{max+1} \} - s_{med} \right| \qquad (4.28)$$

$$d_2 = 2 \left| \frac{1}{2} (s_{max} + \min \{ s_{max-1}, s_{max+1} \}) - s_{med} \right| \qquad (4.29)$$

where k was the integer that leads to the minimum value of $k | s_{max} / k - s_{med} |$. If $d_1 < d_2$, split s_{max} into k equal-sized pieces; otherwise average s_{max} with its smaller neighbor. Go back to **Step 3**.

4.5.3 R Wave Amplitudes and EDR Signal

The occurrences of R waves in the ECG signal could be located by the corrected RR intervals. The R wave amplitudes were derived as the voltages at the peaks of R waves.

The EDR signal reflected the respiration activities and was derived by processing the original ECG signal with two median filters of 200-ms width and 600-ms width, respectively [91]. The first median filter was intended to remove QRS complexes and P waves and the second median filter was intended to remove T waves. Regarded as the baseline, the resulting signal was then removed from the original ECG signal. A sample point of an EDR was obtained by calculating the area enclosed by the baseline corrected ECG in the region 100 ms beyond the QRS detection point.

4.5.4 Feature Set

Corrected RR intervals, R wave amplitudes, and the EDR signal were segmented minute by minute according to the normal/apnea annotation. Based on the three signals, various features were extracted for each segment as potential predictors of the SVM model to distinguish normal segments from apnea segments. The features are listed and described as follows [91]:

- Mean, standard deviation, skewness, and kurtosis of RR intervals
- The first five serial correlation coefficients of RR intervals
- The NN50 measure (variant 1), defined as the number of pairs of adjacent RR intervals where the first RR interval exceeds the second RR interval by more than 50 ms
- The NN50 measure (variant 2), defined as the number of pairs of adjacent RR intervals where the second RR interval exceeds the first RR interval by more than 50 ms
- Two pNN50 measures, defined as each NN50 measure divided by the total number of RR intervals
- The SDSD measure, defined as the standard deviation of the differences between adjacent RR intervals

- The RMSSD measure, defined as the square root of the mean of the sum of the squares of differences between adjacent RR intervals
- The Allan factor $A(T)$ evaluated at a timescale T of 5, 10, 15, 20, and 25 s where the Allan factor is defined as $A(T) = E\{[N_{i+1}(T) - N_i(T)]^2\}/2E\{N_{i+1}(T)\}$, $N_i(T)$ is the number of QRS detection points occurring in a window of length T stretching from iT to $(i+1)/T$ and E is the expectation operator
- Normalized VLF, LF, HF of RR intervals where the total power is the sum of the three components
- Ratio LF/HF of RR intervals
- Mean, standard deviation, skewness, and kurtosis of R wave amplitudes
- Normalized VLF, LF, HF of R wave amplitudes where the total power is the sum of the three components
- Ratio LF/HF of R wave amplitudes
- Mean, standard deviation, skewness, and kurtosis of EDR signal
- Normalized VLF, LF, HF of EDR signal where the total power is the sum of the three components
- Ratio LF/HF of EDR signal

4.5.5   Classifier Training with Feature Selection

A sequential feature selection procedure was employed to exclude irrelevant features and to reduce the risk of overfitting before implementing classification. The 35 recordings in the released set were divided into 35 folds with 1 recording per fold. A leave-one-out cross-validation (LOOCV) scheme was carried out to evaluate the performance of the classification in feature selection procedure, and the average prediction accuracy was calculated. After selecting the best feature set, the SVM model was trained and could be used for further prediction.

4.6   RESULTS

4.6.1   QRS Detection and RR Correction

All 70 ECG recordings were processed by the automatic QRS detection program and the resulting RR intervals were corrected by the median filter. Figure 4.11 illustrates a segment of RR intervals before and after correction. A significant decrease in unreasonable points was spotted.

4.6.2   Feature Selection

Figure 4.12 illustrates the change of the average prediction accuracy of the cross-validation and the change of the number of selected features, along with the feature selection iteration where in each iteration, the number of selected feature changes by ± 1 as a result of adding or removing a feature.

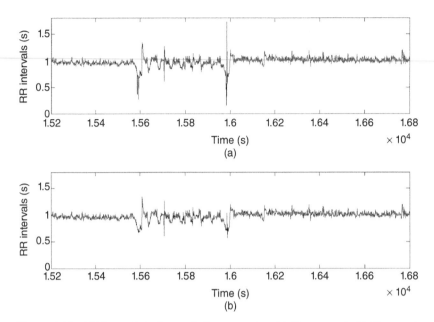

Figure 4.11   RR intervals before and after correction. (a) Uncorrected. (b) Corrected.

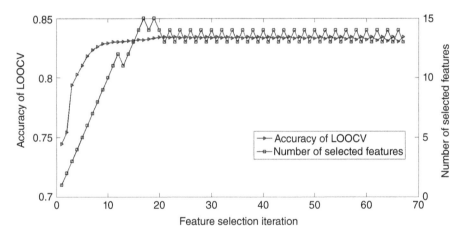

Figure 4.12   Cross-validation accuracy and selected number of features along with feature selection process.

The maximum accuracy, 83.4%, was achieved at iteration 21 with 13 features. Thus, features at iteration 21 were selected as the best feature subset. The selected features are listed as follows

1. Mean value of RR intervals.
2. The second and third correlation coefficients.

3. The pNN50 measure (variant 2).

4. The SDSD measure.

5. The Allan factor evaluated at a timescale of 5 s.

6. Normalized VLF and LF of RR intervals.

7. Skewness and kurtosis of R wave amplitudes.

8. Normalized LF of R wave amplitudes.

9. Normalized VLF and LF of EDR signal.

4.6.3 OSA Detection

The 35 recordings with a total of 17,268 segments were used to evaluate the performance of the SVM model. This SVM model correctly recognized 4848 out of 6550 apnea segments and 9139 out of 10,718 normal segments. Therefore, the sensitivity was 74.0% and the specificity was 85.3% with the overall accuracy 81.0%. Figure 4.13 depicts the receiver operating characteristic (ROC) curve of per-segment OSA detection, and the area under the curve (AUC) is 0.882.

The model could also be used to distinguish between healthy suspects with apnea patients since the result of the per-segment classification could be combined to produce a prediction of AHI for a recording. For the recordings with a prediction of AHI more than 5, they were classified as "apnea" and the others were classified as "healthy." Our model successfully recognized all the "apnea" recordings and 83.3% of the "healthy" recordings, with the overall accuracy of 94.3%.

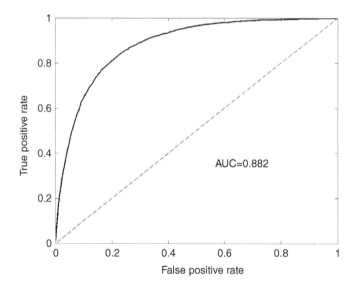

Figure 4.13 ROC curve of SVM model.

4.7 CONCLUSIONS AND DISCUSSIONS

In this example, single-lead ECG signals were statistically analyzed for OSA monitoring and detection. RR intervals were derived by QRS detection algorithm from the original ECG signals and corrected by designed median filter. R wave amplitudes and EDR signal were also derived before segment-by-segment feature extraction. After feature selection, an SVM model was established based on the selected best feature subset. The model was evaluated on the withheld set, achieving a segment prediction accuracy of 81.0% and a recording classification accuracy of 94.3%.

The study of physiological signals is an important part in healthcare informatics. Tools based on various physiological signals are developed in both real clinical diagnosis and research fields. The requirement of efficiency and automation for current healthcare industry calls for more reliable physiological signals together with accurate diagnosis tools, especially in the area of early disease detection. The purpose of this chapter is to review the main ECG modeling approaches and the associated statistical tools for patient monitoring and diagnosis. A brief illustration of physiological operation of heart circulatory system is presented to explain the physical mechanism of generation of ECG signals. As a critical aspect of ECG, the morphological components such as P wave, QRS complex, and ST segment are introduced. A typical procedure for ECG modeling is presented, which include ECG signal denoising, waveform detection, feature selection, and disease diagnosis approaches. This chapter finally provides an example of OSA detection to explain the procedures of monitoring and diagnosis of subjects based on ECG signals.

REFERENCES

[1] Luna D, Bayés A. *Basic Electrocardiography: Normal and Abnormal ECG Patterns*. John Wiley & Sons; 2008.

[2] Einthoven W. Un nouveau galvanometre. Arch Neerl Sc Ex Nat 1901;6:625–633.

[3] Holter NJ, Generelli JA. Remote recording of physiological data by radio. Rocky Mt Med J 1949;46(9):747–751.

[4] Waller AD. A demonstration on man of electromotive changes accompanying the heart's beat. J Physiol 1887;8(5):229–234.

[5] Einthoven W. Le telecardiogramme. Arch Int de Physiol 1906;4:132–164.

[6] James WB, Williams HB. The Electrocardiogram in Clinical Medicine: II The electrocardiogram in some familiar diseases of the heart. Am J Med Sci 1910;140(5):644–668.

[7] Pipberger HV, Arms RJ, Stallmann FW. Stallmann, automatic screening of normal and abnormal electrocardiograms by means of a digital electronic computer. Exp Biol Med 1961;106(1):130–132.

[8] Mirvis DM, Goldberger AL. *Electrocardiography, Heart Disease: A Textbook of Cardiovascular Medicine*. 6th ed. Philadelphia: WB Saunders; 2001. p 126–167.

[9] Morris F, Brady WJ, Camm J. *ABC of Clinical Electrocardiography*. Vol. 93. John Wiley & Sons; 2009.

[10] Goldberger AL. *Clinical Electrocardiography: A Simplified Approach.* Elsevier Health Sciences; 2012.

[11] Surawicz B, Knilans T. *Chou's Electrocardiography in Clinical Practice: Adult and Pediatric.* Elsevier Health Sciences; 2008.

[12] Yang H, Bukkapatnam STS, Trung L, Komanduri R. Identification of myocardial infarction (MI) using spatio-temporal heart dynamics. Med Eng Phys 2011;34(4):485–497.

[13] Bukkapatnam STS, Komanduri R, Yang H, Rao P, Lih W, Malshe M, Raff LM, Benjamin BA, Rockley M. Classification of atrial fibrillation (AF) episodes from sparse electrocardiogram (ECG) datasets. J Electrocardiol 2008;41(4):292–299.

[14] Joshi SL, Vatti RA, Tornekar RV. A survey on ECG signal denoising techniques, communication systems and network technologies (CSNT), 2013 International Conference, 60–64; 2013.

[15] Teich MC et al. Heart rate variability: Measures and models. Nonlinear Biomed Signal Process 2000;2:159–213.

[16] Chavan MS, Agarwala RA, Uplane MD. Design and implementation of digital FIR equiripple notch filter on ECG signal for removal of power line interference. WSEAS Trans Sign Process 2008;4(4):221–230.

[17] Ling B, et al. Fuzzy rule based multiwavelet ECG signal denoising, Fuzzy Systems, 2008, FUZZ-IEEE 2008. (IEEE World Congress on Computational Intelligence). IEEE International Conference, 1064–1068; 2008.

[18] Yang H, Bukkapatnam STS, Komanduri R. Nonlinear adaptive wavelet analysis of electrocardiogram signals. Phys Rev E 2007;76(2):026214.

[19] Khan M et al. Wavelet based ECG denoising using signal-noise residue method, Bioinformatics and Biomedical Engineering,(iCBBE) 2011 5th International Conference, 1–4; 2011.

[20] Lee J et al. Automatic motion and noise artifact detection in Holter ECG data using empirical mode decomposition and statistical approaches. Biomed Eng 2012;59(6):1499–1506.

[21] Jenitta J, Rajeswari A. Denoising of ECG signal based on improved adaptive filter with EMD and EEMD, Information & Communication Technologies (ICT), 2013 IEEE Conference, 957–962; 2013.

[22] Xin Y, Chen Y, Hao WT. ECG baseline wander correction based on mean-median filter and empirical mode decomposition. Biomed Mater Eng 2014;24(1):365–371.

[23] Singh O, Sunkaria RK, et al. ECG signal denoising based on empirical mode decomposition and moving average filter, Signal Processing, Computing and Control (ISPCC), 2013, IEEE International Conference, 1–6; 2013.

[24] Chang K, Liu S. Gaussian noise filtering from ECG by Wiener filter and ensemble empirical mode decomposition. J Sign Process Syst 2011;64(2):249–264.

[25] Das MK, Ari S. Analysis of ECG signal denoising method based on S-transform. IRBM 2013;34(6):362–370.

[26] Barros AK, Mansour A, Ohnishi N. Removing artifacts from electrocardiographic signals using independent components analysis. Neurocomputing 1998;22(1):173–186.

[27] Daubechies I. The wavelet transform, time-frequency localization and signal analysis. Inf Theory 1990;36(5):961–1005.

[28] Heil CE, Walnut DF. Continuous and discrete wavelet transforms. SIAM Rev 1989;31(4):628–666.

[29] Alfaouri M, Daqrouq K. ECG signal denoising by wavelet transform thresholding. Am J Appl Sci 2008;5(3):276.

[30] Rilling G et al. On empirical mode decomposition and its algorithms. IEEE-EURASIP Workshop Nonlinear Sign Image Process 2003;3:8–11.

[31] Huang NE et al. The empirical mode decomposition and the Hilbert spectrum for nonlinear and non-stationary time series analysis. Proc R Soc London Ser A 1998;454(1971):903–995.

[32] Kohler B, Hennig C, Orglmeister R. The principles of software QRS detection. Eng Med Biol Mag 2002;21(1):42–57.

[33] Mart I, Nez JP, et al. A wavelet-based ECG delineator: Evaluation on standard databases. Biomed Eng 2004;51(4):570–581.

[34] Burte R, Ghongade R. Advances in QRS detection: Modified wavelet energy gradient method. Int J Emer Trends Sign Process 2012;1(1):23–29.

[35] Sayadi O, Shamsollahi MB. ECG denoising with adaptive bionic wavelet transform. Conference Proceedings: Annual International Conference of the IEEE Engineering in Medicine and Biology Society. IEEE Engineering in Medicine and Biology Society Conference, 6597–6600; 2005.

[36] Arzeno NM, Deng Z, Poon C. Analysis of first-derivative based QRS detection algorithms. Biomed Eng 2008;55(2):478–484.

[37] Pan J, Tompkins WJ. A real-time QRS detection algorithm. Biomed Eng 1985;3:230–236.

[38] Li C, Zheng C, Tai C. Detection of ECG characteristic points using wavelet transforms. Biomed Eng 1995;42(1):21–28.

[39] Xue Q, Hu YH, Tompkins WJ. Neural-network-based adaptive matched filtering for QRS detection. Biomed Eng 1992;39(4):317–329.

[40] Lin KP, Chang WH. QRS feature extraction using linear prediction. Biomed Eng 1989;36(10):1050–1055.

[41] Coast DA et al. An approach to cardiac arrhythmia analysis using hidden Markov models. Biomed Eng 1990;37(9):826–836.

[42] Ruha A, Sallinen S, Nissila S. A real-time microprocessor QRS detector system with a 1-ms timing accuracy for the measurement of ambulatory HRV. Biomed Eng 1997;44(3):159–167.

[43] Benitez D et al. The use of the Hilbert transform in ECG signal analysis. Comput Biol Med 2001;31(5):399–406.

[44] Gritzali F. Towards a generalized scheme for QRS detection in ECG waveforms. Sign Process 1988;15(2):183–192.

[45] Trahanias P, Skordalakis E. Syntactic pattern recognition of the ECG. Pattern Anal Mach Intell 1990;12(7):648–657.

[46] Acharya UR et al. Heart rate variability: A review. Med Biol Eng Comput 2006;44(12):1031–1051.

[47] Cerutti S, Goldberger AL, Yamamoto Y. Recent advances in heart rate variability signal processing and interpretation. Biomed Eng 2006;53(1):1–3.

[48] Buccelletti E et al. Heart rate variability and myocardial infarction: Systematic literature review and metanalysis. Eur Rev Med Pharmacol Sci 2009;13(4):299–307.

[49] Tapanainen JM et al. Fractal analysis of heart rate variability and mortality after an acute myocardial infarction. Am J Cardiol 2002;90(4):347–352.

[50] Huikuri HV et al. Fractal correlation properties of RR interval dynamics and mortality in patients with depressed left ventricular function after an acute myocardial infarction. Circulation 2000;101(1):47–53.

[51] Quintana M et al. Heart rate variability as a means of assessing prognosis after acute myocardial infarction: A 3-year follow-up study. Eur Heart J 1997;18(5):789–797.

[52] Chattipakorn N et al. Heart rate variability in myocardial infarction and heart failure. Int J Cardiol 2007;120(3):289–296.

[53] Cripps TR et al. Prognostic value of reduced heart rate variability after myocardial infarction: Clinical evaluation of a new analysis method. Br Heart J 1991;65(1):14–19.

[54] Vaishnav S et al. Relation between heart rate variability early after acute myocardial infarction and long-term mortality. Am J Cardiol 1994;73(9):653–657.

[55] Bigger JT et al. The ability of several short-term measures of RR variability to predict mortality after myocardial infarction. Circulation 1993;88(3):927–934.

[56] Stein PK et al. Traditional and nonlinear heart rate variability are each independently associated with mortality after myocardial infarction. J Cardiovasc Electrophysiol 2005;16(1):13–20.

[57] Acharya R, Kannathal N, Krishnan SM. Comprehensive analysis of cardiac health using heart rate signals. Physiol Meas 2004;25(5):1139.

[58] Karim N, Hasan JA, Ali SS. Heart rate variability: A review. J Basic Appl Sci 2011;7:71–77.

[59] Logan D, Mathew J. Using the correlation dimension for vibration fault diagnosis of rolling element bearings – I Basic concepts. Mech Syst Sign Process 1996;10(3): 241–250.

[60] Iasemidis LD, Sackellares JC. The evolution with time of the spatial distribution of the largest Lyapunov exponent on the human epileptic cortex, Measuring chaos in the human brain, 49–82; 1991.

[61] Brennan M, Palaniswami M, Kamen P. Do existing measures of Poincare plot geometry reflect nonlinear features of heart rate variability? Biomed Eng 2001;48(11):1342–1347.

[62] Richman JS, Moorman JR. Physiological time-series analysis using approximate entropy and sample entropy. Am J Physiol 2000;278(6):2039–2049.

[63] Chen S, Teixeira JE. Structure and fractal dimension of protein-detergent complexes. Phys Rev Lett 1986;57(20):2583.

[64] Pincus SM. Approximate entropy as a measure of system complexity. Proc Natl Acad Sci 1991;88(6):2297–2301.

[65] Zhang H, Zhu Y, Wang Z. Complexity measure and complexity rate information based detection of ventricular tachycardia and fibrillation. Med Biol Eng Comput 2000;38(5):553–557.

[66] Vikman S et al. Altered complexity and correlation properties of RR interval dynamics before the spontaneous onset of paroxysmal atrial fibrillation. Circulation 1999;100(20):2079–2084.

[67] Hornero R et al. Utility of approximate entropy from overnight pulse oximetry data in the diagnosis of the obstructive sleep apnea syndrome. Biomed Eng 2007;54(1):107–113.

[68] Peng C et al. Fractal mechanisms and heart rate dynamics: Long-range correlations and their breakdown with disease. J Electrocardiol 1995;28:59–65.

[69] Peng C et al. Quantification of scaling exponents and crossover phenomena in nonstationary heartbeat time series. Chaos 1995;5(1):82–87.

[70] Amaral LISA et al. Scale-independent measures and pathologic cardiac dynamics. Phys Rev Lett 1998;81(11):2388.

[71] Chang WH, Lin K, Tseng S. ECG analysis based on Hilbert transform descriptor, Engineering in Medicine and Biology Society, 1988. Proceedings of the Annual International Conference of the IEEE, 36–37; 1988.

[72] Afonso VX, Tompkins WJ. Detecting ventricular fibrillation. Eng Med Biol Mag 1995;14(2):152–159.

[73] Khadra L, Al-Fahoum AS, Al-Nashash H. Detection of life-threatening cardiac arrhythmias using the wavelet transformation. Med Biol Eng Comput 1997;35(6):626–632.

[74] Polat K, Güneş S. Detection of ECG Arrhythmia using a differential expert system approach based on principal component analysis and least square support vector machine. Appl Math Comput 2007;186(1):898–906.

[75] Ge D, Srinivasan N, Krishnan SM. Cardiac arrhythmia classification using autoregressive modeling. Biomed Eng Online 2002;1(1):5.

[76] Homaeinezhad MR et al. ECG arrhythmia recognition via a neuro-SVM–KNN hybrid classifier with virtual QRS image-based geometrical features. Exp Syst Appl 2012;39(2):2047–2058.

[77] Dayhoff JE, DeLeo JM. Artificial neural networks. Cancer 2001;91(S8):1615–1635.

[78] Chen Y, Yang H. Self-organized neural network for the quality control of 12-lead ECG signals. Physiol Meas 2012;33(9):1399–1418.

[79] Srinivasan N, Wong MT, Krishnan SM. A new phase space analysis algorithm for cardiac arrhythmia detection, Engineering in Medicine and Biology Society, 2003. Proceedings of the 25th Annual International Conference of the IEEE, 1, 82–85; 2003.

[80] Wang Y et al. A short-time multifractal approach for arrhythmia detection based on fuzzy neural network. Biomed Eng 2001;48(9):989–995.

[81] Chakroborty S. Accurate arrhythmia classification using auto-associative neural network, Engineering in Medicine and Biology Society (EMBC), 2013 35th Annual International Conference of the IEEE, 4247–4250; 2013.

[82] Ham FM, Han S. Classification of cardiac arrhythmias using fuzzy ARTMAP. Biomed Eng 1996;43(4):425–429.

[83] Zuo, WM, et al. Diagnosis of cardiac arrhythmia using kernel difference weighted KNN classifier, Proceedings of Computers in Cardiology, IEEE, 253–256; 2008.

[84] Jadhav SM, Nalbalwar SL, Ghatol AA. Modular neural network based arrhythmia classification system using ECG signal data. Int J Inf Technol Knowl Manage 2011;4(1):205–209.

[85] Ramirez-Rodriguez, C, Hernandez-Silveira, M. Multi-thread implementation of a fuzzy neural network for automatic ECG arrhythmia detection. Proceedings of Computers in Cardiology, IEEE, 297–300; 2001.

[86] Mohamad FN, et al. Principal component analysis and arrhythmia recognition using Elman neural network, Control and System Graduate Research Colloquium (ICSGRC), 2013 IEEE 4th, 141–146; 2013.

[87] Khandoker AH, Palaniswami M, Karmakar CK. Support vector machines for automated recognition of obstructive sleep apnea syndrome from ECG recordings. Inf Technol Biomed 2009;13(1):37–48.

[88] Song MH et al. Support vector machine based arrhythmia classification using reduced features. Int J Control Autom Syst 2005;3(4):571.

[89] Young T et al. Population-based study of sleep-disordered breathing as a risk factor for hypertension. Arch Intern Med 1997;157(15):1746.

[90] BioSig. 2014 Available at http://biosig.sourceforge.net/. Accessed 2014 Mar 14.

[91] De Chazal P et al. Automated processing of the single-lead electrocardiogram for the detection of obstructive sleep apnoea. Biomed Eng 2003;50(6):686–696.

5

MODELING AND SIMULATION OF MEASUREMENT UNCERTAINTY IN CLINICAL LABORATORIES

VARUN RAMAMOHAN

School of Industrial Engineering, Purdue University, West Lafayette, IN, USA

JAMES T. ABBOTT

School of Industrial Engineering, Roche Diagnostics Corporation, Indianapolis, IN, USA

YUEHWERN YIH

School of Industrial Engineering, Purdue University, West Lafayette, IN, USA

5.1 INTRODUCTION

In 2011, the net healthcare expenditure of the United States accounted for 17.7% of the GDP, and it is expected that healthcare expenditure will increase to up to 19.8% of the GDP by 2020 [1]. Globally, among the countries that make up the Organization for Economic Cooperation and Development (OECD), the United States spends the largest percentage of its GDP on healthcare [2]. Further, $810 billion, approximately 5% of the 2013 US GDP, is wasted every year in the United States due to inefficient use of resources, medical errors, and the prescription of unnecessary procedures.

A significant proportion of these unnecessary procedures include repetition of clinical laboratory tests used to assess a patient's body function. These laboratory tests are typically repeated when a patient moves between hospitals and laboratories, and because the attending doctor does not have access to information regarding the quality of a laboratory test that was performed in another laboratory.

Healthcare Analytics: From Data to Knowledge to Healthcare Improvement, First Edition.
Edited by Hui Yang and Eva K. Lee.
© 2016 John Wiley & Sons, Inc. Published 2016 by John Wiley & Sons, Inc.

In this chapter, we address the issue of quality of a clinical laboratory measurement process by describing the previous and current research in the field, and present a methodology to model and estimate the uncertainty associated with these measurement processes. A statement of uncertainty about the result of a measurement provides information that describes the quality of the measurement process. Information that describes the quality of the measurement result is vital for clinical laboratory test results, since they inform every stage of medical decision making, from diagnostic and prognostic assessment to determining and prescribing drug dosages. The United States Congress has recognized this need in its passage of the Clinical Laboratory Improvement Amendments Act in 1988. This Act requires laboratories to validate laboratory procedures and establish valid quality control systems. Information regarding the current level of quality delivered by the laboratory is required in order to establish valid quality control systems, and this information is provided by estimates of measurement uncertainty.

Currently, clinical laboratories typically perform minimal testing in order to verify measurement performance in terms of the possible range of values that can be reported by the laboratory test, measurement accuracy with respect to samples of a known analyte concentration, and reproducibility using one lot of reagents and one operator, which does not adequately describe the system performance. In this chapter, we present a methodology that combines mathematical modeling and simulation and enables the estimation of the uncertainty associated with a clinical laboratory measurement process. The methodology involves the development of a physics-based mathematical model that expresses the measurement result as a function of the sources of uncertainty that operate within the measurement process, and then uses the Monte Carlo method to simulate the long-term behavior of the measurement process. The use of the Monte Carlo method also enables the simulation and optimization of various aspects of the laboratory measurement process in terms of its effect on measurement uncertainty. The estimates of uncertainty provided by the model, used in conjunction with the performance information collected in the laboratory, can be used to establish quality control systems that bridge the disparity between clinically required performance and that observed in the laboratory.

The chapter is organized as follows: in Section 5.2, we provide background information regarding clinical laboratory measurement processes and an overview of the recent research that has been conducted regarding the modeling and estimation of measurement uncertainty in the clinical laboratory. In Section 5.3, we provide a brief description of some general guidelines for developing mathematical models of measurement uncertainty. In Section 5.4, we illustrate the implementation of these guidelines by developing a mathematical model of the uncertainty associated with the measurement of the enzyme alkaline phosphatase (ALP) in the clinical laboratory and then use the model to estimate the contributions of each source of uncertainty operating within the process to the net measurement uncertainty. Finally, in Section 5.5, we discuss the validation of the model, the limitations and advantages of the modeling methodology, and outline possible avenues for future research in the field.

5.2   BACKGROUND AND LITERATURE REVIEW

A clinical laboratory measurement process is typically divided into three stages: the preanalytical stage, which deals with patient sample collection, transportation, storage, preparation, and so on; the analytical stage, which involves analysis of the patient sample using a calibrated instrument; and the postanalytical stage, which deals with recording, reporting, and interpreting the result of the measurement. Each of these stages has uncertainty associated with it, and the uncertainty of a given stage of the measurement process arises from multiple sources of variation operating within that stage. Identifying all the sources of variation associated with each stage is often impractical [3]; however, a list of important sources of variation associated with each stage is provided in Table 5.1 [4].

The methodology presented in this chapter involves identifying and characterizing the sources of uncertainty operating within the analytical stage of the process and estimates the uncertainty of this stage using the Monte Carlo method. As can be seen in Table 5.1, there are numerous sources of uncertainty associated with the preanalytical stage, and characterizing the variation of these sources merits a separate discussion in its own right and is beyond the scope of the methodology in its current form. The postanalytical stage does not generally contribute to measurement uncertainty; however, human errors may occur in the reporting and interpretation of measurement results. These errors are, by definition, out of the scope of this chapter.

TABLE 5.1   Sources of Uncertainty Operating within the Measurement Process

Stage of the Process	Sources of Uncertainty
Preanalytical	Identification of the patient
	Preparation of the patient
	Venipuncture site selection
	Preparation of venipuncture site
	Tourniquet application and time
	Proper venipuncture technique
	Order of draw
	Proper tube mixing
	Correct specimen volume
	Proper tube handling and specimen processing
	Centrifugation
	Special handling for blood specimens
	Storage and transportation temperature stability
Analytical	Calibrators or Certified Reference Materials
	Reagents
	Instrument(s)
Postanalytical	Recording of measurement result
	Reporting of measurement result
	Interpretation of measurement result

5.2.1   Measurement Uncertainty: Background and Analytical Estimation

In this section, we provide a brief introduction to modeling measurement uncertainty, in general, and describe some simple rules for the analytical modeling and estimation of measurement uncertainty that are applicable to all measurement systems, including those in clinical laboratories.

In 1978, the *Comite International des Poids et Mesures* (CIPM) entrusted the *Bureau International des Poids et Mesures* (BIPM) to work in collaboration with national standards laboratories with the purpose of developing internationally accept- able standards for the expression of uncertainty in measurement. The BIPM con- vened a meeting with the purpose of arriving at a uniform and generally acceptable procedure for the expression of uncertainty in measurement, and this was attended by delegates from 11 national standards laboratories. The attendees at this meeting formed the Working Group on the Statement of Uncertainties, and they developed Recommendation INC-1 in 1980 [5], Expression of Experimental Uncertainties. It was approved by the CIPM in 1981 and later reaffirmed in 1986.

According to the Recommendation INC-1 [5], the uncertainty associated with a measurement result is typically a function of the uncertainties of several components. The methods of estimation of the uncertainties of these components can be classified into two categories:

1. Components for which experimental data is available, and whose uncertainty is estimated by applying appropriate statistical methods to this data. This method of characterization is known as the "Type A" method.
2. Components that are characterized by other less rigorous ad hoc methods, which often rely on the judgment of experts. This method of characterization is known as the "Type B" method.

It was also emphasized in the Recommendation INC-1 that the classification of different components of uncertainty into "random" and "systematic" uncertainties, as was previously used, is to be avoided, and in particular, the term "systematic uncertainty" may even be misleading as to the nature of the variation in the result of a measurement. Further, it was recommended that the net uncertainty of the mea- surement result be estimated by applying the usual method for the combination of variances and expressed in the form of a standard deviation.

In addition to the Recommendation INC-1, the CIPM entrusted the task of devel- oping a comprehensive guide for the specification of the uncertainty of measurement to the International Organization for Standardization. Six organizations partnered with the ISO Technical Advisory Group, and they developed the Guide to the Expres- sion of Measurement in Uncertainty in 1993, referred to hereafter as the GUM (1993) [6]. The GUM (1993) is now accepted worldwide as the definitive document on the conception, specification, and estimation of the uncertainty associated with the result of a measurement.

The GUM (1993) establishes guidelines for the modeling and estimation of the uncertainty of measurement. The term "uncertainty of measurement" is formally defined in the GUM as follows: "parameter, associated with the result of a measurement, that characterizes the dispersion of the values that could reasonably be attributed to the measurand." The term measurand refers to the quantity being measured.

In most cases, based on the guidelines in the Recommendation INC-1 (1980), the standard deviation is the parameter used to characterize the dispersion of the result of measurement. In the clinical assay model presented in Section 5.4, we also use the standard deviation as a measure of uncertainty associated with both the components of uncertainty and the measurand of the system under consideration. The uncertainty associated with a component may be characterized by one of the two methods described in the Recommendation INC-1 (1980), the Types A and B methods of uncertainty estimation. The GUM (1993) methodology for the evaluation of uncertainty associated with a measurement system involves the following steps. First, a mathematical model relating the different components of the measurement system to the measurand is developed. Next, the uncertainties associated with the different components of the model are characterized by either a Type A or a Type B method. A first-order Taylor's series expansion of a function, referred to as the law of propagation of uncertainty, is then used to compute the combined uncertainty associated with the system. This expression is as follows:

$$u(y) = \sqrt{\sum_{i=1}^{n} \left(\frac{\partial f}{\partial x_i}\right)^2 * u^2(x_i) + 2\sum_{i=1}^{n-1}\sum_{j=i+1}^{n} \left(\frac{\partial f}{\partial x_i}\right) * \left(\frac{\partial f}{\partial x_j}\right) * u(x_i, x_j)} \qquad (5.1)$$

Here, f represents the model of the measurement system; $u(y)$ denotes the uncertainty of the measurand y; the x_i denote the components of the system and the $u(x_i)$ their individual uncertainties; and the $u(x_i, x_j)$ represent the pairwise covariances between the components of the measurement system. The partial derivatives $\frac{\partial f}{\partial x_i}$ are referred to as the sensitivity coefficients for each of the x_i and are evaluated at the expectations of the x_i. The above-mentioned expression is a general rule for combining individual measurement uncertainties. We now describe some examples of its application to simpler measurement systems.

If the model of the measurement system is linear, it can be represented by the following expression:

$$y = f(x_1, x_2, \ldots, x_n) = \sum_{i=1}^{n} a_i x_i + b$$

Here, the a_i and b are constants $\in \mathbb{R}$. For such a measurement system, the law of propagation of uncertainty simplifies to the following standard expression for the variance of a linear function of random variables:

$$u(y) = \sqrt{\sum_{i=1}^{n} a_i^2 u^2(x_i) + 2\sum_{i=1}^{n-1}\sum_{j=i+1}^{n} a_i a_j u(x_i, x_j)} \qquad (5.2)$$

If the relationship between the measurand y and the components of the system x_i is multiplicative and can be expressed as $y = b\, x_1^{a_1} x_2^{a_2} \ldots x_n^{a_n}$, then the combined uncertainty of the measurement system is estimated using the following expression:

$$\frac{u(y)}{y} = \sqrt{\sum_{i=1}^{n} \left[\frac{a_i u(x_i)}{x_i} \right]^2} \tag{5.3}$$

The x_i and y in the above-mentioned expression represent their expected values or means, respectively. The two simplifications of the law of propagation of uncertainty described in Equations 5.2 and 5.3 can be used together to estimate the combined uncertainty associated with most simple measurement systems. An example of such a calculation is now described. Consider a measurement system with measurand y, which is a function of its components x_1, x_2, x_3, x_4, and x_5. Let their individual uncertainties be denoted by $u(x_1), u(x_2), u(x_3), u(x_4)$, and $u(x_5)$. The functional relationship is given as follows:

$$y = x_1 + \frac{x_2\, x_3}{x_4 + x_5} \tag{5.4}$$

Equation 5.3 can be used to estimate the combined uncertainty of the numerator $(x_2\, x_3)$ of the fractional term in the right-hand side of Equation 5.4, and Equation 5.2 can be used for the denominator $(x_4 + x_5)$ of the same fractional term. If we replace the numerator and denominator of the fractional term by the variables x_{23} and x_{45} with the corresponding uncertainties represented by $u(x_{23})$ and $u(x_{45})$, then Equation 5.4 becomes

$$y = x_1 + \frac{x_{23}}{x_{45}}$$

The uncertainties of x_{23} and x_{45} are given by the following equations:

$$u(x_{23}) = x_{23} \sqrt{\left[\frac{u(x_2)}{x_2} \right]^2 + \left[\frac{u(x_3)}{x_3} \right]^2}$$

$$u(x_{45}) = \sqrt{u^2(x_4) + u^2(x_5)}$$

The expected values of x_{23} and x_{45} are estimated by appropriately convolving the distributions of the corresponding individual random variables. Equation 5.3 can now be applied to estimate the combined uncertainty of the simplified fractional term in the above-mentioned expression. This yields a further simplification of Equation 5.4 given by $y = x_1 + x_{2345}$. The uncertainty of $u(x_{2345})$ is given by the following equation:

$$u(x_{2345}) = x_{2345} \sqrt{\left[\frac{u(x_{23})}{x_{23}} \right]^2 + \left[\frac{u(x_{45})}{x_{45}} \right]^2}$$

Finally, Equation 5.2 can be applied to yield the combined uncertainty of the measurement system $u(y)$, as given below:

$$u(y) = \sqrt{u^2(x_1) + u^2(x_{2345})}$$

In order to simplify the process of estimating the net uncertainty of a measurement system using the law of propagation of uncertainty, Kragten [7] developed a spreadsheet program that automated the process of computing the combined standard uncertainty using the law of propagation of uncertainty. Further, the EURACHEM group published the document "Quantifying Uncertainty in Analytical Measurements" in 1995 to guide the implementation of principles of the GUM (1993) for analytical measurements in laboratories.

An updated edition of the GUM (1993) was published in 2008 by the Joint Committee for Guides in Metrology [8], with some minor corrections to the 1993 version. Several publications supplemental to the GUM (1993) [9–12] have also been published.

The application of the law of propagation of uncertainty and its simplifications is appropriate when the model of the measurement system is simple, as in the example described earlier. However, in practice, useful models of measurement systems are often complex in that the number of components (and therefore, the number of variables in the model of the measurement system) is large or in that there are significant nonlinearities in the model. Often, both cases are simultaneously true of the measurement system model. The presence of significant nonlinearities in the model, such as exponential or logarithmic terms, high-degree polynomials, and so on, requires the addition of higher-order terms to the law of propagation of uncertainty, which then makes its use cumbersome. In such cases, the Monte Carlo method is most often used to estimate the combined uncertainty of the measurement system model.

Recognizing this, in 2008, the JCGM also published a supplement that advocates for the use of the Monte Carlo method to model the propagation of uncertainty through a measurement process, and it outlines the statistical conditions that must be satisfied if the Monte Carlo method is to be used for estimating the combined measurement uncertainty [9]. These conditions are listed below.

1. The model f must be continuous in the neighborhood of the best estimates of all the independent variables x_i.
2. The distribution function for the measurand y must be continuous and strictly increasing.
3. The PDF for the measurand y is as follows:
   a. continuous as well as positive over the interval under consideration;
   b. unimodal;
   c. strictly increasing to the left of the mode and strictly decreasing to the right of the mode.
4. $E(y)$ and $V(y)$ exist.
5. A sufficiently large number of Monte Carlo iterations are used.

The model of measurement uncertainty presented in Section 5.4 satisfies all of the above-mentioned conditions. Further, since the components of the measurement process that are subject to variability typically follow the Gaussian distribution, they are characterized by a probability distribution with the expected value and the standard deviation as parameters, with the standard deviation used as the parameter describing the uncertainty of measurement.

5.2.2 Uncertainty in Clinical Laboratories

In this section, we describe the research that has been conducted on the modeling and estimation of uncertainty in clinical laboratories.

The need for ascertaining information about the reliability of analytical methods used in the laboratory was recognized by Aronsson et al. as early as 1974 [13]. Further, the authors proposed conducting a systems analysis to determine the contribution of various components of the analytical procedure to, in their terms, the "quality" of the result. They conclude that systems analysis is a valuable tool for minimizing the effect of the contributing components and to inform the design of analytical assays that are optimal with respect to the existing laboratory conditions.

This study was followed by Tietz [14], who proposed a model to quantify the accuracy and reliability of clinical measurements so as to support the interlaboratory comparison of clinical laboratory tests. The author discussed the traceability of a clinical laboratory measurement termed as a "field method" by the author – to the most accurate method, designated by the author as a "definitive method."

Following the publication of the GUM (1993), Kristiansen et al. [15] applied the principles in the Guide to estimate the uncertainty of the atomic absorption spectrometry technique, which is used to determine the amount of lead in the blood. The uncertainty associated with each component of the process was characterized and integrated into a net measurement uncertainty using the law of propagation of uncertainty. Validation of their estimates was carried out by comparing the estimated uncertainty with experimentally obtained data. Two of the above authors also published a treatise on traceability and uncertainty in analytical measurements in 1998 [16].

Kallner, in 1999 [17], utilized the principles of the GUM (1993) and the first edition of the EURACHEM guide [18] to estimate the net measurement uncertainty associated with an analytical assay. The author suggested that the uncertainty estimates obtained in this manner be used to set quality specifications for such analytical assays in laboratory medicine. The author used a spreadsheet program, similar to that used by Kragten in 1994 [7] to automate the uncertainty estimation using the law of propagation of uncertainty. The study presented in this paper provided some valuable insights into the estimation of uncertainty in laboratory medicine and in our development of a systems simulation approach toward the estimation and analysis of uncertainty for clinical laboratory measurement systems.

Kallner and Waldenstrom, also in 1999 [19], obtained uncertainty estimates for glucose measurements and investigated the clinical utility of uncertainty around decision levels for the diagnosis of diabetes. They also applied the procedures described in the GUM (1993) to the steps of sampling and measurement and identified the measurement procedure as the major source of uncertainty, followed by the prean-alytical sources. They arrive at the conclusion that presently available procedures do not allow identification of individuals at high risk for diabetes.

Dybkaer [20] published a general paper that stressed the need for quality manage-ment, certification, and accreditation of medical laboratories. The author maintains that while the costs of achieving accreditation may be high, its rewards include the development of an open system, smoother work, satisfied stakeholders, and emphasis on the prevention of mistakes.

Fuentes-Arderiu [21] raised a few pertinent questions about standardizing the practice of providing uncertainty statements for calibrator materials, the establish-ment of a relationship between metrological standard deviation and concentration level, and the question of whether preanalytical variation can be accurately quantified. As illustrated in Section 5.4, we attempt to answer some of these questions.

Kristiansen, in 2001 [22], published an important paper wherein he describes the development of a generally applicable methodology for the estimation of uncertainty in clinical laboratories. The methodology involves the following steps: (i) specifi-cation, which involves the establishment of a functional relationship between the measurand and the quantities on which it depends; (ii) identification, which entails the listing of all the possible sources of uncertainty; (iii) quantification, which involves the estimation of the uncertainties of all the sources of uncertainty, and finally (iv) combination, wherein all the sources of uncertainty are combined according to the law of propagation of uncertainty and its special cases for independent, linear, and uncorrelated components. The author implemented these guidelines to estimate the uncertainty of the human serum prolactin assay.

Petersen et al. [23] studied three models in 2001: a linear model, a squared model based on the GUM (1993), and a combined model for the development of analytical quality specifications – for handling and combining random and systematic variations/errors according to their purpose, their application, and the validity of their assumptions. The authors conclude that each model possesses specific advantages compared to the other models and should be applied according to its suitability for the assay under consideration.

In 2001, Petersen et al. [24] also investigated the utility of estimating systematic and random uncertainties in setting quality specifications for the laboratory tests used in the diagnosis of type 2 diabetes mellitus. Further, they also investigated the effect of the then current WHO and ADA recommendations on the diagnosis of type 2 diabetes mellitus and the implications of their estimates of measurement uncertainty on the same.

Linko et al. [3] implemented the GUM (1993) guidelines to evaluate the uncer-tainty associated with routine clinical chemistry measurements and, in particular, estimated the uncertainty of the serum calcium and glucose assays. The evaluation focuses on the analytical stage, but they introduce empirical terms to account for the preanalytical phase and other patient-related issues.

Krouwer, in 2002 [25], conducted a review of the literature to reconcile three dif-ferent approaches to the estimation of total analytical error for diagnostic assays: the simple combination model, the distribution of differences model, and a simulation approach. The author concludes that total analytical error should be estimated either using the distribution of differences method or by simulation. The author also mentions that the use of outlier rate estimates from large studies could also help assess assay quality.

Further, Krouwer argues in 2003 [26] that the methodology proposed in the GUM (1993) does not provide mechanisms to deal with outliers. Also, the author suggests that the GUM (1993) methodology does not deal with systematic errors, particularly in the case of calibrators. Due to these reasons, Krouwer suggests that the principles laid out in the GUM (1993) are not suitable for the evaluation of uncertainty in diagnostic assays. Kristiansen [27] counters this argument by suggesting that external quality control data can be used to estimate calibrator uncertainty and then applying the law of propagation of uncertainty for the estimation of combined uncertainty, as illustrated in the author's earlier publication [22]. Further, the author counters Krouwer's argument regarding outliers by suggesting that the estimation of an uncertainty interval for the measurement result is in itself sufficient to identify outliers and indicate the need for further investigation.

There have been several attempts at the estimation of uncertainty in analytical laboratory measurement systems, prominent among them being Fuentes-Arderiu and Dot-Bach [28], Petersen et al. [24], Patriarca et al. [29], Burns and Valdivia [30], Canalias et al. [31], Leung et al. [32], Middleton and Vaks [33], Sundvall et al. [34], Fuentes-Arderiu and Dot-Bach [35], and Chen et al. [36]. A very useful survey of the research on the estimation and analysis of uncertainty in various fields, including method validation and QC, clinical chemistry, health, fitness and sports sciences, and so on, was conducted by Burns [37]. In addition, commentaries of the evolution of metrology in chemistry by Kipphardt et al. [38] and a review treatment of bias and systematic error in analytical measurements by Hibbert [39] have been found useful in developing a perspective of how variation has been handled in analytical and clinical laboratories.

5.2.3 Uncertainty in Clinical Laboratories: A System Approach

Among the publications discussed earlier, the work done in Kallner and Waldenstrom [19], Kallner [17], Kristiansen [22], and Krouwer [25] was found to be particularly useful to the development of general guidelines for the estimation of uncertainty in clinical laboratory measurement systems. While Kristiansen (2001) was one of the first to explicitly outline a broadly applicable model for the estimation of the uncertainty for clinical assays, the guidelines proposed in Section 5.3 of this chapter are developed from a different perspective. In this chapter, we present the conceptualization of the clinical measurement process as a system with inputs and outputs, and describe the development of a mathematical model of the measurement system that combines descriptions of the physical and chemical phenomena underlying the measurement as well as the operational aspects of the measurement process. The use of the Monte Carlo method for the estimation of the uncertainty associated with the output of the system is then described. These general guidelines for the development of models of measurement uncertainty are described in detail in Section 5.3.

The choice of using the Monte Carlo method for estimating the uncertainty associated with such systems was made due to the following reasons. The most widely used method for computing the uncertainty associated with a measurement system is based on the law of propagation of uncertainty, as described in the GUM (1993). However, the Monte Carlo method becomes more appropriate to use for uncertainty estimation when the model of the measurement system possesses one or more of the following characteristics, as described by Cox et al. [40]:

1. The measurand is nonlinear.
2. The distribution of the measurand is not Gaussian.
3. Estimating the degrees of freedom for the sources of uncertainty is not possible. This is typically the case when the variation of the sources of uncertainty is characterized using Type B methods.

The models of measurement uncertainty developed using the methodology presented in the chapter have typically been nonlinear in the sources of uncertainty. The sources of uncertainty are also characterized using Type B methods, and hence these models meet conditions 1 and 3 described earlier. Therefore, the use of the Monte Carlo method to estimate measurement uncertainty becomes appropriate for the models developed using this methodology.

Further, using the general law of uncertainty propagation to compute uncertainties becomes tedious [41] when one or more of the following scenarios occur: (i) the model function is complex or nonlinear or both; (ii) there are a large number of sources of uncertainty; and (iii) there are a large number of correlated sources of uncertainty. Monte Carlo simulation has been considered as a tool of choice to overcome these limitations (Technical Report, 2004, National Physical Laboratory, UK). Monte Carlo simulation has also been used to estimate measurement uncertainty in analytical chemistry [42] and for the evaluation of assigned value uncertainty for complex calibrators [33], and hence the natural extension to clinical laboratory measurement systems as a whole.

The primary advantage, however, of using this methodology is that it lends itself to the development of a simulation model and, therefore, facilitates conducting simulation experiments and extracting information about the measurement process that would otherwise require controlled experimentation in laboratory settings. The mathematical model itself will not be written out in its entirety for complex systems [9]; expressions representing each step of the process are usually provided, thereby further encouraging the use of simulation for characterizing the stochastic behavior of such systems.

The use of the Monte Carlo simulation model to simulate and analyze a clinical measurement process is illustrated in Section 5.4. The methodology presented in this chapter and its uses for the estimation of the contributions of the sources of uncertainty operating within the system on the net measurement uncertainty, and for the simulation and optimization of calibration protocols, have been published by the authors in both methodological and clinical journals [4, 43–45].

5.3   MODEL DEVELOPMENT GUIDELINES

The guidelines described in this section for the development of the mathematical model are applicable to any clinical measurement process irrespective of whether the Monte Carlo method or the law of propagation of uncertainty is used to estimate the combined measurement uncertainty.

5.3.1   System Description and Process Phases

In the analytical stage of a clinical measurement process, the measuring instrument analyses the patient sample and determines the value of the measurand. A distinction is made here between the terms analyte and measurand: the *analyte* is the substance or chemical constituent determined in an analytical procedure, whereas the *measurand* represents the amount of the analyte in the patient sample. In general, there are two types of measurands: direct measurands, wherein the amount of analyte is directly measured by the instrument, and indirect measurands, wherein the instrument measures a property of the analyte, and the value of this property is converted into the measurand value using a calibration function. In most measurement systems, the instrument first analyzes known standards, and a calibration function is established. This phase of the analytical process, wherein a calibrator or Certified Reference Material (CRM) is analyzed by the instrument to characterize the calibration function, is termed the *calibration phase*. Three major components of the system are involved in the calibration phase: the calibrator or reference material, the instrument, and the reagents. There are uncertainties associated with each of these three components, and they are calibrator uncertainty, reagent uncertainty, and instrument uncertainty. These combine to yield the uncertainty associated with this phase, *calibration uncertainty*.

The calibrated instrument then analyzes the patient sample and provides the value of the measurand as system output. This phase of the analytical process – where the patient sample analysis takes place – is termed the *sample analysis phase*. Three principal components of the system are involved in this phase, the patient sample, the reagents, and the measuring instrument. The uncertainty associated with the patient sample is referred to as the specimen uncertainty, and the uncertainties associated with the reagents and the instrument are, as before, reagent uncertainty and instrument uncertainty. These combine to yield the uncertainty associated with this phase, sample analysis uncertainty. Calibration uncertainty and sample analysis uncertainty combine to form the net system uncertainty, which is the uncertainty associated with the measurand. The division of the analytical stage of the measurement process into phases provides intuitive structure to the modeling process and facilitates an understanding of the contribution of different stages of the measurement process to the net measurement uncertainty. This conceptualization is illustrated in Figures 5.1 and 5.2.

A few important points must be mentioned here. (i) Even though certain components are present in both phases, the uncertainty associated with each phase is unique. (ii) Specimen uncertainty represents uncertainty that affects the concentration of the analyte in the patient specimen before analysis on the instrument, and hence it is the uncertainty associated with the preanalytical stage. (iii) While a majority of

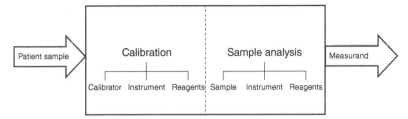

Figure 5.1 Clinical laboratory measurement process: system conceptualization.

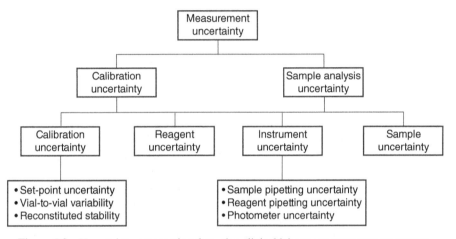

Figure 5.2 Uncertainty propagation through a clinical laboratory measurement process.

commonly used laboratory tests involve a chemical reaction requiring the use of reagents, some do not involve a chemical reaction; and hence do not have reagents as a principal component. An example of such an assay is the manual differential leukocyte count.

5.3.2 Modeling Guidelines

The first step in estimating the uncertainty associated with a clinical laboratory measurement system involves identifying the different components of the measurement system. As mentioned previously, the principal components of most clinical laboratory measurement systems are (i) the calibrator/CRM; (ii) the measuring instrument; (iii) the reagents; and (iv) the patient sample. Once the components of the system are identified, the next step is to identify the factors that contribute to the variation inherent in each component. To this end, the subcomponents of the principal components, if any, must be identified. As an example, the measuring instrument may have individual subcomponents with attendant uncertainties. These factors, which contribute to the uncertainty of each component and hence to the net measurement uncertainty, represent the sources of uncertainty operating within the measurement system.

Once the sources of uncertainty are identified, the next step involves character-izing their variation with an appropriate distribution. Here, a Type A or a Type B characterization of the sources of uncertainty can be carried out [6]. Following this, a mathematical model is developed that accurately describes the relationship between the measurand and the system components. Developing the mathematical model gen-erally involves the following: (i) understanding the role that each component of the system plays in estimating the value of the measurand; (ii) understanding the chemical reaction involved, if applicable, and the physical principle underlying the measure-ment; and (iii) understanding the calibration process. The calibration function often serves as a convenient starting point for the development of the mathematical model because each term in the calibration function represents the uncertainty associated with a specific stage of the measurement process. The calibration function relates to the process phases as follows: the uncertainty associated with the parameters repre-sents uncertainty in the calibration phase; the uncertainty associated with the inde-pendent variable(s) represents the uncertainty of the sample analysis phase, including preanalytical uncertainty; and the net measurement uncertainty is that associated with the dependent variable. Once the mathematical model is developed, the measurand can be evaluated for different values of each source of uncertainty by using the Monte Carlo method. The behavior of the measurand under uncertainty can thus be charac-terized and the uncertainty associated with the measurement system is thus estimated.

A key advantage of using the Monte Carlo method is that it enables the representa-tion of the measurement process in a manner that most closely resembles day-to-day laboratory operations. Therefore, the simulation must be organized in a manner that is, to the extent possible, exactly the same as the laboratory operation of interest. For instance, if 100 ALP measurements are carried out in a given day and the instru-ment is calibrated every 5 days, then the simulation must be organized in exactly the same way – that is, a calibration is performed every 500 measurements. Further, sources of uncertainty that vary with time can also be incorporated. For instance, if time-dependent drift is present in a sample or reagent pipette, then the expected value of the distribution describing this source of uncertainty can be incremented every day (or once every appropriate time unit). Since recalibration of the instrument nullifies the effect of drift in an instrument component, the simulation model can be used to determine the maximum time allowable between successive calibrations.

Since the Monte Carlo method enables accurate representation of laboratory oper-ations, including calibration, the model can be used to simulate, evaluate, and opti-mize laboratory operating protocols and calibration policies in terms of minimizing the net measurement uncertainty. For instance, as a sensitivity analysis exercise, the simulation model can be used to estimate the contributions of each component or source of uncertainty to the net measurement uncertainty by changing the parameters of the distribution of that source of uncertainty. Another example involves using the simulation model to determine the minimum number of optical absorbance measure-ments used as part of the calibration process that achieves the maximum reduction in net measurement uncertainty.

In the following section, we describe the development of the mathematical model of the ALP clinical assay. We then describe the use of the Monte Carlo method to estimate the uncertainty of the assay and to estimate the contributions of each source of uncertainty to the net measurement uncertainty as well as the effect of uncertainty in the calibration process on the net measurement uncertainty

5.4 IMPLEMENTATION OF GUIDELINES: ENZYME ASSAY UNCERTAINTY MODEL

In this section, we implement the guidelines outlined in the previous section by describing the development of a model of the uncertainty associated with the measurement of the ALP enzyme in the clinical laboratory. Elevated levels of the ALP enzyme may indicate liver function abnormalities, bone disease, as well as the presence of some cancers such as lymphoma and leukemia [46]. This model was first described in Ramamohan et al. [47].

We model the ALP assay that is performed on the Roche Diagnostics P-Modular Analytics measurement platform. The assay consists of conducting a chemical reaction between reactants supplied by two reagents. The chemical reaction is catalyzed by the enzyme supplied by the patient sample, and the amount of enzyme in the patient sample is characterized by its acceleration of the rate of the reaction. The rate of the reaction is a function of the amount of the reaction product formed per unit time, and the optical absorbance of the reaction mixture at a given point in time is proportional to the amount of product present in the reaction mixture at that point in time. The optical absorbance of the reaction mixture is recorded at regular intervals of time in order to estimate the rate of the reaction. The calibration function then converts the measured rate of the reaction into the "activity level" of the enzyme, which quantifies the amount of enzyme in the patient sample. The most widely used unit of enzyme activity is enzyme unit per liter (denoted as U/l), which is defined as the amount of enzyme that catalyzes the conversion of one micro mole of the substrate into the reaction product per minute.

The chemical reaction catalyzed by the ALP enzyme, and thereby forming the basis of the ALP assay, is given below:

$$p\text{-nitrophenyl phosphate} + H_2O \xrightarrow{\text{ALP}} p\text{-nitrophenol} + \text{phosphate} \qquad (5.5)$$

This chemical reaction yields the product of interest, p-nitrophenol, and the optical absorbance of the reaction mixture at a given point in time is directly proportional to the concentration of the p-nitrophenol.

Two reagents are added as part of the ALP assay: R_1, containing the metal-ion buffer necessary for the reaction, and R_2, containing the reactant p-nitrophenyl phosphate. The patient sample supplies the ALP enzyme that catalyzes the reaction. In the description of the model that follows, we use the term "substrate" to refer to the p-nitrophenyl phosphate supplied by the reagent R_2 and "reagent" to refer to the metal-ion buffer supplied by the reagent R_1. The volumes of the reagent and the substrate are denoted by V_{r1} and V_{r2}, respectively. The volume of the patient sample containing the ALP is denoted by V_s. The concentration of a species is represented by enclosing its symbol within square brackets.

The ALP activity level is linearly proportional to the rate of the reaction (rate of change of absorbance with time) and is estimated using the calibration equation, specified below:

$$[E]_x = K(m_x - m_b) \tag{5.6}$$

Here $[E]_x$ denotes the ALP activity level in the patient sample; K the calibration parameter, and m_b represents the rate of the reaction (absorbance/min) for a blank sample. The value of m_b is zero. Further, all properties (absorbance, activity level, etc.) of the patient sample with unknown enzyme activity level will be denoted using the subscript x in this document.

K, the calibration parameter, is computed as follows:

$$K = \frac{[E]_2 - [E]_1}{m_2 - m_1} \tag{5.7}$$

Here, $[E]_1$ and $[E]_2$ represent the desired (error-free) lower and higher activity levels of the ALP enzyme in the calibrators 1 and 2, respectively. n absorbance readings, recorded at equal intervals of time and denoted by $A_1, A_2, ..., A_n$, are used to derive a linear relationship between absorbance and time. The rate of the reaction m is estimated by fitting a linear regression function using these n absorbance readings, that is,

$$m = \frac{\sum_i t_i A_i - \frac{1}{n} \sum_i t_i \sum_i A_i}{\sum_i t_i^2 - \frac{1}{n}(\sum_i t_i)^2} \tag{5.8}$$

5.4.1 Calibration Phase

In the calibration phase, the values of K and m_b are estimated. A two-point calibration is performed since the sample activity level is a linear function of the rate of change of absorbance. Three sources of uncertainty are identified as affecting the value of the calibrator activity level: calibrator set point uncertainty (u_{c1}), vial-to-vial variability (u_{c2}) and calibrator reconstituted stability ($u_{c3(t)}$). The first, calibrator set-point uncertainty, involves the uncertainty in the calibrator activity level during manufacture and prior to its use in the laboratory. The second source of calibrator uncertainty, vial-to-vial variability, represents the uncertainty introduced in the sample activity in the laboratory while preparing different vials of the calibrator from the batch supplied by the manufacturer. The third source of uncertainty, calibrator reconstituted stability, quantifies the deterioration (percentage decrease in activity per day) of the sample when the calibrator vial is stored and reconstituted after each use. When these sources of uncertainty are introduced into the model, the values of E_1 and E_2 change according to the following equation:

$$[E]_1' = [E]_1 (1 + u_{c1}) (1 + u_{c2}) \prod_{t=1}^{N}(1 + u_{c3(t)}) \tag{5.9a}$$

$$[E]_2' = [E]_2 (1 + u_{c1}) (1 + u_{c2}) \prod_{t=1}^{N}(1 + u_{c3(t)}) \tag{5.9b}$$

We assume a multiplicative model for the combination of these sources of uncertainty because the sources of calibrator uncertainty are introduced into the calibration process one after the other and, therefore, serially change the concentration of the calibrator. The variation of these sources of uncertainty, along with the others identified as operating within the measurement process, is characterized by fitting suitable distributions to the specifications provided by Roche Diagnostics for each source of uncertainty. As an illustration, specifications for vial-to-vial variability were provided by the instrument manufacturer in the form of a coefficient of variation (CV) of 1.5%. After discussion with the manufacturers, a Gaussian distribution with a mean of 0% and a standard deviation of 1.5% was assumed to characterize the variation in the calibrator activity levels due to vial-to-vial variability. The expected value of the distribution was assumed to be 0%, as systematic errors in the calibrator manufacturing process were ruled out based on the manufacturer's recommendation. Therefore, at a desired (error-free) calibrator enzyme activity level of 200 units/liter, the activity level in practice would be described by a Gaussian distribution with an expected value of 200 U/l and a standard deviation of 3 U/l.

The activity values of the calibrator also change due to the sources of instrument uncertainty. Three sources of uncertainty are associated with the instrument: sample pipetting uncertainty, reagent pipetting uncertainty, and photometer uncertainty. Sample and reagent pipetting uncertainty describe the uncertainty in the volumes of the sample and reagents pipetted into the reaction cell, hence resulting in a change in the total volume of the reaction mixture and the number of enzyme and reactant molecules in the reaction mixture before the reaction begins. Therefore, their effect on the measurand occurs at time $t = 0$. However, photometer uncertainty changes each of the 15 optical measurements recorded during the course of the reaction. The variations of the sources of instrument uncertainty are also characterized in a manner similar to that of the sources of calibrator uncertainty, and hence are also described by Gaussian distributions. The parameters of the distributions used to characterize the sources of uncertainty are summarized in Table 5.2.

We now derive the effect of sample and reagent pipetting uncertainty on each optical absorbance measurement recorded during the reaction. We begin with the assumption that the optical absorbance at time t, denoted by A_t, is linearly proportional to the concentration of the product p-nitrophenol in the reaction mixture at

TABLE 5.2 Characterization of Sources of Uncertainty

Source of Uncertainty	Distribution	Mean (%)	SD (%)	Notes
Calibrator set-point uncertainty	Gaussian	0.00	0.10	
Vial-to-vial variability	Gaussian	0.00	1.50	
Reconstituted stability	Gaussian	−1.25	0.42	Decrease of enzyme activity per day
Sample pipetting uncertainty	Gaussian	0.00	1.50	
Reagent pipetting uncertainty	Gaussian	0.00	4.00	
Photometer uncertainty	Gaussian	0.00	0.15	

time t (denoted by $[P]_t$), that is,

$$A_t = k[P]_t + A_{0(t)} \tag{5.10}$$

Here, k represents the molar extinction coefficient, $A_{0(t)}$ represents the absorbance at time t when the p-nitrophenol concentration at time t is zero. This assumption is based on the Beer–Lambert law, which states that the optical absorbance of a solution is proportional to the concentration of the absorbing species – in this case the product of the reaction. It is reasonable to assume that the optical absorbance at time t at zero p-nitrophenol concentration is equal to the optical absorbance at time $t = 0$ at zero p-nitrophenol concentration. The p-nitrophenol concentration will be zero if the chemical reaction does not take place; in other words, it can correspond to a configuration wherein a water blank is used. In this case, the optical absorbance will be independent of time, and the measurements recorded at regular time intervals will remain constant. Therefore, we replace the intercept term $A_{0(t)}$ by a more general intercept term A_0 to denote optical absorbance of a sample with zero enzyme activity. Equation 5.10 can then be rewritten as

$$A_t = k[P]_t + A_0 \tag{5.11}$$

In order to derive the relationship between the concentration $[P]_t$ of p-nitrophenol, time t, and the initial concentration of the substrate $[S]_0$, we consider the fact that reaction 5.5 belongs to the class of enzyme reactions that follow the following reaction mechanism:

$$E + S \underset{k_{-1}}{\overset{k_1}{\rightleftharpoons}} ES \xrightarrow{k_2} E + P \tag{5.12}$$

Here, E represents to the enzyme ALP, S to the substrate p-nitrophenyl phosphate, ES to the enzyme–substrate complex formed during the reaction, and P to the product p-nitrophenol. The rate constants for the forward reactions are represented by k_1 and k_2, and the rate constant for the reverse reaction is k_{-1}. We now recall that the patient sample supplies the enzyme E, reactant R_2 supplies the substrate S, and the product P refers to p-nitrophenol.

Applying the law of mass action to each of the terms in reaction 5.12, which states that the rate of a reaction, represented by the rate of formation or consumption of a species in the reaction, is proportional to the product of the concentrations of the reactants, we obtain the following system of nonlinear differential equations:

$$\frac{d[S]}{dt} = -k_1 [E] [S] + k_{-1} [ES] \tag{5.13a}$$

$$\frac{d[E]}{dt} = -k_1 [E] [S] + (k_{-1} + k_2) [ES] \tag{5.13b}$$

$$\frac{d[ES]}{dt} = k_1 [E] [S] - (k_{-1} + k_2) [ES] \tag{5.13c}$$

$$\frac{d[P]}{dt} = k_2 [ES] \tag{5.13d}$$

The initial conditions for this system are as follows:

$$([E], [S], [ES], [P])_{t=0} = ([E]_0, [S]_0, 0, 0) \tag{5.13e}$$

There are two conservation laws applicable to this system. First, the sum of the concentrations of the free substrate $[S]$, enzyme–substrate complex $[ES]$, and product $[P]$ must be equal to the initial substrate concentration $[S]_0$. Second, the sum of the enzyme concentration $[E]$ and the enzyme–susbtrate complex concentration $[S]$ must be equal to the initial free enzyme concentration $[E]_0$. Mathematically, these are represented as follows:

$$[S] + [ES] + [P] = [S]_0 \tag{5.14a}$$

$$[E] + [ES] = [E]_0 \tag{5.14b}$$

Applying Equation 5.14a and b to the system of coupled differential Equation 5.13a–e results in reducing the system of four equations to the following:

$$\frac{d[S]}{dt} = -k_1 \left([E]_0 - [ES]\right) [S] + k_{-1} [ES] \tag{5.15a}$$

$$\frac{d[ES]}{dt} = k_1 \left([E]_0 - [ES]\right) [S] - (k_{-1} + k_2) [ES] \tag{5.15b}$$

Briggs and Haldane [48] developed a mathematical framework, based on the work by Michaelis and Menten [49], for the analysis of enzyme kinetics that expressed the initial velocity of the reaction as a function of the initial enzyme concentration as well as the initial substrate concentration (at time $t = 0$). They postulated that the concentration of the enzyme–substrate complex will rapidly reach at a constant value, which enables the following steady-state approximation to be applied to Equation 5.15b:

$$\frac{d[ES]}{dt} = 0 = k_1 \left([E]_0 - [ES]\right) [S] - (k_{-1} + k_2) [ES] \tag{5.16}$$

Solving for the enzyme–substrate complex concentration $[ES]$, we have the following expression:

$$[ES] = \frac{k_1 [E]_0 [S]_0}{k_{-1} + k_2 + k_1 [S]_0} \tag{5.17}$$

The initial velocity of the reaction is defined by Equation 5.13d, as the rate of formation of the product. Substituting the expression for $[ES]$ developed in Equation 5.13d, we have

$$\frac{d[P]}{dt} = \frac{k_2 k_1 [E]_0 [S]_0}{k_{-1} + k_2 + k_1 [S]_0} \tag{5.18}$$

Upon dividing the right-hand side of the above-mentioned equation by k_1, the equation can be rewritten as following:

$$\frac{d[P]}{dt} = \frac{v_{\max} [S]_0}{K_m + [S]_0} \tag{5.19}$$

Now we write $\frac{k_2+k_{-1}}{k_1}$ as K_m and replace the term $k_2\,[E]_0$ by v_{max}. K_m is also known as the Michaelis constant and v_{max} is the maximum rate – the reaction velocity at which all the enzyme molecules are in the enzyme–substrate complex form. Now, when $[S]_0 = K_m$, we find that the rate of the reaction, as defined by Equation 5.19 is equal to $\frac{1}{2}v_{max}$, and therefore the Michaelis constant represents the value of the initial substrate concentration at which the reaction attains half its maximum velocity.

We can use Equation 5.19 to determine the relationship between product concentration $[P]$ and time as follows:

$$\int_0^{[P]_t} d[P] = \int_0^t \frac{v_{max}\,[S]_0}{K_m + [S]_0}\,dt \tag{5.20}$$

That is,

$$[P]_t = \left(\frac{v_{max}\,[S]_0}{K_m + [S]_0} \right) t \tag{5.21}$$

Substituting the above-mentioned expression for $[P]_t$ in Equation 5.10, we obtain the relationship between optical absorbance and the initial enzyme and substrate concentrations and time.

$$A_t = k \left(\frac{v_{max}\,[S]_0}{K_m + [S]_0} \right) t + A_0 \tag{5.22}$$

For the purpose of maintaining economy of notation in the rest of the derivation, we express the product concentration at time t as a function f of the initial substrate and enzyme concentrations and time t as follows:

$$[P]_t = f([S]_0, [E]_0, t)$$

Therefore, Equation 5.22 now becomes

$$A_t = k\,f([S]_0, [E]_0, t) + A_0 \tag{5.23}$$

Now, at $t = 0$, substrate concentration in the reaction mixture can be written as the ratio of the number of moles of the substrate $N_{S(0)}$ to the volume of the reaction mixture V. That is, the above equation can be written as

$$A_t = k\,f\left(\frac{N_{S(0)}}{V}, [E]_0, t \right) + A_0 \tag{5.24}$$

Further, the number of moles of the substrate $N_{S(0)}$ can also be written as the product of the substrate concentration $[S]_{r2}$ in R_2 and its volume V_{r2}. The distinction between the terms $[S]_0$ and $[S]_{r2}$ must be emphasized here: the former refers to the desired substrate concentration in the reaction mixture at time $t = 0$, and the latter to the desired substrate concentration in the reagent R_2 before it is added to the reaction mixture. Therefore, the above-mentioned equation can be written as

$$A_t = k f \left(\frac{[S]_{r2} \, V_{r2}}{V}, [E]_0, t \right) + A_0 \tag{5.25}$$

The total volume of the reaction mixture V is the sum of the sample and reagent volumes V_s, V_{r1}, and V_{r2}. We now introduce pipetting uncertainty into the model. Let the fractional change in sample volume due to sample pipetting uncertainty be x, the fractional change in reagent volumes due to reagent pipetting uncertainty be y_1 and y_2, and the fractional change in total reaction mixture volume be denoted by z. Then,

$$V_s + \delta V_s = V_s(1 + x) \tag{5.26a}$$

$$V_{r1} + \delta V_{r1} = V_{r1}(1 + y_1) \tag{5.26b}$$

$$V_{r2} + \delta V_{r2} = V_{r2}(1 + y_2) \tag{5.26c}$$

$$V + \delta V = V(1 + z) \tag{5.26d}$$

Now, using the fact that $V = V_s + V_{r1} + V_{r2}$, we have

$$V + \delta V = V_s(1 + x) + V_{r1}(1 + y_1) + V_{r2}(1 + y_2) \tag{5.27a}$$

That is,

$$V + \delta V = V_s + V_{r1} + V_{r2} + xV_s + y_1 V_{r1} + y_2 V_{r2} \tag{5.27b}$$

and

$$\delta V = xV_s + y_1 V_{r1} + y_2 V_{r2} \tag{5.27c}$$

Uncertainty in the instrument can also manifest itself as an error in the time at which the absorbance measurement is recorded. This in turn can change the extent to which the reaction has occurred, and therefore the optical absorbance is measured ostensibly at time t. We refer to this uncertainty in time of measurement as *clock uncertainty*. We denote this error in the time of measurement as δt and the fractional change in the desired time of measurement t as u_t. If we denote the change in optical absorbance measured at time t as δA_t, then the optical absorbance after the incorporation of pipetting and clock uncertainty can be written as

$$A_t + \delta A_t = k f \left(\frac{[S]_{r2} \, (V_{r2} + \delta V_{r2})}{(V + \delta V)}, [E]_0, (t + \delta t) \right) + A_0 \tag{5.28}$$

Using Equation 5.26a–d, we obtain

$$A_t + \delta A_t = k f \left(\frac{[S]_{r2} \, V_{r2} \, (1 + y_2)}{V \, (1 + z)}, [E]_0, t \, (1 + u_t) \right) + A_0 \tag{5.29}$$

Subtracting Equation 5.25 from Equation 5.29, we obtain the change in absorbance due to instrument uncertainty.

$$\delta A_t = k \left[f\left(\frac{[S]_{r2}\, V_{r2}\, (1+y_2)}{V\,(1+z)}, [E]_0, t\,(1+u_t) \right) - f\left(\frac{[S]_{r2}\, V_{r2}}{V}, [E]_0, t \right) \right] \quad (5.30)$$

We denote the fractional change in optical absorbance at time t due to pipetting and clock uncertainty, $\frac{\delta A_t}{A_t}$, by the term $u_{pc(t)}$. Now, Equation 5.30 denotes the change in absorbance at time t from the desired value that occurs before the measurement is performed. When the measurement is performed, the uncertainty due to the photometer changes the absorbance further by the fractional amount $u_{p(t)}$. Therefore, the final expression for optical absorbance after incorporating pipetting and clock uncertainty into the model is as follows:

$$A'_t = A_t(1 + u_{pc(t)})(1 + u_{p(t)}) \quad (5.31)$$

The above-mentioned expression denotes the value of absorbance after all sources of uncertainty affecting the optical absorbance measurement have been incorporated into the model. This process is repeated for all absorbance measurements recorded during the chemical reaction. Therefore, the corresponding rate of the reaction is estimated as follows:

$$m_{int} = \frac{\sum_i t_i A'_i - \frac{1}{n}\sum_i t_i \sum_i A'_i}{\sum_i t_i^2 - \frac{1}{n}(\sum_i t_i)^2} \quad (5.32)$$

Now, since the patient sample supplies the enzyme ALP that catalyzes the assay reaction, a change in the volume of the patient sample due to sample pipetting uncertainty changes the number of enzyme molecules available to catalyze the reaction. The change in the rate of the reaction due to a change in sample volume is linearly proportional to the change in volume; therefore, an $x\%$ change in the sample volume would cause the same $x\%$ change in the rate of the reaction. Therefore, the final rate of the reaction after all the sources of uncertainty operating within the calibration process is given by

$$m' = m_{int}(1 + x) \quad (5.33)$$

This process of incorporating uncertainty into the calibration process is applied to both calibrators E_1 and E_2 and their corresponding desired reaction rates m_1 and m_2. Therefore, after incorporating the uncertainty introduced by the calibration process, this results in the estimation of the calibration factor as

$$K' = \frac{[E]'_2 - [E]'_1}{m'_2 - m'_1} \quad (5.34)$$

In the case of most clinical enzyme assays, one of the calibrators is a water blank, and hence only the slope of the calibration line, the calibration factor, is estimated.

5.4.2   Sample Analysis Phase

After the value of the calibration factor is estimated, the process moves into the sample analysis phase. In terms of the calibration line, the uncertainty of this phase is that associated with the independent variable m; that is, the absorbance measurements recorded as part of the analysis of the patient sample. Instrument uncertainty is the primary source of uncertainty operating within this phase.

The effect of instrument uncertainty on net measurement uncertainty has been dealt with in the previous section, and we denote the fractional change in optical absorbance at time t due to pipetting uncertainty and clock uncertainty in the sample analysis phase as $u_{\mathrm{pc}(t,x)}$. If we denote the "true" error-free enzyme activity level of the sample as $[E]_x$ and the corresponding absorbance at time t as $A_{x(t)}$, the absorbance obtained after the incorporating sample and instrument uncertainty is expressed as

$$A'_{x(t)} = A_{x(t)}(1 + u_{\mathrm{pc}(t,x)})(1 + u_{p(t,x)}) \tag{5.35}$$

Here A'_x represents the absorbance after the uncertainty of the measurement phase is introduced into the process. The process of incorporating instrument uncertainty is followed for each absorbance measurement, and the rate of the reaction corresponding to the patient sample (denoted by $m_{\mathrm{int}(x)}$) is estimated as the following:

$$m_{\mathrm{int}(x)} = \frac{\sum_i t_i A'_{x(i)} - \frac{1}{n}\sum_i t_i \sum_i A'_{x(i)}}{\sum_i t_i^2 - \frac{1}{n}(\sum_i t_i)^2} \tag{5.36}$$

The above value of the rate of the reaction is further changed due to sample pipetting uncertainty as follows:

$$m'_x = m_{\mathrm{int}(x)}\,(1 + x) \tag{5.37}$$

The term m'_x denotes the value of the rate of the reaction after all sources of uncertainty operating within the measurement process are incorporated into the model. When this value of the rate of the reaction is input into the calibration line, we get the ALP activity of the sample as

$$[E]'_x = K' m'_x \tag{5.38}$$

The uncertainty associated with the model is estimated by generating patient sample activity levels (in the current implementation, 1000, since it corresponds to the average number of tests conducted on the P-modular analytics platform in a day in a hospital) for different sets of realizations of the sources of uncertainty and then computing the standard deviation of these 1000 activity levels. After each set of 1000 measurements, the instrument is calibrated again. The average measurement uncertainty observed for the ALP assay is computed by estimating the mean of the uncertainties recorded for each of 30 sets of 1000 measurements. We note here that while the model accounts for clock uncertainty, it was decided not to include it in the implementation of the model upon the recommendation of the manufacturer, as it is negligible in practice.

5.4.3   Results and Analysis

The model was programmed in Python with the NumPy and SciPy packages. Values of the rate constant k_2 (34/s) and the Michaelis constant K_m (4.48 mmol/L) were estimated from the BRENDA Comprehensive Enzyme Information System [50]. The measurement uncertainties (coefficients of variation (CVs)) estimated for a range of patient sample activity levels between 120 and 360 U/l varied from 3.63% to 2.11%. In order to estimate the measurement uncertainty at different activity levels, the simulation model was used to develop an empirical function, referred to as the uncertainty profile, that generates an estimate of measurement uncertainty at a given activity level. The uncertainty profile is constructed by generating uncertainty estimates at enzyme activity levels, across the possible range of patient sample activity levels, and then identifying the function that is the best statistical fit to the data. For the uncertainty profile, the sample activity level (in U/l) is the independent variable, and the standard deviation (in U/l) of the distribution of the measurement result is the dependent variable. The uncertainty profile for the ALP assay is shown in Figure 5.3. A sample activity level range of 120–360 U/l, traversed in increments of 5 U/l, was used to construct the uncertainty profile. The coefficients of variation used in constructing the uncertainty profile were generated by organizing the simulation in the same manner as described in the previous section. That is, CVs were estimated by computing the mean of 30 values of measurement uncertainty, each of which was estimated from a set of 1000 measurements.

One of the principal uses of such an uncertainty model is to estimate the contribution of each individual source of uncertainty in both the calibration and sample

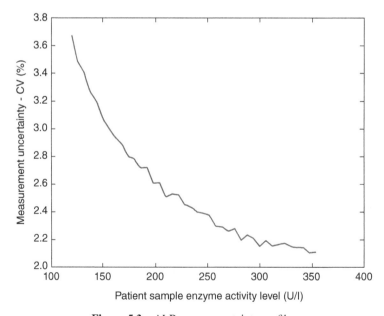

Figure 5.3   ALP assay uncertainty profile.

TABLE 5.3 Contribution of Sources of Uncertainty in the Sample Analysis Phase to Net Measurement Uncertainty

Source of Uncertainty	Measurement Uncertainty with All Sources Operating (CV, %)	Measurement Uncertainty with Source Removed (CV, %)	% Contribution to Net Measurement Uncertainty
Sample pipette	2.50	2.02	19.20
Reagent pipette	2.50	2.31	7.60
Photometer	2.50	1.78	28.80

analysis phase of the measurement process. The contribution of a given source of uncertainty in a phase is estimated by nullifying its variation (setting its mean and standard deviation of its distribution to zero) and then re-estimating the net measurement uncertainty. The difference between the value of the measurement uncertainty estimated without the source under consideration and the value estimated with all sources of uncertainty quantifies its contribution to the net measurement uncertainty.

First, the contributions of the sources of uncertainty operating within the sample analysis phase are estimated. Only the sources of instrument uncertainty operate within this phase, and their individual contributions to the net measurement uncertainty within the sample analysis phase are listed in Table 5.3. It is evident that the photometer and the sample pipette are the largest contributors to the net measurement uncertainty, and that reducing the variation in their operation would lead to a substantial decrease in net measurement uncertainty. For instance, a decrease in 50% of photometer uncertainty (from an SD of 0.15% to 0.075%) reduces the net measurement uncertainty by 20%.

Next, the contributions of the sources of calibrator uncertainty are estimated. Since these sources operate within the calibration phase, their contribution is estimated not by studying the effect of nullifying their variation on the net measurement uncertainty, but by studying the distribution of the calibration parameter K'. The effect of these sources of uncertainty on the distribution of K' is estimated by nullifying the variation of these sources of uncertainty in the calibration phase alone and then re-estimating the net measurement uncertainty.

Uncertainty in K' shifts the expected value of the distribution of the measurement result. We refer to this shift in the expected value of the measurement result distribution as *bias* and estimate the worst-case bias of the measurand due to each source of uncertainty operating within the calibration phase. We define the worst-case bias of the measurand as the absolute value of the percentage deviation in the expected value of the measurand distribution from the desired error-free enzyme activity level when the calibration parameter is at +3 standard deviations from its expected value. The estimates of the worst-case bias due to each source of uncertainty operating within the calibration phase are provided in Table 5.4.

It is clearly seen from Table 5.4 that the sources of uncertainty operating within the calibration phase do not have a significant effect on the expected value of K'. This can

TABLE 5.4   Contribution of Individual Sources of Uncertainty in the Calibration Phase

Source of Uncertainty Removed	Mean of Calibration Parameter K'(U-s/l)	CV of Calibration Parameter K'(%)	Worst-Case Bias (%)
None	0.002094	2.560	7.269
Calibrator set-point uncertainty	0.002093	2.553	7.169
Vial-to-vial variability	0.002093	2.537	7.093
Reconstituted stability	0.002093	2.480	6.970
All calibrator sources	0.002095	2.506	7.077
Sample pipetting uncertainty	0.002093	2.088	5.924
Reagent pipetting uncertainty	0.002093	2.341	6.616
Photometer uncertainty	0.002093	1.796	5.185

be attributed to the fact that the expected values of all the sources of uncertainty are assumed to be zero, except for reconstituted stability. It is also clear that the sources of calibrator uncertainty, including reconstituted stability, do not have a significant effect on the distribution of K'. Among the sources of calibrator uncertainty, reconstituted stability has the largest effect on the worst-case bias, with a reduction of 4.11% when its variation is set to zero. The effect of the sources of instrument uncertainty dominates that of the sources of calibrator uncertainty on the calibration parameter, and therefore on the measurand distribution. Once again, photometer uncertainty has the largest effect on the measurand distribution, with a reduction of approximately 30% in the CV of K' and a reduction of approximately 29% in the worst-case bias as compared to the case when all sources of uncertainty are operating within the measurement system. The dominance of photometer uncertainty in its effect on the measurand distribution can be attributed to the fact that multiple absorbance measurements are made within the assay analysis process – 15 within each phase in the current configuration of the ALP assay.

As is evident from this section, such models can be used to estimate the effect of the sources of uncertainty operating within both the calibration phase and the measurement phase on the distribution of the measurement result.

5.5   DISCUSSION AND CONCLUSIONS

Two categories of assumptions are made in developing such models of measurement uncertainty: physical assumptions that form the basis of the mathematical model of the measurement system; and statistical assumptions made regarding the probability distributions of the sources of uncertainty operating within the system. Both sets of assumptions must be valid if the model is to accurately describe the measurement process. Experimentally verifying these assumptions made in building the ALP assay model was not possible due to limitations of access to experimental equipment.

However, a minimum level of validation was conducted by comparing estimates of uncertainty obtained from the model with uncertainty estimates provided by the instrument manufacturer. These estimates of uncertainty from the instrument manufacturer were provided in the form of an upper bound of 4% for the CV for ALP activity levels greater than 75 U/l. As can be seen from Figure 5.3, this condition is satisfied for all enzyme activity levels greater within the range of enzyme activity levels considered in the model. This comparison is not an adequate substitution for validation via controlled experimentation; however, it serves to indicate that the model provides estimates of uncertainty comparable to that seen in the laboratory.

We would like to emphasize here that for the purpose of comparison of model estimates of uncertainty with estimates of uncertainty from experimental data, the organization of the Monte Carlo simulation must be the same as that of the experimental data. For instance, consider a data set consisting of 50 sets of 20 measurements each (all at the same desired enzyme activity level), with the instrument being calibrated after every 20 measurements. Estimates of uncertainty must be computed for each of these 20 sets, and then the mean uncertainty must be computed from these 50 estimates of uncertainty. Then the estimates of uncertainty from the simulation model must also be obtained in exactly the same way, with the mean uncertainty computed from 50 estimates of uncertainty, each of which is computed from a set of 20 measurements.

A few important points require consideration while developing such models of measurement uncertainty. It is imperative that the mathematical model developed be accurate and adequately representative of the clinical laboratory testing system. Some potential sources of uncertainty, although not included currently in the study, require investigation, an example being the sources of preanalytical uncertainty. To this end, a close working relationship with both the clinical laboratorians and the instrument manufacturers is required. These considerations imply that this simulation approach would be useful for clinicians and instrument manufacturers as a design tool to set quality specifications and to estimate and understand the contribution of the different sources of uncertainty to the net system uncertainty (as shown in [4]). The authors have previously explored the use of these models to simulate and evaluate the effect of existing and new calibration protocols on the net system uncertainty, such as the use of multiple replicate measurements or calibrators in establishing the calibration function [43].

The use of the model, as demonstrated in the previous section, in determining the largest contributors to net measurement uncertainty demonstrates the utility of the model as an alternative or aid to conducting controlled experiments in the laboratory. In our estimation, such models would best be developed by the instrument manufacturer during the conceptualization stage of the instrument design process. The instrument manufacturer would have the best access to information regarding the performance of the subcomponents of the instrument, which would be required to parameterize the distributions of the sources of uncertainty, and also to the resources required to experimentally validate the physical assumptions made in the development of the model.

   Estimates of measurement uncertainty and the contribution of individual sources of uncertainty to the net measurement uncertainty can provide guidance to the instrument designers as to which subcomponent should be the target of their design efforts. Based on the information provided by clinicians across different hospitals, instrument manufacturers can simulate and evaluate commonly used calibration and quality control protocols and make recommendations to clinicians regarding optimal operating policies. Clinicians can use the models supplied by the instrument manufacturers to specify quality control limits for regular evaluation of the measurement process and also experiment with alternative operating protocols that suit their laboratory's needs.

   Further, such models of measurement uncertainty can be built for general linear and nonlinear calibration systems, and general guidelines for developing such models have been described in [4]. Building an adequately representative model of a measurement system requires understanding and modeling the physical principle underlying the measurement process, and then introducing uncertainty into the model by treating the relevant parameters of the model as random variables. The calibration function therefore serves as a convenient starting point for developing the uncertainty model. Uncertainty in the calibration process can be incorporated into the variation in the parameters of the calibration function, and the uncertainty associated with the analysis of the sample can be incorporated into the variation of the independent variable. After the mathematical model is developed and the sources of uncertainty are characterized by appropriate distributions, the model can then be used to simulate, analyze, and optimize the measurement process.

REFERENCES

[1] Keehan SP, Sisko AM, Truffer CJ, Poisal JA, Cuckler GA, Madison AJ, Lizonitz JM, Smith SD. National health spending projections through 2020: economic recovery and reform drive faster spending growth. Health Aff 2011;30(8):1594–1605.

[2] Anderson GF, Frogner BK, Johns RA, Reinhardt UE. Health care spending and use of information technology in OECD countries. Health Aff 2006;25(3):819–831.

[3] Linko S, Ornemark U, Kessel R, Taylor PDP. Evaluation of uncertainty of measurement in routine analytical chemistry – applications to determination of the substance concentration of calcium and glucose in serum. Clin Chem Lab Med 2002;40(4):391–398.

[4] Ramamohan V, Chandrasekar V, Abbott J, Klee GG, Yih Y. A Monte Carlo approach to the estimation and analysis of uncertainty in clinical laboratory measurement processes. IIE Trans Healthc Syst Eng 2012;2(1):1–13.

[5] BIPM, CIPM, and Working Group. *Expression of Experimental Uncertainties*. Sevres: ISO; 1980.

[6] BIPM, IEC, IFCC, ISO, IUPAC, IUPAP, and OIML. *Guide to the Expression of Uncertainty in Measurement*. Geneva: ISO; 1993.

[7] Kragten J. Calculating standard deviations and confidence intervals with a universally applicable spreadsheet technique. Analyst 1994;119:2161–2165.

[8] BIPM. Evaluation of Measurement Data – Guide to the Expression of Uncertainty in Measurement. Technical report JCGM-100, BIPM; 2008.

[9] BIPM. Evaluation of Measurement Data – Supplement 1 to the "Guide to the Expression of Uncertainty in Measurement" – Propagation of Distributions Using a Monte Carlo Method. Technical report JCGM-101, BIPM; 2008.

[10] BIPM. Evaluation of Measurement Data – Supplement 2 to the "Guide to the Expression of Uncertainty in Measurement" – Extension to Any Number of Output Quantities. Technical report JCGM-102, BIPM; 2011.

[11] BIPM. Evaluation of Measurement Data – The Role of Measurement Uncertainty in Conformity Assessment. Technical report JCGM-106, BIPM; 2012.

[12] BIPM. Evaluation of Measurement Data – An Introduction to the "Guide to the Expression of Uncertainty in Measurement" and Related Documents. Technical report JCGM-104, BIPM; 2009.

[13] Aronsson T, de Verdier C-H, Groth T. Factors influencing the quality of analytical methods: a systems analysis, with use of computer simulation. Clin Chem 1974;20(7):738–748.

[14] Tietz NW. A model for a comprehensive measurement system in clinical chemistry. Clin Chem 1979;25(6):833–839.

[15] Kristiansen J, Christensen JM, Nielsen JL. Uncertainty of atomic absorption spectrometry: application to the determination of lead in blood. Microchim Acta 1996;123(1-4):241–249.

[16] Kristiansen J, Christensen JM. Traceability and uncertainty in analytical measurements. Ann Clin Biochem 1998;35:371–379.

[17] Kallner A. Quality specifications based on the uncertainty of measurement. Scand J Clin Lab Invest 1999;59(7):513–516.

[18] EURACHEM. EURACHEM, Quantifying Uncertainty in Analytical Measurement. Technical report, London: Laboratory of the Government Chemist; 1995. ISBN: 0-948926-08-2.

[19] Kallner A, Waldenstrom J. Does the uncertainty of commonly performed glucose measurements allow identification of individuals at high risk for diabetes? Clin Chem Lab Med 1999;37:907–912.

[20] Dybkaer R. Quality management, certification and accreditation in medical laboratories – the view of ECLM. Accredit Qual Assur 1999;4(3):90–92.

[21] Fuentes-Arderiu X. Uncertainty of measurement in clinical laboratory sciences. Clin Chem 2000;46(9):1437–1438.

[22] Kristiansen J. Description of a generally applicable model for the evaluation of uncertainty of measurement in clinical chemistry. Clin Chem Lab Med 2001;39(10):920–931.

[23] Petersen PH, Stöckl D, Westgard JO, Sandberg S, Linnet K, Thienpont L. Models for combining random and systematic errors. Assumptions and consequences for different models. Clin Chem Lab Med 2001;39(7):589–595.

[24] Petersen PH, Brandslund I, Jorgensen L, Stahl M, Olivarius NdeFine, Borch-Johnsen K. Evaluation of systematic and random factors measurements of fasting plasma glucose as the basis for analytical quality specifications in the diagnosis of diabetes. 3. Impact of the new WHO and ADA recommendations on diagnosis of diabetes mellitus. Scand J Clin Lab Invest 2001;61:191–204.

[25] Krouwer J. Setting performance and evaluating total analytical error for diagnostic assays. Clin Chem Lab Med 2002;48(6):919–927.

[26] Krouwer JS. Critique of the guide to the expression of uncertainty in measurement method of estimating and reporting uncertainty in diagnostic assays. Clin Chem 2003;49(11):1818–1821.

[27] Kristiansen J. The guide to expression of uncertainty in measurement approach for estimating uncertainty an appraisal. Clin Chem 2003;49(11):1822–1829.

[28] Fuentes-Ardeiru X, Dot-Bach D. Measurement uncertainty in manual differential leukocyte counting. Clin Chem Lab Med 1999;47(2):112–115.

[29] Patriarca M, Castelli M, Corsetti F, Menditto A. Estimate of uncertainty of measurement from a single-laboratory validation study: application to the determination of lead in blood. Clin Chem 2004;50(6):1396–1405.

[30] Burns M, Valdivia H. A procedural approach for the identification of sources of uncertainty associated with gm quantification and real-time quantitative PCR measurements. Eur Food Res Technol 2007;226(1-2):7–18.

[31] Canalias F, Camprubí S, Sánchez M, Gella F-J. Metrological traceability of values for catalytic concentration of enzymes assigned to a calibration material. Clin Chem Lab Med 2006;44(3):333–339.

[32] Leung GNW, Ho ENM, Kwok WH, Leung DKK, Tang FPW, Wan TSM, Wong ASY, Wong CHF, Wong JKY, Yu NH. A bottom-up approach in estimating the measurement uncertainty and other important considerations for quantitative analyses in drug testing for horses. J Chromatogr A 2007;1163(1):237–246.

[33] Middleton J, Vaks JE. Evaluation of assigned-value uncertainty for complex calibrator value assignment processes: a prealbumin example. Clin Chem 2007;53(4):735–741.

[34] Sundvall J, Laatikainen T, Hakala S, Leiviska J, Alfthan G. Systematic error of serum triglyceride measurements during three decades and the effect of fasting on serum triglycerides in population studies. Clin Chim Acta 2008;397:55–59.

[35] Fuentes-Arderiu X, Braga-Fernandez S, Freire-Campo L, Garcia-Lario JV, García-Martín M-I, Jorde-Andrés JL, Largo-Caballerizo E, Lugo-Arocena J, Pardo-Laseca C, Villanueva-Curto S, Juve-Cuxart S. Comparison of measurement uncertainties in direct plasma low-density lipoprotein cholesterol method of measurement and indirect estimation according to Friedewald equation. Accredit. Qual. Assur. 2009;14(2):179–183.

[36] Chen H, Deng X-L, Bi X-Y, Yang P, Zhang L-P, Chen H-C. Study on measurement uncertainty for total cholesterol in routine clinical laboratory. Chin J Clin Lab Sci 2010;5:p. 206. Available at: http://en.cnki.com.cn/Article_en/CJFDTotal-LCJY201005026.htm.

[37] Burns M. Current practice in the assessment and control of measurement uncertainty in bio-analytical chemistry. TrAC, Trends Anal Chem 2004;23(5):393–398.

[38] Kipphardt H, Matschat R, Panne U. Metrology in chemistry – a rocky road. Microchim Acta 2008;162(1-2):35–41.

[39] Hibbert DB. Systematic errors in analytical measurement results. J Chromatogr A 2007;1158(1):25–32.

[40] Cox M, Harris P, Siebert BR-L. Evaluation of measurement uncertainty based on the propagation of distributions using Monte Carlo simulation. Meas Tech 2003;46(9):824–833.

[41] Herrador M, Asuero AG, González AG. Estimation of the uncertainty of indirect measurements from the propagation of distributions by using the Monte Carlo method: an overview. Chemom Intell Lab Syst 2005;79(1):115–122.

[42] Ángeles Herrador M, González AG. Evaluation of measurement uncertainty in analytical assays by means of Monte Carlo simulation. Talanta 2004;64(2):415–422.

[43] Ramamohan V, Abbott J, Klee GG, Yih Y. Application of mathematical models of system uncertainty to evaluate the utility of assay calibration protocols. Clin Chem Lab Med 2012;50(4):1945–1951.

[44] Ramamohan V, Abbott JT, Klee G, Yih Y. Modeling, analysis and optimization of calibration uncertainty in clinical laboratories. Measurement 2014;50:175–185.

[45] Ramamohan V, Yih Y, Abbott JT, Klee GG. Category-specific uncertainty modeling in clinical laboratory measurement processes. Clin Chem Lab Med 2013;51(12):2273–2280.

[46] Dugdale DC. ALP-Bloodtest: Medlineplus Medical Encyclopedia; Feb. 2014.

[47] Ramamohan V, Abbott JT, Yih Y. Modeling and analysis of the uncertainty of clinical enzyme measurement processes. Proceedings of the Industrial and Systems Engineering Research Conference; 2014.

[48] Briggs GE, Haldane JBS. A note on the kinetics of enzyme action. Biochem J 1925;19(2):338.

[49] Michaelis L, Menten ML. Die kinetik der invertinwirkung. Biochem Z 1913;49(333-369):352.

[50] Schomburg I, Chang A, Söhngen SPC, Rother M, Lang M, Munaretto C, Ulas S, Stelzer M, Grote A. BRENDA in 2013: integrated reactions, kinetic data, enzyme function data, improved disease classification: new options and contents in BRENDA. Nucleic Acids Res 2013;41(D1):D764–D772.

6

PREDICTIVE ANALYTICS: CLASSIFICATION IN MEDICINE AND BIOLOGY

Eva K. Lee

Center for Operations Research in Medicine and HealthCare, Atlanta, GA, USA;
NSF I/UCRC Center for Health Organization Transformation, Industrial and Systems
Engineering, Atlanta, GA, USA;
Georgia Institute of Technology, Atlanta, GA, USA

6.1 INTRODUCTION

Classification is a fundamental machine learning task whereby rules are developed for the allocation of independent entities to groups. Classic examples of applications include medical diagnosis – the allocation of patients to disease classes based on symptoms and laboratory tests, and credit screening – the acceptance or rejection of credit applications based on applicant data. Data are collected concerning entities with known group membership. These *training data* are used to develop rules for the classification of future entities with unknown group membership.

Cognitive science is the science of learning, knowing, and reasoning. *Pattern recognition* is a broad field within cognitive science that is concerned with the process of recognizing, identifying, and categorizing input information. These areas intersect with computer science, particularly in the closely related areas of *artificial intelligence, machine learning*, and *statistical pattern recognition*. Artificial intelligence is associated with constructing machines and systems that reflect human abilities in cognition. Machine learning refers to how these machines and systems replicate the learning process, which is often achieved by seeking and discovering patterns in data, or statistical pattern recognition.

Healthcare Analytics: From Data to Knowledge to Healthcare Improvement, First Edition.
Edited by Hui Yang and Eva K. Lee.
© 2016 John Wiley & Sons, Inc. Published 2016 by John Wiley & Sons, Inc.

Discriminant analysis is the process of discriminating between categories or between populations. Associated with discriminant analysis as a statistical tool are the tasks of determining the features that best discriminate between populations and the process of classifying new entities based on these features. The former is often called *feature selection*, and the latter is referred to as *statistical pattern classification*.

Supervised learning is the process of developing classification rules based on entities for which the classification is already known. Note that the process implies that the populations are already well defined. *Unsupervised learning* is the process of discovering patterns from unlabeled entities and thereby discovering and describing the underlying populations. *Semisupervised learning* falls between supervised and unsupervised learning that uses a large collection of unlabeled entities jointly with a few labeled entities for improving classification performance. Models derived using supervised learning can be used for both functions of discriminant analysis – feature selection and classification. The model that we consider is a method for supervised learning, so we assume that populations are previously defined.

A fundamental problem in discriminant analysis, or supervised learning, concerns the classification of an entity into one of several *a priori*, mutually exclusive groups based on k-specific measurable features of the entity. Typically, a discriminant (predictive) rule is formed from data collected on a sample of entities for which the group classifications are known. New entities, whose classifications are unknown, will then be classified based on this rule. Such an approach has been applied in a variety of domains, and a large body of literature on both the theory and applications of discriminant analysis exists (e.g., see the bibliography in [1]).

In experimental biology and in medical research, very often, experiments or tests are performed and measurements are recorded under different conditions. A critical analysis involves the discrimination of different features under different conditions that will reveal potential predictors for biological and medical phenomena. Hence, classification techniques play an extremely important role in biological analysis, as they facilitate systematic correlation and classification of different biological and medical phenomena. A resulting predictive rule can assist in early health risk and disease prediction and diagnosis, identifying new target therapeutic sites (genomic, cellular, and molecular) for drug delivery, disease prevention and early intervention, optimal treatment design, and treatment outcome prediction.

There are five fundamental steps in discriminant analysis: (i) determine the data for input and the predictive output classes; (ii) gather a training set of data (including output class) from human experts or from laboratory experiments. Each element in the training set is an entity with the corresponding known output class; (iii) determine the input attributes to represent each entity; (iv) identify discriminatory attributes and develop the predictive rule(s); and (v) validate the performance of the predictive rule(s).

In our Center for Operations Research in Medicine and Healthcare, we have developed a general-purpose machine learning framework that incorporates an optimization-based discriminant analysis model and a rapid solution engine for large-scale complex biological and biomedical informatics analyses. Our classification model, the first discrete support vector machine, offers these distinct features simultaneously: (i) it can classify any number of distinct groups; (ii) it allows incorporation of heterogeneous, continuous, and temporal features as input; (iii) it utilizes a high-dimensional data transformation to minimize noise and errors; (iv) it incorporates a reserved-judgment region that provides a safeguard against overtraining; and (v) it enables successive multistage classification capability [2–7].

Studies involving vaccine immunity prediction, early detection of MCI and Alzheimer's disease, CpG island aberrant methylation in human cancer, ultrasonic cell disruption in drug delivery, tumor volume identification; predicting early atherosclerosis using biomarkers; and fingerprinting native and angiogenic microvascular networks using functional perfusion data demonstrate that our approach is adaptable and can produce effective and reliable predictive rules for a broad variety of biomedical applications [4–6, 8–17].

Section 6.2 briefly describes the background of discriminant analysis. Section 6.3 describes the optimization-based multistage discriminant analysis predictive models for classification. The use of the predictive models on various biological and medical applications is presented in Section 6.4. This is followed by a brief summary in Section 6.5.

6.2 BACKGROUND

The main objective in discriminant analysis is to derive rules that can be used to classify entities into groups. Discriminant rules are typically expressed in terms of variables representing a set of measurable attributes of the entities in question. Data on a sample of entities for which the group classifications are known (perhaps determined by extraordinary means) are collected and used to derive rules that can be used to classify new yet-to-be-classified entities. Often there is a trade-off between the discriminating ability of the selected attributes and the expense of obtaining measurements on these attributes. Indeed, the measurement of a relatively definitive discriminating feature may be prohibitively expensive to obtain on a routine basis, or perhaps impossible to obtain at the time that classification is needed.

Thus, a discriminant rule based on a selected set of feature attributes will typically be an imperfect discriminator, sometimes misclassifying entities. Depending on the application, the consequences of misclassifying an entity may be substantial. In such a case, it may be desirable to form a discrimination rule that allows less specific classification decisions, or even nonclassification of some entities to reduce the probability of misclassification.

To address this concern, a number of researchers have suggested methods for deriving *partial discrimination rules* [18–22]. A partial discrimination rule allows an entity to be classified into some subset of the groups (i.e., rule out membership in the remaining groups) or be placed in a "reserved-judgment" category. An entity is considered misclassified only when it is assigned to a nonempty subset of groups not containing the true group of the entity. Typically, methods for deriving partial discrimination rules attempt to constrain the misclassification probabilities (e.g., by enforcing an upper bound on the proportion of misclassified training sample entities). For this reason, the resulting rules are also sometimes called *constrained discrimination rules*.

Partial (or constrained) discrimination rules are intuitively appealing. A partial discrimination rule based on relatively inexpensive measurements can be tried first. If the rule classifies the entity satisfactorily according to the needs of the application, then nothing further needs to be done. Otherwise, additional measurements – albeit more expensive – can be taken on other, more definitive, discriminating attributes of the entity.

One disadvantage of partial discrimination methods is that there is no obvious definition of optimality among any set of rules satisfying the constraints on the misclassification probabilities. For example, since some correct classifications are certainly more valuable than others (e.g., classification into a small subset containing the true group versus a large subset), it does not make sense simply to maximize the probability of correct classification. In fact, to maximize the probability of correct classification, one would simply classify every entity into the subset consisting of all the groups – clearly this is not an acceptable rule.

A simplified model, whereby one incorporates only the reserved-judgment region (i.e., either an entity is classified as belonging to exactly one of the given *a priori* groups, or it is placed in the reserved-judgment category), is amenable to reasonable notions of optimality. For example, in this case, maximizing the probability of correct classification is meaningful. For the two-group case, the simplified model and the more general model are equivalent. Research on the two-group case is summarized in [1]. For three or more groups, the two models are not equivalent, and most work has been directed towards the development of heuristic methods for the more general model (e.g., see [18, 19, 21–23]).

Assuming that the group density functions and prior probabilities are known, [24] showed that an optimal rule for the problem of maximizing the probability of correct classification subject to constraints on the misclassification probabilities must be of a specific form when discriminating among multiple groups with a simplified model. The formulae in Anderson's result depend on a set of parameters satisfying a complex relationship between the density functions, the prior probabilities, and the bounds on the misclassification probabilities. Establishing a viable mathematical model to describe Anderson's result, and finding values for these parameters that yield an optimal rule are challenging tasks. Gallagher et al. [3] presented the first computational model for Anderson's results.

A variety of mathematical programming models have been proposed for the discriminant analysis problem [25–44]. None of these studies deal formally with measuring the performance of discriminant rules specifically designed to allow allocation to a reserved-judgment region. There is also no mechanism employed to explicitly constrain the level of misclassifications for each group, although some researchers manage to include it within their objective functions.

Many different techniques and methodologies have contributed to advances in classification, including artificial neural networks, decision trees, kernel-based learning, machine learning, mathematical programming, statistical analysis, boosting, and support vector machines [45–53]. There are some review papers for classification problems with mathematical programming techniques. Stam [54] summarized basic concepts and ideas and discusses potential research directions on classification methods that optimize a function of the L_p-norm distances. The paper focuses on continuous models and includes normalization schemes, computational aspects, weighted formulations, secondary criteria, and extensions from two-group to multigroup classifications. Wilson [55] presented a series of integer programming formulations for statistical classification problems and compared their performance on sample data. Zopounidis and Doumpos [56] reviewed the research conducted on the framework of the multicriteria decision aiding, covering different classification models. Mangasarian [57] and Bradley et al. [58] gave an overview of using mathematical programming approaches to solve data mining problems. Byvatov and Schneider [59] provided an overview on the theory and basic principles of support vector machine and their application to bioinformatics. Lee et al. [60] and Lee and Wu [61] provided a comprehensive overview of continuous and discrete mathematical programming models for classification problems and their usage within medicine.

6.3 MACHINE LEARNING WITH DISCRETE SUPPORT VECTOR MACHINE PREDICTIVE MODELS

In our computational center, we have been developing and advancing a general-purpose machine-learning framework for classification in medicine and biology. The system consists of a pattern recognition module, a feature selection module, and a classification modeler and rapid solver module. The pattern recognition module involves automatic image analysis, "omic" pattern recognition, spectrum pattern extractions, and unstructure text-mining capabilities. The feature selection module consists of a combinatorial selection algorithm where discriminatory patterns are extracted from among a large set of pattern attributes. These modules are wrapped around the classification modeler and solver into a machine learning framework. Our system is applicable to a wide variety of applications, including biological, biomedical, and logistics problems. Utilizing the technology of large-scale discrete optimization and support vector machines, our classification model includes the following features within a single modeling framework: (i) the ability to classify any number of distinct groups; (ii) the ability to incorporate heterogeneous and temporal type of attributes as input; (iii) a high-dimensional data transformation that reduces noise and errors; (iv) constraints to limit the rate of misclassification, and a reserved-judgment region that provides a safeguard against overtraining (which tends to lead to high misclassification rates from the resulting predictive rule); and (v) successive multistage classification capability to handle data points placed in the reserved-judgment region. Based on the description in Gallagher et al. [2, 3], Lee et al. [7], and Lee [4–6], we summarize below some of the classification models that we have developed.

6.3.1   Modeling of Reserved-Judgment Region for General Groups

When the population densities and prior probabilities are known, the constrained rules with a reject option (reserved judgment), based on Anderson's results, calls for finding a partition $\{R_0, \ldots, R_G\}$ of $\mathfrak{R}^k$ that maximizes the probability of correct allocation subject to constraints on the misclassification probabilities; that is,

$$\text{maximize } \sum_{g=1}^{G} \pi_g \int_{R_g} f_g(w) dw \tag{6.1}$$

$$\text{subject to } \int_{R_g} f_h(w) dw \leq \alpha_{hg}, h, \; g = 1, \ldots, G, \; hg, \tag{6.2}$$

where f_h, $h = 1, \ldots, G$, are the group conditional density functions, π_g denotes the prior probability that a randomly selected entity is from group g, $g = 1, \ldots, G$, and α_{hg}, $h \neq g$, are constants between zero and one. Under quite general assumptions, it was shown that there exist unique (up to a set of measure zero) nonnegative constants λ_{ih}, $i, h \in \{1, \ldots, G\}$, $i \neq h$, such that the optimal rule is given by

$$R_g = \{x \in \mathfrak{R}^k : L_g(x) = \max_{h \in \{0,1,\ldots G\}} L_h(x)\}, \; g = 0, \ldots, G \tag{6.3}$$

where

$$L_0(x) = 0 \tag{6.4}$$

$$L_h(x) = \pi_h f_h(x) - \sum_{\substack{i=1 \\ i \neq h}}^{G} \lambda_{ih} f_i(x), h = 1, \ldots, G \tag{6.5}$$

For $G = 2$, the optimal solution can be modeled rather straightforward. However, finding optimal λ_{ih}'s for the general case, $G \geq 3$, is a difficult problem, with the difficulty increasing as G increases. Our model offers an avenue for modeling and finding the optimal solution in the general case. It is the first such model to be computationally viable [2, 3].

Before proceeding, we note that R_g can be written as $R_g = \{x \in \mathfrak{R}^k : L_g(x) \geq L_h(x)$ for all $h = 0, \ldots, G\}$. So, since $L_g(x) \geq L_h(x)$ if, and only if, $(1/\sum_{t=1}^{G} f_t(x)) L_g(x) \geq (1/\sum_{t=1}^{G} f_t(x)) L_h(x)$, the functions L_h, $h = 1, \ldots, G$, can be redefined as

$$L_h(x) = \pi_h p_h(x) - \sum_{\substack{i=1 \\ i \neq h}}^{G} \lambda_{ih} p_i(x) \; h = 1, \ldots, G \tag{6.6}$$

where $p_i(x) = f_i(x) / \sum_{t=1}^{G} f_t(x)$. We assume that L_h is defined as in Equation 6.6 in our model.

6.3.2 Discriminant Analysis via Mixed-Integer Programming

Assume that we are given a training sample of N entities whose group classifications are known; say n_g entities are in group g, where $\sum_{g=1}^{G} n_g = N$. Let the k-dimensional vectors x^{gj}, $g = 1, \ldots, G$, $j = 1, \ldots, n_g$, contain the measurements on k available characteristics of the entities. Our procedure for deriving a discriminant rule proceeds in two stages. The first stage is to use the training sample to compute estimates $\widehat{f}_h$, either parametrically or nonparametrically, of the density functions f_h (e.g., see [1]) and estimates $\widehat{\pi}_h$, of the prior probabilities π_h, $h = 1, \ldots, G$. The second stage is to determine the optimal λ_{ih}'s given these estimates. This stage requires being able to estimate the probabilities of correct classification and misclassification for any candidate set of λ_{ih}'s. One could, in theory, substitute the estimated densities and prior probabilities into Equation 6.5 and directly use the resulting regions R_g in the integral expressions given in Equations 6.1 and 6.2. This would involve, even in simple cases such as normally distributed groups, the numerical evaluation of k-dimensional integrals at each step of a search for the optimal λ_{ih}'s. Therefore, we have designed an alternative approach. After substituting the $\widehat{f}_h$'s and $\widehat{\pi}_h$'s into Equation 6.5, we simply calculate the proportion of training sample points that fall in each of the regions $R_1, \ldots, R_G$. The mixed-integer programming (MIP) models discussed below attempt to maximize the proportion of training sample points correctly classified while satisfying constraints on the proportions of training sample points misclassified. This approach has two advantages. First, it avoids having to evaluate the potentially difficult integrals in Equations 6.1 and 6.2. Second, it is nonparametric in controlling the training sample misclassification probabilities. That is, even if the densities are poorly estimated (by assuming, e.g., normal densities for nonnormal data), the constraints are still satisfied for the training sample. Better estimates of the densities may allow a higher correct classification rate to be achieved, but the constraints will be satisfied even if poor estimates are used. Unlike most support vector machine models that minimize the sum of errors, our objective is driven by the number of correct classifications and will not be biased by the distance of the entities from the supporting hyperplane. Hence, our model returns a robust classifier.

A word of caution is in order. In traditional unconstrained discriminant analysis, the true probability of correct classification of a given discriminant rule tends to be smaller than the rate of correct classification for the training sample from which it was derived. One would expect to observe such an effect for the method described herein as well. In addition, one would expect to observe an analogous effect with regard to constraints on misclassification probabilities – the true probabilities are likely to be greater than any limits imposed on the proportions of training sample misclassifications. Hence, the α_{hg} parameters should be carefully chosen for the application in hand.

Our first model is a nonlinear 0/1 MIP model with the nonlinearity appearing in the constraints. Model 1 maximizes the number of correct classifications of the given N training entities. Similarly, the constraints on the misclassification probabilities are modeled by ensuring that the number of group g training entities in region R_h is less than or equal to a prespecified percentage, α_{hg} $(0 < \alpha_{hg} < 1)$, of the total number, n_g, of group g entities, $h, g \in \{1, \ldots, G\}, h \neq g$.

For notational convenience, let $\mathbf{G} = \{1, \ldots, G\}$ and $\mathbf{N_g} = \{1, \ldots, n_g\}$, for $g \in \mathbf{G}$. Also, analogous to the definition of p_i, define $\hat{p}_i$ by $\hat{p}_i(x) = \hat{f}_i(x) / \sum_{t=1}^{G} \hat{f}_t(x)$. In our model, we use binary indicator variables to denote the group classification of entities. Mathematically, let u_{hgj} be a binary variable indicating whether or not x^{gj} lies in region R_h; that is, whether or not the jth entity from group g is allocated to group h. Then Model 1 can be written as follows:

DAMIP:

$$\text{Maximize} \sum_{g \in G} \sum_{j \in N_g} u_{ggj}$$

Subject to

$$L_{hgj} = \hat{\pi}_h \hat{p}_h(x^{gj}) - \sum_{i \in G \backslash h} \lambda_{ih} \hat{p}_i(x^{gj}) \quad h, g \in \mathbf{G}, j \in \mathbf{N_g} \tag{6.7}$$

$$y_{gj} = \max\{0, L_{hgj} : h = 1, \ldots, G\} \quad g \in \mathbf{G}, j \in \mathbf{N_g} \tag{6.8}$$

$$y_{gj} - L_{ggj} \leq M(1 - u_{ggj}) \quad g \in \mathbf{G}, j \in \mathbf{N_g} \tag{6.9}$$

$$y_{gj} - L_{hgj} \geq \varepsilon(1 - u_{hgj})h, \quad g \in \mathbf{G}, j \in \mathbf{N_g}, h \neq g \tag{6.10}$$

$$\sum_{j \in N_g} u_{hgj} \leq \lfloor \alpha_{hg} n_g \rfloor \quad h, g \in \mathbf{G}, h \neq g \tag{6.11}$$

$$-\infty < L_{hgj} < \infty, \, y_{gj} \geq 0, \lambda_{ih} \geq 0, u_{hgj}\{0, 1\}$$

Constraint (6.7) defines the variable L_{hgj} as the value of the function L_h evaluated at x^{gj}. Therefore, the continuous variable y_{gj}, defined in constraint (6.8), represents $\max\{L_h(x^{gj}): h = 0, \ldots, G\}$; and consequently, x^{gj} lies in region R_h if, and only if, $y_{gj} = L_{hgj}$. The binary variable u_{hgj} is used to indicate whether or not x^{gj} lies in region R_h; that is, whether or not the jth entity from group g is allocated to group h. In particular, constraint (6.9), together with the objective, forces u_{ggj} to be 1 if, and only if, the jth entity from group g is correctly allocated to group g; and constraints (6.10) and (6.11) ensure that at most $\lfloor \alpha_{hg} n_g \rfloor$ (i.e., the greatest integer less than or equal to $\alpha_{hg} n_g$) group g entities are allocated to group h, $h \neq g$. One caveat regarding the indicator variables u_{hgj} is that although the condition $u_{hgj} = 0$, $h \neq g$, implies (by constraint (6.10)) that $x^{gj} \notin R_h$, the converse need not hold. As a consequence, the number of misclassifications may be overcounted. However, in our preliminary numerical study we found that the actual amount of overcounting is minimal. One could force the converse (thus, $u_{hgj} = 1$ if and only if $x^{gj} \in R_h$) by adding constraints $y_{gj} - L_{hgj} \leq M(1 - u_{hgj})$, for example. Finally, we note that the parameters M and ε are extraneous to the discriminant analysis problem itself, but are needed in the model to control the indicator variables u_{hgj}. The intention is for M and ε to be, respectively, large and small positive constants.

6.3.3 Model Variations

We explore different variations in the model to grasp the quality of the solution and the associated computational effort.

A first variation involves transforming Model 1 to an equivalent linear mixed-integer model. In particular, Model 2 replaces the N constraints defined in Equation 6.8 with the following system of $3GN + 2N$ constraints:

$$y_{gj} \geq L_{hgj} \quad h, g \in \mathbf{G}, j \in \mathbf{N_g} \tag{6.12}$$

$$\widetilde{y}_{hgj} - L_{hgj} \leq M\left(1 - v_{hgj}\right) \quad h, g \in \mathbf{G}, j \in \mathbf{N_g} \tag{6.13}$$

$$\widetilde{y}_{hgj} \leq \hat{\pi}_h \hat{p}_h(x^{gj}) v_{hgj} \quad h, g \in \mathbf{G}, j \in \mathbf{N_g} \tag{6.14}$$

$$\sum_{h \in G} v_{hgj} \leq 1 \quad g \in \mathbf{G}, j \in \mathbf{N_g} \tag{6.15}$$

$$\sum_{h \in G} \widetilde{y}_{hgj} = y_{gj} \quad g \in \mathbf{G}, j \in \mathbf{N_g} \tag{6.16}$$

where $\widetilde{y}_{hgj} \geq 0$ and $v_{hgj} \in \{0,1\}, h, g \in \mathbf{G}, j \in \mathbf{N_g}$. These constraints, together with the nonnegativity of y_{gj}, force $y_{gj} = \max\{0, L_{hgj}: h = 1, \ldots, G\}$.

The second variation involves transforming Model 1 to a heuristic linear MIP model. This is done by replacing the nonlinear constraint (6.8) with $y_{gj} \geq L_{hgj}, h, g \in \mathbf{G}, j \in \mathbf{N_g}$, and including penalty terms in the objective function. In particular, Model 3 has the objective

$$\text{Maximize} \sum_{g \in G} \sum_{j \in N_g} \beta u_{ggj} - \sum_{g \in G} \sum_{j \in N_g} \gamma y_{gj},$$

where β and γ are positive constants. This model is heuristic in that there is nothing to force $y_{gj} = \max\{0, L_{hgj}: h = 1, \ldots, G\}$. However, since in addition to trying to force as many u_{ggj}'s to one as possible, the objective in Model 3 also tries to make the y_{gj}'s as small as possible, and the optimizer tends to drive y_{gj} toward $\max\{0, L_{hgj}: h = 1, \ldots, G\}$. We remark that β and γ could be stratified by group (i.e., introduce possibly distinct $\beta_g, \gamma_g, g \in \mathbf{G}$) to model the relative importance of certain groups to be correctly classified.

A reasonable modification to Models 1, 2, and 3 involves relaxing the constraints specified by (6.11). Rather than placing restrictions on the number of type g training entities classified into group h, for all $h, g \in \mathbf{G}, h \neq g$, one could simply place an upper bound on the *total* number of misclassified training entities. In this case, the $G(G-1)$ constraints specified by (6.11) would be replaced by the single constraint

$$\sum_{g \in G} \sum_{h \in G \setminus \{g\}} \sum_{j \in N_g} u_{hgj} \leq \lfloor \alpha N \rfloor \tag{6.17}$$

where α is a constant between 0 and 1. We will refer to Models 1, 2, and 3, modified in this way, as Models 1T, 2T, and 3T, respectively. Of course, other modifications are also possible. For instance, one could place restrictions on the total number of type g points misclassified for each $g \in \mathbf{G}$. Thus, in place of the constraints specified in

(6.17), one would include the constraints $\sum_{h \in G \setminus \{g\}} \sum_{j \in N_g} u_{hgj} \leq \lfloor \alpha N \rfloor$, $g \in \mathbf{G}$, where $0 < \alpha_g < 1$.

We also explore a heuristic linear model of Model 1. In particular, consider the linear program (DALP):

$$\text{Minimize} \sum_{g \in G} \sum_{j \in N_g} (c_1 w_{gj} + c_2 y_{gj}) \tag{6.18}$$

subject to

$$L_{hgj} = \hat{\pi}_h \hat{p}_h(x^{gj}) - \sum_{i \in G \setminus h} \lambda_{ih} \hat{p}_i(x^{gj}) \quad h, g \in \mathbf{G}, \ j \in \mathbf{N_g} \tag{6.19}$$

$$L_{ggj} - L_{hgj} + w_{gj} \geq 0 \quad h, g \in \mathbf{G}, h \neq g, j \in \mathbf{N_g} \tag{6.20}$$

$$L_{ggj} + w_{gj} \geq 0 \quad g \in \mathbf{G}, j \in \mathbf{N_g} \tag{6.21}$$

$$-L_{hgj} + y_{gj} \geq 0 \quad h, g \in \mathbf{G}, j \in \mathbf{N_g} \tag{6.22}$$

$$-\infty < L_{hgj} < \infty, \ w_{gj}, y_{gj}, \lambda_{ih} \geq 0$$

Constraint (6.19) defines the variable L_{hgj} as the value of the function L_h evaluated at x^{gj}. As the optimization solver searches through the set of feasible solutions, the λ_{ih} variables will vary, causing the L_{hgj} variables to assume different values. Constraints (6.20–6.22) link the objective-function variables with the L_{hgj} variables in such a way that correct classification of training entities and allocation of training entities into the reserved-judgment region are captured by the objective-function variables. In particular, if the optimization solver drives w_{gj} to zero for some g, j pair, then constraints (6.20) and (6.21) imply that $L_{ggj} = \max\{0, L_{hgj}: h \in \mathbf{G}\}$. Hence, the jth entity from group g is correctly classified. If, on the other hand, the optimal solution yields $y_{gj} = 0$ for some g, j pair, then constraint (6.22) implies that $\max\{0, L_{hgj}: h \in \mathbf{G}\} = 0$. Thus, the jth entity from group g is placed in the reserved-judgment region. (Of course, it is possible for both w_{gj} and y_{gj} to be zero. One should decide prior to solving the linear program how to interpret the classification in such cases.) If both w_{gj} and y_{gj} are positive, the jth entity from group g is misclassified.

The optimal solution yields a set of λ_{ih}'s that best allocates the training entities (i.e., "best" in terms of minimizing the penalty objective function). The optimal λ_{ih}'s can then be used to define the functions L_h, $h \in \mathbf{G}$, which in turn can be used to classify a new entity with feature vector $x \in \mathfrak{R}^k$ by simply computing the index at which $\max\{L_h(x): h \in \{0, 1, ..., G\}\}$ is achieved.

Note that Model DALP places no *a priori* bound on the number of misclassified training entities. However, since the objective is to minimize a weighted combination of the variables w_{gj} and y_{gj}, the optimizer will attempt to drive these variables to zero. Thus, the optimizer is, in essence, attempting either to correctly classify training entities ($w_{gj} = 0$) or to place them in the reserved-judgment region ($y_{gj} = 0$). By varying the weights c_1 and c_2, one has a means of controlling the optimizer's emphasis for correctly classifying training entities versus placing them in the reserved-judgment region. If $c_2/c_1 < 1$, the optimizer will tend to place a greater emphasis on driving the w_{gj} variables to zero than driving the y_{gj} variables to zero (conversely, if $c_2/c_1 > 1$).

TABLE 6.1 Model size

Model	Type	Constraints	Total Variables	0/1 Variables
1	Nonlinear MIP	$2GN + N + G(G-1)$	$2GN + N + G(G-1)$	GN
2	Linear MIP	$5GN + 2N + G(G-1)$	$4GN + N + G(G-1)$	$2GN$
3	Linear MIP	$3GN + G(G-1)$	$2GN + N + G(G-1)$	GN
1T	Nonlinear MIP	$2GN + N + 1$	$2GN + N + G(G-1)$	GN
2T	Linear MIP	$5GN + 2N + 1$	$4GN + N + G(G-1)$	$2GN$
3T	Linear MIP	$3GN + 1$	$2GN + N + G(G-1)$	GN
DALP	Linear program	$3GN$	$NG + N + G(G-1)$	0

Hence, when $c_2/c_1 < 1$, one should expect to get relatively more entities correctly classified, fewer placed in the reserved-judgment region, and more misclassified than when $c_2/c_1 > 1$. An extreme case is when $c_2 = 0$. In this case, there is no emphasis on driving y_{gj} to zero (the reserved-judgment region is thus ignored), and the full emphasis of the optimizer is to drive w_{gj} to zero.

Table 6.1 summarizes the number of constraints, the total number of variables, and the number of 0/1 variables in each of the discrete support vector machine models and in the heuristic LP model (DALP). Clearly, even for moderately sized discriminant analysis problems, the MIP instances are relatively large. Also, note that Model 2 is larger than Model 3, both in terms of the number of constraints and the number of variables. However, it is important to keep in mind that the difficulty of solving an MIP problem cannot, in general, be predicted solely by its size; problem structure has a direct and substantial bearing on the effort required to find optimal solutions. The LP relaxation of these MIP models pose computational challenges as commercial LP solvers return (optimal) LP solutions that are infeasible, due to the equality constraints, and the use of big M and small ε in the formulation.

It is interesting to note that the set of feasible solutions for Model 2 is "tighter" than that for Model 3. In particular, if F_i denotes the set of feasible solutions of Model i, then

$$F_1 = \{(L, \lambda, u, y) : \text{ there exists } \widetilde{y}, v \text{ such that } (L, \lambda, u, y, \widetilde{y}, v) \in F_2\}\} \subseteq F_3 \quad (6.23)$$

The novelties of the classification models developed herein include the following: (i) they are suitable for discriminant analysis given any number of groups, (ii) they accept heterogeneous types of attributes as input, (iii) they use a parametric approach to reduce high-dimensional attribute spaces, and (iv) they allow constraints on the number of misclassifications, and utilize a reserved judgment to facilitate the reduction of misclassifications. The latter point opens the possibility of performing multistage analysis.

Clearly, the advantage of an LP model over an MIP model is that the associated problem instances are computationally much easier to solve. However, the most important criterion in judging a method for obtaining discriminant rules is how the rules perform in correctly classifying new unseen entities. Once the rule is developed, applying it to a new entity to determine its group is trivial. Extensive computational experiments have been performed to gauge the qualities of solutions of different models ([3–7]).

6.3.4   Theoretical Properties and Computational Strategies

Theoretically and empirically, DAMIP has many appealing characteristics including that the resulting classification rule is (i) *strongly universally consistent*, given that the Bayes optimal rule for classification is known [62, 63]; (ii) the misclassification rates using the DAMIP method are consistently lower than other classification approaches in both simulated data and real-world data; (iii) the classification rules from DAMIP appear to be insensitive to the specification of prior probabilities, yet capable of reducing misclassification rates when the number of training entities from each group is different; (iv) the DAMIP model generates stable classification rules regardless of the proportions of training entities from each group.

The DAMIP model and its variations described herein offer a computational avenue for numerically estimating optimal values for the λ_{ih} parameters in Anderson's formulae. However, it should be emphasized that MIP problems are themselves difficult to solve. Anderson himself noted the extreme difficulty of finding an optimal set of λ_{ih}'s [24]. Indeed, DAMIP is proven to be *NP-complete* when the number of groups is greater than 2 [62]. Nevertheless, due to the fact that integer variables – and in particular, 0/1 variables – are a powerful modeling tool, a wide variety of real-world problems have been modeled as mixed-integer programs. Consequently, much effort has been invested in developing computational strategies for solving MIP problem instances.

The numerical work reported in Section 6.4 is based on an MIP solver, which is built on top of a general-purpose in-house MIP solver. The general-purpose solver integrates state-of-the-art MIP computational devices such as problem preprocessing, primal heuristics, global and local reduced-cost fixing, and cutting planes into a branch-and-bound framework [64, 65]. The solver has been shown to be effective in solving a wide variety of large-scale real-world instances [66]. For our MIP instances, special techniques including variable aggregation, a heuristic branching scheme, and hypergraphic cut generations are employed [3, 62, 63, 67].

6.4   APPLYING DAMIP TO REAL-WORLD APPLICATIONS

The main objective in discriminant analysis is to derive rules that can be used to classify entities into groups. Computationally, the challenge lies in the effort expended to develop such a rule. Feasible solutions obtained from our classification models correspond to predictive rules. Empirical results [3, 7] indicate that the resulting classification model instances are computationally very challenging and even intractable by competitive commercial MIP solvers. However, the resulting predictive rules prove to be very promising, offering correct predictive accuracy on new unknown data ranging from 80% to 100% on various types of biological/medical problems. Our results indicate that the general-purpose classification framework that we have designed has the potential to be a very powerful predictive method for clinical setting.

The choice of MIP as the underlying modeling and optimization technology for our support vector machine classification model is guided by the desire to simultaneously incorporate a variety of important and desirable properties of predictive models within a general framework. MIP itself allows for incorporation of continuous and discrete variables, and linear and nonlinear constraints, providing a flexible and powerful modeling environment.

6.4.1 Validation of Model and Computational Effort

We performed 10-fold cross-validation and designed simulation and comparison studies on our preliminary models. The results, reported in Gallagher et al. [3] and Lee et al. [7], show that the methods are promising, based on applications to both simulated data and real-application data sets from the machine learning database repository [68]. Furthermore, our methods compare well to existing methods, often producing better results when compared to other approaches such as artificial neural networks, quadratic discriminant analysis, tree classification, and other support vector machines.

6.4.2 Applications to Biological and Medical Problems

Our mathematical modeling and computational algorithmic design show great promise. The resulting predictive rules are able to produce higher rates of blind prediction accuracy on new data (with unknown group status) compared to existing classification methods. The resulting classification rules are robust and are insensitive to imbalance in sample size. This is partly due to the transformation of raw data via the set of constraints in Equation 6.7, and the distinct features that occur simultaneously in a single modeling framework. While most support vector machines (summarized in [60, 61]) directly determine the hyperplanes of separation using raw data, our approach transforms the raw data via a probabilistic model before the determination of the supporting hyperplanes. Furthermore, the separation is driven by maximizing the sum of binary variables (representing correct classification or not of entities), instead of minimizing a sum of errors (representing distances of entities from hyperplanes), as in other support vector machines. The combination of these two strategies offers better and robust classification capability. Noise in the transformed data is not as profound as in raw data. And the magnitudes of the errors do not skew the determination of the separating hyperplanes, as all entities have "equal" importance when correct classification is being counted. To highlight the broad applicability of our approach, we briefly summarize the application of our predictive models and solution algorithms to seven different biological and medical problems. These projects were carried out in close partnership with experimental biologists and clinical investigators. We also include multigroup classification using the UCI Repository of machine learning databases. Applications to finance and other industry applications are described elsewhere [3, 7, 69, 70].

6.4.2.1 *Quick Test to Predict Immune Responses to Flu Shots [16, 17]* Vaccines have drastically reduced the mortality and morbidity of many diseases. However, vaccines have historically been developed empirically, and recent development of vaccines against current pandemics such as HIV and malaria has been met with difficulty.

The path to licensure of candidate vaccines involves very lengthy and expensive clinical trials to assess their efficacy and safety. These trials involve thousands of subjects and can cost hundreds of millions of dollars to complete. As a result, very few vaccine concepts are tested.

A major challenge in vaccinology is that the effectiveness of vaccination can only be ascertained after vaccinated individuals have been exposed to infection. The ability to identify early predictive signatures of vaccine responses and novel and robust correlates of protection from infection will play an instrumental role in developing rationally designed, next-generation vaccines. It will facilitate rapid design and evaluation of new and emerging vaccines, and the identification of individuals who are unlikely to be protected by a vaccine. This work focuses on predicting the immunity of a vaccine without exposing individuals to infection. The study addresses a long-standing challenge in the development of vaccines – that of only being able to determine immunity or effectiveness long after vaccination and, often, only after being exposed to infection.

Three studies involving nine trials of patient subjects were carried out. The first study aims to predict the body's ability shortly after immunization to stimulate a strong and enduring immunity against yellow fever. Healthy individuals were vaccinated with YF-17D, and T cell and antibody responses in their blood were captured for 30 days. These blood samples were studied with genomic signatures characterized. There was a striking variation in these responses between individuals. Analysis of gene expression patterns in white blood cells revealed that in majority of the individuals the vaccine induced a network of genes involved in the early innate immune response against the viruses. DAMIP takes in these gene expression data and uses it to uncover discriminatory gene signatures to establish the classification rule that can classify the T cell and the antibody responses induced. To validate its predictive accuracy, and whether these gene signatures could actually predict immune response, a second group of individuals were vaccinated for independent blind predication.

To analyze the generalizability of this approach, we apply DAMIP to predict the effectiveness of other vaccines, including flu vaccines. The second study is based on a series of clinical studies during the annual flu seasons in 2007, 2008, and 2009. Healthy young adults were vaccinated with a standard flu shot (trivalent inactive vaccine). Others were given live attenuated vaccine nasally. Comprehensively surveyed, the activity levels of all human genes in blood samples from the volunteers revealed that the activities of many genes involved in innate immunity, interferon, and reactive oxygen species signaling were changing after flu vaccination. Biological analysis also identified genes in the "unfolded protein response," necessary for cells to adapt to the stress of producing high levels of antibodies. These genomic expression data are then input into our DAMIP model to identify discriminatory gene signatures that can classify patients who respond positively to the vaccine versus those who do not.

The yellow fever study offered a groundbreaking work in vaccine immunogenicity. DAMIP identified signatures of gene expression in the blood of healthy humans a few days after vaccination that could predict with up to 90% accuracy of the strength of the immune response, weeks or months after yellow fever vaccination. In the flu analysis, being named 2011 Paper of the Year by the International Society of Vaccine, we extended this approach to the seasonal influenza vaccines over the course of three influenza seasons. By studying gene expression patterns in the blood a few days after vaccination, we were able to identify "signatures" that were capable of predicting the magnitude of the later immune response, with >90% accuracy. Importantly one of the genes in the signature, CAMK4 whose expression was negatively correlated with antibody titers, revealed an unappreciated role for CAMK4 in B-cell responses. This landmark study demonstrates the use of DAMIP in predicting vaccine efficacy and highlights one of the ways for the future of vaccinology – use of systems biology tools to perform sophisticated human studies that in turn returns specific hypothesis to be tested experimentally.

Encouragingly, some of the genes identified in the seasonal flu study were also predictors of the antibody response to vaccination against yellow fever. Furthermore, DAMIP facilitates discovery of new functions for genes, even when scientists previously did not suspect their involvement in antibody responses.

6.4.2.2 Predictive Model for Early Detection of Mild Cognitive Impairment and Alzheimer's Disease [14]

The number of people affected by Alzheimer's disease is growing at a rapid rate, and the subsequent increase in costs will have significant impacts on the world's economies and healthcare systems. Alzheimer's disease, the sixth leading cause of death in the United States, is a progressive and irreversible brain disease causing memory loss and other cognitive dysfunction severe enough to affect daily life. It is estimated that one in eight elderly Americans suffer from Alzheimer's. The number of AD victims is briskly rising, with an estimated 35 million people worldwide currently living with Alzheimer's or forms of dementia. AD is currently incurable. Drugs are used to manage the symptoms, but no treatments to prevent or meaningfully slow the disease's progression are known to exist.

Since changes in the brain triggered by AD develop slowly over many years and symptom onset coincides with advanced neurodegeneration, the need to identify new and noninvasive diagnostics before any symptoms occur has become a public health imperative. Creating new opportunities for early intervention is vital. System's predictive analyses on noninvasive tests that can identify people who are at-risk but currently have no symptoms are critical to curtail the rapid rise of this illness.

Neuropsychological tests are inexpensive, noninvasive, and can be incorporated within an annual physical examination. Thus, they can serve as a baseline for early cognitive impairment or Alzheimer's disease-risk prediction. We apply the DAMIP machine learning framework for early detection of MCI and Alzheimer's disease. Anonymous data of neuropsychological tests from 35 subjects were collected at Emory Alzheimer's Disease Research Center from 2004 to 2007. Eighteen types of neuropsychological tests were applied to the subjects, but only four of them were applied to all subjects, thus being used in our predictive model. These tests included Mini Mental State Examination (MMSE), Clock drawing test, Word list memory tasks by the Consortium to Establish a Registry for Alzheimer's Disease (CERAD), and Geriatric depression scale (GDS).

The MMSE is a screening tool for cognitive impairment, which is brief, but covers five areas of cognitive function, including orientation, registration, attention and calculation, recall, and language. The clock drawing test assesses cognitive functions, particularly visuospatial abilities and executive control functions. The CERAD word list memory tasks assess learning ability for new verbal information. The tasks include word list memory with repetition, word list recall, and word list recognition. The GDS is a screening tool to assess the depression in older populations.

There were 153 features including raw data from the four neuropsychological tests as well as subjects' age. Raw data from tests contained answers to individual questions in the tests. Discarding features that contained missing values or that were nondiscriminating (i.e., features which contained almost the same value among all subjects), 100 features were used for feature selection and classification. The clinicians also summarize performance of subtotal scores in different tests, resulting in nine scores for each patient.

Using two trials of patients with Alzheimer's disease (AD), MCI, and control groups, we show that one can successfully develop a classification rule based on the data from neuropsychological tests to predict AD, MCI, and normal subjects where the blind prediction accuracy is over 90%. Table 6.2 illustrates one predictive rule obtained for this study. Furthermore, our study strongly suggests that raw data of neuropsychological tests have higher potential to predict subjects from AD, MCI, and control groups than preprocessed subtotal score-like features, as contrasted in Table 6.3. When applying our predictive rule to a third trial of 200 patients, over 88% blind prediction accuracy is achieved. The classification approach and the results offer

TABLE 6.2   Classification Results of Emory Data: 10-Fold Cross-Validation and Blind Prediction

	10-Fold Cross-Validation						Blind Prediction					
	AD	MCI	Ctl	AD	MCI	Ctl		AD	MCI	Ctl	AD	MCI	Ctl
AD	4	1	0	0.80	0.20	0.00	AD	2	0	0	1.00	0.00	0.00
MCI	0	11	0	0.00	1.00	0.00	MCI	1	4	0	0.20	0.80	0.00
Ctl	0	0	8	0.00	0.00	1.00	Ctl	0	0	4	0.00	0.00	1.00
	Unbiased estimate accuracy: 96%							Blind prediction accuracy: 91%					

Five discriminatory features were selected (among the 100 features): MMSE – cMMtotal, WordList – cWL2Butter, WordList – cWL2Queen, WordList – cWL2Ticket, GDS – GDS13.

TABLE 6.3   Classification Results of the Same Emory Data: 10-Fold Cross-Validation and Blind Prediction from Nine Score-Type Features Instead of Raw Data

	10-Fold Cross-Validation						Blind Prediction					
	AD	MCI	Ctl	AD	MCI	Ctl		AD	MCI	Ctl	AD	MCI	Ctl
AD	4	1	0	0.80	0.20	0.00	AD	1	1	0	0.50	0.50	0.00
MCI	1	9	1	0.09	0.82	0.09	MCI	0	5	0	0.00	1.00	0.00
Ctl	0	2	6	0.00	0.25	0.75	Ctl	0	1	3	0.00	0.25	0.75
Unbiased estimate accuracy: 79%							Blind prediction accuracy: 82%					

Two discriminatory features were selected: MMSE – cMMtotal, Word List – cWLcorTotal.

the potential for development of a clinical decision-making tool for early detection. Further study must be conducted to validate its clinical significance and its predictive accuracy among various demographic groups and across multiple sites.

6.4.2.3 Predicting Aberrant CpG Island Methylation in Human Cancer [9, 10]

Epigenetic silencing associated with aberrant methylation of promoter region CpG islands is one mechanism leading to loss of tumor suppressor function in human cancer. Profiling of CpG island methylation indicates that some genes are more frequently methylated than others, and that each tumor type is associated with a unique set of methylated genes. However, little is known about why certain genes succumb to this aberrant event. To address this question, Restriction Landmark Genome Scanning (RLGS) is used to analyze the susceptibility of 1749 unselected CpG islands to *de novo* methylation driven by overexpression of DNMT1. We found that although the overall incidence of CpG island methylation was increased in cells overexpressing DNMT1, not all loci were equally affected. The majority of CpG islands (69.9%) were resistant to *de novo* methylation, regardless of DNMT1 overexpression. In contrast, we identified a subset of methylation-prone CpG islands (3.8%) that were consistently hypermethylated in multiple DNMT1 overexpressing clones. Methylation-prone and methylation-resistant CpG islands were not significantly different with respect to size, CpG content, CpG frequency, chromosomal location, or gene or promoter association. To discriminate methylation-prone from methylation-resistant CpG islands, we developed a novel DNA pattern recognition model and algorithm [71] and coupled our DAMIP predictive model described herein with the patterns found. We were able to derive a classification function based on the frequency of seven novel sequence patterns that was capable of discriminating methylation-prone from methylation-resistant CpG islands with 90% correctness upon cross-validation, and 85% blind prediction accuracy when applied to blind CpG islands unknown to us on the methylation status. The data indicate that CpG islands differ in their intrinsic susceptibility to *de novo* methylation and suggest that the propensity for a CpG island to become aberrantly methylated can be predicted based on its sequence context.

The significance of this research is twofold. First, the identification of sequence pattern/attributes that can discriminate methylation-prone CpG islands will lead to a better understanding of the basic mechanisms underlying aberrant CpG island methylation. Because genes that are silenced by methylation are otherwise structurally sound, the potential for reactivating these genes by blocking or reversing the methylation process represents an exciting new molecular target for chemotherapeutic intervention. A better understanding of the factors that contribute to aberrant methylation, including the identification of sequence elements that may act to target aberrant methylation, will be an important step in achieving this long-term goal. Second, the classification of more than 29,000 known (but as yet unclassified) CpG islands in human chromosomes will provide an important resource for the identification of novel gene targets for further study as potential molecular markers that could impact on both cancer prevention and treatment. Extensive RLGS fingerprint information (and thus potential training sets of methylated CpG islands) already exists for a number of human tumor types, including breast, brain, lung, leukemias, hepatocellular carcinomas, and PNET [72–75]. Thus, the methods and tools developed are directly applicable to CpG island methylation data derived from human tumors. Moreover, new microarray-based techniques capable of "profiling" more than 7000 CpG islands have been developed and applied to human breast cancers [76–78]. Indeed, we have shown that using the predictive rule established from the breast cancer cell line and applying it to lung cancer cells, the blind prediction accuracy reaches over 80% [15]. We are uniquely poised to take advantage of the tumor CpG island methylation profile information that will likely be generated using these techniques over the next several years. Thus, our general-purpose predictive modeling framework has the potential to lead to improved diagnosis and prognosis and treatment design for cancer patients.

6.4.2.4   *Ultrasonic Assisted Cell Disruption for Drug Delivery [13]*   Although biological effects of ultrasound must be avoided for safe diagnostic applications, ultrasound's ability to disrupt cell membranes has attracted interest as a method to facilitate drug and gene delivery. This preliminary study seeks to develop rules for predicting the degree of cell membrane disruption based on specified ultrasound parameters and measured acoustic signals. Too much ultrasound destroys cells, while cell membranes will not open up for absorption of macromolecules when too little ultrasound is applied. The key is to increase cell permeability to allow absorption of macromolecules and to apply ultrasound transiently to disrupt viable cells so as to enable exogenous material to enter without cell damage. Thus, our task is to uncover a "predictive rule" of ultrasound-mediated disruption of red blood cells using acoustic spectra and measurements of cell permeability recorded in experiments.

DAMIP is applied to data obtained from a sequence of experiments on bovine red blood cells. For each experiment, the attributes consist of four ultrasound parameters, acoustic measurements at 400 frequencies, and a measure of cell membrane disruption. To avoid overtraining, various feature combinations of the 404 predictor variables are selected when developing the classification rule. The results indicate that the variable combination consisting of ultrasound exposure time and acoustic signals measured at the driving frequency and its higher harmonics yields the best rule. Furthermore, our method compares favorably with classification tree and other *ad hoc* approaches, with correct classification rate of 80% upon cross-validation and 85% blind prediction accuracy when classifying new unknown entities. Our methods used for deriving the prediction rules are broadly applicable and could be used to develop prediction rules in other scenarios involving different cell types or tissues. These rules and the methods used to derive them could be used for real-time feedback about ultrasound's biological effects. For example, it could assist clinicians during a drug delivery process or could be imported into an implantable device inside the body for automatic drug delivery and monitoring.

6.4.2.5   *Identification of Tumor Shape and Volume in Treatment of Sarcoma [12]*
This project involves the determination of tumor shape for adjuvant brachytherapy treatment of sarcoma based on catheter images taken after surgery. In this application,

the entities are overlapping consecutive triplets of catheter markings, each of which is used for determining the shape of the tumor contour. The triplets are to be classified into one of two groups: Group 1 = [triplets for which the middle catheter marking should be bypassed], and Group 2 = [triplets for which the middle marking should not be bypassed]. To develop and validate a classification rule, we used clinical data collected from 15 soft tissue sarcoma (STS) patients. Cumulatively, this comprised 620 triplets of catheter markings. By careful (and tedious) clinical analysis of the geometry of these triplets, 65 were determined to belong to Group 1, the "bypass" group, and 555 were determined to belong to Group 2, the "do-not-bypass" group.

A set of measurements associated with each triplet is then determined. The choice of what attributes to measure to best distinguish triplets as belonging to Group 1 or Group 2 is nontrivial. The attributes involved distance between each pair of markings, angles, curvature formed by the three triplet markings. Based on the selected attributes, DAMIP was used to develop a classification rule. The resulting rule provides 98% correct classification on cross-validation and was capable of correctly predicting 95% of the shape of the tumor on new patients' data. We remark that the current clinical procedure requires manual outline based on markers in films of the tumor volume. This study was the first to use automatic construction of tumor shape for sarcoma adjuvant brachytherapy [12].

6.4.2.6 *Discriminant Analysis of Biomarkers for Prediction of Early Atherosclerosis [4]* Oxidative stress is an important etiologic factor in the pathogenesis of vascular disease. Oxidative stress results from an imbalance between injurious oxidant and protective antioxidant events in which the former predominate [79, 80]. This results in the modification of proteins and DNA, alteration in gene expression, promotion of inflammation, and deterioration in endothelial function in the vessel wall, all processes that ultimately trigger or exacerbate the atherosclerotic process [81, 82]. It was hypothesized that novel biomarkers of oxidative stress would predict early atherosclerosis in a relatively healthy nonsmoking population who are free from cardiovascular disease. One hundred and twenty-seven healthy nonsmokers, without known clinical atherosclerosis, had carotid intima media thickness (IMT) measured using ultrasound. Plasma oxidative stress was estimated by measuring plasma lipid hydroperoxides using the determination of reactive oxygen metabolites (d-ROMs) test. Clinical measurements include traditional risk factors including age, sex, low-density lipoprotein (LDL), high-density lipoprotein (HDL), triglycerides, cholesterol, body mass index (BMI), hypertension, diabetes mellitus, smoking history, family history of CAD, Framingham risk score, and Hs-CRP.

For this prediction, the patients are first clustered into two groups: (Group 1: IMT ≥ 0.68, Group 2: IMT < 0.68). Based on this separator, 30 patients belong to Group 1 and 97 belong to Group 2. Randomly selecting 90 patients from these two groups as a training set, DAMIP trains and learns and returns the most discriminatory patterns among the 14 clinical measurements, ultimately resulting in a prediction rule based on age, sex, BMI, HDLc, Fhx CAD < 60, hs-CRP, and d-ROM as discriminatory attributes. The resulting rule provides 80% and 89% blind prediction accuracy on the remaining 37 patients into Groups 1 and 2, respectively. The importance of d-ROM as a discriminatory predictor for IMT status was confirmed during the machine learning process, this biomarker was selected in every iteration as the "machine" learned and trained to develop a predictive rule to correctly classify patients in the training set. We also performed predictive analysis using Framingham Risk Score and d-ROM; in this case the unbiased correct classification rates for Groups 1 and 2 are 77% and 84%, respectively. This is the first study to illustrate that this measure of oxidative stress can be effectively used along with traditional risk factors to generate a predictive rule that can potentially serve as an inexpensive clinical diagnostic tool for predicting early atherosclerosis.

6.4.2.7 Fingerprinting Native and Angiogenic Microvascular Networks through Pattern Recognition and Discriminant Analysis of Functional Perfusion Data [4]   The cardiovascular system provides oxygen and nutrients to the entire body. Pathological conditions that impair normal microvascular perfusion can result in tissue ischemia, with potentially serious clinical effects. Conversely, development of new vascular structures fuels the progression of cancer, macular degeneration, and atherosclerosis. Fluorescence microangiography offers superb imaging of the functional perfusion of new and existent microvasculature, but quantitative analysis of the complex capillary patterns is challenging. We developed an automated pattern recognition algorithm to systematically analyze the microvascular networks and then apply DAMIP to generate a predictive rule. The pattern recognition algorithm identifies the complex vascular branching patterns, and the predictive rule demonstrates 100% and 91% correct classification on perturbed (diseased) and normal tissue perfusions, respectively. We confirmed that transplantation of normal bone marrow to mice in which genetic deficiency resulted in impaired angiogenesis eliminated predicted differences and restored normal tissue perfusion patterns (with 100% correctness). The pattern recognition and DAMIP offer an elegant solution for the automated fingerprinting of microvascular networks that could contribute to a better understanding of angiogenic mechanisms and be utilized to diagnose and monitor microvascular deficiencies. Such information would be valuable for early detection and monitoring of functional abnormalities before they produce obvious and lasting effects, which may include improper perfusion of tissue or support of tumor development.

The algorithm can be used to discriminate between the angiogenic response in a native healthy specimen and the groups with impairment due to age, or chemical or other genetic deficiency. Similarly, it can be applied to analyze angiogenic responses as a result of various treatments. This will serve two important goals. First, the identification of discriminatory patterns/attributes that distinguish angiogenesis status will lead to a better understanding of the basic mechanisms underlying this process. Because therapeutic control of angiogenesis could influence physiological and pathological processes such as wound and tissue repairing, cancer progression and metastasis, or macular degeneration, the ability to understand it under different conditions will offer new insight into developing novel therapeutic interventions, monitoring, and treatment, especially in aging and heart disease. Thus, our study and the results form the foundation of a valuable diagnostic tool for changes in the functionality of the microvasculature and for discovery of drugs that alter the angiogenic response. The methods can be applied to tumor diagnosis, monitoring, and prognosis. In particular, it will be possible to derive microangiographic fingerprints to acquire specific microvascular patterns associated with early stages of tumor development. Such "angioprinting" could become an extremely helpful early diagnostic modality, especially for easily accessible tumors such as skin cancer.

6.4.2.8 Applying DAMIP to UCI Repository of Machine Learning Databases [68]

Determining the Type of Erythemato-squamous Disease   The differential diagnosis of erythemato-squamous diseases is an important problem in dermatology. They all share the clinical features of erythema and scaling, with very little differences. The six groups are psoriasis, seboreic dermatitis, lichen planus, pityriasis rosea, chronic dermatitis, and pityriasis rubra pilaris. Usually, a biopsy is necessary for the diagnosis, but unfortunately these diseases share many histopathological features as well. Another difficulty for the differential diagnosis is that a disease may show the features of another disease at the beginning stage and may have the characteristic features at the following stages.

The six groups consist of 366 subjects (112, 61, 72, 49, 52, 20, respectively) with 34 clinical attributes. Patients were first evaluated clinically with 12 features. Afterwards, skin samples were taken for the evaluation of 22 histopathological features. The values of the histopathological features are determined by an analysis of the samples under a microscope. The 34 attributes include the following: (i) clinical attributes: erythema, scaling, definite borders, itching, koebner phenomenon, polygonal papules, follicular papules, oral mucosal involvement, knee and elbow involvement, scalp involvement, family history, age; and (ii) histopathological attributes: melanin incontinence, eosinophils in the infiltrate, PNL infiltrate, fibrosis of the papillary dermis, exocytosis, acanthosis, hyperkeratosis, parakeratosis, clubbing of the rete ridges, elongation of the rete ridges, thinning of the suprapapillary epidermis, spongiform pustule, munro microabscess, focal hypergranulosis, disappearance of the granular layer, vacuolization and damage of basal layer, spongiosis, saw-tooth appearance of retes, follicular horn plug, perifollicular parakeratosis, inflammatory mononuclear infiltrate, band-like infiltrate.

Using 250 randomly selected subjects to develop the rule, our multigroup DAMIP model selected 27 discriminatory attributes and successfully classified the patients into six groups, each with an unbiased correct classification of greater than 93% (with 100% correct rate for groups 1, 3, 5, 6) with an average overall accuracy of 98%. Blind prediction on the remaining 116 patients yields a prediction accuracy of 91% for each group.

Predicting Presence/Absence of Heart Disease   The four databases concerning heart disease diagnosis were collected by Dr Janosi of Hungarian Institute of Cardiology, Budapest; Dr Steinbrunn of University Hospital, Zurich; Dr Pfisterer of University Hospital, Basel, Switzerland; and Dr Detrano of V. A. Medical Center, Long Beach and Cleveland Clinic Foundation. Each database contains the same 76 attributes. The "goal" field refers to the presence of heart disease in the patient. The classification attempts to discriminate *presence* (values 1, 2, 3, 4, involving a total of 509 subjects) from *absence* (value 0, involving 411 subjects). The attributes include demographics, physiocardiovascular conditions, traditional risk factors, family history, personal lifestyle, and cardiovascular exercise measurements. This data set has posed some challenges to past analysis via various classification approaches, resulting in less than 80% unbiased classification accuracy. Applying our classification model without reserved judgment, we obtain 79% and 85% correct classification for each group, respectively. To gauge the usefulness of multistage analysis, we apply two-stage classification. In the first stage, 14 attributes were selected as discriminatory. One hundred and thirty-five Group *absence* subjects were placed into the reserved-judgment region, with 85% of the remaining were classified as Group *absence* correctly; while 286 Group *presence* subjects were placed into the reserved judgment region, and 91% of the remaining classified correctly into the Group *presence*. In the second stage, 11 attributes were selected with 100 and 229 classified into Group *absence* and *presence*, respectively. Combining the two stages, we obtained a correct classification of 82% and 85%, respectively, for diagnosis of absence or presence of heart disease. Figure 6.1 illustrates the two-stage classification.

Using 600 of them as training via multistage DAMIP classification results in 85% and 84% accuracy for 10-fold cross-validation. Blind prediction on the remaining 320 patients results in 85% and 83% prediction accuracy.

Prediction of Protein Localization Sites   The protein localization database consists of 8 groups with a total of 336 instances (143, 77, 52, 35, 20, 5, 2, 2, respectively) with

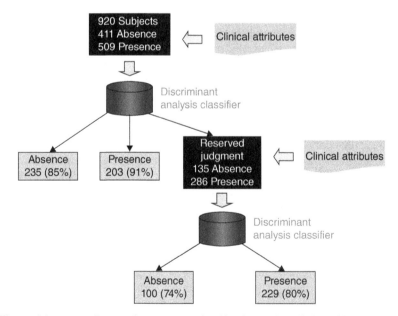

Figure 6.1   A tree diagram for two-stage classification and prediction of heart disease.

7 attributes. The 8 groups are 8 localization sites of protein including cp (cytoplasm), im (inner membrane without signal sequence), pp (periplasm), imU (inner membrane, uncleavable signal sequence), om (outer membrane), omL (outer membrane lipoprotein), imL (inner membrane lipoprotein), imS (inner membrane, cleavable signal sequence). However, the last 4 groups are taken out from our classification experiment since the population sizes are too small to ensure significance.

The 7 attributes include mcg (McGeoch's method for signal sequence recognition), gvh (von Heijne's method for signal sequence recognition), lip (von Heijne's Signal Peptidase II consensus sequence score), chg (Presence of charge on N-terminus of predicted lipoproteins), aac (score of discriminant analysis of the amino acid content of outer membrane and periplasmic proteins), alm1 (score of the ALOM membrane spanning region prediction program), and alm2 (score of ALOM program after excluding putative cleavable signal regions from the sequence).

In the classification we use 4 groups, 307 instances, with 7 attributes. Our classification model selected the discriminatory patterns mcg, gvh, alm1, and alm2 to form the predictive rule with unbiased correct classification rates of 89%, compared to the results of 81% by other classification models [83]. Using only 200 instances to train, the prediction accuracy on the remaining 107 instances reaches over 90% for each of the 4 groups.

Pattern Recognition in Satellite Images for Determining Types of Soil The satellite database consists of the multispectral values of pixels in 3×3 neighborhoods in a satellite image and the classification associated with the central pixel in each neighborhood. The aim is to predict this classification, given the multispectral values. In the sample database, the class of a pixel is coded as a number. There are 6 groups with 4435 samples in the training data set and 2000 samples in testing dataset; and each sample entity has 36 attributes describing the spectral bands of the image.

The original Landsat Multispectral Scanner image data for this database was generated from data purchased from NASA by the Australian Centre for Remote Sensing. The Landsat satellite data are one of the many sources of information available for a scene. The interpretation of a scene by integrating spatial data of diverse types and resolutions including multispectral and radar data, maps indicating topography, land use, and so on, is expected to assume significant importance with the onset of an era characterized by integrative approaches to remote sensing (e.g., NASA's Earth Observing System commencing this decade).

One frame of Landsat MSS imagery consists of four digital images of the same scene in different spectral bands. Two of these are in the visible region (corresponding approximately to green and red regions of the visible spectrum) and two are in the (near) infrared. Each pixel is an eight-bit binary word, with 0 corresponding to black and 255 to white. The spatial resolution of a pixel is about $80\,m \times 80\,m$. Each image contains 2340×3380 such pixels.

The database is a (tiny) subarea of a scene, consisting of 82×100 pixels. Each line of data corresponds to a 3×3 square neighborhood of pixels completely contained within the 82×100 subarea. Each line contains the pixel values in the four spectral bands (converted to ASCII) of each of the nine pixels in the 3×3 neighborhood and a number indicating the classification label of the central pixel. The number is a code for the following six groups: red soil, cotton crop, gray soil, damp gray soil, soil with vegetation stubble, very damp gray soil. Running the DAMIP model, 17 discriminatory attributes were selected to form the classification rule, producing a prediction accuracy of 85%.

6.5 SUMMARY AND CONCLUSION

In the article, we summarize a class of general-purpose predictive models that we have developed based on the technology of large-scale optimization and support vector machines [3–7]. Our models seek to maximize the correct classification rate while constraining the number of misclassifications in each group. The models incorporate the following features simultaneously: (i) the ability to classify any number of distinct groups; (ii) allow incorporation of heterogeneous and temporal types of attributes as input; (iii) a high-dimensional data transformation that reduces noise and errors in biological data; (iv) constraining the misclassification in each group and a reserved-judgment region that provides a safeguard against overtraining (which tends to lead to high misclassification rates from the resulting predictive rule); and (v) successive multistage classification capability to handle data points placed in the reserved-judgment region. The performance and predictive power of the classification models is validated through a broad class of biological and medical applications.

Classification models are critical to medical advances as they can be used in genomic, cell, molecular, and system-level analyses to assist in early-risk prediction, diagnosis and detection of disease, intervention and monitoring, and treatment outcome prediction. As shown in the vaccine immunity prediction, the predictive signatures can guide the rapid development of vaccines against emerging infections and aid in the monitoring of suboptimal immune responses in the elderly, infants, or people with weakened immune systems. Neuropsychological tests are inexpensive, noninvasive, and can be incorporated within an annual physical examination. Our study on Alzheimer's disease shows that they offer potential predictive capability for earliest diagnosis. Identifying individuals who are at-risk but currently have no symptoms are critical to curtail the rapid rise of this illness. In the CpG island study for human cancer, such prediction and diagnosis open up novel therapeutic sites for early intervention. The ultrasound application illustrates its application to a novel drug delivery mechanism, assisting clinicians during a drug delivery process, or in devising implantable devices into the body for automated drug delivery and monitoring. Prediction of the shape of a cancer tumor bed provides a personalized treatment design, replacing manual estimates by sophisticated computer predictive models. Prediction of early atherosclerosis through inexpensive biomarker measurements and traditional risk factors can serve as a potential clinical diagnostic tool for routine physical and health maintenance, alerting doctors and patients to the need for early intervention to prevent serious vascular disease. Fingerprinting of microvascular networks opens up the possibility for early diagnosis of perturbed systems in the body that may trigger disease (e.g., genetic deficiency, diabetes, aging, obesity, macular degeneracy, tumor formation), identify target sites for treatment, and monitor prognosis and success of treatment. Determining the type of erythemato-squamous disease and the presence/absence of heart disease helps clinicians to correctly diagnose and effectively treat patients. Thus, classification models can serve as a basis for predictive health/medicine where the desire is to diagnose early and provide personalized target intervention. This has the potential to reduce healthcare costs, improve success of treatment, and improve quality of life of patients.

The modeling framework of the discrete support vector machines, DAMIP, offers great flexibility, enabling one to simultaneously incorporate the features as listed earlier, as well as many other features. Further theoretical study will be performed on these models to understand their characteristics and the sensitivity of the predictive patterns to model/parameter variations. We note that deriving the predictive rules for such problems can be computationally demanding due to the *NP-hard* nature of MIP. We continue to work on improving optimization algorithms utilizing novel cutting plane and branch-and-bound strategies, fast heuristic algorithms, and parallel algorithms.

ACKNOWLEDGMENTS

This research was partially supported by the National Institutes of Health and the National Science Foundation.

REFERENCES

[1] McLachlan GJ. *Discriminant Analysis and Statistical Pattern Recognition*. New York: Wiley; 1992.

[2] Gallagher RJ, Lee EK, Patterson D. An optimization model for constrained discriminant analysis and numerical experiments with iris, thyroid, and heart disease datasets. In: Cimino JJ. Ed. Proceedings of the 1996 American Medical Informatics Association, 209–213; 1996.

[3] Gallagher RJ, Lee EK, Patterson DA. Constrained discriminant analysis via 0/1 mixed integer programming. Ann Oper ResSpecial Issue on Non-Traditional Approaches to Statistical Classification and Regression 1997;74:65–88.

[4] Lee EK. Large-scale optimization-based classification models in medicine and biology. Ann Biomed Eng 2007;35(6):1095–1109.

[5] Lee EK. Optimization-based predictive models in medicine and biology. In: Alves CJS, Pardalos PM, Vicente LN, editor. *Optimization in Medicine*. New York: Springer; 2008. p 127–151.

[6] Lee EK. Machine learning framework for classification in medicine and biology. In: Van Hoeve WJ, Coban E, editor. *Integration of AI and OR Techniques in Constraint Programming for Combinatorial Optimization Problems*. Berlin, Heidelberg: Springer; 2009. p 1–7.

[7] Lee EK, Gallagher RJ, Patterson D. A linear programming approach to discriminant analysis with a reserved judgment region. INFORMS J Comput 2003;15(1):23–41.

[8] Cao K, Lailler N, Zhang Y, Kumar A, Uppal K, Liu Z, Lee EK, Wu H, Medrzycki M, Pan C, Ho PY, Cooper GP Jr, Dong X, Bock C, Bouhassira EE, Fan Y. High-resolution mapping of h1 linker histone variants in embryonic stem cells. PLoS Genet 2013;9(4):1–16.

[9] Feltus FA, Lee EK, Costello JF, Plass C, Vertino PM. Predicting aberrant CpG island methylation. Proc Natl Acad Sci 2003;100(21):12253–12258.

[10] Feltus FA, Lee EK, Costello JF, Plass C, Vertino PM. DNA signatures associated with CpG island methylation states. Genomics 2006;87:572–579.

[11] Koczor CA, Lee EK, Torres RA, Boyd A, Vega JD, Uppal K, Yuan F, Fields EJ, Samarel AM, Lewis W. Detection of differentially methylated gene promoters in failing and non-failing human left ventricle myocardium using computation analysis. Physiol Genomics 2013;45(14):597–605.

[12] Lee EK, Fung AYC, Brooks JP, Zaider M. Automated tumor volume contouring in soft-tissue sarcoma adjuvant brachytherapy treatment. Int J Radiat Oncol Biol Phys 2002;47(11):1891–1910.

[13] Lee EK, Gallagher R, Campbell A, Prausnitz M. Prediction of ultrasound-mediated disruption of cell membranes using machine learning techniques and statistical analysis of acoustic spectra. IEEE Trans Biomed Eng 2004;51(1):1–9.

[14] Lee EK, Wu TL, Goldstein F, Levey A. Predictive model for early detection of mild cognitive impairment and Alzheimer's disease. In: Pardalos PM, Coleman TF, Xanthopoulos P, editor. *Optimization and Data Analysis in Biomedical Informatics*. New York: Springer; 2012. p 83–97.

[15] McCabe MT, Lee EK, Vertino PM. A multifactorial signature of DNA sequence and polycomb binding predicts aberrant CpG island methylation. Cancer Res 2009;69(1):282–291.

[16] Nakaya HI, Wrammert J, Lee EK, Racioppi L, Marie-Kunze S, Haining WN, Means AR, Kasturi SP, Khan N, Li GM, McCausland M, Kanchan V, Kokko KE, Li S, Elbein R, Mehta AK, Aderem A, Subbarao K, Ahmed R, Pulendran B. Systems biology of seasonal influenza vaccination in humans. Nat Immunol 2011;12(8):786.

[17] Querec TD, Akondy RS, Lee EK, Cao W, Nakaya HI, Teuwen D, Pirani A, Gernert K, Deng J, Marzolf B, Kennedy K, Wu H, Bennouna S, Oluoch H, Miller J, Vencio RZ, Mulligan M, Aderem A, Ahmed R, Pulendran B. Systems biology approach predicts immunogenicity of the yellow fever vaccine in humans. Nat Immunol 2009;10(1):116–125.

[18] Broffit JD, Randles RH, Hogg RV. Distribution-free partial discriminant analysis. J Am Stat Assoc 1976;71:934–939.

[19] Gessaman MP, Gessaman PH. A comparison of some multivariate discrimination procedures. J Am Stat Assoc 1972;67:468–472.

[20] Habbema JDF, Hermans J, Van Der Burgt AT. Cases of doubt in allocation problems. Biometrika 1974;61:313–324.

[21] Ng T-H, Randles RH. Distribution-free partial discrimination procedures. Comput Math Appl 1986;12A:225–234.

[22] Quesenberry CP, Gessaman MP. Nonparametric discrimination using tolerance regions. Ann Math Stat 1968;39:664–673.

[23] Beckman RJ, Johnson ME. A ranking procedure for partial discriminant analysis. J Am Stat Assoc 1981;76(375):671–675.

[24] Anderson JA. Constrained discrimination between k populations. J R Stat Soc B 1969;31:123–139.

[25] Bajgicr SM, Hill AV. An experimental comparison of statistical and linear programming approaches to the discriminant problems. Dec Sci 1982;13:604–618.

[26] Bal H, Örkcü HH. A new mathematical programming approach to multi-group classification problems. Comput Oper Res 2011;38(1):105–111.

[27] Bennett KP, Bredensteiner EJ. A parametric optimization method for machine learning. INFORMS J Comput 1997;9:311–318.

[28] Bennett KP, Mangasarian OL. Multicategory discrimination via linear programming. Optim Methods Software 1993;3:27–39.

[29] Cavalier TM, Ignizio JP, Soyster AL. Discriminant analysis via mathematical programming: Certain problems and their causes. Comput Oper Res 1989;16:353–362.

[30] Freed N, Glover F. A linear programming approach to the discriminant problem. Dec Sci 1981;12:68–74.

[31] Freed N, Glover F. Evaluating alternative linear programming models to solve the two-group discriminant problem. Dec Sci 1986;17:151–162.

[32] Gehrlein WV. General mathematical programming formulations for the statistical classification problem. Oper Res Lett 1986;5:299–304.

[33] Glen JJ. Integer programming methods for normalisation and variable selection in mathematical programming discriminant analysis models. J Oper Res Soc 1999;50:1043–1053.

[34] Glover F. Improved linear programming models for discriminant analysis. Dec Sci 1990;21:771–785.

[35] Glover F, Keene S, Duea B. A new class of models for the discriminant problem. Dec Sci 1988;19:269–280.

[36] Gochet W, Stam A, Srinivasan V, Chen S. Multigroup discriminant analysis using linear programming. Oper Res 1997;45:213–225.

[37] Koehler GJ, Erenguc SS. Minimizing misclassifications in linear discriminant analysis. Dec Sci 1990;21:63–85.

[38] Liittschwager JM, Wang C. Integer programming solution of a classification problem. Manage Sci 1978;24:1515–1525.

[39] Mangasarian OL. Mathematical programming in neural networks. ORSA J Comput 1993;5:349–360.

[40] Mangasarian OL, Street WN, Wolberg WH. Breast cancer diagnosis and prognosis via linear programming. Oper Res 1995;43:570–577.

[41] Nakayama H, Kagaku N. Pattern classification by linear goal programming and its extensions. J Global Optim 1998;12(2):111–126.

[42] Pavur R, Loucopoulos C. Examining optimal criterion weights in mixed integer programming approaches to the multiple-group classification problem. J Oper Res Soc 1995;46:626–640.

[43] Stam A, Joachimsthaler EA. Solving the classification problem in discriminant analysis via linear and nonlinear programming. Dec Sci 1989;20:285–293.

[44] Stam A, Ragsdale CT. On the classification gap in mathematical-programming-based approaches to the discriminant problem. Nav Res Logist 1992;39:545–559.

[45] Bishop CM. *Neural Networks for Pattern Recognition*. Oxford: Oxford University Press; 1995.

[46] Breiman L, Friedman J, Olshen RA, Stone CJ. *Classification and Regression Trees.* Wadsworth; 1984.

[47] Cristianini N, Shawe-Taylor J. *An Introduction to Support Vector Machines and Other Kernel-Based Learning Methods.* Cambridge University Press; 2000.

[48] Duda RO, Hart PE, Stork DG. *Pattern Classification.* 2nd ed. Wiley; 2001.

[49] Dreiseitl S, Ohno-Machado L. Logistic regression and artificial neural network classification models: A methodology review. J Biomed Inform 2002;35(5):352–359.

[50] Freund Y, Schapire R, Abe N. A short introduction to boosting. J Jpn Soc Artif Intell 1999;14(771–780):1612.

[51] Lim TS, Loh WY, Shih YS. A comparison of prediction accuracy, complexity, and training time of thirty-three old and new classification algorithms. Mac Learn 2000;40:203–228.

[52] Müller KR, Mika S, Rätsch G, Tsuda K, Schölkopf B. An introduction to kernel-based learning algorithms. IEEE Trans Neural Netw 2001;12(2):181–201.

[53] Vapnik V. *The Nature of Statistical Learning Theory.* Springer-Verlag; 1999.

[54] Stam A. Nontraditional approaches to statistical classification: Some perspectives on L_p-norm methods. Ann Oper Res 1997;74:1–36.

[55] Wilson JM. Integer programming formulations of statistical classification problems. Omega 1996;24(6):681–688.

[56] Zopounidis C, Doumpos M. Multicriteria classification and sorting methods: A literature review. Eur J Oper Res 2002;138:229–246.

[57] Mangasarian OL. Mathematical programming in data mining. Data Min Knowl Discovery 1997;1(2):183–201.

[58] Bradley PS, Fayyad UM, Mangasarian OL. Mathematical programming for data mining: Formulations and challenges. INFORMS J Comput 1999;11:217–238.

[59] Byvatov E, Schneider G. Support vector machine applications in bioinformatics. Appl Bioinformatics 2002;2(2):67–77.

[60] Lee EK, Wu TL, Brooks JP. Optimization in medicine and biology (Chapter 1). In: Lim GJ, Lee EK, editor. *Classification and Disease Prediction via Mathematical Programming.* Boca Raton, FL: Auerbach Publications, Taylor, Francis Group; 2008. p 3–60.

[61] Lee EK, Wu TL. Classification and disease prediction via mathematical programming. Handb Optim Med 2009;26:381–430.

[62] Brooks JP, Lee EK. Analysis of the consistency of a mixed integer programming-based multi-category constrained discriminant model. Ann Oper Res 2010;174(1):147–168.

[63] Brooks JP, Lee EK. Solving a multigroup mixed-integer programming-based constrained discrimination model. INFORMS J Comput 2014;26(3):567–585.

[64] Mitchell JE. Branch-and-cut algorithms for combinatorial optimization problems. In: Pardalos PM, Resende MGC, editor. *Handbook of Applied Optimization.* Oxford University Press; 2002. p 65–77.

[65] Savelsbergh MW. Preprocessing and probing techniques for mixed integer programming problems. ORSA J Comput 1994;6(4):445–454.

[66] Lee EK, Zaider M. Operations research advances cancer therapeutics. Interfaces 2008;38(1):5–25.

[67] Easton T, Hooker K, Lee EK. Facets of the independent set polytope. Math Program B 2003;98:177–199.

[68] Murphy PM, Aha DW. *UCI Repository of Machine Learning Databases*. Irvine, California: Department of Information and Computer Science, University of California; 1994.

[69] Brooks JP, Lee EK. Solving a mixed integer programming formulation of a multi-category constrained discrimination model. In: Proceedings of the 2006 INFORMS Workshop on Artificial Intelligence and Data Mining, 1–6; 2006.

[70] Brooks JP, Lee EK. Mixed integer programming constrained discrimination model for credit screening. In Proceedings of the 2007 Spring Simulation Multiconference, Business and Industry Symposium, 1–6, Norfolk, VA, Mar 2007. ACM Digital Library; 2006.

[71] Lee EK, Easton T, Gupta K. Novel evolutionary models and applications to sequence alignment problems. Oper Res Med 2006;148:167–187.

[72] Costello JF, Fruhwald MC, Smiraglia DJ, Rush LJ, Robertson GP, Gao X, Wright FA, Feramisco JD, Peltomaki P, Lang JC, Schuller DE, Yu L, Bloomfield CD, Caligiuri MA, Yates A, Nishikawa R, Su HH, Petrelli NJ, Zhang X, O'Dorisio MS, Held WA, Cavenee WK, Plass C. Aberrant CpG-island methylation has non-random and tumour-type-specific patterns. Nat Genet 2000;24:132–138.

[73] Costello JF, Plass C, Cavenee WK. Aberrant methylation of genes in low-grade astrocytomas. Brain Tumor Pathol 2000;17:49–56.

[74] Fruhwald MC, O'Dorisio MS, Rush LJ, Reiter JL, Smiraglia DJ, Wenger G, Costello JF, White PS, Krahe R, Brodeur GM, Plass C. Gene amplification in NETs/medulloblastomas: mapping of a novel amplified gene within the MYCN amplicon. J Med Genet 2000;37:501–509.

[75] Rush LJ, Dai Z, Smiraglia DJ, Gao X, Wright FA, Fruhwald M, Costello JF, Held WA, Yu L, Krahe R, Kolitz JE, Bloomfield CD, Caligiuri MA, Plass C. Novel methylation targets in de novo acute myeloid leukemia with prevalence of chromosome 11 loci. Blood 2001;97:3226–3233.

[76] Brock GJ, Huang TH, Chen CM, Johnson KJ. A novel technique for the identification of CpG islands exhibiting altered methylation patterns (ICEAMP). Nucleic Acids Res 2001;29:E123.

[77] Yan PS, Chen CM, Shi H, Rahmatpanah F, Wei SH, Caldwell CW, Huang TH. Dissecting complex epigenetic alterations in breast cancer using CpG island microarrays. Cancer Res 2001;61:8375–8380.

[78] Yan PS, Perry MR, Laux DE, Asare AL, Caldwell CW, Huang TH. CpG island arrays: An application toward deciphering epigenetic signatures of breast cancer. Clin Cancer Res 2000;6:1432–1438.

[79] McCord JM. The evolution of free radicals and oxidative stress. Am J Med 2000;108:652–659.

[80] Sies H. Oxidative stress: Introductory comments. In: Sies H, editor. *Oxidative Stress*. Academic Press, INC; 1985. p 1–8.

[81] Chevion M, Berenshtein E, Stadtman ER. Human studies related to protein oxidation: Protein carbonyl content as a marker of damage. Free Radic Res 2000;33(Suppl):S99–S108.

[82] Tahara S, Matsuo M, Kaneko T. Age-related changes in oxidative damage to lipids and DNA in rat skin. Mech Ageing Dev 2001;122:415–426.

[83] Horton P, Nakai K. A probabilistic classification system for predicting the cellular localization sites of proteins. Proc Int Conf Intell Syst Mol Biol 1996;4:109–115.

7

PREDICTIVE MODELING IN RADIATION ONCOLOGY

HAO ZHANG

Department of Radiation Oncology, University of Maryland School of Medicine, Baltimore, MD, USA

ROBERT MEYER

Computer Sciences Department, University of Wisconsin, Madison, WI, USA

LEYUAN SHI

Department of Industrial and Systems Engineering, University of Wisconsin, Madison, WI, USA

WEI LU AND WARREN D'SOUZA

Department of Radiation Oncology, University of Maryland School of Medicine, Baltimore, MD, USA

7.1 INTRODUCTION

Cancer is a leading cause of death worldwide and can affect people at all ages. There will be over 1.6 million new cases of cancer diagnosed in the United States in 2014, and many times that number in other countries. About 60% of US cancer patients are treated with radiation therapy, and increasingly complex radiation delivery procedures are being developed in order to improve treatment outcomes. A key goal of radiation therapy is to determine appropriate values for a large set of delivery parameters in order to ensure that as large a fraction as possible of the radiation that enters the

Healthcare Analytics: From Data to Knowledge to Healthcare Improvement, First Edition.
Edited by Hui Yang and Eva K. Lee.
© 2016 John Wiley & Sons, Inc. Published 2016 by John Wiley & Sons, Inc.

patient is delivered to the tumor as opposed to depositing it in adjacent noncancerous organs that can be damaged by radiation (the latter are termed organs-at-risk (OARs)). As complex as cancer is, radiation therapy is also a complicated process. Analytics tools are becoming critical for clinicians and scientists for improvements to the treatment and a better understanding of the disease. Computational techniques such as predictive modeling using machine learning (ML) have been increasingly used in radiation therapy to help accurately localize the tumors in images, precisely target the radiation to the tumors, analyze treatment outcomes, and improve treatment quality and patient safety.

Machine learning tools are commonly used to extract implicit, previously unknown, and potentially useful information from data. This information, which is expressed in a comprehensible form, can be used for a variety of purposes. The idea is to build programs or models that sift through raw data automatically, seeking regularities or patterns. Strong patterns, if found, will likely generalize to yield accurate predictions with respect to future data. Machine learning algorithms need to be robust enough to cope with imperfect data and to extract regularities that are inexact but useful. In order to achieve this, machine learning algorithms typically involve solving rigorous mathematical optimization (linear or nonlinear) programs to obtain the coefficients for describing regression models or to derive rules, trees, and networks for classification.

Recently, machine learning has gained great popularity in many aspects of cancer research, including tumor localization, prediction of radiotherapy response and image processing, and pattern recognition. Regression methods are essential to any cancer data analysis that attempts to describe the relationship between a response variable (outcome) and any number of predictor variables (input features). Regression analysis helps us understand how the typical value of the outcome changes when any one of the predictor variables is varied, while the other predictor variables are held fixed. Most commonly used methods include linear regression and ordinary least squares regression, in which the regression function is defined in terms of a finite number of unknown coefficients that are estimated from the data.

Frequently in medical applications, situations involving discrete variables arise. In this circumstance, machine learning still plays an essential role, because objects such as lesions, cancer foci, and organs in medical images cannot be modeled accurately by simple equations. Thus, it is natural that tasks in medical analysis require essentially "learning from examples." Logistic regression (LR) analysis extends the techniques of multiple regression analysis to research situations in which the outcome variable is categorical, that is, taking on two or more possible values. In cancer research, the goal of logistic regression analysis is to find the best fitting and most parsimonious, yet biologically reasonable, model to describe the relationship between an outcome and a set of predictor or explanatory variables. But logistic regression requires many data points to ensure the stability of the model and has a disadvantage with respect to interpretability of the model in the face of multicollinearity.

One of the most popular uses of machine learning in Radiation Oncology is the classification of objects into certain categories (e.g., abnormal or normal, lesions or nonlesions). This class of machine learning uses features (e.g., diameter, contrast, and circularity) extracted from segmented objects as information for classifying objects.

Most commonly used techniques include artificial neural networks (ANN), support vector machines (SVM), and decision trees. These methods involve solving an optimization problem in which the objective function has a measure of the errors in the model (e.g., squared error) and may include a term that measures the complexity of the model (e.g., norm of the weights of input features). An example of one such technique is the use of a sequential optimization algorithm for "training" a support vector regression model, which employs a quadratic data-fitting problem whose objective function comprises a weighted combination of two terms: the first term is a quadratic error measure and the second is a model complexity term defined by a norm of the weights selected for the input features. The latter term aids in the prevention of overfitting of data. Training an SVM is accomplished by the solution of a large constrained quadratic programming (QP) optimization problem in order to determine the optimal weights of those linear terms in the model.

The rest of the chapter is organized as follows: First, brief tutorials of four predictive modeling techniques are given. Then, we provide a summary of recent advances of predictive modeling applications in three major areas: medical image processing and diagnostics, real-time tumor localization, and radiotherapy response prediction. After that, the authors' previous work is used to provide detailed examples of predictive modeling approaches to radiation therapy. Section 7.4 demonstrates how to construct predictive models using comprehensive tumor features for the evaluation of tumor response to neoadjuvant chemoradiotherapy (CRT) in patients with esophageal cancer. Section 7.5 shows ML applications in predicting radiation-induced complications: xerostomia (dry mouth) in head and neck cancer and rectal bleeding in whole pelvis/prostate cancer. Section 7.6 shows utilization of an ML method in localizing thorax tumor motion in radiation therapy.

7.2 TUTORIALS OF PREDICTIVE MODELING TECHNIQUES

Depending on the application area, there exist many predictive modeling techniques that can be utilized. It is not the goal of this chapter to give a comprehensive introduction of these techniques. We only give brief tutorials of several widely used techniques.

7.2.1 Feature Selection

Before applying any predictive modeling techniques, feature selection is often used to remove redundant or irrelevant features. Here, we demonstrate an SVM-based feature ranking method [1]. For a training set $\{x_1, x_2, \ldots, x_i, \ldots, x_l\}$ with corresponding labels $\{y_1, y_2, \ldots, y_i, \ldots, y_l\}$, the SVM algorithm is as follows:

$$\text{Minimize}_{\alpha_i} \quad \frac{1}{2} \sum_{hi} y_h y_i \alpha_h \alpha_i (x_h \cdot x_i + \lambda \delta_{hi}) - \sum_i \alpha_i$$

$$\text{subject to} \quad 0 \leq \alpha_i \leq C \quad \text{and} \quad \sum_i \alpha_i y_i = 0$$

The summations run over all training data x_i that are n-dimensional feature vectors. $x_h \cdot x_i$ denotes the scalar product, y_i encodes the class label as a binary value $+1$ or -1, δ_{hi} is the Kronecker symbol ($\delta_{hi} = 1$ if $h = i$ and 0 otherwise), and λ and C are positive constants, which ensure convergence even when the problem is nonlinearly separable or poorly conditioned. In such cases, some of the support vectors may not lie on the margin. The resulting decision function of an input vector x is $D(x) = w \cdot x + b$ with $w = \sum_i \alpha_i y_i x_i$. The weight vector w is a linear combination of training data. The training data with nonzero weights are support vectors. Those with weight satisfying the strict inequality $0 < \alpha_i < C$ are marginal support vectors. The bias value b is an average over marginal support vectors. The final feature ranking is achieved by recursively removing features with the lowest weight until all features are removed. To avoid feature selection bias, a frequency distribution of the top-ranked features after k-fold cross-validation can be obtained. An optimal feature set can be identified as the most frequently selected certain number of features from the frequency distribution.

7.2.2 Support Vector Machine

One of the most commonly used predictive modeling techniques is SVM. In an SVM, a kernel is used to transform the selected features from $x_1, \ldots, x_m$ space into $\tilde{x}_1, \ldots, \tilde{x}_m$ space, so that the two classes become linearly separable. A hyperplane that represents the largest separation between the closest members (support vectors) of the two classes in multidimension is determined, providing a classification rule or model $y = f(\tilde{x}_1, \ldots, \tilde{x}_m)$, which classify a new or testing data based on its y value. One method to train the SVM is the construction of a linear model $f(x) = w \cdot \Phi(x) + b$ via a sequential minimal optimization (SMO) algorithm [2, 3].

$$\min \frac{1}{2} \|w\|^2 + C \sum_i (\alpha_i + \beta_i)$$

$$\text{s.t.} - (\varepsilon + \alpha_i) \le w \cdot z_i + b - d_i \le \varepsilon + \beta_i$$

$$\alpha_i, \beta_i \ge 0$$

The SMO algorithm utilizes the simplest linear model of the form $w \cdot z_i + b$ where z_i denotes the vector of input variables, and w and b denote the fitting parameters (w is a vector, b is a scalar) to be generated by SMO. d_i is the label. Training the SVM is accomplished by the solution of this constrained quadratic programming (QP) optimization problem in order to determine the optimal weights of those linear terms. In support vector regression, an accuracy threshold ε (0.001) is set so that model prediction errors that are below this threshold yield a penalty of 0 in the objective function. C is a weighting factor for the sum of errors terms and 2-norm is used for model complexity measure.

Rather than working directly with the primal quadratic weight optimization problem, SMO adopts the more efficient approach of initially solving the dual of this problem [3], which is derived from optimality conditions and defined in terms of the Lagrange or dual variables and may be formulated as a large QP problem.

After defining the Lagrange multipliers λ as $w(\lambda, \lambda') = \sum_i (\lambda_i - \lambda_i') z_i$ and using Wolfe duality theory, the dual problem is

$$\max \sum_i d_i(\lambda_i - \lambda_i') - \varepsilon \sum_i (\lambda_i + \lambda_i') - \frac{1}{2} \|w(\lambda, \lambda')\|^2$$

$$\text{s.t.} \quad \sum_i (\lambda_i - \lambda_i') = 0$$

$$\lambda_i, \lambda_i' \in [0, C]$$

SMO divides this latter problem into a series of small QP problems involving only two variables each, which are solved sequentially and analytically. After obtaining λ_i and λ_i', the primal variables w and b can be determined by using the KKT conditions.

7.2.3   Logistic Regression

Logistic regression (LR) is one the most widely used predictive modeling techniques in healthcare applications. LR first transformed the response variable into $\Pr[\text{YES}|x_1, \dots, x_m]$, a probability variable corresponding to the "YES" class given features $x_1, \dots, x_m$. A logit transformation, $\log\{\Pr[\text{YES}|x_1, \dots, x_m]/(1 - \Pr[\text{YES}|x_1, \dots, x_m])\}$, is then applied so that the resulting variable lies between negative infinity and positive infinity. The transformed variable is approximated using a linear function of input features (linear regression). The resulting model is $\Pr[\text{YES}|x_1, \dots, x_m] = 1/[1 + \exp(-w_0 - w_1 x_1 - \cdots - w_m x_m)]$ with weight w. The weights are obtained by fitting the model to the training set using maximum log-likelihood estimation.

7.2.4   Decision Tree

Another binary classification method in predicting modeling is an optimized decision tree, whose generation process via supervised learning is outlined here. Referencing Figure 7.1, note that the nonleaf nodes (i.e., the nodes that have successor nodes below them, shown as ellipses in Fig. 7.1) represent univariate inequality tests that

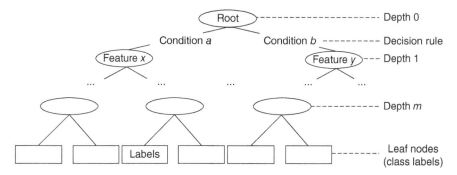

Figure 7.1   Optimized decision tree algorithm schematic.

are followed by further tests at lower nodes until the final tests leading to the leaf nodes (shown as rectangles in Fig. 7.1) yield classification decisions [4, 5].

A general approach to the construction of decision trees starts with the selection of a branching test at the root node at the top of the tree and can be summarized as following:

1. Choose an attribute–value pair that leads to the best partition of the training instances with respect to the output attribute.
2. Create a separate branch for each range of value of the chosen attribute.
3. Divide the instances into subgroups corresponding to the attribute–value range of the chosen node.
4. For each subgroup, terminate the attribute partitioning process if:
   a. All members of a subgroup have the same value for the output attribute.
   b. No further distinguishing attributes can be determined. Label the branch with the output value seen by the majority of remaining instances.
5. Else, for each subgroup created in 3 for which the attribute partitioning process is not terminated in 4 at a leaf, repeat the above branching process.

This stage of the algorithm is based on the training data, and generally produces a large and complex decision tree that correctly classifies all of the training instances. In the second stage of the tree generation process, this decision tree is then pruned by considering the test data and removing parts of the tree that have a relatively high error rate or provide little gain in statistical accuracy.

7.3   REVIEW OF RECENT PREDICTIVE MODELING APPLICATIONS IN RADIATION ONCOLOGY

Optimization-based analytics approaches have been widely applied in medicine and biology fields [6]. In recent years, there have been special sessions dedicated to applications in Radiation Oncology at international machine learning conferences. Even in national medical conferences (e.g., the 2010 American Association of Physicists in Medicine annual meeting), there have been special sessions dedicated to machine learning applications. It is therefore appropriate to survey advancements in this area.

7.3.1   Machine Learning for Medical Image Processing

Machine learning plays an essential role in medical image analysis because objects such as lesions and organs in medical images cannot be modeled accurately by simple equations; thus, tasks in medical image analysis require essentially "learning from examples." One of the most popular uses of machine learning in medical image analysis is the classification of objects such as lesions into certain categories (e.g., abnormal or normal, lesions or nonlesions). This class of machine learning uses features (e.g., diameter, contrast, and circularity) extracted from segmented objects as information for classifying the objects. Machine learning techniques in this class include linear discriminant analysis, k-nearest neighbor classifiers, ANN, and SVM.

Early uses of ML were by Wolberg et al. [7, 8] of the Wisconsin group. They built an interactive computer system via ML to evaluate and diagnose breast cancer based on cytologic features derived directly from a digital scan of fine-needle aspirate (FNA) slides. FNA accuracy is traditionally limited by, among other factors, the subjective interpretation of the aspirate. The authors increased breast FNA accuracy by coupling digital image analysis methods with ML techniques. The ML approach captured nuclear features that were prognostically more accurate than estimates based on tumor size and lymph node status. The method was tested on consecutive series of 569 patients. A 166-patient subset provided the data for the prognostic study. An additional 75 consecutive, new patients provided samples to test the diagnostic system. The projected prospective accuracy of the diagnostic system was estimated to be 97% by 10-fold cross-validation, and the actual accuracy on 75 new samples was 100%. The projected prospective accuracy of the prognostic system was estimated to be 86% by leave-one-out testing.

Based on the evidence suggesting that ML can help improve the diagnostic performance of radiologists in their image interpretations, many investigators have continued the research in developing schemes for detection/diagnosis of lesions in medical images, such as detection of lung nodules in chest radiographs [9, 10], and thoracic CT [11], detection of microcalcifications or masses in mammography, breast MRI, and detection of polyps in CT colonography [12, 13].

For example, a supervised lesion segmentation method based on a massive training artificial neural network (MTANN) filter in a computer-aided diagnostic scheme for detection of lung nodules in CT was developed by Suzuki et al. [14]. Tested on 71 instances of lung cancer patient data, the MTANN filter yielded a sensitivity of 80.3% (57/71), with a rate of 4.8 false positives per patient. Overall, the MTANN-based segmentation method was effective in segmenting lesions in medical images with improved sensitivity and specificity.

In mammography, ML classifiers were proposed for breast cancer diagnosis [15]. The method was evaluated to classify feature vectors extracted from segmented regions (pathological lesion or normal tissue) on craniocaudal (CC) and/or mediolateral oblique (MLO) mammography image views, providing BI-RADS diagnosis (BI-RADS stands for breast imaging reporting and data system, which is a scheme for putting the findings of mammograms into a small number of well-defined categories). Appropriate combinations of image processing and normalization techniques were applied to reduce image artifacts and increase mammogram details. Two hundred and eighty-six cases extracted from an image repository, where specialized radiologists segmented regions on CC and/or MLO images (biopsies provided the golden standard), were evaluated. Around 20,000 ML configurations were tested with different parameter combinations, obtaining classifiers achieving an AUC, defined as the area under receiver operating characteristic (ROC) curves, of 0.996 when combining feature vectors extracted from CC and MLO views of the same case.

7.3.2   Machine Learning in Real-Time Tumor Localization

In recent years, the substantial risks of surgical resection of tumors in the lungs, liver, and pancreas, and the fact that a large percentage of patients are not surgical candidates because their disease is too far advanced or their health is poor, have motivated the investigation of stereotactic body radiation therapy. Stereotactic body radiation therapy involves delivery of a high dose of radiation that conforms precisely to the tumor volume in just a few fractions with the objective of tumor ablation.

However, a significant challenge is the delivery of very precise treatments to moving targets during respiration. Therefore, methods to track tumors during normal respiration need to be developed. The extent of respiratory motion for tumors in various organs is observed with technologies such as fluoroscopy, surrogate markers (spirometry, fiducials), 4D-CT, and dynamic MRI. Then a tumor motion compensation method can be employed. A number of real-time technologies are being developed to account for respiratory motion. These systems require real-time radiation target position information for both respiratory gating and tracking. Classification schemes based on machine learning techniques such as ANN [16] and SVM [17] were used to separate the fluoroscopic images into beam on or off classes. ML regression models have also been proposed to localize tumor position in real time as shown in Section 7.6.

A traditional technique to account for tumor motion is to expand the treatment target with margins. The undesirable outcome of these margins is higher doses to the surrounding normal tissue and the increased risk of toxicity. ML methods, such as neural networks, have been used for real-time spatial and temporal tracking of radiotherapy treatment targets during free breathing [18–21]. These techniques will allow the reduction and possible elimination of dose-limiting motion margins in external-beam radiation delivery plans. Murphy has shown that, despite the widely varying characteristics of 27 test examples of breathing, a neural network based ML technique was able to make temporal predictions 300 ms into the future with high accuracy [22], which enabled its use in radiotherapy for motion tracking.

Ruan and Keall [23] extended ML methods from a single dimension to multidimensional processing. However, the amount of data required for such extensions grows exponentially with the dimensionality of the problem. They investigated a multidimensional prediction scheme based on kernel density estimation in an augmented covariate-response space. Principal component analysis (PCA) was utilized to construct a proper low-dimensional feature space, where kernel density estimation is feasible with the limited training data. The dimension reduction idea proposed in their work was closely related to feature selection used in ML, particularly SVMs. To test the performance of their method, 159 lung target motion traces were obtained with a Synchrony respiratory tracking system. Prediction performance of the low-dimensional feature learning-based multidimensional prediction method was compared against an independent prediction method where prediction was conducted along each physical coordinate independently. The proposed method showed uniformly better performance and reduced the case-wise 3D root-mean-squared prediction error by about 30–40%.

While tracking implanted fiducial markers has been shown to provide good accuracy with respect to tumor motion prediction, this procedure may not be widely accepted due to the risk of pneumothorax. Cui et al. [17] proposed a gating method that includes formulating the problem as a classification problem and generating the gating signals from fluoroscopic images without implanted fiducial markers via template matching methods [24]. The classification problem (gating the beam to be ON or OFF) was solved by SVM. The ground truth was the reference gating signal, which was manually determined by a radiation oncologist. The proposed technique was tested on five sequences of fluoroscopic images from five lung cancer patients and compared to template matching method alone. SVM was slightly more accurate on average (1–3%) than using template matching by itself with respect to delivering the target dose. SVM is thus a potentially precise and efficient algorithm for generating gating signals for radiotherapy.

In order to compensate for the shortcomings of template matching methods, which may fail when the tumor boundary is unclear in fluoroscopic images, Lin et al. [25] proposed a framework of markerless gating and tracking based on machine learning algorithms. A similar two-class classification tracking problem was solved by PCA and ANN. The tracking problem was formulated as a regression task, which employs the correlation between the tumor position and nearby surrogate anatomic features in the image. Proposed methods were tested on 10 fluoroscopic image sequences of 9 patients. For gating, the target coverage (the precision) ranged from 90% to 99%, with the mean of 96.5%. For tracking, the mean localization error was about 2.1 pixels and the maximum error at 95% confidence level was about 4.6 pixels (pixel size is about 0.5 mm). Following the same framework, different combinations of dimensionality reduction techniques (PCA and four nonlinear manifold-learning methods) and two machine learning classification methods (ANN and SVM) were evaluated later [16]. PCA combined with either ANN or SVM achieved a better performance than the other nonlinear manifold-learning methods. Overall, ANN combined with PCA is a better candidate than other combinations for real-time gated radiotherapy. Generalized linear discriminant analysis (GLDA) was recently applied to the same problem [26]. The fundamental difference relative to conventional dimensionality reduction techniques is that GLDA explicitly takes into account the label information available in the training set and therefore is efficient for discrimination among classes. It was demonstrated that GLDA outperformed PCA in terms of classification accuracy and target coverage at a lower nominal duty cycle.

7.3.3 Machine Learning for Predicting Radiotherapy Response

Radiation-induced outcomes are determined by complex interactions between treatment techniques, cancer pathology, and patient-related physiological and biological factors. A common obstacle to building maximally predictive treatment outcome models for clinical practice in radiation oncology is the failure to capture this complexity of heterogeneous variable interactions and the ability to adapt outcome models across different institutions. Methods based on ML can identify data patterns, variable interactions, and higher order relationships among prognostic variables. In addition, they have the ability to generalize to unseen data [27]. In this section, we briefly summarize the research in ML for predicting radiotherapy response.

As in the case of our example of using constraints to build treatment plan surface to predict organ complications (Section 7.5), Buettner et al. [28] proposed to predict radiation-induced rectal bleeding and loose stools using Bayesian logistic regression with high-order interactions. Binary features (constraint satisfied or failed) were used as predictive variables in multivariate logistic regression to build the probabilistic model. The 10-fold cross-validation of the model for loose stools resulted in an average AUC of 0.72 with a standard deviation of 0.11. For rectal bleeding an AUC of 0.64 ± 0.08 was achieved. From the results of these models, they were able to derive a new type of geometrical dosimetric constraint that showed more predictive power than traditional constraints. Similarly, Bayesian logistic regression together with feature selection was also applied to predict esophagitis and xerostomia [29].

In addition to applications in tumor motion localization, neural networks and decision trees have also been utilized in predicting radiotherapy response because of their ability to detect nonlinear patterns in the data. In particular, neural networks were used to model postradiation treatment outcomes for cases of lung injury [30, 31] and prostate cancer [32]. However, these studies have mainly focused on using a single class of neural networks, namely feedforward neural networks with different types of activation functions. A different neural network architecture, referred to as generalized regression neural network, was shown to outperform classical neural networks [33]. The major drawback of using neural network methods was that they are based on greedy heuristic algorithms with no guarantee of global optimality or robustness, in addition to the extensive computational burden associated with them. This drawback led to introduction of SVM methods from medical imaging applications [34, 35] to the area of response modeling [36].

The Washington University group applied ML techniques for the prediction of radiation pneumonitis in lung cancer patients [37]. The authors compared several widely used classification algorithms in the machine learning field, including SVM, decision trees, random forest, and naïve Bayes, to distinguish between different risk groups for pneumonitis. The performance of these classification algorithms was evaluated in conjunction with several feature selection strategies (SVM-recursive feature elimination, correlation based, chi-square, and information gain based feature selections), and the impact of the feature selection on performance was further evaluated. In conclusion, kernel-based SVMs showed greatly higher Matthew's correlation coefficient values (a metric that is widely used as a performance measure) than not only linear SVM but also other competing classification algorithms after correction for imbalance.

Oh and El Naqa [38] continued research along this line for lung cancer patients. Instead of SVM, a Bayesian network was applied to not only predict the probability that a given treatment plan for a patient will result in a treatment complication but also for developing better understanding of the clinical decision-making process. Feature selection was used to reduce the time and space complexity associated with Bayesian structure learning. The authors demonstrated that a Bayesian network was able to identify the relationship between the dose-volume parameters and pneumonitis (distinguishing the control group from the disease group based on the trained Bayesian network).

Das et al. [39] provided a simple hybrid ML method, in which they fuse the results of four different machine learning models (boosted decision trees, neural networks, SVM, self-organizing maps) to predict the risk of lung pneumonitis in patients undergoing thoracic radiotherapy. Fusion was achieved by simple averaging of the 10-fold cross-validated predictions for each patient from all four models. The AUC for the fused cross-validated results was 0.79, higher than the individual models and with lower variance.

Lung cancer has been the most frequent tested disease site utilizing ML, especially via neural networks [40] and SVM [41, 42]. However, Bayesian networks were hypothesized to have an advantage with respect to handling missing data. Dekker et al. [43] provided a comparison between an SVM and Bayesian network model regarding the handling of missing data for predicting survival in lung cancer. A Bayesian network model outperformed the SVM model in the case of missing data. If an important feature was missing that could not be inferred by the Bayesian model, a strong change in AUC was noticed (AUC from the Bayesian network went from 0.72 to 0.82 while AUC from SVM went from 0.68 to 0.76) when the patients with missing data are removed from the validation set.

To emphasize the advantage of ML in dealing with heterogeneous data from multiple institutions, El Naqa et al. [44] described an ML methodology that can screen for nonlinear relations among prognostic variables and generalize to unseen data. An independent RTOG data set from multiple institutions was used for model validation. The database contained different cancer disease sites including complications such as esophagitis, pneumonitis, and xerostomia. The distribution of patient groups was analyzed using PCA to uncover potential nonlinear behavior. Results suggested that an SVM kernel method provided superior performance on leave-one-out testing compared to logistic regression and neural networks in cases in which the data exhibited nonlinear behavior on PCA. In prediction of esophagitis and pneumonitis endpoints, 21% and 60% improvement was reported, respectively.

7.4 MODELING PATHOLOGIC RESPONSE OF ESOPHAGEAL CANCER TO CHEMORADIOTHERAPY

Trimodality therapy, which consists of concurrent neoadjuvant CRT followed by surgery, has been the most common treatment for locally advanced cancers. However, it was recently suggested that not all patients benefit from surgery after the induction of CRT and that definitive CRT (CRT alone) could also become an option [45]. Evidence suggests that surgery after CRT can significantly improve local control [46, 47]. These improvements in local control, however, have been tempered by the increased mortality (9–12%) and morbidity (30%) compared to CRT alone (mortality, 0.8–3.5%). Several studies have shown that tumor response to CRT remains an important predictor of both local control and overall survival [45–47]. Complete pathologic responders to CRT appear to have superior outcomes, regardless of whether they undergo surgical resection. These data also support that the addition of resection can improve outcomes for patients who are discovered to have residual tumor following completion of CRT. Given the added mortality and morbidity of surgery after CRT, as well as the high local failure rate for CRT alone, it is critical to accurately identify patients who respond to CRT so that surgery may be safely deferred. It is equally important to accurately identify patients who do not respond to CRT so that early surgical salvage can be initiated. A preliminary study with 20 locally advanced esophageal cancer patients was conducted to predict the tumor response to CRT [48].

7.4.1 Input Features

Sixteen clinical parameters and demographic features were extracted from patients' charts. Clinical parameters included differentiation stage, T stage, N stage, M stage, distant metastasis, type of chemotherapy, radiotherapy dose, treatment with concomitant boost, location of tumor, tumor involves gastroesophageal junction, histology, total extent of disease, and extent of disease >4 cm. Demographic features included age and gender.

Comprehensive spatiotemporal positron emission tomography (PET) features were extracted from pre-CRT and post-CRT PET/CT images, which characterize the tumor standardized uptake value (SUV) intensity distribution, spatial variations (texture), geometry, and their associated changes resulting from CRT. Nine intensity features, 8 Haralick texture features, 15 geometry features, and 1 volume-intensity feature were extracted. After incorporating temporal changes and excluding quantitatively identical features, a total of 137 features were obtained for each tumor.

The resected surgical specimen was submitted to the pathologist for evaluation and was used as modeling ground truth. The specimen was microscopically examined and semiquantitatively categorized into one of three groups: pathologic complete response (pCR), microscopic residual disease (mRD), or gross residual disease (gRD), according to the amount of residual viable carcinoma observed in relation to areas of fibrosis [49]. In this study, both pCR and mRD were considered as "responders," because they have been shown to have similar survival rates [50], while gRD was considered as "nonresponder."

7.4.2 Feature Selection and Predictive Model Construction

Four groups of tumor features were examined: (i) 16 conventional PET/CT response measures; (ii) 16 clinical parameters and demographics as described earlier; (iii) 137 spatiotemporal PET features; and (iv) all 169 combined features. Since there were many features, a feature selection process as described in Section 7.2.1 with cross-validation (Fig. 7.2) was applied first within each feature group for each tested predictive model.

Ten-, five-, and twofold cross-validations were repeatedly used for both feature selection and model accuracy evaluation. Our goal was to model pathologic tumor

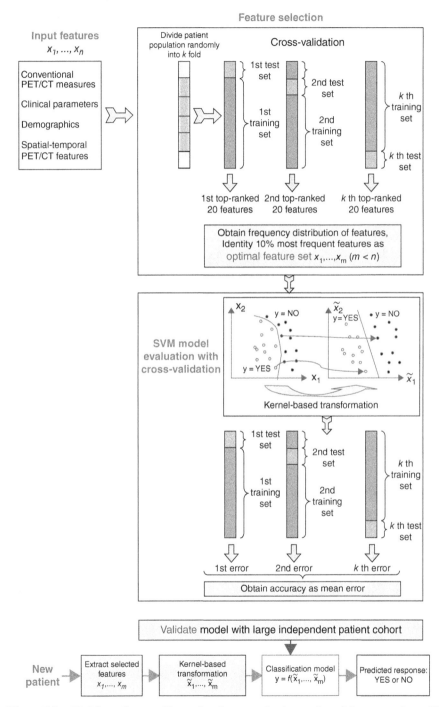

Figure 7.2 Workflow diagram illustrating feature selection and model construction with cross-validations for prediction of tumor response.

response to CRT as a function (f) of each of the four groups of tumor features so that:

Pathologic tumor response

$$= f\left(\text{conventional PET}\Big/\begin{array}{l}\text{CT measures, or clinical parameters and demographics,}\\ \text{or spatiotemporal PET features, or all combined features}\end{array}\right)$$

$$(7.1)$$

We used two machine learning models, LR and SVM, to obtain functions f. Figure 7.2 illustrates the modeling process using SVM with all tumor features as an example.

The outputs of the ML models were the predicted pathologic response represented as a binary variable (yes or no), which corresponded to "responder" or "nonresponder," respectively (Fig. 7.2). The accuracy of using each feature group and each model to predict the pathologic tumor response was quantified using the AUC. In addition, the sensitivity and specificity of each model were calculated and compared using the unpaired t-test at a significance level of 0.05. Model precision was evaluated with the 95% confidence intervals (CI).

7.4.3   Results

Because LR and SVM are two distinct models, our feature selection process resulted in different optimal feature sets for each model. The optimal feature set for SVM always contained the optimal feature set for LR, except when applied to clinical parameters and demographics, where histology was the only feature selected for SVM.

Figure 7.3 shows the model accuracy (AUC) and precision (95% CI) obtained from repeating the 10-, 5-, and 2-fold cross-validations. The best prediction was obtained using the SVM model with 17 features from all combined features (SVM_{all}). All patients within the testing set were correctly classified during the repetition of 10-fold cross-validations, resulting in a mean AUC of 1.00 (100% sensitivity, 100% specificity). SVM_{all} contained 1 conventional PET/CT measure, "residual metabolic tumor volume (i.e., $\text{SUV} \geq 2.5$) post-CRT"; 2 clinical parameters, "whether tumor involves gastroesophageal junction" and "T stage"; and 14 spatiotemporal PET (3 intensity, 8 texture, 2 geometry, and 1 volume-intensity) features, suggesting that all 3 groups of tumor features and all 4 categories of spatiotemporal PET features contained useful predictors of response. The model performance was stable when leaving more patients out with five- and two-fold cross-validations compared to 10-fold cross-validation. Only a small reduction in mean AUC (from 1.00 to 0.99 and 0.92) was observed.

Figure 7.3 also shows the sensitivity and specificity obtained from each model using different groups of features. When the SVM model was used with 10-fold cross-validation, significantly higher sensitivity was achieved by using all features including spatiotemporal PET features (100%) than by using conventional PET/CT

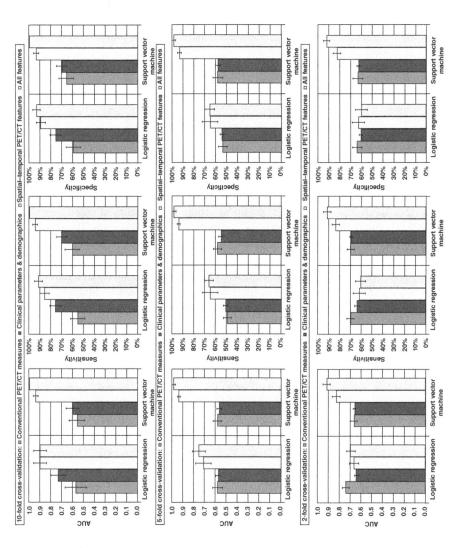

Figure 7.3 Response modeling accuracy and reliability: mean AUC, sensitivity, and specificity of 10-, 5-, 2-fold cross-validations. Error bars indicate 95% confidence intervals.

measures (60%) or clinical parameters and demographics (70%) alone ($P < 0.001$). Significantly higher specificity ($P < 0.001$) was achieved as well. Similar results were obtained when the LR model was used (92% sensitivity, 94% specificity; both $P < 0.001$).

For 10-fold cross-validation, the differences between SVM and LR models were not significant when using any of the four groups of features ($P > 0.06$). However, when using selected spatiotemporal PET features or using all features in five- and two-fold cross-validations, the SVM models demonstrated significantly better results than the LR models ($P < 0.0001$ and $P < 0.0002$, respectively).

7.4.4 Discussion

Analytical predictive models using all features include spatiotemporal PET features accurately and precisely predicted pathologic tumor response to CRT in 20 patients with esophageal cancer. It has the potential to be used to safely defer surgery or to give a higher dose in definitive CRT for patients who respond to CRT. This will ultimately improve patient's quality of life while reducing costs.

When using the same feature group and comparing the performance of LR and SVM models, the results varied from group to group. SVM achieved significantly higher accuracy than LR when using spatial–temporal PET feature group. The reason is that this group contained more candidate features, whose complementary relationship for response prediction is hard to identify with LR. On the other hand, SVM has been proven to be able to extract complex relationships among a large number of features [51]. Because the candidate feature group of the conventional PET/CT measures or clinical parameters and demographics contained only 16 features and because only 1 or 4 features were selected into the optimal subset, LR resulted in better results than SVM. The reason is that with this small number of selected features, it would be difficult for SVM to achieve high accuracy.

Another important aspect of constructing predictive models is to avoid model overfitting. To test this, we used different number of patients to train and test our models, namely 10-, 5-, and 2-fold cross-validations. When leaving more patients out of training set, the prediction accuracy decreased. However, the AUC was still above 0.90 for SVM$_{all}$ model, suggesting that it was not notably affected by overfitting. The LR model was not as stable as the SVM model in this case (AUC dropped from 0.90 to below 0.70).

The limitation is that it is a retrospective analysis of a small patient cohort. Although 10-, 5-, and 2-fold cross-validations showed that the model was not notably affected by overfitting, the predictive accuracy and stability of the models should be validated in a larger, independent patient cohort as shown in Figure 7.2. Validation is also needed to confirm that the selected features are indeed meaningful measures and important for response evaluation in esophageal cancer. When the model is validated, it can be used to more appropriately select patients for surgery, thus avoiding the mortality and morbidity of surgery in responders for whom surgery can be safely deferred. The methodology can also be applied to evaluate response during CRT, which will provide the opportunity for early adjustments to treatment strategies that are as follows: giving a higher dose in definitive CRT to responders, changing the type of chemotherapy, or performing surgery earlier in nonresponders.

7.5   MODELING CLINICAL COMPLICATIONS AFTER RADIATION THERAPY

Radiation treatment planning requires consideration of competing objectives: maximizing the radiation delivered to the planning target volume (PTV) and minimizing the amount of radiation delivered to all other tissues. A limitation of the current planning approach is that the relationship between the achieved plan dose-volume (DV) or dose levels and the DV or dose constraint settings is not known *a priori*. Furthermore, the current planning approach does not allow for inferential determination of the ideal DV constraint settings that will yield desired outcomes (plan-related complication levels).

We have previously described a multiplan framework, which provides for the generation of many plans that differ in their DV constraint settings [52]. The rationale is via the computation of a limited number of plans combined with suitable modeling tools that could enable the construction of a *plan surface*, representing achieved DV levels for a given OAR as a function of DV constraint settings corresponding to *all* involved OARs. The purpose of this section is to describe an approach to guide the selection of DV constraint settings by predicting plan-related OAR complications (and achieved DV levels as an intermediate step) as a function of DV constraint settings directly without explicit plan computation [53, 54]. We hypothesize that such a prediction is possible using predictive modeling. We selected two frequently encountered OAR complications: xerostomia (dry mouth) in head and neck radiotherapy and rectal bleeding in prostate radiotherapy.

7.5.1   Dose-Volume Thresholds: Relationship to OAR Complications

Previous research has described the relationships (derived retrospectively) between plan DV levels and OAR complications. These data served as the *"ground truth"* for the actual calculation of OAR complications against which our prediction of OAR complications is compared. A large knowledge base was generated for one head and neck case (125 plans were generated by varying the DV constraints on the left parotid, right parotid, and spinal cord) and one prostate case (256 plans were generated by varying the DV constraints on the rectum, bladder, and small bowel).

For xerostomia, retrospective studies have shown that specific volumes of the parotid glands (66%, 45%, and 24%) receiving specific doses (15, 30, and 45 Gy) (Gy is the symbol for Gray, which is unit of absorbed radiation dose of ionizing radiation) correlated with posttreatment saliva flow rate [55–57]. Chao et al. [57] presented an equivalent uniform dose (EUD)-based model to calculate posttreatment saliva flow rate, which we use as the *ground truth* for each of the 125 plans. The saliva flow rate (ml/min) is normalized to that before treatment. The model is

$$F = [\exp(-A \cdot \text{EUD}_R - B \cdot \text{EUD}_R^2) + \exp(-A \cdot \text{EUD}_L - B \cdot \text{EUD}_L^2)]/2 \qquad (7.2)$$

where A and B are fitted parameters (0.0315 and 0.000168, respectively), F is the expected resulting fractional saliva output, and EUD is the EUD to the left (L) and right (R) parotids as defined in Equation 7.3.

$$\text{EUD} = \left(\frac{1}{N} \sum_{i=1}^{N} D_i^a \right)^{1/a} \tag{7.3}$$

where N is the total number of voxels corresponding to a given structure, D_i is the dose to the ith voxel, and a is a structure-specific parameter that describes the dose-volume effect.

For rectal bleeding, retrospective studies have shown a correlation between rectal bleeding and 25–70% of the rectal volume receiving 60–75 Gy [58–63]. We used a threshold of 25%/70 Gy to determine a binary classification for the plans in the prostate case.

7.5.2 Modeling the Radiation-Induced Complications via Treatment Plan Surface

Our goal is to predict OAR complications (referred to as *labels*) during the treatment planning process as a function of the DV constraint settings (referred to as *features*) corresponding to all involved OARs. In some cases, in order to accurately predict treatment-related complications, an intermediate step of modeling achieved plan DV levels (referred to as *plan properties*) corresponding to one OAR as a function of DV constraint settings (*features*) for the full set of OARs is employed (Eq. 7.4):

$$\text{plan properties}_{\text{OAR}i} = f(\text{features}_{\text{OAR}1}, \text{features}_{\text{OAR}2}, \dots, \text{features}_{\text{OAR}n}) \tag{7.4}$$

where i corresponds to the OAR whose plan properties are being modeled and n corresponds to the number of involved OARs. This intermediate modeling step was utilized in the head and neck case. *Plan properties* (specifically dose to 24%, 45%, and 66% of the parotids) were modeled as a function of the input constraint settings (*features*) using quadratic functions and employing linear programming data-fitting tools as described in [52].

The quadratic model of a PTV or OAR property p_j would have the following algebraic form:

$$p_j \sim k_j + l_j u + u' M_j u \tag{7.5}$$

where j indexes the plan properties; u is a vector of variables corresponding to the constraint settings that were varied to generate the knowledge base; and k_j (a scalar), l_j (a vector), and M_j (a symmetric matrix) are fitting parameters. This is a second-order Taylor approximation of a multivariate function representing the property as a function of the constraint settings. The fitting parameters were computed using linear programming optimization to minimize the maximum relative error of the fit of the p_j values of the plans. (We minimized the maximum relative error instead of minimizing the sum of squared errors because the former limits the largest error in comparison with minimizing average-squared error.) Thus, the quadratic model includes terms of the form mu_k^2 and $\mu u_k u_l$, where m and μ correspond to entries of the matrix M_j.

These terms yield a second-order model that takes into account the combined effects of the interaction of pairs of constraint settings.

The problem of determining the model parameters that minimize the maximum relative error is stated as an unconstrained optimization problem:

$$\text{Minimize} \left\{ \max_i \left(\left| p_j^i - k_j + l_j u^i + u^{i\prime} M_j u^i \right| / p_j^i \right) \right\} \qquad (7.6)$$

where i denotes a plan index and the optimization is performed with respect to the set of variables consisting of the unknown model parameters k_j, l_j, and M_j. This problem can be solved by applying standard linear programming software (such as CPLEX) to the equivalent problem:

$$\text{Minimize } y$$

$$\text{such that} - y \leq \left(p_j^i - k_j + l_j u^i + u^{i\prime} M_j u^i \right) / p_j^i \leq y$$

$$\text{for } i = 1, \ldots, N$$

where N is the number of plans. Linear programming problems of the corresponding size are solved in a fraction of a second with current software.

Then we use ML algorithms to predict treatment-related complications for an OAR as a function of DV constraint settings (*features*) corresponding to all involved OARs and *modeled* achieved dose and dose-volume levels (*plan properties*) corresponding to the OAR in question if necessary as input (Eq. 7.7).

$$\text{Complications}_{\text{OAR}i} = g(\text{features}_{\text{OAR}1}, \ldots, \text{features}_{\text{OAR}n}, \text{plan properties}_{\text{OAR}i})$$

$$= g(\text{features}, f(\text{features})) \qquad (7.7)$$

The goal of ML in this research is to build and validate the numerical prediction or decision models (described in Eq. 7.7) from the knowledge base. The knowledge base is the collection of plans arising from our multiplan framework coupled with properties of those plans. In summary, 11 inputs (5 *features* and 3 predicted *plan properties* for each parotid) were used to predict saliva flow rate in the head and neck case and 5 inputs (5 *features*) were used to predict Grade 2 rectal bleeding complication in the prostate case using ML. These inputs to the ML algorithms are summarized in Table 7.1.

The SVM algorithm and decision tree method as described in previous section were used for predictive modeling. Although both approaches were tested for each of the two cases, it was determined that SVMs yielded superior results in predicting saliva flow rate and decision trees yielded superior results in predicting rectal bleeding.

TABLE 7.1   Input Variables Used in Modeling the Achieved Dose-volume and Dose Levels in the Head and Neck Case and the OAR Complications in the Head and Neck and Whole Pelvis Case

	Input Variables (Dose Settings at Following Volume Levels)				
Head and neck	33% Left parotid	66% Left parotid	33% Right parotid	66% Right parotid	Maximum Cord
Pelvis/prostate	25% Bladder	50% Bladder	25% Rectum	50% Rectum	30% Bowel

7.5.3   Modeling Results

The results for predicted saliva flow rate using the SMO algorithm are shown in Figure 7.4. The x-axis was the actual flow rate (normalized to the pretreatment saliva flow rate) for each of the 125 plans in the knowledge base (plans were sorted according to increasing saliva flow rate). The actual saliva flow rate was obtained using Equation 7.2. The y-axis was the mean predicted saliva flow rate obtained from the twofold cross-validation process. From Figure 7.4, it can be seen that the normalized saliva flow rate ranged from 20% to 30% for the case considered. The further a point is from the diagonal (which represents equality of actual and predicted values), the larger the prediction error is. The mean absolute error (averaged over cross-validations) for saliva flow rate prediction compared with the ground truth

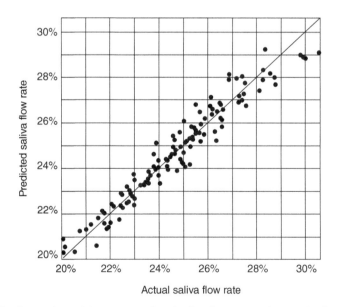

Figure 7.4   Comparison of the mean-predicted saliva flow rate to the actual saliva flow rate.

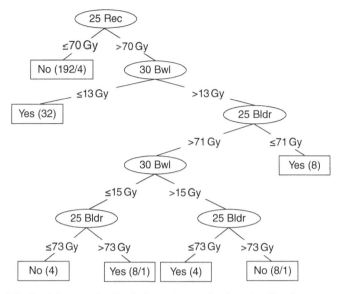

Figure 7.5   Decision tree for Grade 2 rectal complication classification – an example.

obtained from the EUD-exponential model in Equation 7.3 was 0.42% with a 95% confidence interval [0.41%, 0.43%].

Figure 7.5 shows a representative decision tree resulting from twofold cross-validation method applied to the 256 prostate treatment plans. Each decision node of the tree represents one dose-volume histogram (DVH) constraint, which is an input to the planning system. For example, *25Bldr* is the DVH constraint setting for 25% of the bladder volume. The number on the branches shows the dose-level partitions. Each leaf node represents a classification result, and the number in parenthesis is the number of instances that were classified correctly/incorrectly. Each leaf node corresponds to the set of inequalities on the path from the top-most node to that leaf. Using twofold cross-validation 50 times, we achieved an average classification accuracy of 97.04% with a 95% confidence interval of [96.67%, 97.41%] for Grade 2 rectal bleeding.

Figure 7.6 shows an example of the resulting plan surface for the prediction of normalized saliva flow rate as a function of the DV constraints using the approach described in this work. The contours in each plot correspond to the percentage saliva flow rate normalized to the pretreatment saliva flow rate as a function of DV constraint settings for two of the OARs and a fixed constraint setting for the third OAR. It can be observed that the plot for saliva flow rate as a function of the DV constraint settings on one parotid gland (left or right) and the maximum dose constraint to the spinal cord for a fixed DV constraint setting for the other parotid gland is near linear or near quadratic.

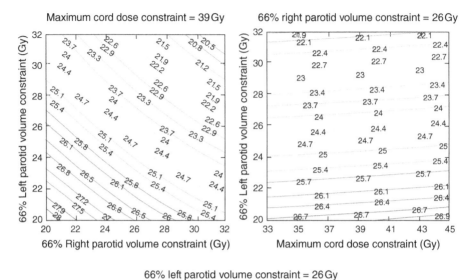

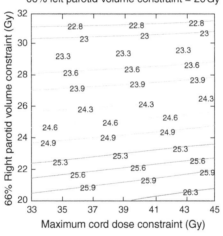

Figure 7.6 Prediction of saliva flow rate as a function of the dose constraint settings for the three OARs: (a) fixed cord constraint, ranges for left parotid (LP) and right parotid (RP), (b) fixed RP constraint, ranges for cord and LP, and (c) fixed LP constraint, ranges for cord and RP.

Figure 7.7 shows an example of the resulting plan surface for the prediction of Grade 2 rectal complications. The shaded region in the plot corresponds to the complication region for a range of DV constraint settings for two OARs and a fixed constraint setting for the third OAR. We attribute the unshaded region (lack of rectal bleeding) in Figure 7.7 corresponding to an increase in the bladder and bowel settings to an associated dose transfer to the bladder and bowel and reduced dose to the rectum. These results are examples of how the prediction of OAR complications can guide the selection of DV constraint settings for all OARs.

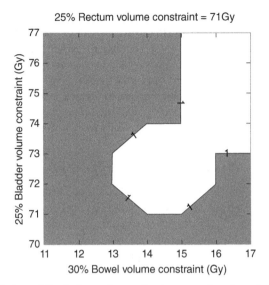

Figure 7.7   Prediction of Grade 2 rectal complications as a function of the dose constraint settings when fixing rectum constraint and ranging for bladder and bowel.

7.6 MODELING TUMOR MOTION WITH RESPIRATORY SURROGATES

Advances in radiation therapy for cancer have made it possible to deliver conformal doses to the tumor while sparing normal healthy tissues. However, one of the difficulties radiation oncologists face is targeting moving tumors, such as those in the thorax, which can change position during normal respiration. Tumor motion can be determined by directly monitoring tumor position using continuous X-ray imaging or electromagnetic transponders placed in the tumor that emit a signal. These approaches require potentially unnecessary radiation to the patient or acquisition of expensive technology. Alternatively, one can image the patient intermittently to determine tumor location and external markers placed on the patient's torso. The external surrogates can then be used to determine an inferential model that would determine the tumor position as a function of external surrogates. These external surrogates can be monitored continuously in order to determine the real-time position of the tumor. In order to do that, it is necessary to know whether the relationship between internal tissue motion and external tissue motion is constant during a single treatment fraction. In this section, we evaluate a machine learning algorithm for inferring intrafraction tumor motion from external markers using a database obtained via the Cyberknife Synchrony™ system [64].

7.6.1 Cyberknife System Data

The Cyberknife Synchrony system intermittently localizes fiducials implanted in or near the tumor using fluoroscopy and models tumor positions from continuously tracked optical marker positions. We analyzed a database of Cyberknife system files comprising 128 treatment fractions from 62 lung cancer patients, 10 treatment fractions from 5 liver cancer patients, and 48 treatment fractions from 23 pancreas cancer patients. The Cyberknife files for each fraction included both the 3D positions of three optical markers affixed to the abdomen and/or chest and the 3D positions of the centroid of a set of three fiducial markers implanted in or near the tumor (determined through fluoroscopic imaging). Each fraction contained 40–112 (mean = 62) stereoscopic radiographs acquired over a mean treatment fraction of 64 min.

7.6.2   Modeling for the Prediction of Tumor Positions

In this tumor position prediction context, the knowledge base is the collection of positions from different external markers coupled with properties of those markers (actual position of the tumor). The model that is constructed below for numerical prediction (real coordinates) employs multivariate quadratic functions (whose input features are coordinates of external markers). The outputs of the model are the properties that are of interest – in this case, true position of tumor represented by fiducial markers. The method that we used to predict the continuous value of positions is SMO for training a support vector regression model as described in previous section.

We also performed an empirical approach to reduce the knowledge base size (i.e., number of fluoroscopic image acquisitions) based on machine learning approaches. The size of the training data corresponds to the knowledge base, the number of fluoroscopic image acquisitions required to obtain the model. We used 50%, 25%, 12.5%, 6% of the full knowledge base as training data and the rest of knowledge base as testing data. For each fractional value, 20 random samples of the corresponding size were used as training sets. Mean absolute prediction errors in millimeter (mm) were reported.

7.6.3   Results of Tumor Positions Modeling

We tested our method on three motion directions of tumors (superior–inferior (SI), medial–lateral (ML), and anterior–posterior (AP)) of the three types of cancer: lung, liver, and pancreas. Each motion direction was modeled separately. The detailed results are shown in Table 7.2. From Table 7.2, we can see that the predicted errors using machine learning increased monotonically when using fewer data points in the training set. We can achieve less than 2–3 mm error with 5–15 training data points for all three tumor sites. Based on real-time application experience, we believe that using 12.5% of the full knowledge base (eight data points on average) can provide enough prediction accuracy, which corresponds to eight fluoroscopic image acquisitions.

Figure 7.8 shows the details of prediction errors when using about eight data points as training set in machine learning algorithm. We can see that tumor motions on the medial–lateral directions can be predicted with the highest accuracy. Prediction accuracy on anterior–posterior directions is the second highest and on superior–inferior direction is the lowest. From Figure 7.8, there is no clear evidence showing which of the three tumor sites could be modeled more accurately.

TABLE 7.2   Tumor Motion Prediction Error Summary (in mm)

	Lung			Liver			Pancreas		
	SI	ML	AP	SI	ML	AP	SI	ML	AP
50%	0.8	0.7	0.8	0.9	0.5	0.6	0.9	0.8	0.8
25%	0.9	0.8	0.9	1.1	0.6	0.6	1.0	0.9	0.9
12.5%	1.2	0.9	1.1	1.5	0.8	0.9	1.3	1.1	1.1
6%	2.1	1.7	2.0	3.0	1.4	1.6	2.2	1.8	1.8

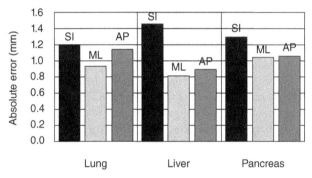

Figure 7.8   Prediction summary using 12.5% of full knowledge base as a training set for lung, liver, and pancreas cases.

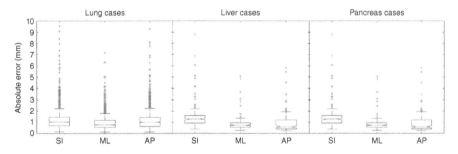

Figure 7.9   Prediction error distributions with 12.5% of full knowledge base as a training set.

We further investigated the results by looking at the distributions of the prediction errors. Figure 7.9 shows the box plot of these errors. The lines in the middle of each box in the figure were the median of the errors of the predictions, and the lower and upper edges of boxes represented 25% and 75% quantiles. The whiskers were estimated extreme ranges of the predictions (not considering outliers). The points outside the whiskers were outliers. The notches within the boxes were 95% confidence intervals on the median. From Figure 7.9, we see that the stability of machine learning algorithm varied when applied to different tumor sites: there were more outliers for

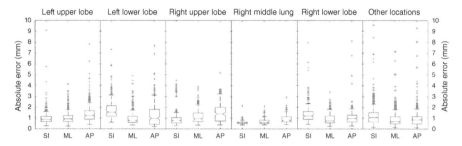

Figure 7.10   Error distributions of lung tumor position prediction within different locations.

the lung cases than liver and pancreas cases, and the outliers ranged from more than 2 mm to 1 cm.

Because more prediction outliers occurred for lung patients, we plotted the error distributions for different tumor locations within the lung patients (Fig. 7.10). From Figure 7.10, we noticed that for the left and right lower lobe the outliers were less than 8 mm, for the right upper lobe the outliers were less than 5 mm and for the right middle lung the outliers were less than 3 mm. For other locations, the outliers spread to 1 cm. Most outliers occurred for the left upper lobe and other locations. This provided information about which tumor location in the lung had a better chance to be modeled accurately.

7.6.4   Discussion

Our aim for this initial research was to investigate predictive modeling as a method for creating models of instantaneous tumor positions based on a limited number of fluoroscopic image acquisitions. By minimizing image acquisitions, we decrease the in-room time for the patient and improve the efficiency of treatment delivery. We were able to achieve accurate intrafraction motion modeling using eight (mean error less than 2 mm) samples corresponding to individual image acquisitions. Thus, our results indicate that ML algorithm shows potential for use in intrafraction motion modeling in real-time systems.

In practice, model errors could increase over time due to tumor–surrogate relationship changes. This effect could be overcome by updating the model during the treatment fraction. Intrafraction model updates have been utilized by tracking systems such as Cyberknife Synchrony, but model updates are not common in clinical treatment protocols. The ML algorithm represents the state of the art in indirect tumor localization algorithms. In addition to its accuracy, ML requires only milliseconds to derive tumor position from surrogate data. This shows that it can be an ideal candidate for real-time applications. Decreased measurement precision in either gold-standard tumor localizations or external surrogate measurements was found to have considerable impact on model accuracy.

We also evaluated the patient-specific, fraction-specific, and site-specific factors. The results did not differ between lung, liver, and pancreas cancers. Furthermore, the model error was not found to be significantly associated with fraction index. Patient index, on the other hand, was significantly associated with model accuracy. The practical implication of these results is that the design of a study to evaluate tumor motion models should use a large enough group of patients to obtain statistically significant results; multisite and interfraction data are less important unless a model will be applied without revision on multiple treatment days.

7.7 CONCLUSION

We live in an era of "Big Data": rapid development in science and technology from genomics and proteomics research is available to researchers and clinicians. With high-throughput/high-performance computing power, we are capable of delivering societal expectations of personalized patient care. This is especially relevant in the clinical management of cancer. Cancer is a leading cause of death worldwide, and most patients go through radiation therapy during their treatment. As complex as cancer is, we have shown that the predictive modeling technique has the ability to provide information to physicians for better diagnostic, more accurate treatment delivery and to predict radiotherapy response so that personalized treatment can be developed.

In conclusion, this book chapter provides an up-to-date review of the state of the art in several key elements of applied predictive modeling in Radiation Oncology, which is of special importance for the treatment of cancer. It makes the case for collaborative efforts between technical and scientific disciplines, such as operations research, healthcare informatics, data analytics, machine learning, and, beyond them, the clinical arena.

REFERENCES

[1] Guyon I, Weston J, Barnhill S, Vapnik V. Gene selection for cancer classification using support vector machines. Mach Learn 2002;46:389–422.

[2] Platt JC. Fast training of support vector machines using sequential minimal optimization. In: Bernhard S, Burges CJC, Smola AJ, editors. *Advances in Kernel Methods: Support Vector Learning.* Cambridge, MA: MIT Press; 1999. p 185–208.

[3] Shevade SK, Keerthi SS, Bhattacharyya C, Murthy KK. Improvements to SMO algorithm for SVM regression. IEEE Trans Neural Netw 2000;11:1188–1193.

[4] Quinlan J. *C4.5: Programs for Machine Learning.* Morgan Kaufmann Publishers; 1993.

[5] Witten I, Frand E, Hall M. *Data Mining: Practical Machine Learning Tools and Techniques.* 3rd ed. San Francisco: Morgan Kaufmann; 2011.

[6] Lee EK. Optimization-based predictive models in medicine and biology. Optim Med-Springer Optimization and Its Applications 2008;12:127–151.

[7] Wolberg W, Street W, Mangasarian O. Machine learning techniques to diagnose breast cancer from image-processed nuclear features of fine needle aspirates. Cancer Lett 1994;77:163–71.

[8] Wolberg W, Street W, Mangasarian O. Image analysis and machine learning applied to breast cancer diagnosis and prognosis. Anal Quant Cytol Histol 1995;17:77–87.

[9] Suzuki K, Li F, Sone S, Doi K. Computer-aided diagnostic scheme for distinction between benign and malignant nodules in thoracic low-dose CT by use of massive training artificial neural network. IEEE Trans Med Imaging 2005;24:1138–1150.

[10] Suzuki K, Shiraishi J, Abe H, MacMahon H, Doi K. False-positive reduction in computer-aided diagnostic scheme for detecting nodules in chest radiographs by means of massive training artificial neural network. Acad Radiol 2005;12:191–201.

[11] Arimura H, Katsuragawa S, Suzuki K, Li F, Shiraishi J, Sone S, Doi K. Computerized scheme for automated detection of lung nodules in low-dose computed tomography images for lung cancer screening. Acad Radiol 2004;11:617–629.

[12] Suzuki K, Yoshida H, Nappi J, Dachman A. Massive-training artificial neural network (MTANN) for reduction of false positives in computer-aided detection of polyps: Suppression of rectal tubes. Med Phys 2006;33:3814–3824.

[13] Suzuki K, Yoshida H, Nappi J, Armato S, Dachman A. Mixture of expert 3D massive-training ANNs for reduction of multiple types of false positives in CAD for detection of polyps in CT colonography. Med Phys 2008;35:694–703.

[14] Suzuki K, Armato S, Li F, Sone S, Doi K. Massive training artificial neural network (MTANN) for reduction of false positives in computerized detection of lung nodules in low-dose CT. Med Phys 2003;30:1602–1617.

[15] Ramos-Pollán R, Guevara-López M, Suárez-Ortega C, Díaz-Herrero G, Franco-Valiente J, Rubio-Del-Solar M, González-de-Posada N, Vaz MA, Loureiro J, Ramos I. Discovering mammography-based machine learning classifiers for breast cancer diagnosis. J Med Syst 2012;36:2259–2269.

[16] Lin T, Li R, Tang X, Dy J, Jiang S. Markerless gating for lung cancer radiotherapy based on machine learning techniques. Phys Med Biol 2009;54:1555–1563.

[17] Cui Y, Dy J, Alexander B, Jiang S. Fluoroscopic gating without implanted fiducial markers for lung cancer radiotherapy based on support vector machines. Phys Med Biol 2008;53:N315–N327.

[18] Murphy M, Jalden J, Isaksson M. Adaptive filtering to predict lung tumor breathing motion during image-guided radiation therapy. Proceedings of 16th Intern Congress on Computer Assisted Radiology and Surgery, 539–544; (2002).

[19] Sharp G, Jiang S, Shimizu S, Shirato H. Prediction of respiratory tumour motion for real-time image-guided radiotherapy. Phys Med Biol 2004;49:425–440.

[20] Isaakson M, Jalden J, Murphy M. On using an adaptive neural network to predict lung tumor motion during respiration for radiotherapy applications. Med Phys 2005;32:3801–3809.

[21] Murphy M, Dieterich S. Comparative performance of linear and nonlinear neural networks to predict irregular breathing. Phys Med Biol 2006;51:5903–5914.

[22] Murphy M. Using Neural Networks to Predict Breathing Motion. Proceedings of 7th International Conference on Machine Learning and Applications, 528–532; (2008).

[23] Ruan D, Keall P. Online prediction of respiratory motion: Multidimensional processing with low-dimensional feature learning. Phys Med Biol 2010;55:3011–3025.

[24] Cui Y, Dy J, Sharp G, Alexander B, Jiang S. Robust fluoroscopic respiratory gating for lung cancer radiotherapy without implanted fiducial markers. Phys Med Biol 2007;52:741–755.

[25] Lin T, Cerviño L, Tang X, Vasconcelos N, Jiang S. Fluoroscopic tumor tracking for image-guided lung cancer radiotherapy. Phys Med Biol 2009;54:981–992.

[26] Li R, Lewis J, Jiang S. Markerless fluoroscopic gating for lung cancer radiotherapy using generalized linear discriminant analysis. Proceedings of 8th International Conference on Machine Learning and Applications, 468–472; (2009).

[27] El Naqa I. Machine learning as new tool for predicting radiotherapy response. Med Phys 2010;37:3396.

[28] Buettner F, Gulliford S, Webb S, Partridge M. Using bayesian logistic regression with high-order interactions to model radiation-induced toxicities following radiotherapy. Proceedings of 8th International Conference on Machine Learning and Applications, 451–456; (2009).

[29] El Naqa I, Bradley J, Blanco A, Lindsay P, Vicic M, Hope A, Deasy J. Multivariable modeling of radiotherapy outcomes, including dose-volume and clinical factors. Int J Radiat Oncol Biol Phys 2006;64:1275–1286.

[30] Munley M, Lo J, Sibley G, Bentel G, Anscher M, Marks L. A neural network to predict symptomatic lung injury. Phys Med Biol 1999;44:2241–2249.

[31] Su M, Miften M, Whiddon C, Sun X, Light K, Marks L. An artificial neural network for predicting the incidence of radiation pneumonitis. Med Phys 2005;32:318–325.

[32] Lennernas B, Sandberg D, Albertsson P, Silen A, Isacsson U. The effectiveness of artificial neural networks in evaluating treatment plans for patients requiring external beam radiotherapy. Oncol Rep 2004;12:1065–1070.

[33] El Naqa I, Bradley J, Deasy J. Machine Learning Methods for radiobiological outcome modeling. Med Phys 2005;32:2037.

[34] El Naqa I, Yang Y, Wernick M, Galatsanos N, Nishikawa R. A support vector machine approach for detection of microcalcifications. IEEE Trans Med Imaging 2002;21:1552–1563.

[35] El Naqa I, Yang Y, Galatsanos N, Nishikawa R, Wernick M. A similarity learning approach to content based image retrieval: application to digital mammography. IEEE Trans Med Imaging 2004;23:1233–1244.

[36] El Naqa I, Bradley J, Deasy J. Nonlinear kernel-based approaches for predicting normal tissue toxicities. Proceedings of 7th International Conference on Machine Learning and Applications, 539–544; (2008).

[37] Oh J, Al-Lozi R, El Naqa I. Application of machine learning techniques for prediction of radiation pneumonitis in lung cancer patients. Proceedings of 8th International Conference on Machine Learning and Applications, 478–483; (2009).

[38] Oh J, El Naqa I. Bayesian network learning for detecting reliable interactions of dose-volume related parameters in radiation pneumonitis, Proceedings of 8th International Conference on Machine Learning and Applications, 484–488; (2009).

[39] Das S, Chen S, Deasy J, Zhou S, Yin F, Marks L. Decision fusion of machine learning models to predict radiotherapy-induced lung pneumonitis. Proceedings of 7th International Conference on Machine Learning and Applications, 545–550; (2008).

[40] Chen S, Zhou S, Zhang J, Yin F, Marks L, Das S. A neural network model to predict lung radiation-induced pneumonitis. Med Phys 2007;34:3420–3427.

[41] Chen S, Zhou S, Yin F, Marks L, Das S. Investigation of the support vector machine algorithm to predict lung radiation-induced pneumonitis. Med Phys 2007;34:3808–3814.

[42] Dehing-Oberije C, Yu S, De Ruysscher D, Meersschout S, Van Beek K, Lievens Y, Van Meerbeeck J, De Neve W, Rao B, van der Weide H, Lambin P. Development and external validation of prognostic model for 2-year survival of non-small-cell lung cancer patients treated with chemoradiotherapy. Int J Radiat Oncol Biol Phys 2009;74:355–362.

[43] Dekker A, Dehing-Oberije C, De Ruysscher D, Lambin P, Hope A, Komati K, Fung G, Yu S, De Neve W, Lievens Y. Survival prediction in lung cancer treated with radiotherapy – Bayesian networks vs. support vector machines in handling missing data. Proceedings of 8th International Conference on Machine Learning and Applications, 494–497; (2009).

[44] El Naqa I, Bradley J, Lindsay P, Hope A, Deasy J. Predicting radiotherapy outcomes using statistical learning techniques. Phys Med Biol 2009;54:S9–S30.

[45] Monjazeb AM, Riedlinger G, Aklilu M, Geisinger KR, Mishra G, Isom S, Clark P, Levine EA, Blackstock AW. Outcomes of patients with esophageal cancer staged with [(18)F]fluorodeoxyglucose positron emission tomography (FDG-PET): Can postchemoradiotherapy FDG-PET predict the utility of resection? J Clin Oncol 2010;28:4714–4721.

[46] Stahl M, Stuschke M, Lehmann N, Meyer H, Walz MK, Seeber S, Klump B, Budach W, Teichmann R, Schmitt M, Franke C, Wilke H. Chemoradiation with and without surgery in patients with locally advanced squamous cell carcinoma of the esophagus. J Clin Oncol 2005;23:2310–2317.

[47] Bedenne L, Michel P, Bouche O, Milan C, Mariette C, Conroy T, Pezet D, Roullet B, Seitz JF, Herr JP, Paillot B, Arveux P, Bonnetain F, Binquet C. Chemoradiation followed by surgery compared with chemoradiation alone in squamous cancer of the esophagus: FFCD 9102. J Clin Oncol 2007;25:1160–1168.

[48] Zhang H, Tan S, Chen W, Kligerman S, Kim G, D'Souza D, Suntharalingam M, Lu W. Modeling pathologic response of esophageal cancer to chemo-radiotherapy using spatial-temporal FDG-PET features, clinical parameters and demographics. Int J Radiat Oncol Biol Phys 2014;88:195–203.

[49] Mandard AM, Dalibard F, Mandard JC, Marnay J, Henry-Amar M, Petiot JF, Roussel A, Jacob JH, Segol P, Samama G. Pathologic assessment of tumor regression after preoperative chemoradiotherapy of esophageal carcinoma. Clinicopathologic correlations. Cancer 1994;73:2680–2686.

[50] Koshy M, Greenwald BD, Hausner P, Krasna MJ, Horiba N, Battafarano RJ, Burrows W, Suntharalingam M. Outcomes after trimodality therapy for esophageal cancer: The impact of histology on failure patterns. Am J Clin Oncol 2011;34:259–264.

[51] Kotsiantis SB. Supervised machine learning: A review of classification techniques. Informatica 2007;31:249–268.

[52] Meyer R, Zhang H, Goadrich L, Nazareth D, Shi L, D'Souza W. A multi-plan treatment planning framework: A paradigm shift for IMRT. Int J Radiat Oncol Biol Phys 2007;68:1178–1189.

[53] Zhang H, D'Souza W, Shi L, Meyer R. Modeling plan-related clinical complications using machine learning tools in a multiplan IMRT framework. Int J Radiat Oncol Biol Phys 2009;74:1617–1626.

[54] Zhang H, Meyer R, Shi L, D'Souza W. The minimum knowledge base for predicting organ-at-risk dose-volume levels and plan-related complications in IMRT planning. Phys Med Biol 2010;55:1935–1947.

[55] Eisbruch A, Ten Haken R, Kim H, Marsh L, Ship J. Dose, volume, and function relationships in parotid salivary glands following conformal and intensity-modulated irradiation of head and neck cancer. Int J Radiat Oncol Biol Phys 1999;45:577–587.

[56] Eisbruch A, Ship J, Kim H, Ten Haken R. Partial Irradiation of the Parotid Gland. Semin Radiat Oncol 2001;11:234–239.

[57] Chao K, Deasy J, Markman J, Haynie J, Perez C, Purdy J, Low D. A prospective study of salivary function sparing in patients with head-and-neck cancers receiving intensity-modulated or three-dimensional radiation therapy: initial results. Int J Radiat Oncol Biol Phys 2001;49:907–916.

[58] Boersma L, van den Brink M, Bruce A, Shouman T, Gras L, te Velde A, Lebesque J. Estimation of the incidence of late bladder and rectum complications after high-dose (70–78 Gy) conformal radiotherapy for prostate cancer, using dose-volume histograms. Int J Radiat Oncol Biol Phys 1998;41:83–92.

[59] Jackson A. Partial irradiation of the rectum. Semin Radiat Oncol 2001;11:215–223.

[60] Jackson A, Skwarchuk M, Zelefsky M, Cowen D, Venkatraman E, Levegrun S, Burman CM, Kutcher GJ, Fuks Z, Liebel SA, Ling C. Late rectal bleeding after conformal radiotherapy of prostate cancer (II): Volume effects and dose-volume histograms. Int J Radiat Oncol Biol Phys 2001;49:685–698.

[61] Yorke E. Biological indices for evaluation and optimization of IMRT, intensity-modulated radiation therapy: The state of the art. AAPM Med Phys Monogr 2003;29:77–114.

[62] Fiorino C, Sanguineti G, Cozzarini C, Fellin G, Foppiano F, Menegotti L, Piazzolla A, Vavassori V, Valdagni R. Rectal dose-volume constraints in high-dose radiotherapy of localized prostate cancer. Int J Radiat Oncol Biol Phys 2003;57:953–962.

[63] Cozzarini C, Fiorino C, Ceresoli G, Cattaneo G, Bolognesi A, Calandrino R, Villa E. Significant correlation between rectal DVH and late bleeding in patients treated after radical prostatectomy with conformal or conventional radiotherapy (66.6–70.2 Gy). Int J Radiat Oncol Biol Phys 2003;55:688–694.

[64] D'Souza W, Malinowski K, Zhang H. Machine learning for intra-fraction tumor motion modeling with respiratory surrogates. Proceedings of 8th International Conference on Machine Learning and Applications, 463–467; (2009).

8

MATHEMATICAL MODELING OF INNATE IMMUNITY RESPONSES OF SEPSIS: MODELING AND COMPUTATIONAL STUDIES

CHIH-HANG J. WU, ZHENSHEN SHI, AND DAVID BEN-ARIEH

Department of Industrial and Manufacturing Systems Engineering, Kansas State University, Manhattan, KS, USA

STEVEN Q. SIMPSON

Division of Pulmonary Diseases and Critical Care Medicine, University of Kansas, Kansas City, KS, USA

8.1 BACKGROUND

Sepsis, currently defined as a systemic inflammatory response (SIR) in the presence of an infectious agent or trauma, is increasingly being considered an exaggerated, poorly regulated innate immune response to microbial products [1, 2]. The progression to severe sepsis is marked by the generalized hypotension, tissue hypoxia, and coagulation abnormality [1]. Severe sepsis can further develop into septic shock under the long-lasting severe hypotension [1] and ultimately lead to death.

Severe sepsis and septic shock during an infection are the major causes of death in an intensive care setting [3]. There is an average of 250,000 deaths per year in the United States caused by sepsis [4]. Among patients in intensive care units (ICUs), it ranks as the second highest cause of mortality [5] and the 10th leading cause of death overall in the United States [6]. Average of 750,000 sepsis cases happen

Healthcare Analytics: From Data to Knowledge to Healthcare Improvement, First Edition.
Edited by Hui Yang and Eva K. Lee.
© 2016 John Wiley & Sons, Inc. Published 2016 by John Wiley & Sons, Inc.

annually and is increasing [5]. In addition, the quality of life for sepsis survivors is significantly reduced [5, 7]. Care of patients with sepsis costs can be as much as $60,000 per patient. This cost results in a significant healthcare burden of nearly $17 billion annually in the United States alone [8]. The development of sepsis in a hospitalized patient can lead to a longer length of stay in the hospital, which implies stiffer financial burden. Cross and Opal [9] in their research pointed out "the availability of rapid and reliable assays that could be used to quickly identify the stage or severity of sepsis and to monitor therapy may optimize the use of immunomodulatory therapy." However, no such assays are available because the complex nature of the inflammatory response and the unpredictable nature of septic shock in individual patients render the effect of targeting isolated components of inflammation with supportive therapy difficult to predict [9, 10].

The human immune response evolves to protect the body from infection by harmful pathogens found in the environment [11]. This response is characterized by the activation and mobilization of white blood cells, the release of cytokines, and the modification of the vascular and lymphoid tissue [12, 13]. Unfortunately, the activation of the immune system can become dysregulated and the immune responses or acute inflammatory responses (AIR) can become pathogenic. Indeed, an uncontrolled AIR may lead to possible sepsis or septic shock. Whether a patient will progress to sepsis, severe sepsis, or even septic shock is determined by a cascade of immune system components. These include pro-inflammatory cytokines such as tumor necrosis factor-α (TNF-α); interferon gamma (IFN-γ); interleukins (IL)-1, IL-6, IL-8; and high motility group box-1 (HMGB-1) [9, 14]. These cytokines are released to recruit more activated phagocytes to the location of infection to help eliminate the causal pathogen(s). Unfortunately, this process likely causes tissue damage [15]. In addition, anti-inflammatory cytokines such as IL-1ra, IL-4, IL-10, IL-6 and transforming growth factor-β (TGF-β) are also released to serve as negative regulators of the response [15, 16].

Recent data indicate that the interactions between anti-inflammatory responses and pro-inflammatory responses determine the prognosis of AIR [16, 17]. More specifically, the presence of HMGB-1, which reaches its peak concentrations around 8–12 h after it is induced by TNF-α, may be a key component in the progression of AIR. If the level of HMGB-1 remains elevated for long periods of time, the patient may be at risk for more severe AIR or developing sepsis [18–20]. Also, clinical experiments have demonstrated that monoclonal antibody therapy against HMGB-1 elevation can prevent septic patients from organ damage and subsequent organ dysfunction in trials of both animals and humans [21–25]. Anti-inflammatory cytokines such as IL-4, IL-10, IL-13, and IL-14 also play crucial roles in inhibiting the production of pro-inflammatory cytokines and in turn slowing down the progression of AIR [26, 27]. For example, circulating levels of IL-6 can be used to predict the severity of acute respiratory distress syndrome, sepsis, and the associated acute pancreatitis [28]. Clearly, the levels of pro- and anti-inflammatory mediators are closely linked to the development of severe sepsis and septic shock.

As mentioned earlier, the levels of cytokines and their presence over time play very important roles in AIR and the development of sepsis; however, there is little data on the quantitative relationships of the cytokine network, which can be used to predict the progression of disease. Kumar et al. [29] presented a simplified three-equation SDMM to describe mathematical relationships between pathogen, early pro-inflammatory mediators, and late pro-inflammatory mediators, respectively. However, the model is overly simplified and fails to represent the overall prognosis of AIR. It lacks several key components including phagocytes, anti-inflammatory cytokines, and the resultant tissue damage. Later, Reynolds et al. [30] proposed a mathematical model for AIR that included a time-dependent, anti-inflammatory response in an attempt to provide insights into a variety of clinically relevant scenarios associated with the inflammatory response to infection. However, this model missed essential mathematical expression of early and late pro-inflammatory mediators (TNF-α) and (HMGB-1) that are important biomarkers used in the progression of sepsis during treatments.

The collective disadvantage of current existing mathematical models is that they are incomplete. They only represent some of the essential factors in AIR. Therefore, to improve on current models, we have developed a 14-equation SDMM in an attempt to incorporate the most critical variables involved in the development of the septic response and the innate immune system during the AIR. In particular, we have included equations to represent pathogen load, phagocyte (including neutrophils and monocytes) activation, early and late pro-inflammatory cytokine mediators, tissue damage, and anti-inflammatory cytokine mediators.

8.2   SYSTEM DYNAMIC MATHEMATICAL MODEL (SDMM)

A mathematical model currently being developed as a dynamic knowledge representation may be a powerful tool to help understand the complex local and global dynamics of AIR and the development of sepsis. Using a series of known and hypothesized kinetics of biochemical and immunological components from the existing literature, this approach provides a comprehensive attempt to model the progression of sepsis. This method combines conventional logistics dynamics, the laws of mass action, Michaelis–Menten kinetics, and their nonlinear transformations into ordinary differential equations. We propose this modeling technique to describe AIR and the SIR processes by measuring either the steady state or changes of the various components during simulated inflammatory responses.

The first step in our analysis was to create a mathematical model to reflect the global dynamics of sepsis. The variables were selected based on what is known about the molecular and physiological mediators that are important to the development of sepsis. We initially validated the mathematical model by comparing the model outcomes to data from actual experiments. If the results did not match, equations were rewritten or the model was reconfigured to adjust relationships between the components (indicators). After the initial validation, we conducted sensitivity and stability analyses (based on bifurcation theory). The goal was to identify which parameters and processes were critical in influencing modeled outcomes. We believe that construction of the mathematical model for exhibiting various outcomes and facilitating the

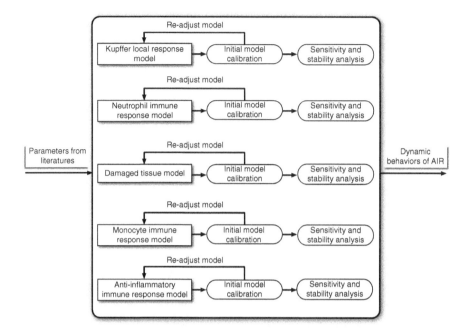

Figure 8.1   Framework of the system dynamic mathematical model.

understanding of complex interactions between various components in AIR and SIR response will be one of the most difficult and fundamental steps of using the mathematical model in the future as a platform to generate experiment-dependent results by incorporating a large amount of experimental data. In order to help on reading, we have summarized a framework of the mathematical model in Figure 8.1.

8.3   PATHOGEN STRAIN SELECTION

We chose *Salmonella* as a "targeted" pathogen strain in our mathematical model and simulated immune responses to *Salmonella* in the liver of mice. We chose *Salmonella* because it is Gram-negative bacteria and *Salmonella* sepsis widely impacts developing countries, commonly occurring in young children [31]. Furthermore, immune responses to *Salmonella* sepsis have been investigated in mice experiments for the past several years [32–37], and hence it is effective for us to get either data or evidence support for our mathematical model.

8.3.1   Step 1: Kupffer Local Response Model

Macrophages are one of first lines of the innate host defense system against bacterial pathogens. They are important because not only are they antimicrobicidal cells but also they play a role in the initiation of the adaptive immune response [38]. Therefore, macrophages often determine the outcomes of an infection [38]. In septic responses, the liver frequently plays a major role in host defense [39]. Furthermore, hepatic macrophages (also known as Kupffer cells or resident liver macrophages) constitute 80–90% of tissue resident macrophages in the body and significantly influence the propagation of liver inflammation [40, 41]. Majority of bacteria that enter the blood stream are taken up and eliminated by Kupffer cells within the liver [42]. During the initial stage of an AIR, Kupffer cells will eliminate the pathogens, specifically *Salmonella*, during the local immune responses.

The Kupffer cell-related local immune response was defined as the interactions between the pathogen and Kupffer cells [40] and was modeled as follows:

$$\frac{dP}{dt} = k_{pg}P\left(1 - \frac{P}{P_\infty}\right) - r_{pmk}\frac{[P^n]}{[P^n + k_{c1}^n]}M_{kf}P^* \tag{8.1}$$

$$\frac{dM_{kf}}{dt} = k_{mk}M_{kf}\left(1 - \frac{M_{kf}}{K_\infty}\right) + k_{mkub}M_{kb} - \frac{[P^n]}{[P^n + k_{c1}^n]}M_{kf}P^* - u_{mk}M_{kf} \tag{8.2}$$

$$\frac{dM_{kb}}{dt} = \frac{[P^n]}{[P^n + k_{c1}^n]}M_{kf}P^* - k_{mkub}M_{kb} \tag{8.3}$$

In Equation 8.1, P denotes the pathogen load. k_{pg} represents a constant growth rate for pathogens and P_∞ represents maximum carrying capacity of the pathogen. The parameter r_{pmk} represents phagocytosis rate of Kupffer cells when Kupffer cells start to engulf pathogens. Although phagocytosis rate is dependent on time in a slow S-shaped curve [43], the phagocytosis rate changes only slightly per hour if we assume that the phagocytosis rate versus time is linear, and therefore we relaxed this condition in our model and assumed it was constant [43]. Equation 8.2 represents the changes of the Kupffer cells over a unit time period, and M_{kf} denotes the amount of Kupffer cells resided in the liver available for pathogen binding. The parameter term, k_{mk}, represents a constant proliferation (replenishment) rate for Kupffer cell population and K_∞ represents the maximum carrying capacity of Kupffer cells. The parameter term, k_{mkub}, represents the unbinding rate of binding Kupffer cells and u_{mk} represents the killing rate of free Kupffer cells induced by binding to intruding pathogens.

Here, a standard logistic function is used to model the pathogen population growth with limited maximal carrying capacity, which is the first term $\left(k_{pg}P\left(1 - \frac{P}{P_\infty}\right)\right)$ in Equation 8.1 [44]. The second term of Equation 8.1 models the local Kupffer cell responses, the decrease in pathogen population phagocytized by initial tissue resident macrophages (Kupffer cells). This process includes two steps: pathogen–ligand binding to the receptors of Kupffer cells and the actual phagocytosis by Kupffer cells. We used a Hill-type function and receptor–ligand kinetics to model the two basic steps [34, 38, 40, 45–47]. First, we define the rate of pathogen binding to Kupffer cells as a Hill-type function ($\frac{[P^n]}{[P^n+k_{c1}^n]}$). Here, n represents a strong affinity of pathogen binding to Kupffer cells and k_{c1} is the pathogen concentration occupying half of Kupffer cell receptors. Second, we modeled pathogen to Kupffer cell receptors using receptor–ligand kinetics ($\frac{[P^n]}{[P^n+k_{c1}^n]}M_{kf}P^*$), where P^* represents pathogen concentration. We determined the pathogen concentration using the number of pathogens divided by the maximum carrying capacity of pathogen (10^8 cells in mouse [37]). The final variable to determine the pathogen is the phagocytosis rate of pathogens by Kupffer cells (represented by r_{pmk}) times the portion of pathogens binding to Kupffer cells ($\frac{[P^n]}{[P^n+k_{c1}^n]}M_{kf}P^*$).

We assumed that Kupffer cells population growth followed a standard logistic growth pattern with a constant proliferation (replenishment) rate denoted as k_{mk}, and a maximal carrying limit, K_∞, represented by the first term $\left(k_{mk}M_{kf}\left(1 - \frac{M_{kf}}{M_\infty}\right)\right)$ in Equation 8.2. Since the binding of a pathogen did not preclude the phagocytosis of additional bacteria after the completion of phagocytosis, we used receptor–ligand kinetics to model the release of Kupffer cells from the binding complex, which is represented by the second term ($k_{mkub}M_{kb}$) in Equation 8.2, and k_{mkub} representing the rate of the *motile enterobacteria* (i.e., *Salmonella*) are phagocytosed by the free Kupffer cells and are made available for additional interactions with *motile enterobacteria*. The decreasing number of free Kupffer cells is due to two things: the free Kupffer cells binding to pathogen, which is described by the third term $\left(\frac{[P^n]}{[P^n+k_{c1}^n]}M_{kf}P^*\right)$, also the natural decay of free Kupffer cells represented by the fourth term ($u_{mk}M_{kf}$) in Equation 8.2. The free Kupffer cells become binding Kupffer cells once they bind to pathogen, which is described by the first term $\left(\frac{[P^n]}{[P^n+k_{c1}^n]}M_{kf}P^*\right)$ in Equation 8.3. The second term ($k_{mkub}M_{kb}$) in Equation 8.3 measures decreasing (releasing) portion of binding Kupffer cells. The definition of parameters and the corresponding experimental data for each system parameter in Kupffer local response model are summarized in Table 8.1.

Experimental results show that 50% *Salmonella* are phagocytosed by Kupffer cells in liver, and we used this fact to determine the number of Kupffer cells that phagocytoses half of *Salmonella* equal to the number of Kupffer cells in the liver [35]. Experimental data also show that *Salmonella* ingestion can kill macrophages, and such macrophages will no longer return to the active state for pathogen binding if they are killed [36]. Our assumption was that the "dissociation" rate of Kupffer cells is equivalent to 1-infected rate of Kupffer cells. This is based on data showing that Kupffer cell activity could range from 0.1 to 0.77 from known infection rates [36]. Other parameters are either directly derived from published observations in the literature or will be estimated from our model. Our sensitivity analysis revealed that this system is highly sensitive to the proliferation (replenishment) rate of Kupffer cells (k_{mk}).

The data are represented by plotting the number of motile enterobacteria and Kupffer cells (arbitrary units) versus time (hours) based on the variation in the proliferation rate (including the growth rate of Kupffer cells, as well as the recruitment rate of monocytes from the blood vessels) of Kupffer cells (k_{mk}) in Figure 8.2a and b.

Figure 8.2 indicates that Kupffer cells alone are not able to resolve an infection when the "proliferation rate" of Kupffer cells is less than 0.5/h. In this simulation, all

TABLE 8.1   Definition of Parameters and Experimental Values in Kupffer local Response Model

Parameters	Description	Value	References
k_{pg}	*Salmonella* growth rate	1.2–3.6/h	[33]
P_∞	*Salmonella* carrying capacity	10^8 cells	[37]
r_{pmk}	Rate at which pathogens are killed by Kupffer cells	0.03/Kupffer cell/h	[35]
n	The extent of *Salmonella* binding to Kupffer cells	2	Estimated
k_{c1}	Number of Kupffer cells that phagocytose half of *Salmonella*	0.03 cells/h	[35]
k_{mk}	Proliferation rate of Kupffer cells under inflammation	0.015–2/h	Estimated
K_∞	Kupffer cells carrying capacity	$\dfrac{(16\text{–}20) \times 10^6 \text{cells}}{\text{g liver}}$	[48]
k_{mkub}	Unbinding rate of binding Kupffer cells	0.1–0.77/h	[36]
u_{mk}	Killing rate of free Kupffer cells induced by binding to pathogens	0.23–0.9/h	[36]

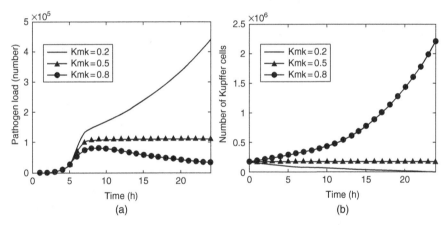

Figure 8.2   (a) Concentration of *pathogen* load versus time, for three different proliferation rates of *Kupffer cells* in Kupffer local response model. (b) Concentration of *Kupffer cells* versus time, for three different proliferation rates of *Kupffer cells* in the Kupffer local response model. The horizontal axes represent the time in hours, and the vertical axes represent concentration in arbitrary units.

Kupffer cells are phagocytosing pathogens and there are no Kupffer cells available to phagocytose additional motile enterobacteria, and hence phagocytosis fails to continue. However, the pathogen could be cleared completely if Kupffer proliferation rate is set relatively high. In our model, we assume that the proliferation rate of Kupffer cells in the liver comprises two parts: the natural growth rate of Kupffer cells and the recruiting rate of monocytes from the nearby blood vessels. The results of the experimental studies show that the local growth rate of Kupffer cells is low and stable with 0.015/h [49, 50]. Therefore, we conclude that the increase in proliferation rate of Kupffer cells is due to the increasing recruitment rate of monocytes from blood vessels, with those recruited monocytes contributing to the clearance of local infection. Based on our simulation results, we could further inference that Kupffer cells are not a major responder to resolve an overwhelming AIR episode, which allows us to model the effects of other immune cells during AIR such as neutrophils and monocytes.

8.3.2   Step 2: Neutrophils Immune Response Model

The results in the Kupffer immune response model show that Kupffer cells may not be sufficient to eliminate the infection, especially when the local infection is overwhelming. The Kupffer cells in local immune response release pro-inflammatory cytokines such as TNF-α, which contribute to the recruitment of neutrophils in the circulation and accumulation of neutrophils in the liver (transmigration) [51–53]. The transmigration can be mediated by a chemokine gradient (e.g., TNF-α, IL-1, CXC chemokines, and PAF) established toward the hepatic parenchyma that generally involves the adhesion molecules on neutrophils (β_2 integrins) and on endothelial cells (intracellular adhesion molecules, ICAM-1). After transmigration, neutrophils adhere to distressed hepatocytes through their β_2 integrins and ICAM-1 expressed on hepatocytes. Neutrophils contact with hepatocytes mediate oxidative killing of hepatocytes by the initiation of respiratory burst and neutrophil degranulation leading to hepatocellular oncotic necrosis. Neutrophils, as a double-effect mediator, will either phagocytose pathogens or induce tissue damages by killing distressed hepatocytes [53]. Furthermore, activated neutrophils (priming) will release TNF-α and therefore recruit even more neutrophils to the site of infection [54]. The release of cytokines follows trafficking machinery, and the cytokines are released via protein–protein interactions initiated by the ligand binding to the receptors [55, 56]. The mechanism of cytokine release is depicted in Figure 8.3.

During the process of cytokine release, R-SNARE protein complex on the membrane of the secretory organelle will interact with Q-SNARE protein complex on the membranes of different types of immune cells, which allows membrane fusion and extrusion of cytokines from the granule interior [55]. We model a protein–protein interaction as Michaelis–Menten kinetics [57] and derive our neutrophil immune response model as follows.

$$\frac{dP}{dt} = k_{\text{pg}}P\left(1 - \frac{P}{P_\infty}\right) - r_{\text{pmk}}\frac{[P^n]}{[P^n + k_{c1}^n]}M_{\text{kf}}P^* - r_{\text{pn}}\frac{[P^n]}{[P^n + k_{c2}^n]}(N_f + N_b)P^*$$

$$\tag{8.4}$$

$$\frac{dM_{\text{kf}}}{dt} = k_{\text{mk}}M_{\text{kf}}\left(1 - \frac{M_{\text{kf}}}{K_\infty}\right) + k_{\text{mkub}}M_{\text{kb}} - \frac{[P^n]}{[P^n + k_{c1}^n]}M_{\text{kf}}P^* - u_{\text{mk}}M_{\text{kf}} \tag{8.5}$$

$$\frac{dM_{\text{kb}}}{dt} = \frac{[P^n]}{[P^n + k_{c1}^n]}M_{\text{kf}}P^* - k_{\text{mkub}}M_{\text{kb}} \tag{8.6}$$

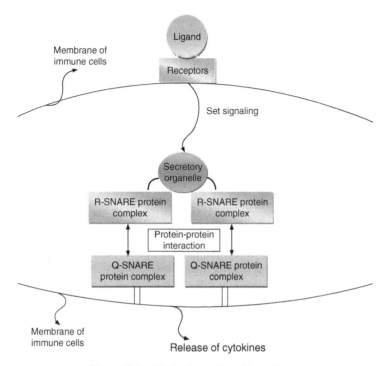

Figure 8.3 Mechanism of cytokine release.

$$\frac{dT}{dt} = \left(\frac{r_{t1\max}M_{kb}}{m_{t1} + M_{kb}}\right) M_{kb} + \left(\frac{r_{t2\max}N_b}{m_{t2} + N_b}\right) N_b - u_t T \tag{8.7}$$

$$\frac{dN_R}{dt} = k_{rd}N_R\left(1 - \frac{N_R}{N_S}\right) - r_1 N_R(T + P)^* - \mu_{nr}N_R \tag{8.8}$$

$$\frac{dN_f}{dt} = r_1 N_R(T + P)^* + k_{nub}N_b - \frac{[P^n]}{[P^n + k_{c2}^n]}N_f P^* - \mu_n N_f \tag{8.9}$$

$$\frac{dN_b}{dt} = \frac{[P^n]}{[P^n + k_{c2}^n]}N_f P^* - k_{nub}N_b \tag{8.10}$$

$$\frac{dr_1}{dt} = k_{r1}(1 + \tanh(N_f^*)) - \mu_{r1}r_1 \tag{8.11}$$

Equation 8.4 is further derived from Equation 8.1 in the Kupffer local immune response by incorporating the phagocytotic effects of neutrophils, which is represented by term $r_{pn}\frac{[P^n]}{[P^n + k_{c2}^n]}(N_f + N_b)P^*$. Details about parameters are defined in Table 8.2. Equations 8.5 and 8.6 are cited from Equations 8.2 and 8.3.

Equation 8.7 represents the changes of the pro-inflammatory cytokines (denoted by T) such as TNF-α, released by binding both tissue resident Kupffer cells (M_{kb}) and

TABLE 8.2   Definition of Parameters and Experimental Values in Neutrophils Immune Response Model

Parameters	Description	Value	References
r_{pn}	Rate at which pathogens are killed by neutrophils	20–100/ neutrophil/h	[58]
r_{t1max}	The maximum number of TNF-α being released by Kupffer cells per enzyme molecule per hour	10/h	Estimated
r_{t2max}	The maximum number of TNF-α being released by neutrophils per enzyme molecule per hour	1,000/h	Estimated
m_{t1}	Number of Kupffer cells at which the reaction rate is half of maximal production rate	10,000 cells	Estimated
m_{t2}	Number of activated neutrophils at which the reaction rate is half of maximal production rate	10,000 cells	Estimated
k_{c2}	Concentration of neutrophils which phagocytose half of *Salmonella*	About $1.5 \times \frac{10^{-4}}{h}$	[59]
u_t	Degradation rate of TNF-α	0.025–0.5/h (measured in kidney)	[60]
k_{rd}	Influx rate of neutrophils into blood vessel	0.1–0.72/h	[61]
N_s	Maximum amount of neutrophils in liver	3.5×10^5	[42]
μ_{nr}	Apoptotic rate of resting neutrophils	0.069–0.12/h	[62]
μ_n	Apoptotic rate of activated neutrophils	0.05/h	[62]
k_{nub}	Unbinding rate of activated neutrophils	0.01–0.5/h	Estimated
k_{r1}	Auxiliary parameter associated with the activation rate of resting neutrophils	3/h	Estimated
u_{r1}	Degradation rate of parameter r_1 to maintain a slow saturation curve	0.003/h	Estimated

activated neutrophils (N_b) along with a constant degradation rate (u_t). Since TNF-α was released after pathogens binding to the receptors of tissue resident macrophages or neutrophils, we model the process of TNF-α release as a combination of Michaelis–Menten kinetics and receptor–ligand kinetics [12]. In Equation 8.7, the release of TNF-α from Kupffer cells is initiated by a receptor–ligand kinetics and secondly following enzymatic kinetics (Michaelis–Menten) represented by the term $\left(\frac{r_{t1max}M_{kb}}{m_{t1}+M_{kb}} \right)$ where r_{t1max} represents the maximal production rate of TNF-α by binding Kupffer cells. It is well known that the release of TNF-α is a combined effect of both receptor–ligand kinetics and enzymatic kinetics, therefore, we incorporate both terms together $\left(\frac{r_{t1max}M_{kb}}{m_{t1}+M_{kb}} \right) M_{kb}$ in the model to represent the combined effects of the TNF-α releasing processes. Similarly, we use the same principle to model the release of TNF-α contributed by activated neutrophils in the second term in

Equation 8.7. The third term in Equation 8.7, $u_t T$, measures the degradation of TNF-α, with u_t representing the degradation rate of TNF-α.

In Equation 8.8, the first term $k_{rd} N_R \left(1 - \frac{N_R}{N_S}\right)$ is a standard logistic function to measure the increase in number of resting neutrophils per time unit (hour), which is represented by the influx of neutrophils into blood vessel per hour. The second term $r_1 N_R (T + P)^*$ describes that the decrease in the number of resting neutrophils per time unit is due to neutrophils' activation process promoted by pro-inflammatory mediator TNF-α where T^* denotes the concentration of TNF-α and P^* denotes the concentration of pathogens [52–54]. The third term in Equation 8.8 $\mu_{nr} N_R$ represents the natural decay of resting neutrophils, and u_{nr} is defined as the apoptotic rate of resting neutrophils per time unit in hours. In Equation 8.9, the first term exactly equals to the second term in Equation 8.8 since the increase in the population of activated neutrophils results directly from the population of resting neutrophils being activated. The second term of Equation 8.9 used mass action kinetics ($k_{nub} N_b$) to model the release of activated phagocytes from the binding complex and make activated phagocytes available for additional interaction with pathogens, where N_b represents the binding complex and k_{nub} represents the rate of activated phagocytes releasing from the binding complex. The third term of 8.9, similar to the third term in Equation 8.8 models the natural apoptosis of activated neutrophils.

Equation 8.10 is similar to the derivation of Equation 8.3 in Kupffer local response model. We used a hyperbolic tangent function in Equation 8.11 to represent a slow-saturation influx rate of neutrophils into hepatic parenchyma and therefore represent the rate of resting neutrophils being activated. The definition and the corresponding experimental data for newly added system parameters in the immune response model of neutrophils are summarized in Table 8.2.

By substituting the above-mentioned experimental data into our neutrophil immune response model, we plot the pathogen loads, TNF-α, resting neutrophils, activated neutrophils versus time (hours) using Mathematica, and the computed results are shown in Figure 8.4a–d.

Compared to the result in Figure 8.2a, the result in Figure 8.4a shows that pathogen load peaks out and decreases significantly in a short time period (around 10 h from our neutrophil immune response model) if the effects of neutrophils are incorporated. Regardless of the overall effects of immune cells in the liver, experimental studies have shown that mice at 6 h after infection exhibit a large decrease (0.6log$_{10}$) in bacteria correlating with the influx of neutrophils [42]. The bulk of clearance of bacteria or pathogen is largely due to influx of neutrophils and their programmed mechanism to ingest bacteria and other harmful microorganisms [63]. Being one of the major immune cells arrived early at the site of infection, neutrophils play an essential role in the initial stage of AIR and further influence the downstream progression of AIR. Also, previously activated neutrophils release pro-inflammatory cytokines such as TNF-α, and newly released TNF-α helps to recruit more neutrophils from blood vessels to the site of infection. Our neutrophil immune response model recapitulates the patterns of TNF-α reported in the literature that TNF-α concentration in the liver increases to a peak at 6 h after infection and trends down toward baseline by 24 h (Fig. 8.4b) [64]. From our simulation results, the highest level of activated

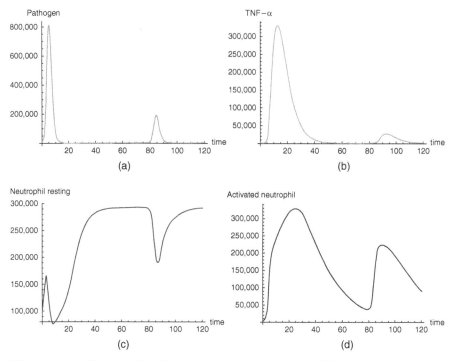

Figure 8.4   (a) Concentration of *pathogen* versus time in neutrophil immune response model at the first 100 h of simulation. (b) Concentration of *TNF-α* versus time in neutrophil immune response model at the first 100 h of simulation. (c) Concentration of *resting neutrophils* versus time in neutrophil immune response model at the first 100 h of simulation. (d) Concentration of *activated neutrophils* versus time in neutrophil immune response model at the first 100 h of simulation.

neutrophils occurs around 10 hours after infection, which is later than the highest level occurred for TNF-α, and its level decreases toward zero around 3 days (72 h) after the infection (Fig. 8.4d). Furthermore, the observed infection is "oscillated" during first 500 h of simulation, which matches to biological experimental data in the literature [63]. The relationships among pathogen, TNF-α, and activated neutrophils, shown in Figure 8.5, are interconnected based on our model.

Figure 8.5 provides a simple logistic chart to illustrate the interactions between each component in our neutrophil immune response model. An increase in pathogen (denoted as P in Figure 8.5) will induce the production of TNF-α and further help to recruit more activated neutrophils (denoted as N in Figure 8.5), which contribute to the decrease in pathogen load. We conclude that the clearance of pathogen is more dependent on the effects of infiltrating neutrophils in the liver than on the Kupffer cells in the liver after comparing the results from both models.

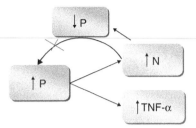

Figure 8.5   Interactions between *pathogen, activated neutrophils*, and *TNF-α*.

8.3.3   Step 3: Damaged Tissue Model

The complexity in AIR is due to the multiple effects induced by inflammatory cells. We show that the recruitment of neutrophils helps to clear local pathogen level; however, those inflammatory cells are harmful at the same time because they release toxic molecules such as reactive oxygen species (ROS), which could cause damage to the host tissue [53, 54]. Recent experimental results show that neutrophils' β_2 integrins adhere to the ICAM-1 receptors of hepatocytes and accelerate the killing process of distressed hepatocytes [65]. We assume that the binding process of neutrophils to hepatocytes also follows ligand–receptor kinetics and derive the following damaged tissue model.

$$\frac{dD}{dt} = r_{hn}\frac{[D^n]}{[D^n + k_{c3}^n]}N_f D^* \left(1 - \frac{D}{A_\infty}\right) - r_{ah}D \tag{8.12}$$

In Equation 8.12, D denotes the number of apoptotic hepatocytes or dead hepatocytes), r_{hn} represents the rate of apoptotic hepatocytes killed by activated neutrophils and r_{ah} represents the recovery rate of apoptotic hepatocytes. The ligand–receptor kinetics $\frac{[D^n]}{[D^n+k_{c3}^n]}N_f D^*$ is used to represent the amount of apoptotic hepatocytes that bind to activated neutrophils, with the binding rate being modeled as a Hill-type function $\frac{[D^n]}{[D^n+k_{c3}^n]}$. The activated neutrophils have recently been found to kill the apoptotic hepatocytes [65]. After neutrophil adhered to apoptotic hepatocytes, the neutrophils release ROS and proteases, which accelerate the death of apoptotic hepatocytes [65, 66]. Multiplying $\frac{[D^n]}{[D^n+k_{c3}^n]}N_f D^*$ by r_{hn}, the entire first term in Equation 8.12 represents the number of apoptotic hepatocytes killed by activated neutrophils per hour, which is the total number of dead hepatocytes per hour. The maximal number of apoptotic or dead hepatocytes will not exceed the total number of hepatocytes in liver (represented by A_∞). In addition, we use r_{ah} to represent the recovery rate of apoptotic hepatocytes, and the second term in Equation 8.12 is defined as the amount of recovering apoptotic hepatocytes. The definition of parameters and the corresponding experimental data in damaged tissue model are summarized in Table 8.3, and Figure 8.6 shows the concentration of dead hepatocytes versus time (hours).

TABLE 8.3   Definition of Parameters and Experimental Values in Damaged Tissue Model

Parameters	Description	Value	References
A_∞	Number of hepatocytes in liver	3.2×10^8 cells/h	Mouse phenome database
r_{hn}	Rate at which activated neutrophils kill apoptotic hepatocytes	9000/ neutrophil/h	Estimated
k_{c3}	Concentration of activated neutrophils that phagocytose half of apoptotic hepatocytes	0.04 cells/h	Estimated
r_{ah}	Recovery rate of apoptotic hepatocytes	0.5–2/h	[67]

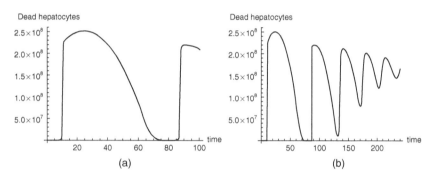

Figure 8.6 (a). Concentration of *dead hepatocytes* versus time in damaged tissue model at the first 100 h of simulation. (b) Concentration of *dead hepatocytes* versus time in damaged tissue model at the first 240 h of simulation. X-axes represent time (in hours) and Y-axes represent concentration in arbitrary units.

Our simulation result shows that the population of dead hepatocytes significantly increases by 12 h. The dead hepatocytes are defined as accumulated apoptotic hepatocytes over time. In the Gal/ET shock model [66], neutrophils extravasate in response to 15–20% of hepatocytes undergoing apoptosis at 6 h, and the neutrophil attack expands the tissue damage to 40–50% of hepatocytes by 7 h. Our simulation results correspond to the evidence that about 15% of hepatocytes are undergoing apoptosis at 9 h and the tissue damage is expanding to around 40% of hepatocytes by 10 h with the attack of neutrophils.

8.3.4   Step 4: Monocytes Immune Response Model

Recent biological experiments from the literature [68, 69] have shown that monocyte, recruited by the presence of HMGB-1, plays an essential role in the liver inflammation and liver fibrosis. Upon liver injury, the inflammatory Ly6cC (Gr1C) monocyte subset as precursors of tissue macrophages in blood vessel near the infected site will be attracted and recruited to the injured liver via CCR2-dependent bone marrow egress. The chemokine receptor CCR2 and its ligand MCP-1/CCL2 promote monocyte subset infiltration upon liver injury and further promote the progression of liver fibrosis [40, 70]. Since evidence showed that tumor necrosis factor-α (TNF-α) induced a marked increase in CCL2/MCP-1 production in dose- and time-dependent manners [71], we assume the influx of monocytes from the blood vessel to the liver is induced by effects of both HMGB-1 and TNF-α and model the influx of monocytes similar to the kinetics of neutrophils' influx. According to existing literature, HMGB-1 is released by necrotic cells and activated monocytes in response to TNF-α simulation [20, 71, 72]. Hence, we model the release of HMGB-1 using receptor–ligand kinetics as well as enzymatic kinetics, similar to the release of TNF-α, by incorporating the effects of necrotic cells and activated monocytes.

$$\frac{dP}{dt} = k_{pg}P\left(1 - \frac{P}{P_\infty}\right) - r_{pmk}\frac{[P^n]}{[P^n + k_{c1}^n]}M_{kf}P^* - r_{pn}\frac{[P^n]}{[P^n + k_{c2}^n]}(N_f + N_b)P^*$$

$$- r_{pm}\frac{[P^n]}{[P^n + k_{c4}^n]}(M_f + M_b)P^* \tag{8.13}$$

$$\frac{dN_b}{dt} = \frac{[P^n]}{[P^n + k_{c2}^n]}N_f P^* - u_{mn}N_b M_f^* - k_{nub}N_b \tag{8.14}$$

$$\frac{dM_R}{dt} = k_{mr}M_R(1 - M_R/M_s) - r_2 M_R(H + T)^* - \mu_{mr}M_R \tag{8.15}$$

$$\frac{dM_f}{dt} = r_2 M_R(H + T)^* + k_{umb}M_b - \frac{[P^n]}{[P^n + k_{c4}^n]}M_f P^* - \mu_m M_f \tag{8.16}$$

$$\frac{dM_b}{dt} = \frac{[P^n]}{[P^n + k_{c4}^n]}M_f P^* - k_{umb}M_b \tag{8.17}$$

$$\frac{dH}{dt} = \left(\frac{r_{h1max}(M_b + D)}{mh_1 + M_b + D}\right)(M_b + D) - u_h H \tag{8.18}$$

In Equation 8.13, we incorporate the effect of phagocytosis by monocytes into Equation 8.4 since monocytes phagocytose Gram-negative bacteria by a CD14-dependent mechanism [73]. We recall Hill-type function equation ($\frac{[P^n]}{[P^n + k_{c4}^n]}$) to represent the receptor–ligand binding kinetics between pathogens and activated monocytes. Since binding-activated neutrophils are engulfed by infiltrating monocytes [74], we use $u_{mn}N_b M_f^*$ to calibrate the killing process of binding-activated neutrophils by activated monocytes, which modify Equation 8.10 to Equations 8.14–8.17, and describe the activation and migration of resting monocytes from blood vessel to infected tissue. In Equations 8.15–8.17, M_R, M_f, and M_b represent the resting monocytes, free activated monocytes, and binding-activated monocytes, respectively. The principles used to build those three equations are similar to the principle used to build Equations 8.8–8.10 for the neutrophil immune response model. Equation 8.18 calibrates the release of HMGB-1 per hour by activated monocytes (monocytes-derived macrophage) and apoptotic hepatocytes, and the process of releasing HMGB-1 is similar to the process of releasing TNF-α. Most experiments in the literature have shown that HMGB-1 is a delayed pro-inflammatory cytokine and is released late in the course of AIR [19, 20, 75]. The definition of parameters and the corresponding experimental data in the monocyte immune response model are summarized in Table 8.4.

We plot the population size of resting monocytes in blood vessel, the activated monocytes in liver and concentration of TNF-α, and HMGB-1 versus time (hours) in Figure 8.7a–d.

From Figure 8.7b, the recruitment of monocytes to the liver reaches it maximal level around 40 h after the introduced infection in our model, compared with 3 days in an experimental model [77], which demonstrates that monocytes arrive later to the site of infection, following the recruitment of neutrophils. Our simulation results correspond to the evidence from experimental study that serum HMGB1 levels were not significantly altered for the first 10 h and then significantly increased at 18 h after the introduced infection as shown in Figure 8.7d [19, 21]. Comparing the peak level of

TABLE 8.4   Definition of Parameters and Experimental Values in Monocytes Immune Response Model

Parameters	Description	Value	References
k_{mr}	Influx rate of monocytes into blood vessel	0.5/h	[61]
r_{pm}	Rate at which pathogens are killed by inflammatory monocytes	7/monocyte/h	[76]
r_2	Influx rate of monocytes in liver	80/h	[77]
M_s	Maximum amount of inflammatory monocytes in liver	50,000	[51]
μ_{mr}	Apoptotic rate of resting monocytes	0.2	Estimated
μ_m	Apoptotic rate of activated monocytes (monocytes-derived macrophage)	0.08	[78]
r_{h1max}	The maximum number of HMGB-1 being released by monocytes per enzyme molecule per hour	0.001	Estimated
m_{h1}	Number of monocytes generate half of maximal HMGB-1 production rate	10,000	Estimated
n	Hill-type coefficient associated with monocytes	2	Estimated
k_{c4}	Number of monocytes that phagocytose half of *Salmonella*	0.002 cells/h	[76]
k_{umb}	Unbinding rate of binding activated monocytes	0.4	[21]
u_h	Degradation rate of HMGB-1	0.5–3	Estimated
u_{mn}	Rate at which activated neutrophils are killed by inflammatory monocytes	200	Estimated

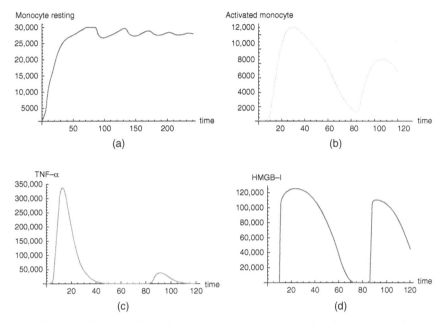

Figure 8.7 (a) Concentration of *resting monocytes* versus time in monocyte immune response model at the first 240 h of simulation. (b) Concentration of *activated monocytes* versus time in monocyte immune response model at the first 120 h of simulation. (c) Concentration of *TNF-α* versus time in monocyte immune response model at the first 120 h of simulation. (d) Concentration of *HMGB-1* versus time in monocyte immune response model at the first 120 h of simulation. Horizontal axes represent time (in hours), and vertical axes represent concentrations in arbitrary units.

HMGB-1 with the peak level of TNF-α, the peak level of HMGB-1 is smaller and the release time of HMGB-1 is slower than the release time of TNF-α (10 vs. 6 h postinfection). Furthermore, our simulation results show that HMGB-1 is readily detectable at 10 h and is maintained at peak, plateau levels from 18 to 32 h after infection, which is similar to the results from experimental studies [19]. Our simulation results suggest that HMGB-1, as a late pro-inflammatory cytokine, downregulates the AIR induced by TNF-α production.

8.3.5 Step 5: Anti-inflammatory Immune Response Model

IL-10 is an anti-inflammatory cytokine. Plasma levels are elevated in animal models of endotoxemia and inhibit the release of pro-inflammatory cytokine (TNF-α, IL-1β, and IL-6) from monocytes/macrophages, thus preventing subsequent tissue damage [79]. This anti-inflammatory mediator is produced by macrophages, dendritic cells (DC), B cells, and various subsets of CD4 and CD8_T cells [80] and follows the same mechanism as pro-inflammatory (TNF-α and HMGB-1) release. Since our main focus in this chapter is to model the innate immune responses, we ignore the release of IL-10 by B cells and T cells during the adaptive immune responses. Hence, we model the release of IL-10 in a similar way as pro-inflammatory cytokine release.

$$\frac{dC_A}{dt} = \left(\frac{r_{\text{camax}} M_b}{C_{\text{Ah}} + M_b} \right) M_b - u_{ca} C_A \tag{8.19}$$

In Equation 8.19, C_A represents the concentration of anti-inflammatory cytokine (IL-10) during AIR. $\left(\frac{r_{\text{camax}} M_b}{C_{\text{Ah}} + M_b} \right)$ represents the release rate of anti-inflammatory cytokine (IL-10) by activated monocytes, derived from enzymatic kinetics. The first term in Equation 8.19 calibrates the increase in the number of anti-inflammatory cytokines every hour and the second term $u_{ca} C_A$ calibrates the decrease in number of anti-inflammatory cytokines every hour due to a natural degradation. The corresponding parameters and their values are defined in Table 8.5.

We plot the concentration of TNF-α, HMGB-1, and IL-10 versus time (hours) in Figure 8.8a–c.

Experimental studies in mice have shown that early predominance of pro-inflammatory cytokines transitions to anti-inflammatory predominance at 24 h [17, 64]. Figure 8.8a–c shows that the time to approach the peak levels of

TABLE 8.5   Definition of Parameters and Experimental Values in Anti-inflammatory Immune Response Model

Parameters	Description	Value	References
r_{camax}	The maximum number of IL-10 being released by monocytes per enzyme molecule per hour	10,000	Estimated
C_{Ah}	Number of monocytes generate half of maximal HMGB-1 production rate	10,000	Estimated
n	Hill-type coefficient associated with monocytes	2	Estimated
u_{ca}	Degradation rate of IL-10	0.02	Estimated

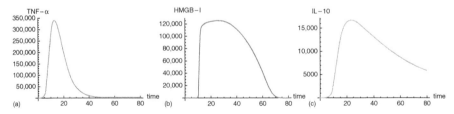

Figure 8.8   (a) Concentration of *TNF-α* versus time in anti-inflammatory immune response model at the first 80 h of simulation. (b) Concentration of *HMGB-1* versus time in anti-inflammatory immune response model at the first 80 h of simulation. (c) Concentration of *IL-10* versus time in anti-inflammatory immune response model at the first 80 h of simulation. Horizontal axes represent time (in hours) and vertical axes represent concentration in arbitrary unit.

TNF-α, HMGB-1, and IL-10 are 6, 18, and 24 h, respectively, and demonstrates that anti-inflammatory responses will follow pro-inflammatory responses and play a role in the later phase of AIR. In the following section, we will discuss the inhibiting effects of anti-inflammatory cytokines and the comprehensive structure of our mathematical model of innate immunity in the AIR.

8.4 MATHEMATICAL MODELS OF INNATE IMMUNITY OF AIR

8.4.1 Inhibition of Anti-inflammatory Cytokines

Before we incorporate mathematical models of subsystems into a comprehensive mathematical model of innate immunity in AIR, we will review the mechanism of inhibition of anti-inflammatory cytokines to the course of infection. IL-10 was found to inhibit protein kinase activation (IKK activity) induced by LPS binding to the CD14 receptor and to consequently block the downstream Ras signaling pathway [81]. Furthermore, IL-10 inhibits both TNF-α and LPS-induced NF-κB DNA binding, gene transcription, and cytokine synthesis [82–84]. The mechanism of IL-10 inhibition of protein production is shown in Figure 8.9.

By IKK activity, NF-κB as a protein complex is released from cytoplasm into the cell nucleus and binds to DNA in order to accomplish NF-κB-dependent DNA transcription [85]. We assume the NF-κB protein complex binding to DNA as an enzyme kinetics, since DNA-binding proteins, such as transcription factors, have recently been found to exhibit enzymatic activity during the process of transcription [86]. Furthermore, we assume and model IL-10 inhibition as an enzyme inhibition process, since IL-10 inhibits the process of DNA–protein binding, as well as transcription. The mathematical formation of IL-10 inhibition will, therefore, follow simplified competitive enzyme kinetics (α denoted as adjustment) as follows:

$$f(C_A, x) = \frac{\alpha x}{\left(1 + \frac{C_A}{C_\infty}\right)}$$

After incorporating the inhibition function of IL-10, we derive a comprehensive mathematical model for innate immunity of AIR, and C_∞ represents the dissociation rate of IL-10 with initial estimated value equivalent to 0.02.

8.4.2 Mathematical Model of Innate Immunity of AIR

$$\frac{dP}{dt} = k_{pg}P\left(1 - \frac{P}{P_\infty}\right) - r_{pmk}\frac{[P^n]}{[P^n + k_{c1}^n]}M_{kf}P^* - r_{pn}\frac{[P^n]}{[P^n + k_{c2}^n]}(N_f + N_b)P^*$$

$$- r_{pm}\frac{[P^n]}{[P^n + k_{c4}^n]}(M_f + M_b)P^* \tag{8.20}$$

$$\frac{dM_{kf}}{dt} = k_{mk}M_{kf}\left(1 - \frac{M_{kf}}{K_\infty}\right) + k_{mkub}M_{kb} - \frac{[P^n]}{[P^n + k_{c1}^n]}M_{kf}P^* - u_{mk}M_{kf} \tag{8.21}$$

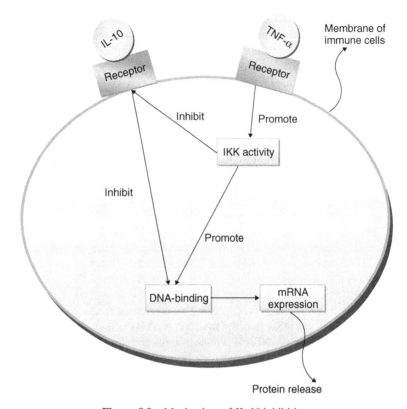

Figure 8.9   Mechanism of *IL-10* inhibition.

$$\frac{dM_{kb}}{dt} = \frac{[P^n]}{[P^n + k_{c1}^n]} M_{kf} P^* - k_{mkub} M_{kb} \tag{8.22}$$

$$\frac{dT}{dt} = \left(\frac{r_{t1max} M_{kb}}{m_{t1} + M_{kb}} \right) M_{kb} + \left(\frac{r_{t2max} N_b}{m_{t2} + N_b} \right) N_b - u_t T \tag{8.23}$$

$$\frac{dN_R}{dt} = k_{rd} N_R \left(1 - \frac{N_R}{N_S} \right) - r_1 N_R (T + P)^* - \mu_{nr} N_R \tag{8.24}$$

$$\frac{dN_f}{dt} = \frac{r_1 N_R (T + P)^*}{\left(1 + \frac{C_A}{C_\infty} \right)} + k_{nub} N_b - \frac{[P^n]}{[P^n + k_{c2}^n]} N_f P^* - \mu_n N_f \tag{8.25}$$

$$\frac{dN_b}{dt} = \frac{[P^n]}{[P^n + k_{c2}^n]} N_f P^* - u_{mn} N_b M_f^* - k_{nub} N_b \tag{8.26}$$

$$\frac{dr_1}{dt} = k_{r1}(1 + \tanh(N_f^*)) - \mu_{r1} r_1 \tag{8.27}$$

$$\frac{dD}{dt} = r_{hn}\frac{[D^n]}{[D^n + k_{c3}^n]}N_fD^* \left(1 - \frac{D}{A_\infty}\right) - r_{ah}D \tag{8.28}$$

$$\frac{dM_R}{dt} = k_{mr}M_R(1 - M_R/M_s) - r_2M_R(H + T)^* - \mu_{mr}M_R \tag{8.29}$$

$$\frac{dM_f}{dt} = \frac{r_2M_R(H + T)^*}{\left(1 + \frac{C_A}{C_\infty}\right)} + k_{umb}M_b - \frac{[P^n]}{[P^n + k_{c4}^n]}M_fP^* - \mu_mM_f \tag{8.30}$$

$$\frac{dM_b}{dt} = \frac{[P^n]}{[P^n + k_{c4}^n]}M_fP^* - k_{umb}M_b \tag{8.31}$$

$$\frac{dH}{dt} = \left(\frac{r_{h1max}(M_b + D)}{mh_1 + M_b + D}\right)(M_b + D) - u_hH \tag{8.32}$$

$$\frac{dC_A}{dt} = \left(\frac{r_{camax}M_b}{C_{Ah} + M_b}\right)M_b - u_{ca}C_A \tag{8.33}$$

8.4.3   Stability Analysis

To study the model behaviors under various parameter settings and initial conditions, stability analyses are conducted for each subsystem during model construction using bifurcation diagrams. Bifurcation diagrams are graphical tools to visualize the behaviors of dynamic system change with parameters, which are generated by Matcont in this chapter. Matcont is a Matlab continuation package with a graphic user interface (GUI) for the interactive numerical study of parameterized nonlinear ODEs. It allows to compute curves of equilibria, limit points, Hopf point, limit cycles, fold, torus, and branch point bifurcation of limit cycles and so on [87].

In bifurcation diagrams, the Y-axis represents the equilibrium of state variable and the X-axis represents the value of system parameter that generates equilibrium. Therefore, bifurcation diagrams reflect change in equilibrium of dynamic system (either change in number of equilibrium or change in numerical value of equilibrium) in relation to the change in numerical value of system parameter. We analyzed stability of dynamic system by identifying types of bifurcation point in bifurcation diagrams since bifurcation points are defined as points where stability changes from stable to unstable. In our bifurcation diagrams, there are two typical bifurcation points: limit point (marked as "LP" in Matcont) and Hopf point (marked as "H" in Matcont). Neutral Saddle Point is marked as "NS" in bifurcation diagram; however, it is not a bifurcation point for the equilibrium since it is identified as a hyperbolic saddle. Figure 8.10 shows stability of equilibria of state variable *pathogens* change in relation to system parameters change in neutrophil subsystem.

8.4.3.1 *Neutrophil Subsystem Stability Analysis* LPs in bifurcation diagrams of neutrophil subsystem appear when two equilibria merge into one equilibrium, and thus, the number of equilibrium of dynamic system changes when LPs are detected. LPs are also turning points at which dynamic system changes from stability to instability. In Figure 8.10a, there is stable equilibrium of *pathogen* when system parameter k_{pg} increases from 0 to 4.93, when k_{pg} equals to 4.93, LP is identified and unstable equilibrium of *pathogen* is generated as k_{pg} decreases from 4.93 to 0. Therefore, equilibrium of *pathogen* of our neutrophil subsystem is bistable when k_{pg} is from 0 to 4.93. Similarly, equilibrium of *pathogen* in Figure 8.10b is bistable when system parameter r_{pn} is from 25 to 200. In Figure 8.10c, equilibrium of *pathogen* before LP is stable and the equilibrium is bistable when u_n is from 0.05 to 0.21.

A Hopf bifurcation, identified in Figure 8.10d, is a periodic bifurcation in which a new limit cycle is born from a stationary solution. Hopf point is a point in a turning point for periodic orbits, and Hopf point is detected when system parameter r_{f2max} changes. The detected Hopf point in Figure 8.10d is used to start a limit cycle continuation, where two cycles collide and disappear. Since the first Lyapunov coefficient

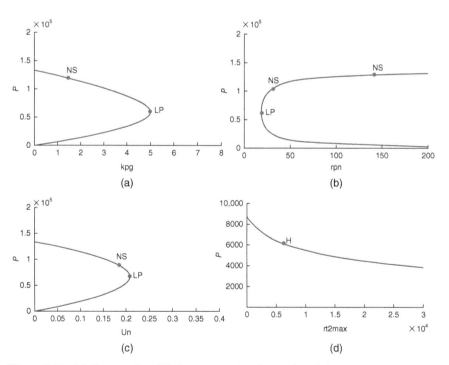

Figure 8.10 (a) Computed equilibrium curve of *pathogens* in relation to system parameter k_{pg} in neutrophil subsystem. (b) Computed equilibrium curve of *pathogens* in relation to system parameters r_{pn} in neutrophil subsystem. (c) Computed equilibrium curve of *pathogens* in relation to system parameters u_n in neutrophil subsystem. (d) Computed equilibrium curve of *pathogens* in relation to system parameters r_{f2max} in neutrophil subsystem.

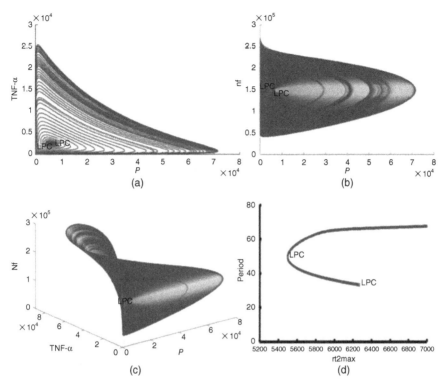

Figure 8.11 (a) Family of limit cycles bifurcating from the Hopf point in *TNF-α* and *pathogen* plane. (b) Family of limit cycles bifurcating from the Hopf point in N_f and *pathogen* plane. (c) Equilibria and limit cycles in (N_f, *pathogen*, and *TNF-α*)-space. (d) Period of the cycle as function of r_{t2max}.

[88] is positive, there exists an unstable limit cycle, bifurcating from this equilibrium. Figure 8.11a and b shows the family of limit cycles bifurcating from detected Hopf point in Figure 8.10d. The family of limit cycles is represented using limit cycle planes such as *TNF-α–pathogen plane* and N_f–*pathogen* plane. Figure 8.11c shows a limit cycle sphere represented by a *TNF-α*, N_f, and *pathogen* plane. Figure 8.11d indicates that the presence of two limit cycles occurs when r_{t2max} equal to 5495.6394 or 6265.0029

In Figure 8.11c, the first family of limit cycle (a dark gray small cycle in the center of sphere) spiral outward as system parameter r_{t2max} decreases, and the second family of limit cycle appears when r_{t2max} decreases to 5495.6394 (a dark gray cycle line appears). As r_{t2max} increases from 5495.6394, the second family of limit cycle spiral outward again, when r_{t2max} increases to 6265.0029, an unstable equilibrium is detected in Figure 8.12. If value of r_{t2max} is between 5495.6394 and 6265.0029, the equilibria of neutrophil subsystem are stable and converged shown by Figure 8.13.

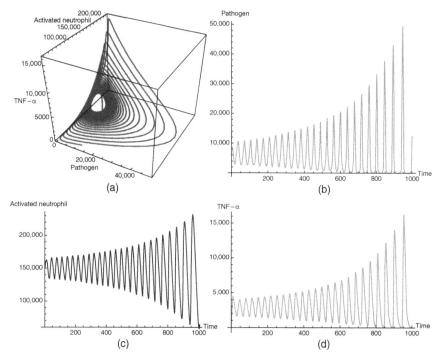

Figure 8.12 (a) Numerical relationships between N_f, *pathogen*, and *TNF-α* in unstable neutrophil subsystem at equilibrium when r_{t2max} is equal to 6265.0029. (b) *Pathogen* diverges in unstable neutrophil subsystem at equilibrium when r_{t2max} is equal to 6265.0029. (c) *Activated neutrophils* diverge in unstable neutrophil subsystem at equilibrium when r_{t2max} is equal to 6265.0029. (d) *TNF-α's* diverge in unstable neutrophil subsystem at equilibrium when r_{t2max} is equal to 6265.0029.

To conclude, we have detected system parameters k_{pg}, r_{pn}, and r_{t2max} contributing to bistability of our neutrophil subsystem. Furthermore, we observe system parameter r_{t2max} (the maximum release rate of TNF-α by activated neutrophils) is essential for generating a closed trajectory of neutrophil subsystem. A significant unstable infection oscillation occurs when r_{t2max} increases to 6265.0029.

8.4.3.2 Monocyte Subsystem Stability Analysis Continued stability analysis on monocyte subsystem indicates a change in system parameters k_{rd}, u_{nr}, and u_n, inducing bistability of monocyte subsystem. From Figure 8.14a–c, we know monocyte subsystem is bistable if at least one of the three conditions meets: k_{rd} is between 0 and 0.32, u_{nr} is between 0 and 0.28, and u_n is between 0 and 0.21. Specifically, we have observed that r_{t2max} (the maximum release rate of TNF-α by activated neutrophils) and m_{t2} (the number of activated neutrophils releasing half of TNF-α) are essential for oscillated monocyte subsystem. Limit cycles are bifurcating from Hopf point, shown in Figure 8.14d and e, similar to neutrophil subsystem. Therefore, we conclude that

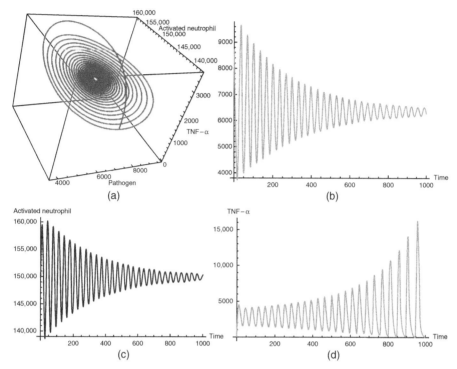

Figure 8.13 (a) Numerical relationships between N_f, *pathogen*, and *TNF-α* in stable neutrophil subsystem at equilibrium when r_{t2max} is between 5495.6394 and 6265.0029. (b) *Pathogen* converges in stable neutrophil subsystem at equilibrium when r_{t2max} is between 5495.6394 and 6265.0029. (c) *Activated neutrophils* converge in stable neutrophil subsystem at equilibrium when r_{t2max} is between 5495.6394 and 6265.0029. (d) *TNF-α* converges in stable neutrophil subsystem at equilibrium when r_{t2max} is between 5495.6394 and 6265.0029.

the oscillated infection is significantly dependent on the amount of released TNF-$α$ and further recruited neutrophils in AIR. However, the released monocytes and the associated cytokines, such as HMGB-1, play no roles in contributing to oscillation in AIR progression.

8.4.3.3   Full Model Stability Analysis   Built upon monocyte subsystem, our full model incorporating the effect of anti-inflammatory cytokines and our stability analysis shows that the stability of our full model is significantly dependent on the effect of anti-inflammatory cytokines, especially when medium effect of anti-inflammatory cytokines are incorporated (dissociation rate of IL-10 equal to logarithm 4). Our stability analysis, in Figure 8.15, shows that the Hopf points move forward as r_{t2max} and m_{t2} increases when medium effect of anti-inflammatory cytokines is incorporated.

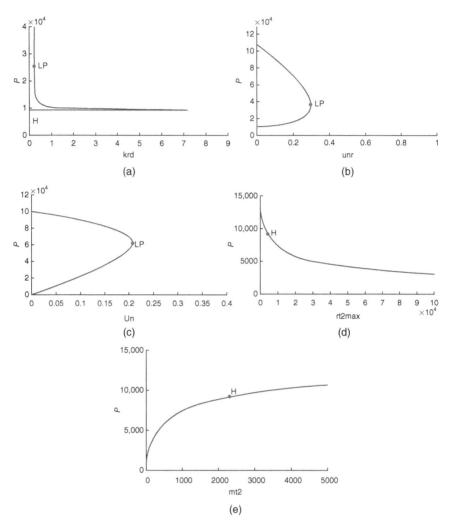

Figure 8.14 (a) Computed equilibrium curve of *pathogens* in relation to system parameter k_{rd} in monocyte subsystem. (b) Computed equilibrium curve of *pathogens* in relation to system parameters u_{nr} in monocyte subsystem. (c) Computed equilibrium curve of *pathogens* in relation to system parameters u_n in monocyte subsystem. (d) Computed equilibrium curve of *pathogens* in relation to system parameters r_{t2max} in monocyte subsystem. (e) Computed equilibrium curve of *pathogens* in relation to system parameters m_{t2} in monocyte subsystem.

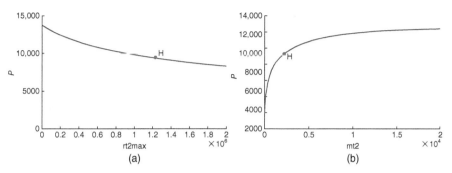

Figure 8.15 (a) Computed equilibrium curve of *pathogens* in relation to system parameter r_{f2max} if medium effect of anti-inflammatory cytokine is incorporated. (b) Computed equilibrium curve of *pathogens* in relation to system parameters m_{f2} if medium effect of anti-inflammatory cytokine is incorporated.

8.4.3.4 Medium Effect of Anti-inflammatory Cytokines

In Figure 8.15a and b, comparing to Figure 8.14d and e, we see the Hopf point is detected when r_{f2max} and m_{f2} increases to a bigger value since the anti-inflammatory cytokines inhibit the activation of phagocytic cells (neutrophils and monocytes). This trend indicates that the infection oscillation requires, with the medium effect of anti-inflammatory cytokines, more pro-inflammation (including TNF-α and activated neutrophils) compared to our monocyte subsystem without including the effect of anti-inflammatory cytokines. The strengthened (increased r_{f2max} and m_{f2}) pro-inflammatory immune responses could also induce stable or unstable equilibria, and therefore leads to a dampened oscillated infection or diverged infection, similar to our observations in Figures 8.12 and 8.13. However, we have observed that our AIR progression, if high effect of anti-inflammatory cytokine is incorporated (dissociation rate equal to logarithm 6) at the beginning of infection, will induce a stable overwhelming pathogen load. These observations inspire us that the effects of anti-inflammatory cytokines play a vital role in AIR progression and could be either positive or negative to AIR progression dependent on levels of anti-inflammatory cytokines.

8.5 DISCUSSION

8.5.1 Effects of Initial *Pathogen* Load on Sepsis Progression

Using our system dynamic mathematical model, we analyzed the impact of effect of bacteria load on phagocytic cells, inflammatory cytokines, and damaged tissue at low, medium, and high level during innate immunity of AIR. The computed results are shown in Figures 8.16–8.18.

8.5.1.1 *Low Initial Load of* **Pathogen** (**p**(0) = 100)

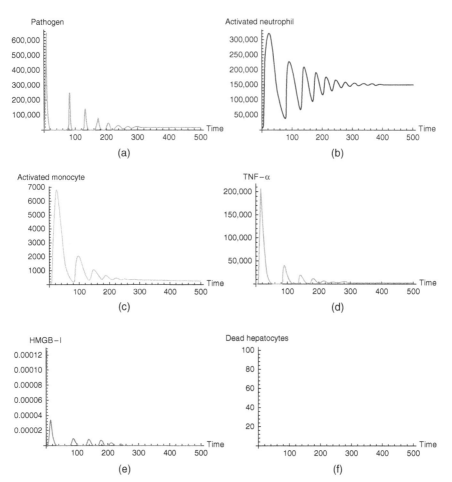

Figure 8.16   (a) Concentration of *pathogen* in the presence of low initial load of *pathogen*. (b) Concentration of *activated neutrophils* in the presence of low initial load of *pathogen*. (c) Concentration of *activated monocytes* in the presence of low initial load of *pathogen*. (d) Concentration of *TNF-α* in the presence of low initial load of *pathogen*. (e) Concentration of *HMGB-1* in the presence of low initial load of *pathogen*. (f) Concentration of *dead hepatocytes* in the presence of low initial load of *pathogen*. Horizontal axes represent time (in hours) and vertical axes represent concentration in arbitrary units.

8.5.1.2 Medium Initial Load of Pathogen (p(0) = 10,000)

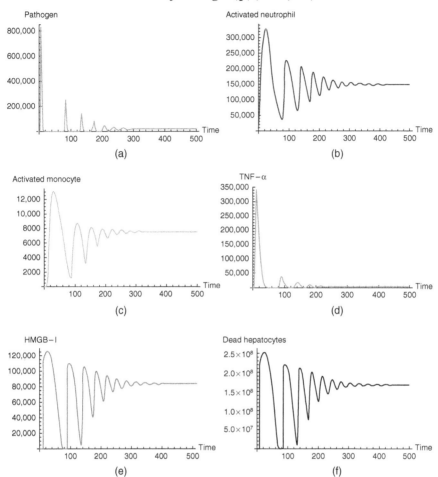

Figure 8.17 (a) Concentration of *pathogen* in the presence of medium initial load of *pathogen*. (b) Concentration of *activated neutrophils* in the presence of medium initial load of *pathogen*. (c) Concentration of *activated monocytes* in the presence of medium initial load of *pathogen*. (d) Concentration of *TNF-α* in the presence of medium initial load of *pathogen*. (e) Concentration of *HMGB-1* in the presence of medium initial load of *pathogen*. (f) Concentration of *dead hepatocytes* in the presence of medium initial load of *pathogen*. Horizontal axes represent time (in hours) and vertical axes represent concentration in arbitrary units.

8.5.1.3 High Initial Load of Pathogen (p(0) = 100,000)

Based on our computed results, we conclude a resolved healthy state, pathogen falls below threshold during the oscillation as well as other phagocytic cells and inflammatory cytokines, when initial pathogen load is low. We recognize a persistent infection pattern happening, when initial pathogen load is medium, if inflammatory responses are still active (damaged tissue oscillates during infection). If initial pathogen load is high, an overwhelming bacteria load occurs eventually, leading to a high risk of death.

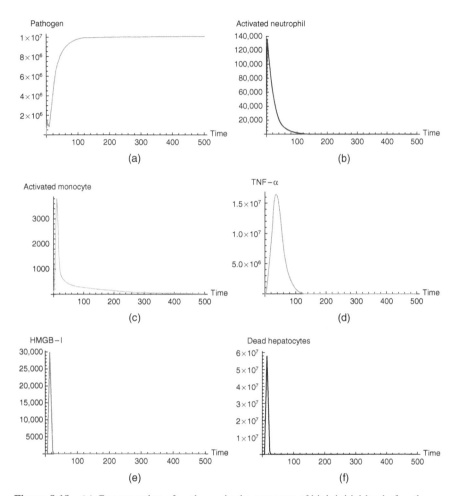

Figure 8.18   (a) Concentration of *pathogen* in the presence of high initial load of *pathogen*. (b) Concentration of *activated neutrophils* in the presence of high initial load of *pathogen*. (c) Concentration of *activated monocytes* in the presence of high initial load of *pathogen*. (d) Concentration of *TNF-α* in the presence of high initial load of *pathogen*. (e) Concentration of *HMGB-1* in the presence of high initial load of *pathogen*. (f) Concentration of *dead hepatocytes* in the presence of high initial load of *pathogen*. Horizontal axes represent time (in hours) and vertical axes represent concentration in arbitrary units.

8.5.2   Effects of Pro- and Anti-inflammatory Cytokines on Sepsis Progression

Interactions and balances between pro-inflammatory cytokines and anti-inflammatory cytokines are essential to the progression of the AIR. Previous experiments on mice [17] have found a close link between severity of sepsis and the balance and time course of inflammatory cytokines. Experiments from existing literature showed that excess production of pro-inflammatory cytokines has been associated with multiple organ system dysfunction (severe sepsis), postfluid resuscitation hypertension (septic shock), and mortality [16]. Based on our simulation results, the response of TNF-α is maximal at an early stage of AIR. Following TNF-α, the late pro-inflammatory HMGB 1 and the anti-inflammatory IL-10 will typically dominate AIR progression and ultimately determine the possible outcomes of AIR. Therefore, local TNF-α level elevation may not end with multiple organ system dysfunctions and anti-TNF-α treatment alone could be ineffective in the early stages of AIR, consistent with clinical trials [79].

Biological results show that effect with IL-10 increases mortality in the murine model [64]. In general, effectiveness of IL-10 on sepsis progression is inconsistent in experimental studies. A group of experimental studies showed that IL-10 improved the outcome of mice undergoing cecal ligation and puncture (CLP), while antibody against IL-10 contributed to worsened outcome or even mortality [17, 89]. In contrast, other investigators failed to confirm the improvement by showing no difference on survival rate between pretreatment with IL-10 and non-pretreatment with IL-10 in mice after CLP [90]. Using our system dynamic mathematical model, we analyzed the impact of effect of IL-10 (measured by system parameter C_A) on bacteria load, phagocytic cells, and damaged tissue at high, medium, and low level during innate immunity of AIR. The computed results are shown in Figures 8.19–8.21.

8.5.2.1 High Effect of Anti-inflammatory Cytokines

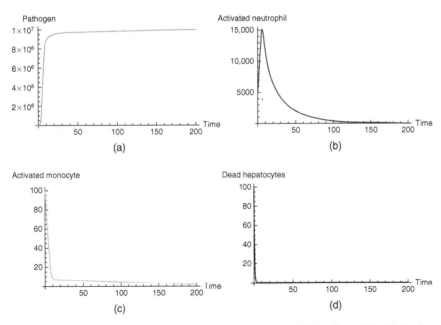

Figure 8.19 (a) Concentration of *pathogen* in the presence of high effect of *IL-10*. (b) Concentration of *activated neutrophils* in the presence of high effect of *IL-10*. (c) Concentration of *activated monocytes* in the presence of high effect of *IL-10*. (d) Concentration of *dead hepatocytes* in the presence of high effect of *IL-10*. Horizontal axes represent time (in hours) and vertical axes represent concentration in arbitrary units.

8.5.2.2   *Medium Effect of Anti-inflammatory Cytokines*

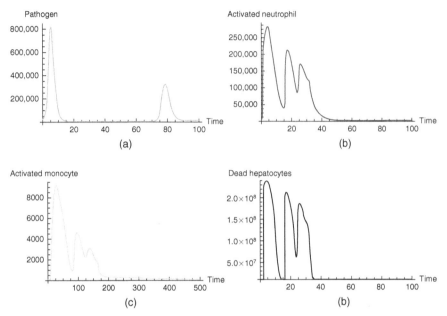

Figure 8.20   (a) Concentration of *pathogen* in the presence of medium effect of *IL-10*. (b) Concentration of *activated neutrophils* in the presence of medium effect of *IL-10*. (c) Concentration of *activated monocytes* in the presence of medium effect of *IL-10*. (d) Concentration of *dead hepatocytes* in the presence of medium effect of *IL-10*. Horizontal axes represent time (in hours) and vertical axes represent concentration in arbitrary units.

8.5.2.3   *Low Effect of Anti-inflammatory Cytokines*   Our simulation results have

shown that the high effect of anti-inflammatory cytokine (*IL-10*) inhibits the release of activated immune cells (activated neutrophils and activated monocytes) as well as subsequent cytokine production. The levels of damaged tissue significantly decrease with the presence of the anti-inflammatory cytokine, which in turn moderates the progression of the AIR and reduces the risks of the sepsis development. Our quantitative results are supported by an abundance of experimental studies in the literature, which have shown that IL-10 downregulates the production of secreted cytokines by inhibiting the various behaviors of activated immune cells [26, 27, 91]. Moreover, existing experimental results have suggested that anti-inflammatory mediator inhibits the activation of phagocytes and reduces the ability of activated phagocytes to attack pathogen [24] and therefore is associated with mortality and severity of infection in sepsis [64, 92]. Based on the above-mentioned evidence, our computed results suggest that the high effect of anti-inflammatory cytokines is a "double-edged sword" for AIR since it would either decrease the mortality associated with tissue damage or increase the mortality associated with high load of bacteria.

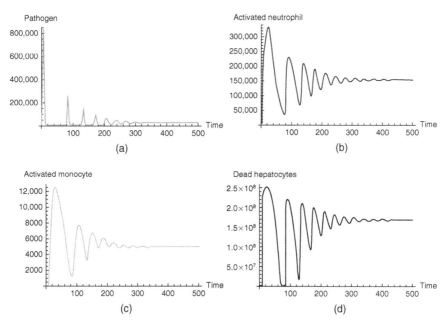

Figure 8.21 (a) Concentration of *pathogen* in the presence of low effect of *IL-10*. (b) Concentration of *activated neutrophils* in the presence of low effect of *IL-10*. (c) Concentration of *activated monocytes* in the presence of low effect of *IL-10*. (d) Concentration of *dead hepatocytes* in the presence of low effect of *IL-10*. Horizontal axes represent time (in hours) and vertical axes represent concentration in arbitrary units.

With the low effect of anti-inflammatory cytokines, our computed results have shown that low effect of anti-inflammatory cytokine (*IL-10*) fails to inhibit the release of activated immune cells (activated neutrophils and activated monocytes) as well as subsequent cytokine production. The levels of damaged tissue significantly accumulate during the first 500 h (about 20 days) of infection. In the presence of low effect of the anti-inflammatory cytokine, AIR is at a high risk of development to organ dysfunction and eventually progression to septic shock.

To further investigate the effects of anti-inflammatory cytokines, we simulate a medium effect of anti-inflammatory cytokines and compare simulated results to both high effect of anti-inflammatory cytokines and low effect of anti-inflammatory cytokines. Our computed results show bacteria load decreases during the first 100 h of infection, together with the total amount of dead hepatocytes. Furthermore, we have observed the production of both activated neutrophils and activated monocytes declines to baseline near 0 at the end of simulation, which indicates a positive trend of sepsis progression to a healthy pattern. Thus, we conclude that the level of anti-inflammatory cytokines plays a vital role in determining the direction of sepsis progression, and the levels of anti-inflammatory cytokines and the time of intervention of anti-inflammatory cytokines will largely influence the outcomes of AIR.

8.6 CONCLUSION

In this chapter, we propose a system dynamic mathematical model and show that the model has significant potential to help predict the possible pathogenesis of AIR based on a patient's physiological conditions. Also, we show that the model is able to give insight into the innate immunity of sepsis progression by exploring various combinations of levels of phagocytes and cytokines. Our focus is especially on the effects of anti-inflammatory cytokines on pathogen load, phagocytic cells, and tissue damage. We observed that the outcomes of sepsis progression could be improved in presence of IL-10 at a medium level at an early stage of infection. Furthermore, our model quantitatively measures the levels of phagocytes (neutrophils and monocytes), compared with existing mathematical models, which provide qualitative estimates.

One of the assumptions of our model is that we currently only include innate immunity, and therefore the results of our model could only represent an early stage of AIR. Adaptive immunity occurs following the innate immune response and includes B-cells, T-cells, and antibodies released from B-cells, which contribute to pathogen clearance [93]. IL-10 is known to be released by various subsets of T-cells, which may lead to overproduction of the anti-inflammatory cytokines by the compensatory anti-inflammatory response and, eventually, an increased risk of secondary infection and poor prognosis [80, 93]. For further research, we expect to explore the prominent effects of anti-inflammatory mediators on the outcomes of AIR progression by incorporating adaptive immunity and its effects on anti-inflammatory cytokine. Also, we propose an agent-based model of sepsis progression and compare the results from the system dynamic mathematical model and the agent-based model.

The system dynamic mathematical model proposed in this chapter is a robust and accurate representation of the comprehensive innate immune responses within an AIR/sepsis episode. This underlining model is general enough and flexible enough that it can be further used to predict the possible outcomes and prognosis for different patient demographics with different model parameters using the experimental data from the literature.

REFERENCES

[1] Bone RC, Balk RA, Cerra FB, Dellinger RP, Fein AM, Knaus WA. Definitions for sepsis and organ failure and guidelines for the use of innovative therapies in sepsis. Chest 1992;101:1644–1655.

[2] Glauser MP. Pathophysiologic basis of sepsis: Considerations for future strategies of intervention. Crit Care Med 2000;28:84–88.

[3] Sharma S, Kumar A. A septic shock, multiple organ failure, and acute respiratory distress syndrome. Curr Opin Pulm Med 2003;9:199–209.

[4] Angus DC, Linde-Zwirble WT, Lidicker J, Clermont G, Carcillo J, Pinsky MR. Epidemiology of severe sepsis in the United States: analysis of incidence, outcome, and associated costs of care. Crit Care Med 2001;29:1472–1474.

[5] Parrillo JE, Parker MM, Natanson C. Septic shock in humans: Advances in the understanding of pathogenesis, cardiovascular dysfunction, and therapy. Ann Int Med 1990;113:227–242.

[6] Hoyert DL, Arias E, Smith BL, Murphy SL, Kochanek KD. Deaths: Final data for 1999. Natl Vital Stat Rep 2001;49(8):1–113. Hyattsville, MD: National Center for Health Statistics, 2001. (DHHS publication no. (PHS) 2001–1120 PRS 01–0573.).

[7] Perl TM, Dvorak L, Hwang T. Wenzel RP: Long-term survival and function after suspected gram-negative sepsis. JAMA 1995;274:338–345.

[8] Rangel-Frausto MS, Pittet D, Costigan M. The natural history of the systemic inflammatory response syndrome (SIRS): A prospective study. JAMA 1995;273:117–123.

[9] Cross A, Opal S. A new paradigm for the treatment of sepsis: It is time to consider combination therapy. Ann Intern Med 2003;138:502–505.

[10] Riedemann NC, Guo RF, Ward PA. Novel strategies for the treatment of sepsis. Nat Med 2003;9:517–524.

[11] Parham P. *The Immune System*. New York: Garland Science, Taylor and Francis Group; 2009.

[12] Janeway C, Shlomchik M, Walport M, Travers P. *Immunobiology: The Immune System in Health and Disease*. New York: Garland Science Publishing; 2005.

[13] Kindt TJ, Goldsby RA, Osborne BA. *Kuby Immunology*. W.H. Freeman and Company; 2007.

[14] Aderem A, Ulevitch RJ. Toll-like receptors in the induction of the innate immune response. Nature 2000;406:782–787.

[15] Janeway CA, Medzhitov R. Innate immune recognition. Annu Rev Immunol 2002;20:197–216.

[16] Gogos CA, Drosou E, Bassaris HP, Skoutelis A. Pro- versus anti-inflammatory cytokine profile in patients with severe sepsis: A marker for prognosis and future therapeutic options. J Infect Dis 2000;181:176–180.

[17] Walley KR, Lukacs NW, Standiford TJ, Strieter RM, Kunkel SL. Balance of inflammatory cytokines related to severity and mortality of murine sepsis. Infect Immun 1996;64:4733–4738.

[18] Sundén-Cullberg J, Norrby-Teglund A, Msci AR, Rauvala H, Msci GH, Tracey KJ, Lee ML, Andersson J, Tokics L, Treutiger CJ. Persistent elevation of high mobility group box-1 protein (HMGB1) in patients with severe sepsis and septic. Shock 2005;33:564–573.

[19] Wang H, Bloom O, Zhang MH, Vishnubhakat JM, Ombrellino M, Che JT, Frazier A, Yang H, Lvanova S, Borovikova L, Manogue KR, Faist E, Abraham E, Andersson J, Andersson U, Molina PE, Abumrad NN, Sama A, Tracey KJ. HMGB-1 as a late mediator of endotoxin lethality in mice. Science 1999;285:248–251.

[20] Wang H, Yang H, Tracey KJ. Extracellular role of HMGB1 in inflammation and sepsis. J Intern Med 2004;255:320–331.

[21] Yang H, Ochani M, Li JH, Qiang XL, Tanovic M, Harris HE, Susarla SM, Ulloa L, Wang H, DiRaimo R, Czura CJ, Wang HC, Roth J, Warren HS, Fink MP, Fenton MJ, Anderson U, Tracey KJ. Reversing established sepsis with antagonists of endogenous high-mobility group box 1. Proc Natl Acad Sci USA 2004;101:296–301.

[22] Mantell LL, Parrish WR, Ulloa L. HMGB-1 as a therapeutic target for infectious and inflammatory disorders. Shock 2006;25:4–11.

[23] Qin SX, Wang HC, Yuan RQ, Li H, Ochani M, Ochani K, Rosas-Ballina M, Czura CJ, Huston JM, Miller E, Lin XC, Sherry B, Kumar A, LaRosa G, Newman W, Tracey KJ, Yang H. Role of HMGB1 in apoptosis-mediated sepsis lethality. J Exp Med 2006;203:1637–1642.

[24] Tsukaguchi K, de Lange B, Boom WH. Differential regulation of IFN-gamma, TNF-alpha, and IL-10 production by CD4 (+) alphabetaTCR+ T cells and vdelta2 (+) gammadelta T cells in response to monocytes infected with Mycobacterium tuberculosis-H37Ra. Cell Immunol 1999;194:12–20.

[25] Bacon GE, Kenny FM, Murdaugh HV, Richards C. Prolonged serum half-life of cortisol in renal failure. Johns Hopkins Med J 1973;132:127–131.

[26] Fiorentino DF, Zlotnik A, Mosmann TR, Howard M, O'garra A. IL-10 inhibits cytokine production by activated macrophages. J Immunol 1991;147:3815–3822.

[27] Chan CS, Ming-Lum A, Golds GB, Lee SJ, Anderson RJ, Mui AF. Interleukin-10 inhibits lipopolysaccharide-induced tumor necrosis factor: Translation through a SHIP1-dependent pathway. J Biol Chem 2012;287:38020–38027.

[28] Bhatia M, Moochhala S. Role of inflammatory mediators in the pathophysiology of acute respiratory distress syndrome. J Pathol 2004;202:145–156.

[29] Kumar R, Clermont G, Vodovotz Y, Chow CC. The dynamics of acute inflammation. J Theor Biol 2004;230:145–155.

[30] Angela R, Jonathan R, Gilles C, Judy D, Yoram V, Ermentrout GB. A reduced mathematical model of the acute inflammatory response: I. Derivation of model and analysis of anti-inflammation. J Theor Biol 2006;242:220–236.

[31] Graham SM. Salmonellosis in children in developing and developed countries and populations. Curr Opin Infect Dis 2002;15:507–512.

[32] Jotwani R, Tanaka Y, Watanabe K, Tanaka K, Kato N, Ueno K. Cytokine stimulation during *Salmonella typhimurium* sepsis in Ity mice. J Med Microbiol 1995;42:348–352.

[33] Beuzón CR, Salcedo SP, Holden DW. Growth and killing of a *Salmonella* enteric serovar Typhimurium sifA mutant strain in the cytosol of different host cell lines. Microbiology 2002;148:2705–2715.

[34] de Jong HK, Parry CM, van der Poll T, Wiersinga WJ. Host–pathogen interaction in invasive salmonellosis. PLoS One 2012;8:1–9.

[35] Friedman RL, Moon RJ. Hepatic clearance of *Salmonella typhimurium* in silica-treated mice. Infect Immun 1977;16:1005–1012.

[36] Gog JR, Murcia A, Osterman N, Restif O, McKinley TJ, Sheppard M, Achouri S, Wei B, Mastroeni P, Wood JN, Maskell DJ, Cicuta P, Bryant CE. Dynamics of Salmonella infection of macrophages at the single cell level. J R Soc Interface 2012;9:2696–2707.

[37] Hess J, Ladel C, Miko D, Kaufmann SH. Salmonella typhimurium and aroA-infection in gene-targeted immunodeficient mice: Major role of CD4+ TCR-alpha beta cells and IFN-gamma in bacterial clearance independent of intracellular location. J Immunol 1996;156:3321–3326.

[38] Rosenberger CM, Finlay BB. Phagocyte sabotage: Disruption of macrophage signaling by bacterial pathogens. Mol Cell Biol 2003;4:385–396.

[39] Dhainaut JF, Marin N, Mignon A, Vinsonneau C. Hepatic response to sepsis: Interaction between coagulation and inflammatory processes. Crit Care Med 2001;29:S42–S47.

[40] Zimmermann HW, Trautwein C, Tacke F. Functional role of monocytes and macrophages for the inflammatory response in acute liver injury. Front Physiol 2012;3:1–18.

[41] Ishibashi H, Nakamura M, Komori A, Migita K, Shimoda S. Liver architecture, cell function, and disease. Semin Immunopathol 2009;31:399–409.

[42] Gregory SH, Sagnimeni AJ, Wing EJ. Bacteria in the bloodstream are trapped in the liver and killed by immigrating neutrophils. J Immunol 1996;157:2514–2520.

[43] Russell DG, VanderVen B, Glennie S, Mwandumba H, Heyderman R. The macrophage marches on its phagosome: Dynamic assays of phagosome function. Nat Rev Immunol 2009;9:594–600.

[44] Otto SP, Day T. *A Biologist's Guide to Mathematical Modeling in Ecology and Evolution.* New Jersey: Princeton University Press; 2007.

[45] Lauffenburger DA, Linderman JJ. *Receptors: Models for Binding, Trafficking, and Signaling.* New York: Oxford University Press; 1993.

[46] Morelock MM, Ingraham RH, Betageri R, Jakes S. Determination of receptor-ligand kinetic and equilibrium binding constants using surface plasmon resonance: Application to the Zck SH2 domain and phosphotyrosyl peptides. J Med Chem 1995;38:1309–1318.

[47] Gesztelyi R, Zsuga J, Kemeny-Beke A, Varga B, Juhasz B, Tosaki A. The Hill equation and the origin of quantitative pharmacology. Arch Hist Exact Sci 2012;66:427–438.

[48] Bouwens L, Baekeland M, De Zanger R, Wisse E. Quantitation, tissue distribution and proliferation kinetics of Kupffer cells in normal rat liver. Hepatology 1986;6:718–722.

[49] Diesselhoff-Den Dulk MMC, Crofton RW, Van Furth R. Origin and kinetics of Kupffer cells during an acute inflammatory response. Immunology 1979;37:7–14.

[50] Natio M, Hasegawa G, Ebe Y, Yamamoto T. Differentiation and function of Kupffer cells. Med Electron Microsc 2004;37:16–28.

[51] Gallin JI, Goldstein IM, Snyderman R. *Inflammation Basic Principles and Clinical Correlates.* New York: Raven Press; 1992.

[52] Hewett JA, Jean PA, Kunkel SL, Roth RA. Relationship between tumor necrosis factor-alpha and neutrophils in endotoxin-induced liver injury. Am J Physiol Gastrointest Liver Physiol 1993;265:G1011–G1015.

[53] Ramaiah SK, Jaeschke H. Role of neutrophils in the pathogenesis of acute inflammatory liver injury. Toxicol Pathol 2007;35:757–766.

[54] Wright HL, Moots RJ, Bucknall RC, Edwards SW. Neutrophil function in inflammation and inflammatory diseases. Rheumatology 2010;49:1618–1631.

[55] Lacy P, Stow JL. Cytokine release from innate immune cells: Association with diverse membrane trafficking pathways. Blood 2011;118:9–18.

[56] Stanley AC, Lacy P. Pathways for cytokine secretion. Physiology 2010;25:218–229.

[57] Lehninger AL, Nelson DL, Cox MM. *Lehninger Principles of Biochemistry.* New York: W.H. Freeman and Company; 2005.

[58] Stossel TP, Mason RJ, Hartwlg J, Vaughan M. Quantitative studies of phagocytosis by polymorphonuclear leukocytes: Use of emulsions to measure the initial rate of phagocytosis. J Clin Invest 1972;51:615–624.

[59] Hampton MB, Vissers MCM, Winterbourn CC. A single assay for measuring the rates of phagocytosis and bacterial killing by neutrophils. J Leukoc 1994;55:147–152.

[60] Bemelmans MH, Gouma DJ, Buurman WA. Influence of hephrectomy on tumor necrosis factor clearance in a murine model. J Immunol 1993;150:2007–2017.

[61] Boxio R, Bossenmeyer-Pourié C, Steinckwich N, Dournon C, Nüße O. Mouse bone marrow contains large numbers of functionally competent neutrophils. J Leukoc Biol 2004;75:604–611.

[62] Coxon A, Tang T, Mayadas TN. Cytokine-activated endothelial cells delay neutrophil apoptosis in vitro and in vivo. A role for granulocyte/macrophage colony-stimulating factor. J Exp Med 1999;190:923–934.

[63] Drescher B, Bai FW. Neutrophil in viral infections, friend or foe? Virus Res 2013;171:1–7.

[64] Ashare A, Power LS, Bulter NS, Doerschug KC, Monick MM, Hunninghake GW. Anti-inflammatory response is associated with mortality and severity of infection in sepsis. Am J Physiol Lung Cell Mol Physiol 2004;288:L633–L640.

[65] Jaeschke H. Mechanisms of liver injury. II. Mechanisms of neutrophil-induced liver cell injury during hepatic ischemia-reperfusion and other acute inflammatory conditions. Am J Physiol Gastrointest Liver Physiol 2006;290:G1083–G1088.

[66] Jaeschke H, Fisher MA, Lawson JA, Simmons CA, Farhood A, Jones DA. Activation of caspase 3 (CPP32)-like proteases is essential for TNF-alpha-induced hepatic parenchymal cell apoptosis and neutrophil-mediated necrosis in a murine endotoxin shock model. J Immunol 1998;160:3480–3486.

[67] Dos Santos SA, de Andrade DR, de Andrade DR. TNF-alpha production and apoptosis in hepatocytes after Listeria monocytogenes and Salmonella typhimurium invasion. Rev Inst Med Trop Sao Paulo 2011;53:107–112.

[68] Schiraldi M, Raucci A, Muñoz M, Livoti E, Celona B, Venereau E, Apuzzo T, De Marchis F, Pedotti M, Bachi A, Thelen M, Varani L, Mellado M, Proudfoot A, Bianchi ME, Uguccioni M. HMGB1 promotes recruitment of inflammatory cells to damaged tissues by forming a complex with CXCL12 and signaling via CXCR4. J Exp Med 2012;209:551–563.

[69] Karlmark KR, Weiskirchen R, Zimmermann HW, Gassler N, Ginhoux F, Weber C, Merad M, Luedde T, Trautwein C, Tacke F. Hepatic recruitment of the inflammatory Gr1_ Monocyte subset upon liver injury promotes hepatic fibrosis. Hepatology 2009;50:261–274.

[70] Tacke F. Functional role of intrahepatic monocyte subsets for the progression of liver inflammation and liver fibrosis in vivo. Fibrogenesis Tissue Repair 2012;5:S27.

[71] Chen GQ, Li JH, Ochani M, Rendon-Mitchell B, Qiang XL, Susarla S, Ulloa L, Yang H, Fan SJ, Goyert SM, Wang P, Tracey KJ, Sama AE, Wang HC. Bacterial endotoxin stimulates macrophages to release HMGB1 partly through CD14- and TNF-dependent mechanisms. J Leukoc Biol 2004;76:994–1001.

[72] Willenbrock S, Braun O, Baumgart J, Lange S, Junghanss C, Heisterkamp A, Nolte I, Bullerdiek J, Escobar HM. TNF-a induced secretion of HMGB1 from non-immune canine mammary epithelial cells (MTH53A). Cytokine 2012;57:210–220.

[73] Grunwald U, Fan XL, Jack RS, Workalemahu C, Kallies A, Stelter F, Schütt C. Monocytes can phagocytose gram-negative bacteria by a CD14-dependent mechanism. J Immunol 1996;157:4119–4125.

[74] Savill JS, Wyllie AH, Henson JE, Walport MJ, Henson PM, Haslett C. Macrophage phagocytosis of aging neutrophil in inflammation. Programmed cell death in the neutrophil leads to its recognition by macrophages. J Clin Invest 1989;83:865–875.

[75] Kokkola R, Sundberg E, Ulfgren AK, Palmblad K, Li J, Wang H, Ulloa L, Yang H, Yan XJ, Furie R, Chiorazzi N, Tracey KJ, Andersson U, Erlandsson H. High mobility group box chromosomal protein 1 a novel proinflammatory mediator in synovitis. Arthritis Rheum 2002;46:2598–2603.

[76] Nagl M, Kacani L, Müllauer B, Lemberger EM, Stoiber H, Sprinzl GM, Schennach H, Dierich MP. Phagocytosis and killing of bacteria by professional phagocytes and dendritic cells. Clin Diagn Lab Immunol 2002;9:1165–1168.

[77] Shi C, Velázquez P, Hohl TM, Leiner I, Dustin ML, Pamer EG. Monocyte trafficking to hepatic sites of bacterial infection is chemokine independent and directed by focal intercellular adhesion molecule-1 expression. J Immunol 2010;184:6266–6274.

[78] Lund PK, Namorkb E, Brorsonc SH, Westvika ÅB, Joøa B, Øvstebøa R, Kierulf P. The fate of monocytes during 24 h of culture as revealed by flow cytometry and electron microscopy. J Immunol Methods 2002;270:63–76.

[79] Bhatia M, Brady M, Shokuhi S, Christmas S, Neoptolemos JP, Slavin J. Inflammatory mediators in acute pancreatitis. J Pathol 2000;190:117–125.

[80] Kevin NC, Daniel GB, Eleanor MR. IL-10: The master regulator of immunity to infection. J Immunol 2008;180:5771–5777.

[81] Geng Y, Gulbins E, Altman A, Lotz M. Monocyte deactivation by interleukin 10 via inhibition of tyrosine kinase activity and the Ras signaling pathway. Proc Natl Acad Sci 1994;91:8602–8606.

[82] Wang P, Wu P, Siegel M, Egan RW, Billah MM. IL-10 inhibits transcription of cytokine genes in human peripheral blood mononuclear cells. J Immunol 1994;153:811–816.

[83] Wang P, Wu P, Siegel MI, Egan RW, Billah MM. Interleukin (IL)-10 inhibits nuclear factor κB (NFκB) activation in human monocytes. J Biol Chem 1995;270:9558–9563.

[84] Schottelius AJG, Mayo MW, Sartor RB, Baldwin AS. Interleukin-10 signaling blocks inhibitor of κB kinase activity and nuclear factor κB DNA binding. J Biol Chem 1999;274:31868–31873.

[85] Wan FY, Lenardo MJ. Specification of DNA binding activity of NF-kB proteins. Cold Spring Harb Perspect Biol 2009;1:a000067.

[86] Figuera-Losada M, LoGrasso PV. Enzyme kinetics and interaction studies for human JNK1β1 and substrates activating transcription factor 2 (ATF2) and c-Jun N-terminal kinase (c-Jun). J Biol Chem 2012;287:13291–13302.

[87] Dhooge A, Govaerts W, Kuznetsov YA. Numerical continuation of fold bifurcations of limit cycles in MATCONT. Comput Sci 2003;2657:701–710.

[88] Hassard B, Wan YH. Bifurcation formulae derived from center manifold theory. J Math Anal Appl 1978;63:297–312.

[89] Van der Poll T, Marchant A, Buurman WA. Endogenous IL-10 protects mice from death during septic peritonitis. J Immunol 1995;155:5397–5401.

[90] Remick DG, Garg SJ, Newcomb DE. Exogenous interleukin-10 fails to decrease the mortality or morbidity of sepsis. Crit Care Med 1998;26:895–904.

[91] Demols A, Goldman M, Moine OL, Geerts A, Deviére J. Interleukin-10 controls neutrophilic infiltration, hepatocyte proliferation, and liver fibrosis induced by carbon tetrachloride in mice. Hepatology 1998;28:1607–1615.

[92] Brooks DG, Trifilo MJ, Edelmann KH, Teyton L, McGavern DB, Oldstone MBA. Interleukin-10 determines viral clearance or persistence in vivo. Nat Med 2006;12:1301–1309.

[93] Aziz M, Jacob A, Yang WL, Matsuda A, Wang P. Current trends in inflammatory and immunomodulatory mediators in sepsis. J Leukoc Biol 2013;93:1–14.

PART II

ANALYTICS FOR HEALTHCARE DELIVERY

9

SYSTEMS ANALYTICS: MODELING AND OPTIMIZING CLINIC WORKFLOW AND PATIENT CARE

Eva K. Lee

Center for Operations Research in Medicine and HealthCare, Atlanta, GA, USA; NSF I/UCRC Center for Health Organization Transformation, Industrial and Systems Engineering, Atlanta, GA, USA; Georgia Institute of Technology, Atlanta, GA, USA

Hany Y. Atallah

Grady Health System, Atlanta, GA, USA; Department of Emergency Medicine, Emory University School of Medicine, Atlanta, GA, USA

Michael D. Wright

Grady Health System, Atlanta, GA, USA

Calvin Thomas IV

Health Ivy Tech Community College, Indianapolis, IN, USA

Eleanor T. Post

Rockdale Medical Center, Conyers, GA, USA

Daniel T. Wu

Grady Health System, Atlanta, GA, USA; Department of Emergency Medicine, Emory University School of Medicine, Atlanta, GA, USA

Leon L. Haley Jr

Grady Health System, Atlanta, GA, USA; Department of Emergency Medicine, Emory University School of Medicine, Atlanta, GA, USA

9.1   INTRODUCTION

The US healthcare system is considered the most expensive in the world ($8508 per capita). Unfortunately, the United States consistently underperforms relative to other western industrialized countries on many fronts, including quality, access, efficiency, equity, and healthy lives. The reforms brought about by the Affordable Care Act can be expected to boost access and equity by providing health insurance to some of the 50 million people who previously lacked it. However, many problems of our healthcare system remain challenging and pervasive, and it will take more than better access and equity to resolve them.

Over the years, the Institute of Medicine has highlighted longstanding systemic inefficiencies in US health care, with ongoing reports of inadequate safety, variable quality, and runaway costs. In its 2001 report, "Crossing the Quality Chasm: A New Health System for the 21st Century" (IOM [1]), it designated "efficiency" and "timeliness" as two of six key aims for improvement in health care. The recent report to the President "Better health care and lower costs: Accelerating improvement through systems engineering" offers glimpses of successes and encouraging steps; it also emphasizes the urgent need for further advances from the research and the practice communities [2].

This chapter focuses on recent advances on "timeliness," "efficiency," and "quality" of patient care that our team has helped to implement in several hospitals in the United States. In the writing, we focus our discussion on emergency departments (EDs). However, the methods are generalizable and have been applied successfully in other units including intensive care, pharmacy, the operating room, the step-down, primary care, and some specialty settings.

Over the past two decades, ED crowding and delays have become serious issues for hospitals and health systems in the United States. ED visits have increased by more than 2 million per year, characterized by patients who were older and sicker, and thus required more complex, time-consuming workups (i.e., complete medical examinations, including medical history, physical exam, laboratory tests, X-rays, and analysis) and treatments, and by nonurgent patients who use the ED in place of primary care facilities. The National Hospital Ambulatory Medical Care survey [3] reported 130 million ED visits in 2010. Despite increased demand, 19 hospitals closed in 2011. In 2012, hospitals reported that more than 40% of ED patient visits were for nonurgent care, contributing to long waiting times, decreased quality and timeliness of care, and decreased patient satisfaction. Numerous reports have questioned the ability of US EDs to handle this increasing demand for emergency services [4–10].

This chapter summarizes our work on advancing clinic workflow and patient care that was named second prize for the 2013 INFORMS Daniel H. Wagner Prize for Excellence in Operations Research Practice [11] and a finalist for the 2014 INFORMS Franz Edelman Award Achievement in Operations Research [12].

The content of this chapter, starting from the following paragraph, is excerpted from the Interfaces Edelman–Wagner published article [12].

This project showcases the transformation that can happen when operations research (OR) is applied to improve a hospital's ED operations. Working with Grady Memorial Hospital (also referred to as Grady Hospital or Grady), we devised a customizable model and decision-support system that couples machine learning, simulation, and optimization to help hospitals improve effectiveness in their EDs. Part of the Grady Health System, Grady Hospital is the fifth largest safety net hospital in the United States; these hospitals provide a disproportionate amount of care to vulnerable populations (US Department of Health and Human Services [13]). Grady implemented our decision-support system with beneficial results, such as reduced length of stay (LOS), patient waiting times, and readmissions (i.e., repeat admissions related to an initial admission), and improved efficiencies and throughput, all without investing additional funds or resources. Subsequently, 20 other hospitals implemented our system and also achieved beneficial results.

Grady's ED, which is a level 1 trauma center, operates the country's largest hospital-based ambulance service. Its ED receives more than 125,000 patient visits per year, more than 20,000 of whom are trauma patients. Grady provides critical services to Georgia's health system. It is home to Georgia's only poison control center, the area's first primary stroke center, and Georgia's first cancer center for excellence. Its extended trauma facilities include surgical suites, burn units, the LifeFlight, and AngelFlight air medical transport programs; Angel II neonatal transport units; and an emergency medical service ambulance program.

Grady serves a large population of uninsured patients and diverse socioeconomic groups. Of more than 621,000 annual patient visits, only 8% of these patients are privately insured (vs 50% nationally). In 2007, Grady "was in desperate need of more than $200 million to remain solvent. Grady's financial collapse has serious consequences not just for metro Atlanta – its crisis could reverberate across the state ... Experts say its inefficient customer service and general administration have created this financial crisis of epic proportions" [14]. In the midst of this financial crisis, a new management team came on board to rescue the hospital and transform its operations. The new leadership was committed to serious ED system transformation and initiated a joint collaboration with our team of operations researchers. Through extensive data collection and vigorous OR analytical advances and recommendations, Grady adopted the transformative steps, which included addressing readmissions, quality, and efficiency of care before the Affordable Care Act and its associated penalties were put in place.

The ED crisis is being experienced across the nation. In January 2014, the American College of Emergency Physicians ranked [nationwide] ED access as D+ to reflect "that hospitals are not getting the necessary support in order to provide effective and efficient emergency care" [15]. Grady feels a more-than-average burden; it treats all patients, whether or not they have insurance. For each service that it provides, it incurs costs for which it will be reimbursed only a small portion. In addition, many critically ill patients (including referrals from other EDs) are routed to Grady because of the excellent specialty care that it provides.

The novelty of our Edelman–Wagner prize work with Grady has five main aspects. To the best of our knowledge, these have not been incorporated in previous methods or studies.

1. We optimize within the ED system simulation, rather than relying on a scenario-based method, so that the results more closely approach global optima. The global solution involves aligning and consolidating operations, optimizing staffing, and optimizing processes.
2. We dynamically and stochastically incorporate treatment patterns and patient characteristics within an agent-based simulation, while focusing on ED operations and quality improvement.
3. We model ED readmissions using data that simultaneously encompass demographics, socioeconomic status, clinical information, hospital operations, and disease behavioral patterns.
4. We explicitly model the interdependencies to and from the ED with numerous other hospital departments, capturing inefficiencies in those processes.
5. We integrate machine learning within the simulation–optimization framework.

We also note that in our work, all medical terms and related metrics are defined as is customary in the medical community.

From a hospital's perspective, healthcare leaders have acknowledged that this work advances ED operations in several ways, which we describe in Section 9.6. From an OR perspective, the collaboration this project engendered and the challenges it presented have led to both theoretical and computational advances in optimization and simulation.

9.2 BACKGROUND

Crowded ED conditions have sparked research on several fronts. Eitel et al. [16] discussed different methods for improving ED quality and flow, including demand management, critical pathways, process mapping, emergency severity-index triage, bedside registration, and lean and six sigma management methods [17]. Popovich et al. [18] developed a volume-driven protocol and implemented it through the use of published evidence, which focused on essential endpoints of measurement. Wiler et al. [19] evaluated interventions, such as immediate bedding, bedside registration, advanced triage, physician and (or) practitioner at triage, and dedicated fast-track service lines, all of which are considered potential solutions to streamline the front-end processing of ED patients. Ashby et al. [20] optimized patient flow throughout the inpatient units, while modeling and observing the impacts on other interdependent parts of the hospital, such as the ED and operating rooms. Kolker [21] tried to establish a quantitative relationship between ED performance characteristics, such as percentage of time on ambulance diversion and the number of patients in queue in the waiting room, and the upper limits of patient LOS. Moskop et al. [22] identified and described operational and financial barriers to resolving the crisis of ED crowding; they also proposed a variety of institutional and public policy strategies to overcome those barriers. Nugus et al. [23] used an ethnographic approach, which involves direct observation of on-the-ground behaviors, observing interactions among physicians and nurses, emergency clinicians, and clinicians from other hospital departments to identify indicators of and responses to pressure in the day-to-day ED work environment. DeFlitch et al. [24] reported provider-directed queuing for improving ED operations. McCarthy et al. [25] used discrete-time survival analysis to determine the effects of crowding on ED department waiting room, treatment, and boarding times (i.e., the time spent in the ED after the decision has been made to admit the patient to the hospital) across multiple sites and acuity levels. Sturm et al. [26] identified predictors that can influence nonurgent pediatric ED utilization.

9.3 CHALLENGES AND OBJECTIVES

Although some of the ED advances have been successful, the improvement is often not sustainable, or it redirects inefficiencies from one area of the ED to another, or to other hospital divisions. Poor results from these approaches are partly because the requisite data are very time consuming to collect, often resulting in poor data being entered into a model. In addition, a model may be flawed if important elements and system dependencies are overlooked in its design.

Readmissions are a key challenge in ED performance. In particular, avoidable readmissions (i.e., readmissions resulting from an adverse event that occurred during the initial admission or from inappropriate care coordination following discharge) through the ED have become a major burden on the US health system (see [27]). Recent research shows that nearly one in five patients are readmitted to the discharging hospital within 30 days of discharge; these readmissions accounted for $17.8 billion in Medicare spending in 2004 [28].

Numerous studies have been conducted to identify frequently readmitted patients' characteristics and construct patient profiles to aid hospitals in predicting these patients. These studies have identified a number of demographic and clinical factors that are thought to significantly correlate with readmission. Other factors concerning hospital operations have also been investigated. Various statistical tools have been used to identify patient factors that are associated with readmissions [29–32]. Westert et al. [33] conducted an international study, including three US states and three countries, to find patterns in the profiles of readmitted patients. The findings are divided into demographic and social factors, clinical factors [30, 34], and hospital operations factors [33, 35–39]. A study of 26 readmission risk-prediction models concluded that after reviewing 7843 citations, none of the models analyzed could suitably predict future hospital readmissions [40]. Allaudeen et al. [41] noted that healthcare personnel could not accurately predict the readmission of patients discharged from their own hospitals; however, conclusions from these studies may be premature, given that much of the analyses were performed via logistic regression on only subsets of data.

We recently published a readmission study in which, for the first time, a predictive model can incorporate comprehensive factors related to demographics and socioeconomic status, clinical and hospital resources, operations and utilization, and patient complaints and risk factors for global prediction [42]. Our approach empowers healthcare providers with good predictive capability, which we generalized for this Grady study.

The Affordable Care Act, its influence on Medicaid and Medicare payments, the high cost of emergency care, the persistent nonurgent visits, and the penalties imposed because of inappropriate readmissions and hospital-related health problems demand transformation of ED patient care and workflow.

The Edelman–Wagner project focuses on large-scale systems' modeling and decision analytics for modeling and optimizing the workflow for an ED [12]. Specifically, we aim to improve workflow, reduce wait time, improve quality and timeliness of care, and reduce the number of avoidable readmissions. Although most studies incorporate simulation to model ED operations and perform scenario-based improvement (e.g., [43]), we believe that our model is the first to intertwine machine learning, simulation, and optimization into one system in which (i) the ED patient characteristics are analyzed and patterns uncovered, and (ii) operations and workflow are modeled and resources optimized within the system to achieve the best performance outcome.

Grady began an ED process transformation with our OR team in 2008. At that time, the average patient LOS in its ED exceeded 10 h. LOS represents the time between a patient's arrival at the ED and the time that patient is discharged from the ED or admitted to the hospital. Thus, LOS includes the door-to-provider time, the time the patient waits for the service and receives care, and the boarding time. Hence, LOS is often dominated by long stretches of nonservice times. Grady's goal was to achieve an LOS of close to 7 h and reduce its readmissions rate by 25%. We refer to the period from the beginning of the study in 2008 to the time of the sustained improved performance (July 2011) as Phase I. As a result of the Phase I improvements, the hospital was able to use sponsored funds to open a walk-in center for low-acuity patients, further driving down costs and LOS [44]. In addition, the implementation of an electronic medical record (EMR) system in October 2010 has enabled the administration to better track hospital operations. Because of the alternative care options and the addition of a new dedicated 15-bed trauma center, the dynamics of ED patient visits have changed. Phase II captures the period of ED advances from 2011 to the present. This chapter is excerpted from the Edelman–Wagner paper that summarizes the OR analytic, system-driven advances in the ED, and their associated performance outcomes during these two phases. By design, the two phases overlap.

9.4   METHODS AND DESIGN OF STUDY

Figure 9.1 highlights the study schema and the interdependencies of our methods. The human-centered computational modeling environment comprises data analytics served by innovative OR predictive decision tools. We simultaneously explore patterns of patient behavior and care characteristics, provider decision and process

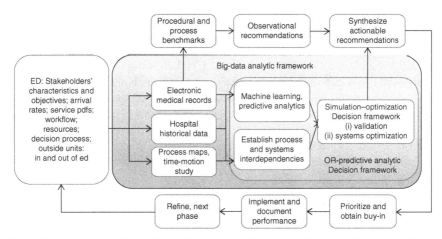

Figure 9.1 This figure shows the study schema and interdependencies of the analytic framework that we use. These interdependencies are crucial to achieving a valid description of the actual processes. Reproduced from Lee et al. [12] with permission of the Institute for Operations Research and the Management Sciences.

workflow, facility-layout design, and staffing, where resource allocation, cognitive human behavior, and care patterns are optimized globally for best outcomes, as measured by LOS and readmissions. Uncovering patterns in patient care helps to appropriately align resources with demands and enables providers to better anticipate needs. Exploring facility design provides decision makers with the envisioned improvement before they embark on an expensive layout redesign effort.

In the following, we detail the major steps in our study.

9.4.1 ED Workflow and Services

Patients who visit the ED for care are evaluated first at the triage area to determine the severity of their injuries and (or) conditions. They are assigned an acuity level based on the emergency severity index (ESI), a five-level index for prioritizing ED patients for care, ranging from level 1 (emergent and requiring multiple resources) to level 5 (nonurgent and least resource intensive). The ESI is unique among triage tools because it categorizes ED patients by both acuity and resource needs.

At Grady, the blue zone is used to treat high-acuity patients (levels 1 and 2) and all prisoners, except those with significant trauma. (Note that a detention area for prisoners is located inside the blue zone, and prisoner patients are registered in the blue-zone treatment area.) A major resuscitation room anchors this area, which also includes eight critical care rooms, seven respiratory isolation rooms, and several general-patient care areas. The red zone is used to treat general patients. This area has general-care rooms; an orthopedic room; a gynecology evaluation room; and an eye, ear, nose, and throat room. All rooms in the blue and red zones are capable of cardiac monitoring. In 2010, based on our Phase I results, Grady added a clinical decision unit. This unit provides an alternative to admission to the main hospital by providing observation services for those patients who have already received treatment in the ED. All patients in the clinical decision unit are evaluated by a case manager who helps coordinate care, provide education, and ensure appropriate follow-up. A patient who is not improving is sent to the hospital's main building for admission.

The mission of the patient ambulatory care express (PACe) area is to treat patients with relatively minor conditions. The PACe facility operates 24 h a day, 7 days a week, and is staffed primarily by nurse practitioners and physician assistants. The trauma center is designed to treat patients with trauma levels 1, 2, and 3, as categorized by the American Trauma Society [45]. Trauma operating rooms are staffed 24 h a day year-round.

Patients arriving in an ambulance or other vehicle enter the ED through the ambulance arrival area, which is separate from the walk-in area. Here, patients determined to be ESI level 1 or 2 will be triaged and sent directly to the blue or red zone. Levels 3 and 4 patients are triaged, sent to the ED waiting room, and enter the same queue as the patients in the walk-in area to wait for a bed in either zone. Walk-in patients, some of whom may not be assigned an acuity level, are treated by the walk-in triage physician and discharged from there.

Table 9.1 summarizes the ED patient care and resources, excluding the walk-in. Figure 9.2a–d shows the workflow process maps at the start of our study.

9.4.2 Data Collection and Time-Motion Studies

In this section, we discuss the two phases of our study.

9.4.2.1 Phase I From August 2008 through February 2009, multiple trained observers collected ED data by reviewing files and charts and conducting interviews and time-motion studies related to services at various stations, as guided by the process maps. The data collected in this manner contain 45,983 data fields covering 2509 patients. In addition, the hospital maintained vital statistics, including acuity level, LOS, and discharge data. Grady also provided readmission status for 42,456 patients. Furthermore, we received more than 40,000 individual service times for laboratory turnaround – the amount of time between the time a laboratory receives a specimen and the time that the results are available.

9.4.2.2 Phase II In Phase II, data from 16,217 patient visits from October 28, 2010 to December 31, 2010 were pulled from the EMR system. For each visit, data include patient information, ED admission time, hospital discharge time, acuity level, ED zones, diagnosis, and insurance type. The EMR records also include time stamps for relevant events, including registration, triage, laboratory orders and results, doctor assessment, observation, and discharge. We supplemented the EMR ED data with observations and time-motion studies at the triage and registration areas, and sampled treatment time and wait time inside the rooms by shadowing various care providers.

TABLE 9.1   Zones, Patient and Worker Types, and Resource Availability

	Patient Type	Space/Beds		Worker Type		
		2008	2010	Attending Physicians	Mid-Level Providers	Nurses
Triage	All			Yes	Nurse practitioners, physician assistants	Yes
Blue zone (acuity levels 1 and 2)	High-acuity patients and all prisoners without significant trauma	34	37	Yes	Residents	Yes
Red zone (acuity levels 2 and 3)	General patients	25	21	Yes	Residents	Yes
Clinical decision unit	Treated ED patients who need observation	0	7	Yes	No	Yes
PACe (acuity levels 4 and 5)	Patients with relatively minor conditions	8	8	No	Nurse practitioners, physician assistants	Yes
Trauma center	Patients who meet either trauma level 1, 2, 3 criteria, in addition to any child involved in a traumatic accident, any patient arriving on a backboard, all gunshots and stab victims, and patients with complex extremity injuries or burns	4	15	Yes	Residents	Yes

Source: Reproduced from Lee et al. [12] with permission of the Institute for Operations Research and the Management Sciences.

By identifying the responsibilities of each type of worker via shadowing in the ED and reviewing the EMR system patient timeline, we found variability and randomness in arrival and treatment processes and workers' responsibilities. The variability emerges from the delivery practices of the nurses, mid-level practitioners, and attending physicians. Our model may not describe each case in the ED; however, it represents more than 93% of the cases.

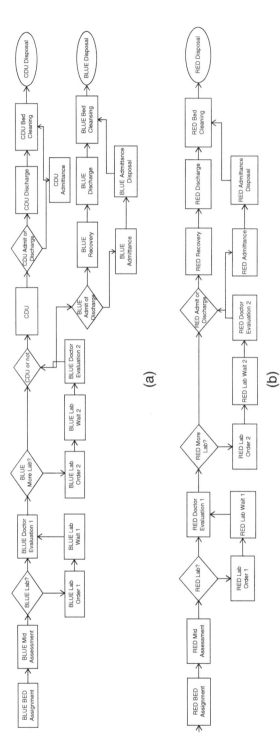

Figure 9.2 (a) The flowchart shows the workflow process map for the blue zone. Reproduced from Lee et al. [12] with permission of the Institute for Operations Research and the Management Sciences. (b) The flowchart shows the workflow process map for the red zone. Reproduced from Lee et al. [12] with permission of the Institute for Operations Research and the Management Sciences. (c) The flowchart shows the workflow process map for the PACe. Reproduced from Lee et al. [12] with permission of the Institute for Operations Research and the Management Sciences. (d) The flowchart shows the workflow process map for the trauma center. Reproduced from Lee et al. [12] with permission of the Institute for Operations Research and the Management Sciences.

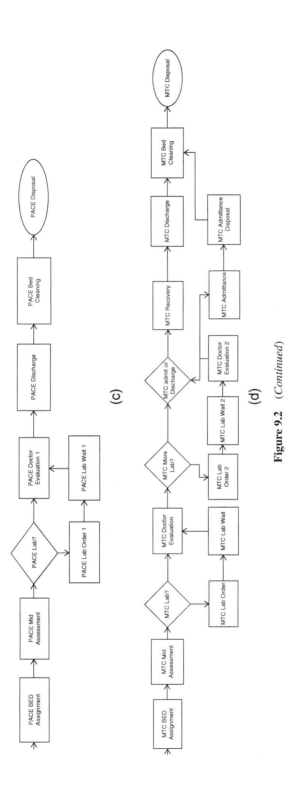

Figure 9.2 (*Continued*)

9.4.3   Machine Learning for Predicting Patient Characteristics and Return Patterns

Armed with comprehensive data, we first developed machine learning techniques to uncover patient characteristics, including resource needs, treatment outcome, LOS and readmission patterns, and to establish predictive rules. A significant contribution of our work is that it is the first study in which demographics, socioeconomic status, clinical information, hospital operations, and disease behavioral patterns are employed simultaneously as attributes within a machine learning framework.

The computational design of our machine learning framework utilizes a wrapper approach; specifically, we apply pattern recognition based on our recent advances on text mining for unstructured clinical notes to the input attributes [46]. Next, we couple a combinatorial attribute-selection algorithm with a discriminant analysis via a mixed-integer program (DAMIP) learning and classification module. The attribute selection, classification, and cross-validation procedures are wrapped so that the attribute-selection algorithm searches through the space of attribute subsets using the cross-validation accuracy from the classification module as a measure of goodness. The small subset of attributes returned from the machine learning analysis can be viewed as critical patient and clinical and (or) hospital variables that drive service characteristics. This provides feedback to clinical decision makers for prioritization and intervention of patients and tasks.

In the Edelman–Wagner ED study, entities correspond to patients. The input attributes for each patient include comprehensive demographics, socioeconomic status, clinical information, hospital resources and utilization, and disease behavioral patterns. The machine learning uncovers patient disease patterns, associated resource needs, and factors influencing treatment characteristics and outcome. For readmission, there are two statuses for patients: they come back to the hospital for visits (return group), or they do not come back (nonreturn group). The classification aims to uncover from the set of all attributes a set of discriminatory attributes that can classify each patient into the return or nonreturn group. We seek to identify the rule that offers the best predictive capability.

In this supervised classification approach, the status of each patient in the training set is known. The training set consists of a group of patients extracted from the hospital database whose status (e.g., returned within 72 h after the first visit or within 30 days after the first visit) is known. The training data are input into the machine learning framework. Through the attribute-selection algorithm, a subset of attributes is selected to form a classification rule. This rule is then used to perform 10-fold cross-validation on the training set to obtain an unbiased estimate.

In 10-fold cross-validation, the training set is randomly partitioned into 10 roughly equal subsets. Of the 10 subsets, 1 subset is retained as the validation data for testing the model, and the remaining 9 subsets are used as training data. The cross-validation process is then repeated 10 times (the folds), with each of the 10 subsets used exactly once as the validation data. The 10 results from the folds can then be added to produce an unbiased estimation. The advantage of this method over repeated random subsampling is that all observations are used for both training and validation, and each observation is used exactly once for validation.

To gauge the predictive power of the rule, we perform blind prediction on an independent set of patients; these patients have never been used in attribute selection. We run each patient through the rule, which returns a status. We then give the hospital personnel the predicted status of each patient, which they check against the patient's actual status. Hence, we always compare our prediction with the actual outcome in measuring predictive accuracy.

Once our machine learning system sends a trigger that a particular patient is highly likely to return, an expert human (usually a nurse) places this patient on a to-observe list. That our predictions are not 100% accurate is understandable; however, the first pass is critical because it narrows down the return to a very small subset of patients, allowing the human expert to focus on them to determine which patients in this selected set should be observed in the clinical decision unit. Learning is continuous because human experts may identify attributes that they will use in their second pass of selection. These attributes will then be incorporated into our system for learning and refinement. Lee et al. [47], Lee [48], Lee and Wu [49], Brooks and Lee [50], and Brooks and Lee [51] detail the DAMIP modeling and its theoretical and computational contributions. In the following, we include the mathematical formulation and a brief explanation of how it works within this ED study.

Optimization-Based Classifier: Discriminant Analysis via Mixed-Integer Program (DAMIP) We assume there are n entities (e.g., patients) from K groups (e.g., returning or nonreturning) with m features. Let $\mathcal{G} = \{1, 2, \dots, K\}$ be the group index set, $\mathcal{O} = \{1, 2, \dots, n\}$ be the entity index set, and $\mathcal{F} = \{1, 2, \dots, m\}$ be the feature index set. Also, let $\mathcal{O}_k$, $k \in \mathcal{G}$, and $\mathcal{O}_k \subseteq \mathcal{O}$, be the entity set that belongs to group k. Moreover, let $\mathcal{F}_j$, $j \in \mathcal{F}$, be the domain of feature j, which could be the space of real, integer, or binary values. The ith entity, $i \in \mathcal{O}$, is represented as $(y_i, x_i) = (y_i, x_{i1}, \dots, x_{im}) \in \mathcal{G} \times \mathcal{F}_1 \times \cdots \times \mathcal{F}_m$, where y_i is the group to which entity i belongs, and $(x_{i1}, \dots, x_{im})$ is the feature vector of entity i. The classification model finds a function $\psi : (\mathcal{F}_1 \times \dots \times \mathcal{F}_m) \to \mathcal{G}$ to classify entities into groups based on a selected set of features.

Let π_k be the prior probability of a randomly chosen entity being in group k and $f_k(x)$ be the group conditional probability density function for the entity $x \in \mathbb{R}^m$ of group k, $k \in \mathcal{G}$. Also let n_h denote the number of entities from group h, and $\alpha_{hk} \in (0, 1)$, $h, k \in \mathcal{G}$, $h \neq k$, be the upper bound for the misclassification percentage that group h entities are misclassified into group k. DAMIP seeks a partition $\{P_0, P_1, \dots, P_K\}$ of $\mathbb{R}^K$, where P_k, $k \in \mathcal{G}$, is the region for group k, and P_0 is the reserved-judgment region with entities for which group assignment are reserved (for potential further exploration).

Let u_{ki} be the binary variable to denote if entity i is classified to group k. Mathematically, DAMIP can be formulated as follows [47, 48]:

$$\text{Max} \quad \sum_{i \in \mathcal{O}} u_{y_i i} \tag{D1}$$

$$\text{subject to} \quad L_{ki} = \pi_k f_k(x_i) - \sum_{h \in \mathcal{G}, h \neq k} f_h(x_i)\lambda_{hk}, \qquad \forall i \in \mathcal{O}, k \in \mathcal{G} \tag{D2}$$

$$u_{ki} = \begin{cases} 1 & \text{if } k = \arg\max\{0, L_{hi} : h \in \mathcal{G}\} \\ 0 & \text{otherwise} \end{cases}, \quad \forall i \in \mathcal{O}, k \in \{0\} \cup \mathcal{G} \quad \text{(D3)}$$

$$\sum_{k \in \{0\} \cup \mathcal{G}} u_{ki} = 1 \qquad\qquad\qquad \forall i \in \mathcal{O} \qquad\qquad \text{(D4)}$$

$$\sum_{i: i \in \mathcal{O}_h} u_{ki} \le \lfloor \alpha_{hk} n_h \rfloor, \qquad\qquad \forall h, k \in \mathcal{G}, h \ne k \qquad \text{(D5)}$$

$$u_{ki} \in \{0, 1\}, \qquad\qquad\qquad \forall i \in \mathcal{O}, \ k \in \{0\} \cup \mathcal{G}$$

$$L_{ki} \text{ unrestricted in sign}, \qquad\qquad \forall i \in \mathcal{O}, k \in \mathcal{G}$$

$$\lambda_{hk} \ge 0, \qquad\qquad\qquad \forall h, k \in \mathcal{G}, h \ne k$$

The objective function (D1) maximizes the number of entities classified into the correct group. Constraints (D2) and (D3) govern the placement of an entity into each of the groups in $\mathcal{G}$ or the reserved-judgment region. Thus, the variables L_{ki} and λ_{hk} provide the shape of the partition of the groups in the $\mathcal{G}$ space. Constraint (D4) ensures that an entity is assigned to exactly one group. Constraint (D5) allows the users to pre-set the desirable misclassification levels, which can be specified as overall errors for each group, pairwise errors, or overall errors for all groups together. With the reserved judgment in place, the mathematical system ensures that a solution that satisfies the preset errors always exists.

Mathematically, we have proven that DAMIP is *NP-hard* and that the resulting classification rule is strongly universally consistent, given that the Bayes optimal rule for classification is known [50, 51]. In addition, DAMIP model generates stable and robust classification rules, regardless of the proportions of training entities from each group. Computationally, DAMIP is the first multiple-group classification model that includes a reserved judgment and the ability to constrain the misclassification rates simultaneously within the model. Furthermore, we have demonstrated in real-world applications that DAMIP works well on biomedical applications [26, 42, 47–53]. In Brooks and Lee [50, 51], we have shown that DAMIP is difficult to solve, and we applied the hypergraphic structures that Lee and Maheshwary [54] and Lee et al. [55] derived to efficiently solve these instances. Empirically, DAMIP can handle imbalanced data well; thus, it is suitable for the ED readmission analysis, when compared against other classification approaches [42].

The predictive model maximizes the number of correctly classified cases; therefore, it is robust and not skewed by errors committed by observation values. The associated optimal decision variable values (L_{ki} and λ_{hk}) form the classification rule, which consists of the discriminatory attributes; examples include patient chief complaint, diagnosis, whether IV antibiotics were ordered, trainee and (or) resident involved, primary nurse, time when the patient received an ED bed to time until first medical doctor arrived. Using this rule, blind prediction of whether a new patient will return to the ED can be performed in real time.

One can use alternative objectives, for example, by placing different weights on each group. In Lee [48], we discuss various alternative objectives that take into account differences in the relative cost of different types of classification errors [42]. We tested these alternatives on the Grady data and report the best combination in the Edelman–Wagner ED paper [12].

9.4.4 The Computerized ED System Workflow Model

To establish a framework for modeling and optimizing the ED workflow, including ED processes and dependencies on other hospital divisions when discharging patients from the ED, we use the RealOpt© simulation–optimization decision-support environment [56–62]. RealOpt was developed at Georgia Tech for the purpose of optimizing operations, throughput, and resource allocation for public health resources, in particular for emergency response and public health medical preparedness. It includes easy-to-use drawing tools to permit users to enter the workflow via mouse clicks and keystrokes. It also allows incorporation of the stochastic nature of human behavior (both the servers and patients) in workflows and processes and provides a method to model fatigue and stress factors. In the background, it translates the workflow into a computerized simulation model in which resources can be optimized to achieve the best throughput and system performance. Figure 9.3a shows the (simplified) clinic workflow and service zones for Grady's ED, as entered into RealOpt via its graph-drawing panel.

Figure 9.3b shows the average total time to admit a patient from the ED to different units of the hospital. Note that until the patient is admitted elsewhere, ED resources (in particular, the patient's bed) are not free to assign to a new patient. This information forms part of our RealOpt model for systems optimization.

Within RealOpt, optimization is performed to ensure the best operations and system performance (e.g., throughput, wait time, queue length, utilization). The resource allocation is modeled via a nonlinear mixed-integer program (NMIP). Resources include labor, equipment, and beds, and so on. Constraints in the model include (i) maximum limits on wait time and queue length, which are dictated by the capacity of the waiting room in most EDs, and the desire to quickly service patients; (ii) range of utilization desired at each station; (iii) for each resource group, assignability and availability of resource types at each station (i.e., the skill set and the number of skilled personnel available); and (iv) maximum limit on the cycle time of the individual (i.e., ED LOS). In the following, we briefly describe the resource allocation model [12, 56, 57, 60, 61].

Nonlinear Mixed-Integer Program for Multiple-Resource Allocation The NMIP used in allocating resources was built on top of the nonlinear MIP formulated in Lee et al. [57] and solved using the simulation–optimization framework described in Lee et al. [56].

Mathematically, the model parameters are defined as follows:

- R: the set of resource groups;
- T_r: the set of resource types in resource group r, $r \in R$;
- S: the set of services in the process flow;
- $S_{ir} \subseteq S$: the set of services in which resource type i in resource group r can be assigned. This models the assignability of the resource (e.g., based on skills of workers);
- k_{ijr}: the cost of assigning a resource of type i in resource group r to station j. $r \in R, i \in T_r, j \in S_{ir}$;
- $\overline{m_{ijr}}$ and $\underline{m_{ijr}}$: the maximum and minimum number of resources of type i in resource group r that may be assigned to station j. $r \in R, i \in T_r, j \in S_{ir}$;

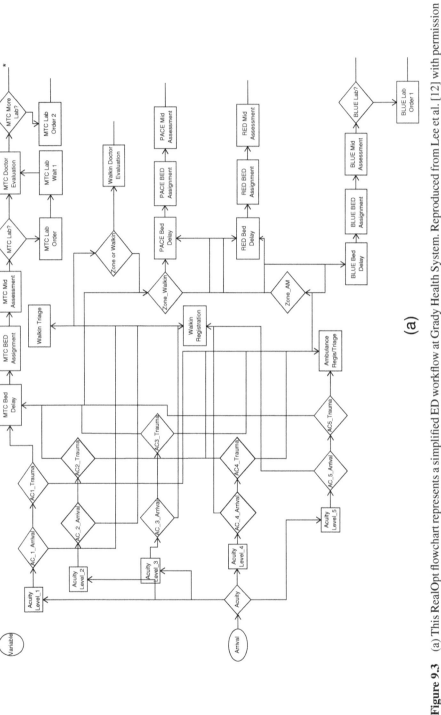

Figure 9.3 (a) This RealOpt flowchart represents a simplified ED workflow at Grady Health System. Reproduced from Lee et al. [12] with permission of the Institute for Operations Research and the Management Sciences. (b) The figure shows discharge destinations for October 2009 ED patients and the time taken from ED disposition to actual departure for each destination. Destinations are the telemedicine sign-up, intensive care unit, floor (normally staffed inpatient unit), isolation unit, and the step-down unit (provides intermediate care between the ICU and floor). Reproduced from Lee et al. [12] with permission of the Institute for Operations Research and the Management Sciences.

(a)

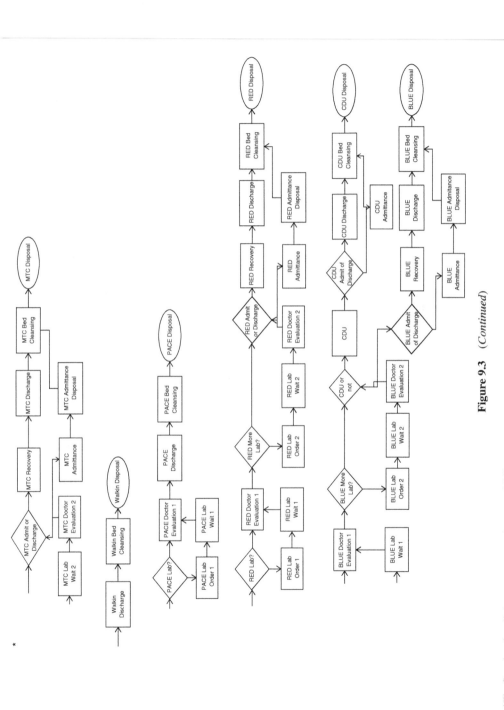

Figure 9.3 (*Continued*)

*The flowchart is split in two pages to enhance readability.

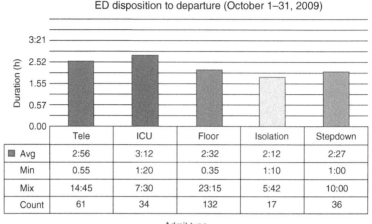

ED disposition to departure (October 1–31, 2009)

	Tele	ICU	Floor	Isolation	Stepdown
■ Avg	2:56	3:12	2:32	2:12	2:27
Min	0.55	1:20	0.35	1:10	1:00
Mix	14:45	7:30	23:15	5:42	10:00
Count	61	34	132	17	36

Admit type

(b)

Figure 9.3 *(Continued)*

- n_{ir}: the number of available resources of type i in resource group r. $r \in \mathbf{R}$, $i \in \mathbf{T}_r$;
- w_j, q_j, and u_j: the average wait time, average queue length, and average utilization rate, respectively, at station j. $j \in \mathbf{S}$;
- c: the average cycle time (i.e., the length of time a customer spends in the system); and
- θ: the average throughput (number of customers served in a specified period).

The decision variables for this problem are $x_{ijr} \in \mathbf{Z}_+$: the number of resources of type i in resource group r assigned to station j. $r \in \mathbf{R}$, $i \in \mathbf{T}_r$, $j \in \mathbf{S}_{ir}$.

We can represent the cost at each station j as $g_j(\sum_{(i,r) \in \Omega_j} k_{ijr} x_{ijr}, w_j, q_j, u_j)$, $j \in \mathbf{S}$, where $\Omega_j = \{(i,r)|r \in \mathbf{R}, i \in \mathbf{T}_r, j \in \mathbf{S}_{ir}\}$. The total system cost depends on the cost at each station and on system performance variables, such as cycle time and throughput. Thus, we can represent the total cost as $f\left(\sum_{j \in \mathbf{S}} g_j, c, \theta\right)$. Here, g_j and f are functions that are not necessarily expressible in closed form. We can formulate a general representation of the multiple-resource allocation problem as

$$\text{Min } z = f\left(\sum_{j \in \mathbf{S}} g_j, c, \theta\right) \tag{N0}$$

$$\text{subject to } \quad m_{ijr} \leq x_{ijr} \leq \overline{m_{ijr}}, \qquad \forall r \in \mathbf{R}, i \in \mathbf{T}_r, j \in \mathbf{S}_{ir} \tag{N1}$$

$$\sum_{j \in \mathbf{S}_{ir}} x_{ijr} \leq n_{ir}, \qquad \forall r \in \mathbf{R}, i \in \mathbf{T}_r \tag{N2}$$

$$w(x)_j \leq w_{max}$$

$$q(x)_j \leq q_{max}, \qquad\qquad \forall j \in \mathbf{S} \qquad\qquad (N3)$$

$$u_{min} \leq u(x)_j \leq u_{max}$$

$$\theta(x) \geq \theta_{min}$$

$$c(x) \leq c_{max} \qquad\qquad\qquad\qquad\qquad\qquad (N4)$$

$$x_{ijr} \in \mathbf{Z}_+, \qquad\qquad \forall r \in \mathbf{R}, i \in \mathbf{T}_r, j \in \mathbf{S}_{ir} \qquad (N5)$$

(N0)–(N2), (N3), (N4), (N5) form an NMIP problem for cost minimization under the constraints of multiple-resource allocation and stochastic system performance. For (N3), (N4), these are system parameters in the simulation and performance variables in the optimization. Due to the fact that some functions in the objective and constraints are not necessarily expressible in closed form, the problem is proven intractable by commercial systems. RealOpt© is designed to overcome such computational bottlenecks by interweaving rapid system simulation and optimization [56, 61, 63].

In all three papers [12, 56, 61], an initial solution is obtained via a fluid model as a warm start to a resource optimization model; the results of the optimization are entered into a simulation model that estimates the system's average wait time, queue length, and utilization. If the solution satisfies all the input ranges, this solution is returned. Otherwise, the system looks for violated constraints (from among wait time, queue length, and cycle time) and determines violated service blocks. Service blocks are all the services and (or) processes that a patient might undergo in an ED visit, including triage, registration, PACe examination, walk-in, and laboratory tests. Once these blocks are identified, optimization will be performed on them. This time, however, the objective is to minimize a total violation penalty. The process continues until convergence.

There are two key distinctions between this work and the earlier work by Lee (e.g., [56, 61]). First, machine learning that predicts patient pattern and treatment characteristics is integrated into the simulation–optimization decision framework. Second, this work models multiple-resource groups at each station. The optimization within each simulation step maximizes throughput without exceeding the existing resources and includes weights on how to use staff skills. For example, if a nurse and a physician can both perform a specific task, it may be more expensive to use a physician than a nurse (or vice versa). The user ranks them in the input, and we use these ranks as weights in the optimization process.

Integrating Machine Learning within the RealOpt Simulation–Optimization Environment As we describe earlier, machine learning is used to identify discriminatory attributes that can predict whether a patient will return to the ED. Within the simulation, an individual patient is simulated thoroughly, including medical conditions, arrival times, zones visited, and treatments received. Hence, in addition to modeling the hospital operations, it also characterizes each individual by disease type, risk factors, demographics, and payor types – knowledge that the machine learning analysis uncovers. Upon completion of a patient's treatment and before discharge, the machine learning classification rule is used within the simulation environment to predict whether that patient will return. If it predicts that the patient will return, it triggers an alarm; a nurse then determines whether the patient should be sent to the clinical decision unit for observation.

One of the novelties in the Edelman–Wagner ED work is the incorporation of patient characteristics and care patterns that the machine learning framework uncovers within the RealOpt simulation–optimization environment. Hence, agents (representing patients) within the simulation present disease symptoms that challenge the care providers. They mimic the behavior of returning patients for whom certain symptoms may not have been diagnosed properly during previous ED visits. Furthermore, the model captures more than 200 processes, including ED connected environments (e.g., discharge destinations and factors external to ED), which contribute to delays in the ED workflow. The optimization component connects the multiple-resource allocation, as we describe earlier, with process and operations optimization over the entire ED process network. The multiple-objective function values are evaluated through the simulation process.

9.4.5   Model Validation

Using the data collected, we simulated the hospital environment and operations and validated the simulation results against an independent set of 3 months of hospital data. The model returned ED LOS, throughput, wait time, queue length, and other system statistics that are useful for performance measurement and comparison. For brevity, Table 9.2 includes only LOS and throughput comparisons. The simulation results accurately reflect the existing ED system performance, with outcome metrics and performance statistics consistent with their actual hospital values.

The average characteristics of Grady's ED patients differ markedly from national averages, especially because so few have private insurance. In 2009 at Grady, only 8% of the ED patients had private insurance; more than 50% self-paid for the service, and Medicaid and Medicare paid for 36%. In contrast, nationally, approximately 50% of ED patients have private insurance. Moreover, Grady is burdened by return visits from uninsured individuals who use the ED as their primary care facility. Table 9.3a shows Grady's ED readmission statistics for November to December 2009, which were close to the national average.

Our goal in predicting readmissions is twofold: (i) capture the characteristics of the disease and treatment patterns of readmitted patients to incorporate their behavior within the simulation–optimization environment; and (ii) provide real-time guidance to ED providers to identify individuals (for observation) before discharge to mitigate the number of avoidable readmissions. Reducing the number of readmissions improves quality of care and provides financial and resource savings.

We apply the machine learning framework using a training set of 42,456 patients and blind predict using an independent set of 18,464 patients to gauge the predictive accuracies. Table 9.3b summarizes the results. We select those results in which both the specificity and sensitivity are above 70%. Note that for self-pay and Medicaid patients, the accuracy is below 70%. We also observe that predicting insured

TABLE 9.2 Actual and Simulated 30-Day Average LOS and Throughput at Grady Hospital

	Phase I: Train: August 2008–February 2009 Validate: March–May 2009				Phase II: Train: October–December 2010 Validate: January–March 2011			
	Hospital Statistics		Simulated Values		Hospital Statistics		Simulated Values	
ED zone	LOS (h)	Patient Volume[a]	LOS (h)	Patient Volume	LOS (h)	Patient Volume	LOS (h)	Patient Volume
Overall	10.59	8274	10.49	8446	7.97	8421	8.02	8398
Blue zone	14.54	2141	13.90	2137	11.40	2107	11.78	2126
Red zone	12.54	2097	11.96	2140	8.98	2083	8.37	2133
Trauma center[b]	7.85	271	7.98	251	6.80	268	6.86	259
Detention	13.85	437	12.93	407	10.90	441	10.53	432
PACe	7.90	2037	8.60	1983	5.10	1920	5.60	1983
Walk-in	3.20	990	3.30	992	2.50	950	2.88	940

[a]Remainder patients: 301 of the patients in this column include those who left before being seen, transferred to another facility, or provided no information.
[b]Remainder patients: These are airlift level 1 trauma patients. Grady treats roughly 1542 trauma patients per month; many enter through the ED and are treated in the blue zone.

Source: Reproduced from Lee et al. [12] with permission of the Institute for Operations Research and the Management Sciences.

TABLE 9.3a   ED Readmission Statistics for the Period from November to December 2009

November–December 2009		72-h Return		30-Day Return	
Acuity Level	Number of Visits	Number of Revisits	Percentage of Revisits	Number of Revisits	Percentage of Revisits
Total	15,168	824	5.43	3279	21.62
1: Immediate	367	17	4.63	56	15.26
2: Emergent	2,793	157	5.62	651	23.31
3: Urgent	6595	385	5.84	1531	23.21
4: Less urgent	3310	147	4.44	651	19.67
5: Nonurgent	1531	90	5.88	294	19.20
None – missing	572	28	4.90	96	16.78

Source: Reproduced from Lee et al. [12] with permission of the Institute for Operations Research and the Management Sciences.

TABLE 9.3b   Tenfold Cross-Validation Results and Blind-Prediction Accuracy for 72-h Returns and 30-Day Returns

Acuity Level	72-h Return		30-Day Return	
	10-Fold Cross-Validation (%)	Blind-Prediction Accuracy (%)	10-Fold Cross-Validation (%)	Blind-Prediction Accuracy (%)
1: Immediate	83.9	82.7	78.3	75.4
2: Emergent	70.0	70.0	79.7	79.0
3: Urgent	70.1	70.5	78.5	78.5
4: Less urgent	71.1	70.1	80.2	80.0
5: Nonurgent	70.5	70.5	77.0	78.5
None – missing	75.3	74.7	89.8	91.1
Overall	71.0	71.1	79.3	78.7
Payment type				
Private insurance	86.5	85.9	84.7	84.8
Self-pay	67.1	67.3	76.9	76.6
Medicare	70.1	70.9	77.5	77.9
Medicaid	66.1	67.4	76.5	76.7

The percentage represents the percentage of patients with correct predictions.
Source: Reproduced from Lee et al. [12] with permission of the Institute for Operations Research and the Management Sciences.

individuals yields the highest accuracy because insured individuals use the ED only when necessary. Obtaining high prediction accuracy for patients who are not privately insured (e.g., self-pay, Medicaid, Medicare) is difficult. We also note that for 72-h returns, prediction accuracy is highest for acuity level 1 patients, because their symptoms and conditions are generally more conspicuous; in addition, 72-h returns and 30-day returns show variations.

9.5 COMPUTATIONAL RESULTS, IMPLEMENTATION, AND ED PERFORMANCE COMPARISON

9.5.1 Phase I: Results

We performed systems optimization of the overall ED processes. In addition to the ED processes, the system model included other units in which ED patients are being discharged, for example, the ICU, step-down, floor, isolation unit, and telemedicine sign-up. In Table 9.4a, we summarize the operational performance according to improvement options using LOS and throughput. When we optimized over the existing ED layout, the system returned a global solution, which comprises Options 1–4. When we relaxed the layout restriction and optimized, it returned Options 1, 2, and 5 as the solution. Although these global solutions include a collection of changes and recommendations that together result in the best overall operations improvement, we split the solution into individual options and individually simulated the effects of these changes to allow for prioritization and selection by hospital management for implementation.

Specifically, we separated the global solution into five options according to change potential and analyzed the anticipated ED operations improvement. In the following, we describe the five options and their predicted impact.

Option 1: Combining registration and triage decreases the LOS of blue-zone and red-zone patients by more than 1 h, with more significant gains by the most severe (i.e., blue zone) patients. Detention patients are registered separately; thus, they do not benefit from the change. We find no change in how trauma patients are admitted. This is marginal improvement for less urgent patients.

Option 2: Reducing laboratory and X-ray turnaround time (by 15 min) drastically reduces blue-zone, red-zone, and detention patients' LOS by more than 2 h. These savings are realized because 59% of these patients require one laboratory order and 40% require two orders. The gain is also realized for trauma patients, although to a lesser extent. PACe and walk-in patients seldom require laboratory or X-ray orders. The time reduction is achieved via bin-tracking on orders and improved scheduled pickup and delivery between the ED and the laboratory.

Option 3: Optimizing staffing in blue and red zones reduces the LOS of blue-zone and red-zone patients by more than 1 h, with more significant reductions observed by red-zone patients, because nurses originally operated at about 80% capacity in the blue zone and at 91% in the red zone. Detention-patient LOS also decreases because of using blue-zone resources.

Option 4: Optimizing staffing in triage, walk-in, and PACe areas reduces LOS by about 30 min for blue-zone and red-zone patients; as expected, it has a major impact on PACe and walk-in patients, reducing LOS by 3.8 h (−49%) and 42 min (−22%), respectively.

Option 5: Combining blue-zone and red-zone layouts with optimized staffing offers substantial operational efficiency. Before the ESI was introduced,

TABLE 9.4a ED LOS and Throughput Comparisons for Various Systems Improvement Strategies

		Actual Hospital Operations March–May 2009			Simulation Systems Performance Systems Improvement				
		Actual Hospital Statistics	Simulation Output (Using August–December 2008 Observed Data for Training)	System Solution (Options 1–4)	Option 1 Combine Registration and Triage	Option 2 Reduce Lab/X-ray Turnaround (−15 min)	Option 3 Optimize Staffing in Blue and Red Zones	Option 4 Optimize Staffing in Triage, Walk-In, and PACe	Option 5 Combine Blue and Red Zones with Optimized Staffing
Overall	Patient volume	8274	8446	8413	8433	8324	8392	8401	8331
	LOS	10.59 h	10.49 h	7.33 h	10.02 h	9.22 h	9.84 h	9.49 h	7.68 h
	Average total wait time	4.51 h	4.34 h	1.39 h	3.95 h	2.50 h	3.87 h	3.64 h	1.76 h
Blue zone	Patient volume	2141	2137	2135	2138	2139	2145	2139	4273
	LOS	14.54 h	13.9 h	11.08 h	12.89 h	11.83 h	13.38 h	14.00 h	8.70 h
Red zone	Patient volume	2097	2140	2129	2142	2137	2145	2140	See above
	LOS	12.54 h	11.96 h	8.64 h	11.34 h	10.34	10.62 h	12.01 h	See above
Trauma	Patient volume	271	251	251	250	249	251	251	271
	LOS	7.85 h	7.98 h	6.94 h	7.51 h	7.49 h	7.74 h	7.98 h	7.70 h
Detention	Patient volume	437	407	410	411	410	408	411	401
	LOS	13.85 h	12.93 h	10.17 h	13.95 h	11.36 h	12.46 h	13.95 h	9.16 h
PACe	Patient volume	2037	1983	1970	1988	1966	2001	1979	1989
	LOS	7.90 h	8.60 h	3.64 h	8.60 h	7.95 h	7.74 h	4.03 h	6.63 h
Walk-in	Patient volume	990	992	989	997	996	990	998	971
	LOS	3.20 h	3.30 h	1.9 h	3.31 h	2.86	3.2 h	2.49 h	2.94 h

Source: Reproduced from Lee et al. [12] with permission of the Institute for Operations Research and the Management Sciences.

patients were sent to each color zone for similar complaints and (or) severity, as set forth by hospital personnel, to streamline the treatment process, to be assigned to appropriate providers, or to anticipate complexity of treatment. This also made revisits easier because patients would recall their previously assigned color zone. With the establishment of the ESI and sophisticated triage, patients are assigned an acuity level to assist in the treatment process. The color zones no longer serve their original purpose, although the hospital retains them (and appropriately uses them to accommodate the ESI). At Grady, the blue and red zones are adjacent to each other and share the same labor resources. Providers spend a good part of each day walking back and forth between these two zones to tend to patients. Our combined layout with optimized staffing provides operational efficiency because it reduces LOS by over 5 and 3 h for the blue and red zones, respectively, and reduces more than 40% of blue-zone LOS and 30% of red-zone LOS. Detention patients use blue-zone resources and achieve an LOS reduction of about 26%. As expected, LOS for trauma patients improves only slightly.

In addition to the systems optimization, our time-motion studies and machine learning analysis also led us to make the following recommendation to hospital management:

Option 6: Allocate a separate area for walk-in patients to be assigned a bed instead of at the ambulance triage area.

Option 7: Eliminate batching patients from the walk-in area to a zone or PACe. Instead of accumulating enough patients and taking a group of them to a zone or PACe, service each patient based on his (her) arrival time.

Option 8: Eliminate batch discharges. Discharge paperwork is performed for each patient whenever that patient is ready for discharge, rather than discharging them in groups.

Option 9: Create a clinical decision unit to observe patients before formal discharge to reduce avoidable readmissions as a result of insufficient care, discrepancies in diagnosis, or premature discharge. This option arises from the machine learning analysis that predicts patients who would be readmitted; providers then observe them to mitigate the readmission probability. This area is created by system optimization, which repurposes three beds from the blue zone and four beds from the red zone. Since 2003, Grady had an observation unit with six beds to manage ED patients for whom extra time is required to determine discharge or hospital admission. The repurposed seven beds increase Grady's ED observation capacity.

Option 10: Redirect nonurgent or walk-in patients to an alternative care facility.

9.5.2   Phase I: Adoption and Implementation

Grady management adopted Options 1–4, 7, and 8 for implementation, but made a minor alteration to Option 1 – it combined the registration and triage only at the ambulance arrival area. These changes, which required no extra resources, were implemented by July 2009.

At that time, Option 9 was under discussion for implementation because we recommended reallocating or reoptimizing existing resources (i.e., labor, space, equipment). Option 10 was under consideration to raise funds to help pay for establishing the alternative care facility.

Subsequently, based on follow-up time-motion studies and independent best-practice benchmarking tools that Grady employs (e.g., CMS core measures, National Association of Public Hospitals (NAPH) quality indicators, Press Ganey, and Leapfrog quality indicators), the changes implemented by July 2009 led to an LOS reduction of about 3 h (from more than 10 h to slightly more than 7 h), as Table 9.4b shows for the Phase I adoption and implementation. In January 2011, the hospital implemented the recommended clinical decision unit for observation, using the machine learning prediction to trigger the targeted treated ED patients for observation. Figure 9.4 shows the actual reduction of 72-h and 30-day return patients. For acuity levels 1 and 2, 72-h returns decreased by more than 30% and 7%, respectively. For 30-day returns, the reductions for these two levels were 24% and 9%, respectively. Our Grady ED transformation was timely. As a result of requirements in the Affordable Care Act, the hospital does not receive payment for return visits; in addition, it must pay a penalty. Hence, reducing avoidable readmissions represents improved care quality and provides financial savings.

These improvements raised confidence in our recommendations and prompted the hospital to use $1 million of a donation from Kaiser Permanente to act on Option 10 of our recommendations – to open an alternative care facility, a walk-in center for low-acuity patients. This facility opened in August 2011 [44]. With confidence in improved ED efficiency, in October 2011, Grady also unveiled the Marcus trauma center, which increases the number of trauma beds from 4 to 15 [64]. Based on the improved ED efficiency, our study recommended only one additional attending physician.

9.5.3   Phase II: Results

In conjunction with the walk-in-center option and the increase of beds in the trauma center from 4 to 15, the hospital gained an attending physician; however, the ED demand also increased. The hospital observed a slight increase in LOS from 7.9 h to more than 8 h. Understanding that system improvement is an ongoing effort in aligning demand with resources, the team embarked on Phase II of the system optimization effort using existing resources.

In our summary below, we omit the performance report for the PACe and walk-in because the system output from the various strategies offers only marginal LOS differences compared to the larger improvements observed from Phase I.

TABLE 9.4b Thirty-Day Average LOS and Throughput Performance Following the Initial Phase I Implementation

ED Zone	Original		Phase I: Comparison of ED Performance (Actual Hospital Monthly Statistics)					
			Implementation of Recommendations					
			Options 1–4, 7, 8		Options 1–4, 7–9 (Clinical Decision Unit for Observation)		Options 1–4, 7–10 (Redirect Nonurgent Visits to Walk-In Center)	
	March–May 2009		July 2009–December 2010		January–August 2011		September 2011–December 2011	
	LOS (l^*) (h)	Patient Volume	Reduction in LOS ($l-l^*$) (h)	Patient Volume	Reduction in LOS ($l-l^*$) (h)	Patient Volume	Reduction in LOS ($l-l^*$) (h)	Patient Volume
Overall	10.59	8274	−3.00	8395	−2.86	8421	−2.29	8364
Blue zone	14.54	2141	−3.26	2525	−3.14	2317	−3.22	2603[a]
Red zone	12.54	2097	−3.78	2109	−3.80	2230	−3.60	2254
Trauma center	7.85	271	−1.01	252	−1.19	283	−1.22	305[a]
Detention	13.85	437	−3.12	420	−2.95	446	−3.01	445
PACe	7.90	2037	−3.02	2104	−3.18	2098	−3.60	2083
Walk-in	3.20	990	−1.0	945	−0.85	970	−1.2	510[b]

[a]The new trauma center was opened in November 2011.
[b]A significant number of nonurgent ED patients have been redirected to the new walk-in center since August 19, 2011, thus resulting in a significant decrease in ED walk-in patients.
Source: Reproduced from Lee et al. [12] with permission of the Institute for Operations Research and the Management Sciences.

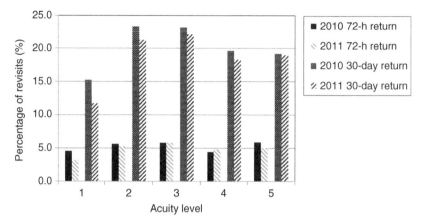

Figure 9.4   The graph compares the percentage of ED revisits in 2010 and 2011. Note the significant reduction in 72-h and 30-day returns following the installation of the clinical decision unit in 2011. Reproduced from Lee et al. [12] with permission of the Institute for Operations Research and the Management Sciences.

Table 9.5a summarizes the anticipated results based on simulation and optimization. Specifically, globally optimizing the system resulted in an overall LOS reduction of 90 min. This entails global resource allocation and changes in ED layout. The improvement is considerable, with major LOS reductions in the blue and red zones (44% and 30%, respectively). Although the trauma center significantly increased its bed capability, it added only one attending physician. As a result, trauma LOS improved by only about 10 min, because the new facility had a significant increase in trauma patients. Nevertheless, for trauma patients, particularly those who suffer from traumatic brain injury, 10 min can have a tremendous impact on outcome (e.g., survival, disablement, death) and is vital to the survival and quality of life of these patients.

Splitting the global strategies into Option 11 (optimal staffing) and Option 12 (optimal layout) resulted in similar minor LOS improvements in trauma patients. However, blue-zone and red-zone patients continued to enjoy significant LOS reductions.

9.5.4   Phase II: Adoption and Implementation

Table 9.5b contrasts the ED performance before and after the Phase II Option 11 implementation. Using existing resources and facility layout, Grady gained efficiency and timeliness of care by simply globally optimizing resources across the ED. The net LOS reduction of 4 h for high-severity patients (i.e., blue zone) is substantial and could translate to better quality of care and outcomes. Even minor improvements in timeliness of care for trauma patients could make a difference between life and death and have a significant impact on quality of life for these patients.

TABLE 9.5a   Phase II Comparisons of Potential ED Performance Showing Efficiency Improvements Using Different Strategies

	Actual Hospital Operations August–December 2011	Simulation Systems Performance		
		Global Strategy: System Optimization (Resource + Layout)	Option 11: Optimize Worker Allocation	Option 12: Combine Blue and Red zones
Overall LOS (h)	8.30	6.79 (−1.51)	7.21 (−1.09)	6.94 (−1.36)
Blue zone (h)	11.32	6.24 (−5.08)	6.66 (−4.66)	6.61 (−4.71)
Red zone (h)	8.94	6.24 (−2.70)	6.19 (−2.75)	6.61 (−2.33)
Trauma center (h)	6.63	6.46 (−0.17)	6.16 (−0.47)	6.47 (−0.16)

Source: Reproduced from Lee et al. [12] with permission of the Institute for Operations Research and the Management Sciences.

TABLE 9.5b   The 30-Day Average LOS and Throughput Performance Improved as a Result of the Phase II Implementation

		Phase II: Comparison of ED Performance (Actual Hospital Monthly statistics)		
		Original (from Phase I Improvement)	Implementation of Phase II Recommendations	
			Option 11 (Optimizing Overall ED Staffing)	
		September 2011– December 2011		January– December 2013
ED Zone		LOS (l^{**})	2012 Reduction in LOS ($l–l^{**}$)	Reduction in LOS ($l–l^{**}$)
Patient volume		8364	8920	9060
Overall LOS		8.30 h	−1.00 h	−1.16 h
Blue zone		11.32 h	−3.95 h	−4.05 h (−36%)
Red zone		8.94 h	−2.70 h	−2.52 h (−30%)
Trauma center	6.63 h	−0.35 h	−0.30 h (−5%)	

Source: Reproduced from Lee et al. [12] with permission of the Institute for Operations Research and the Management Sciences.

Combining blue and red zones is viable because all patients entering either zone require a consultation and generally require multiple resources or extensive diagnostic testing. However, such layout redesign may not be desirable because commingling patients with different acuity levels may have detrimental effects on the treatment process; for example, care providers may not be as focused. The net gain of combining the zones, even with optimizing resource usage across all areas, is less substantial for trauma patients. The hospital executives carefully weighed this option and are now confident that combining the zones will have an overall positive impact.

At the time of this writing, the hospital has received $77 million of sponsored funding and has embarked on the ED facility-layout redesign.

To monitor the performance of the clinical decision unit, Figure 9.5 contrasts the 72-h and 30-day return performance for 2010 through 2013. Between Phases I and II, the 30-day return reduction shows substantial gain, especially among severe-acuity patients. Nonurgent patients (level 5) return to ED at high rates because it is often their only means of access to health care. Such nonurgent readmission is unavoidable because some patients come in with unrelated health complaints. In contrast, although level 1 patients demand the most urgent care, their diagnosis is typically very specific; upon discharge, they are well counseled with regard to follow-up care with their primary care providers, resulting in lower returns to the ED. Mid-level acuity patients have higher rates of return because of the less-specific nature of their complaints and (or) diagnosis.

Figure 9.6 shows LOS trends for the ED zones through the various stages of implementation. Specifically, adoption of the initial optimization of overall staffing and process consolidation significantly reduced LOS across all zones (from the first to the second bar). This implementation did not require additional resources or financial investment. When the clinical decision unit was established in 2011, Grady experienced a marginal increase in LOS across all zones because some patients were selected for observation to reduce potential returns (third bar). This also very slightly affected the LOS of the blue and red zones because space and labor resources were repurposed for the clinical decision unit. In September 2011, the alternative walk-in center was opened, drastically reducing LOS for ED walk-in patients (fourth bar). The difference in LOS across other zones was marginal; however, overall LOS increased slightly because the number of walk-in patients decreased significantly. Although the throughput in the ED and trauma center increased steadily over the years (by approximately 16.2%), the LOS from 2012 to the present stayed close to constant, indicating that the earlier improvement was being sustained. The clinical decision unit reduced potential avoidable returns, thus helping to save hospital resources, reduce penalties, and improve the quality of patient care. Since November 2013, the unit has expanded to 15 beds. The walk-in center has helped to relieve Grady's large healthcare burden of Medicaid and Medicare patients. By redirecting nonurgent ED patients, the hospital saved valuable resources and reduced the costs needed to unnecessarily treat these patients in the ED. This has also reduced the number of patients who leave without being seen by more than 32%.

9.6   BENEFITS AND IMPACTS

The Edelman–Wagner OR analytical work and the subsequent implementation and successes are extremely important to Grady. As a safety net healthcare provider, Grady must make transformative changes to improve efficiencies and reduce expenses so that it can continue to provide care to a significant segment of the population that

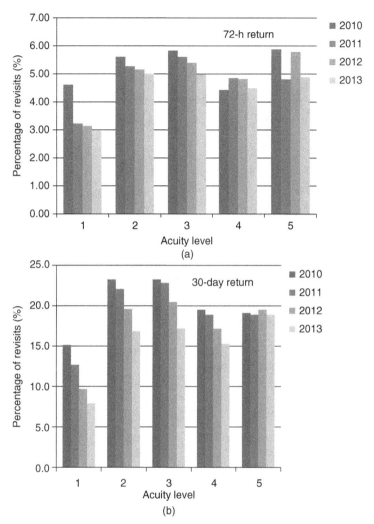

Figure 9.5 (a, b) The graphs compare the percentage of ED revisits in 2010 (no intervention), 2011 (Phase I), and 2012–2013 (Phase II). Note the significant drop in 72-h and 30-day returns following the Phase I implementation. The machine learning tool learns from revisit patterns and improves progressively as it adapts through the years. The levels 4 and 5 patients who use the ED as their primary care service (i.e., super-utilizers) remain a challenge, especially for 72-h returns. Reproduced from Lee et al. [12] with permission of the Institute for Operations Research and the Management Sciences.

is underserved medically. The goal of our work is to significantly improve the efficiency and timely delivery of quality care to Grady's ED patients. In the opinion of Grady executives and medical staff members, our OR analytical work made possible and substantially facilitated the following benefits and impacts listed.

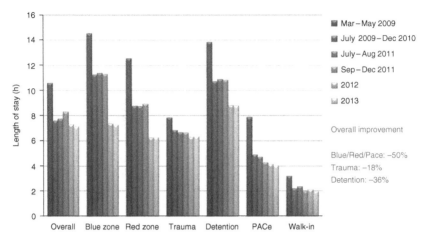

Figure 9.6   The graph compares LOS from 2009 to the present. Grady has sustained a steady ED LOS since the 2009 system improvement implementation. The graph shows the following: March–May 2009 (original performance, first bar), July 2009–December 2010 (after Phase I implementation, second bar), January–August 2011 (after implementation of the clinical decision unit for observation, third bar), September–December 2011 (after implementation of the walk-in center to redirect nonurgent patients, and expansion of the trauma center, fourth bar), and 2012–2013 (after Phase II implementation, fifth and sixth bars). The overall average LOS in 2013 was 7.14 h. Reproduced from Lee et al. [12] with permission of the Institute for Operations Research and the Management Sciences.

9.6.1   Quantitative Benefits

Our work has improved the timeliness of emergency care. From the beginning of Phase I to the present, the overall average LOS decreased by 33% (10.59 to 7.14 h), while average total waiting time decreased by 70%. This contrasts with an ED LOS of 8–11 h in comparable safety net hospitals (see Table 9.6). The reductions are most significant for high-acuity patients: LOS decreased by more than 50% for both the blue and red zones (−7.27 and −6.28 h, respectively); the LOS in the trauma zone decreased by 20% (−1.52 h). In the following, we list quantitative improvements.

9.6.1.1   Improved Efficiency of Emergency Care   Facilitated by the creation of the walk-in center, the improvements allowed Grady to increase its ED annual throughput (i.e., number of patients treated) by more than 7.8% (+8114), its trauma volume by 8.4% (+1664), and its volume of severe trauma cases (i.e., patients facing life-and-death situations) by 14% (+417) and reduce the number of patients who leave without being seen by more than 30% (−5553). Moreover, it made these improvements without increasing its ED staff or facilities. The use of the clinical decision unit decreased avoidable 72-h and 30-day readmissions among the acuity levels 1–3 patients by 28% (−602). This produced direct financial and resource savings for the

TABLE 9.6   Comparison of LOS in Major Safety Net Hospitals (http://www.Hospitalcompare.hhs.gov)

Hospital	LOS for ED Patients Discharged to Hospital (h)	LOS for ED Patients Discharged Home (h)	Average ED LOS (h)
LAC/USC (Los Angeles)	17.8	6.7	8–11
Cook County (Chicago)	15.0	6.0	
Parkland (Dallas)	11.1	5.3	
Grady (2014)	9.3	6.7	7.1
Grady (before) 2008	13.5	10.0	10.6

Source: Reproduced from Lee et al. [12] with permission of the Institute for Operations Research and the Management Sciences.

hospital and had a positive impact on patient-care quality measures. The alternative walk-in center serviced more than 32% of the nonurgent ED cases outside the ED treatment area, thus reducing the hospital's financial burden (by treating these patients in a lower cost area) and ensuring proper ED resource usage.

9.6.1.2   Annual Financial Savings and Revenues   From 2008 to 2012, the reduction in revisits resulted in $7.5 million of savings in penalties. The walk-in center for nonurgent conditions reduced ED costs by $21.6 million and resulted in $12.5 million in additional revenue. ED and trauma efficiency increased the revenue by $96.6 million. Expansion of trauma care resulted in $51.8 million in revenue. For a critical safety net hospital with $1.5 billion of annual economic impact, only 8% of which is paid by private insurance, the $190 million financial gains have a tremendous impact on maintaining Grady's financial health.

The ED, often called the front door to a hospital, serves as a source of hospital inpatient admissions, which on average generate more revenue than ED-only admissions. For Grady hospital, the ED provides about 75% of inpatient admissions. Thus, the ED's increased throughput and other improvements played a major role in the significant revenue increases shown in Grady's annual financial reports.

9.6.1.3   Encouragement of External Sponsorship   In part, as a result of the rigorous OR-driven recommendations, Grady has been able to document success in timeliness of care and operational efficiencies, thus facilitating increased philanthropic donations. The Kaiser Foundation contributed $1 million [44] to establish an alternative care site (walk-in center) for low-acuity patients. A $20 million gift from the Marcus Foundation [64] enabled Grady to create a world-class stroke and neuroscience center and a state-of-the-art trauma center. The OR advances and the subsequent ED transformation give investors confidence in sponsoring projects that will benefit the hospital and its patients.

TABLE 9.7   Estimates of Potential Death and Disability Reductions Resulted from Increasing Patient Volumes at Grady in 2013

ED Service	2013 Volume	Increase in Volume	Reduced Death and Disability
Airlift trauma patients	3395 Patients	417 Patients (+14%)	All need immediate care for life-and-death situations
Trauma patients	15,992	1665 (+8.4%)	Death ~ 56 Disability ~ 160
Comprehensive care	39,059	2001 (+5.52%)	Disability ~ 390
Extended care	29,645	902 (+2.9%)	Disability ~ 296

Volume increases shown compare 2013 and 2012.
Source: Reproduced from Lee et al. [12] with permission of the Institute for Operations Research and the Management Sciences.

9.6.2   Qualitative Benefits

Our work has saved lives, reduced morbidity, and reduced disabilities. Efficient ED operations allow the ED to more quickly treat patients with time-sensitive conditions. The shortened LOS demonstrates that patients move from the ED and receive appropriate care in the appropriate setting in a timelier manner. For high-acuity patients, quicker response during the golden hour of treatment (i.e., a period of about 1 h following traumatic injury) during which prompt medical treatment will likely prevent death can mean the difference between life and death, disability, or returning to a normal life. Faster door-to-computerized-tomography (CT) scan and door-to-tissue-plasminogen-activator (a clot-dissolving drug) administration for stroke patients, and faster door-to-antibiotics for pneumonia patients have decreased long-term disability and death. More acute trauma patients can be treated, saving more lives. Improved timeliness and service quality directly translate to improved quality of life for patients and decreased morbidity and mortality and make a difference in whether a patient is treated and released, or is admitted to the hospital (see Table 9.7).

9.6.2.1   *Health Cost Reductions*   ED timeliness and efficiency of care have a broad impact on patient quality of life and on healthcare spending. Timeliness and improved quality of care improve outcomes and consequently lead to indirect savings of hundreds of millions of dollars in ongoing care and management of patients. In addition, reducing disability allows patients to lead normal lives. The estimate of the value of one life in the United States is $50,000 to $100,000 per year of life saved [65]. We emphasize that although quality and systems efficiency have been our focus, the monetary savings (for both the providers and the patients) are real and are critical to our national healthcare system. This is especially true for safety net hospitals such as Grady, which feel the burden more acutely than other hospitals, given that many of its service costs are not reimbursed.

9.6.2.2 Continuous Improvement and Adaptive Advances The hospital has been able to achieve its targeted goal of ED LOS of 7 h and sustain overall improvement for over 5 years. With ED demand continuing to grow, maintaining a culture of continuous improvement is key to sustaining good performance.

9.6.2.3 Improved Quality of Care in Other Facilities The model can be generalized and has been tested and successfully implemented in 10 other EDs. The benefits across these EDs are consistent with the substantial benefits Grady achieved. The ED volumes at these 10 sites range from 30,000 to 80,000 patients per year. Upon implementation, they have experienced a total throughput increase of 15–35%, a reduction of revisits of severe acute patients of 19–41%, an LOS reduction of 15–38%, and a reduction in the number of patients who leave without being treated of 35–50%.

Grady has applied the technology in other units, including medication error analysis for the pharmacy and hospital-acquired conditions (HACs) in the ED, operating room, and intensive care units. HAC is one of the 10 major causes of death in the United States. Our surgical site infection (SSI) study at Grady involved reducing mediastinitis after cardiac surgery. Nationwide, the 700,000 open-heart surgeries performed each year result in infection rates of 0.5–5%. Of those infected, the mortality rate is 40%. On average, an additional 30 days of hospital LOS and (or) one extra surgical procedure are required. The SSI rate at Grady was 23% in 2010. The team implemented transformative changes, including strategic preoperative procedures for both inpatients and outpatients and optimal timing and dosing of preoperative antibiotics in July 2011. The infection rate decreased to 1.5% between July 2011 and January 2012 and has been 0% since February 2012. The team is now conducting a study on joint surgeries, bloodstream infection, and catheter-induced urinary-tract infection.

9.7 SCIENTIFIC ADVANCES

The collaborative effort between hospital researchers and OR scientists resulted in scientific advances on two fronts:

9.7.1 Hospital Care Delivery Advances

The new system couples machine learning, and simulation and optimization decision support to improve the efficiency and timeliness of care in the ED, while reducing avoidable readmissions. The model allows a hospital to globally optimize its ED workflow, taking into account the uncertainty of human disease characteristics and care patterns, to drive the patient LOS and wait time to a minimum. It provides a comprehensive analysis of the entire patient flow from registration to discharge and enables a decision maker to understand the complexities and interdependencies of individual steps in the process sequence; ultimately, it allows a hospital to perform systems optimization to achieve the most optimum performance.

The model focuses on system optimization that results in improvements in LOS and waiting time through resource allocation, system consolidation, and operations optimization without attempting to change the behavior of healthcare providers or patients. Rather, the system captures the human behavior and optimizes the workflow process to achieve optimal results. Although changing human behavior can result in significant gains, we understand that such changes may be more costly in terms of training and altering habits; this is particularly true for teaching hospitals at which rotations of residents and healthcare trainees are common. The potential to introduce new errors also exists. Thus, we accept the variability in human behavior and services and incorporate these elements into our model to reflect workflow and human characteristics.

9.7.2   OR Advances

The novelty of our OR-driven analytical work includes performing systems optimization within the ED simulation environment; incorporating treatment patterns and patient characteristics dynamically and stochastically within the ED operations and quality–improvement framework; modeling ED readmission using – simultaneously – demographics, socioeconomic status, clinical information, hospital operations, and disease behavioral patterns; modeling ED interdependencies involving other hospital units; and integrating a machine learning framework within the simulation–optimization environment.

We acknowledge the computational challenges of such large-scale complex models in data collection for model validation, parameter estimation, and global system optimization. The machine learning framework and the DAMIP model have been proven to be NP-hard [51]; hence, they require both theoretical and computational breakthroughs [47–51, 54, 55]. However, once the predictive rule has been established, it can analyze and predict patient return patterns in nanoseconds, opening up real-time target patient intervention. We derived polyhedral theory and applied it to the solution strategies for DAMIP [50, 51, 54, 55].

Because of the complexity of simultaneously simulating dynamic system behavior and optimizing operational performance, solving within our simulation–optimization framework remains a challenge. We caution that our solutions, although obtained rapidly, are not proven to be optimal. Nevertheless, our investigations indicate that the solutions are close to optimal.

Related photos, presentations, hospital-insider notes, and an Institute of Medicine/National Academy of Engineering letter concerning the significance of the work are available at http://www2.isye.gatech.edu/medicalor/EDadvances.

ACKNOWLEDGMENTS

The majority of this chapter is excerpted from the Edelman–Wagner ED study that was published in Interfaces 2015 [12]. The work was partially supported by the National Science Foundation. The authors would like to thank C. Allen, C. Girard, S. Lahlou, D. Meagh, J. Phillips, A. Widmaier, F. Yuan, R.L. Zhou, and

H.Z. Zhang from Georgia Tech for performing the time-motion study on this project. Special thanks go to Grady's caretakers: Deborah Western, Manuel Patterson, Nadia Ralliford, Jill Cuestas, and all the nurses for their support of this project and for helping with data collection and interviews.

REFERENCES

[1] Institute of Medicine. *Crossing the Quality Chasm: A New Health System for the 21st Century*. Committee on Quality of Health Care in America, Institute of Medicine. Washington, DC: National Academy Press; 2001.

[2] President's Council of Advisors on Science and Technology: Report to the President. 2014. Better health care and lower costs: Accelerating improvement through systems engineering. Available at http://www.whitehouse.gov/sites/default/files/microsites/ostp/ PCAST/pcast_systems_engineering_in_healthcare_-_may_2014.pdf. Accessed 2014 Jun 30.

[3] Centers for Disease Control. 2010. National hospital ambulatory medical care survey: 2010 emergency department summary tables. Available at http://www.cdc.gov/nchs/data/ ahcd/nhamcs_emergency/2010_ed_web_tables.pdf. Accessed 2014 Aug 20.

[4] Derlet RW. Overcrowding in emergency departments: Increased demand and decreased capacity. Ann Emerg Med 2002;39(4):430–432.

[5] Derlet RW, Richards JR. Overcrowding in the nation's emergency departments: Complex causes and disturbing effects. Ann Emerg Med 2000;35(1):63–68.

[6] Derlet RW, Richards JR. Emergency department overcrowding in Florida, New York, and Texas. South Med J 2002;95(8):846–849.

[7] Derlet RW, Richards JR, Kravitz R. Frequent overcrowding in US emergency departments. Acad Emerg Med 2001;8(2):151–155.

[8] Lewin Group. 2002. Emergency department overload: A growing crisis. Available at http://www.aha.org/content/00-10/EdoCrisisSlides.pdf. Accessed 2014 Oct 1.

[9] Richardson LD, Hwang U. America's health care safety net: Intact or unraveling? Acad Emerg Med 2001;8(11):1056–1063.

[10] Taylor TB. Threats to the health care safety net. Acad Emerg Med 2001;8(11):1080–1087.

[11] Robinson R. Special issue editors' note: Wagner prize second-place winner Lee et al. Grady health system. Interfaces 2014;44(5):444.

[12] Lee EK, Atallah HY, Wright MD, Post ET, Thomas C IV, Wu DT, Haley LL Jr. Transforming hospital emergency department workflow and patient care. Interfaces 2015;45(1):58–82.

[13] United States Department of Health and Human Services. 2014. A policy framework for targeting financially vulnerable safety net hospitals. Available at http://aspe.hhs.gov/ health/reports/02/dsh/ch2.htm. Accessed 2014 Aug 18.

[14] de Moura HC. 2007. Financial crisis at Atlanta's Grady hospital Available at http://www .gpb.org/healthdesk/financial-crisis-at-atlantas-grady-hospital. Accessed 2014 Sep 20.

[15] American College of Emergency Physicians. 2014. National report card press release: Nation's grade drops to a dismal d+ for failure to support emergency patients. Available at http://www.emreportcard.org/Content.aspx?id=534. Accessed 2014 Sep 7.

[16] Eitel DR, Rudkin SE, Malvehy MA, Killeen JP, Pines JM. Improving service quality by understanding emergency department flow: A white paper and position statement prepared for the American Academy of Emergency Medicine. J Emerg Med 2010;38(1):70–79doi: 10.1016.

[17] Bahensky JA, Roe J, Bolton R. Lean sigma – will it work for healthcare? J Healthc Inf Manage 2005;19(1):39–44.

[18] Popovich MA, Boyd C, Dachenhaus T, Kusler D. Improving stable patient flow through the emergency department by utilizing evidence-based practice: One hospital's journey. J Emerg Nurs 2012;38(5):474–478.

[19] Wiler JL, Gentle C, Halfpenny JM, Heins A, Mehrotra A, Mikhail MG, Fite D. Optimizing emergency department front-end operation. Ann Emerg Med 2010;55(2):142–160.

[20] Ashby M, Ferrin D, Miller M, Shahi N. 2008. Discrete event simulation: Optimizing patient flow and redesign in a replacement facility. Available at http://www.informs-sim.org/wsc08papers/200.pdf. Accessed 2014 Sep 7.

[21] Kolker A. Process modeling of emergency department patient flow: Effect of patient length of stay on ED diversion. J Med Syst 2008;32(5):389–401.

[22] Moskop JC, Sklar DP, Geiderman JM, Schears RM, Bookman KJ. Emergency department crowding, part 2 – Barriers to reform and strategies to overcome them. Ann Emerg Med 2009;53(5):612–617.

[23] Nugus P, Holdgate A, Fry M, Forero R, McCarthy S, Braithwarte J. Work pressure and patient flow management in the emergency department: Findings from an ethnographic study. Acad Emerg Med 2011;18(10):1045–1052.

[24] DeFlitch C, Eitel D, Geeting G, Cherukuri R, Escott M, Smith J, Arnold J, Paul SA. Physician directed queuing (PDQ) improves health care delivery in the ED: Early results. Ann Emerg Med 2007;50(3):S125–S126.

[25] McCarthy ML, Zeger SL, Ding R, Levin SR, Desmond JS, Lee J, Aronsky D. Crowding delays treatment and lengthens emergency department length of stay, even among high-acuity patients. Ann Emerg Med 2009;54(4):492–503, e4.

[26] Sturm JJ, Hirsh DA, Lee EK, Massey R, Weselman B, Simon HK. Practice characteristics that influence nonurgent pediatric emergency department utilization. Acad Pediatr 2010;10(1):70–74.

[27] Minott J. 2008. Reducing hospital readmissions. Available at http://www.academyhealth.org/files/publications/ReducingHospitalReadmissions.pdf. Accessed 2014 Oct 1.

[28] Osei-Anto A, Joshi M, Audet AM, Berman A, Jencks S. 2010. Health care leader action guide to reduce avoidable readmissions. Available at http://www.hret.org/care/projects/resources/readmissions_cp.pdf. Accessed 2014 Oct 1.

[29] Allaudeen N, Vidyarthi A, Maselli J, Auerbach A. Redefining readmission risk factors for general medicine patients. J Hosp Med 2011;6(2):54–60.

[30] Billings J, Dixon J, Mijanovich T, Wennberg D. Case finding for patients at risk of readmission to hospital: Development of algorithm to identify high risk patients. BMJ 2006;333(7563):327.

[31] Hasan O, Meltzer DO, Shaykevich BCM, Kaboli PJ, Auerbach AD, Wetterneck TB, Arora VM, Zhang J, Schnipper JL. Hospital readmission in general medicine patients: A prediction model. J Gen Intern Med 2010;25(3):211–219.

[32] Kirby SE. Dennis SM, Jayasinghe UW, Harris MF. 2010. Patient related factors in frequent readmissions: The influence of condition, access to services and patient choice. Available at http://www.biomedcentral.com/content/pdf/1472-6963-10-216.pdf. Accessed 2014 Dec 1.

[33] Westert GP, Lagoe RJ, Keskimäki I, Leyland A, Murphy M. An international study of hospital readmissions and related utilization in Europe and the USA. Health Policy 2002;61(3):269–278.

[34] Southern DA, Quan HG, William A. Comparison of the Elixhauser and Charlson/Deyo methods of comorbidity measurement in administrative data. Med Care 2004;42(4): 355–360.

[35] Benbassat J, Taragin M. Hospital readmissions as a measure of quality of health care: Advantages and limitations. Arch Intern Med 2000;160(8):1074–1081.

[36] Davidson G, Moscovice I, Remus D. *Hospital Size, Uncertainty and Pay-for-Performance*. Working paper. Minneapolis: Upper Midwest Rural Health Research Center; 2007.

[37] Joynt KE, Orav EJ, Jha AK. Thirty-day readmission rates for medicare beneficiaries by race and site of care. J Am Med Assoc 2011;305(7):675–681.

[38] Scuteri J, Fodero L, Pearse J. Determining a threshold hospital size for the application of activity-based funding. BMC Health Serv Res 2011;10(Supp.1):A10.

[39] VanSuch M, Naessens JM, Stroebel RJ, Huddleston JM, Williams AR. Effect of discharge instructions on readmission of hospitalised patients with heart failure: Do all of the joint commission on accreditation of healthcare organizations heart failure core measures reflect better care? Qual Saf Health Care 2006;15(5):414–417.

[40] Kansagara D, Englander H, Salanitro A, Kagen D, Theobald C, Freeman M, Kripalani S. Risk prediction models for hospital readmission. J Am Med Assoc 2011; 306(15):1688–1698.

[41] Allaudeen N, Schnipper JL, Orav EJ, Wachter RM, Vidyarthi AR. Inability of providers to predict unplanned readmissions. J Gen Intern Med 2011;26(7):771–776.

[42] Lee EK, Yuan F, Hirsh DA, Mallory MD, Simon HK. 2012. A clinical decision tool for predicting patient care characteristics: Patients returning within 72 hours in the emergency department. Available at http://www.ncbi.nlm.nih.gov/pmc/articles/PMC3540516. Accessed 2014 Oct 1.

[43] Medeiros DJ, Swenson E, DeFlitch C. Improving patient flow in a hospital emergency department. In: Mason S, Hill R, Rose O, Moünch L, editors. *Proc. 2008 Simulation Conf*. Washington, DC: Institute of Electrical and Electronics Engineers; 2008. p 1526–1531.

[44] Williams M. 2011. Grady to open ER alternative offering lower costs. Available at http://www.ajc.com/news/news/local/grady-to-open-er-alternative-offering-lower-costs/nQKxb/. Accessed 2014 Oct 1.

[45] American Trauma Society. 2014. Trauma center levels explained. Available at http://www.amtrauma.org/?page=TraumaLevels. Accessed 2014 Aug 18.

[46] Hagen MS, Jopling JK, Buchman TG, Lee EK. 2013. Priority queuing models for hospital intensive care units and the impacts to severe case patients. Available at http://www.ncbi.nlm.nih.gov/pmc/articles/PMC3900220. Accessed 2014 Oct 1.

[47] Lee EK, Gallagher RJ, Patterson D. A linear programming approach to discriminant analysis with a reserved judgment region. INFORMS J Comput 2003;15(1):23–41.

[48] Lee EK. Large-scale optimization-based classification models in medicine and biology. Ann Biomed Eng 2007;35(6):1095–1109.

[49] Lee EK, Wu TL. Classification and disease prediction via mathematical programming. In: Seref O, Kundakcioglu OE, Pardalos PM, editors. *Data Mining, Systems Analysis and Optimization in Biomedicine*. Melville, NY: American Institute of Physics; 2007. p 1–42.

[50] Brooks JP, Lee EK. Analysis of the consistency of a mixed integer programming-based multi-category constrained discriminant model. Ann Oper Res Data Mining 2010; 174(1):147–168.

[51] Brooks JP, Lee EK. Solving a multigroup mixed-integer programming-based constrained discrimination model. INFORMS J Comput 2014;26(3):567–585.

[52] Koczor CA, Lee EK, Torres RA, Boyd A, Vega JD, Uppal K, Yuan F, Fields EJ, Samarel AM, Lewis W. Detection of differentially methylated gene promoters in failing and non-failinghuman left ventricle myocardium using computational analysis. Physiol Genomics 2013;45(14):597–605.

[53] Nakaya HI, Wrammert J, Lee EK, Racioppi L, Marie-Kunze S, Haining WN, Means AR, et al. Systems biology of seasonal influenza vaccination in humans. Nat Immunol 2011;12(8):786–795.

[54] Lee EK, Maheshwary S. Facets of conflict hypergraphs. SIAM J Optim 2013. Accepted.

[55] Lee EK, Surana V, Shapoval A. Facets for generalized conflict hypergraphs. SIAM J Optim 2014. Submitted.

[56] Lee EK, Pietz F, Benecke B. Service networks for public health and medical preparedness: Medical countermeasures dispensing and large-scale disaster relief efforts. In: Herrmann J, editor. *Handbook of Operations Research for Homeland Security*. NL: Springer; 2013. p 167–196.

[57] Lee EK, Chen CH, Pietz F, Benecke B. Modeling and optimizing the public health infrastructure for emergency response. Interfaces 2009;39(5):476–490.

[58] Lee EK, Maheshwary S, Mason J, Glisson W. Large-scale dispensing for emergency response to bioterrorism and infectious disease outbreak. Interfaces 2006;36(6):591–607.

[59] Lee EK, Maheshwary S, Mason J, Glisson W. Decision support system for mass dispensing of medications for infectious disease outbreaks and bioterrorist attacks. Ann Oper Res 2006;148(1):25–53.

[60] Lee EK, Yang AY, Pietz F, Benecke B. Public health and medical preparedness. In: Yih Y, editor. *Handbook of Healthcare Delivery Systems*. Boca Raton, FL: CRC Press; 2011, Chapter 41.

[61] Lee EK, Chen CH, Brown N, Handy J, Desiderio A, Lopez R, Davis B. Designing guest flow and operations logistics for the dolphin tales. Interfaces 2012;42(5):492–506.

[62] RealOpt. 2012. Realopt user manual. Avaiable at http://www2.isye.gatech.edu/medicalor/realopt/. Accessed 2012 Dec 1.

[63] Lee EK, Pietz F, Benecke B, Mason J, Burel G. Advancing public health and medical preparedness with operations research. Interfaces 2013;43(1):79–98.

[64] PRNewswire. 2014. The Marcus foundation gives $20 million to Grady health system. Available at http://www.prnewswire.com/news-releases/the-marcus-foundation-gives-20-million-to-grady-health-system-61849312.html. Accessed 2014 Oct 1.

[65] Owens DK. Interpretation of cost-effectiveness analyses. J Gen Intern Med 1998; 13(10):716–717.

10

A MULTIOBJECTIVE SIMULATION OPTIMIZATION OF THE MACROLEVEL PATIENT FLOW DISTRIBUTION

YUNZHE QIU AND JIE SONG

Department of Industrial Engineering & Management, College of Engineering, Peking University, Beijing, China

10.1 INTRODUCTION

The imbalance development of public healthcare system and patients' demand has grown into a worldwide problem. Patients desire fast and high-quality healthcare service with less expense, but not all of the hospitals provide effective and timely service. In the United States, patients with un-emergent illness also visit Emergency Departments (ED) for faster treatment, while in China patients with minor illness still prefer General Hospitals (GH) for higher quality healthcare service. Although ED and GH play different roles in their own indigenous healthcare system, they are facing the same problem that the demand exceeds service capacity.

Components of the hierarchical healthcare system currently in urban China include Community Healthcare Centers (CHCs) and GHs. CHCs are faster to deal with ailments, but the service quality, the skill of physicians, and medical devices are far behind high-level hospitals. The GH always covers several communities, even a district or a whole city. The service quality is usually better in GH, but patients have a long access time to healthcare service. Statistics from Ministry of Health in China show that 73.9% of patients choose GHs for the first attendance. However, 65% of

Healthcare Analytics: From Data to Knowledge to Healthcare Improvement, First Edition.
Edited by Hui Yang and Eva K. Lee.

outpatients currently in GH could also be well treated by CHC. In a word, patients' blindness of seeking healthcare service causes the irrational patient flow distribution.

The Chinese government has been conscious of the severity and proposed a series of incentive policies to guide the patient flow. Among them, the "Two-Way Referral Policy" (TWRP) is the most important one. The TWRP consists of two parts. The "Upward Referral" part states that CHC patients (those choosing CHC for first healthcare attendance) whose acuteness exceeds the CHC's ability can be transferred to higher-level hospitals directly without extra waiting in GH. It aims to encourage patients to choose CHCs for the first diagnosis so as to release GH's pressure from outpatients. Another part of the TWRP is the "Downward Referral" policy. It announces that the inpatient in GHs, whose health condition has been controlled but still needs further observation, is encouraged to move to the CHC. Similar to the "Upward Referral" part, the "Downward Referral" part is used to reduce the high utilization of bed resources from inpatients at the recovery stage. Therefore, we build a two-level healthcare system consisting of several CHCs and a GH connected according to the TWRP.

This study is aimed at optimizing the performance of a hierarchical urban healthcare system by adjusting the patient flow distribution among different level healthcare facilities. Different from previous researches in the healthcare system, it focuses on the quantitative analysis to the patient flow distribution among the two-level urban healthcare system, with the intention to develop a decision-making supported tool for the government to determine the optimal patient flow distribution. Our method integrates the discrete-event simulation (DES), multiobjective optimization, and simulation optimization. There are three control variables describing the patient flow distribution, and eight system performance measures functioned as objectives in the optimization model. Since the stochastic healthcare service processes are too complicated to be modeled by mathematical tools, we use DES to model the healthcare system. In addition, we develop two simulation optimization algorithms to find the optimal patient flow distribution. One is based on Random Search (RS) and the Ranking and Selection (R&S), and the other is a variant algorithm based on Stochastic Approximation (SA) and improved by the Response Surface Method (RSM). We finally carry out a case study on the background of the Peking University Third Hospital (PUTH) and 15 CHCs in Beijing, China, to implement our method. Based on the analysis of the results, we conclude recommendations to improve the patient flow distribution in the current urban healthcare system. A comparison between the two algorithms from the aspects of efficiency and accuracy is also discussed in this case.

The main contribution of our work is that we propose a multiobjective simulation optimization method in a policy-driven healthcare problem. Simulation is used to describe the relationship between decision variables and objective functions in the multiobjective optimization model. Two improved algorithms have been designed to determine the optimal patient flow distribution. A typical case study demonstrates how to implement our approach. To our best knowledge, this work is the first chapter considering the macrolevel patient flow distribution in a hierarchical healthcare delivery system based on multiobjective simulation optimization.

This chapter is structured as follows. Section 10.2 reviews the previous research on improving patient flow distribution and simulation optimization in the field of healthcare. In Section 10.3, the macrolevel patient flow problem is studied as a multiobjective optimization model, and the two-level healthcare delivery system is simulated. In Section 10.4, we introduce simulation optimization approaches to solve the multiobjective model, and the developed algorithms are also included. Section 10.5 is the case study, in which our approach is implemented, and the two developed simulation optimization algorithms are compared. Section 10.6 is the conclusion to our approach along with policy recommendations to the government. In the end, the limitation of our approach and future study directions are also pointed out.

10.2   LITERATURE REVIEW

With respect to the objective of improving patient flow, relevant literatures associated with patient flow, multiobjective optimization, and simulation optimization are reviewed. Section 10.2.1 briefly reviews previous researches on patient flow optimization problem. Section 10.2.2 provides existing literatures on multiobjective optimization problems in the field of healthcare. In Section 10.2.3, literatures on simulation optimization are reviewed.

10.2.1   Simulation Modeling on Patient Flow

Most existing researches on patient flow planning focus on one or several certain departments at a microlevel. Among them, the allocation of crew and facilities, including the doctors, nurses, beds, medical devices, are mainly investigated, and the patients' length of stay (LOS), utilizations of medical resources, and the throughput of the system are chosen as the performance measures. Coelli et al. [1] develop a discrete-event computation simulation model, based on an existing public sector clinic of the Brazilian Cancer Institute, for the analysis of a mammography clinic performance. And they successfully prove that small-capacity configurations help to abridge the patient waiting time. Mallor et al. [2] develop a simulation model combined with generalized regression models to study bed occupancy levels in Intensive Care Unit (ICU). The beds and specialized staff are re-planned to meet the patients' requirement. Kumar [3] designs a surgical delivery process to optimize the patient flow in a country hospital in the United States. The bed capacity is adjusted by building a system simulation model. Venkatadri et al. [4] use simulation-based alternatives at the cardiac catheterization lab to improve the overall patient care process by reducing patient turnaround time.

Researches on patient flow congestion are also investigated. Raunak et al. [5] uses executable process definitions and separate components for specifying resources to support DES so as to improve efficiency of hospital Emergency Department. Powell et al. [6] conduct a cross-sectional computer modeling analysis to test three policies and choose the best-performed one to implement. In order to reduce the waiting time in ED, Konrad et al. [7] uses DES modeling to support the implementation of a split-flow process improvement in an ED. Statistical analysis of data taken before and after the implementation indicates that the waiting time is significantly improved and overall patient LOS is reduced.

Patients sometimes move from one healthcare facility to another. A few literatures investigate the healthcare system consisting of several levels of hospitals and referrals among them. Koizumi et al. [8] use a queuing network with blocking to model the patient flow in a mental health system in Pennsylvania. The system consists of three types of psychiatric institutions: extended acute hospitals, residential facilities, and supported housing, and the in-flows and out-flows between them are also considered. Farinha et al. [9] use a stochastic discrete-event simulation model to study the organization of primary and secondary care services. Original services are re-organized, and improvement in efficiency and quality healthcare delivery is achieved. Abo-Hamad and Arisha [10] develop a methodology using the DES to evaluate the entire emergency medical system of Belo Horizonte in Brazil.

10.2.2 Multiobjective Patient Flow Optimization Problems

Another criterion to classify the researches on patient flow distribution is the objective(s) they choose. Most of the researches only optimize one objective. Some are concerned about the service time represented by LOS [7, 11–13], and some are aimed to reduce Leave-Without-Being-Seen (LWBS) rate or to improve the throughputs [14–16], but only a few focus on the utilization of severs [17].

However, considering only one objective sometimes cannot improve the system in all directions, and thus the optimization to multiple objectives is required. Common methods of multiobjective programming include the objective dimensionality reduction, preference-based multiobjective optimization, and ideal multiobjective optimization [18].

The objective dimensionality reduction is to set benchmarks to secondary objectives and only optimize one primary objective instead. In this method, secondary objectives are transformed into constraints and primary objective retains as the objective function. Ahmed and Alkhamis [19] transform the average waiting time and costs to an ED unit into constraints of the programming model. Only the system throughput chosen as the single-objective function is optimized. Santibáñez et al. [20] use simulation to redesign the scheduling strategy of ACU process under several scenarios at an ambulatory care in Canada. In this research, a waiting time criteria is defined, and the utilization of ACU should be maximized. Popovich et al. [21] reduce the patients' LWBS rate in hospital emergency services by firstly making total LOS meets national benchmarks. Zhang et al. [22] carry out a research to long-term care capacity planning in Canada. They aim to find the minimal capacity planning satisfying the standard service level for patients' waiting time expressed as the probability that a patient exceeds the given target waiting time.

Another way to transform a multiobjective into single objective is the preference-based multiobjective optimization method [18]. The procedure is as follows:

(i) determining a preference vector representing the weight of each objective based on the higher-level information to construct the composite single-objective function, and (ii) using single-objective optimization algorithms to find the optimal solution(s). Oddoye et al. [23] describe a detailed simulation model for healthcare planning in a medical assessment unit and optimize five objectives including the patient queue length for nurses, for doctors, the total length of queues in the system, the total waiting time, and the number of beds. They use the weighted goal programming technique to construct the objective function where the weights are derived from the elicited preferences of the medical assessment unit management. Cardoen et al. [24] study a multiobjective combinatorial optimization problem to determine the sequence of patients within the operating rooms of a freestanding ambulatory surgical center. They study six objectives including the travel distance, the LOS in recovery area, the peak number of bed space, and the surgery scheduling of different types of patients. The chapter introduces each objective a weight and then sums the values of all weighted objectives.

An appropriate preference vector can be determined by Analytic Hierarchy Process (AHP), developed by Thomas Saaty's [25], and its variants, fuzzy AHP and Monte Carlo AHP, which have been used in the healthcare field. Abo-Hamad and Arisha [10] use AHP to aggregate conflicting objectives of providing wide accessibility and delivering high-quality services together as single objective, after their simulation model based on the exported outputs in the emergency department.

The ideal multiobjective optimization is as follows: (i) finding the set of trade-off (nondominated Pareto) optimal solutions by considering all objectives, (ii) using higher-level qualitative considerations to make a choice in the optimal solution set [18]. Baesler and Sepúlveda [26] develop a methodology integrating simulation and Genetic Algorithm (GA) for a cancer treatment center to optimize the performance of four objectives. They solves a two-objective operating room scheduling problem by the combination of simulation and Random Key Genetic Algorithm (RKGA).

10.2.3 Simulation Optimization

With the development of computing technology, the power of computer simulation becomes much stronger. Simulation nowadays can not only be used to describe a system but also to solve optimization problem to support decision making. Fu [27] introduces the theory of simulation optimization and summarizes several common methodologies.

Similar with deterministic optimization, methodologies in simulation optimization applied in healthcare area can be divided into several groups: (i) nonintelligent search; (ii) metaheuristic; and (iii) gradient search. A critical difference between deterministic optimization and simulation optimization is the randomness of outputs. Among all the methods in the field of simulation optimization, R&S is the most basic one that provides the comparison and ordinal theory to random simulation outputs based on statistical techniques. So R&S always functions as the auxiliary method to others in the researches on simulation optimization (i.e., [28–30], and [31]).

Both of exhaustive search and RS are functioned as nonintelligent global search strategies in simulation and optimization. They are usually used under discrete and countable settings, but exceptions also exist. Taboada et al. [32] use agent-based simulation (ABS) model to test the effects of different patients' derivation policies to the patients' LOS in ED. Six scenarios are tested separately, and the best-performed one is obtained as the optimal patient arrival pattern. Cabrera et al. [33] integrate ABS and exhaustive search optimization to find out the optimal ED staff configuration, which is modeled as a multidimensional problem. Several optimization methods based on RS, such as the Stochastic Ruler (SR) algorithm [34], the stochastic comparison (SC) algorithm [35], have also been proposed, but few of them is used in the healthcare area.

Metaheuristic methods are also used in discrete settings. Compared with exhaustive search and RS, metaheuristic methods search the definition domain with more wisdom. Another superiority of metaheuristic methods is their applicability in multiobjective optimization problems. Pareto optimal set can be found instead of determining weights of each objective to translate the problem into a single objective. Literatures on GA used in simulation optimization have been mentioned in Section 10.2.2. Other metaheuristic methods, such as Tabu search [36], Simulated Annealing [37], and Artificial Neural Network [38], have also been used in simulation optimization.

SA is based on gradient-search mechanism, which is often used in continuous settings, when the solution or scenario of the problem is noncountable. In these cases, procedure of SA runs much more efficiently than traditional random or exhaustive search. As a gradient-search algorithm, SA is not as widely used as methodologies mentioned earlier because the algorithm of SA is easily trapped in local optimality. Spall [39], Alrefaei and Diabat [40], and Broadie et al. [41] used SA in simulation optimization, and both of them obtained satisfied results. Another gradient-search algorithm RSM combines stochastic tool with simulation optimization, which provides regression model between the inputs and outputs of simulation [42–44].

10.3   PROBLEM DESCRIPTION AND MODELING

10.3.1   Problem Description

China's urban healthcare system in this chapter consists of a GH and several CHCs, in which all of the hospitals are accessible to patients. Because of the TWRP, referrals have higher priority in registration queues. Through the observation of the patient movement process, we obtain the patient flow chart of the two-level healthcare system as shown in Figure 10.1.

In this model, patients from the community choose CHC or GH for the first attendance with constant probabilities. The patient flow and service processes in CHC are modeled as follows. Before receiving the treatment, the current congestion level of CHC is judged. If the CHC is too crowded, patients abandon the service and leave

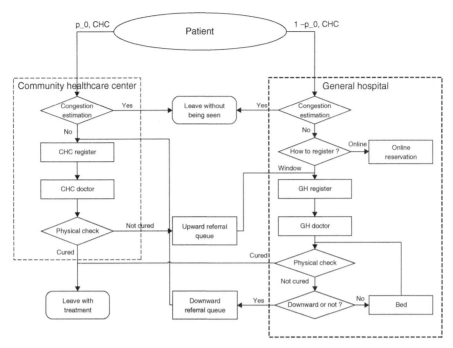

Figure 10.1 Patient flow and service processes in the two-level healthcare system.

the system with service failure. Otherwise, they sequentially go through the "CHC Register," the "CHC Doctor" servers for treatment. Patients who have finished the diagnosis are inspected whether they are cured in the "Physical Check" server. Cured patients leave the system with successful service, while others enter the "Upward Referral" queue, waiting to enter the GH part.

The GH part in this model is more complex, it includes three ways for registration: the registrations for upward referrals, the online reservation, and the window register for walk-in patients. The sum of all the registrations is fixed. The upward referrals have categorical priority in the registration queue. As for the "Online Reservation," patients request the appointment dates according to their preference and receive an appointment on the nearest available date after the day they want instead. Once the registration capacity runs out, patients do not get the admission and leave the system directly, which indicates the service is failed. Treatment process of GHs is similar to the CHCs. However, CHCs in China hardly have beds, and only GHs provide bed for hospitalization service to patients. So most of the GH patients leave the system with successful healthcare service, while the rest of them turn into inpatients. After a course of treatment, patients go back to the "Physical Check" server for another inspection to their health condition. And they also need another judgment module called "Downward or not" to choose a proper place for recovery.

10.3.2   System Modeling

The aim of our research is to optimize the system performances by adjusting the patient flow distribution. We choose three controllable variables with significant impacts on the patient flow distribution, which appeal much attention from the government as decision variables:

$p_{0,CHC}$ denotes the CFAR (Community First Attendance Ratio)
$p_{CHC,GH}$ denotes the upward referral ratio
$p_{GH,CHC}$ denotes the downward referral ratio.

We formulate the multiobjective functions containing the LOS, the throughput, the service efficacy represented by the LWBS rate, and the resources utilization. We define

T_{CHC} and T_{GH} as the average LOS in CHC and GH
T_{Upward} as the average LOS of upward referrals in the system
H as the number of cured patients in a day
L_{CHC} and L_{GH} as the service LWBS rate in CHC and GH
U_{CHC} and U_{GH} as the average utilization of resources in CHC and GH.

Then we get a series of multiobjective functions as follows:

$$\text{Minimize} \quad T_{CHC} = T_1(p_{0,CHC}, p_{CHC,GH}, p_{GH,CHC}) \tag{10.1}$$

$$\text{Minimize} \quad T_{GH} = T_2(p_{0,CHC}, p_{CHC,GH}, p_{GH,CHC}) \tag{10.2}$$

$$\text{Minimize} \quad T_{Upward} = T_3(p_{0,CHC}, p_{CHC,GH}, p_{GH,CHC}) \tag{10.3}$$

$$\text{Maximize} \quad H = H(p_{0,CHC}, p_{CHC,GH}, p_{GH,CHC}) \tag{10.4}$$

$$\text{Minimize} \quad L_{CHC} = L_1(p_{0,CHC}, p_{CHC,GH}, p_{GH,CHC}) \tag{10.5}$$

$$\text{Minimize} \quad L_{GH} = L_2(p_{0,CHC}, p_{CHC,GH}, p_{GH,CHC}) \tag{10.6}$$

$$\text{Maximize} \quad U_{CHC} = U_1(p_{0,CHC}, p_{CHC,GH}, p_{GH,CHC}) \tag{10.7}$$

$$\text{Maximize} \quad U_{GH} = U_2(p_{0,CHC}, p_{CHC,GH}, p_{GH,CHC}) \tag{10.8}$$

Subject to

$$0 \leq p_{0,CHC} \leq 1 \tag{10.9}$$

$$0 \leq p_{CHC,GH} \leq 0.1 \tag{10.10}$$

$$0 \leq p_{GH,CHC} \leq 0.05 \tag{10.11}$$

where $T_1(\cdot), T_2(\cdot), T_3(\cdot), H(\cdot), S_1(\cdot), S_2(\cdot), U_1(\cdot), U_2(\cdot)$ are the multiobjective functions determined by the three decision variables.

We use simulation to discover the value of functions 10.1–10.8. Constraints 10.9–10.11 are the policy limit, which also give the range of the decision variables. To solve the linear programming, we transform the multiobjective functions into a composite single-objective function using expression 10.12:

$$\text{Maximize } J(p_{0,\text{CHC}}, p_{\text{CHC,GH}}, p_{\text{GH,CHC}}) = w \cdot Y \qquad (10.12)$$

where $w = (w_1, w_2, \ldots, w_8)$ is the preference vector and Y is the linear standardized multiobjective vector.

(a) *Linear standardization* From the output of our simulation model, the orders of magnitude of the outputs are varied from 10^{-1} to 10^3, which destroy the fairness of the objective functions. In this paper, we target to develop a decision-support tool for the policy makers to justify the value of the multiobjective optimization model. The standardized output values of objective functions ranging from [0,100] are easy for the policy makers to understand the quantitative effect of the multiobjective optimization model. The expressions of $y_i(\hat{\mu}_i)$ are

$$y_i(\hat{\mu}_i) = \alpha_i \hat{\mu}_i + \beta_i \qquad (10.13)$$

where α_i, β_i are the one-stage coefficient and constant coefficients and $\hat{\mu}_i$ is the observed value of ith performance measure.

The method of undetermined coefficients is used to determine α_i, β_i. We should figure out the Upper Bound (UB) and Lower Bound (LB) of each objective at first by simulating under extreme circumstances. We define $\overline{\hat{\mu}_i}$ as the UB of ith performance measure and $\underline{\hat{\mu}_i}$ as the LB, and we then obtain equation sets to find α_i, β_i:

As for positive objectives, which should be maximized, such as $H, U_{\text{CHC}}, U_{\text{GH}}$, we define $y_i = 100$ when $\hat{\mu}_i = \overline{\hat{\mu}_i}$, and $y_i = 0$ when $\hat{\mu}_i = \underline{\hat{\mu}_i}$.

$$\begin{cases} \alpha_i \underline{\hat{\mu}_i} + \beta_i = 0 \\ \alpha_i \overline{\hat{\mu}_i} + \beta_i = 100 \end{cases}$$

On the contrary, as for negative objectives, we define $y_i = 0$ when $Y_i = \overline{Y}_i$, and $y_i = 100$ when $Y_i = \underline{Y}_i$.

$$\begin{cases} \alpha_i \underline{\hat{\mu}_i} + \beta_i = 100 \\ \alpha_i \overline{\hat{\mu}_i} + \beta_i = 0 \end{cases}$$

(b) *Determining preference vector* Some of the previous researches on healthcare service quality used AHP methodology ([45, 46], Arisha 2012) to determine the importance of factors. AHP is an easier method to carry out when the decision-making group is small and considers both the absolute and relative weights of the objectives as an entire system, which determines the weights comprehensively. The procedures of AHP are as follows: (i) proposing the hierarchy model; (ii) constructing the pairwise comparison matrix; (iii) figuring out the weights vector; and (iv) checking the consistency.

10.4 METHODOLOGY

The methodology structure of the multiobjective optimization is based on the preference-based multiobjective optimization procedure [18] as follows:

- Use higher-level information to determine the preference vector and the composite single-objective function;
- Find a single trade-off optimal solution by a single-objective optimization algorithm.

Distinguished from deterministic optimization, the value of objective variables is observed by the simulation model. The flow chart of multiobjective simulation optimization algorithm is shown in Figure 10.2.

10.4.1 Simulation Model Description

We used Arena 14.0.0 developed by Rockwell company to construct our simulation model. The logical of the patient flow chart in the simulation model is the same as described in Figure 10.1. In order to have easier observations and calculations, we raise the following assumptions in the DES simulation model:

- Patients are categorized into three groups: (i) CHC patients, who enter CHC for diagnosis and leave the system after finishing all the processes in CHC; (ii) GH

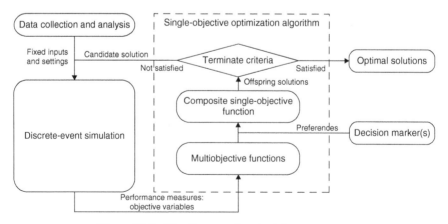

Figure 10.2 The diagram of methodology structure.

patients, who enter GH directly; (iii) upward patients, who enter CHC at first, but go upward to GH for further treatment after finishing all the processes in CHC. Since the number of downward referrals is too small to analyze and the difference of the average LOS between GH patients and downward referrals are not significant, we do not differentiate downward referrals with GH patients.

- As a macrolevel patient flow simulation optimization research, more detailed processes of diagnosis and treatment, such as physical tests, payment, prescription, and pharmacy, are included in the "CHC Doctor" and "GH Doctor" servers for model simplification.
- Upward patients need GH-level healthcare service and will finish their treatments in GH ultimately. Therefore, they are included in the throughputs of GH.

10.4.2 Optimization

With the development of computing technology, simulation has been used to construct and analyze complex systems for a couple of years. The integration of simulation model and optimization techniques is now accessible for decision making, and several simulation optimization approaches have been put forward. Fu [27] introduces simulation optimization, as well as five common approaches including R&S, SA, RSM, RS algorithm, and SPO (Sample Path Optimization). After that, some more chapters discuss the theories and applications of simulation optimization [1, 19, 22, 47].

Each simulation optimization approach has its own pros and cons. In order to design a more effective and efficient framework, we develop two improved integrated algorithms. Algorithm 1 is based on RS algorithm, and R&S is used to determine the number of simulation replications. The second one is gradient-search algorithm based on SA and improved by the RSM to regress the local surface.

10.4.2.1 Algorithm 1: RS + R&S RS is one of the most common approaches of simulation optimization because of the existence of theoretical convergence [48–51]. It is appropriate for both discrete and continuous inputs. A candidate solution randomly chosen by procedure each time is substituted into simulation model as decision variables. After computing the value of objective functions, the procedure makes a comparison between the current optimal solution and the candidate solution, and chooses the better one as new optimal solution.

Algorithm 1

Step 1 Initiation: Define $\hat{\theta}_*$ as the initial solution. Then define $i = 1$, and i_{max} as the maximum iteration times. Plug $\hat{\theta}_*$ into the simulation model and run the simulation. We get the mean value of objective $\hat{J}(\hat{\theta}_*)$ by running the replication for m times.

Step 2 Iteration: Generate another $\theta_i \in \Omega$ (Ω is the feasible domain) and plug it into the simulation model. Run the replication for m times to obtain the value of objective $\hat{J}(\theta_i)$. Compare $\hat{J}(\hat{\theta}_*)$ and $\hat{J}(\theta_i)$. Update $\hat{\theta}_*$, i as follows:

$$\hat{\theta}_* = \begin{cases} \theta_i & \hat{J}(\hat{\theta}_*) > \hat{J}(\theta_i) \\ \hat{\theta}_* & \hat{J}(\hat{\theta}_*) \leq \hat{J}(\theta_i) \end{cases}$$

$$i = i + 1 \tag{10.14}$$

Step 3 Optimal solution: when the terminal criteria $i > i_{\max}$ is satisfied, return $\hat{\theta}_*$.

One of the challenges of Algorithm 1 is to identify the performance of input $\hat{\theta}_*$ and θ_i. The value of outputs collected by simulation is with uncertainty, we can only infer its distribution by repeated observations. However, determining the sample size has a dilemma that more samples guarantee the accuracy of results, while the speed of algorithm decreases with increasing replications. Therefore, we introduce R&S to determine the sample size that is statistically optimal.

Before that, we firstly introduce two concepts: indifference zone δ and confidence level α [52]. The indifference zone expresses the precision level of the selection, and the confidence level means the probability to make a correct selection. Briefly, we claim $\overrightarrow{\theta_1}$, $\overrightarrow{\theta_2}$ to be indifferent in zone δ at a confidence level α if

$$\text{Prob}[|J(\overrightarrow{\theta_1}) - J(\overrightarrow{\theta_2})| < \delta] \geq \alpha \tag{10.15}$$

After knowing indifference zone δ, confidence level α, sample standard deviation σ, the number of candidate solutions k, and the number of optimal solutions t, we can figure out the proper sample size n according to single-stage procedure which is determined by

$$n = \left(\frac{c_{\alpha,k,t}\sigma}{\delta}\right)^2 \tag{10.16}$$

where $c_{\alpha,k,t}$ exists in the lookup table [53].

10.4.2.2 Algorithm 2: SA + RSM   Compared with RSA, SA is much more effective on searching the optimal solution. SA is a greedy algorithm that each iteration of candidate solution moves forward to a greedy direction so as to maximize the improvements of objective function [54]. As for a MINIMIZE problem, θ_n denotes the input of nth iteration, the iteration formulation is

$$\theta_{n+1} = \Pi_\Theta(\theta_n - a_n \hat{\nabla} J(\theta_n)) \tag{10.17}$$

where function Π_Θ is used to guarantee the feasibility of new candidate point, a_n is the step multiplier, and $\hat{\nabla} J$ indicates the gradient of current point.

The key point of SA is finding the gradient. According to Fu [27], no direct gradient is available because there is no mathematical relationship between inputs and outputs. In this case, one-sided finite difference (FD) or two-sided symmetric difference

(SD) estimation is used to figure out the approximate gradient. However, neither approach is accurate enough since the response surface of this problem seems relatively complex and nonlinear. Therefore, we bring in RSM to obtain approximate functional relationship between decision variables and objective function near candidate points so as to figure out the gradient [55]. One-stage and two-level linear regression models are used in RSM. Considering the trade-off of effectiveness and efficiency of the algorithm, we only use one-stage regression model as follows:

$$J(\vec{\theta}) = \alpha_0 + \alpha_1 p_{0,CHC} + \alpha_2 p_{CHC,GH} + \alpha_3 p_{GH,CHC} + \varepsilon \qquad (10.18)$$

where $J(\vec{\theta})$ denotes objective function (response), $\alpha_i (0 \leq i \leq 3)$ denotes the undetermined coefficient, $p_{0,CHC}, p_{CHC,GH}, p_{GH,CHC}$ are the decision variables (factors), and ε is the random disturbance that cannot be explained by our model.

Algorithm 2

- **Step 1 Initiation**: Assign the current value of $\vec{\theta} = (p_{0,CHC}, p_{CHC,GH}, p_{GH,CHC})$ as the initial candidate point of the model. According to Resolution-III full factorial design with center points, choose 27 extreme and center points of area Ω:

$$\Omega = \{p_{0,CHC} - \delta_1 \leq p'_{0,CHC} \leq p_{0,CHC} + \delta_1, p_{CHC,GH} - \delta_2 \leq p'_{CHC,GH}$$
$$\leq p_{CHC,GH} + \delta_2, p_{GH,CHC} - \delta_3 \leq p'_{GH,CHC} \leq p_{0,CHC} + \delta_3\}$$

as the sample of experiment, where δ_i is the width of the area on dimension i. Then we can obtain a sample set sized $27*m$, after simulating each point for m times.

- **Step 2 Regression**: Regress the sample in order to obtain the one-stage linear model between factors and response shown as

$$J(\vec{\theta}) = a p_{0,CHC} + b p_{CHC,GH} + c p_{GH,CHC} + J_0 \qquad (10.19)$$

  Figure out the gradient as following:

$$\nabla J(\vec{\theta}) = \left(\frac{\partial J}{\partial p_{0,CHC}}, \frac{\partial J}{\partial p_{CHC,GH}}, \frac{\partial J}{\partial p_{GH,CHC}} \right) = (a, b, c) \qquad (10.20)$$

- **Step 3 Iteration**: Calculate the length of gradient

$$|\nabla J(\vec{\theta})| = \sqrt{a^2 + b^2 + c^2} \qquad (10.21)$$

If $|\nabla J(\vec{\theta})|$ is relatively small, or the area Ω does not fit the one-stage linear regression model, or the value of objective function is worse than the previous one, the algorithm ends and return

$$\vec{\theta} = \arg \max_{\theta \in \Theta} n_\theta$$

Otherwise, move forward by one step α along the direction of gradient, and update the candidate point by

$$\vec{\theta} = \left(p_{0,\text{CHC}} + \frac{a\alpha}{|\nabla J(\vec{\theta})|}, \ p_{\text{CHC,GH}} + \frac{b\alpha}{|\nabla J(\vec{\theta})|}, p_{\text{GH,CHC}} + \frac{c\alpha}{|\nabla J(\vec{\theta})|} \right) \tag{10.22}$$

- **Step 4**: Return to step 1.

There are few chapters discussing the value of α, and no rigorous method has been derived to determine α. In this chapter, we alternate several values of α, and choose the best-performed one to recommend in the following case study.

10.5   CASE STUDY: ADJUSTING PATIENT FLOW FOR A TWO-LEVEL HEALTHCARE SYSTEM CENTERED ON THE PUTH

10.5.1   Background and Data

The PUTH, located in Haidian district, Beijing, is one of the most famous GHs, providing healthcare service not only for nearby residential communities but also for patients all over the country. There are 15 CHCs keeping long-term partnerships with PUTH. Due to its fame, a huge number of outpatients come to PUTH for medical service, but only a few go to the CHC. To solve this problem, we model the real two-level healthcare system and use our proposed simulation optimization approach to find an optimal patient flow distribution that maximize the system multiple performances.

The data sources of this case study include Haidian District Community Health Reporting System (HDCHRS), Beijing Registration Reservation Platform (BRRP), and China Health Statistics Yearbook 2012 (CHSY 2012) [56]. Unfortunately, not all data could be obtained directly through these sources mentioned earlier, that is, the service time distribution of register windows at CHC. So these microcosmic data are collected through field research. Parameters are classified into two types: fixed parameters keeping constant throughout the simulation optimization, and decision variables need dynamic adjustment. The current values of all parameters (by April 4, 2013) are shown in Tables 10.1 and 10.2.

As mentioned in Section 10.3.2, to complete the simulation optimization model, we transform the multiobjective functions into a single one. The first step is to linearly standardize all the objectives (outputs) distributed in [0, 100]. Through the simulation under extreme conditions, we obtain the upper and lower bounds of each objective. According to linear standardize expression, we figure out α_i, β_i as shown in Table 10.3.

The second step is to determine the weights w_i of each objective. We invited several experts in healthcare area to weight the significance of all of the objectives and measured them by the AHP template (Table 10.4).

TABLE 10.1   The Current Value of Fixed Parameters

	Variable	Value
λ	Total customer arrival rate (person/h)	1894
μ_r	Service rate of CHC register window (person/h)	103
μ_C	Service rate of CHC doctor (person/h)	6.43
μ_R	Service rate of GH register window (person/h)	103
μ_G	Service rate of GH doctor (person/h)	2.90
T_B	Average LOS in hospital (day)	6.64
P	The probability of patients in hospital (%)	10.05
n_{cr}	The number of register windows in CHCs	30
n_{cd}	The number of CHC doctors	88
n_{gr}	The number of register windows in GH	12
n_{gd}	The number of GH doctors	552
m	The number of beds in GH	1463
K	The number of registrations released by GH each day	8077
K'	The number of GH registrations reserved online each day	4038
N	The time limit of online reserving (day)	7

TABLE 10.2   The Current Value of Decision Variables

	Variables	Value
$p_{0,CHC}$	The CFAR (Community First Attendance Ratio) (%)	4.94
$p_{CHC,GH}$	The upward referral ratio (%)	1.13
$p_{GH,CHC}$	The downward referral ratio (%)	0.1

TABLE 10.3   Bounds of Each Objective and Value of α_i, β_i

	Upper Bound	Lower Bound	α_i	β_i
T_{CHC}	2	0.17	−54.6448	109.2896
T_{GH}	18	8	−4.3478	134.7826
T_{Upward}	13	2.5	−9.5238	123.8095
H	13,000	4200	0.0113	−47.7273
L_{CHC}	0.73	0	−136.9863	136.9863
L_{GH}	0.48	0	−208.3333	208.3333
U_{CHC}	0.835	0	119.7605	0.0000
U_{GH}	0.767	0	130.3781	0.0000

TABLE 10.4   The Weight of Each Objective

w_i	Value
w_1	0.1094
w_2	0.0640
w_3	0.1559
w_4	0.2584
w_5	0.1658
w_6	0.1527
w_7	0.0381
w_8	0.0558

We feed the value of α_i, β_i into linear standard expressions and then feed both $y_i()$ and w_i into expression 10.12 to obtain the composite objective function as shown in expression 10.24.

$$\text{Maximize}\ \ J(p_{0,\text{CHC}}, p_{\text{CHC,GH}}, p_{\text{GH,CHC}}) = -5.9758\text{T}_{\text{CHC}} - 0.2782\text{T}_{\text{GH}}$$

$$- 1.4846\text{T}_{\text{Upward}} + 0.002936\text{H} - 22.7185\text{L}_{\text{CHC}} - 31.8027\text{L}_{\text{GH}}$$

$$+ 4.5580\text{U}_{\text{CHC}} + 7.2753\text{U}_{\text{GH}} + 82.0764 \tag{10.23}$$

10.5.2   Simulation under Current Situation

10.5.2.1   Results of System Simulation   We input the data in Tables 10.1 and 10.2 to our simulation model and define the length of each day to be 8 h (equal to the real work-hour), the length of simulation to be 30 days. The simulation runs for 100 times, and we finally obtain the simulation results.

(a) *LOS*   Since the number of downward patients is very little, in this section, we only consider the LOS of three types of patients: the CHC patients, the GH patients, and the upward referrals. The timing of LOS starts once the patient enters the system and ends when the patient leaves.

As shown in Figure 10.3, the LOS of CHC patient is much shorter than the other two. More details in the simulation process shows that the congestion rate in CHC is quite low because of the small arrival rate of CHC patients. The average length of queues in CHC is very short, indicating that most of the CHC patients' demand can be received without delay. Another discovery is that the LOS of GH patients is almost three times that of upward referrals, which is regarded as a positive effect of the TWRP.

(b) *Throughputs and LWBS Rates*   These performances reflect the service capacity and quality of hospitals. From Figure 10.4, the GH's throughput is over 10 times of CHCs', in other words, over 90% patients are cured in GH. The LWBS rate of CHC is 0, but the service success rate in GH is that nearly half of GH patients leave the system without successful treatments. The poor performance in GH

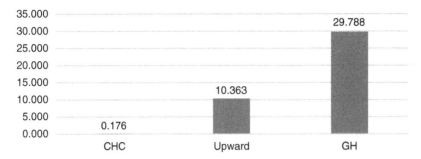

Figure 10.3 The LOS of three kinds of patients under current situation.

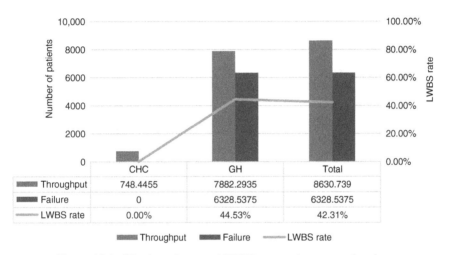

Figure 10.4 The throughputs and LWBS rates under current situation.

hugely influences the whole healthcare system that most of the service occurs in GH, making the total LWBS rate exceed 40%.

(c) *Resources' Utilizations* The utilizations of all the resources are shown in Figure 10.5, and we find doctors in GH are three times busier than those in CHC. The register windows in GH are even busier than doctors, while the register windows in CHC are idle most of the time. The bottleneck in GH is the bed server. Beds in GH are always occupied according to the simulation results, which is consistent with the data shown in CHSY 2012.

10.5.2.2 Analysis and System Estimation We obtain that the value of composite objective function is 51.91 after inputting the simulation results to expression 10.24. The original value and the standardized score (belongs to interval [0,100]) of each objective are shown in Table 10.5.

The objectives of T_{CHC}, L_{CHC} are nearly full marks, which means that CHC patients can receive fast and guaranteed service, but U_{CHC} does not perform well.

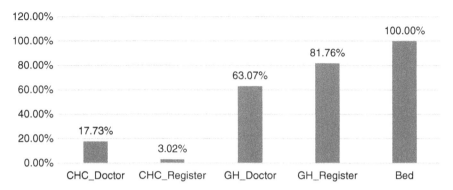

Figure 10.5 The resources' utilizations under current situation.

TABLE 10.5 The Value and Score of Objective Variables under Current Situation

	Value	Score
T_{CHC}	0.176	99.65
T_{GH}	29.788	5.27
T_{Upward}	10.363	25.11
H	8630.7	49.80
L_{CHC}	0.00%	100
L_{GH}	44.53%	7.22
U_{CHC}	14.79%	17.71
U_{GH}	76.02%	99.11
Sum		51.91

This is because the patients that go to CHC for healthcare service is in the minority, making resources in CHC always idle. On the contrary, blocking and congestion in GH are severe. The score of U_{GH} is high, but of the T_{GH}, L_{GH}, and T_{Upward} are low. Though servers in GH are made full use of to meet the huge demand, the service time and LWBS rate cannot reach a satisfied level. Obviously, the simulation results is consistent with the current situation of urban healthcare system in China. The unmatched situation between patient flow and the medical resource allocation brings a series of problems mentioned in the introduction part to the system. In Section 10.5.4, we introduce our approach to optimize the patient flow by readjusting $P_{0,CHC}$, $P_{CHC,GH}$, $P_{GH,CHC}$ to improve the performance of current system.

10.5.3 Model Validation

To validate the simulation model, we compare simulation results collected in Section 10.5.3 to the authoritative data published by the Ministry of Health (MOH).

TABLE 10.6   The Comparison between Statistics Published by MOH and Simulation Results

	Statistics	Simulation Results	Error
Ratio of throughputs between GH and CHC	9.901	10.537	6.42%
Utilization (%) of beds in hospitals	104.2	100	−4.03%
Daily visits per doctor in CHC	7.9	8.5	7.59%
Daily visits per doctor in GH	20	19.705	−1.48%
Throughputs of PUTH per day	7977	7882	−1.1%

As shown in Table 10.6, most of the performances of our simulation system are consistent with the statistics.

10.5.4   Optimization through Algorithm 1

10.5.4.1 Defining Variables   We firstly derive the value of the indifferent zone δ, the confidence level α, the sample standard deviation σ, the number of candidate points k, and the number of optimal solution t in order to determine the sample size according to the R&S approach. In step (b) of Algorithm 1 (seen from Section 10.4.2.1), the comparison only occurs between the newly generated point θ_i and the current optimal point θ_*. Therefore, we set $k = 2$, $t = 1$. Through the preliminary experiment, we found the sample standard deviation varied from 0.35 to 0.84. By convention, we set $\delta = 0.1$, $\alpha = 0.05$, and plug them into expression 10.19, so that we have

$$n = \left(\frac{2.3262 \times 0.84}{0.1} \right)^2 = 382 \tag{10.24}$$

Since the effective simulation length is 20 days (removing the 10-day warm-up time), the replication time of simulation should be $m = \frac{n}{20} = 20$. Limited by the hardware capability, we defined the number of iteration times $N = 1000$ as the end condition that 1000 randomly generated points in definition domain are tested. Hence, the total duration of the algorithm lasts $30 \times 20 \times 1000 = 6 \times 10^5$ simulation days.

10.5.4.2 Optimization Result   The optimization decision variables found by Algorithm 1 is $\hat{\theta}_* = (0.4798, 0.01032, 0.016805)$, which is significantly different from the current value of $\theta_0 = (0.0494, 0.0113.0.0010)$, especially the $p_{0,CHC}$ and $p_{GH,CHC}$. The values and scores of objectives under the optimal scenario $\hat{\theta}_*$ are shown in Table 10.7.

Compared with Table 10.6, the value of composite objective function expressed by formulation 10.24 in Table 10.7 improves by nearly 50%. The huge increase of $p_{0,CHC}$ reverse the unbalanced allocation of CHC patients and GH patients. More details are contained in Table 10.7 that the objectives T_{GH} and L_{GH} almost reach the full score, which means that the crowd in GH is released. In addition, the U_{CHC} and U_{GH}

TABLE 10.7   The Value and Score of Objective Variables under Optimal Solution of Algorithm 1

	Value	Score
T_{CHC}	0.981	55.66
T_{GH}	8.274	98.81
T_{Upward}	6.363	63.21
H	11,901.9	87.53
L_{CHC}	42.24%	42.14
L_{GH}	0.34%	99.29
U_{CHC}	83.41%	99.89
U_{GH}	75.09%	97.90
Sum		76.29

also obtain high scores, especially U_{CHC}, leading to the increase of throughputs in CHC and the whole system. The average number of cured patients each day increases by over 3000, in other words, the service capability of the whole system significant increases by 38%. However, the optimal solution sacrifices T_{CHC} and L_{CHC} to the improvement of GH because the scores of T_{CHC} and L_{CHC} decrease to some extent.

10.5.4.3   Outputs Analysis   We record the outputs of all of the 1000 points generated in Algorithm 1 to analyze the relationship between three decision variables and the composite objective function value. The correlation tests between the composite objective function and one-dimension factors $p_{0,CHC}$, $p_{CHC,GH}$, $p_{GH,CHC}$, along with two-dimension factors $(p_{0,CHC}, p_{CHC,GH})$, $(p_{GH,CHC}, p_{0,CHC})$, $(p_{CHC,GH}, p_{GH,CHC})$ are carried out, but only $p_{0,CHC}$ has significant effects on the objective value. The scatters of one-dimension factors and the composite objective function are shown in Figure 10.6.

Figure 10.6a shows that there are two local maxima all over the domain of $p_{0,CHC}$ located near 0.26 and 0.47. Through segmented tests, we find that the curves between a maximum (minimum) and its adjacent minimum (maximum) are all linear. The insight of Figure 10.6a contains that when $p_{0,CHC} \in [0, 0.26)$ or $[0.28, 0.47)$, the value of objective function and $p_{0,CHC}$ increase synchronously, while when $p_{0,CHC} \in [0.26, 0.28)$ or $[0.47, 1.00]$, the value of objective function decreases as $p_{0,CHC}$ increases. Figure 10.6b and c shows that the relationships between $p_{CHC,GH}$, $p_{GH,CHC}$ and the composite objective function are not significant.

10.5.5   Optimization through Algorithm 2

Since the domain of decision variables is relatively small, as well as the number of iterations, we only discussed the iteration step with a fixed length. According to constraints 10.9–10.11, the widths of definition domain are $D_{0,CHC} = 1$, $D_{CHC,GH} = 0.1$, $D_{GH,CHC} = 0.05$. We defined $\delta_i = \frac{\min(D_i)}{50} = 1 \times 10^{-3}$,

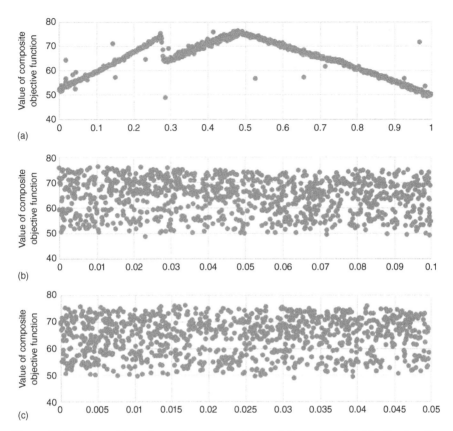

Figure 10.6 The scatters of one-dimension factors and the composite objective function. (a) $p\_(0, \text{CHC})$, (b) $p\_(\text{CHC}, \text{GH})$, and (c) $p\_(\text{GH}, \text{CHC})$

the replication times $m = 10$, the length of simulation to be 20 days, with a 10-day warm-up time, and the original point $\vec{\theta}_0 = (0.0494, 0.0113, 0.001)$ from the performance of existing system.

10.5.5.1   Step Length $\alpha = 0.02$ The procedure of Algorithm 2 stops after 29 iterations, lasting 156,600 workdays in simulation. During the procedure, two peaks $(0.2605, 0.02437, 0.006447)$ and $(0.4773, 0.01168, 0.04979)$ are discovered, consistent to the results of Algorithm 1. By comparing the objective function value at these two points, we found the latter one is better, at which the objective function equaled to 76.90, a bit larger than the maximal value 76.29 discovered by Algorithm 1.

The iteration path of candidate solutions is shown in Figure 10.7, and the arrow shows the direction that the candidate solution evolves. Figure 10.7a is the three-dimensional plot of iteration path and the iteration paths in Figure 10.7b–d are two-dimensional projections in plane $p_{0,\text{CHC}} - p_{\text{CHC},\text{GH}}$, $p_{\text{GH},\text{CHC}} - p_{\text{CHC},\text{GH}}$, and $p_{0,\text{CHC}} - p_{\text{GH},\text{CHC}}$. Part figures (a), (b), and (d) of Figure 10.7 all show that the value of $p_{0,\text{CHC}}$ increase as the procedure goes forward until the procedure stops, while

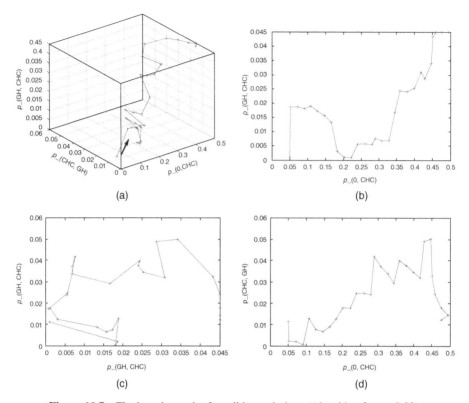

(a)   (b)

(c)   (d)

Figure 10.7   The iteration path of candidate solutions (Algorithm 2, $\alpha = 0.02$).

the values of $p_{CHC,GH}$ and $p_{GH,CHC}$ move irregularly. These properties indicate that
the evolution of the composite objective function is mainly driven by the increase of
$p_{0,CHC}$. Therefore, we can get the similar insights with Section 10.5.4.3 that $p_{0,CHC}$
is the main factor influencing the objective function.

Figure 10.8 shows the evolution of the composite objective function during the
procedure. The value increases continuously until the 13th step. After two-step adjustment, the procedure finds another rising path, and the objective function increases
until the 29th step. The procedure ends at that time because no rising path could be
found. For more details, we discuss the evolution of each objective in the following.

According to the evolution curve of the composite objective function, we divide
the iteration process into three stages: (i) the 1st to 13th step, (ii) the 13th to 15th step,
and (iii) the 15th to 29th step. The evolution curves of individual objective functions
are shown in Figures 10.9–10.11. In the first stage, the CHC is idle, but the GH is
overloaded. The increase of the CFAR $p_{0,CHC}$ lead to the increase of the utilization of
resources and the throughput in CHC. Along with the decrease of arrivals at GH, the
service failure in GH reduces at the same time. That is why the value of the composite
objective function increases at this stage. When the procedure comes to the 14th step,

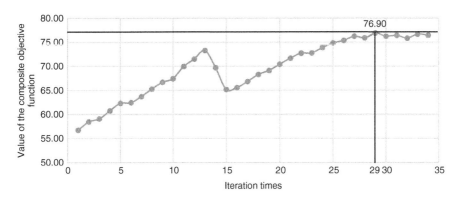

Figure 10.8 The evolution of the composite objective function (Algorithm 2, $\alpha = 0.02$).

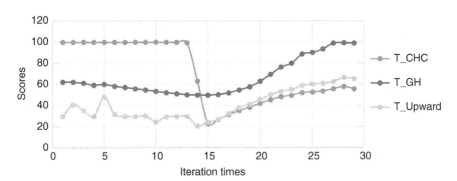

Figure 10.9 The evolution of the LOS of each type of patients (Algorithm 2, $\alpha = 0.02$).

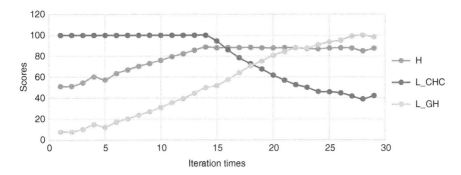

Figure 10.10 The evolution of the throughputs and LWBS rate (Algorithm 2, $\alpha = 0.02$).

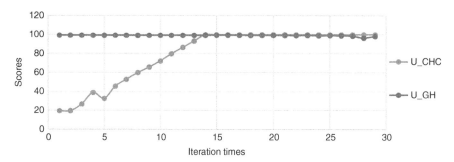

Figure 10.11 The evolution of the average utilization of resources in CHC and GH (Algorithm 2, $\alpha = 0.02$).

the CHC is saturated with patients, which makes the LOS of CHC patients increases sharply, and the score of T_{CHC} decreases. The composite objective function is hugely influenced by the change of T_{CHC}, and starts to decrease at this moment. In the last stage, both of CHC and GH run at the full speed, so that the values of U_{CHC}, U_{GH}, and H keep steady. Although L_{CHC} starts to decrease, the increase of other objectives including T_{CHC}, T_{GH}, T_{Upward}, and H helps to improve the composite objective function. At this time, T_{GH} and T_{Upward} are shortened under the effects of increasing $p_{GH,CHC}$, which leads to the reduction of GH patients' LOS in bed. Meanwhile, L_{GH} increases at the beginning of the procedure and reaches the upper bound 100 finally. Comparing the scores of L and L_{GH} at the end of iteration, we find that the CHC is overloaded, but the GH is just saturated. Since the arrival rate of the whole system exceeds the service rate, the LWBS rates of CHC and GH cannot reach 0 at the same time. Therefore, sacrificing one of them is an acceptable choice.

10.5.5.2 Step Length $\alpha = 0.05$ and $\alpha = 0.1$ In order to check the influence of step length toward output, we then set the step length α as 0.05 and run the procedure of Algorithm 2. The procedure stops after 10 iterations, lasting 54,000 workdays in simulation. Similar to the results shown in Section 10.5.5.1, two peaks (0.2771, 0.02372, 0.02295) and (0.4779, 0.004649, 0.02718) are found. The objective function obtained the maximum 76.60 at point $\hat{\theta}_* = (0.4779, 0.004649, 0.02718)$. By comparing the iteration path and the evolution of composite objective function with Figures 10.7 and 10.9, we find that the shapes of the curves are similar. The procedure of Algorithm 2 with a 0.1-step length has similar results with a six-step iteration, lasting 32,400 workday in simulation. The optimal solution is $\hat{\theta}_* = (0.4686, 0.000255, 0.04954)$, where the value of final objective function equals to 76.86.

The values of final objective function identified by procedures of Algorithm 2 with different step lengths are quite close. Result obtained by procedure with the step length of 0.02 is the best, and the point $\vec{\theta} = (0.4773, 0.01168, 0.04979)$ is the optimal solution of Algorithm 2. The value and score of objectives are shown in Table 10.8.

TABLE 10.8 The Value and Score of Objective Variables under Optimal Solution of Algorithm 2

	Value	Score
T_{CHC}	0.984	55.54
T_{GH}	8.280	98.78
T_{Upward}	6.070	66.00
H	11,938.1	87.94
L_{CHC}	42.09%	42.34
L_{GH}	0.27%	99.44
U_{CHC}	83.41%	99.90
U_{GH}	75.45%	98.37
Sum		76.90

10.5.6 Comparison of the Two Algorithms

Both of the two algorithms have their own pros and cons. On the one hand, the theoretical convergence of Algorithm 1 guarantees the use in almost all the simulation optimization problems. On the other hand, the greedy mechanism of Algorithm 2 helps to promote the efficiency of procedure by eliminating iterations from many noneffective points. As for this case, we recommend Algorithm 2 according to the comparison shown in Table 10.9. We estimate the convergence rate of two algorithms by using the simulation running time (workdays), because for a simulation optimization problem, most of the computation time is spent on simulation. The simulation time for each point in Algorithm 1 is $30 \times 20 = 600$ workdays, and the procedure test 1000 points. However, for Algorithm 2, the simulation running time for each iteration is $27 \times 20 \times 10 = 5400$ workdays, and the effective iteration times for Algorithm 2 with different step sizes are 29, 10, and 6. The running time of Algorithm 1 is much longer than Algorithm 2, almost three times longer than the Algorithm 2 with α equals to 0.02, and 18 times longer than the Algorithm 2 with α equals to 0.1. However, the performance of optimal solution under Algorithm 1 is not as good as Algorithm 2.

TABLE 10.9 The Comparison between Algorithms 1 and 2

	Algorithm 1	Algorithm 2 (SA + RSM)		
	(RSA + R&S)	$\alpha = 0.02$	$\alpha = 0.05$	$\alpha = 0.1$
Running time	600,000	156,600	54,000	32,400
Optimal solution	(0.4798, 0.01032, 0.016805)	(0.4773, 0.01168, 0.04979)	(0.4779, 0.004649, 0.02718)	(0.4686, 0.000255, 0.04954)
Maximum of objective function	76.29	76.90	76.60	76.86

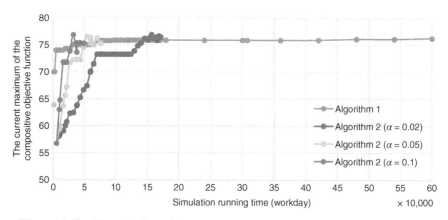

Figure 10.12 The evolutions of the current maximum of composite objective function.

From another aspect, the curves in Figure 10.12 show the evolutions of current maximum of objective function. For Algorithm 1, the value of current maximum does not change much after 60,000 simulation workdays, while the curves of Algorithm 2 rise steadily before reaching a peak.

Unfortunately, Algorithm 2 is always available. First of all, both the SA method and the RSM can only be used on continuous problems, that is, both the decision variable (input) and objective function (output) should be continuous. In addition, the number of peaks on response surface greatly influences the efficiency of procedure. Each time after reaching a peak, the program must spend a couple of iterations searching for a path to a new peak or to prove there is not any more peak in the domain. If there are more than 10 peaks throughout the definition domain, the efficiency of Algorithm 2 will substantially decrease. The step length in SA method is the key to determine the accuracy and efficiency of the algorithm. In the PUTH case, the 0.1 step length is recommended considering both the accuracy and efficiency. However, if the accuracy of the optimal solution is more important, the shorter step length will be needed.

10.5.7 Managerial Insights and Recommendations

The case study is aimed to ameliorate the awkward situation of healthcare system in Haidian. On the other hand, it helps to confirm the practicability of our decision-support approach. Insights from the comparison between current situation and the optimal solution are as follows:

- The practical CFAR now in CHC is 4.94%, only one-tenth of the optimal solution of 47.69%. Such a low CHC arrival rate prevents the full use of healthcare resources in CHC. We recommend our government to strive to develop CHC, especially the technical and skill levels of CHC.
- The current ratio of upward referral (1.13%) is almost the same as the optimal solution (1.17%), which indicates that the upward part of TWRP has been

brought into effect in the real-world system. However, since the optimal CFAR in CHC increases hugely, the actual number of upward referrals increases at the same time. The transferring passage for upward referrals should be consolidated.

Different from the upward referral part, the downward referral part of TWRP is not fully used. According to the optimal solution, the value of $p_{GH,CHC}$ reaches the upper bound, which means that transferring treatment downward should be strongly advocated.

From the simulation results, the CHC is indeed much more convenient than GH in terms of short waiting time and high success service rate. It is important that patients can have a diagnosis to their disease in advance, so that they can choose a proper healthcare facility to receive treatment. By comparing the current and optimal values of objective variables, we obtained the following insights:

- The LOS of patients treated in GH is shortened sharply (from 3.724 days to 1.034 days), and the LOS of upward referrals also decreases by 39% because of the quicker service in GH, which is still shorter than the LOS in GH. The only bad effect is that the LOS in CHC increases from 11 min to nearly an hour.
- The utilization of resources in CHC increases by five times under the premise of keeping the utilization of GH constant. It improves the throughput of the entire two-level system 38% each day.

The LWBS rate in GH decreases from 44.53% to 0.34%, making almost all the GH patients received successfully, but the CHC's service of LWBS rate increases. As aforementioned in Section 10.5.5.1, sacrificing L_{CHC} to fulfill other objectives' improvement is acceptable.

10.6 CONCLUSIONS AND THE FUTURE WORK

This chapter proposes a novel methodology for the adjustment of patient flow in the two-level urban healthcare system. Our approach integrates statistical analysis, discrete-event simulation, multiobjective programming, and simulation optimization. We use the mathematical programming technique to model the problem, the simulation tool to describe the healthcare system, and the simulation optimization to find the optimal solution. We also carry out a real-world case of the PUTH, which helps to confirm the operational applicability of our approach. Two modified simulation optimization algorithms are designed to our approach, and we compare both of their efficiency and effectiveness in the case study.

From a methodological perspective, the main innovation of this chapter is the combination of multiobjective optimization and simulation optimization methods. We model the patient flow problem aimed at the optimization of service time (LOS), service capacity (throughputs), service quality (LWBS rate), and resources' utilization. We use the preference-based multiobjective optimization combined with AHP to integrate the objective function and use the single-objective optimization algorithm to find the optimal solution of the composite objective function. We develop two algorithms (RSA + R&S and SA + RSM) for this research to find the unique optimal solution of the macrolevel patient flow distribution.

From a practical perspective, the multiobjective simulation optimization is a rigorous approach to estimate the system performance and to adjust the patient flow that makes the system perform better. The result of our approach improves the system by finding a trade-off between CHC and GH to reduce the waiting time and improve the total service throughput and quality. Our work verifies the positive effect of the TWRP and also provides quantitative recommendations of readjusting patient flow to decision makers. More detailed insights are explained as follows:

- A general problem to Chinese urban healthcare system is the insufficient use of CHCs. The government should encourage more patients to choose CHC for their first diagnosis.

- The promotion to the downward part of TWRP should be strengthened compared with the upward part. In addition, the bed in hospital is the bottleneck of the system.

- There are several simulation optimization methods. Each of them has its own pros and cons. In the PUTH case, the method based on SA and RSM is the best-performed method. If the problem is continuous and the number of peaks in the definition domain is small, SA and RSM are much quicker. Nevertheless, if the decision variable space of the problem is discrete and the shape of response surface is complex, the method based on RSA is recommended.

This research also has several further directions concerning the patient flow in hierarchical healthcare system. First of all, we only figure out the optimal patient flow of the system, but not how to achieve these. Behavioral operations research is an important direction to discover the influence of changing price, service quality, and waiting time on the patients' choice of hospital. By combining those two parts, we can develop a more intelligent decision-support system for policy makers to put forward the proper incentives. Another shortage of our approach is that it does not classify the patients by gender, age, and other demographic characters. They should be classified as heterogeneous patients groups lead to the variant healthcare requirements and different behaviors in the system. Furthermore, we use multiagent-based simulation in order to treat every patient in the system as separate entity. They can make decisions by themselves according to other entities' behaviors and the current performance of the system. The multiobjective optimization can be improved by finding the nondominated Pareto solution set that is another interesting direction of further work.

ACKNOWLEDGMENTS

This work was partially supported by National Science Foundation of China (NSFC) under the grant 71301003 and Specialized Research Fund for the Doctoral Program of Higher Education (SRFDPH) 20130001120007.

REFERENCES

[1] Coelli FC et al. Computer simulation and discrete event models in the analysis of a mammography clinic patient flow. Comput Methods Programs Biomed 2007;87(3):201–207.

[2] Mallor F, Azcárate C. Combining optimization with simulation to obtain credible models for intensive care units. Ann Oper Res 2011;221(1):255–271.

[3] Kumar S. Modeling hospital surgical delivery process design using system simulation: Optimizing patient flow and bed capacity as an illustration. Technol Health Care 2011;19(1):1–20.

[4] Venkatadri V, Raghavan VA, Kesavakumaran V, Lam SS, Srihari K. Simulation based alternatives for overall process improvement at the cardiac catheterization lab. Simul Model Pract Theory 2011;19(7):1544–1557.

[5] M Raunak, et al. Simulating patient flow through an emergency department using process-driven discrete event simulation. Software Engineering in Health Care, 2009. SEHC'09. ICSE Workshop on, IEEE; (2009).

[6] Powell ES, Khare RK, Venkatesh AK, Van Roo BD, Adams JG, Reinhardt G. The relationship between inpatient discharge timing and emergency department boarding. J Emer Med 2012;42(2):186–196.

[7] Konrad R et al. Modeling the impact of changing patient flow processes in an emergency department: Insights from a computer simulation study. Oper Res Health Care 2013;2(4):66–74.

[8] Koizumi N et al. Modeling patient flows using a queuing network with blocking. Health Care Manage Sci 2005;8(1):49–60.

[9] Farinha R, Duarte Oliveira M, de Sá AB. Networks of primary and secondary care services: how to organise services so as to promote efficiency and quality in access while reducing costs. Qual Primary Care 2008;16(4):249–258.

[10] Abo-Hamad W, Arisha A. Simulation-based framework to improve patient experience in an emergency department. Eur J Oper Res 2013;224:154–166.

[11] Horwitz LI et al. US emergency department performance on wait time and length of visit. Ann Emerg Med 2010;55(2):133–141.

[12] Wang J et al. A system model of work flow in the patient room of hospital emergency department. Health Care Manage Sci 2013;16(4):341–351.

[13] Zeng Z et al. A simulation study to improve quality of care in the emergency department of a community hospital. J Emerg Nurs 2012;38(4):322–328.

[14] Cochran JK, Broyles JR. Developing nonlinear queuing regressions to increase emergency department patient safety: Approximating reneging with balking. Comput Indus Eng 2010;59(3):378–386.

[15] Cochran JK, Roche KT. A multi-class queuing network analysis methodology for improving hospital emergency department performance. Comput Oper Res 2009;36(5):1497–1512.

[16] Kennedy M et al. Review article: Leaving the emergency department without being seen. Emerg Med Aust 2008;20(4):306–313.

[17] Behr JG, Diaz R. A system dynamics approach to modeling the sensitivity of inappropriate emergency department utilization. Adv Soc Comput 2010;6007:52–61.

[18] Deb K. *Multi-Objective Optimization: Search Methodologies*. Springer; 2014. p 403–449.

[19] Ahmed MA, Alkhamis TM. Simulation optimization for an emergency department healthcare unit in Kuwait. Eur J Oper Res 2009;198(3):936–942.

[20] Santibáñez P et al. Reducing patient wait times and improving resource utilization at British Columbia Cancer Agency's ambulatory care unit through simulation. Health Care Manage Sci 2009;12(4):392–407.

[21] Popovich MA et al. Improving stable patient flow through the emergency department by utilizing evidence-based practice: One hospital's journey. J Emerg Nurs 2012;38(5):474–478.

[22] Zhang Y et al. A simulation optimization approach to long-term care capacity planning. Oper Res 2012;60(2):249–261.

[23] Oddoye JP et al. Combining simulation and goal programming for healthcare planning in a medical assessment unit. Eur J Oper Res 2009;193(1):250–261.

[24] Cardoen B et al. Optimizing a multiple objective surgical case sequencing problem. Int J Prod Econ 2009;119(2):354–366.

[25] Saaty TL. *What is the Analytic Hierarchy Process?* Springer; 1988.

[26] Baesler FF, Sepúlveda JA. Multi-objetive simulation optimization for a cancer treatment center. Proceedings of the Winter Simulation Conference 2001;2:1405–1411.

[27] Fu MC. Optimization for simulation: Theory vs. practice. INFORMS J Comput 2002;14(3):192–215.

[28] Alrefaei MH, Diabat AH. A simulated annealing with ranking and selection for stochastic optimization. Adv Mater Res 2012;488:1335–1340.

[29] Frazier PI. *Decision: Theoretic Foundations of Simulation Optimization*. Wiley Encyclopedia of Operations Research and Management Science; 2010.

[30] Sriver TA et al. Pattern search ranking and selection algorithms for mixed variable simulation-based optimization. Eur J Oper Res 2009;198(3):878–890.

[31] Yang M et al. The call for equity: simulation optimization models to minimize the range of waiting times. IIE Trans 2013;45(7):781–795.

[32] Taboada M, Cabrera E, Epelde F, Iglesias ML, Luque E. Using an agent-based simulation for predicting the effects of patients derivation policies in emergency departments. Procedia Comput Sci 2013;18:641–650.

[33] Cabrera E, Taboada M, Iglesias M, Epelde F, Luque E. Simulation optimization for healthcare emergency departments. Procedia Comput Sci 2012;9:1464–1473.

[34] Yan D, Mukai H. Stochastic discrete optimization. SIAM J Control Optim 1992;30(3):594–612.

[35] Gong W-B, Ho Y-C, Zhai W. Stochastic comparison algorithm for discrete optimization with estimation. SIAM J Optim 2000;10(2):384–404.

[36] Niu Q, Peng Q, ElMekkawy TY. Improvement in the operating room efficiency using Tabu search in simulation. Bus Process Manage J 2013;19(5):799–818.

[37] Zhu JC, Ramanathan R, Ramanathan U. Measuring service quality using SERVQUAL and AHP: An application to a Chinese IT company and comparison. Int J Serv Oper Manage 2011;8(4):418–432.

[38] Xu M, Jin B, Yu Y, Shen H, Li W. Using artificial neural networks for energy regulation based variable-speed electrohydraulic drive. Chin J Mech Eng 2010;23(3):327–335.

[39] Spall JC. Implementation of the simultaneous perturbation algorithm for stochastic optimization. Aerosp Electron Syst 1998;34(3):817–823.

[40] Alrefaei MH, Diabat AH. A simulated annealing technique for multi-objective simulation optimization. Appl Math Comput 2009;215(8):3029–3035.

[41] Broadie M et al. General bounds and finite-time improvement for the Kiefer-Wolfowitz stochastic approximation algorithm. Oper Res 2011;59(5):1211–1224.

[42] Chang K-H et al. Stochastic trust-region response-surface method (STRONG)-a new response-surface framework for simulation optimization. INFORMS J Comput 2013;25(2):230–243.

[43] Dellino G et al. Robust optimization in simulation: Taguchi and response surface methodology. Int J Prod Econ 2010;125(1):52–59.

[44] Shankar TJ et al. A case study on optimization of biomass flow during single-screw extrusion cooking using genetic algorithm (GA) and response surface method (RSM). Food Bioprocess Technol 2010;3(4):498–510.

[45] Danner M et al. Integrating patients' views into health technology assessment: Analytic hierarchy process (AHP) as a method to elicit patient preferences. Int J Technol Assess Health Care 2011;27(04):369–375.

[46] Pecchia L et al. Analytic hierarchy process (AHP) for examining healthcare professionals' assessments of risk factors. Methods Inf Med 2010;49:435–444.

[47] Swisher JR, Jacobson SH. Evaluating the design of a family practice healthcare clinic using discrete-event simulation. Health Care Manage Sci 2002;5:75–88.

[48] Andradóttir S. A review of simulation optimization techniques. Proceedings of the 30th conference on Winter simulation, IEEE Computer Society Press; 1998.

[49] Andradóttir S. An overview of simulation optimization via random search. Handb Oper Res Manage Sci 2006;13:617–631.

[50] Azadivar F. Simulation optimization methodologies. Proceedings of the 31st conference on Winter simulation: Simulation – a bridge to the future – Volume 1, ACM; 1999.

[51] Grefenstette JJ. Optimization of control parameters for genetic algorithms. Syst Man Cyber 1986;16(1):122–128.

[52] Ólafsson S, Kim J. Simulation optimization: simulation optimization. Proceedings of the Winter Simulation Conference 2002;79–84.

[53] Bechhofer RE. A single-sample multiple decision procedure for ranking means of normal populations with known variances. Ann Math Stat 1954;25(1):16–39.

[54] Haddock J, Mittenthal J. Simulation optimization using simulated annealing. Comput Indus Eng 1992;22(4):387–395.

[55] Pflug GC. *Optimization of Stochastic Models: The Interface Between Simulation and Optimization*. Boston: Kluwer Academic; 1996.

[56] Ministry of Health of the PRC. *China Health Statistics Yearbook 2012*. 2012.

11

ANALYSIS OF RESOURCE INTENSIVE ACTIVITY VOLUMES IN US HOSPITALS

SHIVON BOODHOO

Albert Dorman Honors College, Mechanical & Industrial Engineering, New Jersey Institute of Technology, Newark, NJ, USA

SANCHOY DAS

Healthcare Systems Management Program, Newark College of Engineering, New Jersey Institute of Technology, Newark, NJ, USA

11.1 INTRODUCTION

Hospitals are the primary provider of medical services and are in a sense the factories of the healthcare industry. About a third of all US healthcare costs are hospital related. Hospitals typically evaluate performance in two dimensions: clinical outcomes (quality of care/process of care) and financial stability (reimbursement rates and profitability). The well-known *US News and World Report* ranking evaluates performance on the three interlocking dimensions of healthcare: structure, process, and outcomes [1]. Today, these rankings are generally accepted as a surrogate measure for clinical performance and identifying the best hospitals in the US. In contrast, there are only a limited number of broadly applicable evaluation metrics or even studies that focus on hospital operations productivity and efficiency. A classical measure of productivity is resources used to provide or create a unit of output, which in most cases is standardized (e.g. mid-sized automobile). A key obstacle to hospital productivity measurement is defining a standard unit of healthcare output

Healthcare Analytics: From Data to Knowledge to Healthcare Improvement, First Edition.
Edited by Hui Yang and Eva K. Lee.

because every patient is different in terms of diagnosis, response to medical care, and their acuity level. From an analytical perspective, the hospital patient input is heterogeneous; hence, simple counts of patients or patients' days are not sufficient for inter-hospital comparisons.

Traditionally used units of hospital output have been inpatient days, adjusted patient days (APD), and adjusted discharge, all of which are reasonable estimators of hospital output activity. When combined with total cost or total patient revenue, they can be used to derive the nominal resource efficiency (e.g., Total Cost/APD or Total Revenue/Adjusted Discharge). These metrics are, however, assumed that patient profiles are generally equivalent across hospitals. Clearly this is not the case and as a result comparative assessments across hospitals cannot be made effectively. It is therefore difficult to identify an operationally excellent hospital, even though one can today identify the best hospitals in terms of clinical outcomes. As an example consider two hospitals with the same volume of APD and the same level of clinical outcomes, but one has an operating budget that is 20% more than the other. One cannot conclude that the hospital with the larger budget has a lower operational productivity. This inability to compare hospital operational productivity limits many healthcare cost reduction efforts and national health policy initiatives. We can only search for system-wide cost reductions, as opposed to focusing improvement on the less productive parts of the system. What is needed are data analysis methods and measures that help identify hospital operational excellence, allowing these practices to be replicated across the weaker units of the healthcare system.

Even in the face of the above-mentioned analytical challenges, there is an extensive literature on methods and models for measuring the productivity or efficiency of hospitals and a detailed review is provided in Section 11.3. These research methods employ a range of approaches for measuring the hospital healthcare output including inpatient days, outpatient visits, case complexity, number of patient admissions, number of surgeries, and number of discharges. The Hospital Unit of Care (HUC) model [2] provides an activity-based approach to modeling hospital resource use and, thus, is independent of the patient acuity profiles. The HUC model can then be used to determine different activity components of any hospital, which in turn can be used to estimate resource use productivity. Tiemann and Schreyögg [3] note that in an environment of rising healthcare costs, hospitals, in particular, are increasingly being held accountable for their efficiency and financial performance. A key assumption made by the HUC model is that all hospitals provide acceptable or higher levels of quality patient care, that is, as required by the patient's condition and specified by acceptable process of care. The research here therefore does not address variances in quality of care between hospitals.

In this chapter, we utilize the HUC model to characterize hospitals based on their operational activity profiles. For our data set of 1000+ hospitals, we show that resource use profiles vary significantly between states and within states. The profiles are then used to define HUC resource use peer groups or λ-Types. Each group includes hospitals with a similar positive bias in a specific HUC component. Group distribution by state is shown to vary significantly, and specific differences are discussed. Clearly, operational initiatives and productivity benchmarks cannot be generalized for all hospitals, but should be focused on their specific resource use profiles. First, we describe the structural classification of US hospitals since resource use and activity sets tend to vary across this classification. A key component of a data analytics is the data source, and in the following we describe the Medicare databases used in this project. Next, the HUC model for quantifying hospital output is introduced and the derivation of the first HUC component is presented. Following that in the next section, we introduce the data analysis underlying the HUC model and also describe the functional relationship of the model to the MEDPAR database. Subsequently, the resources usage analysis is developed and the associated hospital data are presented.

11.2 STRUCTURAL CLASSIFICATION OF HOSPITALS

To better evaluate the operational use of resources in hospitals, it is first necessary to understand the structural classification of hospitals. Just as in any other industry, specific hospitals will vary from the general group due to specific characteristics in their individual profiles. A data analytical study such as this will attempt to study the factorial relationships between specific structural characteristics and the analytical results, in this case the use of different resources. We find that the most common structural factor for hospitals is "size" or number of beds, which are classified as shown in Figure 11.1. Many hospital systems studies focus on medium- and large-sized hospitals as hospitals of this size offer a more homogeneous suite of service activities. Smaller hospitals, particularly those with less than 70 beds, frequently offer only a subset of services and tend to have very different resource use patterns. The economics and operational behavior of small size hospitals are known to be quite different from other size hospitals.

A second structural classification is the type of care delivered – short-term acute care or long-term rehabilitation and psychiatric care. Healthcare systems engineering efforts are usually focused on short-term acute care hospitals. There are 5723 general and specialty hospitals registered as members of the American Hospital Association. These hospitals may be further separated by the type of control as in Figure 11.2.

Size Class	Number of Beds (Range)	% US Hospitals
Small	Less than 100	47
Medium	100 to 300	38
Large	300 to 500	10
Very large	500+	5

Figure 11.1 Hospital Size in the United States.

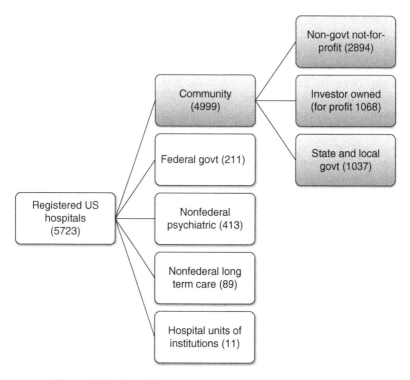

Figure 11.2   United States hospital count by the type of control.

Community hospitals are all nonfederal, short-term general, and special hospitals (obstetrics and gynecology; eye, ear, nose, and throat; rehabilitation; orthopedic; and other defined specializations). Many data analysis projects will exclude hospitals not accessible by the general public, such as prison hospitals or veteran's hospitals. Resource usage is closely related to the functional relationships between different areas of a hospital. A typical acute care hospital involves an interaction among (i) bed-related inpatient functions, (ii) outpatient-related functions, (iii) diagnostic and treatment functions, (iv) administrative functions, (v) service functions (food, supply, etc.), and (vi) research and teaching functions (Fig. 11.3). The hospital's care profile as well as its physical configuration, transportation, and logistics systems is inextricably intertwined as shown in the flow diagram in Figure 11.4, which illustrates the movement and communication of people, materials, and waste.

The operational resources required to deliver hospital care will vary by the hospital's structural and/or care profile. This is a key factor in the analysis of hospital productivity, since hospitals may be limited by an inherited operational structure and/or regulatory environment. In this project, we focus on comparing the resource usage of hospitals between states. The motivation for this stems from the common regulatory environment in which hospitals within a state operate.

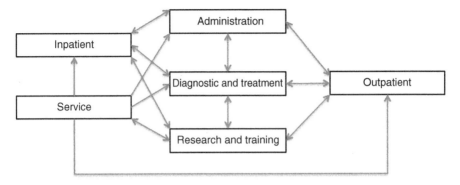

Figure 11.3 Functional relationships in a hospital [4].

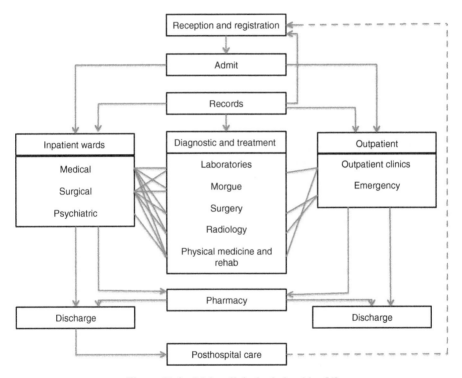

Figure 11.4 Major clinical relationships [4].

11.3 PRODUCTIVITY ANALYSIS OF HOSPITALS

A classical productivity measure is given by resources used per unit output. The only flow entities in a hospital system are the patients who spend time at a hospital during which they receive a range of healthcare services. In the context of a hospital, the

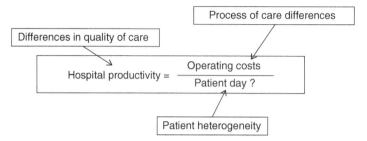

Figure 11.5   Hospital productivity and analytical challenges.

productivity relationship is then described in Figure 11.5. In the application of this productivity relationship, we find three key analytical challenges. All of these relate to standardization of the three equation elements:

Patient Heterogeneity. Differences in case-mixes, disease profile, disease acuity, available support groups, and so on. Makes it impossible to achieve patient equivalency, hence impatient days are not the same across hospitals.

Process of Care Differences. Hospital may follow different approaches in terms of procedures, tests, and care services for the same diagnosis. These are then billed different resulting in operating cost variances.

Quality of Care Differences. The expectation is that all hospitals provide an equivalent quality of care. Put just like in any other service industry, there are differences in the quality of the services provided.

Hollingsworth [5] notes that in contrast to manufacturers with standardized production lines, hospitals confront considerable variations in how and what outputs are produced, thus limiting the productivity analysis. The simplest measure of hospital output is patient volume measured by the total annual inpatient days. Progressively there has been a shift away from this approach, and MacLean and Mix [6] recommended that APD provided a more accurate measure of hospital output. APD is an outpatient revenue ratio adjustment from inpatient days. For a long time, APD has been the predominant measure of hospital care volume and is widely used in the hospital productivity research literature. Current research postulates that APD is no longer a reliable approach for benchmarking hospital output. The APD count can be extended by factoring in the "service-mix" and "case-mix" indices. Hospital output measurement has rarely been tackled directly. Typically, such work has been secondary to the principal research objectives, which have related to the study of hospital cost structure and economies of scale. Soderlund et al. [7] and Miller et al. [8] found that case-mix differences accounted for 77% of the cost variance between healthcare providers emphasizing the need for factoring case-mix in hospital output. More recently, Cleverley and Cleverley [9] suggest a new output metric, equivalent patient units (EPU), given by

$$EPU = \text{Equivalent discharges} + (\text{Payment ratio} \times \text{Equivalent visits})$$

where

Equivalent discharges = Number of discharges × Average case-mix index (CMI)

Equivalent visits = Number of outpatient visits × Relative weights (RW)

Payment ratio = Reimbursement for outpatient visit at RW = 1/inpatient discharge at CMI = 1

There is an extensive literature on methods and models for measuring the productivity or efficiency of hospitals. Huerta et al. [10] provide a detailed summary of the methods and note that they are all built on the same basic principle: the "transformation" of inputs to outputs. The two classical approaches followed by most hospital productivity research are (i) DEA – Data Envelopment Analysis, and (ii) SCFA – Stochastic Cost Frontier Analysis. Of these, the dominant research method for studying hospital performance or resource efficiency is DEA. The output metric most frequently used in these studies has been APD. For example, Zhivan and Diana [11] propose a cost-efficiency measure for hospitals as a function of the price of labor, number of discharges, number of outpatient visits, and price of capital that is normalized by the price of labor. Other studies have used stochastic frontier analysis to estimate the cost function and then evaluate hospital efficiency, and a comprehensive review is provided by Hollingsworth [5]. An application of this method to US hospitals is reported by Greene [12].

The HUC model provides an alternative approach to measuring hospital output and can therefore be easily integrated with existing DEA approaches. A range of approaches for measuring output are also seen including inpatient days, outpatient visits, case complexity, number of patient admissions, number of surgeries, and number of discharges. In a review of several studies, McGlynn et al. [13] identify patient discharges and inpatient days as two of the most commonly used outputs. Most studies though use adjusted patient revenue, number of discharges, and number of inpatient days that is equivalent to APD. Some recent examples include Rosko and Mutter [14] who reported a DEA-based hospital efficiency study, which used APD for the output, and Zhivan and Diana [11] who proposed a cost-efficiency measure in which output is defined as a function of the number of discharges and the number of outpatient visits. In an analysis of hospital productivity growth using the Luenberger indicator, Barros et al. [15] assume that hospitals produce four outputs: (i) number of patients that leave the hospital, (ii) length of stay, (iii) consultations, and (iv) emergency cases. These four have been the measured outputs in most hospital productivity studies.

11.4 RESOURCE AND ACTIVITY DATABASE FOR US HOSPITALS

To successfully implement data analytics projects in the context of hospitals, it impor-tant to first determine the available data sources and their formats. Clinical data sets that focus on disease statistics are formally recorded and readily available to research groups. Hospital operational data sets, on the other hand, are difficult to obtain and even when available tend to be unstructured and not standardized. Researchers must evaluate both healthcare operation flows and data availability before building analytical models. This will allow for better validation and applicability of the models.

Figure 11.6 identifies possible hospital operation data sources. A common approach is the "create your own" pathway. As a note of caution it is difficult, if not impossible, to create reliable data sets for hospital activity using direct feeds from individual hospitals. Despite the fact that hospitals collect and store a myriad of data elements at the local level, every patient encounter generates a mountain of paperwork: timestamps, patient chart, medication record, scans, labs, nursing notes, surgeon notes, and prescription information just to name the major elements. Even a relatively small hospital with 2000 or 3000 annual discharges will have an extremely large data set. Although large, this data set is typically unusable for cross-hospital comparisons as few hospitals use a common definition for data elements since this is not required by regulatory and accreditation bodies. Even at the local level, many hospitals keep all patient records on paper charts in files not easily accessible to analysts. In fact, the norm has become for hospitals to hire an entire department devoted to "chart abstractions" – clinical support staff whose job is to comb through patient records to provide data for regulatory audits and billing.

Most US hospitals with electronic health records (EHRs) have multiple electronic patient systems that do not "talk to each other" so data remains in silos across the organization. Under these circumstances, many large hospitals do not routinely perform operational analysis or even root cause analysis for adverse events unless there are legal ramifications for not investigating specific cases. A good source of hospital-specific data would be payers such as insurance companies. These entities require detailed reports on patient care – diagnoses, comorbidities, services

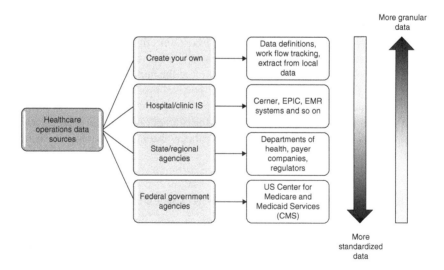

Figure 11.6   Data sources for hospital operations analysis.

rendered, and procedures delivered – a wealth of information, which could be used to understand the full range of patient treatment. Unfortunately, in most cases, there is no true link between hospital charges and payer reimbursements. The reimbursement rates are also typically a well-guarded secret as these "contractual discounts" are all based on negotiated rates per hospital. As a result, "Big Data" sets for hospital operations are rare. The only truly national, publicly accessible "Big Data" class hospital information is the Medicare database. The analysis reported here utilizes this publicly available data set.

11.4.1   Medicare Data Sources for Hospital Operations

In the United States, the Center for Medicare and Medicaid Services (CMS) maintains several databases [16] that can be utilized for healthcare analytics research. These databases provide detailed activity reports for all US hospitals. These files are updated annually and represent the most comprehensive "Big Data" class hospital data set available to researchers in the United States. The two specific data sets used here are as follows:

Healthcare Cost Report Information System (HCRIS). Medicare-certified providers are required to submit an annual cost report to a Medicare Administrative Contractor (MAC). The report contains provider information such as facility characteristics, utilization data, cost, and charges by cost center as well as quality of care and financial statement data segmented for Medicare and the facility as a whole. HCRIS includes reports for the various subclasses of providers, each with its own cost report – Hospital Cost Report, Skilled Nursing Facility (SNF) Cost Report, Home Health Agency (HHA) Cost Report, Renal Facility Cost Report, Health Clinic Cost Report, and the Hospice Cost Report.

Medicare Provider Analysis and Review (MEDPAR). The MEDPAR file contains data from claims for services provided to beneficiaries admitted to Medicare-certified inpatient hospitals and SNF. This file contains a detailed record of claims stemming from a beneficiary's stay record. A single hospital stay may generate a single or multiple claims. The MEDPAR file contains beneficiary demographic characteristics, diagnosis and surgery information, use of hospital or SNF resources, accommodation and departmental charge data, days of care, and entitlement data [2].

This HUC project focused its analysis on the approximately 5000 short-term acute care and specialty hospitals in the United States. The HUC model was built to match the available data sets to ensure implementation feasibility. The MEDPAR and HCRIS data are organized into multiple categories including financial, inpatient activity, outpatient activity, quality of care, and department activity. Figure 11.7 illustrates the MEDPAR data structure for ICU services while Figure 11.8 shows a sample data snapshot for ICU services. The HUC model then is designed to

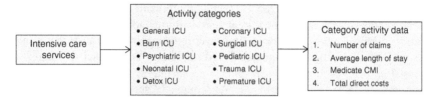

Figure 11.7   MEDPAR data structure for ICU services.

match this data structure. Specifically the HUC model utilizes the four-activity data elements as input parameters.

In this data analysis project, 318 unique data points were extracted from the HCRIS and MedPAR databases for each hospital. Proprietary programs were developed for the extraction process. A series of qualifying filter that identified and removed hospitals, which had missing data elements and special characteristics (e.g., psychiatric care), was developed. Note that most data are for Medicare patients only, typically between 25% and 50% of inpatients days at most US hospitals. Where necessary the data must then be extrapolated to account for the total hospital population. The extracted data quantify all healthcare activities at each hospital and form the basis for deriving the HUC model as described in the following section.

11.5   ACTIVITY-BASED MODELING OF HOSPITAL OPERATIONS

11.5.1   Direct Care Activities

Patient care in hospitals can be modeled as a series of healthcare-related activities that are designed to provide the needed quality of care for the specific disease. We define a healthcare activity as a patient-centric activity prescribed by physicians, requiring the direct use of hospital resources. These resources include (i) clinical staff, (ii) nonclinical staff, (iii) equipment, (iv) supplies, and (v) facilities plus other indirect resources. Hospitals are typically compensated by insurance companies for a specific activity or a care process, which includes a defined set of activities. Healthcare activities are, therefore, the basic element of the measurable output that a hospital provides to its patients.

Consider two admitted patients with the same diagnosis and different acuity levels but with the same length of stay. The care may involve different activities; hence, they will consume different levels of hospital resources. Presumably the patient with higher acuity will require higher units of care output for the hospital. By a simple count of inpatient days, the two patients would be equivalent. But a more accurate and effective output measure must track the difference in activity and resource usage.

Figure 11.9 describes the activity-based view of hospital operations adopted in the HUC model. This view postulates that patient care can be modeled as a series of healthcare-related activities that are needed to provide the quality of care for

Hospital	General ICU (j=1) Number of Days (M1)	General ICU- Total Costs	Coronary Care Unit (j=2) Number of Days (M2)	Coronary Care Unit- Total Costs	Burn ICU (j=3) Number of Days (M3)	Burn ICU- Total Costs	Surgical ICU (j=4) Number of Days (M4)	Surgical ICU- Total Costs	Neonatal ICU (j=7) Number of Days (M7)	Neonatal ICU- Total Costs
Torrance Memorial Medical Center	8,759	$17,881,658	NA	NA	1,895	$3,853,327	NA	NA	5,092	$7,601,260
Tri-City Medical Center	5,639	$12,046,428	NA	NA	NA	NA	NA	NA	5,187	$9,077,425
UCLA Medical Center, Santa Monica	6,150	$22,595,400	NA	NA	NA	NA	NA	NA	3,032	$8,567,693
University of California Irvine Medical	14,131	$42,166,884	3,249	$7,370,741	2,548	$7,886,454	NA	NA	10,009	$21,478,976
University of California Davis Medical	10,780	$35,399,044	2,719	$9,107,616	4,282	$15,959,392	7,085	$23,768,420	9,046	$26,276,640
University of California, San Diego Me	NA	NA	7,459	$25,539,770	5,187	11,529,815	1,177	$33,402,916	12,857	$22,027,004

Figure 11.8 Sample data for ICU services.

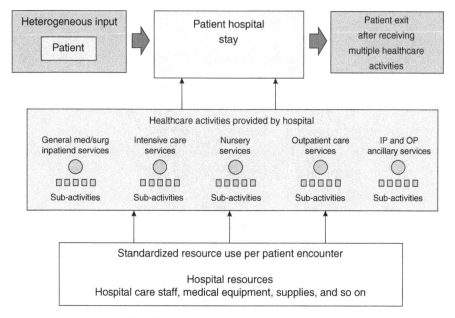

Figure 11.9 Hospital productivity view of inputs and outputs.

the specific disease. A healthcare activity is a patient-centric activity prescribed by physicians, and here there is a many-to-many relationship between diseases and activities. Translating from a patient-centric to an activity-centric view, the HUC model considers healthcare activities as the basic measurable output of a hospital. To formulate the HUC output measure, it is necessary to make a standardization assumption. That is, the resources required to complete a specific healthcare activity are generally independent of the patient acuity and/or diagnosis. For instance, the resources used to conduct a chest X-ray will be the same regardless of patient type or acuity, and arguably should be the same at any US hospital. Then similar to other industries, difference in resource usage can be attributed to differences in worker skill and/or differences in process design.

An activity-based approach must track all healthcare activities in the hospital and equate them to resource usage. Then an indexed or weighted summation of the activities would be functionally equivalent to the total medical care output of a hospital. Figure 11.9 translates the classical productivity input–output model to patient flow operations in a hospital. Key attributes of this activity-centric flow model are as follows:

Patients. The primary flow entity in a hospital and the focus of all resources. Patients are heterogeneous and there is a great variance in resource utilization. This variance will depend on multiple factors including patient acuity, case-mix, treatment options and strategies, and resource availability at the hospital.

Activities. The hospital provides a large range of healthcare activities all of which are intended to provide a health-related service to the patient. Key activity groups are shown in Figure 11.2. Within each group, MEDPAR defines a standardized list of subactivities. For example, in Outpatient Care Services, there are 45 subactivities including pharmacy orders, IV therapy, surgical supplies, CT scans, and pathological lab orders. Specific subactivities that patient will access are prescribed to meet the required process of care to achieve accepted quality of care standards for their diagnosis.

Resources. Each healthcare activity will require or consume one or more resources at varying levels. Resources include staff, equipment, supplies, utilities, and numerous other items. Altogether these represent both the direct and indirect costs of operating the hospital. All resources are quantified into a common dollar scale, and the HCRIS database will track the resource expenditures by activity group and subactivity.

Discharge. Patients exiting from the hospital after having received the accepted quality of care, which is defined by a set of healthcare activities.

11.5.2   The Hospital Unit of Care (HUC) Model

The HUC model was developed by Boodhoo and Das [2] using the above-described activity-based view of a hospital. They define a baseline HUC as the resources required for delivery of one general medical-acute care inpatient day, which includes the needed healthcare staff, ancillary, and support services and facilities to deliver the required (acceptable quality) continuum of care. Frequently, this is referred to as a general medical/surgical inpatient day or the provision of a bed with routine care. The baseline HUC measure does not include outpatient care and services, specialty or intensive care, surgeries, prescribed services, prescribed diagnostics, enhanced facilities, patient complexity, and so on. They then expand the HUC to account for all additional care/service activities that the hospital provides by deriving an equivalency value for all activities. For example, it may be estimated that 1 Intensive Care Patient Day = 2.3 Hospital Units of Care. This approach provides a function to roll-up all the reported hospital direct patient care activities into a unified activity or output measure, which can be standardized across hospitals.

While hospitals collect and store a myriad of data elements at the local level, these data are typically unusable for cross-hospital comparisons as few hospitals use a common definition set. Furthermore, HIPPA regulations make it restrictive for analytical groups to get data directly from hospitals. Clearly, developing a measure that is dependent on unavailable or typically unrecorded data is unlikely to be implemented. An effective healthcare data analysis project must be based on data that is readily available and when possibly scalable to a large set of hospitals. For many hospital data analytics research projects, this can be the biggest challenge. The implementation strategy is to develop a measure, which can readily be applied to an available data set. The only truly national, publicly accessible hospital operations information is the MedPAR database. The HUC model was designed to be compatible to the MedPAR and HCRIS databases, allowing analysis of almost every US hospital.

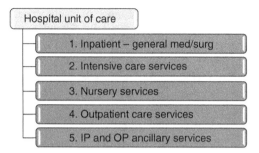

Figure 11.10   HUC output activity components.

Development of the HUC measure involved several research activities including (i) review of patient activity process flows for different hospitals, both from onsite studies and those reported in the literature; (ii) review of Medicare billing and payment procedures and the link to direct patient activity; and (iii) review of the Medicare maintained data sets to identify data elements that relate to identified activities. The HUC measure comprises five components (Fig. 11.10), each of which represents a different set of patient care activities for the hospital.

Brief definitions of the five HUC components follow, the HUC units for each are denoted by Ω_n where $n = 1$–5 is the component number as identified below:

1. *Inpatient General Med/Surg* (Ω_1). The general inpatient ward in a hospital caters to a mix of cases in a hospital. This mix reflects the diversity and clinical complexity of the population of inpatients served by the hospital. The base line HUC measure is simply the number of inpatient days. This component factors the difference in resource usage as a function of the patient case-mix to derive the adjusted number of inpatient days. Medicare tracks patient volumes in different medical service categories; examples are Cardiology, Gynecology, and Neurology. Each category is based on groupings of patient diagnosis-related groups (DRGs) and is assigned a case-mix index (CMI) for the hospital. The CMI indicates the mix of patient severity levels. Higher severity levels will consume relatively more hospital resources.

2. *Intensive Care Services* (Ω_2). Intensive care is an integral part of a hospital's operations, consuming a significant proportion of all resources and of the hospital-operating budget [17, 18]. Intensive Care Units (ICUs) provide specialized care to critically ill patients and are typically characterized by additional resource requirements due to services being rendered at a heightened level of care. Maintenance of the ICU location and its operating personnel is the most costly component of ICU services. This component factor in the additional resources required to provide ICU services. Several types of ICU services are possible, and Medicare requires hospitals to track and report patient volumes in 10 ICU categories, including General ICU, Coronary ICU, and Neonatal ICU.

3. *Nursery Services* (Ω_3). This component factors the additional load placed on hospital resources by caring for newborns in the nursery. Newborns are not considered in the traditional "inpatient days" count but nonetheless consume resources. Typically, the newborn is taken to the nursery, which does not count "beds" hence does not appear in many output measures, but certainly incurs its own costs. Any special care for the newborn such as neonatal ICU is treated separately as part of the ICU adjustment factor. Only when a newborn enters a special care unit does it become an identified patient, and the associated resources are directly tracked.

4. *Outpatient Care Services* (Ω_4). In recent years, there has also been rapid growth in the number of patients seeking care as outpatients through both hospital outpatient departments and emergency rooms. The Centers for Disease Control trend analysis indicates that the volume of outpatients is approaching almost seven times the number of inpatients. In many cases, outpatients now account for larger portions of a hospital's resource utilization. This component accounts for the resource usage by the hospital's outpatient population. Medicare tracks a mix of 45 different healthcare services provided to outpatients. Example services include pharmacy orders, IV therapy, surgical supplies, CT scans, and pathological laboratory orders.

5. *IP and OP Ancillary Services* (Ω_5). Hospitals provide a range of additional or ancillary services that are delivered to both inpatients and outpatients. Ancillary services are considered to be supplemental services provided to patients and typically fall into one of three categories. (i) *Diagnostic*: Provided in support of physician services and includes audiology, radiology, pulmonary testing services, and clinical lab services. (ii) *Therapeutic*: Focus on treatment of illness or disease and includes medications, dialysis, and rehabilitation. (iii) *Custodial*: Primary focus on hospice, home health, and nursing home care. These services should not be confused with routine services that patients receive. For example, inpatients receive basic nursing care and noncharge medicine such as aspirin as part of "routine services" provided to all patients. For outpatients, any services administered beyond those covered in the basic care for a particular diagnosis are considered ancillary. Medicare tracks 23 different ancillary services provided to patients. An X-ray of an injured leg for an inpatient would be considered a diagnostic ancillary service. Physical therapy in the hospital on that leg would be an example of therapeutic ancillary service.

As noted earlier, all of the above six HUC output activity components can be derived from data reported by hospitals to Medicare for a given year. An example calculation for the CMI adjustment is shown here.

i = Medical service categories ($i = 1$–16)

N_i = Number of Medicare patients (annual) in this category for hospital

L_i = Average inpatient length of stay (LOS) in this category for hospital

C_i = Medicare assigned CMI for this category at this hospital
V_{IN} = Total (Medicare plus non-Medicare) inpatient volume for hospital
Ψ_{IN} = Inpatient volume coefficient $V_{IN}/\sum_i N_i$ for hospital
ρ = CMI scaling coefficient

$$\text{Inpatient General Med Surg CMI Days} = \Omega_1 = \psi_{IN} \sum_i N_i L_i \, \text{Min}\{C_i, \, 1 + \rho(C_i - 1)\}$$

Since data are reported only for Medicare patient volumes, the coefficient ψ_{IN} scales the data for the total hospital patient volume. The assumption here is that the case-mix profile of Medicare and non-Medicare patients is the same. The CMI is indicative of the additional resources required to care for the patient. Part of these resources are included in the other activities associated with the patient. The factor ρ is introduced to account only for a portion of the resources beyond CMI = 1 that are included in this HUC component. Based on an analysis of data for hospital data of 1000 US hospitals, here we set $\rho = 0.33$. Observe that depending on the patient severity mix at a hospital, Ω_1 could be greater or less than the baseline $(N_i L_i)$.

Equations for all other HUC components are reported in Boodhoo and Das [2]. The total HUC units delivered by a specific hospital are thus given by

$$\text{Total delivered HUC per year} = \Omega_1 + \Omega_2 + \Omega_3 + \Omega_4 + \Omega_5$$

The measurement unit of the HUC is inpatient-days equivalency, the same unit as APD. The HUC value will change from year to year for a specific hospital.

11.5.3 HUC Component Results by State

Table 11.1 provides a summary of the HUC data analysis for 1009 US hospitals, representing all 70+ bed hospitals in 16 states. Note that the data analysis continues, and in the future a similar analysis will be available for all 52 states. The total HUC units show that four states (California, Florida, New York, and Texas), clearly the most populated states, have very large resource intensive activities in their hospitals. In contrast, four states (Nebraska, South Dakota, Oregon, and Utah) have activity levels that are less than 10% of the large states. The HUC data now allow a more extensive data analysis to be conducted at the per capita level and also perform productivity analysis across the set of hospitals. With productivity being defined as the cost per delivered HUC unit.

Table 11.1 data also provides insights into how hospital resources are distributed across the components. We see that for the set of 1009 hospitals, 42.9% of resources are assigned to ancillary services. The current research literature has only occasional mention of ancillary services, but this analysis shows that when accounted for as an explicit entity it is the most resource significant part of a hospital.

TABLE 11.1   HUC Component Activity Levels by State

				HUC Distribution Ratio				
#	State	Hospitals	Total HUC units	$\Omega_1 -$ CaseMix (%)	$\Omega_2 -$ IntCare (%)	$\Omega_3 -$ Nursery (%)	$\Omega_4 -$ Outpatient (%)	$\Omega_5 -$ Ancillary (%)
1	AZ	34	6,635,249	36.3	10.3	1.2	14.0	38.2
2	CA	207	34,551,159	35.9	11.6	1.2	10.0	41.2
3	CT	21	4,821,575	32.7	7.2	0.8	15.3	44.1
4	FL	125	28,631,206	35.0	9.9	0.8	12.7	41.5
5	IL	85	16,173,424	31.0	8.8	1.1	13.9	45.3
6	MA	39	10,214,560	28.5	7.8	1.0	19.6	43.1
7	NE	12	2,079,149	30.2	7.9	1.0	9.8	51.1
8	NJ	57	12,800,336	34.0	9.5	1.5	14.0	41.0
9	NY	136	34,155,088	34.5	8.5	0.8	15.9	40.2
10	PA	95	23,161,162	30.4	8.2	0.6	14.8	46.0
11	SD	6	1,049,730	31.5	8.0	0.6	12.7	47.1
12	WA	26	6,007,042	29.0	10.2	1.2	15.0	44.6
13	TX	119	29,379,282	30.6	10.9	1.6	14.8	42.1
14	CO	22	4,264,448	30.5	9.8	1.4	13.1	45.2
15	OR	14	2,800,968	35.9	9.8	1.0	11.0	42.3
16	UT	11	2,140,025	24.7	8.4	1.7	17.8	47.4
All states		1009	218,864,403	32.9	9.6	1.1	13.9	42.4

11.6   RESOURCE USE PROFILE OF HOSPITALS FROM HUC ACTIVITY DATA

In the analysis of large data sets where multiple organizations are involved, an effective strategy is to separate the organizations into peer groups. This allows for deriving reliable conclusions that are specific to each peer group, additionally comparisons between the peer groups are possible. In the evaluation of multihospital data, the most common peer group classification criteria are structural in nature. These include (i) Hospital size – number of beds; (ii) Patient volume – annual inpatient days; (iii) Geographical location – urban, suburban, or rural; and (iv) Ownership – profit, nonprofit, or county. There are few studies that characterize hospitals based on an operational characteristic, primarily due to the difficulty in accessing operations data in a standardized format. The development of the HUC model allows the creation of hospital peer groups. We introduce the following peer group definition consistent with the HUC operations data.

> *Hospital HUC Resource Use Group (λ-Type)*. Hospitals with a similar positive bias, as measured by the percentage of healthcare activities in a specific HUC component, are classified into a common group. Six groups or *λ-Types* 1–6 are identified.

Classification into λ-*Type* is based on the HUC component data for each hospital as introduced earlier in Section 11.2. We introduce the following notation:

$\Pi_{n,i}$ Proportionate activity level of HUC component n relative to the total HUC activity of hospital i, which is derived as follows:

$$\Pi_{n,i} = \Omega_{n,i}\Big/\sum_n \Omega_{n,i}$$

S Set of reference hospitals against which the hospital is evaluated. For the purpose of this study, S is defined by state. That is $S = \{NJ\}$ represents all hospitals in the state of New Jersey.

$\mu(\Pi_n)_S$ Mean of $\Pi_{n,i}$ for all hospitals in set S. Note that $i \in S$ if hospital i is located in state S.

$\sigma(\Pi_n)_S$ Standard deviation of $\Pi_{n,i}$ for all hospitals in set S.

$\sigma(\Pi_n)_G$ Standard deviation of $\Pi_{n,i}$ for all hospitals in all S, that is, the global data set.

The classification groups then are as follows:

λ-*Type* = 1 **Intensive Care** – Significantly higher than state average
λ-*Type* = 2 **Outpatient Care Services** – Significantly higher than state average
λ-*Type* = 3 **Ancillary Services** – Significantly higher than state average
λ-*Type* = 4 **Nursery Care** – Significantly higher than state average
λ-*Type* = 5 **Basic Inpatient Care** – Significantly higher than state average
λ-*Type* = 6 **General** – No significant difference from state average

The λ-*Type* classification rules are then as follows. These are applied to each hospital i to derive the corresponding λ_i:

1. If $\Pi_{2,i} > \mu(\Pi_2)_S + 0.4\sigma(\Pi_2)_S + 0.6\sigma(\Pi_2)_G$ then set $\lambda_i = 1$ and quit rules, else go to next rule.
2. If $\Pi_{4,i} > \mu(\Pi_4)_S + 0.4\sigma(\Pi_4)_S + 0.6\sigma(\Pi_4)_G$ then set $\lambda_i = 2$ and quit rules, else go to next rule.
3. If $\Pi_{5,i} > \mu(\Pi_5)_S + 0.4\sigma(\Pi_5)_S + 0.6\sigma(\Pi_5)_G$ then set $\lambda_i = 3$ and quit rules, else go to next rule.
4. If $\Pi_{3,i} > \mu(\Pi_3)_S + 0.4\sigma(\Pi_3)_S + 0.6\sigma(\Pi_3)_G$ then set $\lambda_i = 4$ and quit rules, else go to next rule.
5. If $\Pi_{1,i} > \mu(\Pi_1)_S + 0.4\sigma(\Pi_1)_S + 0.6\sigma(\Pi_1)_G$ then set $\lambda_i = 5$ and quit rules, else go to next rule.
6. Else set $\lambda_i = 6$

Bias is detected in the above rules when the proportionate activity level in a HUC component exceeds the state average by 40% of the state standard deviation plus 60%

of the global standard deviation. The bias rules are thus anchored to variance in both state and global data. In the data analysis, we experimented with other multiplier levels ranging from 0.3 to 1.0 for $\sigma(\Pi_n)_S$, but observed that at higher levels the classification rules are triggered a very low levels. While at lower levels, it tends to skew toward the early rules.

Note that the rules prioritize the HUC component by which classification is determined. Top priority is given to intensive care ($n = 2$). These priorities were determined by the resource complexity as assessed by healthcare professionals. It is important in healthcare data analysis to seek and establish necessary links with the practitioners. This will ensure that where subjective data are involved, the relevant conclusions can be drawn. In the absence of these linkages, the data analysis results may lose relevance to the practitioner community.

11.6.1 Comparing the Resource Use Profile of States

A key step in data analysis is identifying reference data sets for performance comparison. The approach followed here and the HUC study, in general, is to define the reference groups by state. Since all hospitals in a state experience equivalent wage rates, patient demographics, legal and regulatory requirements, and associated infrastructures, any differences in resource use are less likely to be due to these reasons. Presented here (Table 11.2) are results of the application of the resource use data analysis of hospitals in 16 US states. The analytical results show that there are key differences in the resource use profiles between states and within states.

1. *Intra-state Differences*: Some states have large differences between hospitals as indicated by high values of $\sigma(\Pi_n)_S$. CA is the most diverse state in hospital operations behavior, in particular both $\sigma(\Pi_1)_S$ and $\sigma(\Pi_5)_S$ are significantly higher than other states. Intuitively, the expectation would be that all large states would show diversity, but that is not necessarily the case. For instance, large states such as TX and FL have much lower $\sigma(\Pi_n)_S$ values, indicating that hospitals are quite similar in the activity profiles. In contrast OR, a small state, also exhibits a diverse hospital profile.

2. *Inter-state Difference*: A key research question is whether the hospital resource use activity profile as described by the vector $\{\mu(\Pi_n)_S \mid n = 1 \text{ to } 5\}$ is consistent across the states. A data scan indicates that some states are quite different in that $\mu(\Pi_n)_S$ is significantly greater than that for other states. For all components, we can identify at least one state where it this true: Case Mix, OR; Intensive Care, CA; Nursery, UT; Outpatient, MA; and Ancillary, SD. Further research can identify the causal factors for these differences.

Ideally we would want to do an *F*-test to confirm that the observed HUC-based resource use behavior is not the same for all states in the study. That is, for each n, we would evaluate if $\mu(\Pi_n)_S$ is the same for all s. But the data set is unbalanced in that the max–min standard deviation ratio is greater than two plus the population sizes are unequal. Instead we limit the analysis to graphical evaluation of the box plot, as shown in Figure 11.11.

TABLE 11.2 HUC Component Data by State

#	State S	$\mu(\Pi_n)_S$ – HUC Component Mean					$\sigma(\Pi_n)_S$ – HUC Component SD				
		Ω_1 – CaseMix (%)	Ω_2 – IntCare (%)	Ω_3 – Nursery (%)	Ω_4 – Outpatient (%)	Ω_5 – Ancillary (%)	Ω_1 – CaseMix (%)	Ω_2 – IntCare (%)	Ω_3 – Nursery (%)	Ω_4 – Outpatient (%)	Ω_5 – Ancillary (%)
1	AZ	36.4	9.7	1.2	14.6	38.1	5.9	3.9	1.0	4.6	6.1
2	CA	39.7	11.8	1.4	9.4	37.7	*17.1*	*7.9*	1.2	5.4	*17.7*
3	CT	35.5	6.2	0.7	15.6	41.9	14.9	3.4	0.4	6.4	9.9
4	FL	35.1	9.4	0.7	12.6	42.2	8.3	3.9	0.7	5.7	9.1
5	IL	32.5	8.2	1.1	14.2	44.1	10.2	4.2	0.8	4.9	10.5
6	MA	29.6	8.9	1.1	20.0	40.4	8.1	15.2	0.8	6.8	11.0
7	NE	29.5	7.0	1.1	9.9	52.4	6.2	2.3	0.4	3.6	8.5
8	NJ	35.1	8.8	1.4	13.9	40.9	7.8	5.7	0.9	4.8	9.0
9	NY	34.9	8.6	0.9	16.7	39.1	11.3	5.2	0.7	*10.0*	13.4
10	PA	32.4	7.7	0.7	17.1	42.1	8.5	3.1	0.7	6.4	11.1
11	SD	29.2	6.6	0.9	12.6	50.7	6.1	2.4	0.4	*1.5*	6.7
12	WA	29.8	9.3	1.2	15.3	44.4	6.1	4.8	0.9	5.4	7.4
13	TX	30.7	10.2	1.8	14.5	42.8	7.4	4.2	1.6	6.2	8.6
14	CO	30.8	9.3	1.5	12.5	45.9	4.6	4.1	0.9	3.4	6.6
15	OR	38.5	8.8	1.1	9.8	41.8	15.4	4.4	0.4	5.2	13.8
16	UT	23.8	7.3	1.8	17.1	50.0	5.3	4.2	0.5	3.6	7.4

Italic terms show the subscripts.

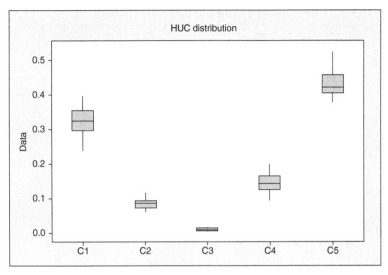

Figure 11.11   Box plot of $\mu(\Pi_n)_S$ by component.

11.6.2   Application of the Hospital Classification Rules

An example λ-*Type* classification using the above-defined rules for three California hospitals of different sizes (as measured by adjusted inpatient days) is shown in
Table 11.2. What we demonstrate here is the use of the HUC model to classify hospitals using data analysis, as opposed to the more peer-assessment approach. The first
hospital, Hollywood Community, is classified as $\lambda = 5$ or basic inpatient care. This
hospital has no nursery service, marginal levels of outpatients services provide very
limited advanced healthcare services as evidenced by low $\Pi_{2,i}$ and $\Pi_{5,i}$ values. We see
from Table 11.2 that $\mu(\Pi_4)_{CA} = 5.4\%$ while for the second hospital in Table 11.3, UC
San Diego, $\Pi_{4,i}$ is much larger classifying the hospital as $\lambda = 4$. Clearly, operational
initiatives and productivity benchmarks established for the first hospital should not
be immediately applied to the second hospital. Since the two hospitals have different resource use profiles, they should be evaluated according to their peer group. The
HUC analysis, therefore, allows not only aggregate analysis but also specific analysis
at the hospital level.

Distributions of hospitals by λ-*Type* for the data set are shown in Figures 11.12
and 11.13. Overall, the dominant hospital type is $\lambda = 5$ implying that 62% of hospitals have a resource use profile similar to the mean behavior for their state. But
operationally 38% of hospitals have a signifcantly different resource use profile. Furthermore, as seen in Figure 11.4, the overall distribution of hospital types is not been
consistent across states, and in many cases quite contrasting.

TABLE 11.3   Classification for a Sample of California Hospitals

Hospital	Adj Inpatient Days	Ω_1 – CaseMix (%)	Ω_2 – IntCare (%)	Ω_3 – Nursery	Ω_4 – Outpatient (%)	Ω_5 – Ancillary (%)	λ-Type
Hollywood Community Hospital	42,277	*80.2*	7.2	0.0	2.0	10.4	**5**
UC San Diego Medical Center	254,062	32.5	15.3	0.63	*16.0*	35.4	**2**
Valley Presbyterian Hospital	99,922	40.7	15.1	*3.43*	13.9	27.6	**4**

The maximum values in the columns are given in italics.
Bold terms show the subscripts.

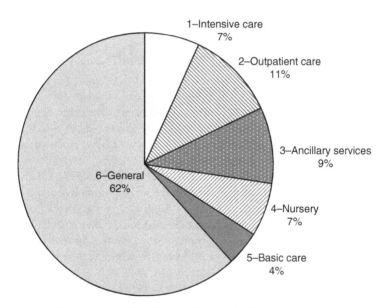

Figure 11.12   Distribution of hospital λ-*Type* full data set.

In combination with the HUC component data, key insights into operational characteritics can be gleaned. Consider the case of CA, which has only five $\lambda = 1$ hospitals but $\mu(\Pi_2)_{CA} = 11.8\%$ higher than most states. This indicates that intensive care activities are more widespread in CA hospitals although the variance is high. In contrast, PA has fewer $\lambda = 6$ hospitals, indicating that operationally many hospitals have a bias to one of the HUC components.

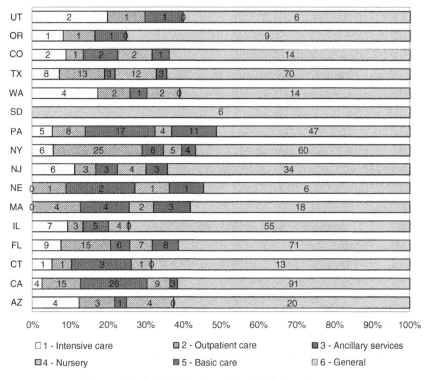

Figure 11.13 Distribution of hospital λ-*Type* by state.

11.7 SUMMARY

The application of the HUC model to extract key operational behavior about hospitals from the "Big Data" sets maintained by Medicare has been demonstrated. This application confirms that large-scale cross-hospital productivity analysis involving multiple states can be done from available databases. This is in contrast to most current studies that are limited to one hospital or a small subset of hospitals. Research groups are encouraged to further leverage these database sources for data analysis studies that focus on hospital operations.

The analytical results have identified and quantified the resource intensive activity behavior of hospitals, a key factor in productivity analysis. The resource use profile across the five HUC components was shown to vary significantly both inter-state and intra-state. Supporting the common view that there is a lack of operational commonality between hospitals, the dominance of ancillary services as resources was identified, although these services are addressed only briefly in the research literature. Many studies focus on the operations of Emergency Rooms (ER), but an ER is a collection of multiple activities and this analysis shows the volume of these activities individually. The results of this analysis allows for more focussed performance improvement initiatives. Using the resource activity volume ratios, a λ-*Type* hospital classification system was developed. In contrast to structural classification systems, this is first method for classifying hospitals strictly on the basis of activity and resource usage profiles. Analysis of the data reveals significant different in λ-*Type* distribution between states.

REFERENCES

[1] US News & World Report. 2012. Best Hospitals 2012–2013: The Honor Roll, these 17 medical centers are standouts in half a dozen or more specialties. Available at http://health .usnews.com/best-hospitals/rankings. Accessed 2015 Dec 22.

[2] Boodhoo, S, Das, SK. A productivity output measure for a hospital unit of care, Ph.D. Dissertation Report, New Jersey Institute of Technology, Newark, NJ; 2013.

[3] Tiemann O, Schreyögg J. Changes in hospital efficiency after privatization. Health Care Manag Sci 2012;15(4):310–326.

[4] Carr RF. *Design Guidance for Healthcare Facilities – Hospitals* http://www.wbdg. org/design/hospital.php. National Institute for Building Sciences; 2011.

[5] Hollingsworth B. The measurement of efficiency and productivity of health care delivery. Health Econ 2008;17(10):1107–1128.

[6] MacLean M, Mix P. Measuring hospital productivity and output: The omission of outpatient services. Health Rep 1983;3(3):229–244.

[7] Soderlund N, Milne R, Gray A, Raftery J. Differences in hospital case mix and the relationship between casemix and hospital costs. J Public Health Med 1995;17(1):25–32.

[8] Miller M, Sulvetta MB, Englert E. Service mix in the hospital outpatient department: Implications for Medicare payment reform. Health Serv Res 1995;30:59–77.

[9] Cleverley WO, Cleverley JO. A better way to measure volume and benchmark costs. Healthc Financ Manage 2011;65:78–82.

[10] Huerta TR, Ford EW, Ford WF, Thompson MA. Realizing the value proposition: A longitudinal assessment of hospitals total factor productivity. J Healthc Eng 2011;2(3):285–302.

[11] Zhivan NA, Diana ML. U.S. hospital efficiency and adoption of health information technology. Health Care Manag Sci 2012;15(1):37–47.

[12] Greene W. Distinguishing between heterogeneity and efficiency: Stochastic frontier analysis of the World Health Organisation's panel data on national health care systems. Health Econ 2004;13:959–980.

[13] McGlynn, EA, et al. Identifying, Categorizing, and Evaluating Health Care Efficiency Measures. Final Report, AHRQ Publication No. 08-0030, Agency for Healthcare Research and Quality: Rockville, MD; 2008.

[14] Rosko MD, Mutter RL. Stochastic frontier analysis of hospital inefficiency: A review of empirical issues and an assessment of robustness. Med Care Res Rev 2008;65:131–166.

[15] Barros CP, Menezes AG, Peypoch N, Solonandrasana B, Vieira JC. An analysis of hospital efficiency and productivity growth using the Luenberger indicator. Health Care Manag Sci 2008;11(4):373–381.

[16] MEDPAR. 2012. Medicare Provider Analysis and Review (MEDPAR) File, Available at http://www.cms.gov/Research-Statistics-Data-and-Systems/Files-for-Order/IdentifiableDataFiles/MedicareProviderAnalysisandReviewFile.html. Accessed 2015 Dec 22.

[17] American Hospital Association. 2011. The cost of caring: Drivers of spending on hospital care, Trendwatch. Available at http://www.aha.org/research/reports/tw/11mar-tw-costofcaring.pdf. Accessed 2015 Dec 22.

[18] Tachell W. Measuring hospital output: A review of the service mix and case mix approaches. Soc Sci Med 1983;17:871–883.

12

DISCRETE-EVENT SIMULATION FOR PRIMARY CARE REDESIGN: REVIEW AND A CASE STUDY

XIANG ZHONG

Department of Industrial and Systems Engineering, University of Wisconsin, Madison, WI, USA

MOLLY WILLIAMS

University of Wisconsin Medical Foundation, Middleton, WI, USA

JINGSHAN LI

Department of Industrial and Systems Engineering, University of Wisconsin, Madison, WI, USA

SALLY A. KRAFT AND JEFFREY S. SLEETH

University of Wisconsin Medical Foundation, Middleton, WI, USA

12.1 INTRODUCTION

The goal of University of Wisconsin Health (UW Health) primary care redesign efforts is to provide easy and timely access to healthcare, which is culturally sensitive, quality driven, and maximizes the use of education and community resources based on patient needs. To make such a care delivery model successful, it is essential to create a sustainable environment, in which team members work to their highest level of licensure with excellence at all levels of the system of care, and make full use of existing and emerging technologies [1].

Healthcare Analytics: From Data to Knowledge to Healthcare Improvement, First Edition.
Edited by Hui Yang and Eva K. Lee.
© 2016 John Wiley & Sons, Inc. Published 2016 by John Wiley & Sons, Inc.

Redesigning primary care has attracted substantial research effort (see white paper [2], an early paper [3], and review [4–7]). Most of the work in primary care redesign focuses on investigating team work, evaluating physician performance and patient quality, assessing performance-based payments and electronic medical record system, and so on. Qualitative methods have been used prevailingly in many studies.

Many health systems use "small tests of change" to iteratively improve processes. However, when contemplating major changes in systems of care, such as appointment scheduling and staffing, use of the PDCA (plan-do-check-act) model is not appropriate for being disruptive and time consuming. On the other hand, simulation offers an alternative method to "test" changes in practice and to evaluate the impact of those changes on patients and staff. In recent years, discrete-event simulation (DES) dominates the quantitative studies in healthcare delivery research (see reviews [8–10]). The successful implementation areas include emergency department (ED), hospital pharmacy unit, critical care unit (CCU), outpatient clinics, and so on. The objective of this work is to develop a simulation model to support primary care redesign.

In this chapter, we present a review of primary care redesign and healthcare system simulation and introduce a case study conducted at a pediatric and adolescent medicine clinic owned and operated by UW Health in Madison, WI. As one of UW Health's leading pediatric clinics, it provides a comprehensive service to child care from birth to adolescence and offers the entire spectrum of pediatric and adolescent primary health care. The intent of this study is to understand the patient flow in the pediatric clinic and identify the opportunities to minimize patient waiting time and improve the patient outcome. The main objective is to develop a simulation model to analyze patient flow, evaluate its design options, and propose recommendations for improvement. Through identifying the optimal scheduling template and staffing model, managerial alternatives and insights for potential ways to reduce patient average length of stay (LOS) will be investigated.

The remainder of the chapter is structured as follows: The review of relevant literature on both primary care redesign and DES in healthcare is reviewed in Section 12.2. The simulation model of the case study is introduced in Section 12.3. Section 12.4 presents the what–if analyses with respect to changes in scheduling template, patient volume, room assignment, staffing, and so on. Finally, conclusions are given in Section 12.5.

12.2   REVIEW OF RELEVANT LITERATURE

12.2.1   Literature on Primary Care Redesign

12.2.1.1   Reviews   Primary care, as the backbone of the nation's healthcare system, is facing significant challenges and risk of collapse [3, 5]. Bodenheimer [6] discusses the difficulties in primary care, in which a confluence of factors could lead to disaster, such as excessive demands, uneven quality of care, unhappiness with jobs, inadequate reimbursement, and fewer and fewer US medical students choosing to enter the field. To address these challenges, actions on primary care practices (microsystem improvement) and larger healthcare system (macrosystem reform) are needed.

Bodenheimer and Pham [7] review the state of primary care in the United States. They discuss the feature and landscape of primary care practices and resulting difficulty accessing primary care due to multiple factors, including shortage in the primary care practitioner workforce, geographic maldistribution, and organizational issues within primary care practices. Reform strategies are proposed to address the problems of estimating panel size, increasing capacity, mitigating geographic maldistribution, standardizing reimbursement levels to reduce insurance-linked refusal, increasing after-hour access, implementing open access for same-day scheduling, introducing e-mail and telephone visits, and forming primary care teams with nonprofessional team members.

12.2.1.2 Team Work Team work plays a critical role in primary care practice. Lemieux-Charles and McGuire [11] provide a review of healthcare team effectiveness from 1985 to 2004 by comparing team with usual (nonteam) care, examining the impact of team design on effectiveness, and exploring relationships among team context, structure, processes, and outcomes. It is suggested that the type and diversity of clinical expertise involved in team decision making largely accounts for improvements in patient care and organizational effectiveness. Staff satisfaction and perceived team effectiveness are largely influenced by collaboration, conflict resolution, participation, and cohesion.

Through observation studies, Bower et al. [12] discuss team practice structure, process (climate), and outcome (quality of care) in primary care. The results indicate there exist important relationships between team structure, process, and outcome that may be of relevance to quality improvement initiatives in primary care. It is necessary to determine the possible causal mechanisms that might underlie these associations. Grumback and Bodenheimer [13] study how a team with individuals from different disciplines work together to care for the patient. Through research of two primary care sites, it is shown that the team with greater cohesiveness is associated with better clinical outcome and higher satisfaction. The planning and team work in multiple disciplinary care to improve outcomes for patients with chronic disease and complex care needs are presented in paper [14]. It shows that such an effort does improve outcomes. To widespread its implementation in standard practice, complex and targeted strategies are necessary to change patterns of interactions between care providers, alignment of roles, and work practices and change organizational arrangements.

More studies on team work in primary care can be found in [15–17].

12.2.1.3 Data and Information Data in electronic health records (EHR) plays a central role in healthcare delivery, quality control, clinical governance, and provider practices. The adoption of EHR system has been a worldwide trend in healthcare practice. de Lusignan and van Weel [18] review the opportunities of using routinely collected data in primary care research, such as growing volumes, improving data quality, technological progress for processing, and potentials to link clinical and genetic data, and established body of know-how within health informatics community. However, there exist challenges such as limited research methods working with large data sets and inferences of data meaning; lack of reliable unique identifier between health and social care systems; increased pace of change in medicine and technology; and information security, confidentiality, and privacy issues. A comprehensive review of literature on the current state of implementation of health information system in primary care is carried out in paper [19]. It shows that the graphical user interface design quality, feature functionality, project management, procurement, and users' previous experience affect implementation outcomes. Factors such as privacy, patient safety, provider/patient relations, staff anxiety, time factors, quality of care, finances, efficiency, and liability are the major concerns.

In addition, the data quality in electronic patient records (EPRs) in primary care is reviewed in paper [20] based on publications in 1980–2001. Hillestad et al. [21] investigate the impact of electronic medical record systems on transforming primary care and the potential health benefits, savings and costs. From a human factors' engineering perspective, Beasley et al. [22] discuss the concept of information chaos in primary care and explore implications for its impact on physician performance and patient safety.

More studies related to data and information system in primary care are introduced in papers [21, 23–26].

12.2.1.4 *Medical Homes*

The concept of medical home is defined as follows: having a regular doctor or place of care, doctor/staff knowing information about patient's health history, the place being easy to contact by phone, and the doctor/staff coordinating care received from other doctors or source of care [27].

Rosenthal [28] reviews the literature and program on medical homes to assess the usefulness of the model based on several principles, such as personal physician, team-directed medical practice, whole-person orientation, coordinated and integrated care across the healthcare domain, quality, and safety. It is claimed that a reformulation of reimbursement policy is required to institutionalize the medical homes. By arguing that the specialist-dominated US healthcare system results in mediocre quality care with excessive use of costly service but little marginal health benefit, Landon et al. [29] further claim that the patient-centered medical home has become a policy shorthand for rebuilding US primary care capacity. The success will require effective policies in payment reform and certification of medical homes, and proper act to facilitate transformation of existing practices and identify the appropriate linkages of medical homes to other delivery systems. Gilfillan et al. [30] carry out observational study to evaluate the ability of a medical home model in improving the efficiency of care for Medicare beneficiaries. It shows that medical homes in primary care service may increase healthcare value by improving the efficiency of care. It can also help significantly reduce hospital admissions and readmissions for Medicare Advantage members.

Papers [31–34] provide more references addressing medical homes in primary care practice.

12.2.1.5 *Payment System*

Davis et al. [4] introduce seven attributes of the patient-centered primary care to improve care quality: access to care, patient engagement in care, information systems, care coordination, integrated and comprehensive team care, patient-centered care surveys, and publicly available information. They argue that a new primary care payment system to blend monthly patient panel fees, traditional fee-for-service, and new incentives for patient-centered care performance is desirable. As performance-based payments are increasingly common in primary care, Friedberg et al. [35] suggest that pay-for-performance programs should monitor and address the potential impact of performance-based payments on healthcare disparities. To improve the ability of primary care to play its essential role in the healthcare system, Porter et al. [36] offers a framework based on value for patients to sustain and improve primary care practice. It proposes to organize primary care around subgroups of patients with similar needs, and thus team-based services could be provided to each subgroup. The patient's outcome and costs should be measured by subgroup, and payment should be bundled to reimburse for each subgroup. Finally, subgroup teams should be integrated with relevant specialty providers.

Extensive studies in payment-related issues in primary care have been introduced in recent years, such as papers [37–40].

12.2.1.6 Advanced Access

The advanced access, also known as open access or same-day scheduling, in which patients calling to schedule a physician visit are offered an appointment on the same day [41], has been increasingly shown to be helpful to reduce waiting times in primary care. Murray and Berwick [42] summarize six elements of advanced access to make it sustainable: balancing supply and demand, reducing backlog, reducing the variety of appointment types, developing contingency plans for unusual circumstances, working to adjust demand profiles, and increasing the availability of bottleneck resources. Case studies using the advanced access models are presented in paper [43]. By analyzing 462 general practices (GP) in England, Pickin et al. [44] show that advanced access can help practices to improve availability of GP appointments and has been well received by the majority of practices. Another survey in paper [45] also shows that patients are seen more quickly in advanced access practices, but with less flexibility in choice of appointment. Thus, appointment systems need to be flexible to accommodate different needs of different patient groups.

Additional papers studying advanced access in primary care can be found in [46–49].

12.2.1.7 Global Experiences

In paper [27], healthcare experiences for adults in seven countries: Australia, Canada, Germany, the Netherlands, New Zealand, the United Kingdom, and the United States, are compared. It discovers that the accessible medical home can yield significant positive experience. It finds that differences exist between countries, but many concerns are common. However, the United States is standing out in cost-related access and less-efficient care. Four more countries (France, Italy, Norway, and Sweden) are included in a more recent survey [50] from physicians' perspective, which finds wide differences in practice systems, incentives, perceptions of access to care, use of health information technology (IT), and programs to improve quality. It shows that US and Canadian physicians lag in the adoption of IT. More reports on insurance restrictions on obtaining medication and treatment and difficulty with costs for patients are reported in the United States. It is believed that opportunities exist for cross-national learning in disease management, use of teams, and performance feedback to improve primary care globally. Additional studies are presented in papers [51] and [52], which indicate opportunities to learn cross-nationally to improve outcomes and efficiency.

12.2.2   Literature on Discrete-Event Simulation in Healthcare

12.2.2.1   Reviews   In recent years, there has been a significant increase in using computer simulation to study healthcare delivery systems. The rapid development of information technology and data analytics has substantially enhanced and extended the functions of simulation tools. Thus, simulations can be used as an aid for decision making and operation improvement through modeling complex facilities, sophisticated logics, and dynamic schedules, assessing the efficacy of the system, carrying out what–if analysis to evaluate the design, studying the impact of potential changes, and investigating the complex relationships of system variables. A comprehensive review of DES in health care is presented in [8]. In this chapter, simulation studies of single or multifacility healthcare organizations are reviewed, which include outpatient clinics, emergency departments, surgical centers, orthopedic departments and pharmacies, and so on. Similar reviews have been provided in [9, 10, 53]. Gunal and Pidd [10] classify the papers of DES for performance modeling in healthcare according to the areas of applications. They also indicate that there is a lack of generality and explain the rationale why generic approaches are rare and specificity dominates. By reviewing the legacies of simulation modeling in healthcare, Eldabi et al. [9] propose future opportunities to use simulation as a problem-solving technique in healthcare setting. In addition, Wiler et al. [53] focus on emergency department and categorizes the modeling approach of patient flow in emergency department into five categories: formula-based, regression-based, time series analysis, queueing models, and DESs.

12.2.2.2   Emergency Department   As emergency department (ED) is one of the most critical departments in a hospital, and overcrowding becomes a national crisis [54–56], substantial amount of simulation studies have been devoted to ED to reduce crowding (see reviews [53, 57]). Many simulation studies have been used to help reduce patient waiting time, determine ED configuration and resource allocation, and so on, which can effectively simulate changes to the model and its effects on patient flow. For example, Hung et al. [58] construct a patient flow model using DES to test different staffing scenarios in pediatric and emergency departments. Such a model is also used as an analysis tool to assist in physician scheduling. Fanti et al. [59] introduce a Petri net model to simulate emergency cardiology department in Bari, Italy. A simulation study is introduced to model the ED in University of Kentucky Chandler Hospital in paper [60]. It shows that the diagnostic test is the bottleneck in the ED. As a result of this study, a new CT scanner and two more nurses are added in the ED. Similarly, Zeng et al. [61] identify the same procedure as bottleneck at another community hospital in Lexington, KY. It also investigates the impact of limited team nursing policy (i.e., two nurses sharing the work together) on ED efficiency, which shows that such a policy could help reducing patient LOS and waiting time. Similarly, simulation results in paper [62] also show that decreasing lab turnaround time could lead to improvement in ED efficiency, such as ED LOS, throughput, and diversion. In another community hospital study [63], improvement has been achieved by adding a float nurse and integrating registration and triage processes.

Additional simulation studies in emergency departments have been reported in papers [64–68].

12.2.2.3 Other Hospital Units In addition to simulations of EDs, other hospital departments are also studied intensively. A simulation model developed to represent the complex process of radiation therapy and suggest improvements to reduce the planning time and waiting times is described in paper [69]. The operation performance of an endoscopy suite is studied using simulation in paper [70]. The results show that, under a constant room to endoscopist ratio, the maximum number of patients served is linearly related to the number of procedure rooms in the colonoscopy suite. In addition, the procedure room turnaround time has a significant influence on patient throughput, procedure room utilization, and endoscopist utilization. The patient waiting time can be reduced by changing the patient arrival schedule.

As intensive care units (ICUs) are the most critical department in a hospital, ICU simulation has attracted substantial interests. Griffiths et al. [71] simulate the bed-occupancy of the CCU of a large teaching hospital in order to optimize the number of beds available to minimize cancellations of elective surgery and maintain an acceptable level of bed-occupancy. What–if analysis has been carried out to evaluate the impact of increasing bed numbers, "ring-fencing" beds for elective patients, reducing LOS to account for delayed discharge, and changing the scheduling of elective surgery. In paper [72], simulation model is also developed to determine the number of supplementary nurses in an ICU that are required to minimize overall nursing staff costs.

For pharmacies, Lu et al. [73] introduce a simulation study to improve the antineo-plastic medication preparation and delivery performance at a pharmacy department in a large community hospital. It is discovered that by introducing early preparation for the returning patients and dedicating an infusion staff member for medication delivery, patients' waiting time for antineoplastic medications can be reduced sub-stantially. The implementation results have indicated more than 50% reduction in waiting time. Reynolds et al. [74] present a DES study of the hospital pharmacy out-patient dispensing systems at two London hospitals in the United Kingdom. Different scenarios related to prescription workload, staffing levels and skill-mix, and utiliza-tion of the dispensaries' automatic dispensing robots are tested, which are used to support business cases for changes in staffing levels and skill-mix in response to changes in workload.

Moreover, Couchman et al. [75] introduce a computer simulation model to pre-dict the effects of increased workload, replacement of analytical instruments, and changes in working practices at a general hospital's clinical biochemistry laboratory. A simulation model is developed in paper [76] focusing on patient flow analysis, by considering patient classification, blocking effects, time-dependent arrival and departure patterns, and distributions for LOS. Through the application to DeKalb Medical's Women's Center, it is shown that implementation of "swing" rooms (flexible between Antepartum (AP) and Mother–Baby (MB) rooms) could help to balance bed allocation.

Through simplifications, simulation models of a whole hospital have been studied. To balance bed unit utilizations in a 400-bed hospital, Cochran and Bharti [77] use DESs to maximize the flow and cope with the complexity of hospital operations. The study is only limited to bed-related operations. van der Meer et al. [78] study all phases of the musculoskeletal service: an elective patient passing through in orthopedics medicine. It focuses on the reduction of waiting time for elective patients, both for a first outpatient appointment and for the subsequent commencement of inpatient treatment.

More simulation studies on different hospital units (e.g., critical care, surgical, discharge) can be found in [79–83].

12.2.2.4   *Primary Care Outpatient Clinics*

*12.2.2.4   **Primary Care Outpatient Clinics***   In primary care outpatient clinics, scheduling is of substantial importance [84]. Simulations have been used in paper [85] to evaluate the performance of different appointment systems. The results show that patient sequencing has a larger impact on ambulatory care performance than the choice of an appointment rule. In addition, panel characteristics such as walk-ins, no-shows, punctuality, and overall session volume influence the effectiveness of appointment systems. A detailed simulation model is presented in paper [86] for an Ear, Nose, and Throat (ENT) clinic to test different appointment schedules. It is shown that the patients' waiting time can be reduced dramatically through improved appointment schedules without the need for extra resources. In order to utilize the limited and expensive equipment and manpower more efficiently, a patient scheduling approach based on simulation analysis is introduced in paper [87] to determine appropriate scheduling policy under different environmental conditions.

More applications of simulation in primary care clinics can be found. For instance, a simulation-based project to help North Mersey Community National Health Service (NHS) Trust in the United Kingdom to design and plan the operation of an NHS Walk-in Centre is introduced in paper [88]. A simulation study of an orthopedic outpatient clinic is presented by Rohleder et al. [89], which can help identify improvement alternatives such as optimized staffing levels, better patient scheduling, and an emphasis on staff arriving promptly. The implementation results show that waiting-time measures are significantly improved and overall patient time in the clinic is reduced. Moreover, a discrete-event computer simulation model is developed by Coelli et al. [90] to simulate changes in patient arrival rates, number of equipment units, available personnel, equipment maintenance scheduling schemes, and exam repeat rates in a mammography clinic of Brazilian Cancer Institute. Again in the city of Rio de Janeiro, Brazil, a computer simulation model is described in paper [91] to analyze the performance of a standard physiotherapy clinic and investigate the impacts of changes in the number of patients, human resources of the clinic, and the scheduling of patient arrivals. Finally, Reynolds et al. [92] study the design of staffing model for a health clinic for homeless people.

In addition, simulations have been used to analyze and improve the financial performance in radiology procedure scheduling for outpatients and to reduce the number of tests without pre-approvals [93]. Emerging methods in economic modeling of imaging costs and outcomes using DES have been summarized and reported in [94]. It is concluded that DES is playing an increasingly important role in the future modeling of annual screening programs, diagnosis, and treatment of chronic recurrent disease and modeling the utilization of imaging equipment.

More simulation studies on outpatient clinics are described in [95–99].

12.2.3 UW Health Improvement Projects

In UW Health, much effort has been devoted to implementing primary care redesign and simulation modeling. For example, an initiative has been taken to reduce Odana Atrium (OA) overall clinic telephone abandonment rate to 3% or below [100]. Through reallocating staff and rerouting phone calls, the OA communication center is redesigned, and the phone abandonment rate is decreased from 13% to 1.3% within 6 months, which leads to improved physician and staff satisfaction. In addition, colonoscopy capacity analysis through Markovian analysis/pseudosimulation has been carried out to understand the capacities for general colon procedure and designed colon screening at UW Health [101]. Similar improvement projects in CT test center, mammography imaging test laboratory, and Gastroenterology (GI) clinic design in new digestive health center (DHC) have been carried out in UW Health as well [102–105]. Such activities have helped UW Health improve care quality and patient outcome in primary care.

As introduced earlier, simulations have been widely used in many healthcare applications. It can play a significant role in primary care redesign. Following is a case study of pediatric clinic of UW Health using simulations. First, a simulation model is developed and validated. Second, what–if analyses are carried out to investigate the impact of demand variation, scheduling template, staffing level, and room assignment.

12.3 A SIMULATION CASE STUDY AT A PEDIATRIC CLINIC

To develop a simulation model to emulate the patient flow in the pediatric clinic, a detailed analysis of the patient care delivery process is essential.

12.3.1 Patient Flow

The pediatric clinic has a high patient volume with around 20,000 patient visits per year and a staff model consisting of physicians (9.7 full time equivalent (FTE)), registered nurses (RN) (8.5 FTE), and medical assistants (MA) (12.0 FTE). Each pediatrician is working with a dedicated MA and is assigned three to four exam rooms. There

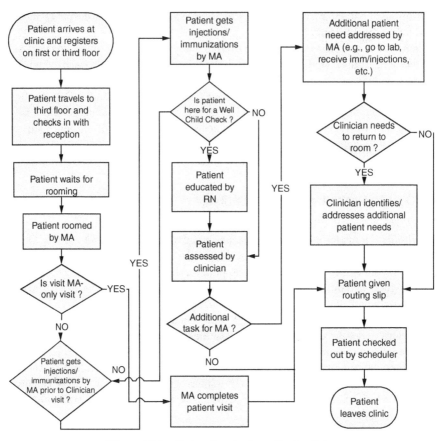

Figure 12.1 Patient flow in the pediatric clinic.

are mainly three types of patient visits: well child (WEL), office visit (OFV), and long office visit (LOV), which includes other longer appointment/consultation visits. In addition to physician appointments, there are also patient appointments with the MA, referred to here as MA-only visits. For those children who have an annual WEL check, an RN is responsible for providing patient education. Daily patient volume varies by physician, generally accommodating 15–25 visits per day. An appointment is scheduled based on a designated template: OFV patients are scheduled every 15 min and WEL patients are scheduled every 30 min in both morning and afternoon sessions. At the end of the day, an LOV patient appointment is scheduled. The current template can accommodate up to 33 patients; however, it is usually not fully filled due to either appointment vacancy or patient no-shows.

The patient flow is illustrated in Figure 12.1. The sequential stages of a patient visit are described as follows:

- A patient arrives at the clinic and registers. The patient checks-in with the receptionist and waits for rooming.

- The patient is roomed by an MA. If it is an MA-only visit, the MA completes the patient visit and the patient is given a routing slip for checkout. If it is a physician visit (WEL/OFV/LOV), the MA completes the rooming workflow and then may administer any needed injections or immunizations prior to the clinician visit, as time allows.
- A WEL patient receives education from an RN prior to the clinician visit.
- Some patients need additional tasks following the clinician visit, usually performed by the MA. These tasks include administration of injections or immunizations, going to laboratory, and so on. After the additional task, there may be a need for the clinician to follow-up with the patient, identify or address additional patient needs.
- Finally, the patient is given a routing slip and checks out at the reception desk.

12.3.2 Model Development

Given the patient flow introduced earlier, a simulation model is developed using SIMUL8, a commercial software tool for planning, design, optimization, and reengineering of production, manufacturing, logistic, or healthcare systems [106]. In this model, each procedure or operation is treated as a "machine" with processing time, required resources, and routing in/out logic. The resources utilized include exam rooms, receptionists, MAs, RNs, and physicians. In the following, each part of the model is introduced.

12.3.2.1 Patient Arrival The parameters in the model are obtained from the UW Health medical record information system, which collects the time stamps of patient arrival and composition, such as scheduled arrival time, actual arrival time, checkin time, first access time by MA and by physician, and checkout time. Additional data were collected through direct observations. To model the arrival, several steps are made to characterize the patient behavior.

Different types of visits are defined in this model. To evaluate the impact of queueing at registration, patients who visit other clinics within the same building are included in the registration process and are referred to as a "Non-Peds visit." Since there are around 200–250 Non-Peds visits each day, a Poisson arrival is used to model this type of arrival. Those patients are set to leave the system directly after registration. For the MA-only visits, the arrival is generated using Poisson distribution with one to two visits daily. For those patients coming for a physician visit, the arrival is generated based on the scheduling template. The sample appointment template is shown in Table 12.1. The first patient is scheduled to arrive at 9:00 AM and the last patient is scheduled no later than 4:30 PM. To incorporate the randomness in arrivals, the deviation of the actual arrival time from the appointment time is captured using field data. It is found that the deviation has a distribution with a negative mean value, which suggests that most of the patients arrive ahead of their scheduled time. This deviation is modeled as a normal distribution with mean -7.1 min and standard deviation 11.4 min, added to the scheduled time. In

TABLE 12.1 Patient Arrival Template

Time (Morning)	Patient Type	Time (Afternoon)	Patient Type
9:00	WEL	13:30	WEL
9:00	OFV	13:30	OFV
9:15	OFV	13:45	OFV
9:30	WEL	14:00	WEL
9:30	OFV	14:00	OFV
9:45	OFV	14:15	OFV
10:00	WEL	14:30	WEL
10:00	OFV	14:30	OFV
10:15	OFV	14:45	OFV
10:30	WEL	15:00	WEL
10:30	OFV	15:00	OFV
10:45	OFV	15:15	OFV
11:00	WEL	15:30	WEL
11:00	OFV	15:30	OFV
11:15	OFV	15:45	OFV
11:30	OFV	16:00	OFV
		16:30	LOV

TABLE 12.2 Appointment Vacancy Probability

Winter	Min (%)	Max (%)	Summer	Min (%)	Max (%)
WEL	0	40	WEL	0	30
Other	5	60	Other	40	80

addition, appointment vacancy and patient no-show are not negligible. To model this scenario, some patients are chosen to leave the system without being served, which is modeled based on a certain appointment vacancy probability distribution varying among patient types and by seasons (summarized in Table 12.2). For example, more children come in for their annual WEL check in summer, while more sick kids require acute visits in winter.

12.3.2.2 Resources In the pediatric clinic, three to four physicians are on duty daily, each working with a designated MA. There are 15 exam rooms in the clinic, each physician is assigned three to four exam rooms. Typically, there will be a lunch break at noon lasting 30–60 min. The responsibilities of the MA include rooming, administrating injections, immunizations, and so on. The RN is mainly responsible for patient education during WEL visits. In addition, MAs and RNs also spend time answering phone calls, scheduling, and handling other paperwork. In addition to seeing patients, physicians also help with teaching the residents and coordinating care with other providers. A receptionist is responsible for patient registration and checkin.

Remark 1 Since all the physicians work independently with their assigned MA and RN and have their own exam rooms to manage, we only track the patient flow for one physician, in order to simplify the model without impairing the properties of the system.

12.3.2.3 Operation Times The operation time of each service is collected either by direct measurement or through estimation by clinic staff. The operation times associated with different clinic staff are provided in Table 12.3. As shown in [92] and [107], the average LOS and other performance measures are practically independent of the distribution type, but are mainly determined by the coefficient of variations. Such a property is also observed in this study. Thus, log-normal distribution characterized by mean and standard deviation is used for modeling operation times.

12.3.2.4 Control Logics The patient routing logistics are designed based on observational data of patients' behavior. In SIMUL8, each patient is assigned a label to characterize the visit type. Such labels determine the patient's routing options within the clinic and the corresponding operation times. Non-Peds patients leave the system directly after checking-in at the registration. After the patient has been roomed, patients' in-room service depends on visit type. Only WEL patients receive nurse education. For a WEL patient, the chance of receiving injections and immunizations is 4% while the probability for an OFV patient is only 1%. Physicians spend more time with LOV patients (see Table 12.4 for more detailed routing probabilities).

12.3.2.5 The Complete Model Using the information discussed earlier, a complete simulation model is developed (Figure 12.2). Three modules are included in the model: pre-rooming service, in-room service, and post-room service.

TABLE 12.3   Operation Times (Minute)

Description	Mean	Std
Registration for pediatric patients	0.5	0.5
Pediatric patients checkin	1.5	1
Rooming for well child	12.19	4.99
Rooming for office visit	10.97	4.12
Rooming for long office visit and consult	10.73	4.23
MA-only visits (immunizations, injections, etc.)	8	5
Immunization or injection prior to MD visit	3	1
RN education (WEL visits only)	13.51	6.03
Well child visit	15.30	6.64
Office visit	12.22	7.03
Long office visit/consult	26.00	10.53
Additional tasks postvisit	3.84	2.95
MD revisit	11.85	6.15
Pediatric patients checkout	0.75	1

TABLE 12.4   Control Logic

Routing	Option	Probability
Entry	Queue for first floor registration	90% Non-Peds 65% Peds
	Queue for third floor registration	10% Non-Peds 35% Peds
Registration	End Non-Peds	100% Non-Peds
	Queue for reception	100% WEL/OFV/LOV
Reception	Queue for MA-Only	100% MA-only visit type
	Queue for rooming	100% WEL, OFV, LOV visit types
Rooming	Dummy WEL split	96% WEL 99% OFV 97% LOV
	Prior immunization/ injection queue	4% WEL 1% OFV 3% LOV
Dummy WEL split	Queue for RN	100% WEL
	Dummy resident split	100% OFV 100% LOV
MD visit	Queue for additional task	40% WEL w/o prior immunization 1% WEL w/ prior immunization 4% OFV 0% LOV
	Queue for checkout	60% WEL w/o prior immunization 99% WEL w/ prior immunization 96% OFV 100% LOV
Additional tasks	Queue for MD revisit	10%
	Checkout queue	90%

- The pre-rooming service process is modeled to include patient arrival, label assignment (characterizing patient identity), and patient routing to different registration/checkin locations. Non-Peds patients leave the system directly while other patients wait for rooming when any exam room and MA become available.

- The in-room service starts with the MA rooming sequence. In some cases, the patient may require an injection or immunization prior to the physician's visit. The MA-only patients will go to checkout directly after their service with the MA. For patients with a physician's appointment, a dummy work center is set to direct WEL patients for RN education. Depending on the patient status, additional activities might be required (such as laboratory work or injections), and finally, the patient might require a physician revisit.

- The post-room service is a quick checkout.

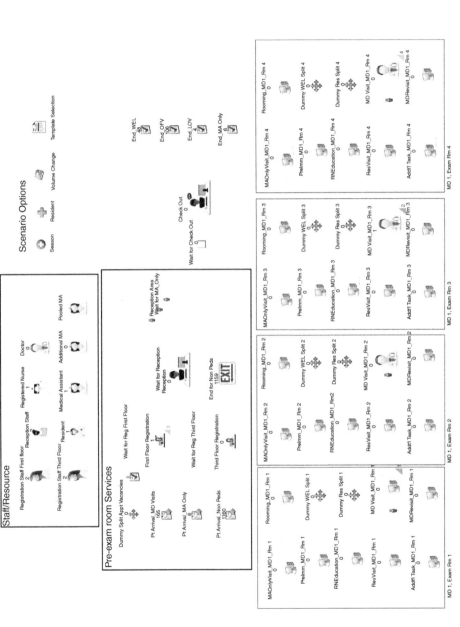

Figure 12.2 Pediatric clinic patient flow simulation model.

TABLE 12.5   Model Validation (Unit: Minute)

Summer	Visit type	LOS^{data}	LOS^{sim}	Δ	ε (%)
	WEL	64.7	65.2	−0.7	−1.1
	OFV	46.2	44.3	1.9	4.1
Winter	Visit type	LOS^{data}	LOS^{sim}	Δ	ε (%)
	WEL	67.1	68.7	−1.6	−2.4
	OFV	51.9	51.4	0.5	0.9

12.3.3   Model Validation

To validate the model developed earlier, observational data are analyzed and the average patient LOS is calculated to compare with simulation results. Let LOS^{data}_{WEL}, LOS^{data}_{OFV}, LOS^{sim}_{WEL}, and LOS^{sim}_{OFV} denote the LOS for WEL and OFV patients obtained by data collection and the simulation model, respectively. The 95% confidence intervals in simulation are typically within 5% of the corresponding measures. Then, the following accuracy measurements are introduced:

$$\Delta_{WEL} = LOS^{\text{data}}_{WEL} - LOS^{\text{sim}}_{WEL},$$

$$\Delta_{OFV} = LOS^{\text{data}}_{OFV} - LOS^{\text{sim}}_{OFV},$$

$$\varepsilon_{WEL} = \frac{LOS^{\text{data}}_{WEL} - LOS^{\text{sim}}_{WEL}}{LOS^{\text{data}}_{WEL}} \cdot 100\%,$$

$$\varepsilon_{OFV} = \frac{LOS^{\text{data}}_{OFV} - LOS^{\text{sim}}_{OFV}}{LOS^{\text{data}}_{OFV}} \cdot 100\%.$$

The results of such comparisons are shown in Table 12.5. As one can see, the differences are typically within 4%. Considering the accuracy of the input data, such a result is acceptable. Therefore, the model is validated and can be used for further analysis.

Remark 2   Note that there are only a few LOV patients' data collected during the observation, hence its comparison is not included.

12.4   WHAT–IF ANALYSES

In this section, several simulation experiments are conducted to accommodate the questions raised by clinicians. By analyzing the simulation results, recommendations are proposed to clinic leadership.

12.4.1   Staffing Analysis

It is of interest to investigate the MA per physician ratio in this system. A 1.2 MA per physician model is proposed. Based on the current model, we add another MA with

20% availability to emulate this scenario. Results show that the reduction in average patient LOS is 4–6 min, which is a moderate deduction. In this case, having more MA FTE does help decrease patient waiting significantly.

Moreover, with 1.2 MA, the clinician utilization is almost the same (from 48% to 47%). The original MA's utilization is reduced from 44% to 34%, while the newly added one is 17.8% busy with the patient.

12.4.2   Resident Doctor

In some cases, a clinician is working with a resident doctor. In such a scenario, the patient is assessed by the resident first and then evaluated by the clinician. The simulation model has been revised to accommodate such changes. The resident service time has a mean of 10 min and standard deviation of 5 min, described by log-normal distribution. Then, the patients' average LOS is increased considerably with the resident's presence. For WEL patients who have seen resident first, the average LOS is increased from 65.2 to 73.9 min, that is, 13.3% increase compared with no resident case. For OFV patients seeing residents, the average LOS is increased from 44.3 to 57.6 min, which is a 30.0% increase. However, clinician working with a resident is not prevailing (1 or 2 half-days per week) in the clinic so that such a case would not have a great impact on the overall clinic performance.

12.4.3   Schedule Template Change

To identify the areas of opportunities for reducing patient's waiting time, several potential schedule templates are proposed by the clinicians for investigation. In addition to the current template, a non-double booking template is proposed and the interarrival time is changed to 10 min, as shown in Table 12.6. Another option is to have a block booking, where the same type of patients are grouped as illustrated in Table 12.7.

Simulation results comparing the three types of templates under the same system settings are shown in Table 12.8 and illustrated in Figure 12.3. Note that the average LOS in current template changes slightly (comparing with the results in Table 12.5). It can be seen that the block booking template's performance is considered to be the least satisfying. For the other two options, different types of patients behave differently in terms of the average LOS. The non-double booking template results in a slightly shorter LOS for OFV visits, while the current template gives the shortest LOS for WEL visits. As block booking template typically results in the longest average LOS, we will emphasize on double and non-double booking templates only in subsequent discussions.

In addition to patient LOS, the staff utilization is also analyzed. It is shown that the MA is busy in serving the patients 44% of the time, while the clinician spends 48% of the time with the patient. Note that such utilizations only represent the time the staff is working face to face with the patient, and typically they have much other work (such as documentation, answering phone calls) to handle.

TABLE 12.6   Non-double Booking Template

Time (Morning)	Patient Type	Time (Afternoon)	Patient Type
9:00	WEL	13:30	WEL
9:10	OFV	13:40	OFV
9:20	OFV	13:50	OFV
9:30	WEL	14:00	WEL
9:40	OFV	14:10	OFV
9:50	OFV	14:20	OFV
10:00	WEL	14:30	WEL
10:10	OFV	14:40	OFV
10:20	OFV	14:50	OFV
10:30	WEL	15:00	WEL
10:40	OFV	15:10	OFV
10:50	OFV	15:20	OFV
11:00	WEL	15:30	WEL
11:10	OFV	15:40	OFV
11:20	OFV	15:50	OFV
11:30	OFV	16:00	OFV
		16:30	LOV

TABLE 12.7   Block Booking Template

Time (Morning)	Patient Type	Time (Afternoon)	Patient Type
9:00	WEL	13:30	WEL
9:10	WEL	13:40	WEL
9:20	WEL	13:50	WEL
9:30	WEL	14:00	WEL
9:40	WEL	14:10	WEL
9:50	OFV	14:20	OFV
10:00	OFV	14:30	OFV
10:10	OFV	14:40	OFV
10:20	OFV	14:50	OFV
10:30	OFV	15:00	OFV
10:40	OFV	15:10	OFV
10:50	OFV	15:20	OFV
11:00	OFV	15:30	OFV
11:10	OFV	15:40	OFV
11:20	OFV	15:50	OFV
11:30	OFV	16:00	OFV
		16:30	LOV

TABLE 12.8   Template Comparison

Patient LOS (Minute)			
WEL	Lower Limit	Average	Upper Limit
Current booking template	57.8	60.4	63.0
Non-double booking template	59.1	61.5	63.9
Block booking template	62.5	65.1	67.7
OFV	Lower limit	Average	Upper limit
Current booking template	41.0	43.5	46.0
Non-double booking template	40.3	42.9	45.9
Block booking template	44.8	47.6	50.3

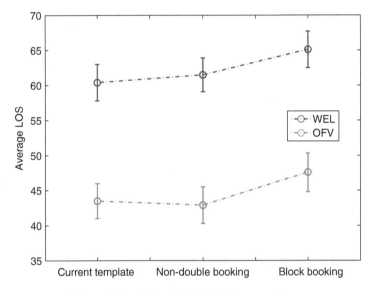

Figure 12.3   Patient LOS for different templates.

12.4.4   Volume Change

Furthermore, we investigate the system performance with 20% increase in patient volume under different templates. The results are shown in Table 12.9. As one can see, the non-double booking template outperforms the other when patient volume is increased by 20%. These results indicate that the clinic should consider changing their current template to non-double booking template to improve the system performance.

12.4.5   Room Assignment

Currently, each physician is assigned three exam rooms, while there are extra exam rooms available. An experiment is conducted to test the impact of having an extra exam room per physician. Here, we compared the system with three exam rooms to

TABLE 12.9   Template Comparison with Increased Patient Volume

Patient LOS (Minute)			
WEL	Lower Limit	Average	Upper Limit
Current template	62.2	64.7	67.3
Non-double booking template	61.5	64.2	69.9
OFV	Lower Limit	Average	Upper Limit
Current template	46.7	49.2	51.7
Non-double booking template	46.3	48.7	51.0

TABLE 12.10   Patient LOS with Different Room Assignment

Patient LOS (Minute)		
WEL	3 Rooms	4 Rooms
Double booking template	60	60.4
Non-double booking template	59.6	61.5
OFV	3 Rooms	4 Rooms
Double booking template	45	43.5
Non-double booking template	44.1	42.9

that of four, under different scheduling templates as proposed. The results are shown in Table 12.10.

The results indicate that the effect of adding an extra room is not the same for different types of patients and different templates. For those visits with a longer stay, having an extra room increases the patient average LOS, for example, WEL patient average LOS is increased by 0.4 minute under current template. However, this change is opposite for those visits with a shorter stay, for example, OFV patient average LOS is decreased by 1.5 min. Such trends are more obvious when using non-double booking (WEL LOS increased by 1.9 min, OFV LOS decreased by 1.2 min). The overall average patient LOS (i.e., count different types of patients) is decreased by 1.2 min by having an extra room using the current template. The LOS remains the same for the non-double booking template. Such reductions are not practically significant. Therefore, it concludes that in this system, there is no need to have more exam rooms, especially if the room operation cost is considerable.

12.4.6   Early Start

In order to reduce patient LOS, new booking templates with early start time (8:45 A.M.) have been proposed and evaluated by the simulation model. Tables 12.11 and 12.12 illustrate the double booking and non-double booking schedules, respectively.

The comparison results with the new templates are shown in Table 12.13. As one can see, the non-double booking template provides slightly shorter average LOS (about 1 min less). In addition, since the templates start at 8:45 A.M., the average LOS decreases in almost all cases comparing with the cases with 9:00 A.M. start.

TABLE 12.11   New Double Booking Template

Time (Morning)	Patient Type	Time (Afternoon)	Patient Type
8:45	WEL	13:30	WEL
8:45	OFV	13:30	OFV
9:00	OFV	13:45	OFV
9:15	WEL	14:00	WEL
9:15	OFV	14:00	OFV
9:30	OFV	14:15	OFV
9:45	WEL	14:30	WEL
9:45	OFV	14:30	OFV
10:00	OFV	14:45	OFV
10:15	WEL	15:00	WEL
10:15	OFV	15:00	OFV
10:30	OFV	15:15	OFV
10:45	WEL	15:30	WEL
11:00	OFV	15:30	OFV
11:15	OFV	15:45	OFV
11:30	OFV	16:00	OFV
		16:30	LOV

TABLE 12.12   New Non-double Booking Template

Time (Morning)	Patient Type	Time (Afternoon)	Patient Type
8:45	WEL	13:30	WEL
8:55	OFV	13:40	OFV
9:05	OFV	13:50	OFV
9:15	WEL	14:00	WEL
9:25	OFV	14:10	OFV
9:35	OFV	14:20	OFV
9:45	WEL	14:30	WEL
9:55	OFV	14:40	OFV
10:05	OFV	14:50	OFV
10:15	WEL	15:00	WEL
10:25	OFV	15:10	OFV
10:35	OFV	15:20	OFV
10:45	WEL	15:30	WEL
11:00	OFV	15:40	OFV
11:15	OFV	15:50	OFV
11:30	OFV	16:00	OFV
		16:30	LOV

TABLE 12.13   **Comparison of Patient LOS Using Templates with Early Start Time**

	Patient LOS (Minute)		
WEL	Lower Limit	Average	Upper Limit
Double booking template	58.5	60.7	62.9
Non-double booking template	57.5	59.8	62.0
OFV	Lower Limit	Average	Upper Limit
Double booking template	39.0	41.8	44.6
Non-double booking template	38.7	41.2	43.7

12.4.7 Additional Observations

Several other questions are also of interest to clinicians and the clinic manager. Some patients complain about experiencing a long wait during registration due to a joint queue with patients scheduled at other clinics within the building. In this analysis, we compare two systems with and without Non-Peds patients. The simulation result suggests that including those Non-Peds patients will not cause a significant change in queueing time at registration. The average queue length at registration is less than one. It can be concluded that the long queue is a rare phenomena and should not be regarded as a constraint for this system.

12.5 CONCLUSIONS

In this chapter, reviews of primary care redesign and DES in healthcare delivery are presented. A simulation model is developed to study the work flow in a pediatric clinic of UW Health. The patient average LOS and staff utilization are evaluated. What–if analyses are carried out to investigate the impacts of different scheduling templates, staffing models, room assignment, and demand change. In the above analyses, the conclusion is reached that the clinic should consider changing the current template to pursue a better system performance. Sharing registration service does not affect the patient LOS significantly. Adding extra MA resources to the system would improve the system performance but cause additional operation cost.

In future work, we plan to generalize the model to redesign other primary care systems. The modeling methods described here are also applicable to other healthcare delivery systems. The results of this work could provide hospital/clinic professionals a quantitative tool to evaluate current system performance, investigate the effects of different configurations, and predict care service efficiency for future redesign plans, which is critical for assisting decision making in healthcare management.

REFERENCES

[1] University of Wisconsin Health. Redesigning Primary Care: Partnering with Patients to Improve Health. UW Health Technical Report. Madison (WI); 2013.

[2] Beasley JW, Carayon P, Smith MA, editors. *Improving the Quality and Efficiency of Primary Care through Industrial and Systems Engineering – A White Paper*. Madison (WI);

2013. Available at: https://www.fammed.wisc.edu/sites/default/files/webfm-uploads/documents/research/i-practise/i-practise-white-paper.pdf.

[3] Ryan R. Primary care redesign. Perm J 1997;1(2):33–36.

[4] Davis K, Schoenbaum SC, Audet A-M. A 2020 vision of patient-centered primary care. J Gen Intern Med 2005;20(10):953957.

[5] American College of Physicians. The Impending Collapse of Primary Care Medicine and its Implications for the State of the Nation's health Care. Washington (DC); 2006.

[6] Bodenheimer T. Primary care – will it survive? N Engl J Med 2006;355:861864.

[7] Bodenheimer T, Pham HH. Primary care: current problems and proposed solutions. Health Aff 2010;29(5):799805.

[8] Jacobson SH, Hall SN, Swisher JR. Discrete-event simulation of health care systems. In: Hall RW, editor. *Patient Flow: Reducing Delay in Healthcare Delivery*. Volume 91. New York: Springer-Verlag; 2006. p 211252.

[9] Eldabi T, Paul RJ, Young T. Simulation modelling in healthcare: reviewing legacies and investigating futures. J Oper Res Soc 2007;58:262270.

[10] Gunal MM, Pidd M. Discrete event simulation for performance modelling in health care: a review of the literature. J Simul 2010;4:4251.

[11] Lemieux-Charles L, McGuire WL. What do we know about health care team effectiveness? A review of the literature. Med Care Res Rev 2006;63(3):263300.

[12] Bower P, Campbell S, Bojke C, Sibbald B. Team structure, team climate and the quality of care in primary care: an observational study. Qual Saf Health Care 2003;12:273279.

[13] Grumback K, Bodenheimer T. Can health care teams improve primary care practice? JAMA 2004;291(10):12461251.

[14] Mitchell GK, Tieman JJ, Shelby-James TM. Multidisciplinary care planning and teamwork in primary care. Med J Aust 2008;188(8):S61S64.

[15] Unutzer J, Katon W, Callahan CM, Williams JW, Hunkeler E, Harpole L, Hoffing M, Penna RDD, Noel PH, Lin EHB, Arean PA, Hegel MT, Tang L, Belin TR, Oishi S, Langston C. Collaborative care management of late-life depression in the primary care setting: a randomized controlled trial. JAMA 2002;288(22):28362845.

[16] Leonard M, Graham S, Bonacum D. The human factor: the critical importance of effective teamwork and communication in providing safe care. Qual Saf Health Care 2004;13:i85i90.

[17] Shaw A, de Lusignan S, Eowlands G. Do primary care professionals work as a team: a qualitative study. J Interprof Care 2005;19(4):396405.

[18] de Lusignan S, van Weel C. The use of routinely collected computer data for research in primary care: opportunities and challenges. Fam Pract 2006;23:253263.

[19] Ludwick DA, Doucettea J. Adopting electronic medical records in primary care: lessons learned from health information systems implementation experience in seven countries. Int J Med Inform 2009;78(1):2231.

[20] Thiru K, Hassey A, Sullivan F. Systematic review of scope and quality of electronic patient record data in primary care. BMJ 2003;326:10701074.

[21] Hillestad R, Bigelow J, Bower A, Girosi F, Meili R, Scoville R, Taylor R. Can electronic medical record systems transform health care? Potential health benefits, savings, and costs. Health Aff 2005;24(5):11031117.

[22] Beasley JW, Wetterneck TB, Temte J, Lapin JA, Smith P, Rivera-Rodriguez AJ, Karsh BT. Information chaos in primary care: implications for physician performance and patient safety. J Am Board Fam Med 2011;24:745751.

[23] Bates DW, Ebell M, Gotlieb E, Zapp J, Mullins HC. A proposal for electronic medical records in U.S. primary care. J Am Med Inform Assoc 2003;10:110.

[24] Wang SJ, Middleton B, Prosser LA, Gardon CG, Spurr CD, Carchidi PJ, Kittlera AF, Goldszer RC, Fairchild DG, Sussman AJ, Kuperman GJ, Bates DW. A cost-benefit analysis of electronic medical records in primary care. Am J Med 2003;114(5):397403.

[25] Wu S, Chaudhry B, Wang J, Maglione M, Mojica W, Roth E, Morton SC, Shekelle PG. Systematic review: impact of health information technology on quality, efficiency, and costs of medical care. Ann Intern Med 2006;144(10):742752.

[26] DesRoches CM, Campbell EG, Rao SR, Donelan K, Ferris TG, Jha A, Kaushal R, Levy DE, Rosenbaum S, Shields AE, Blumenthal D. Electronic health records in ambulatory care – a national survey of physicians. N Engl J Med 2008;359:5060.

[27] Schoen C, Osborn R, Doty MM, Bishop M, Peugh J, Murukutla N. Toward higher-performance health systems: adults' health care experiences in seven countries, 2007. Health Aff 2007;26:W717W734.

[28] Rosenthal TC. The medical home: growing evidence to support a new approach to primary care. J Am Board Fam Med 2008;21(5):427440.

[29] Landon BE, Gill JM, Antonelli RC, Rich EC. Prospects for rebuilding primary care using the patient-centered medical home. Health Aff 2010;29(5):827834.

[30] Gilfillan RJ, Tomcavage J, Rosenthal MB, Davis DE, Graham J, Roy JA, Pierdon SB, Bloom FJ, Graf TR, Goldman R, Weikel KM, Hamory BH, Paulus RA, Steele GD. Value and the medical home: effects of transformed primary care. Am J Manag Care 2010;16(8):607614.

[31] Cooley WC. Redefining primary pediatric care for children with special health care needs: the primary care medical home. Curr Opin Pediatr 2004;16(6):689692.

[32] Cooley WC, McAllister JW. Building medical homes: improvement strategies in primary care for children with special health care needs. Pediatrics 2004;113(S4):14991506.

[33] Cooley WC, McAllister JW, Sherrieb K, Kuhlthau K. Improved outcomes associated with medical home implementation in pediatric primary care. Pediatrics 2009;124(1):358364.

[34] Friedberg MW, Safran DG, Coltin KL, Dresser M, Schneider EC. Readiness for the patient-centered medical home: structural capabilities of massachusetts primary care practices. J Gen Intern Med 2009;24(2):162169.

[35] Friedberg MW, Safran DG, Coltin K, Dresser M, Schneider EC. Paying for performance in primary care: potential impact on practices and disparities. Health Aff 2010;29:926932.

[36] Porter ME, Pabo EA, Lee TH. Redesigning primary care: a strategic vision to improve value by organizing around patients' needs. Health Aff 2013;32:516525.

[37] Gosden T, Forland F, Kristiansen IS, Sutton M, Leese B, Giuffrida A, Sergison M, Pedersen L. Impact of payment method on behaviour of primary care physicians: a systematic review. J Health Serv Res Policy 2001;6(1):4455.

[38] Campbell S, Reeves D, Kontopantelis E, Middleton E, Sibbald B, Roland M. Quality of primary care in England with the introduction of pay for performance. N Engl J Med 2007;357:181190.

[39] Goroll AH, Berenson RA, Schoenbaum SC, Gardner LB. Fundamental reform of payment for adult primary care: comprehensive payment for comprehensive care. J Gen Intern Med 2007;22(3):410415.

[40] Rittenhouse DR, Shortell SM, Fisher ES. Primary care and accountable care – two essential elements of delivery-system reform. N Engl J Med 2009;361:23012303.

[41] Oldham J. *Advanced Access in Primary Care.* Manchester: National Primary Care Development Team; 2001. Available at: http://www.internetgroup.ca/clientnet_new/docs/Advanced

[42] Murray M, Berwick DM. Advanced access: reducing waiting and delays in primary care. JAMA 2003;289(8):10351040.

[43] Murray M, Bodenheimer T, Rittenhouse D, Grumbach K. Improving timely access to primary care: case studies of the advanced access model. JAMA 2003;289(8):10421046.

[44] Pickin M, O'Cathain A, Sampson FC, Dixon S. Evaluation of advanced access in the national primary care collaborative. Br J Gen Pract 2004;54:334340.

[45] Salisbury C, Goodall S, Montgomery AA, Pickin DM, Edwards S, Sampson F, Simons L, Lattimer V. Does advanced access improve access to primary health care? Questionnaire survey of patients. Br J Gen Pract 2007;57:615621.

[46] Salisbury C. Does advanced access work for patients and practices? Br J Gen Pract 2004;54(502):330331.

[47] Newman ED, Harrington TM, Olenginski TP, Perruguet JL, McKinley K. "The rheumatologist can see you now": successful implementation of an advanced access model in a rheumatology practice. Arthritis Care Res 2004;51(2):253257.

[48] Belardi FG, Weir S, Craig FW. A controlled trial of an advanced access appointment system in a residency family medicine center. Fam Med 2005;36(5):341346.

[49] Ostbye T, Yarnall KSH, Krause KM, Pollak KI, Gradison M, Michener JL MD Is there time for management of patients with chronic diseases in primary care? Ann Fam Med 2005;3(3):209214.

[50] Schoen C, Osborn R, Doty MM, Squires D, Peugh J, Applebaum S. A survey of primary care physicians in eleven countries, 2009: perspectives on care, costs, and experiences. Health Aff 2009;28(6):w1171w1183.

[51] Schoen C, Osborn R, Huynh PT, Doty M, Davis K, Zapert K, Peugh J. Primary care and health system performance: adults experiences in five countries. Health Aff 2004;W4:W487W503.

[52] Schoen C, Osborn R, Huynh PT, Doty M, Peugh J, Zapert K. On the front lines of care: primary care doctors office systems, experiences, and views in seven countries. Health Aff 2006;25(6):W555W571.

[53] Wiler JL, Griffey RT, Olsen T. Review of modeling approaches for emergency department patient flow and crowding research. Acad Emerg Med 2011;18(12):13711379.

[54] Burt CW, McCaig LF. Trends in hospital emergency department utilization: United States, 199299. National Center for Health Statistics. Vital Health Stat 2001;13(1):134. Available at: http://www.cdc.gov/nchs/data/series/sr_13/sr13_150.pdf.

[55] Center for Disease Control and Prevention (CDC). CDC Releases Latest Data on Emergency Department Visits; March 18, 2004. Available at: http://www.cdc.gov/nchs/pressroom/04facts/emergencydept.htm.

[56] Pitts SR, Niska RW, Xu J, Burt CW. National Hospital Ambulatory Medical Care Survey: 2006 Emergency Department Summary. National Health Statistics Reports, No. 7; 2008.

[57] Paul SA, Reddy MC, DeFlitch CJ. A systematic review of simulation studies investigating emergency department overcrowding. Simulation 2010;86(8-9):559571.

[58] Hung GR, Whitehouse SR, ONeill C, Gray AP, Kissoon N. Computer modeling of patient flow in a pediatric emergency department using discrete event simulation. Pediatr Emerg Care 2007;23:510.

[59] Fanti MP, Mangini AM, Dotoli M, Ukovich W. A three level strategy for the design and performance evaluation of hospital departments. IEEE Trans Syst Man Cybern Part A 2013;43(4):742756.

[60] Brenner S, Zeng Z, Liu Y, Wang J, Li J, Howard PK. Modeling and analysis of emergency department at University of Kentucky Chandler Hospital using simulations. J Emerg Nurs 2010;36:303310.

[61] Zeng Z, Ma X, Hu Y, Li J, Bryant D. Improving quality of care of emergency department at a community hospital: a simulation study. J Emerg Nurs 2012;38:322328.

[62] Storrow AB, Zhou C, Gaddis G, Han JH, Miller K, Klubert D, Laidig A, Aronsky D. Decreasing lab turnaround time improves emergency department throughput and decreases emergency medical services diversion: a simulation model. Acad Emerg Med 2008;15(11):11301135.

[63] Wang J, Li J, Tussey K, Ross K. Reducing length of stay in emergency department: a simulation study at a community hospital. IEEE Trans Syst Man Cybern Part A 2012;42:13141322.

[64] Connelly LG, Bair AE. Discrete event simulation of emergency department activity: a platform for system level operations research. Acad Emerg Med 2004;11:11771185.

[65] Sinreich D, Marmor Y. Emergency department operations: the basis for developing a simulation tool. IIE Trans 2005;37(3):233245.

[66] Duguay C, Chetouane F. Modeling and improving emergency department systems using discrete event simulation. Simulation 2007;83(4):311320.

[67] Hoot NR, LeBlanc LJ, Jones I, Levin SR, Zhou C, Gadd DS, Aronsky D. Forecasting emergency department crowding: a discrete event simulation. Ann Emerg Med 2008;52:116125.

[68] Kolker A. Process modeling of emergency department patient flow: effect of patient length of stay on ED diversion. J Med Syst 2008;32(5):389401.

[69] Werker G, Sauré A, French J, Shechter S. The use of discrete-event simulation modelling to improve radiation therapy planning processes. Radiother Oncol 2009;92:7682.

[70] Berg B, Denton B, Nelson H, Balasubramanian H, Rahman A, Bailey A, Lindor K. A discrete event simulation model to evaluate operational performance of a colonoscopy suite. Med Decis Making 2010;30(3):380387.

[71] Griffiths JD, Jones M, Read MS, Williams JE. A simulation model of bed-occupancy in a critical care unit. J Simul 2010;4:5259.

[72] Griffiths JD, Price-Lloyd N, Smithies M, Williams JE. Modelling the requirement for supplementary nurses in an intensive care unit. J Oper Res Soc 2005;56:126133.

[73] Lu T, Wang S, Li J, Lucas P, Anderson M, Ross K. Improving performance in the preparation and delivery of antineoplastic medications at a community hospital: a simulation study. J Med Syst 2012;36(5):30833089.

[74] Reynolds M, Vasilakis C, McLeod M, Barber N, Mounsey A, Newton S, Jacklin A, Franklin BD. Using discrete event simulation to design a more efficient hospital pharmacy for outpatients. Health Care Manag Sci 2011;14:223236.

[75] Couchman A, Jones DI, Griffiths KD. Predicting the future performance of a clinical biochemistry laboratory by computer simulation. Simul Model Pract Theory 2002;10(8):473495.

[76] Griffin J, Xia S, Peng S, Keskinocak P. Improving patient flow in an obstetric unit. Health Care Manag Sci 2012;15:114.

[77] Cochran JK, Bharti A. Stochastic bed balancing of an obstetrics hospital. Health Care Manag Sci 2006;9(1):3145.

[78] van der Meer RB, Rymaszewski LA, Findlay H, Curran J. Using OR to support the development of an integrated musculo-skeletal service. J Oper Res Soc 2005;56:162172.

[79] Kreke JE, Schaefer AJ, Roberts MS. Simulation and critical care modeling. Curr Opin Crit Care 2004;10(5):395398.

[80] Stahl E, Rattner D, Wiklund R, Lester J, Beinfeld M, Gazelle GS. Reorganizing the system of care surrounding laparoscopic surgery: a cost-effectiveness analysis using discrete-event simulation. Med Decis Making 2004;24(5):461471.

[81] Ferreira RB, Coelli FC, Pereira WCA, Almeida RMVR. Optimizing patient flow in a large hospital surgical centre by means of discrete-event computer simulation models. J Eval Clin Pract 2008;14(6):10311037.

[82] Zhu Z, Hen BH, Teow KL. Estimating ICU bed capacity using discrete event simulation. Int J Health Care Qual Assur 2012;25(2):134144.

[83] Zeng Z, Xie X, Zhong X, Li J, Liegle B, Sanford-Ring S. Simulation modeling of hospital discharge process. Proceedings of Industrial and Systems Engineering Research Conference; San Juan, Puerto Rico; 2013. p 13831390.

[84] Cayirli T, Veral E. Outpatient scheduling in health care: a review of literature. Prod Oper Manag 2003;12(4):519549.

[85] Cayirli T, Veral E, Rosen H. Designing appointment scheduling systems for ambulatory care services. Health Care Manag Sci 2006;9(1):4758.

[86] Harper PR, Gamlin HM. Reduced outpatient waiting times with improved appointment scheduling: a simulation modelling approach. OR Spectrum 2003;25(2):207222.

[87] Ogulata SN, Cetik MO, Koyuncu E, Koyuncu M. A simulation approach for scheduling patients in the department of radiation oncology. J Med Syst 2009;33:233239.

[88] Ashton R, Hague L, Brandreth M, Worthington D, Cropper S. A simulation-based study of a NHS Walk-in Centre. J Oper Res Soc 2005;56:153161.

[89] Rohleder TR, Lewkonia P, Bischak D, Duffy P, Hendijani R. Using simulation modeling to improve patient flow at an outpatient orthopedic clinic. Health Care Manag Sci 2011;14:135143.

[90] Coelli FC, Ferreira RB, Almeida RMVR, Pereira WCA. Computer simulation and discrete-event models in the analysis of a mammography clinic patient flow. Comput Methods Programs Biomed 2007;87(3):201207.

[91] Villamizar JR, Coelli FC, Pereira WCA, Almeida RMVR. Discrete event computer simulation methods in the optimisation of a physiotherapy clinic. Physiotherapy 2011;97:7177.

[92] Reynolds J, Zeng Z, Li J, Chiang S-Y. Design and analysis of a health care clinic for homeless people using simulations. Int J Health Care Qual Assur 2010;23:607620.

[93] Lu L, Li J, Gisler P. Improving financial performance by modeling and analysis of radiology procedure scheduling at a large community hospital. J Med Syst 2011;35:299307.

[94] Hollingworth W, Spackman DE. Emerging methods in economic modeling of imaging costs and outcomes: a short report on discrete event simulation. Acad Radiol 2007;14(4):406410.

[95] Swisher JR, Jacobson SH. Evaluating the design of a family practice healthcare clinic using discrete-event simulation. Health Care Manag Sci 2002;5(2):7588.

[96] de Angelis V, Felici G, Impelluso P. Integrating simulation and optimisation in health care centre management. Eur J Oper Res 2003;150(1):101114.

[97] Stahl JE, Roberts MS, Gazelle S. Optimizing management and financial performance of the teaching ambulatory care clinic. J Gen Intern Med 2003;18(4):266274.

[98] Rohleder TR, Bischak DP, Baskin LB. Modeling patient service centers with simulation and system dynamics. Health Care Manag Sci 2006;10(1):112.

[99] Vasilakis C, Sobolev BG, Kuramoto L, Levy AR. A simulation study of scheduling clinic appointments in surgical care: individual surgeon versus pooled lists. J Oper Res Soc 2007;58:202211.

[100] Hauschild L, Welnick R, Regnier H, Key S, Micke B, Root A, Calkins C, Hohn T, Hanna D, Goff M, Henry L, Popodi D, Caplan W, Andree C, McGrew M, Fiedler L, Dammen S, Drummond L, Nyeggen A. Odana Atrium: Telecom Improvement Project. UW Health Report; 2008.

[101] University of Wisconsin Health. Colonoscopy Capacity Analysis Summary. UW Health Report; 2008.

[102] Wang J, Quan S, Li J, Hollis A. Modeling and analysis of work flow and staffing level in a computed tomography division of University of Wisconsin Medical Foundation. Health Care Manag Sci 2012;15:108120.

[103] Zhong X, Li J, Ertl SM, Hassemer C, Fielder L. Modeling and analysis of mammography testing process at a breast imaging center of University of Wisconsin Medical Foundation. Proceedings of IEEE International Conference on Automation Science and Engineering; Madison (WI); 2013. p 623628.

[104] Zhong X, Song J, Li J, Ertl SM, Fielder L. Analysis of Gastroenterology (GI) clinic: a systems approach. Proceedings of International Conference on Health Care Systems Engineering, Springer Proceedings in Mathematics & Statistics, Volume 61; Milan, Italy; 2013. p 113125.

[105] Zhong X, Song J, Li J, Fielder L, Ertl SM. Modeling and design of GI clinic in digestive health center using simulations. Proceedings of Industrial and Systems Engineering Research Conference; San Juan, Puerto Rico; 2013. p 25412550.

[106] Hauge JW, Paige KN. *Learning SIMUL8: The Complete Guide*. Bethlingham (WA): Plain Vu Publishers; 2002.

[107] Wang J, Zhong X, Li J, Howard PK. Modeling and analysis of care delivery services within patient rooms: a system-theoretic approach. IEEE Trans Autom Sci Eng 2014;11:379393.

13

TEMPORAL AND SPATIOTEMPORAL MODELS FOR AMBULANCE DEMAND

ZHENGYI ZHOU

Center for Applied Mathematics, Cornell University, Ithaca, NY, USA

DAVID S. MATTESON

Department of Statistical Science, Cornell University, Ithaca, NY, USA

13.1 INTRODUCTION

A primary goal of emergency medical services (EMS) is often to minimize response times to emergencies while managing operational costs. Sophisticated operations research methods have been developed to optimize many management decisions, such as locations of bases, fleet size, staffing, and dynamic deployment strategies [1, 2]. However, these methods require ambulance demand estimates as inputs, and their performances rely critically on the accuracy of these demand estimates. Demand predictions that are too high lead to overstaffing, unnecessary vehicles, and high cost, while estimates that are too low result in slow response times to potentially life-threatening emergencies.

   In practice, two types of demand estimates are of interest: aggregate temporal demand, that is, total expected demand volume, and spatiotemporal demand, or the spatial distribution of demand over time. Temporal aggregate demand estimates inform effective staffing and fleet planning; spatiotemporal estimates are critical for choosing base locations and dynamic deployment strategies. These estimates are ideally needed at high temporal resolution (e.g., 4-h work shifts). Similarly, spatiotemporal estimates at fine spatial granularities are required for accurate

Healthcare Analytics: From Data to Knowledge to Healthcare Improvement, First Edition.
Edited by Hui Yang and Eva K. Lee.
© 2016 John Wiley & Sons, Inc. Published 2016 by John Wiley & Sons, Inc.

dynamic deployment. Therefore, we aim to model aggregate demand bi-hourly and spatiotemporal demand continuously in space over 2-h intervals.

Current EMS industry practice for forecasting ambulance demand in time and space often uses simple averaging models on discretized time and spatial domains. Demand in a small spatial cell over a short time period is typically predicted by averaging a small number of historical counts, from the same location, over the corresponding time intervals from previous weeks or years. For example, the EMS of Toronto, Canada, averages four historical counts in the same hour of the year, over the past 4 years. Another practice mentioned in [3] used by the EMS of Charlotte-Mecklenburg, North Carolina, called the MEDIC method, averages 20 historical counts in the same hour of the preceding 4 weeks for the past 5 years. Averaging so few observations may lead to highly noisy predictions; these methods may also be quite sensitive to how the temporal and spatial domains are partitioned.

We propose methods that estimate ambulance demand accurately on fine scales. Our motivating data set consists of all emergency priority calls from Toronto EMS for which an ambulance was dispatched. Each event contains the time and location that the ambulance was dispatched to. We use training data from February 2007 and test data from March 2007 and February 2008. Altogether, we have 45,730 realized events of ambulance demand. This includes some calls not requiring lights-and-sirens response but does not include scheduled patient transfers. We include only the first event in our analysis when multiple responses are received for the same event. The data were processed to exclude events with no reported location. These removals totaled less than 2% of the data.

We model Toronto's ambulance demand on a continuous spatial domain $S \subseteq \mathbb{R}^2$ and a discrete temporal domain of 2-h intervals $\mathcal{T} = \{1, 2, \cdots, T\}$. Let $\mathbf{s}_{t,i}$ be the ith ambulance demand location occurring at time period t, for $i \in \{1, \cdots, y_t\}$, in which y_t denotes the city-wide aggregate demand for that period. For each time period $t \in \mathcal{T}$, we have a spatial point process $\{\mathbf{s}_{t,i} : i = 1, \cdots, y_t\}$. Since nonhomogeneous Poisson process (NHPP) is a natural model for spatial point process [4–6], we assume $\{\mathbf{s}_{t,i} : i = 1, \cdots, y_t\}$, for each t, independently follow an NHPP over S, with positive intensity function $\lambda_t(\mathbf{s})$. This implies that all demand locations in the point process are independent conditional on the intensity function.

We further decompose the intensity function as

$$\lambda_t(\mathbf{s}) = \delta_t g_t(\mathbf{s}) \tag{13.1}$$

for $\mathbf{s} \in S$. Here, $\delta_t = \int_S \lambda_t(\mathbf{s}) \, d\mathbf{s}$ is the aggregate demand intensity over the spatial domain. Therefore, $g_t(\cdot)$ is the spatial density of the demand at time t, such that $g_t(\mathbf{s}) > 0$ for $\mathbf{s} \in S$ and $\int_S g_t(\mathbf{s}) \, d\mathbf{s} = 1$. Hence, for each t, $y_t | \lambda_t \sim \text{Poisson}(\delta_t)$ and $\mathbf{s}_{t,i} | \lambda_t, y_t \sim g_t(\cdot)$, i.i.d for $i \in \{1, \cdots, y_t\}$.

We thus represent $\{\lambda_t\}$ by separately modeling the aggregate temporal demand intensity and the spatiotemporal demand density. In Section 13.2, we model expected demand counts $\{\delta_t\}$ with a dynamic latent factor structure, imposing covariates in the factor loadings and smoothing the factor levels. Then, we forecast the demand volumes y_t adaptively via an integer-valued time series model in combination with this factor structure. In Section 13.3, we estimate the sequence of spatial densities $g_t(\cdot)$, $t = 1, \cdots, T$. We consider a novel characterization of a time-varying Gaussian mixture model. The mixture distributions are fixed over time to estimate an accurate spatial structure, while the mixture weights are allowed to vary over time. We use the evolution of mixture weights to represent the diverse temporal patterns and dynamics observed in this application. With these models, we obtain accurate temporal aggregate demand estimates and spatiotemporal demand density estimates for the Toronto EMS data.

13.2 TEMPORAL AMBULANCE DEMAND ESTIMATION

In this section, we model the aggregate ambulance demand intensity in Toronto for every 2-h period. Few studies have focused specifically on EMS demand and of those that have proposed methods for time series modeling, most have been based on Gaussian linear models. Even with a continuity correction, this method is highly inaccurate when the observed counts are low, which is typical of EMS demand at the bi-hourly level. For example, Channouf et al. [7] forecast EMS demand by modeling the daily observations as Gaussian, with fixed day-of-week, month-of-year, special day effects, and fixed day–month interactions. They also consider a Gaussian autoregressive moving-average (ARMA) model with seasonality and special day effects. Comparable studies on arrival processes (e.g., call centers) have also considered singular spectrum analysis [8], fixed-effects, mixed-effects and bivariate models [9, 10], Bayesian multiplicative models [11], and singular value decompositions [12, 13].

As we mentioned in Section 13.1, we assume that the observed bi-hourly EMS demand volume y_t has a Poisson distribution with mean δ_t. This allows parsimonious modeling of periods with small counts, conforms with the standard industry assumption [14], and avoids use of variance stabilizing transformations [11, 13]. We also assume that δ_t is a random process, that it may be partitioned into stationary and nonstationary components, and that it can be forecast using previous observations. The demand pattern over the course of a typical day is shown in Figure 13.1.

Each day we observe a distinct shape: demand increases quickly in the late morning, peaks in the early afternoon, and then slowly decreases until it troughs between 4 and 6 AM. In our analysis, we consider an arrival process that has been repeatedly observed over a particular time span, specifically a 12-period day. Let d denote the number of days, let m denote the number of intraday periods, and let

$$\{y_t : t = 1, \cdots, T\} = \{y_{ij} : i = 1, \cdots, d; j = 1, \cdots, m\}$$

denote the sequence of counts, observed in each time period t, which corresponds one-to-one with the jth subperiod of the ith day, such that $T = dm$. Our baseline approach is to model the arrival intensity δ_t for the distinct shape of intraday call arrivals using a small number of smooth curves.

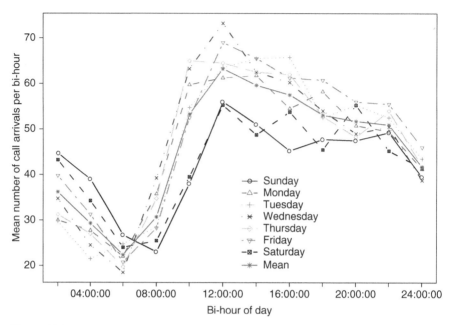

Figure 13.1 Mean number of observations per bi-hour, by day-of-week, for February 2007 in Toronto.

Following [15], we propose to model δ_t using a dynamic latent factor structure. Day-of-week effects are included via simple constraints on the factor loadings. The factor structure allows for a significant reduction in the number of model parameters. Furthermore, it provides a systematic approach to modeling the diurnal pattern observed in intraday counts. Smoothing is used in estimating the factor levels and loadings. Finally, we obtain temporal aggregate demand estimates by combining integer-valued time series models with this factor structure to capture residual dependence and to provide adaptive short-term forecasts. Our estimates are highly accurate and straightforward to implement.

We present some notation in Section 13.2.1, introduce the factor model in Section 13.2.2, and incorporate it into a time series model in Section 13.2.3.

13.2.1   Notation

We consider two disjoint information sets for predictive conditioning. Let $\mathcal{F}_t = (y_1, \cdots, y_t)'$ denote all observed counts through time t, and let $\mathbf{X} = \{\mathbf{X}_1, \cdots, \mathbf{X}_T\}$ denote any available deterministic covariate information about each observation, such as intraday time and day-of-week. We define δ_t as the conditional expectation of y_t given $\mathcal{F}_{t-1}$ and $\mathbf{X}$ and use this as an estimate of y_t. Let $\mu_t = E(y_t; \mathbf{X}) > 0$ denote the expectation of y_t as a function of the nonrandom covariates $\mathbf{X}$, and let

$$\delta_t = E(y_t|\mathcal{F}_{t-1}; \mathbf{X}) = \mu_t E \ (y_t/\mu_t|\mathcal{F}_{t-1}; \mathbf{X}) = \mu_t \eta_t, \tag{13.2}$$

in which $\eta_t > 0$ is referred to as the conditional intensity inflation rate (CIIR). By construction

$$E(\eta_t; \mathbf{X}) = E\{E \ (y_t|\mathcal{F}_{t-1}; \mathbf{X}); \mathbf{X}\}/\mu_t = E(y_t; \mathbf{X})/\mu_t = 1.$$

The CIIR process is intended to model any remaining serial dependence in the observed counts after accounting for available covariates. In the EMS context, we hypothesize that this dependence is due to sporadic events such as inclement weather or unusual traffic patterns. Since information regarding these events may not be available or predictable in general, we argue that an approach such as ours which explicitly models the remaining serial dependence will lead to improved short-term forecast accuracy. In the following, we consider a dynamic latent factor model estimated with smoothing for modeling μ_t and a generalized autoregressive time series model for η_t, conditional on μ_t.

13.2.2 Factor Modeling with Constraints and Smoothing

For notational simplicity, assume m consecutive observations per day are available (e.g., 12) for d consecutive days (e.g., 28) with no omissions in the record. Let $\mathbf{Y} = (y_{ij})$ denote the $d \times m$ matrix of observed counts for each day i and each subperiod j.

Let $\mu_{ij} = E(Y_{ij}; \mathbf{X})$, and let $\mathbf{M} = (\mu_{ij})$ denote the corresponding $d \times m$ latent nonstationary intensity matrix. To reduce the dimension of the intensity matrix $\mathbf{M}$, we introduce a K-factor model.

We assume that the intraday pattern of expected bi-hourly counts on the log scale can be well approximated by a linear combination of K (a small number) factors or functions, denoted by $\mathbf{f}_k$, for $k = 1, \cdots, K$. The intraday arrival rate model $\boldsymbol{\mu}_i$ for day i at subperiod j is given by

$$\log \ ([\boldsymbol{\mu}_i]_j) = [L_{i1}\mathbf{f}_1 + \cdots + L_{iK}\mathbf{f}_K]_j. \tag{13.3}$$

Each of the factors $\mathbf{f}_k$ varies as a function over the periods within a day, but they are constant from one day to the next. Day-to-day changes are modeled by allowing the various factor loadings L_{ik} to vary across days. When K is much smaller than either m or d, the dimensionality of the general problem is greatly reduced. In matrix form, we have

$$\log \ ([\mathbf{M}]_{ij}) = [\mathbf{LF}']_{ij}, \tag{13.4}$$

in which $\mathbf{F} = (\mathbf{f}_1, \cdots, \mathbf{f}_K)$ denotes the K factors and $\mathbf{L}$ denotes the corresponding $d \times K$ full rank matrix of factor loadings. Since neither $\mathbf{F}$ nor $\mathbf{L}$ are observable, the expression (13.4) is not identifiable, in general. We further constrain the columns of $\mathbf{F}$ to be orthonormal.

To further reduce the dimensionality, we impose a set of constraints by way of categorical covariates on the factor loading matrix $\mathbf{L}$. Let $\mathbf{H}$ denote a $d \times n$ full rank matrix ($n < d$) of given constraints and let $\mathbf{B}$ denote an $n \times K$ matrix of unconstrained factor loadings. Specifically, we let $\mathbf{H}$ denote a $d \times 7$ matrix, in which each row $\mathbf{H}_i$ is an incidence vector indicating the day-of-week, and the $7 \times K$ matrix $\mathbf{B}$ contains unconstrained factor loadings for the day-of-week. Hence, the factor model may now be written as

$$\log \left([\mathbf{M}]_{ij}\right) = [\mathbf{LF}']_{ij} = [\mathbf{HBF}']_{ij}.$$

Constraints to assure identifiability are standard in factor analysis. The constraints we now consider incorporate auxiliary information about the rows and columns of the observation matrix $\mathbf{Y}$ to simplify estimation and to improve out-of-sample predictions. Similar constraints have been used in [16] and [17].

We further assume that as the nonstationary intensity process μ_{ij} varies over the hours j of each day i, it does so smoothly. To incorporate smoothness into the model (13.3), we use Generalized Additive Models (GAMs) in the estimation of the common factors $\mathbf{f}_k$. GAMs extend generalized linear models, allowing for more complicated relationships between the response and predictors, by modeling some predictors nonparametrically [cf. [18, 19]]. GAMs have been successfully used for count-valued data in the study of fish populations [cf. [20, 21]]. The factors $\mathbf{f}_k = f_k(j)$ are a smooth function of the intraday time index covariate j. Conditional on the loadings $\mathbf{L}$, Equation (13.3) represents a varying coefficient model [cf. [22]].

Conditional on the factors $\mathbf{F}$, Equation (13.3) represents a generalized linear model. Given the calendar covariates $\mathbf{X}$, let

$$\log \mu_{ij} = \log \mu_i(j) = L_{i1}f_1(j) + \cdots + L_{iK}f_K(j)$$

$$= L_{i1}f_{j1} + \cdots + L_{iK}f_{jK} = \sum_{k=1}^{K} b_k(\mathbf{X}_i)f_{jk}, \qquad (13.5)$$

in which $b_k(\mathbf{X}_i) = [\mathbf{H}_i'\mathbf{B}]_k$ is a piece-wise constant function of the day-of-week in our specification.

To estimate the degree of smoothness for the factors f_k, we apply a *performance* iteration [cf. [23]] versus an *outer* iteration strategy that requires repeated estimation for many trial sets of the smoothing parameters. The performance iteration strategy is much more computationally efficient for use in the estimation algorithm, but convergence is not guaranteed, in general. In particular, *cycling* between pairs of smoothing parameters and coefficient estimates may occur [cf. [19], Section 4.5], especially when the number of factors K is large.

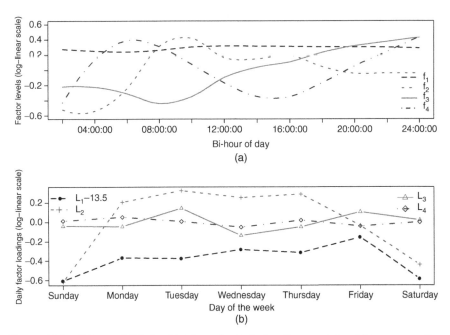

Figure 13.2 February 2007 fitted (a) factor levels f_k (log-linear scale) and (b) corresponding factor loadings $L_{.k}$ (log-linear scale) for a factor model fit with constraints, smoothing, and $K = 4$ factors. $(L_{.1} - 13.5)$ is shown for easier comparison.

The fitted factors f_k applying smoothing are shown (log-linear scale) in Figure 13.2(a), and the corresponding factor loadings $L_{.k}$. (log-linear scale) applying constraints are shown in Figure 13.2(b).

The first factor f_1 is strictly positive and the least variable. It appears to capture the mean diurnal pattern. The factor f_2 appears to isolate the dominant relative differences between weekdays and weekend days. The defining feature of f_3 and f_4 is the large increase late in the day, corresponding closely to the relative increase observed on Friday evenings, in particular. However, f_3 decreases in the morning, while f_4 increases in the morning and decreases in the late afternoon. The much higher loadings $L_{.1}$ on f_1 confirm its interpretation as capturing the overall pattern. The peak on Friday coincides with Friday having the highest average number of calls, as seen in Figure 13.1. Weekdays get a positive loading on f_2, while weekend days get negative loading. Loadings on f_3 are lowest on Wednesdays and loadings on f_4 are largest on Mondays. The estimated intensity process $\hat{\mu}_t$ for a factor model fit with constraints, smoothing, and $K = 4$ factors is shown in Figure 13.3. The curves are smoothed representations of the subperiod sample means as shown in Figure 13.1.

13.2.3 Adaptive Forecasting with Time Series Models

Although the factor model largely removes the strong seasonality exhibited in the observations, see Figure 13.4(a), some additional serial dependence remains.

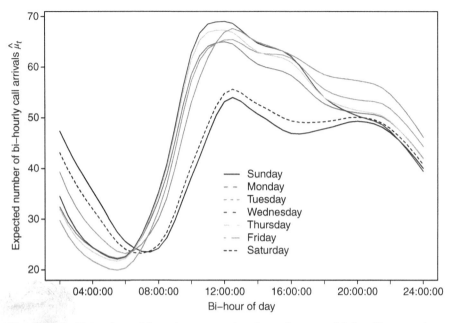

Figure 13.3 The estimated intensity process $\hat{\mu}_t$ using a factor model fit with constraints, smoothing, and $K = 4$ factors; colored by day-of-week for February 2007.

Let $\hat{e}_t = y_t/\hat{\mu}_t$ denote the multiplicative residual in period t implied by the fitted values $\hat{\mu}_t$ from the factor model. We now consider a generalized autoregressive time series model for the latent CIIR process $\eta_t = E(y_t/\mu_t | \mathcal{F}_{t-1}; \mathbf{X})$ to account for this dependence. Additional CIIR models are discussed in [15].

Consider a CIIR model defined by the recursion

$$\eta_t = \omega + \tilde{\alpha}\hat{e}_{t-1} + \tilde{\beta}\eta_{t-1}. \tag{13.6}$$

To ensure positivity, we restrict $\omega > 0$ and $\tilde{\alpha}, \tilde{\beta} \geq 0$. When μ_t is constant with respect to time, the resulting model for y_t is an Integer-GARCH(1,1) (IntGARCH) model [e.g., [24]]. It is worth noting some properties of this model for the constant μ_t case. To ensure the stationarity of η_t, we further require that $\tilde{\alpha} + \tilde{\beta} < 1$, [cf. [25]]. This sum determines the persistence of the process, with larger values of $\tilde{\alpha}$ leading to more adaptability. When this stationarity condition is satisfied, and η_t is initialized from its stationary distribution, the expectation of η_t given $\mathbf{X}$ is

$$E(\eta_t; \mathbf{X}) = \omega/(1 - \tilde{\alpha} - \tilde{\beta}).$$

To ensure $E(\eta_t; \mathbf{X}) = 1$ for the fitted model, we may parametrize $\omega = 1 - \tilde{\alpha} - \tilde{\beta}$.

When μ_t is a nonstationary process, the conditional intensity

$$\delta_t = \mu_t \eta_t$$

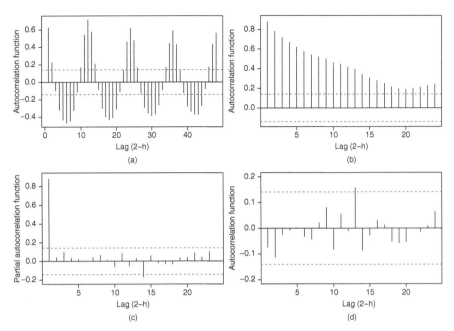

Figure 13.4 (a) Sample autocorrelation function for bi-hourly demand counts y_t during February 2007; the conditional intensity inflation process $\hat{\eta}_t$ (b) autocorrelation and (c) partial autocorrelation functions, given the fitted factor model $\hat{\mu}_t$ with $k = 4$ factors, applying constraints and smoothing; (d) standardized residual $\hat{\epsilon}_t = y_t/\hat{\delta}_t = y_t/(\hat{\mu}_t\hat{\eta}_t)$ autocorrelation function. Dashed horizontal lines give approximate 95% lag-wise confidence intervals about zero.

is also nonstationary. Since $E(\eta_t; \mathbf{X}) = 1$, we interpret η_t as the stationary multiplicative deviation, or inflation rate, between δ_t and μ_t. The sample autocorrelation and partial autocorrelation for the fitted CIIR process $\hat{\eta}_t$ is shown in Figure 13.4(a) and (b), respectively.

The observed bi-hour counts y_t, the fitted factor model $\hat{\mu}_t$ applying constraints and smoothing, and the factor model including the fitted IntGARCH(1,1) model $\hat{\delta}_t$ are shown in Figure 13.5(a). The fitted CIIR process $\hat{\eta}_t$ from the IntGARCH(1,1) model for the same period is shown in Figure 13.5(b). The mean reversion in the $\hat{\eta}_t$ process results in the $\hat{\delta}_t$ process reverting to the $\hat{\mu}_t$ process. Let

$$\hat{\epsilon}_t = y_t/\hat{\delta}_t$$

denote the multiplicative *standardized* residual process given an estimated intensity $\hat{\delta}_t = \hat{\mu}_t\hat{\eta}_t$. If a fitted model defined by Equation (13.6) sufficiently explains the observed linear dependence in $\hat{e}_t$, then an autocorrelation plot of $\hat{\epsilon}_t$ should be statistically insignificant for all lags. As shown in Figure 13.4(d), the standardized residual autocorrelation appears to have been adequately removed.

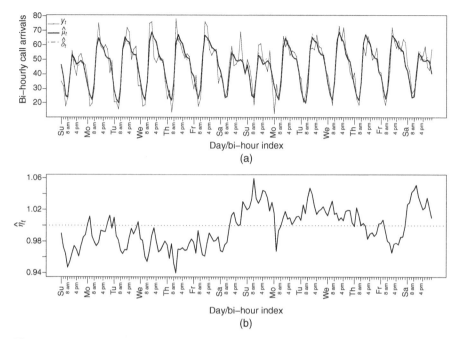

Figure 13.5   First two full weeks of February 2007: (a) observed counts per bi-hour y_t, fitted $K = 4$ dynamic factor model $\hat{\mu}_t$ applying constraints and smoothing, and factor model $\hat{\delta}_t$ including fitted IntGARCH(1,1); (b) the fitted conditional intensity inflation process $\hat{\eta}_t$ from the IntGARCH(1,1) model.

13.3   SPATIOTEMPORAL AMBULANCE DEMAND ESTIMATION

In this section, we estimate a continuous spatial density of demand as it varies across 2-h intervals, that is, we model $g_t(\cdot)$ in Equation (13.1). There are few studies that model spatiotemporal ambulance demand. In [26], the authors apply a nonparametric multiple change point algorithm [27] to spatiotemporal ambulance demand and find many significant changes in the spatial density intraweek. In [3], the authors consider applying artificial neural network (ANN) on discretized domains and compare it to the industry method MEDIC (Section 13.1). While ANN was shown to perform better than the industry practice at low spatial resolutions, both ANN and the industry method produce noisy predictions at high spatial resolutions. We propose a much-needed method for accurate ambulance demand estimation on fine time and location scales.

We see in Section 13.2 that aggregate demand volumes exhibit seasonalities and serial dependence. We explore characteristics of the *spatial density* of this demand in Figure 13.6. We outline the downtown region of Toronto using a rectangle in Figure 13.6(a). For each 2-h period, we compute the proportion of observations that arises from within this rectangle. This proportion is a proxy for the spatial density

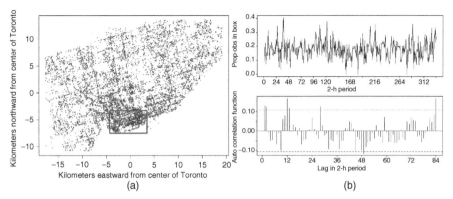

Figure 13.6 (a) The training data from February 2007, with the downtown subregion outlined by a rectangle; (b) time series (top) and autocorrelation function (bottom) of the proportions of observations arising from the rectangle across 2-h periods. Weekly seasonality, daily seasonality, and low-order autocorrelation are observed. Dashed lines depict approximate 95% lag-wise confidence intervals about zero.

at downtown for any time period. We study the sample autocorrelation function of this time series of proportions in Figure 13.6(b). The spatial density at downtown exhibits weekly seasonality (at the 84th time period), daily seasonality (12th period), and short-term serial dependence (first two periods). We also investigate temporal patterns of spatial densities at other locations. We find consistent weekly seasonality, but varying degrees of daily seasonality and short-term serial dependence (stronger at denser areas and weaker at more dispersed areas).

Existing approaches to estimation of spatial or spatiotemporal densities in point processes do not fully address the challenges presented in ambulance demand estimation. Within the framework of NHPP for spatial point processes, Bayesian semiparametric mixture modeling has been used to represent the heterogeneity in the intensity function via Dirichlet processes [28, 29] and Gaussian mixture models with a fixed number of components [30]. However, our data are sparse at the desired temporal granularity for prediction in this industry; the average number of total observations in each 2-h period is only 45. It is difficult to build an accurate mixture model for each time period individually.

Recently, dependent Dirichlet processes have been developed to induce dependence in a collection of dependent distribution [[31, 32], for example]. A similar framework has been used to model correlated spatial densities across discrete time, by letting the stick-breaking proportions of the Dirichlet process evolve in a first-order autoregressive manner [33–36]. However, all components in this Dirichlet process must vary according to the same first-order dependence structure. For EMS data, it is essential to capture a much more complex set of temporal dynamics, including short-term serial dependence as well as daily and weekly seasonalities. Moreover, some of these dynamics vary from location to location. To consider and enforce only the first-order dependence across the entire spatial domain would be very limiting. On the other hand, it is not straightforward to extend the dependent Dirichlet processes to incorporate higher-order serial dependence and multiple seasonalities. It is also not easy to make these dynamics location-specific. Discretizing the spatial domain and imposing different autoregressive parameters on each region would add considerable computational complexity. Furthermore, given the large number of total observations and time periods considered, using an infinite-dimensional Dirichlet process would be computationally intractable.

We propose a novel specification of a time-varying finite mixture model. We fix the distributions of all components in the mixture model through time. This allows for efficient learning of the spatial structure. We let the mixture weights vary in time to capture complex temporal and spatial dynamics in the point process. We represent seasonalities in the spatial densities by incorporating categorical covariate information as constraints on the mixture component weights; we describe location-specific temporal dynamics by applying a separate autoregressive prior on the mixture weights for each component. We introduce our method in Section 13.3.1 and apply it to Toronto EMS data in Section 13.3.2. We demonstrate in Section 13.3.3 that our method compares favorably to industry practice, yielding higher statistical predictive accuracy and lower error in measuring operational performance.

13.3.1   Spatiotemporal Finite Mixture Modeling

Following [37], we estimate $g_t(\cdot)$ in Equation (13.1) using a sequence of bivariate Gaussian mixture models, in which we fix the component distributions across time, but let the mixture weights evolve over time. This promotes efficient information sharing across time to estimate an accurate spatial structure. This is necessary because data per time period is too sparse to describe the spatial structure well. Fixing the component distributions in time is also natural because Toronto has well-established neighborhoods, downtown, and traffic routes. The time-varying mixture weights can capture people's activities and dynamics within the spatial structure over time. Using a fixed number of components C for now, we have for any t

$$g_t(\mathbf{s}; \{p_{t,j}\}, \{\mu_j\}, \{\Sigma_j\}) = \sum_{j=1}^{C} p_{t,j} \, \phi(\mathbf{s}; \mu_j, \Sigma_j), \; \forall \, \mathbf{s} \in S, \qquad (13.7)$$

in which ϕ is the bivariate Gaussian density with mean μ_j and covariance Σ_j, for each $j \in \{1, \cdots, C\}$. Here, the $p_{t,j}$ are the component mixture weights such that $p_{t,j} \geq 0$ for all t and j and $\sum_{j=1}^{C} p_{t,j} = 1$ for all t. The means and covariances remain the same for all time periods, and only the mixture weights change over time.

We observe weekly seasonality in the demand densities throughout Toronto. To capture this weekly seasonality, we can estimate all time periods with the same relative position in a weekly cycle (e.g., all periods corresponding to Monday 8–10 A.M.) to have the same mixture weights, and thus the same density, by introducing a categorical covariate indicating the intraweek subperiod. If B is the cycle length ($B = 84$ for a week in our analysis), we match each $t \in \mathcal{T}$ to a value $b \in \{1, \cdots, B\}$.

Let $\mathbf{x} = (\mathbf{x}_1, \cdots, \mathbf{x}_T)'$, in which each $\mathbf{x}_t$ is a length B incidence vector, which is 0 everywhere except at element $b = t \pmod{B}$, which is 1. Next, for each intraweek period define a length C vector of nonnegative mixture weights $\varpi_b = (\varpi_{b,1}, \cdots, \varpi_{b,C})'$, which sum to 1 for each period b, and let $\varpi = (\varpi_1, \cdots, \varpi_B)'$. Finally, we parametrize the mixture weights $\mathbf{p} = (\mathbf{p}_1, \cdots, \mathbf{p}_T)'$ with $\mathbf{p}_t = (p_{t,1}, \cdots, p_{t,C})'$, as

$$\mathbf{p} = \varpi\mathbf{x}, \quad \text{such that} \quad \mathbf{p}_t = \varpi\mathbf{x}_t,$$

and for $b = t \pmod{B}$, Equation (13.7) becomes

$$g_t(\mathbf{s}; \mathbf{p}, \{\mu_j\}, \{\Sigma_j\}) = g_b(\mathbf{s}; \varpi, \{\mu_j\}, \{\Sigma_j\}) = \sum_{j=1}^{C} \varpi_{b,j} \, \phi(\mathbf{s}; \mu_j, \Sigma_j). \tag{13.8}$$

Such parametrizations on the mixture weights could also be used to group together consecutive time periods with similar characteristics, for example, midnight hours, or indicate special times, for example, holidays. This framework easily extends beyond categorical covariates.

In addition to weekly seasonality, we also find daily seasonality and short-term serial dependence in the demand densities, and such dependence varies in strength at different locations in Toronto. To capture this within the proposed mixture model framework, we can apply a separate conditional autoregressive (CAR) prior on the sequence of mixture weights for each component, that is, on ϖ for each j in Equation (13.8). We can describe any dependence pattern representable by structured time series models. We also have the flexibility to use unique parameters and specifications for each component j. This allows us to efficiently explore location-specific temporal dynamics. Moreover, these autoregressive priors create smoothing, or shrinkage, of the estimated spatial density across discrete time periods, which is desirable since the spatial density is typically believed to vary smoothly across time. Autoregressive priors have been used to smooth parameter estimates at adjacent locations in spatial data [38, 39] and at adjacent times in temporal processes [40, 41].

The intraweek mixture weights $\varpi_{b,j}$ require nonnegativity and sum-to-one constraints across components at every period b. As a result, special care needs to be taken as we impose autoregressive priors and update them. To circumvent this, we transform the $\{\varpi_{b,j}\}$ weights into unconstrained weights $\{\pi_{b,j}\}$ via multinomial logit transformation

$$\pi_{b,r} = \log\left(\frac{\varpi_{b,r}}{1 - \sum_{j=1}^{C-1} \varpi_{b,j}}\right), \quad r \in \{1, \cdots, C-1\} \tag{13.9}$$

We then specify daily seasonality and short-term serial dependence on the unconstrained weights $\{\pi_{b,j}\}$. We assume that the demeaned weights in any period depend on those from four other periods: immediately before and after, to capture short-term serial dependence, and exactly 1 day before and after, for daily seasonality. Specifically, we have the following priors:

$$\pi_{b,r} | \pi_{-b,r} \sim N(c_r + \rho_r[(\pi_{b-1,r} - c_r) + (\pi_{b+1,r} - c_r) + (\pi_{b-d,r} - c_r)$$
$$+ (\pi_{b+d,r} - c_r)], v_r^2),$$
$$c_r \sim N(0, 10^4), \qquad \rho_r \sim U(0, 0.25), \qquad v_r^2 \sim U(0, 10^4) \qquad (13.10)$$

for $r \in \{1, \cdots, C-1\}$ and $b \in \{1, \cdots, B\}$, in which $\pi_{-b,r} = (\pi_{1,r}, \cdots, \pi_{b-1,r}, \pi_{b+1,r}, \cdots, \pi_{B,r})'$, and d is the number of time periods in a day ($d = 12$ in our case).

Here, we have linked $\pi_{B,r}$ with $\pi_{1,r}$, such that $\{\pi_{b,r}\}$ is defined circularly in intraweek time. This is appropriate because we have the same weekly series of spatial densities cycle through time. In the prior of $\{\pi_{b,r}\}$, the intercepts c_r indicate average levels of the weights over time, the autoregressive parameters ρ_r represent persistence of the weights across time, and the variances v_r^2 control for variability of the weights across time. These three parameters are component-specific, and thus location-specific. If $\rho_r \in (-0.25, 0.25)$, then the prior joint distribution of $(\pi_{1,r}, \cdots, \pi_{B,r})'$ is multivariate normal [42]. We restrict ρ_r to take on values in $(0, 0.25)$ because we find positive short-term serial dependence and daily seasonality in our application. As an alternative to the above definition, we could define autoregressive priors by initiating $\{\pi_{1,r}\}$ and letting each $\pi_{b,r}$ depend only on its past. In either case, we can represent a rich set of temporal dynamics.

We follow [43, 44] in defining priors for other parameters. We have the following independent, minimally informative, hierarchical priors

$$\mu_j \sim \text{Normal}(\xi, \kappa^{-1}), \qquad \Sigma_j^{-1} | \beta \sim \text{Wishart}(2\alpha, (2\beta)^{-1}),$$
$$\beta \sim \text{Wishart}(2e, (2h)^{-1}) \qquad (13.11)$$

for $j \in \{1, \cdots, C\}$ and $t \in \{1, \cdots, T\}$. Again following [44], we set $\alpha = 3$, $e = 1$ and

$$\xi = (\xi_1, \xi_2)', \qquad \kappa = \text{diag}(R_1^{-2}, R_2^{-2}), \qquad h = \text{diag}(10R_1^{-2}, 10R_2^{-2})$$

in which ξ_1 and ξ_2 are the medians of all observations in the first and second spatial dimensions, and R_1 and R_2 are the lengths of the ranges of observations in the two dimensions.

To summarize, our model is Equation (13.8) with transformations (13.9) and prior distributions (13.10) and (13.11). We use Markov chain Monte Carlo (MCMC) for estimation. We augment the data with latent component labels $\{z_{t,i}\}$; each $z_{t,i}$ denotes the mixture component to which an observation $s_{t,i}$ belongs [45]. Upon initialization, we update $\{z_{t,i}\}, \{\mu_j\}, \beta$, and $\{\Sigma_j\}$ using their full conditional posterior distribution and update $\{\pi_{b,r}\}, \{c_r\}, \{\rho_r\}$, and $\{v_r\}$ using Metropolis-Hastings random walk.

In this model, we assume a fixed number of mixture components. We can add a refinement to this model by estimating a variable number of components. We can do so through a straightforward generalization of the Birth-and-Death MCMC (BDM-CMC) [44] to the spatiotemporal setting. While the number of components varies across iterations, we assume that it is common to all time periods within any iteration. This is not an unreasonable assumption since the spatial structure of Toronto does not change over such a short amount of time. BDMCMC is a continuous-time alternative to Reversible Jump MCMC (RJMCMC) [43, 46] and is shown to result in even better mixing of all parameters than RJMCMC [44, 47]. Similar to [43, 44], we can put a truncated Poisson prior on the number of components, C, that is, $p(C) \propto \tau^C / C!$, in which $C \in \{1, \cdots, C_{max}\}$ for some fixed τ and C_{max}. However, given the large amount of data, putting a vague prior on C would lead to an infeasibly large number of components in the posterior, and potentially overfitting. A more viable option is to impose a prior on C so as to encourage a small number of components.

13.3.2   Estimating Ambulance Demand

We apply our models to Toronto EMS data from February 2007. First, we use a fixed number of 15 components. Through preliminary analysis, we found 15 components to be able to adequately represent various business, residential, and transportation regions in Toronto, while still being low enough for easy computation. We then use a variable number of components via BDMCMC. We set $C_{max} = 50$ and choose τ such that the posterior average numbers of components are 19 and 24 (with posterior standard deviations of 3 and 5, respectively).

Each MCMC is run for 50,000 iterations, with the first 25,000 discarded as burn-in. The chain length and mixing are deemed sufficient; we obtain Monte Carlo standard errors for the statistical measure for predictive accuracy (detained in Section 13.3.3) that are small enough to yield accuracy of at least three significant figures [48, 49]. The computation time for the mixture model with 15 fixed components is 4 s per iteration on a personal computer, while those for variable components averaging 19 and 24 are 7 and 8 s per iteration, respectively. In practice, estimation only needs to be performed infrequently (at most once a month in our application), and density prediction for any future time period is almost immediate once estimation is complete.

Figures 13.7 and 13.8 show the estimated mixture model using a fixed number of $C = 15$ components. Figure 13.7 presents the posterior means and covariances (ellipses at 90% level) of the 15 components at the last iteration of the MCMC simulation. Ellipses of the first 14 components are each shaded by the posterior mean of the autoregressive parameter ρ_r for that component. Components at the greater downtown and coastal regions of Toronto have higher posterior means of ρ_r. These denser regions exhibit stronger daily seasonality and low-order serial dependence. This indicates that our model can differentiate temporal dynamics based on locations.

Using a fixed number of 15 mixture components, we show in Figure 13.8 the posterior spatial density on the log scale for two different time periods, averaged across the last 25,000 MCMC samples. The ambulance demand is, perhaps not suprisingly, concentrated at the heart of downtown during the mid-afternoon on Wednesday (Figure 13.8(a)) and more spread out throughout the city during the very early hours on Wednesday (Figure 13.8(b)). Our model successfully captures this variation of demand density with time. We also show in Figure 13.9 the posterior

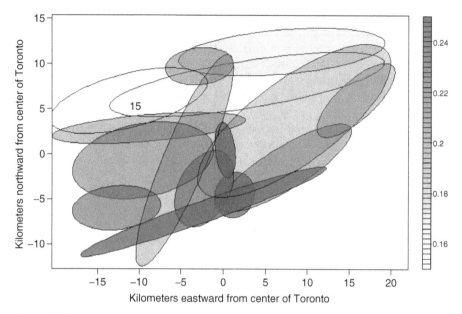

Figure 13.7   Posterior means and covariance ellipses (at 90% level) using our mixture model with 15 fixed components. Each ellipse (except that of the 15th component) is shaded with posterior mean of ρ_r. The greater downtown and coastal regions show stronger daily seasonality and short-term serial dependence.

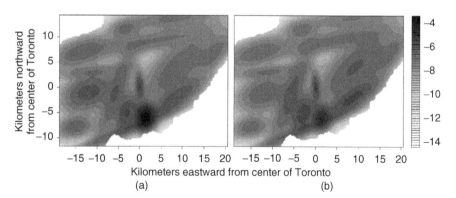

Figure 13.8   Posterior log spatial densities using our mixture model with 15 fixed components: (a) for Wednesday 2:00–4:00 P.M. (demand concentrated at downtown during the day); (b) for Wednesday 2:00–4:00 A.M. (demand more spread out at night).

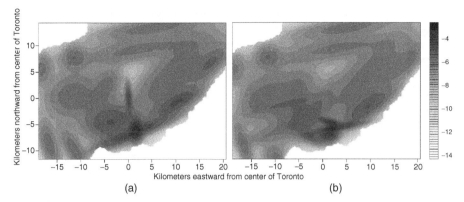

Figure 13.9 Posterior log spatial densities using our mixture model with a variable number of components for Wednesday 2:00–4:00 A.M., when the posterior average number of components are (a) 19 and (b) 24.

log spatial densities during Wednesday night when we fit our mixture model using a variable number of components. These densities are compared to and found similar to that in Figure 13.8(b).

13.3.3 Model Performance

We fit our mixture models on the training data from February 2007 and use the resulting density estimates to predict on two sets of test data, March 2007 and February 2008, respectively. We compare our predictive accuracy to MEDIC, a current industry practice mentioned in Section 13.1, and our proposed extension of MEDIC using kernel density estimation (KDE).

The MEDIC method described in [3] predicts ambulance demand on discretized time and space by averaging 20 corresponding demands in the preceding 4 weeks, for the last 5 years. We implement the MEDIC method as far as we have data. We use a temporal discretization of 2-h intervals and adopt the spatial discretization of 1 km ×1 km used by Toronto EMS. Since our goal is to predict demand densities, we normalize demand volumes at any temporal and spatial bin by the total demand that occurred for that time period. To predict for any 2-h period in March 2007, we average four historical demand densities in the same hours of the preceding 4 weeks. To predict for any 2-h period in February 2008, we average eight historical demand densities in the same hours of the preceding 4 weeks and those of the same 4 weeks in 2007.

We propose an extension of the MEDIC method to predict ambulance demand continuously in space using KDE. We use the kernel density estimate of all data in any 2-h period as the demand density for that period. Here, we use a bivariate

Gaussian kernel and bandwidths chosen by cross-validation using the statistical predictive accuracy measure to be defined in Equation (13.12). Then, we predict demand densities for March 2007 and February 2008 by averaging historical demand densities according to the MEDIC formula. Note that the MEDIC and MEDIC-KDE methods use potentially more data that may be more recent than the proposed mixture models. To ensure fair comparison, we numerically normalize predictive densities produced by all three methods by Toronto's boundary after estimation is complete. This means we predict outside of Toronto with zero probability and elevate the predictive densities within the boundary proportionally. However, we do not normalize to the boundary during estimation because it added little benefit for this application given its additional computational cost. Numerical integration needs to be performed for every Metropolis–Hastings proposal of μ_j and Σ_j for each time period.

We show in Figure 13.10 the log spatial densities produced by MEDIC and MEDIC-KDE for February 6 2008 (Wednesday) at 2:00–4:00 am. These densities are to be compared with those in Figure 13.8(b) and 13.9(a,b), which are the log spatial densities for the same time period using our mixture models. Overall, the MEDIC and MEDIC-KDE estimates appear noisier than those of our mixture models.

To formally measure the statistical predictive accuracies of our mixture models, MEDIC and MEDIC-KDE, we use average logarithmic score [50]. This performance measure is widely used because it is a strictly proper scoring rule closely related to the Bayes factor and BIC, the Bayesian Information Criterion (see details in [51]). It is defined as

$$PA(\{\tilde{\mathbf{s}}_{t,i}\}) = \frac{1}{\sum_{t=1}^{T} y_t} \sum_{t=1}^{T} \sum_{i=1}^{y_t} \log \hat{g}_t(\tilde{s}_{t,i}) \qquad (13.12)$$

in which $\hat{g}_t(\cdot)$ is the density estimate obtained from various methods for the tth period, and $\tilde{s}_{t,i}$ represents the ith test data observation from the tth time period.

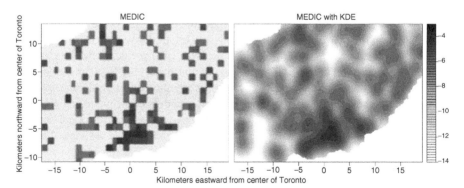

Figure 13.10 Log spatial densities using an industry method (MEDIC) and its extension (MEDIC-KDE) for February 6 2008 (Wednesday) 2:00–4:00 am. Figure 13.8(b) and Figure 13.9(a,b) show the densities for the same period estimated by the mixture models. Compared to mixture models, estimates from the MEDIC and MEDIC-KDE are noisy.

For our mixture models, we use the Monte Carlo estimate of Equation (13.12)

$$\text{PA}_{mix}(\{\tilde{s}_{t,i}\}) = \frac{1}{M} \sum_{m=1}^{M} \left(\frac{1}{\sum_{t=1}^{T} y_t} \sum_{t=1}^{T} \sum_{i=1}^{y_t} \log \ \hat{g}_t(\tilde{s}_{t,i}|\theta^{(m)}) \right) \qquad (13.13)$$

in which $\theta^{(m)}$ are the posterior parameter estimates in the mth iteration of the MCMC simulation, for $m \in \{1, \cdots, M\}$ and some large M.

We show in Table 13.1 the predictive accuracies of various methods for the two test periods. A less negative predictive accuracy indicates better performance. The predictive accuracies of the mixture models are presented with their 95% batch means confidence intervals [52], indicating the accuracy of the MCMC estimates. The mixture models outperform the industry practice and its extension. We note that using a variable number of components only improves the predictive accuracies slightly. Given that the computational expense almost doubles for these modest improvements, we conclude that using a fixed number of 15 components is largely sufficient in this application.

We also translate the statistical predictive advantage of our mixture models over the industry methods to operational advantage in EMS practice. In particular, we show that our mixture model predicts the industry's operational performances much more accurately. The prevalent EMS operational performance is measured by the proportion of events with response times below various thresholds (e.g., 60% responded to within 4 min). This operational performance is usually the optimization objective for management decisions in the EMS industry. It is therefore critical to be able to forecast this performance accurately, and this depends crucially on the accuracy of spatiotemporal demand density forecasts.

First, we generate a time series of 2-h demand density forecasts for each of our two test data sets using the mixture model, MEDIC, and MEDIC-KDE. Using the density forecasts produced by method $\mathcal{M}$ for time period t, we compute the operational performance as the proportion of demand reachable by response time threshold r, $\mathcal{P}_{\mathcal{M},t}(r)$. We do this by numerically integrating the demand density forecasts within all regions that can be covered within time r. Here, we assume a simplified set of

TABLE 13.1 Predictive Accuracies of Mixture Models (with 95% Batch Means Confidence Intervals), MEDIC, and MEDIC-KDE on Test Data from March 2007 and February 2008

	Estimation Method	PA for March 2007	PA for February 2008
Gaussian Mixture	15 components	-6.1378 ± 0.0004	-6.1491 ± 0.0005
	Variable number of comp:		
	average 19 comp	-6.080 ± 0.002	-6.128 ± 0.002
	average 24 comp	-6.072 ± 0.003	-6.122 ± 0.004
Competing Methods	MEDIC	-8.31	-7.62
	MEDIC-KDE	-6.87	-6.56

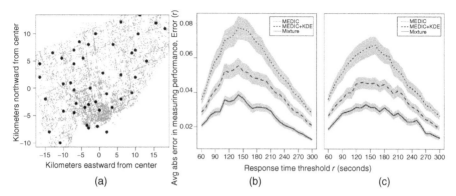

Figure 13.11 (a) The 44 ambulance bases in Toronto; (b) and (c) absolute error in measuring operational performance averaged across time periods, using our mixture model (15 components), MEDIC, and MEDIC-KDE, on test data of March 2007 and February 2008, respectively (with 95% intervals for the averages). Our mixture model reduces this error significantly.

operational strategies: we use the L_1 (Manhattan) distance metric, ambulances always depart from one of the 44 bases in Toronto (see Figure 13.11(a)), and ambulances always travel at the median speed of Toronto EMS trips, 46 km/h. We also calculate the realized operational performance using the test data, $\mathcal{P}_{\text{test},t}(r)$.

Our goal is to assess how close the operational performance $\mathcal{P}_{\mathcal{M},t}(r)$ using each method $\mathcal{M}$ is to the true performance $\mathcal{P}_{\text{test},t}(r)$ for a range of r values. We represent this closeness by the average of absolute prediction errors across time periods, that is, $\text{Error}(\mathcal{M}, r) = \frac{1}{T} \sum_{t=1}^{T} |\mathcal{P}_{\mathcal{M},t}(r) - \mathcal{P}_{\text{test},t}(r)|$. In Figure 13.11 (b) and (c), we plot $\text{Error}(\mathcal{M}, r)$ against r for each method $\mathcal{M}$ (mixture model with 15 components, MEDIC, and MEDIC-KDE), for the test data from March 2007 and February 2008, respectively. We also show the 95% confidence bands for the absolute errors, indicating their variations across time periods.

We find that the mixture model predicts the operational performance much more accurately. Our method reduces error by as much as two-thirds compared to the MEDIC method, even though our method is sometimes trained on less recent data. Although we use a simplified set of operational assumptions here, we expect similar results under different operational strategies.

Finally, we examine the goodness-of-fit of our mixture models, using the model checking method proposed in [36]. We have assumed that our point process follows an NHPP with intensity $\lambda_t(\mathbf{s}) = \delta_t g_t(\mathbf{s})$ for each time period t. Estimates of $\{\delta_t\}$ are obtained by the factor model with covariates and smoothing described in Section 13.2, whereas our mixture models in Section 13.3 offer estimates of $\{g_t(\mathbf{s})\}$. We can marginalize our point process in the first and second spatial dimensions to two one-dimensional NHPPs with intensities $\lambda_{1,t}(\cdot)$ and $\lambda_{2,t}(\cdot)$, obtained by marginalizing $\lambda_t(\cdot)$. We also compute the cumulative marginal intensities $\Lambda_{1,t}(\cdot)$ and $\Lambda_{2,t}(\cdot)$ and order the observations along each marginal for each time period into $\{\bar{s}_{j,1}, \cdots, \bar{s}_{j,y_t}\}$ along each margin $j \in \{1, 2\}$.

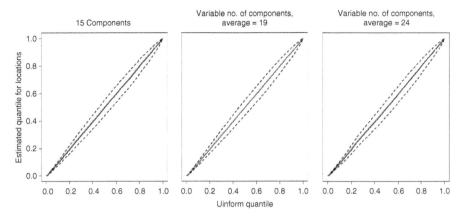

Figure 13.12   Q–Q plots for goodness-of-fit using aggregate intensity estimates from the factor model and spatiotemporal density estimates from various mixture models. The solid lines are the posterior mean Q–Q lines, and the dash lines represent the 95% posterior intervals. All three plots indicate that our models fit the data well.

If our models fit the data perfectly, then $\{\Lambda_{j,t}(\bar{s}_{j,i}) : i = 1, \cdots, y_t\}$ for each margin $j \in \{1,2\}$ and time t follows a homogeneous Poisson process with unit rate. Then the interarrival times along each margin in each time period are i.i.d uniform random variables on $(0,1)$, that is, $u_{i,j,t} = 1 - \exp \{-(\Lambda_{j,t}(\bar{s}_{j,i}) - \Lambda_{j,t}(\bar{s}_{j,i-1}))\} \overset{iid}{\sim} U(0,1)$ for observations $i \in \{2, \cdots y_t\}$, dimensions $j \in \{1,2\}$ and time $t \in \mathcal{T}$. We have a set of $u_{i,j,t}$ using posterior parameter estimates from each MCMC sample. We compare the posterior mean and 95% interval of $u_{i,j,t}$ with the true uniform distribution using quantile–quantile (Q–Q) plots in Figure 13.12. All plots show high goodness-of-fit, suggesting that the factor models and the mixture models, whether with a fixed or a variable number of components, are adequate and appropriate.

13.4   CONCLUSIONS

Predicting ambulance demand accurately at fine temporal and spatial resolutions is critical to optimal ambulance planning. The current industry method and other earlier methods are often simple and do not give accurate predictions. We provide two much-needed and highly accurate methods to predict temporal and spatiotemporal ambulance demand in fine scales. We first model bi-hourly aggregate call arrivals using an integer-valued time series model combined with a factor model that incorporates covariates and smoothing. We then estimate the spatial density of ambulance demand as it varies over 2-h periods by extending Gaussian mixture models. We jointly estimate mixture component distributions over time to promote efficient learning of spatial structures even though data are sparse within each time period. We express a diverse set of location-specific seasonalities and serial dependence typical in the spatial densities of ambulance demand by re-parametrizing the mixture weights and applying conditionally autoregressive priors. We have shown that estimation can be implemented with a fixed or a variable number of components. Both of these methods are parsimonious, flexible, and easy to implement; they also demonstrate substantial advantages over the current industry practice and similar methods. Ultimately, we aim to optimize ambulance planning by providing more accurate spatiotemporal demand estimates.

Our methods utilize the same data used by the current industry methods and do not require any additional data collection. Future work will investigate the use of additional covariates, such as weather, special events, population, and demographic variables, in addition to historical data. A further challenge is to collect and make use of data on population and demographic movement across fine timescales, for example, bi-hourly. For aggregate demand estimation, a nonlinear time series model could be considered, while for spatiotemporal density estimation, a computationally feasible way of incorporating the boundary of Toronto would be an important contribution.

REFERENCES

[1] Goldberg JB. Operations research methods for the deployment of emergency service vehicles. *EMS Manag J* 2004;1:20–39.

[2] Henderson SG. Operations research tools for addressing current challenges in emergency medical services. In: Cochran JJ, Cox LA, Keskinocak P, Kharoufeh JP, Smith JC, editors. *Wiley Encyclopedia of Operations Research and Management Science*. New York: John Wiley and Sons, Inc.; 2009.

[3] Setzler H, Saydam C, Park S. EMS call volume predictions: a comparative study. *Comput Oper Res* 2009;36(6):1843–1851.

[4] Diggle PJ. *Statistical Analysis of Spatial Point Patterns*. 2nd ed. London: Arnold; 2003.

[5] Møller J, Waagepetersen RP. *Statistical Inference and Simulation for Spatial Point Processes*. London: Chapman & Hall/CRC; 2004.

[6] Illian JB, Penttinen A, Stoyan H, Stoyan D. *Statistical Analysis and Modelling of Spatial Point Patterns*. Chichester: John Wiley and Sons, Ltd; 2008.

[7] Channouf N, L'Ecuyer P, Ingolfsson A, Avramidis AN. The application of forecasting techniques to modeling emergency medical system calls in Calgary, Alberta. *Health Care Manag Sci* 2007;10(1):25–45.

[8] Vile JL, Gillard JW, Harper PR, Knight VA. Predicting ambulance demand using singular spectrum analysis. *J Oper Res Soc* 2012;63:1556–1565.

[9] Aldor-Noiman S, Feigin P, Mandelbaum A. Workload forecasting for a call center: methodology and a case study. *Ann Appl Stat* 2009;3(4):1403–1447.

[10] Ibrahim R, L'Ecuyer P. Forecasting call center arrivals: fixed-effects, mixed-effects, and bivariate models. *Manuf Serv Oper Manag* 2013;15(1):72–85.

[11] Weinberg J, Brown LD, Stroud JR. Bayesian forecasting of an inhomogeneous Poisson process with applications to call center data. *J Am Stat Assoc* 2007;102:1185–1199.

[12] Shen H, Huang JZ. Forecasting time series of inhomogeneous Poisson process with application to call center management software. *Ann Appl Stat* 2008;2(2):601–623.

[13] Shen H, Huang JZ. Intraday forecasting and interday updating of call center arrivals. *Manuf Serv Oper Manag* 2008;10(3):391–410.

[14] Whitt W. *Stochastic-Process Limits*, Springer Series in Operations Research. New York: Springer-Verlag; 2002.

[15] Matteson DS, McLean MW, Woodard DB, Henderson SG. Forecasting emergency medical service call arrival rates. *Ann Appl Stat* 2011;5:1379–1406.

[16] Takane Y, Hunter MA. Constrained principal component analysis: a comprehensive theory. *Appl Algebra Eng Commun Comput* 2001;12(5):391–419.

[17] Tsai H, Tsay RS. Constrained factor models. *J Am Stat Assoc* 2010;105(492):1593–1605.

[18] Hastie T, Tibshirani R. *Generalized Additive Models*. London: Chapman and Hall; 1990.

[19] Wood SN. *Generalized Additive Models: An Introduction with R*. New York: CRC Press; 2006.

[20] Borchers DL, Buckland ST, Priede IG, Ahmadi S. Improving the precision of the daily egg production method using generalized additive models. *Can J Fish Aquat Sci* 1997;54(12):2727–2742.

[21] Daskalov G. Relating fish recruitment to stock biomass and physical environment in the black sea using generalized additive models. *Fish Res* 1999;41(1):1–23.

[22] Hastie T, Tibshirani R. Varying-coefficient models. *J R Stat Soc Ser B (Methodological)* 1993;55:757–796.

[23] Gu C. Cross-validating non-Gaussian data. *J Comput Graph Stat* 1992;1(2):169–179.

[24] Ferland R, Latour A, Oraichi D. Integer-valued GARCH process. *J Time Ser Anal* 2006;27:923–942.

[25] Woodard DB, Matteson DS, Henderson SG. Stationarity of generalized autoregressive moving average models. *Electron J Stat* 2011;5:800–828.

[26] Matteson DS, James NA. A nonparametric approach for multiple change point analysis of multivariate data. *J Am Stat Assoc* 2014;109(505):334–345.

[27] James NA, Matteson DS. ecp: An R Package for Nonparametric Multiple Change Point Analysis of Multivariate Data. ArXiv e-prints: 1309.3295 http://arxiv.org/abs/1309.3295, Sept 2013.

[28] Kottas A, Sansó B. Bayesian mixture modeling for spatial Poisson process intensities, with applications to extreme value analysis. *J Stat Plann Inference* 2007;137(10): 3151–3163.

[29] Ji C, Merl D, Kepler TB. Spatial mixture modeling for unobserved point processes: examples in immunofluorescence histology. *Bayesian Anal* 2009;4(2):297–315.

[30] Chakraborty A, Gelfand AE. Analyzing spatial point patterns subject to measurement error. *Bayesian Anal* 2010;5(1):97–122.

[31] Gelfand A, Kottas A, MacEachern S. Bayesian nonparametric spatial modeling with Dirichlet processes mixing. *J Am Stat Assoc* 2005;100:1201–1235.

[32] Duan JA, Guindani M, Gelfand AE. Generalized spatial Dirichlet process models. *Biometrika* 2007;94:809–825.

[33] Taddy MA. Bayesian Nonparametric Analysis of Conditional Distributions and Inference for Poisson Point Processes [PhD thesis]. Santa Cruz, CA: University of California; 2008.

[34] Taddy MA. Autoregressive mixture models for dynamic spatial Poisson processes: application to tracking intensity of violent crime. *J Am Stat Assoc* 2010; 105(492):1403–1417.

[35] Ding M, He L, Dunson D, Carin L. Nonparametric Bayesian segmentation of a multivariate inhomogeneous space-time Poisson process. *Bayesian Anal* 2012;7(2):235–262.

[36] Taddy MA, Kottas A. Mixture modeling for marked Poisson processes. *Bayesian Anal* 2012;7(2):335–362.

[37] Zhou Z, Matteson DS, Woodard DB, Henderson SG, Micheas AC. A spatio-temporal point process model for ambulance demand. *J Am Stat Assoc* 2015;110:6–15.

[38] Besag J, York JC, Mollié A. Bayesian image restoration, with two applications in spatial statistics (with discussion). *Ann Inst Stat Math* 1991;43:1–59.

[39] Banerjee S, Gelfand AE, Carlin BP. *Hierarchical Modeling and Analysis for Spatial Data*. New York: Chapman and Hall; 2003.

[40] Berzuini C, Clayton D. Bayesian analysis on survival on multiple time scales. *Stat Med* 1994;13:823–838.

[41] Knorr-Held L, Besag J. Modelling risk from a disease in time and space. *Stat Med* 1998;17(1):2045–2060.

[42] Besag JE. Spatial interaction and the statistical analysis of lattice systems. *J R Stat Soc Ser B* 1974;36:192–225

[43] Richardson S, Green P. On Bayesian analysis of mixtures with an unknown number of components (with discussion). *J R Stat Soc Ser B* 1997;59(4):731–792.

[44] Stephens M. Bayesian analysis of mixture models with an unknown number of components - an alternative to reversible jump methods. *Ann Stat* 2000;28(1):40–74.

[45] Tanner MA, Wong WH. The calculation of posterior distributions by data augmentation. *J Am Stat Assoc* 1987;82(398):528–540.

[46] Green P. Reversible jump MCMC computation and Bayesian model determination. *Biometrika* 1995;82(4):711–732.

[47] Cappé O, Robert C, Rydé T. Reversible jump MCMC converging to birth-and-death MCMC and more general continuous time samplers. *J R Stat Soc Ser B* 2003;65(3):679–700.

[48] Flegal JM, Haran M, Jones GL. Markov chain Monte Carlo: can we trust the third significant figure? *Stat Sci* 2008;23(2):250–260.

[49] Brooks S, Gelman A, Jones G, Meng X, editors. *Handbook of Markov Chain Monte Carlo*, Handbooks of Modern Statistical Methods. New York: Chapman and Hall/CRC; 2011.

[50] Good IJ. Rational decisions. *J R Stat Soc Ser B* 1952;14:107–114.

[51] Gneiting T, Raftery A. Strictly proper scoring rules, prediction, and estimation. *J Am Stat Assoc* 2007;102(477):359–378.

[52] Jones GL, Haran M, Caffo BS, Neath R. Fixed-width output analysis for Markov chain Monte Carlo. *J Am Stat Assoc* 2006;101(476):1537–1547.

14

MATHEMATICAL OPTIMIZATION AND SIMULATION ANALYSES FOR OPTIMAL LIVER ALLOCATION BOUNDARIES

NAORU KOIZUMI

School of Public Policy, George Mason University, Arlington, VA, USA

MONICA GENTILI

Mathematics Department, University of Salerno, Fisciano, Italy

RAJESH GANESAN

Department of Operations Research, George Mason University, Fairfax, VA, USA

DEBASREE DASGUPTA AND AMIT PATEL

School of Public Policy, George Mason University, Arlington, VA, USA

CHUN-HUNG CHEN

Department of Operations Research, George Mason University, Fairfax, VA, USA

NIGEL WATERS

Department of Geography, George Mason University, Fairfax, VA, USA

KEITH MELANCON

George Washington University Hospital, Washington, DC, USA

Healthcare Analytics: From Data to Knowledge to Healthcare Improvement, First Edition.
Edited by Hui Yang and Eva K. Lee.
© 2016 John Wiley & Sons, Inc. Published 2016 by John Wiley & Sons, Inc.

14.1 INTRODUCTION

Existing studies of organ transplant report various disparities in access to and outcomes in transplantation. Disparities have been found in terms of race, socioeconomic status, insurance type, and the location of candidate's residency. While these disparities tend to coexist, disparity associated with candidates' locations or "geographical disparity" is the first and foremost discussed. Researchers worldwide have repeatedly confirmed that the likelihood of receiving a transplant as well as pre- and posttransplant mortality rates vary significantly from region to region [1–10]. Geographic disparity in transplant access is a persistent issue ever since organ allocation became a regulated process in 1984 under the National Organ Transplant Act (NOTA). As the most important act in the history of the US transplantation, NOTA created the Organ Procurement and Transplantation Network (OPTN) – a public–private network of regional organ allocation offices known as Organ Procurement Organizations (OPOs) [1]. NOTA also authorized the Department of Health and Human Services (HHS) to contract with the United Network for Organ Sharing (UNOS) as the only administrative entity to administer OPTN. At first, all organs were distributed within each OPO's service area in order to limit cold ischemia time (CIT), the interval between organ retrieval, and the time of transplantation during which an organ is preserved in a cold-perfusion solution (ibid). Allocation of organs within each OPO was solely based on the length of time that each candidate had spent waiting for an organ since initial referral. In response to the concern that the waiting time varied significantly by OPO, HHS introduced a new regulation known as the "Final Rule" (42 CFR Part 121) in 1998 to "assure that allocation of scarce organs will be based on common medical criteria, not accidents of geography" (HHS, 1998b) [1].

As per the directives of the Final Rule, the allocation mechanism for a number of vital organs has been rectified to address the criterion of medical necessity. For liver allocation, HHS revised the Code of Federal Regulations that legislate the organ allocation process and, in 2002, the Model for End-Stage Liver Disease (MELD) scoring system was introduced and launched as a way to prioritize the candidates with a higher medical urgency. Until the allocation rule was further revised in 2013, the adult cadaver livers had been distributed, in principle, based on the algorithm summarized in Figure 14.1. Figure 14.2 summarizes the current liver allocation system. As the figures show, the current organ allocation system consists of three hierarchical geographic levels, which are OPO (aka, the Donor Service Area or DSA), UNOS region, and National levels (ibid).

While several changes in allocation rules have been introduced to address the disparities, transplant researchers still report that a number of key elements that determine equity in transplantation vary significantly depending on the location of a patient. Given this background, our study developed a mathematical programming model to redesign liver allocation boundaries. The optimal boundaries were derived to maximize efficiency and geographic equity in access to liver transplantation. Part of this mathematical model also analyzed optimal locations for liver transplant centers. In this analysis, we explored several scenarios to examine whether relocating the 123 liver transplant centers can achieve the objectives specified in the model

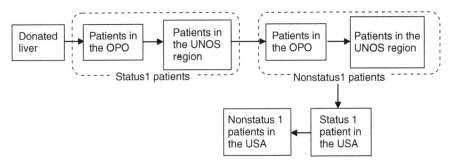

Figure 14.1 Pre-2013 deceased-donor adult liver allocation system.

- Status 1 patient refers to those with fulminant liver failure with a life expectancy without a liver transplant of less than 7 days.
- Within each category of patients (i.e., Status 1, MELD scores ≥ 15, MELD score < 15), a liver is offered, in principle, in the descending order of first MELD score and then waiting time.
- Extra points are added to the MELD score for those patients whose blood type is compatible with that of the available liver and those with specific clinical circumstances such as hepatocellular carcinoma (HCC).

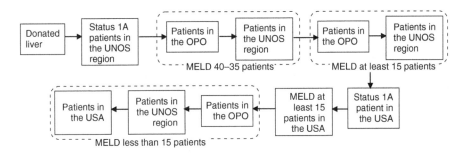

Figure 14.2 Current deceased-donor adult liver allocation system.

more efficiently than locating additional liver transplant centers at the locations of "kidney-only" transplant centers. Using the locations of kidney-only transplant centers as the candidate locations for additional liver transplant centers reflects that most transplant centers start as a kidney transplant center and subsequently add additional transplant program(s) for other organ type(s).

To evaluate the performance of the optimal boundaries in a realistic setting, we developed a discrete-event simulation model that reflects the actual liver–candidate matching and the actual liver allocation protocols practiced until 2013. The primary data used for the analysis is UNOS's Standard Transplant Analysis and Research (STAR) Data set that records the clinical, administrative, demographic, and locational information of 82,020 adult liver transplant candidates and recipients who appeared on the wait-list between 2003 and 2011.

14.2 METHODS

Our mathematical analysis has the twofold objectives of (i) identifying optimal locations for both existing and new liver transplant centers; and (ii) identifying new OPO boundaries as alternatives to the existing OPO boundaries for liver allocation. Once new OPO boundaries were specified, we evaluated the performance of the new boundaries through a series of discrete-event simulations. The simulation approach allowed us to assess the performance of the new boundaries based on a variety of criteria, including those not reflected in the mathematical models.

14.2.1 Mathematical Model: Optimal Locations of Transplant Centers and OPO Boundaries

Two mathematical models are explored to achieve the two aforementioned objectives. The first model (Model 1) addresses the problem of selecting a fixed number p of transplant centers to be opened among a possible set of candidates. With each opened transplant center, an organ acquisition area and a service area are defined. These areas represent, respectively, the set of ZIP codes where donor hospitals provide livers to the center and the set of counties whose recipients can be transplanted an organ in the center. The second model (Model 2) aims at clustering the p selected centers in a predefined number of clusters, each cluster representing an OPO. The union of the acquisition areas and the service areas associated with the transplant centers that belong to the same cluster defines the acquisition area and the service area of the OPO, respectively. Such a clustering is carried out ensuring that the resulting organ acquisition area and service area, associated with each OPO, are balanced both in terms of total acquired and total requested organs and in terms of total number of transplant centers clustered in each OPO. The two models are, respectively, specified below.

14.2.1.1 Model 1 Let $D = \{1, 2, \ldots, m\}$ represent the set of donor hospitals where livers are recovered and let w_j, $j \in D$ be a weight associated with each donor hospital representing the total number of livers recovered at the hospital during our study period. We use "county" as the smallest unit used to represent liver transplant candidates, and thus they are aggregated to the county level to measure the demand per county. Let $C = \{1, 2, \ldots, n\}$ represent the set of counties and h_i, $i \in C$ the total number of candidates waiting for a transplant in county i during the study period. Let $T = \{1, 2, \ldots, q\}$ be the set of potential transplant centers to be opened. We also define the parameter d_{jt}, $j \in D$, $t \in T$ as the Euclidean distance between the donor hospital j and the transplant center t, and f_{it}, $i \in C$, $t \in T$ as the Euclidean distance between the centroid of county i and the transplant center t.

Model 1 solves the problem of selecting p liver transplant centers among the available $|T|$ to be opened and associates a subset of donor hospitals and a subset of counties with each transplant center. The former associations define the *liver acquisition area* of a transplant center while the latter associations define the *patient service area* of a center. The model ensures that each donor hospital and each county are associated with exactly one transplant center. The distance between a donor hospital and each of the transplant centers associated with the donor hospital is such that the corresponding travel time is within a predefined maximum threshold to ensure that livers are transplanted within a certain time length known as the maximum CIT. CIT is defined as the time from the perfusion of an organ by cold solutions until transplantation in the recipient of the organ, and, for liver, the maximum medically accepted CIT is set at 12 h [11]. Similarly, the distance between county centroid and the transplant center assigned to the county is not greater than a predefined maximum threshold to make sure that the distance traveled by a candidate for a transplant is within a realistic range.

Using Model 1, we specifically examined four different scenarios for selecting transplant centers to be activated. The results of these scenarios were compared to the baseline, which represents the current situation. The scenarios are as follows:

- *Scenarios 1-i, 1-ii, and 1-iii.* This scenario selects additional 10 (1-i), 20 (1-ii), and 30 (1-iii) existing "kidney-only" transplant centers to operate as "kidney–liver transplant centers" in addition to the existing 123 liver transplant centers.

- *Scenario 2.* This scenario selects 123 liver transplant centers among the 123 current liver transplant centers and 103 kidney-only transplant centers. In practice, this scenario reflects the situation where some of the existing liver transplant centers are relocated to kidney-only transplant centers.

The proposed model is similar to the model proposed by Bruni et al. [12] in the fact that each selected transplant center is associated with an acquisition area and a service area. However, unlike the model by Bruni et al. [12], we consider an additional set of constraints to ensure that, for each opened transplant center, the ratio between the available organs or "supply" (recovered in the acquisition area) and the total number of recipients or "demand" (in the service area) is greater than a fixed threshold α. The resulting model is specified as follows:

$$\min \sum_{j \in D} \sum_{t \in T} d_{jt} x_{jt} + \sum_{i \in C} \sum_{t \in T} f_{it} y_{it} \tag{14.1}$$

$$\sum_{t \in N_j} x_{jt} = 1, \qquad \forall j \in D \tag{14.2}$$

$$\sum_{t \in N_i} y_{it} = 1, \qquad \forall i \in C \tag{14.3}$$

$$x_{jt} \le z_t, \qquad \forall j \in D \ \forall t \in T \tag{14.4}$$

$$y_{it} \le z_t, \qquad \forall i \in C \ \forall t \in T \tag{14.5}$$

$$\sum_{t \in T} z_t = p \tag{14.6}$$

$$\sum_{j \in D} w_j x_{jt} \le \alpha \sum_{i \in C} h_i y_{it}, \qquad \forall t \in T \tag{14.7}$$

The binary variable x_{jt} assumes a value equal to 1 if the donor hospital j is assigned to the transplant center t and is equal to 0 otherwise; the binary variable y_{it} assumes a value equal to 1 if county i is assigned to the transplant center t and is equal to 0 otherwise. Finally, the binary variable z_t assumes a value equals to 1 if the transplant center t is activated and is equal to 0 otherwise. The objective function 14.1 minimizes the sum of the total Euclidean distance between the donor hospitals and the associated opened transplant centers plus the total distance between the counties and the associated opened transplant centers.

The set $N_j = \{t \in T : d_{jt} \le d_{max}\}$ in constraint 14.2 is the set of transplant centers whose distance from the donor hospital j is less than or equal to a predefined threshold d_{max}. Analogously, the set $N_i = \{t \in T : f_{it} \le f_{max}\}$ in constraint 14.3 is the set of transplant centers whose distance from centroid of county i is less than or equal to a predefined threshold f_{max}. Constraints 14.2 and 14.3 require each donor hospital and each county to be associated with exactly one transplant center that is located within a predefined distance, respectively. Constraints 14.4 and 14.5 are logical constraints that, respectively, ensure a donor hospital and a county are assigned to a transplant center that is open. The total number of transplant centers to be opened must be equal to p, as stipulated by constraint 14.6. Finally, for each opened transplant center, the ratio between the total supply and the total demand must be greater than or equal to a predefined threshold α. If a subset $S \subseteq T$ of transplant centers is already opened, then we would add the constraints: $z_t = 1 \ \forall t \in S$ and we would modify constraint 14.6 accordingly. d_{max} and f_{max} were, respectively, set to 2000 (miles) and 1100 (miles). These values were chosen assuming that recovered livers are transported by helicopter and that recipients drive to their transplant centers for transplantation. Given that the average speed of helicopter is 160 MPH, the value (d_{max}) translates to about 12 h of transportation time or to the aforementioned maximum medically accepted CIT. p was set as 123 for Scenario 2 to reflect the number of liver transplant centers currently existing in the contiguous United States. Scenario 1 tested three different values of p, that is, $123 + 10$, $123 + 20$, and $123 + 30$. Finally, α, the minimum supply/demand ratio, was arbitrary set to 0.4. While there is no organ allocation policy or empirical work that suggests a specific optimal supply/demand ratio, we considered, for this exploratory analysis, $\alpha = 0.4$ can serve as a good representative value, given the minimum ratio observed under the current system is 0.3.

14.2.1.2 Model 2 This model addresses the problem of clustering a set of transplant centers that have been selected to be opened in Model 1 into a predefined number of clusters. Each cluster represents an OPO. The resulting OPOs are defined so that they are balanced both in terms of ratio between supply and demand of livers and in terms of total number of transplant centers that belong to the same OPO. The boundary of each OPO is defined as the union of the service areas of the transplant centers in the OPO. From a practical perspective, one important constraint to take into account when defining the cluster is contiguity of the service areas. Thus, Model 2 takes a graph $G = (V, E)$ as an input where each vertex $i \in V$ is associated with a transplant center, and vertex i and vertex j are connected by two oriented arcs (i,j) and (j,i) if the corresponding service areas have a common border. Two weights, w_i

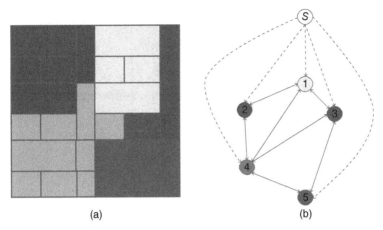

Figure 14.3   Model 2 Illustration.
An example region (a) where each polygon represents a county and polygons with the same shade constitutes the service area associated with an allocated transplant center, and the associated graph (b).

and h_i, are associated with each vertex i of this graph representing, respectively, the total supply and the total demand associated with the transplant center represented by the vertex. A super vertex s is added to the graph and is connected with each vertex of the graph by the set of arcs (s, i), $\forall\, i \in V$. Hence, the resulting graph is such that the total number of vertices is equal to $p+1$, and the total number of arcs depends on the solution returned by Model 1. Figure 14.3 illustrates a region and the associated graph. Each polygon in the region on the left represents a county, and polygons with the same shade constitutes the service area associated with an allocated transplant center. The figure represents an example where five transplant centers are located. The associated graph is depicted on the right: a vertex is associated with each transplant center and the solid arcs in the graphs connect transplant centers whose service areas share a border. The super vertex s is connected with each vertex of the graph (dotted arcs). The resulting graph has $5 + 1$ vertices and 19 arcs.

Model 2 looks for a spanning tree T_s of G rooted in s such that the total number of children of the root is equal to the total number of clusters that need to be defined. In this way, the vertices of each subtree T_i rooted at vertex i (i.e., one of the children of the supervertex s) represent the set of transplant centers that belong to the same cluster. The union of the service areas associated with the transplant centers which belong to the same cluster defines the OPO region boundary. Connection of the subtree ensures contiguity of the service area associated with the cluster. Refer to Figure 14.4 where an example of a possible solution returned by Model 2 is shown with respect to the graph of Figure 14.3. A spanning tree (Fig. 14.3a) is shown to represent a clusterization of the five transplant centers of Figure 14.3 into two clusters. The first cluster contains transplant centers 1, 2, and 3. The second cluster contains

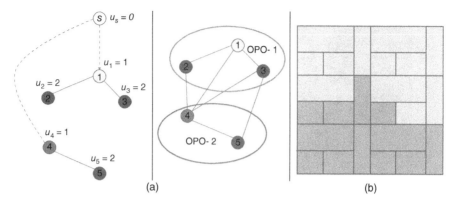

Figure 14.4   An illustration of Model 2 solution.
The spanning tree on the left represents a clusterization of the five transplant centers of Figure 14.3 into two clusters. The two resulting OPO regions are represented on the right.

transplant centers 4 and 5. The two OPO regions corresponding to these two clusters are represented on Figure 14.3b.

Additional constraints in the model ensure that each subtree is such that the ratio between the sum of the weights w_i associated with the vertices of the subtree and the sum of the weights h_i associated with the vertices of the subtree is greater than or equal to a predefined threshold α. The objective function of the model is the minimization of the maximum number of vertices in each of the resulting subtrees, ensuring in this way the resulting clusters are also balanced in terms of the total number of transplant centers that belong to them.

Let $O = \{1, 2, ..., l\}$ be the index set of the clusters that need to be defined. Then, the proposed formulation is a Miller–Tucker–Zemlin (MTZ) formulation [13] where we considered the following set of variables:

- Variable y_{ik} is a binary variable that is equal to one if vertex $i \in V$ belongs to cluster $k \in O$ and is equal to 0 otherwise.
- Variable x_{ijk} is a binary variable that is equal to one if arc $(i,j) \in E$, that connects vertices i and j in the cluster k, is selected to be in the spanning tree and is equal to 0 otherwise.
- Variable u_i, defined on each vertex $i \in V$, assigns a label to each vertex of the graph. In particular, such a labeling ensures any directed arc that belongs to the optimum spanning tree that goes from a vertex with a lower label to a vertex with a higher label.

In Model 2, variables y_{ik} are used to define the clusters, while variables u_i and x_{ijk} are used to define the final spanning tree. In particular, the set of variables u_i defined on each vertex $i \in V$ assigns a label to each vertex of the graph. Such a labeling ensures any directed arc that belongs to the optimum spanning tree that goes from a vertex with a lower label to a vertex with a higher label. Such a label assignment is aimed at subtour elimination. The resulting model is as follows:

$$\min \max_{k \in O} \left(\sum_{i \in V} y_{ik} \right) \tag{14.8}$$

$$\sum_{(s,j) \in E} x_{sjk} = 1, \qquad \forall k \in O \tag{14.9}$$

$$\sum_{k \in O} \sum_{(i,j) \in E} x_{ijk} = 1, \qquad \forall j \in V, j \neq s \tag{14.10}$$

$$\sum_{k \in O} x_{ijk} \leq 1, \qquad \forall (i,j) \in E \tag{14.11}$$

$$x_{ijk} \leq y_{ik}, \qquad \forall (i,j) \in E, \ i \neq s, \ \forall k \in O \tag{14.12}$$

$$y_{ik} \leq \sum_{(i,j) \in E} x_{ijk}, \qquad \forall i \in V, \ i \neq s, \ \forall k \in O \tag{14.13}$$

$$u_s = 0 \tag{14.14}$$

$$1 \leq u_i \leq p, \qquad \forall i \in V, \ i \neq s \tag{14.15}$$

$$(p+1)x_{ijk} + u_i - u_j + (p-1)x_{jik} \leq p, \qquad \forall (i,j) \in E, \ i \neq s, \ \forall k \in O \tag{14.16}$$

$$\sum_{k \in O} y_{ik} = 1, \qquad \forall i \in V, \ i \neq s \tag{14.17}$$

$$\sum_{i \in V, \ i \neq s} w_i y_{ik} \leq \alpha \sum_{i \in V, \ i \neq s} h_i y_{ik}, \qquad \forall k \in O \tag{14.18}$$

$$\sum_{i \in V, \ i \neq s} y_{ik} \geq 1, \qquad \forall k \in O \tag{14.19}$$

The objective function 14.8 minimizes the maximum cardinality of the resulting clusters. Constraint 14.9 ensures that the total number of children of the root s is equal to the total number of clusters that need to be defined. Constraint 14.10 ensures that each vertex has exactly one entering arc. Each arc can be associated with at most one cluster, which is ensured by constraint 14.11. Constraints 14.12 and 14.13 are logical constraints linking the binary variables. The spanning tree is defined by the classical MTZ constraints 14.14–14.16. In particular, these constraints ensure that (i) the root vertex s has label equal to zero (constraint 14.14), (ii) each vertex i in the graph is assigned a label $1 \leq u_i \leq p$ (constraint 14.15), and (iii) each selected arc (i, j) is such that $u_i < u_j$ (constraint 14.16). Note that the MTZ set of constraint 14.16 are such that for a given selected arc (i, j) the labeling variables are such that $u_j = u_i + 1$ (Desrochers and Laporte [14]), so that u_i indicates the position of vertex i in the spanning tree, that is, the number of arcs in the path between the root s and vertex i (see Fig. 14.4). The interested reader could refer to Desrochers and Laporte [14], Gouveia [15], and Carrabs et al. [16] to explore additional lifting constraints and different alternative formulations to define spanning trees. Constraint 14.17 ensures that each vertex belongs exactly to one cluster. The structure of the cluster is defined by constraints 14.18 and 14.19. In particular, each cluster cannot be empty (constraint 14.19) and total supply/demand ratio at each cluster must be greater than or equal to a predefined threshold α (constraint 14.18).

Our model extends a handful of studies [12, 17–20] that investigate optimal boundaries for organ allocation using a mathematical approach. Most previous models [12, 17–20] are based on a set covering mathematical formulation of which feasible sets are represented by all possible regional configurations resulting from different clusters of OPOs. This approach tends to be computationally very demanding. The MTZ formulation we proposed for Model 2 solves a constrained version of the spanning tree problem. This approach enabled us to solve the problem to optimality through the available commercial solvers, Cplex and Gurobi, in a reasonable amount of time. In this study, all mathematical formulations were coded in AMPL and solved using CPLEX 11 and Gurobi 5.1 on a 2.4 GHz Intel Core2 Q6600 processor.

Results of the mathematical analysis were visualized using maps generated in GIS software, ArcView (ArcMap, Ver. 10, ESRI Corp). In addition to the standard tools available in ArcView, a third-party Python program, "Spider Tools" [21], was downloaded and used in ArcView to visualize the associations between donor hospitals and transplant centers. In addition, several statistics were calculated and interpreted to validate the models.

14.2.2 Discrete-Event Simulation: Evaluation of Optimal OPO Boundaries

A series of discrete-event simulations were run to evaluate the performance of the boundaries developed by the mathematical model. The following performance metrics were used to evaluate the new OPO boundaries.

- Mean and median supply/demand ratio per OPO.
- Mean and median waiting time per OPO.
- Mean distance between donor hospitals and transplant centers in each OPO.
- Variation in waiting time for transplant across OPOs.
- Variation in supply/demand ratio across OPOs.

The first two metrics measure patients' access to liver transplantation. The third metric evaluates the new OPO boundaries from the transplant outcome perspective. Longer graft travel distance brings a concomitant increase in CIT, which would in turn increase the likelihood of a graft failure [22, 23]. The last two metrics assess geographic equity in access to liver transplantation.

The key events and the parameters used to frame the simulation were as follows: (i) patient arrival rate, (ii) length of time registered as a transplant candidate, (iii) rate of death and dropout while waiting for an organ, (iv) rate of candidates who receive a transplant, and (v) liver arrival rate. Both livers and patients arrive in the system with certain characteristics used for "match-run" and other purposes. Those characteristics included blood type, MELD score and category, age (below or over 65), and ethnicity.

The first task of baseline simulation was to generate recipient and donor data. Every OPO in the United States covers a group of counties. Every county in the United States has a unique "FIPS" code as its identification. Furthermore, each county has a historical pattern for the number of recipients and donors it generates per year and its arrival rate per day of the year, which also follows the historical proportions for their characteristics. Using the historical numbers and proportions from 2003 to 2009 as described earlier, the simulation was able to generate both recipient and donor data for 2010, which was then validated using the actual data from 2010.

The next step in the simulation was to allocate the donors to the recipients using the current OPO boundaries and using the new OPO boundaries in which the ratio of supply to demand has been balanced between the OPOs. First, a waiting list of candidates as of January 1, 2010 was generated from the actual data from the STAR database. This data set was used to initialize the simulation of liver allocation. Livers were then allocated using the current system of allocation in which status 1 patients were given the top priority followed by patients with MELD > 15 and MELD < 15 (Fig. 14.1). The performance metrics were the waiting time for transplants for status 1, MELD < 15 and MELD > 15 recipients of liver, and the geographical disparity measured in terms of the mean squared error, which captures the deviation of the supply/demand ratio of the OPOs from the mean supply/demand ratio. Since there were about 12,000 candidates on the wait-list on January 1, 2010 and about 10,000 candidates joined the list in 2010, the supply/demand ratio for 5000 donors in 2010 is about 0.23. After accounting for death while waiting (12.8%), the supply/demand ratio is about 0.25 (including both waiting list and new candidates in 2010). However, the supply/demand ratio is about 0.57 considering only the new candidate arrivals of 2010 against the supply of donors in 2010 (after accounting for 12.8% death while waiting). For the evaluation of the new boundaries, we simplified the current allocation system to the two-layered system. Thus, the match-run was first implemented within the OPO where the liver was recovered and then national level match-run was performed if no candidate was found within the OPO. The simulation was written and ran in MATLAB.

14.3   RESULTS

We first validated the mathematical model by preparing maps and calculating basic statistics. The following sections summarize the outputs of our mathematical analysis in terms of the locations of new transplant centers (3.1) and new OPO boundaries (3.2), respectively.

14.3.1   New Locations of Transplant Centers

Figure 14.5a visualizes the results of the Scenario 1 analysis. The black triangles represent the locations of 123 existing liver transplant centers while the circles represent the existing kidney-only transplant centers selected to become kidney–liver transplant

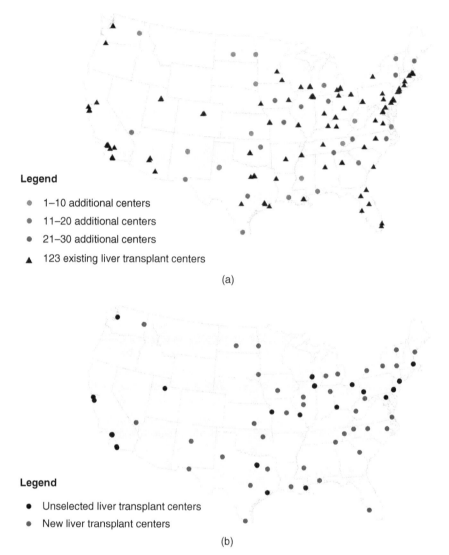

Figure 14.5   (a) Results of Model 1-Scenarios 1-i, 1-ii, and 1-iii: Additional liver transplant centers. (b) Results of Model 1-Scenario 2: New and unselected liver transplant centers.

centers. The shadow of the circles indicates the value of the parameter $p(=10$ (light gray), 20, or 30 (dark gray)) that activated transplant centers that correspond to.

Although Model 1 was run independently to select 10, 20, and 30 locations of additional liver transplant centers, those kidney transplant centers that were selected as the top 10 locations for new liver transplant centers were also part of the top 20 locations. Similarly, the top 20 locations for new liver transplant centers were also part of the top 30 locations. In the figure, the light gray circles correspond to the top

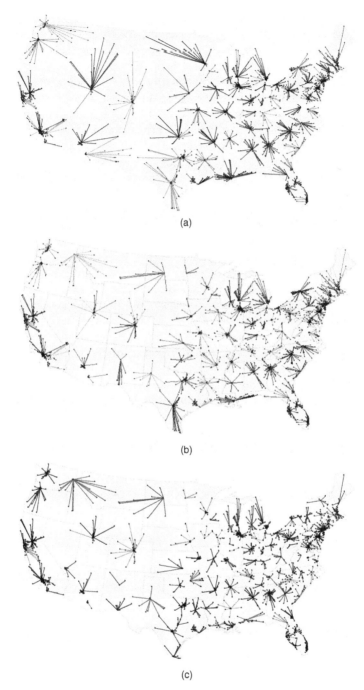

Figure 14.6   (a) Baseline: Donor hospital–transplant center associations. (b) Results of Model 1-Scenario 1-i: Donor hospital–transplant center associations. (c) Results of Model 1-Scenario 2: Donor hospital–transplant center associations.

10 locations for new liver transplant programs (Scenario 1-i), while the gray circles correspond to the second 10 locations (Scenario 1-ii). Finally, the dark gray circles indicate the locations of the third 10 kidney transplant centers selected to become kidney–liver transplant centers (Scenario 1-iii).

The Scenario 2 analysis indicated that, with $p = 123$, replacing 38 existing liver transplant centers with the locations of existing kidney-only transplant centers would optimize the objective function specified in Model 1. Figure 14.5b shows the locations of both unselected existing liver transplant centers (black circles) and kidney-only transplant centers selected to be opened as new liver transplant centers (gray circles). As seen in the Scenario 2 analysis, the locations of the newly activated 38 liver transplant centers included the 30 best locations selected to become kidney–liver transplant centers in Scenario 1-iii.

These results seem to indicate that adding transplant centers in the North Central region (North Dakota, South Dakota, Kansas, and New Mexico) where transplant centers are relatively sparse can most effectively achieve the objective specified in Model 1. In addition, Figure 14.5b indicates that no transplant centers are added in the West Coast region and, moreover, some of the existing liver transplant centers were inactivated in this region as a result of the Scenario 2 analysis.

Figure 14.6a–c exhibit the associations between donor hospitals and liver transplant centers selected in the Scenario 1-i (Fig. 14.6b) and Scenario 2 (Fig. 14.6c) compared to the baseline associations (Fig. 14.6a). The comparisons reveal that graft transfer distance is, on average, shortened by either locating additional liver transplant centers (Scenarios 1-i, 1-ii, 1-iii) or geographically redistributing the locations of existing 123 liver transplant centers (Scenario 2).

Table 14.1 summarizes the average graft transfer distance of 58 OPOs under each scenario. The average distances for all analyzed cases were lower than that of the baseline. In particular, it was found that redistributing the locations of existing liver transplant centers (Scenario 2) was more effective in reducing the average distance than adding 30 additional liver transplant centers, producing more than 40% reduction in average distance compared to the baseline case. The standard deviation, which measures the degree of geographic disparity in terms of graft transfer distance, was also the smallest in Scenario 2.

14.3.2   New OPO Boundaries

Figure 14.7a–d shows the new OPO boundaries for Scenarios 1-i, I-ii, 1-iii, and 2 obtained from Model 2. The gray boundary lines on the maps represent the existing

TABLE 14.1   Average Graft Transfer Distance (km) of 58 OPOs

Scenario	Mean	SD	Min	Max
Baseline	46.39	40.95	0.02	198.81
Scenario 1-i	38.70	34.60	0.00	142.22
Scenario 1-ii	32.10	27.78	0.00	107.37
Scenario 1-iii	28.38	25.93	0.00	128.13
Scenario 2	26.69	20.64	0.70	82.74

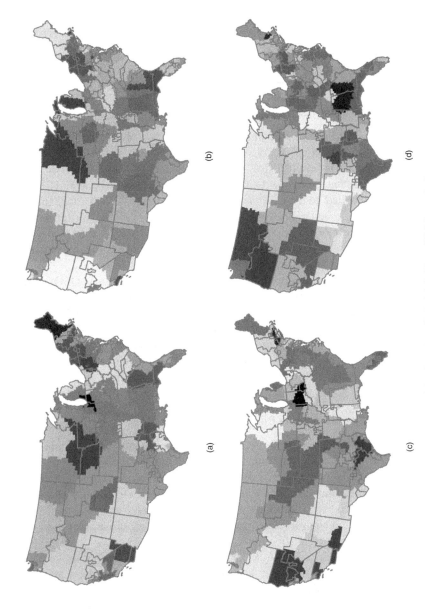

(a)

(b)

(c)

(d)

Figure 14.7 Results of Model 2: New OPO boundaries.

TABLE 14.2   Average Supply/Demand Ratio of 58 OPOs

Scenario	Mean	SD	Min
Baseline	0.64	0.22	0.30
Scenario 1-i	0.62	0.27	0.40
Scenario 1-ii	0.58	0.18	0.40
Scenario 1-iii	0.59	0.18	0.40
Scenario 2	0.63	0.21	0.40

OPO boundaries while the background represents new OPOs obtained as the results of Model 2 in our mathematical model.

The Model 2 analysis revealed that some OPO boundaries were consistent for all scenarios. For instance, the new OPOs covering the states of Maine and Texas remained almost identical to the baseline and across Scenarios 1-i, 1-ii, 1-iii, and 3. In contrast, the OPO boundaries changed significantly in size in the North Central region where the distribution of transplant centers is relatively sparse. Yet, the size of the OPOs in this region is consistently larger than that in other areas as both demand and supply are lower in these relatively low populated areas.

Table 14.2 summarizes the supply/demand ratios of existing and new OPOs. The minimum value of the ratio is 0.4 across the scenarios except the baseline, indicating that the constraint, $\alpha \geq 0.4$, is binding. Comparisons between scenarios indicate that Scenario 2 achieves the highest supply/demand ratio (0.63), although that achieved under Scenario 1-i comes in a close second. Standard deviations are, however, smallest for the baseline and Scenario 1-ii and Scenario 1-iii. The minimum range of the supply/demand ratios across all OPOs is accomplished by Scenario 1-ii.

14.3.3   Evaluation of New OPO Boundaries

The statistics presented earlier reflect neither realistic allocation of livers nor the stochastic nature of liver–candidate matching. As seen in Figures 14.1 and 14.2, the severity level of end-stage liver disease as well as candidate's waiting time and blood type play roles in determining priority level in the queue. Incorporating all factors present in the complex liver allocation system is, however, challenging even if it is possible. The simulation analysis allowed us to evaluate the performance of our new OPO boundaries in a more realistic setting.

To perform the simulation of the donor–recipient matching process in the new OPO boundaries, the following input data were gathered: (i) donor characteristics per county (2003–2009); (ii) recipient characteristics per county (2003–2009); (iii) actual waiting list of candidates as on January 1, 2010; (iv) actual donors in 2010 with their characteristics; (v) actual recipients in 2010 with their characteristics; (vi) the donor hospital transplant center relationship (FIPS and ZIP code information) for all the three OPO boundary scenarios; and (vii) the recipient (demand point) and transplant center accessibility relationship (FIPS and ZIP code information) for all the three OPO boundary scenarios.

Verification of the simulation was done with 30 simulation runs (following standard conventions to ensure statistical significance) for each scenario and, in each run, one full year of donors and candidates was generated along with their characteristics such as FIPS code for location, blood type, MELD score, and so on. The simulation was validated for each scenario using the 2010 actual data on donors and candidates. Since each simulation of the scenarios was run for 1 year, for both verification and validation, the waiting list at the beginning of the year was kept common by using the actual waiting list as on January 1, 2010.

The matching process between the donor and candidate for each simulation followed the layout in Figure 14.1. Death while waiting was excluded (12.8% die while waiting) and patients (candidates) that were too sick for transplant were excluded as well. As mentioned in Section 14.2.2, the liver allocation system under the new OPO boundaries was simplified from the one depicted in Figure 14.1, consisting of two hierarchical layers, that is, OPOs and national.

Figure 14.8 shows the distribution of the (i) number of counties per OPO, (ii) supply per OPO, (iii) demand per OPO, and (iv) supply/demand ratio per OPO for both current (Baseline) and new OPO boundaries (Scenario 2), respectively, using 2010 actual donor and candidate data. By observing the current boundary (Fig. 14.8a) and new boundary (Fig. 14.8b) in Figure 14.8, it can be concluded that there are several OPOs in the current boundary in which the supply (donors) in certain OPOs were disproportionately more than other OPOs when compared to the demand in these OPOs. This is one of the primary causes for geographical disparity. Also as shown in Figure 14.8, with the new boundaries, the number of instances of such disproportionate supply in the OPOs with respect to the demand is much less due to the balancing of the supply/demand ratio in these OPOs.

The statistics on the supply/demand ratio are summarized in Table 14.3. This table shows that supply/demand ratio among OPOs is more uniform with the new OPO boundaries in Scenario 2 compared to the other scenarios. The mean ratio for the new OPO boundaries in Scenario 2 is the closest to 0.57 as described in Section 14.2.2. It can be observed that the standard deviation of the ratios dropped with the new boundaries, in particular for Scenario 2. The mean square error, which is the mean of the squared deviation of errors (error of OPO i = supply/demand ratio of OPO i − mean supply/demand ratio of all OPOs), was the lowest for Scenario 2 compared to the current OPO boundaries (Baseline) and the boundaries under Scenarios 1-i, 1-ii, and 1-iii, confirming that the new OPO boundaries obtained in Scenario 2 have a more uniform supply/demand ratio. From the number of counties per OPO of Figure 14.8, it can be observed that some of the OPOs have a large number of counties, which indicates that these OPOs are large in size. In fact, all OPOs in Scenarios 1-i, 1-ii, 1-iii, and 2 had less than 200 counties while some OPOs in the baseline had more than 200 counties.

Table 14.3 also presents the results of the waiting time for transplant under the current and the new OPO boundaries. The waiting time is for those liver recipients who were chosen by matching process from a pool of candidates that were already

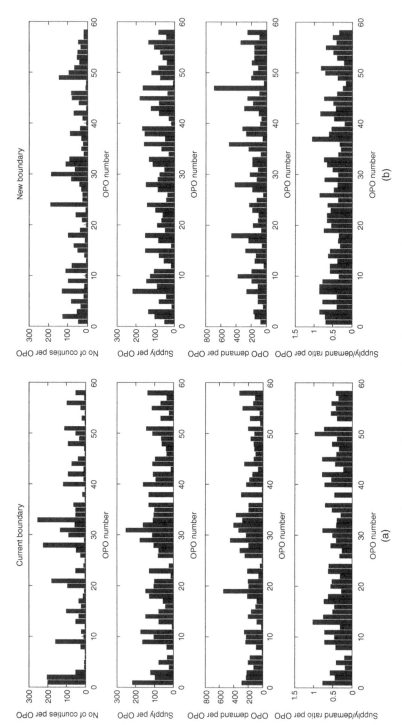

Figure 14.8 Current and new boundary system comparison.

TABLE 14.3 Performance Metrics for 2010 Waiting and New Patient Data: (1) Waiting Time for Transplants and (2) Supply/Demand Ratio

Performance Metric		Scenarios 1-i, 1-ii, and 1-iii			Scenario 2 Optimal Selection
Waiting Time for Transplant (in Days)	Baseline	+10	+20	+30	
Status 1					
Median	1.00	1.00	1.00	1.00	1.00
Mean	1.59	1.55	1.63	1.22	1.23
Standard deviation	2.81	3.09	2.87	1.98	1.62
MELD < 15					
Median	1202.00	1052.50	1269.00	1117.00	1110.50
Mean	1213.82	1218.45	1234.41	1180.59	1172.28
Standard deviation	870.50	885.47	818.60	821.19	857.06
MELD > 15					
Median	279.00	267.00	262.00	255.00	284.00
Mean	498.48	496.06	495.60	495.19	509.42
Standard deviation	567.16	574.28	577.50	579.39	573.06
Geographical disparity 2010					
Supply/demand ratio among 58 OPOs					
Median	0.449	0.449	0.504	0.500	0.515
Mean	0.464	0.457	0.501	0.519	0.534
Standard deviation	0.231	0.221	0.231	0.226	0.201
Maximum	1.013	0.879	1.250	1.250	1.045
Minimum	0.000	0.000	0.000	0.049	0.154
Mean squared error	0.053	0.048	0.053	0.050	0.040

in the queue as on January 1, 2010 and those who arrived in 2010. The waiting time is summarized for each of the severity category (Status 1, MELD < 15, and MELD > 15). It is observed that the mean and the median waiting time for transplants dropped for the new OPOs with most gain coming from Status 1 and MELD<15 categories. In terms of the number of transplants, it is observed that the MELD>15 categories has the highest number of transplants of about 85% of the 5000 donors. In the new OPOs, the mean and median wait time increased for the MELD>15 candidates, although no significant difference was observed in the standard deviation. One can conclude that (i) geographical disparity improved significantly with the new OPO boundaries; and (ii) the overall waiting time for transplants improved for Status 1 and MELD < 15 candidates most significantly while for the MELD < 15 candidates, it increased by about 2%.

Table 14.4 presents waiting time statistics for all three scenarios using only 2010 actual donors and actual candidates. Table 14.3 differs from Table 14.4 because the former uses all data from waiting list as of January 1, 2010 and the new candidates that arrive in 2010, whereas the latter uses only 2010 data. Scenario 2 performed better

TABLE 14.4   Performance Metrics for 2010 Data: Waiting Time for Transplants

Performance Metric		Scenarios 1-i, 1-ii, and 1-iii			Scenario 2 Optimal Selection
Waiting Time for Transplant (in Days)	Baseline	+10	+20	+30	
Status 1					
Median	1.00	1.00	1.00	1.00	1.00
Mean	1.59	1.55	1.63	1.22	1.23
Standard deviation	2.81	3.09	2.87	1.98	1.62
MELD < 15					
Median	108.00	87.00	93.50	126.00	82.00
Mean	116.58	107.41	117.04	129.83	110.31
Standard deviation	88.39	90.66	86.97	95.22	94.80
MELD > 15					
Median	63.00	55.00	63.00	59.00	60.00
Mean	87.46	83.30	86.27	84.28	87.05
Standard deviation	85.01	83.54	81.91	81.15	83.43

TABLE 14.5   Performance Metrics for 2010 Data: Graft Transfer Distance (km) and the Number of Livers Transplanted outside OPO

Performance Metric		Scenarios 1-i, 1-ii, and 1-iii			Scenario 2 Optimal Selection
Graft Transfer Distance	Baseline	+10	+20	+30	
Mean	44.56	37.27	32.17	28.01	26.39
Standard deviation	60.07	48.33	43.06	39.65	38.40
Median	13.94	13.23	12.25	10.26	11.06
Max	448.96	383.90	383.90	383.90	383.90
Min	0	0	0	0	0
No. of livers that were transplanted in an OPO outside the donor OPO among a total of 5076 donated livers in 2010	627	706	784	775	260

than the current situation with the lowest waiting time for MELD < 15 candidates, again confirming that Scenario 2 has a better distribution of transplant centers.

Table 14.5 presents the summary statistics for graft transfer distance measured as the Euclidean distance between the donor hospital that recovered a liver and the transplant center. The actual data on donor and candidate from 2010 were used to obtain the statistics. It can be noticed that the mean values closely match those presented in Table 14.1, which was derived through the location-allocation algorithm.

Scenario 2 achieved the lowest mean of graft transfer distance among all scenarios. The matching process is dynamic and both donors and candidates have their time of arrival in the system. Hence, it is possible that when liver arrived at a donor hospital in a certain OPO, there was no matching candidate in the OPO. In such a case, the liver is given to another eligible candidate outside the donor OPO. This is indicated by the maximum distance that a liver had to travel in Table 14.5. These numbers are much larger than the ideal situation presented in Table 14.1 with no real-time matching process wherein the liver stays in the same OPO. Table 14.5 gives the actual number of livers that would have to be transferred to an OPO outside the donor OPO under each scenario.

14.4   CONCLUSIONS

A mathematical programming approach was used to identify optimal locations of liver transplant centers and to establish liver allocation boundaries that improve transplant outcome and reduce geographic inequity in access to liver transplants. Our discrete-event simulation revealed that the new boundaries are successful in achieving better transplant outcomes and a more equal supply/demand ratio and equitable waiting times across the new OPOs than with the existing boundaries.

As we compared the options between relocating and adding liver transplant centers, we discovered that relocations of the existing liver transplant centers is the most efficient way to remedy geographic inequity in access to transplantation and also to reduce graft transfer distance. It is expected that the administrative and political hurdles would be significant for such relocations, even if they were feasible. While the Center for Medicare & Medicaid Services (CMS) currently acts as the governing authority over transplant centers [24], it does not have the statutory power to direct hospitals and kidney transplant centers to develop liver transplant programs. However, the CMS is currently responsible for monitoring compliance with the set of regulations governing transplant centers and also with the evaluation of transplant centers for recertification (ibid). If a particular liver transplant center falls below a given standard of care, our research may help the agency assess the consequence of closing the transplant program.

Although our results also indicate that altering the existing OPO boundaries can improve the current liver allocation system, their implementation would be equally challenging. However, geographic inequalities in outcome of and access to transplantation are one of the most discussed issues in the transplant community and in transplant research. Furthermore, the allocation systems of various organ types have experienced several modifications in the United States, even after the enactment of the Final Rule in 1998 to achieve further equity among transplant candidates, including the most recent change described in Figure 14.2. If a large body of research reports sufficient merit and if policy makers are convinced, it is possible that boundary restructuring may take place in the future.

From the methodological point of view, our study is one of a handful of studies that investigate optimal boundaries for organ allocation using a mathematical approach. This study extends previous studies [12, 17–20] in several ways. First, the model introduced in this paper is computationally more manageable than those introduced in [17–20]. The previous models are based on a set covering mathematical formulation of which feasible sets are represented by all possible regional configurations that could result from different clusters of OPOs. This approach tends to be computationally very demanding. Second, our mathematical model also analyzed which "kidney-only" transplant centers in the current US system could be activated to improve efficiency and geographic equity of the current liver allocation system. Moreover, our study evaluated the mathematically optimized boundaries dynamically using discrete-event simulation. The approach allowed us to evaluate the performance of the new boundaries in a more realistic setting using additional criteria that are not modeled in the mixed-integer linear programming. For instance, we found that the new OPO boundaries, in general, improve the access to transplants for all categories of disease severity, even though our mathematical model does not differentiate transplant candidates by disease severity.

The usefulness of discrete-event simulation in evaluating organ allocation policies/scenarios is already well established [25–33]. In fact, discrete-event simulation-based software, SAM (Simulated Allocation Model), was developed by the Scientific Registry of Transplant Recipients (SRTR) and has been used to evaluate the impacts of various organ allocation policy alternatives. However, SAM and other existing discrete-event simulation models to analyze organ allocation scenarios are not designed to deal with geography explicitly, thereby limiting their ability to simulate the impacts of boundary changes in detail. This study developed a simulation model that simulates various allocation boundary scenarios in a more direct manner.

Several directions for future research are apparent. Given the current environment that limits the redistribution of liver transplant centers and boundary changes, investigation and evaluation of suboptimal locations of liver transplant centers and OPO boundaries that incur minimum changes to the existing system would be beneficial. Such attempts may be pursued by adding relevant constraints to our mathematical model. Second, the parameters such as d_{max}, f_{max}, α, and p were set rather arbitrarily in this study. Sensitivities of the mathematical model to the values of these parameters need to be tested. Third, this study simplified the current allocation system by looking at only the two allocation layers, that is, OPO and national levels. One of our future studies could explore the possibility to adapt our approach to solve the problem of clustering OPO into UNOS regions to take into account the trade-off between intraregional efficiency and equity in the allocation process as seen in Demirci et al. [17] and Kong et al. [18]. Another natural extension would be to incorporate MELD categories in our optimization modeling as Gentry et al. explored in her model [20]. Another exploratory study may be to perform our mathematical analysis for each MELD category of patients to see if the optimal boundaries vary significantly for each MELD category of patients. Lastly, given that the positive outcomes for the MELD > 15 category of patients are relatively small compared to those seen among Status 1 and MELD < 15 patients, we would like to extend our modeling approach to take into account a measure of the posttransplant outcome resulting from the allocation process [34].

Despite the list of future tasks calling for further investigation, we believe that our results clearly indicate that the current allocation system can be improved through changes to the existing OPO boundaries and the locations of the existing liver transplant centers. Liver transplantation faces the chronic scarcity of organs and lack of alternative treatments, such as the dialysis available to the end-stage renal disease patients. Giving serious consideration to any possible changes that could achieve further equity among transplant candidates and better transplant outcomes would be prudent.

ACKNOWLEDGMENT

This work was partially supported by a R21 grant (DK088368-01) of the National Institutes of Health. The authors alone are responsible for the interpretations of the results.

REFERENCES

[1] Institute of Medicine Committee on Organ Procurement and Transplantation Policy. *Organ Procurement and Transplantation: Assessing Current Policies and the Potential Impact of the DHHS Final Rule.* Washington, DC: National Academic Press; 1999.

[2] Ashby VB, Kalbfleisch JD, Wolfe RA, Lind MJ, Port FK, Leichtman AB. Geographic variability in access to primary kidney transplantation in the United States, 1996–2005. Am J Transpl 2007;7(2):1412–1423.

[3] Barshes NR, Becker NS, Washburn WK, Halff GA, Aloia TA, Goss JA. Geographic disparities in deceased donor liver transplantation within a single UNOS region. Liver Transpl 2007;13:747–751.

[4] Brown KA, Moonka D. Liver transplantation. Curr Opin Gastroenterol 2004;20(3):264–269.

[5] Brown RS, Lake JR. The survival impact of liver transplantation in the MELD era and the future of organ allocation and distribution. Am J Transpl 2005;5(2):203–204.

[6] Ellison MD, Edwards LB, Edwards EB, et al. Geographic differences in access to transplantation in the United States. Transplantation 2003;76(9):1389–1394.

[7] Morris P, Monaco AP, et al. Geographic disparities in access to organ transplantation in France, United States, United Kingdom, Spain and Australia. Transpl Forum 2003;76:1383–1406.

[8] Roberts JP, Dykstra DM, Goodrich NP, Rush SH, Merion RM, Port FK. Geographic differences in event rates by model for end-stage liver disease score. Am J Transpl 2006;6:2470–2475.

[9] Tonelli M, Kalbfleisch JD, Manns B, Culleton B, et al. Residence location and likelihood of kidney transplantation. CMAJ 2006;175(5):478–482.

[10] Yeh H, Smoot E, Schoenfeld DA, Markmann JF. Geographic inequity in access to livers for transplantation. Transplantation 2011;91(4):479–486.

[11] http://www.gao.gov/special.pubs/organ/chapter6.pdf Accessed 2014 April 30

[12] Bruni ME, Conforti D, Sicilia N, Trotta S. A new organ transplantation location-allocation policy: A case study of Italy. Health Care Manage Sci 2006; 9:125–142.

[13] Miller CE, Tucker AW, Zemlin RA. Integer programming formulation of traveling salesman problems. J ACM 1960;7(4):326–329.

[14] Desrochers M, Laporte G. Improvements and extensions to the Miller-Tucker-Zemlin subtour elimination constraints. Oper Res Lett 1991;10:27–36.

[15] Gouveia L. Using the Miller-Tucker-Zemlin constraints to formulate a minimal spanning tree with Hop constraints. Comput Oper Res 1995;22(9):959–970.

[16] Carrabs F, Cerulli R, Gaudioso M, Gentili M. Lower and upper bounds for the spanning tree with minimum branch vertices. Comput Optim Appl 2013;56(2):405–438 ISSN.

[17] Demirci MC, Schaefer AJ, Romeijn HE, Robert MS. An exact method for balancing efficiency and equity in the liver allocation hierarchy. INFORMS J Comput Spring 2012;24(2):260–275.

[18] Kong N, Schaefer AJ, Hunsaker B, Roberts MS. Maximizing the efficiency of the US liver allocation system through region design. Manage Sci 2010;56(12):2111–2122.

[19] Stahl JE, Kong N, Shechter SM, Schaefer AJ, Roberts MS. A methodological framework for optimally reorganizing liver transplant regions. Med Decis Making 2005;25(1):35–46.

[20] Gentry SE, Massie AB, Cheek SW, Lentine KL, Chow EH, Wickliffe CE, Dzebashvili N, Salvalaggio PR, Schnitzler MA, Axelrod DA, Segev DL. Addressing geographic disparities in liver transplantation through redistricting. Am J Transpl 2013;13:2052–2058.

[21] http://resources.arcgis.com/gallery/file/Geoprocessing-Model-and-Script-Tool-Gallery /details?entryID=1C1927D6-1422-2418-8809-3BA43CBD435C Accessed 2014 April 30

[22] Stahl J, Kreke J, Malek F, Schaefer A, Vacanti J. Consequences of cold-ischemia time on primary nonfunction and patient and graft survival in liver transplantation: a meta-analysis. PLoS One 2008;3(6):2468.

[23] Cassuto J, Patel S, Tsoulfas G, Orloff M, Abt P. The cumulative effects of cold ischemic time and older donor age on liver graft survival. J Surg Res 2008;148(1):38–44.

[24] http://www.cms.gov/Regulations-and-Guidance/Guidance/Transmittals/downloads/ R1341CP.pdf Accessed 2014 April 30

[25] Davies R, Rodrick P. Planning resources for renal services throughout UK using simulation. Eur J Oper Res 1998;105(2):285–295.

[26] Feng WX, Kong N, Wan H. A simulation study of cadaveric liver allocation with a single-score ranking formula. J Simul 2013;7:109–125.

[27] Levine GN, McCullough KP, Rodgers AM, Dickinson DM, Ashby VB, Schaubel DE. Analytical methods and database design: Implications for transplant researchers. Am J Transpl 2006;6(2):1228–1242.

[28] Perkins JD, Holldorsen JB, Bakthavatsalam R, Oren KF, Carithers RL Jr, Rayes JD. Should liver transplantation in patients with model for end-stage liver disease scores ≤ 14 be avoided? A decision analysis approach. Liver Transpl 2009;15:242–254.

[29] Pritsker AAB, Martin DL, Reust JS, Wagner MA, Daily OP, Harper AM, Edwards EB, Bennett LE, Wilson JR, Kuhl ME, Roberts JP, Allen MD, Burdick JP. Organ transplantation policy evaluation. In: Proceedings of the 27th Winter Simulation Conference, Arlington, VA. 1341–1323; (1995)

[30] Ratcliffe J, Young T, Buxton M, Eldabi T, Paul R, Burroughs A, Papatheodoridis G, Rolles K. A simulation modeling approach to evaluating alternative policies for the management of the waiting list for liver transplantation. Health Care Manage Sci 2001;4(2):117–124.

[31] Shechter SM, Bryce CL, Alagoz O, Kreke JE, Stahl JE, Schaefer AJ, et al. A clinically based discrete-event simulation of end-stage liver disease and the organ allocation process. Med Decis Making 2005;25(2):199–209.

[32] Thompson D, Waisansen L. Simulating the allocation of organs and transplantation. Health Care Manage Sci 2004;7:331–338.

[33] Zenios SA, Wein LM, Chertow GM. Evidence-based organ allocation. Am J Med 1999;107(1):52–61.

[34] Teng Y, Kong N. An efficient approximation for refining organ geographic distribution in the U.S. liver transplantation and allocation system. Int J Oper Res 2010;7(4):51–65.

15

PREDICTIVE ANALYTICS IN 30-DAY HOSPITAL READMISSIONS FOR HEART FAILURE PATIENTS

SI-CHI CHIN, RUI LIU, AND SENJUTI B. ROY

Institute of Technology, University of Washington Tacoma, Tacoma, WA, USA

Hospitalizations account for more than 30% of the 2 trillion annual cost of health care in the United States. Around 20% of all hospital admissions occur within 30 days of a previous discharge, and 3 out of 20 readmissions are considered preventable. Identifying patients at the higher risk of readmission can guide quality patient care and efficient resource utilization. The task of readmission prediction requires understanding the interplay between multitude of complex factors that cause readmission and appropriate adaptation of advanced analytical models to effectively predict readmissions; added to the complexity is the existence of large volume of noisy data with significant missing values. In this work, we present the application of data mining techniques in predicting 30-day hospital readmission risk for heart failure patients. We describe our proposed solutions end-to-end that involve understanding and exploring complex real-world data, applying and appropriately adapting the state-of-the-art predictive modeling techniques. Moreover, we design principled solutions by learning the structure and parameters of a hierarchical Bayesian network from the available patient data and designing rules to recommend personalized interventions. Finally, we demonstrate the iterative process of using predictive analytics in predicting and managing risk of readmission.

Healthcare Analytics: From Data to Knowledge to Healthcare Improvement, First Edition.
Edited by Hui Yang and Eva K. Lee.

15.1 INTRODUCTION

Heart failure (HF) afflicts about 5.1 million people in the United States, with a median risk-standardized readmission rate of 24.5% [1]. Early readmission is a profound indicator of the quality of care provided by the hospital. The Center for Medicare & Medicaid Services (CMS) recently began reducing payments to hospitals with excess readmissions, effective for discharges beginning on October 1 2012 [2]. The estimated cost of unplanned readmissions was 17 billion annually [3], and more than 27% of them were considered avoidable [4]. Readmission is common and costly. Many hospitals and health care systems are focusing on improving performance and patient outcomes in cardiovascular services. Particular emphases are on how the management of HF can prevent readmissions, decrease the cost per case, and improve the quality and satisfaction for this particular patient population.

Readmission can result from a variety of reasons, including early discharge of patients, improper discharge planning, and poor care transitions. Prior studies have shown that several interventions can effectively reduce the rate of readmission [5-7]. Many interventions are costly and therefore resources are limited. To deliver efficient care, the highest intensity interventions should be targeted to patients who are most likely to benefit. Therefore, identifying patients who have greater risk of readmission can guide implementation of appropriate interventions to prevent these readmissions. Advanced predictive analytics will make progress in the field by bringing two objectives – readmission reduction and intervention recommendations – together into one integrated model.

Suggesting appropriate interventions is closely associated with a patient's current phase. For example, the post-discharge interventions may only be limited to appropriate follow-ups or patient education, while physicians could suggest different procedures or surgery, if the intervention is being administered during her hospital stay. Patient's clinical conditions can progress rapidly. Care providers often need to constantly reexamine patient's clinical conditions and adjust their treatment and intervention strategies. Predictive analytics can aid to this iterative process, providing care providers timely feedback on patient's clinical risk to necessitate appropriate interventions. The development of predictive modeling should also allow the flexibility to accommodate varying availability of clinical information at different stages of care.

This chapter presents solutions to two tasks: (i) predicting the 30-day readmission risk score (or percentage) of heart failure patients at two different stages of care – pre-discharge and post-discharge; (ii) incorporating predictive analytics into clinical care cycle to recommend effective personalized intervention strategies.

Existing research has studied different clinical risk prediction problems in silos. Our work is one of the first efforts to study the risk prediction and management problem in conjunction, providing solutions to facilitate real-time risk prediction and effective intervention recommendations at any point of care.

The rest of the chapter is organized as follows. Section 15.2 presents the process of predicting risk of 30-day hospital readmissions. Our experiment results demonstrate the effectiveness of predicting risk before discharge and shortly after discharge. Section 15.3 describes the integration of risk prediction and intervention recommendations. We construct Bayesian networks to estimate risk of readmission and generate rules of recommendations. Section 15.4 surveys related prior studies of the problem. Section 15.5 summarizes our contributions and outlines future directions.

15.2 ANALYTICS IN PREDICTION HOSPITAL READMISSION RISK

15.2.1 The Overall Prediction Pipeline

Figure 15.1 illustrates the overall pipeline for predicting risk of readmission. The framework involves five major stages: (i) problem definition; (ii) data exploration; (iii) data preprocessing; (iv) predictive modeling; and (v) evaluation. At the first two stages, it requires significant amount of effort to build an interdisciplinary research team to understand the problem thoroughly and explore the data marts as described in our prior work [8]. In this section, we describe the details of data preprocessing (Section 15.2.2), the selected predictive models (Section 15.2.3), and the validation results of our experiments (Section 15.2.4).

15.2.2 Data Preprocessing

Feature Selection In addition to the inputs provided by domain experts (e.g., clinicians), we used Pearson's Chi-square test [9] to perform feature selection. Chi-square is the sum of the squared difference between observed (O) and the expected (E) data divided by the expected data in all possible categories (i.e., the class label Y :

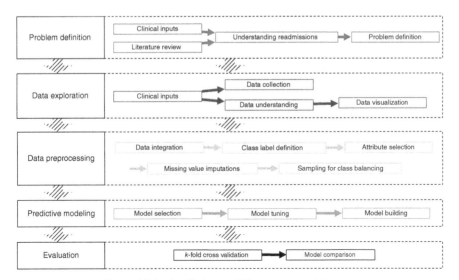

Figure 15.1 Predictive modeling system architecture.

Readmitted within 30 Days ($= 1$) vs. Not Readmitted within 30 Days ($= 0$)). The value of the test statistic is computed as

$$\chi^2 = \sum_{i=1}^{n} \frac{(O_i - E_i)^2}{E_i}$$

where χ^2 is Pearson's cumulative test statistic; O_i is an observed frequency; E_i is an expected frequency; n is the number of cells in the table. We evaluated all our attributes individually with respect to the classes. Numeric features were discretized into intervals. The p-value and the χ^2 revealed whether a feature was informative for predictive modeling.

Missing Value Imputation We used a simple but effective clustering-based technique for imputing missing values. The data set (including instances with missing values) is first divided into a set of clusters using the K-modes clustering method. Then each instance with missing values is assigned to a cluster that is most similar to it. Finally, missing values of an instance are patched up with the plausible values generated from its respective cluster.

Reducing Class Imbalance Once the data are integrated, it is observed that the labeled data set is highly skewed, that is, the number of instances with *No Readmission* label significantly outnumbers the number of instances with class label *Readmission*. To circumvent that problem, we used both oversampling and undersampling. Oversampling works by re-sampling the rare class records [9], while undersampling decreases the number of records belonging to the majority class by randomly eliminating tuples.

15.2.3   Predictive Models

We explore the complex interplay among the magnitude of factors and how they contribute to the hospital readmission for HF patients next and design supervised learning algorithms from the available patient data.

15.2.3.1   Naive Bayesian Classifier Bayesian classifier is a statistical classifier that predicts the class membership probability, in other words, the probability of a given tuple belonging to a particular class. This classifier assumes that the effect of one attribute value on a given class is independent of the values of the other attributes. This assumption is called as *class-conditional independence*, which greatly simplifies the learning process. The basic principle of this classifier is the *Bayes theorem* [9]. Naive Bayesian classification is called "naive" because it assumes class-conditional independence. That is, the effect of an attribute value on a given class is independent of the values of the other attributes. This assumption is made to reduce computational costs, and hence is considered "naive."

Let the number of classes be m, $C_1, C_2, \ldots, C_m$ and $\mathbf{X} = (x_1, x_2, \ldots, x_n)$ be the n dimensional attribute vector for which the prediction has to be done. The naive

Bayesian classifier predicts that $\mathbf{X}$ belongs to the class having the highest posterior probability. In other words, the classifier predicts that the tuple $\mathbf{X}$ belongs to the class C_i only if the below condition is satisfied.

$$P(C_i|\mathbf{X}) > P(C_j|\mathbf{X}) \ for \ 1 <= j <= m, j \neq i$$

The class C_i for which $P(C_i|\mathbf{X})$ is maximized is called the *maximum posteriori hypothesis*. From Bayes theorem:

$$P(C_i|\mathbf{X}) = \frac{P(\mathbf{X}|C_i)P(C_i)}{P(\mathbf{X})} \tag{15.1}$$

Since $P(\mathbf{X})$ is identical for all the classes, so it can be ignored, and so only $P((X)|C_i)P(C_i)$ needs to be maximized. For high-dimensional data, the estimation of $P((X)|C_i)$ from the given set of training tuples is computationally expensive. To make the computation easy, the naive assumption of class-conditional independence is made, which presumes that the attribute values are conditionally independent of one another. Hence,

$$P(\mathbf{X}|C_i) = \prod_{k=1}^{n} P(x_k|C_i) \tag{15.2}$$

With this assumption, naive Bayes classifier simplifies the learning process. In various domains, the performance of naive Bayes classifier is comparable to other sophisticated classifiers such as decision tree and neural network classifiers.

15.2.3.2 Support Vector Machine

SVM searches for a hyperplane that has the maximum distance to the closest points in the training set termed as *support vectors*. This plane is also called *maximum marginal hyperplane* (MMH), which gives the maximum separation between the classes. Let the data set D consists of a set of points $\mathbf{X_i}$ where $i = 1, 2, \ldots, N$, and each point is associated with two class identified by label $y_i \in \{+1, -1\}$. If we consider that the data belonging to two classes are linearly separable, then the separating hyperplane (MMH) can be written as

$$\mathbf{W} \cdot X + b = 0 \tag{15.3}$$

where $\mathbf{W}$ is the weight vector, $\mathbf{W} = w_1, w_2, \ldots, w_n$, n is the number of attributes, and b is a scalar. The MMH can be rewritten as the decision boundary

$$d(\mathbf{X^T}) = \sum_{i=1}^{l} y_i \alpha_i \mathbf{X_i} \mathbf{X^T} + b_0 \tag{15.4}$$

where y_i is the class label of the support vector $\mathbf{X_i}$, $\mathbf{X^T}$ is the test tuple, α_i and b_0 are numeric parameters determined by solving the quadratic optimization problem, and l is the number of support vectors. If the data are not linearly separable, then each input point $\mathbf{X}$ is mapped to another point $\mathbf{Z} = \phi(\mathbf{X})$ of a higher dimensional space. The decision hyperplane in the new space is represented as

$$d(\mathbf{Z}) = \mathbf{W}.Z + b \tag{15.5}$$

15.2.3.3 Adaboost AdaBoost is an algorithm for constructing a "strong" classifier as a linear combination of multiple simple "weak" classifiers. In particular, it makes use of multiple (T) simple-weighted classifiers, each forced to learn a different aspect of the data, to generate a final, comprehensive classifier, which outperforms in terms of mis-classification error rate of any individual classifier with high probability. In particular, if $h_t(x), s.t.t \in T$ is the tth weak classifier, and $H(x)$ is the final strong classifier, then

$$f(X) = \Sigma_{t=1}^{T} \alpha_t h_t(X)$$

$$H(X) = \text{sign}(f(X))$$

In our settings, we used discrete AdaBoost with 2 classes ($\{-1, 1\}$) for a given data set D consisting of a set of points $\mathbf{X_i}$ where $i = 1, 2, \dots, N$. Imagine the class label for each $\mathbf{X_i}$ is Y_i (is either 1 or -1). Initially, each training sample is initialized with uniform weights, that is, $w(i) = 1/N$.

The algorithm runs in T iteration, where in each iteration, it updates the weight function of each training sample and the algorithm stops, when a particular value of the error function is satisfied (e.g., stop when the error is equal or more than 50%, that is, $\varepsilon_t \geq 0.5$). At each iteration t, a weak learner is selected and assigned a coefficient α_t such that the sum training error E_t of the resulting t-stage boost classifier is minimized. At each iteration t of the training process, a weight is assigned to each sample $\mathbf{X_i}$ in the training set equal to the current error $E(F_{t-1}(\mathbf{X_i}))$. Formally, for the tth classifier, we find the weak learner classifier $h_t = \mathcal{X} \rightarrow \{-1, 1\}$ that minimizes the error ε_t with respect to the distribution. Therefore,

$$h_t = \text{argmin}_{\{h_j \in H\}} \varepsilon_j$$

$$\varepsilon_j = \Sigma_{i=1..N} w_t(i)[Y_i \neq h_j \mathbf{X_i}]$$

α_t is computed using the logarithmic function $\alpha_t = 1/2 ln \frac{1-\varepsilon_t}{1+\varepsilon_t}$. Since the error function is exponential, the weight of the ith point is updated as follows:

$$w_{t+1}(i) = w_t(i) e^{-\alpha_t Y_i h_t(X_i)}$$

This way, the output of T weak learners (classifiers) is combined to represent the final output of the boosted classifier.

15.2.4 Experiment and Evaluation

15.2.4.1 Data: Clinical Patient Data This study included patients who have primary diagnosis of heart failure at MultiCare Health Systems (MHS)[1]. Patients who died while in the hospital ($n = 18$) and patients who were discharged less than 30 days ($n = 52$) were excluded from this analysis. The final cohort included 1919 encounters with 1020 unique patients admitted between May 22 2010 and March 07 2014.

---

[1]http://www.multicare.org/.?

TABLE 15.1   Attribute Summary of Heart Failure Cohort

Set	Category	Description
1	Demographics	4 Attributes
2	Admission Abstract	3 Attributes
3	Medical Test	8 Attributes
4	Vital Sign	7 Attributes
5	Diagnosis	17 Attributes
6	Comorbidity	33 Attributes
7	Discharge Abstract	8 Attributes

Patient clinical data were abstracted from MHS hospital records as the attributes for predictive modeling. These attributes were organized into seven sets: (i) Demographics; (ii) Admission Abstract; (iii) Medical Test; (iv) Vital Sign; (v) Diagnosis; (vi) Comorbidity; (vii) Discharge Abstract, as shown in Table 15.1. All the attributes were either suggested by clinicians or selected based on Chi-square test.

Assessing the effect of different types of attributes is critical for clinical understanding of the problem. We therefore designed the experiments to observe the incremental effect of each attribute set based on their characteristics. We conducted seven experiments with different sets of attributes. For each experiment, we add one more set of attributes for the modeling. For example, the first experiment used only attributes from Set 1 and the second experiment used attributes from Sets 1 and 2. Attributes in Set 1 to Set 5 are used in pre-discharge models. However, because Comorbidity and Discharge Abstract are only available after a patient was discharged, we used attributes in Set 6 and Set 7 only in post-discharge models. For each experiment setting, we trained three predictive models – Naive Bayes, SVM, and AdaBoost, as described in Section 15.2.3.

Analyses and predictive modeling were performed using R^2 statistical tool. We performed 10 times 10-fold cross-validation to validate the results. Our evaluation measurements are Area Under ROC curve (AUC), Accuracy (ACC), Precision (PRE), and Recall (RCL).

15.2.4.2   Results   and   Discussions   Experiment   results   are   summarized   in Figure 15.2 and Table 15.2. Prediction results have low variance consistently across different models and across the evaluation metrics. The only exception is the precision for Naive Bayes when the attribute number is limited as shown in Figure 15.2c. Among the three selected models, AdaBoost outperforms SVM and Naive Bayes for most experiment settings. AdaBoost is also shown to be more robust as we introduced more attribute sets, and the data become more noisy. However, SVM has the highest AUC when number of attributes is limited to only Demographics and Admission Abstract. It is observed that the prediction quality decreases for SVM and Naive Bayes when Medical Test and Vital Sign are included. It indicates that

<hr>

[2]http://www.r-project.org/.

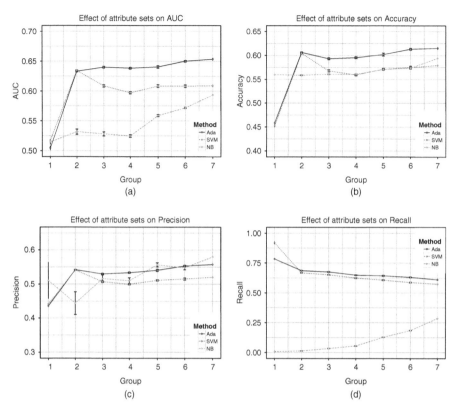

Figure 15.2 Effects of attribute sets to prediction results. (a) AUC, (b) accuracy, (c) precision, and (d) recall.

TABLE 15.2   Prediction Results for Pre-discharge and Post-discharge Modeling

Metric	Model	Pre-discharge					Post-discharge	
		1	1-2	1-3	1-4	1-5	1-6	1-7
AUC	Ada	0.5045	0.6333	0.6399[a]	0.6384[a]	0.6405[a]	0.6501[a]	0.6535[a]
	SVM	0.5172	0.6344	0.6087	0.5972	0.6085	0.6084	0.6090
	NB	0.5145	0.5318	0.5282	0.5246	0.5588	0.5717	0.5935
ACC	Ada	0.4586	0.6064	0.5932[a]	0.5955[a]	0.6020[a]	0.6132[a]	0.6151[a]
	SVM	0.4525	0.6045	0.5677	0.5595	0.5712	0.5749	0.5792
	NB	0.5597	0.5586	0.5607	0.5605	0.5710	0.5738	0.5942
PRC	Ada	0.4361	0.5419	0.5300	0.5335[a]	0.5404	0.5533	0.5576
	SVM	0.4415	0.5413	0.5072	0.4998	0.5111	0.5153	0.5201
	NB	0.5106	0.4438	0.5163	0.5099	0.5565[a]	0.5479	0.5796
RCL	Ada	0.7832	0.6863	0.6749[a]	0.6488[a]	0.6436[a]	0.6308[a]	0.6099[a]
	SVM	0.9179[a]	0.6676	0.6516	0.6243	0.6069	0.5877	0.5737
	NB	0.0072	0.0128	0.0333	0.0549	0.1273	0.1844	0.2857

[a]The model is significantly higher than the other two models.

SVM and Naive Bayes are more sensitive to the noisy introduced by the new added attribute sets.

15.3 ANALYTICS IN RECOMMENDING INTERVENTION STRATEGIES

In this work, we propose a framework by formalizing the intervention recommendation as a structure learning problem [10, 11], where the objective is to *learn the structure of a hierarchical Bayesian network* involving a multitude of factors and how they *contribute* to 30-day readmission risk. Each factor (i.e., socio-demographic, diagnoses, procedures, readmission) in our settings contributes to a node in the network, and the *causal relationship* between two nodes is represented as a weighted (weight represents probability) directed edge, giving rise to a Directed Acyclic Graph (DAG). A sample structure may look like the one presented in Figure 15.4 for the simple case described in Example 15.1 in Section 15.3.2.1.

15.3.1 The Overall Intervention Pipeline

Figure 15.3 illustrates the overall pipeline for intervention recommendations. The framework involves four major stages: (i) Bayesian network construction (Section 15.3.2); (ii) Intervention rules generation (Section 15.3.3); (iii) Intervention rules recommendations (Section 15.3.4); (iv) Evaluations (Section 15.3.5.2).

The underpinning of our proposed framework relies on the following three steps: (i) Since we deal with high-dimensional data involving several hundreds of factors, we first attempt to *learn the structure of the network automatically* from the data itself. For structure learning, we propose several solutions: we use Constraint-Based

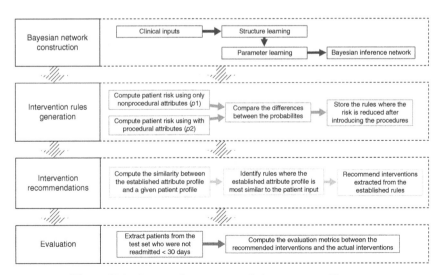

Figure 15.3 Intervention recommendation system architecture.

Bayesian Network Learning Algorithm [12, 13] that uses conditional independence test to detect the Markov Blanket [14] among the factors which in turn induces the network structure. We also apply *Score-Based Learning Algorithm* [14] that uses *Hill-climbing-based greedy search* on the space of the directed graphs for the problem. Finally, we learn the structure using a hybrid algorithm [11], which combines both constraint-based and score-based approaches. (ii) Once the structure is defined, we use parameter learning [15, 16] techniques to compute the probability of the directed edges. (iii) Finally, we propose novel algorithm to generate a set of rules as personalized intervention recommendations.

Our proposed approach is generic to include/exclude additional layers or factors, and the design of the network would satisfy any constraint that the domain expert specifies. Finally, the novelty of the solution lies in nontrivially adapting the Bayesian network to a recommendation task, which is traditionally used for inference learning. We describe our running example next, which will be used throughout the paper.

Example 15.1 Without loss of generality, let us consider a simple setting of the problem, which consists of two socio-demographic factors such as age, gender; three diagnoses (Congestive Heart Failure (CHF) DX4280, Acute Respiratory Failure (ARF) DX51881, Pneumonia (PN) DX486); and three procedures (Continuous Invasive Mechanical Ventilation < 96 h PR9671, Venous Cath NEC PR3893, Packed Cell Transfusion PR9904).[3] These eight factors are predictors and we wish to learn how they relate to the 30-day heart failure readmission problem. The diagnoses, procedures, and the gender are binary variables (factors), whereas age is a continuous variable that has been discretized appropriately. Finally, the dependent variable Readmission is a binary variable, where "Readmission=0" stands for no-30-day readmission, and "Readmission=1" otherwise. For the simplicity of exposition, we consider that only the procedures are actionable. Therefore, our task is to recommend procedures to minimize readmission risk. Furthermore, assume that the domain experts have specified a set of constraints, as follows: (i) there exists causal relationship between the three diagnoses and the two socio-demographic factors; but the two demographic factors are themselves independent; (ii) the diagnoses may themselves be causally related; (iii) there exists causal relationship between the three diagnoses and the three procedures; (iv) there may be causal relationship between the procedures themselves; (v) procedures have causal relationship with readmission; (vi) no edge can exist between two nodes that are not in consecutive layers.

15.3.2 Bayesian Network Construction

15.3.2.1 Structure Learning **Bayesian Network:** A Bayesian network is a graphical model that encodes probabilistic relationships among variables of interest. When used in conjunction with statistical techniques, the graphical model has

---

[3]Each diagnoses procedure has a unique code written after its name, and these procedures are applicable during hospitalization.

several advantages to offer. (1) As the model encodes dependencies among all variables, it readily handles situations where some data entries are missing. (2) A Bayesian network can be used to learn causal relationships, and hence can be used to gain understanding about a problem domain and to predict the consequences of intervention. (3) Because the model has both causal and probabilistic connotations, it is an ideal representation for combining prior knowledge and data. (4) Bayesian statistical methods in conjunction with Bayesian networks offer an efficient and principled approach for avoiding the overfitting. In our work, we leverage this model to understand the causal relationship among different factors (diagnosis, procedures, socio-demographic factors) and how that contribute to readmission risk. Furthermore, we combine the data-based evidence with the prior knowledge to learn the model.

Relevant Notations: Relevant notations and their interpretations are represented in Table 15.3. Bayesian network [10, 11] is a graphical representation of a probability distribution over a set of variables or factors $\mathcal{U} = \{X_1, X_2, \dots, X_n\}$. It consists of two parts:

- The directed network structure as a DAG. Given Example 15.1, a possible structure may look akin to the one described in Figure 15.4.
- A set of probability distribution (i.e., pdf), one on each node or variable, conditional on each value combination of its parents. Altogether with the graph structure, they are sufficient to represent the joint probability distribution of the domain. Any probability distribution could be used to compute the pdf on

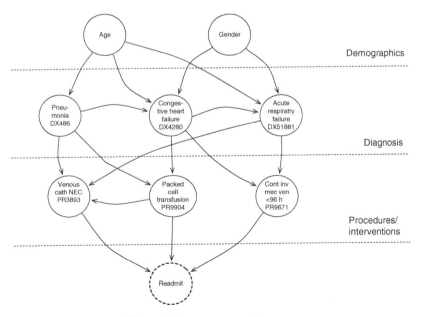

Figure 15.4 System Architecture.

TABLE 15.3   Notations and Interpretations

Notation	Interpretation
D	The data set
N	Number of points in the data set, i.e., $-D-$
X, Y, Z	Three variables
x, y, z	Values of X, Y, Z, respectively
P_a^X	A set of nodes that are parent of X
$\mathcal{X}$	The entire set of predictor variables, or attributes, or factors

each node. More concretely, in our case, the variables are discrete (numeric ones are appropriately discretized) and their respective pdf's are represented using multinomial distributions.

$$\Pr(X_1, X_2, \ldots, X_n) = \prod_{i=1}^{i=n} \Pr(X_i | P_a^{X_i}) \tag{15.6}$$

We now describe our solutions – first for structure learning, then model fitting, and finally recommendation generation.

Our structure learning solution relies upon the *Causal Sufficiency Assumption* and the *Markov Assumption* [17]. The former assumption represents that there does not exist any latent variables (or nodes) that are parent of one or more observed variables, whereas the latter represents that any node in the network is independent of all its non-descendent nodes.

We use *Constraint-Based, Score-Based, and Hybrid* methods to learn the structure of the network. We describe them briefly one by one next.

Constraint-Based Methods.   These methods make use of the conditional independence tests using statistical tests on the data set. We use a computationally efficient algorithm, *Grow and Shrink* [18], which relies on detecting the *Markov blanket* [14] of the variables to induce the network structure. Markov blanket for a node X in a Bayesian network is the set of nodes composed of X's parents, its children, and its children's other parents. It operates by identifying the local neighborhood of each variable in the Bayesian network as a preprocessing step in order to facilitate the recovery of the exact structure around each variable in subsequent steps.

Score-Based Methods.   Score-based method creates several Bayesian network and assigns a score to each candidate of them, typically one that measures how well that Bayesian network describes the data set D. Assuming a structure $\mathcal{R}$, its score is

$$\text{Score}(\mathcal{R}, D) = \Pr(\mathcal{R} | D) = \frac{\Pr(D | \mathcal{R}) \times \Pr(\mathcal{R})}{\Pr(D)}$$

A score-based algorithm attempts to maximize this posterior probability.

As score-based algorithms attempt to optimize this score, returning the structure $\mathcal{R}$ that maximizes it is prohibitively expensive. Since the search space of all possible structures is exponential to the number of variables n, this poses tremendous computational challenges. In our solution, we apply Hill-climbing-based greedy heuristics and use Bayesian information criterion (BIC) [19] to approximate $\Pr(\mathcal{R}|D)$.

Hybrid Approach. We finally apply a hybrid approach to learn the network structure, namely the *max–min Hill-climbing algorithm* [11], which combines ideas from both the score-based approach and constraint-based approach. It first reconstructs the skeleton of a Bayesian network and then performs a Bayesian-scoring greedy Hill-climbing search to orient the edges. The latter phase does not provide any theoretical guarantees. However, this algorithm appears effective in many high-dimensional real-world problems (such as ours) and tackles the limitations posed by the other algorithms.

15.3.2.2 Parameter Learning
After the structure of the network is constructed, the next step is to learn the parameters of the network, given the structure. Using Example 15.1, this step is analogous to creating pdf's to each node in the constructed network to create the conditional probability table at each node. As an example, using the sample network of Figure 15.4, this step will compute all the following probabilities at node PR 9671.

$$\Pr(\text{PR } 9671 = \text{i} \text{— DX } 4280 = 0 \ \& \ \text{DX } 51881 = 0)$$

$$\Pr(\text{PR } 9671 = \text{i} \text{— DX } 4280 = 0 \ \& \ \text{DX } 51881 = 1)$$

$$\Pr(\text{PR } 9671 = \text{i} \text{— DX } 4280 = 1 \ \& \ \text{DX } 51881 = 0)$$

$$\Pr(\text{PR } 9671 = \text{i} \text{— DX } 4280 = 1 \ \& \ \text{DX } 51881 = 1), \forall_{i=0,1}$$

Typically, for parameter learning, a prior distribution is assumed over the parameters of the local pdf's before the data are used (e.g., this can be uniform), or it could be estimated using the given data itself. The distribution of a node X conditional upon its parents may have any form. The conjugacy of this prior distribution is desirable; a distribution family is called conjugate prior to a data distribution when the posterior over the parameters belongs to the same family as the prior, albeit with different parameters.

In our implementation, we use Bayesian parameter estimation [20] to learn the parameter θ. In this method, the prior distribution over θ (i.e., $\Pr(\theta)$) is known. Now the posterior distribution of θ is calculated according to Bayes rule:

$$P(\theta|D) = \frac{\Pr(D|\theta)\Pr(\theta)}{\int \Pr(D|\theta)\Pr(\theta)d\theta}$$

Our objective is to calculate the maximum a posteriori (MAP in short), that is,

$$\hat{\theta}_{\text{MAP}} = \text{argmax}_\theta P(\theta|D) = \text{argmax}_\theta \Pr(D|\theta)\Pr(\theta)$$

The prior $\Pr(\theta)$ is calculated using a Beta distribution for binary variables, which gives rise to a posterior that is also a Beta distribution.

$$\Pr(\theta) = \text{Beta}(\theta|\alpha_1, \alpha_0) = c\theta^{\alpha_1-1}(1-\theta)^{\alpha_0-1}$$

However, for multivalued (i.e., nonbinary) discrete variables, prior $\Pr(\theta)$ is a Dirichlet distribution with $\text{Dir}(\theta|\alpha)$ with hyperparameters α_i's. The posterior would also be a Dirichlet distribution and will have the following form.

$$P(\theta|D) = c\,\Pr(D|\theta)\Pr(\theta)$$

15.3.3 Recommendation Rule Generation

The final step of our proposed framework is to make use of the constructed Bayesian network to generate a set of recommendation rules. While the complex relationship between different factors associated with 30-day heart failure readmission lend themselves to be modeled as a Bayesian network, there does not exist any easy extension to use the learned network to generate recommendation rule. Note that the network constructed in our case may not be *complete*, that is, the constructed network may not consist of all possible edges between the nodes in two successive layers. Consider Example 15.1 again, and note that the variable "Gender" is not connected to all diagnosis nodes. At the same time, it is unrealistic to force the network to have all the edges, given its high dimensionality, because the search space increases exponentially by the addition of edges between the nodes. At the same time, it may not be possible to track back one entire inference path of the network because the network is not complete between two successive levels.

We propose an innovative solution to that end, where the idea is to make use of the inference learning of the network to perform recommendation. Using the constructed network after parameter learning, for each patient record d, we could compute the probability $\Pr(\text{Readmit} = 1|d)$ and $\Pr(\text{Readmit} = 0|d)$. We describe next how to make use of these inference probabilities to generate a set of recommendation rules.

Without loss of generality, let us assume that a total of $|\mathcal{X}'|$ of $|\mathcal{X}|$ factors are nonactionable, and the remaining set $\{\mathcal{X}\} - \{\mathcal{X}'\}$ of factors could be recommended as interventions.

For each patient record d whose actual class label is 0 (i.e., Readmission = 0), we use only $|\mathcal{X}'|$ attributes of record d (denoted as $d(\mathcal{X}')$) and feed it through the constructed network to obtain the inference probability p_1. Then, we use the entire patient record (with both actionable and nonactionable attributes, modulo the class label) and use that to make a second inference probability p_2.

$$p_1 = \Pr(\text{Readmission} = 0|d(\mathcal{X}')), \quad p_2 = \Pr(\text{Readmission} = 0|d)$$

If $p_2 > p_1$ (which indicates that our constructed model infers that the set of procedures associated with the patient input is effective in further bringing down her readmission risk), we store the set of procedures $\{\mathcal{X}\} - \{\mathcal{X}'\}$ associated with d as the generated recommendation, given the values for the nonprocedure attributes. Using Example 15.1, a recommendation rule in our case may look as follows:

Recommendation Rule: 1

if Gender = Female & Age = 64 & diagnosis= PN & diagnosis= ARF & Readmit=0, recommended interventions (i.e., procedures) P1 (PR3893) = 1 & P2 (PR9904) = 0 & P3 (PR9671)= 1.

Similarly, for each patient record d' whose actual class label is 1 (i.e., Readmission = 1), we check if the following condition is satisfied.

$$p_2 = \Pr(\text{Readmission} = 1|d) < p_1 = \Pr(\text{Readmission} = 1|d(\mathcal{X}'))$$

Recommendation Rule: 2

if Gender = Male & Age = 87 & diagnosis= CHF & diagnosis= ARF & Readmit=1, recommended interventions (i.e., procedures) P1 (PR3893) = 1 & P2 (PR9904) = 0 & P3 (PR9671)= 1.

In that case, Rule 2 will be also stored. Following this process, a set of recommendation rules are generated. As we shall see in Section 15.3.5, these recommendation rules are used during the validation phase to evaluate the effectiveness of our proposed framework.

15.3.4 Intervention Recommendation

Given an input patient record (only with nonprocedure attribute) d, we attempt to find out the rule r, which gives rise to the *highest similarity* with the input. In particular, the similarity between the patient record and the nonactionable part of the recommendation rule is treated as binary attributes (e.g., the value of a patient's age is compared with the age value that is present in a recommendation rule and is considered same, if both of these values match, no match otherwise) and is measured using Jaccard index, as follows:

$$\text{Jaccard}(d, r) = \frac{\{d \cap r\}}{\{d \cup r\}}$$

where r denotes the vector comprising of attributes in Groups 1, 2, and 3 described in Table 15.4 for the trained rules and d denotes the input vector (comprising the same set of attributes as r) observed in the test data. This would give rise to a unique set of recommendation rules that are uniquely applicable only to that phase. After that, the rest of the process is akin to what we have described already, that is, the objective is to simply choose the recommendation rule that would give rise to the *highest similarity* for that phase.

TABLE 15.4   Attribute Summary for SID-WA Heart Failure
Cohort

Group	Category	Description
1	Demographics	3 Attributes
2	Comorbidity	21 Attributes
3	Diagnosis	90 Attributes
4	Health services utilization	21 Attributes
5	Procedures	70 Attributes
6	Others	4 Attributes

15.3.5   Experiments

15.3.5.1   Data: Washington State Inpatient Databases   We use the State Inpatient Databases (SID) 4 of Washington State (referred as SID-WA for the rest of the chapter) of years 2010 and 2011. SID are part of the family of databases developed for the Healthcare Cost and Utilization Project (HCUP).[4] The data set is a discharge abstract that includes inpatient discharge records from community hospitals in the State of Washington with all-payer, encounter-level information beginning in 2010 and 2011. SID-WA contains readmissions that occur at any hospital within the State of Washington. SID of 1 year comprises four files that are associated with patients and their encounters in the hospitals. The four files – core file (CORE), charges file (CHGS), diagnosis and procedure groups file (DXPRGRPS), and disease severity measures file (SEVERITY) – provide 596 attributes in total for a single patient encounter. Each inpatient encounter has a unique identifier KEY, which can be used to link records across files. Our initial data set used KEY to join CORE, DXPRGRPS, and SEVERITY files and selected only attributes that are relevant to the clinical aspect of a patient encounter

We use the attribute VisitLink in CORE to identify the same patients in the data. The attribute DaysToEvent is used to compute the days between two consecutive hospital admissions for each patient. In order to determine the number of days since previous hospital discharge, we first calculate the number of days between two hospital admissions and then subtract the length of stay of the first hospital admission. For example, if the two hospital admission for a patient is 37 days and the length of hospital stay for the first admission is 10 days, the number of days since previous hospital discharge would be 27 days, which is considered as a 30-day readmission.

We construct a heart failure cohort based on the initial data set extracted from SID-WA, as described earlier. The cohort contains patients whose primary or secondary ICD9-CM diagnosis codes are listed in [8]. Initially, the cohort contains 3908 distinct diagnosis codes and 2049 procedure codes. In order to resolve the issue of sparsity and high dimensionality of the data, we perform *chi-square* feature selection to filter attributes that are less influential. Table 15.4 summarizes the

---

[4]http://www.hcup-us.ahrq.gov/sidoverview.jsp.

TABLE 15.5 Evaluation Metrics

Jaccard	Accuracy	True Positive Rate
$\dfrac{tp}{tp + fp + fn}$	$\dfrac{tp + tn}{tp + tn + fp + fn}$	$\dfrac{tp}{tp+fn}$

209 attributes used in the cohort. Unless otherwise stated, all 70 procedures are considered as interventions.

The final heart failure cohort contains data extracted from SID-WA 2010 and SID-WA 2011. Our experiments used the 2010 data (67,967 patients) for training and the 2011 data (52,021 patients) for testing.

15.3.5.2 Evaluation Measures We use four metrics to evaluate our experiment results: (i) the number of exact matches from the rules of the test data (HIT); (ii) the Jaccard index between the recommendation procedure vector and the actual observed procedure vector (JAC); (iii) accuracy of the recommendations (ACCY); (iv) true positive rate (TPR). For each pair of a set of recommended procedures and a set of observed procedures, we define a true positive (tp) case, if a recommended procedure appears in the observed procedure set. We define a true negative (tn) case, if a nonrecommended procedure does not appear in the observed procedure set. False positive (fp) occurs when the recommended procedure does not appear in the observed set. False negative (fn) occurs when the nonrecommended procedure actually appears in the observed procedure set. Therefore, we compute the three metrics as shown in Table 15.5.

15.3.5.3 Results We design nine experiments based on three different structure learning algorithms (Hill Climbing (HC), Grow–Shrink (GS), Hybrid (HY)) by varying the number of diagnosis attributes (30, 60, 90). The experimental results for the four aforementioned measures are presented in Figure 15.5. Understandably the HIT values are in the lower side for all the algorithms, while the other three measures (especially Accuracy) are reasonable and demonstrates the effectiveness of our proposed methods.

Interestingly, Figure 15.5 demonstrates that the effectiveness of recommendation slightly increases (or remains same) with increasing number of attributes only for GS. This demonstrates that the number of diagnoses does not have significant effect on the recommendation results, meaning that we can achieve equivalent quality, even using fewer input attributes. On the other hand, the other two algorithms (i.e., HC, HY) exhibit similar behavior. For example, across all quality measures, the algorithms HC and HY remain most effective for 30 attributes, degrade drastically for 60 attributes, and somewhat improve (or remain same) for 90 attributes. We conjecture that the reason of such observation is due to the greedy nature of these Hill-climbing-based heuristics, which can end up in a local optima.

We perform paired t-test to further understand the statistical significance of the obtained results. Table 15.6 enlists the output. The significance level is set to 95%. The

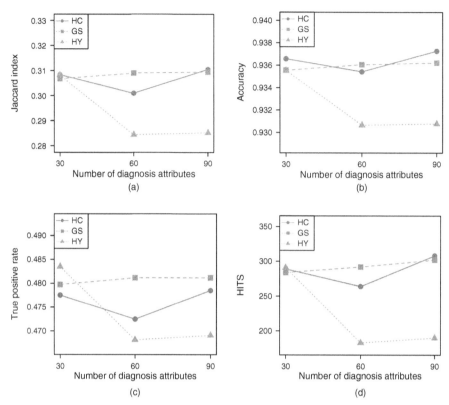

Figure 15.5 Effectiveness of different algorithms for intervention recommendation; x-axis varies the number of diagnoses attributes and y-axis captures the average of a respective quality measure. (a) Jaccard index, (b) accuracy, (c) true positive rate, and (d) hits.

TABLE 15.6 Statistical Significance of Quality Results of Figure 15.5 is further Explained Using Paired *t*-Test

	HC			GS			HY		
	30	60	90	30	60	90	30	60	90
HIT	289	264	308	284	292	302	291	183	190
JAC	0.3083	0.3009	0.3104^{ab}	0.3067	0.3089^{b}	0.3094	0.3082^{a}	0.2843	0.2851
ACCY	0.9365	0.9354	0.9372^{ab}	0.9355	0.9360^{b}	0.9362^{a}	0.9355^{a}	0.9306	0.9307
TPR	0.4775	0.4724	0.4785	0.4797^{b}	0.4811^{b}	0.4811^{b}	0.4834	0.4681	0.4690

[a]The result is significantly better than the others among the three variations of attribute numbers.
[b]The result is significantly better than the others among the three structure learning algorithms.

results show that for Jac, ACCY, and TPR, the results of GS outperforms HC and HY (for the same number of attributes) with statistical significance. On the other hand, the JAC and ACCY results of HC is statistically better for 90 attributes (in comparison to 30 and 60 attributes) and compared to other two algorithms (GS and HY). The results of HY appear to show the least statistical significance. However, the results demonstrate that JAC and ACCY of HY with 30 attributes outperform the other two variants, that is, HY with 60 attributes and HY with 90 attributes. These results corroborate that based on the underlying algorithm and the input diagnoses, the effectiveness of different algorithm varies for the task of intervention recommendation.

15.3.5.4 Case Study: Effect of Iterative Predictions This section presents a case study to demonstrate how predictive analytics can be used to facilitate real-time risk predictions at any point of care. We aim to develop medical interventions and care management strategies to reduce the risk score of an individual. Interventions could take place during hospitalization, at discharge time, or post-discharge. Patients should be treated and/or reached in a unique way in order to minimize the risk score. We construct a predictive model that identifies and selects a subset of intervention factors that are actionable at any stage of care, either during hospitalization, at time of discharge, or post-discharge. After a patient is admitted with HF, a predictive model can be used to evaluate the risk of readmission of the patient. We then suggest interventions that can reduce the risk and their relative effect on risk reduction. Given the updated risk assessment, healthcare provider could then re-evaluate whether the risk is minimized and whether further opportunity for risk reduction exists.

In this case study, we select a patient from our HF cohort and demonstrate the cycle of risk prediction and management. The selected patient is a male Caucasian in the age group of 40–49. The patient is diagnosed with congestive heart failure, renal failure, fluid, and electrolyte disorders. We first predict his risk of readmission and then identify an intervention that would reduce the risk the most. The process repeats until no risk reduction is observed.

Figure 15.6 shows how the risk decreases as we add the selected interventions in order. Based on our model, the first recommendation is the utilization of emergency room (U_ED), followed by nuclear medicine (U_NUCMED), cardiac stress test (U_STRESS), percutaneous abdominal drainage (PR_5941), left heart cardiac catheterization (PR_3722), speech therapy (U_SPEECHTHERAPY), respiratory services (U_RESPTHERAPY), implant procedures (U_OTHIMPLANTS), Chest X-ray (U_CHESTXRAY), and angiocardiography of left heart structures (PR_8853).

15.4 RELATED WORK

Preventing hospitalization is a prominent factor to improve patient outcomes and curb healthcare costs. An increasing body of literature [2] attempts to develop predictive models for hospital readmission risks. A systematic review from [2] shows that these studies range from all-cause readmissions to readmission for specific diseases such as

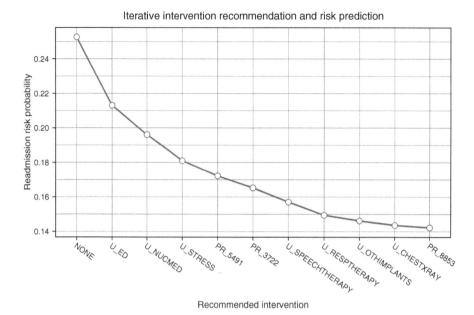

Figure 15.6   Results of risk management cycle.

heart failure, pneumonia, stroke, and asthma. Each of these models exploits various predictor variables (attributes) assessed at various times related to index hospitalization (admission, discharge, first follow-up visit, etc.). However, great majority of prior research applied only regression models to the problem. Research that leverage advanced predictive modeling techniques to predict risk of readmission is still in its infancy. We present one of the earliest effort of applying multiple predictive modeling technique for the problem of predicting 30-day hospital readmissions.

In a closely related research, Yu et al. [23] modeled the readmission risk prediction as a binary classification problem and a prognosis analysis problem. The authors trained SVM model for classification and used Cox regression for prognosis analysis. Compared to existing literature, our work applied multiple predictive modeling technique and presented a complete analytic pipeline for the problem. Moreover, we extend our scope to intervention recommendation problem. To the best of our knowledge, no prior work has investigated the intervention recommendation problem for heart failure.

Several recent research efforts have applied Bayesian network to enable decision support in a clinical and healthcare setting. For example, a recent work has studied the problem of deciding a treatment plan for dental caries based on intercausal association between different sign-symptoms using Bayesian network [24]. The work considers a rather low-dimensional data. Similar modeling effort has been observed to enable decision support for generating treatment plan for other diseases as well, such as coronary diseases [25], ulcers [26], sepsis [27], and depression [28]. Compared to the existing studies, our work addresses the problem of high dimensionality, scale, or multilayered modeling. In addition, we generate recommendation rules and perform large scale validation to enrich clinical knowledge.

15.5   CONCLUSION

In this work, we investigate the problem of predicting the risk of 30-day hospital readmission for heart failure patients and recommending interventions to minimize the risk. The problem is treated as a binary classification problem. Three classification models – Naive Bayes, SVM, and AdaBoost – were selected for our risk prediction experiments. The experiments are designed to understand the incremental effect of different types of attributes. It is shown that AdaBoost is the most stable model and is robust against noises in the data.

Our solution to intervention recommendation for risk management involves learning the structure and parameters of a hierarchical Bayesian network. We use the network to capture the complex interplay between multitude of factors related to heart failure, such as demographic, diagnoses, and procedures and how they contribute to the 30-day heart failure readmission problem. Leveraging the knowledge captured in the Bayesian network, we generate rules of interventions that could lead to risk reduction. Interventions are recommended based on the similarity between the observed patient characteristics (e.g., demographics, diagnoses) and the patient profiles stored in the rule repository. Our case study demonstrates how predictive analytics can be used to integrate risk prediction and intervention recommendation in an iterative process to facilitate the cycle of clinical care.

For future work, we plan to investigate all-cause readmission prediction leveraging the developed risk prediction overall pipeline and predictive models. We also plan to incorporate the objective of cost prediction to the existing modeling. We plan to use predictive analytic techniques to provide personalized recommendations of interventions to prevent readmissions while monitoring the cost of resource use. The outcome of this future research will improve healthcare quality for HF patients as well as enhance cost transparency for the prevention of hospital readmission.

REFERENCES

[1] Go AS, Mozaffarian D, Roger VL, Benjamin EJ, Berry JD, Borden WB, Bravata DM, Dai S, Ford ES, Fox CS, Franco S, Fullerton HJ, Gillespie C, Hailpern SM, Heit JA, Howard VJ, Huffman MD, Kissela BM, Kittner SJ, Lackland DT, Lichtman JH, Lisabeth LD, Magid D, Marcus GM, Marelli A, Matchar DB, McGuire DK, Mohler ER, Moy CS, Mussolino ME, Nichol G, Paynter NP, Schreiner PJ, Sorlie PD, Stein J, Turan TN, Virani SS, Wong ND, Woo D, Turner MB. Heart disease and stroke statistics-2013 update a report from the American heart association. Circulation 2013;127(1):e6–e245. PMID: 23239837.

[2] Englander H, Kansagara D. Risk prediction models for hospital readmission: a systematic review. JAMA 2011;306(15):1688–1698.

[3] Jencks SF, Williams MV, Coleman EA. Rehospitalizations among patients in the medicare fee-for-service program. N Engl J Med 2009;360(14):1418–1428.

[4] van Walraven C, Bennett C, Jennings A, Austin PC, Forster AJ. Proportion of hospital readmissions deemed avoidable: a systematic review. Can Med Assoc J 2011; 183(7):E391E402. PMID: 2144–4623.

[5] Naylor MD, Brooten D, Campbell R, Jacobsen BS, Mezey MD, Pauly MV, Schwartz JS. Comprehensive discharge planning and home follow-up of hospitalized elders: a randomized clinical trial. JAMA 1999;281(7):613–620.

[6] Jack BW, Chetty VK, Anthony D, Greenwald JL, Sanchez GM, Johnson AE, Forsythe SR, O'Donnell JK, Paasche-Orlow MK, Manasseh C, Martin S, Culpepper L. A reengineered hospital discharge program to decreaseRehospitalizationA randomized trial. Ann Intern Med 2009;150(3):178–187.

[7] Hansen LO, Young RS, Hinami K, Leung A, Williams MV. Interventions to reduce 30-day rehospitalization: a systematic review. Ann Intern Med 2011;155(8):520–528.

[8] Zolfaghar K, Meadem N, Sistla D, Chin S-C, Roy SB, Verbiest N, Teredesai A. Exploring preprocessing techniques for prediction of risk of readmission for congestive heart failure patients. Data Mining and Healthcare Workshop; 2013.

[9] Han J, Kamber M. *Data Mining: Concepts and Techniques*. Philadelphia (PA): Morgan Kaufmann Publishers Inc.; 2006.

[10] Neapolitan RE. *Learning Bayesian Networks*. Upper Saddle River (NJ): Pearson Prentice Hall; 2004.

[11] Tsamardinos I, Brown LE, Aliferis CF. The max-min hill-climbing Bayesian network structure learning algorithm. Mach Learn 2006;65(1):3178.

[12] Pearl J, Verma TS. A theory of inferred causation. Stud Logic Found Math 1995; 134:789–811.

[13] Cheng J, Greiner R. Comparing Bayesian network classifiers. Proceedings of the 15th Conference on Uncertainty Inartificial Intelligence; Morgan Kaufmann Publishers Inc.; 1999. p 101–108.

[14] Jensen FV, Nielsen TD. *Bayesian Networks and Decision Graphs*. New York: Springer-Verlag; 2007.

[15] Heckerman D, Geiger D, Chickering DM. Learning Bayesian networks: the combination of knowledge and statistical data. Mach Learn 1995;20(3):197–243.

[16] Box GEP, Tiao GC. *Bayesian Inference in Statistical Analysis*. Volume 40. New York: John Wiley and Sons; 2011.

[17] Spirtes P, Meek C. Learning Bayesian networks with discrete variables from data. KDD; 1995.

[18] Bromberg F, Margaritis D, Honavar V. Efficient Markov network structure discovery using independence tests. SDM; 2006. p 141–152.

[19] Li W, Nyholt DR. Marker selection by Akaike information criterion and Bayesian information criterion. Genet Epidemiol 2000;21:S272–S277.

[20] Kramer SC, Sorenson HW. Bayesian parameter estimation. IEEE Trans Automatic Control 1988;33(2):217–222.

[21] Zolfaghar K, Meadem N, Teredesai A, Roy SB, Chin S-C, Muckian B. Big data solutions for predicting risk-of-readmission for congestive heart failure patients. IEEE Bigdata; 2013.

[22] Zolfaghar K, Verbiest N, Agarwal J, Meadem N, Chin S-C, Roy SB, Teredesai A, Hazel D, Amoroso P, Reed L. Predicting risk-of-readmission for congestive heart failure patients: a multi-layer approach. CoRR, abs/1306.2094, 2013.

[23] Yu S, Esbroeck AV, Farooq F, Fung G, Anand V, Krishnapuram B. Predicting readmission risk with institution specific prediction models. ICHI; 2013. p 415–420.

[24] Bhatia A, Singh R. Using Bayesian network as decision making system tool for deciding treatment plan for dental caries. J Acad Ind Res (JAIR) 2013;2(2):93.

[25] Bittl JA, He Y, Jacobs AK, Yancy CW, Normand S-L. Bayesian methods affirm the use of percutaneous coronary intervention to improve survival in patients with unprotected left main coronary artery disease. Circulation 2013;127(22):2177–2185.

[26] Cho I, Park I, Kim E, Lee E, Bates DW. Using EHR data to predict hospital-acquired pressure ulcers: aprospective study of a Bayesian Network model. Int J Med Inform 2013;82(11):1059–1067.

[27] Gultepe E, Green JP, Nguyen H, Adams J, Albertson T, Tagkopoulos I. From vital signs to clinical outcomes for patients with sepsis: a machine learning basis for a clinical decision support system. J Am Med Inform Assoc 2014;21(2):315–325.

[28] Klein MCA, Modena G. Estimating mental states of a depressed person with Bayesian networks. In: *Contemporary Challenges and Solutions in Applied Artificial Intelligence*. Switzerland: Springer International Publishing; 2013. p 163–168.

16

HETEROGENEOUS SENSING AND PREDICTIVE MODELING OF POSTOPERATIVE OUTCOMES

YUN CHEN

Complex Systems Monitoring, Modeling and Analysis Laboratory, Department of Industrial and Management Systems Engineering, University of South Florida, Tampa, FL, USA

FABIO LEONELLI

Cardiac Electrophysiology Laboratory, James A. Haley Veterans' Hospital, Tampa, FL, USA

HUI YANG

Department of Industrial and Manufacturing Engineering, The Pennsylvania State University, University Park, PA, USA

16.1 INTRODUCTION

US healthcare spending is approximately 17% of GDP (i.e., $2.5 trillion) and will continue the historical upward trend, reaching 19.5% by 2017 [1]. The rapid advancements of biomedical sensing and healthcare information technology have resulted in data-rich environments in hospitals [2, 3]. However, the meaningful information extracted from rich data sets is still limited. Laboratory tests and patient monitoring are two of the primary information sources for estimating clinical statuses of postsurgical patients and optimizing management policies in the Intensive Care Units (ICU) [4]. Traditionally, clinicians make inferences about patient conditions based on most recent test results, ignoring important factors such as historical test

Healthcare Analytics: From Data to Knowledge to Healthcare Improvement, First Edition.
Edited by Hui Yang and Eva K. Lee.
© 2016 John Wiley & Sons, Inc. Published 2016 by John Wiley & Sons, Inc.

results and the relationships among different types of tests. In the general practice of medicine, physicians lack decision-support tools that can help them delineate hidden interactions among different laboratory tests, identify temporal variations of patient conditions, and predict mortality risks.

Although massive data sets are readily available in the healthcare environment, clinicians and nurses are facing significant challenges to improve the current utilization of common measures, for example, laboratory test results and patient monitoring signals. This is even more critical for high-risk patients in ICUs. It is estimated that more than five million patients are admitted to ICUs yearly in the United States and 10–20% of them die in hospitals [5]. Realizing the full potential of postsurgical data sets for ICU decision-making support depends to a great extent on the advancement of information processing methodologies. There is a dire need to go beyond current clinical practice and develop data-driven methods and tools that will enable and assist (i) the extraction of pertinent knowledge about clinical status from heterogeneous healthcare recordings, (ii) the prediction of mortality risks, and (iii) the provision of personalized decision-support systems.

Predicting ICU mortality is critically important to improve the quality of postsurgical healthcare services (e.g., surgical procedures, medication usages, care guidelines, treatment plans, and resource allocations). Furthermore, it provides data-driven performance measures to compare the differences of healthcare facilities and services, thereby eliminating healthcare disparities in the country. In the state of the art, general severity scoring systems that are widely used to describe the acuity levels of ICU patients include Acute Physiology and Chronic Health Evaluation (APACHE), Sequential Organ Failure Assessment (SOFA), and Simplified Acute Physiology Score (SAPS) [6, 7]. However, they have thus far yielded limited successes due to the fewer variables and shorter time period considered.

As shown in Figure 16.1a and b, postsurgical monitoring in ICU leads to a new order-3 tensor form of data sets with unique properties (i.e., variable heterogeneity, patient heterogeneity, and time asynchronization), as opposed to the table form of predictor and response variables commonly seen in predictive modeling. The tensor data and heterogeneous properties pose significant challenges to extract useful and

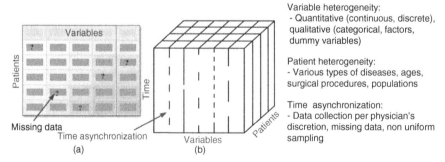

Figure 16.1 (a) Data in traditional table form for predictive modeling and (b) new tensor form data generated in postsurgical sensing.

meaningful knowledge from postsurgical data sets for the optimization of clinical decision making.

1. *Variable Heterogeneity*. In order to capture a complete picture of the recovery process of postsurgical patients, ICU monitoring includes a large number of variables (e.g., laboratory test results, pulse oximetry, blood pressure, and heart rate). Most importantly, there are different types of variables. Some are quantitative (continuous, discrete), while others may be qualitative (categorical, factors, dummy variables). As opposed to the conventional univariate analysis, it is critical to discover risk factors and interactions hidden in heterogeneous types of variables, reducing them to a parsimonious set of sensitive biomarkers that will help in the diagnosis, monitoring, and prediction.

2. *Patient Heterogeneity*. Furthermore, it may be noted that there are also heterogeneous types of patient populations, which may be classified by ages, gender, diseases, surgical types, or ICU types (e.g., coronary care unit, cardiac surgery recovery unit, medical ICU, surgical ICU). This also provides an opportunity to investigate mortality rates for different patient populations.

3. *Time Asynchronization*. It should also be noted that data collection procedures are not standardized in ICU. It is common that the frequency of data measurements is at the physician's discretion. Although each variable has an associated time stamp indicating the time point of data recording, time stamps are often not uniformly distributed along the time axis. During 48-h ICU monitoring, some variables may be recorded in an extremely low-sampling rate while others may be in a high-sampling rate. Missing data problem is also a common property of ICU data sets.

Hence, there is an urgent need to address the issues of variable heterogeneity, patient heterogeneity, and time asynchronization and further develop analytical methods for patient-specific prediction of in-hospital mortality. This chapter focuses on the predictive modeling of postoperative outcomes in ICUs using patient-specific and heterogeneous postsurgical data sets. To cope with the challenges in ICU data sets, we developed the postsurgical decision-support system with a suite of analytical tools, including data categorization, data preprocessing, feature extraction, feature selection, and predictive modeling. As the number of inpatient procedures performed is about 51.4 million every year in the United States [38], such a postoperative decision-support system is particularly timely in helping clinicians and nurses leverage the large and readily available clinical data sets to achieve a substantial boost in smart postoperative management. Realizing a better postoperative care will achieve a remarkable reduction of healthcare costs and improve the health of our society.

The remainder of this paper is organized as follows: Section 16.2 introduces the state of the art in ICU risk-scoring systems. Section 16.3 presents the research methodology of postsurgical data analytics. Section 16.4 provides the details of materials and experimental design. Section 16.5 contains experimental results. Section 16.6 presents the discussion and conclusions arising out of this study.

16.2   RESEARCH BACKGROUND

Scoring systems have been widely used to predict the risk of mortality and treatment outcomes for critically ill patients in intensive care medicine. The APGAR (Appearance, Pulse, Grimace, Activity, Respiration) score is the first of such systems introduced in 1952 to evaluate the effects of obstetric anesthesia on newborn babies [8]. The Glasgow Coma Scale (GCS) is another example of scoring systems that measures the conscious state of a subject [9]. In the field of intensive care, there are a variety of prognostic scoring systems designed for either the general ICU patients or defined subgroups. Examples include APACHE [6, 10–12], SAPS [13–16], MPM [19–21], and SOFA score [20]. In the past few decades, these systems have been continuously updated and widely used in the clinical practice. Standardized mortality ratio (SMR), the ratio of observed to predicted mortality, is a common performance metric for benchmarking the scoring systems. In addition, disease-specific scoring systems were developed to predict ICU outcomes for some disease subgroups such as pancreatitis, hepatic failure, and adult respiratory distress syndrome [21]. This section presents an overview of four ICU scoring systems commonly used in the ICU, namely APACHE, SAPS, MPM and SOFA, and discusses their advantages and limitations in the clinical practice.

16.2.1   Acute Physiology and Chronic Health Evaluation (APACHE)

The APACHE scoring system was first developed in 1981 as a physiologically based classification system to measure severity of illness of ICU patients [10]. APACHE I model derives the acute physiology score (APS) through the weighted summation of 34 physiologic variables. Each variable will be assigned a weight from 0 to 4 based on its amplitude and range. The worst physiologic values, for example, the lowest BP or the highest respiratory rate (RR), will be given a biggest weight. The time period considered is the first 24 h after the ICU admission. The APS provides an indicator of the risk of in-hospital death. A higher APS gives an increased probability in the risk of in-hospital death. However, the APACHE I system requires formal multi-institutional validation and is limited in its capability to handle missing data in 34 physiological variables. In most cases, only the worst values in day 1 of ICU are used. Temporal trends and correlations are not fully utilized in the APACHE I system.

In 1985, APACHE II was developed to mitigate the complexity of APACHE I system and thereafter became the most widely used measurement of the severity of illness for patients admitted to the ICU [6]. Notably, the number of physiologic variables involved is reduced from 34 to 12, namely temperature, mean arterial pressure (MAP), heart rate (HR), respiratory rate (RR), oxygenation, pH arterial, sodium (Na), potassium (K), creatinine, hematocrit, white blood cell count (WCC), and GCS. Reducing the number of involved variables partially overcomes the problem of missing values, as well as concerns about the normal assumption of an unmeasured variable [6]. Similar to APACHE I, these 12 physiologic variables are from the initial 24 h after ICU admission. As shown in Table 16.1, APACHE II optimized the calculation of weighted score for paper schemas through 0–4 scales and reduced the number of

TABLE 16.1 The APACHE II Severity Classification System

	+4	+3	+2	+1	0	+1	+2	+3	+4
Temperature	≥41	39–40.9		38.5–38.9	36–38.4	3–35.9	32–33.9	30–31.9	≤29.9
MAP	≥160	130–159	110–129		70–109		50–69		≤49
HR	≥180	140–179	110–139		70–109		50–69	40–54	≤39
RR	≥50	35–49		25–34	21–24	10–11	6–9		≤5
Oxygenation[a]	≥500	350–499	200–349		<200 >70	61–70		55–60	<55
pH	≥7.7	7.6–7.69		7.5–7.59	7.33–7.49		7.25–7.32	7.15–7.24	<7.15
Na	≥180	160–179	155–159	150–154	130–149		120–129	111–119	≤110
K	≥7	6.6–6.9		5.5–5.9	3.5–5.4	3–3.4	2.5–2.9		<2.5
Creatinine	≥3.5	2–3.4	1.5–1.9		0.6–1.4		<0.6		
Hematocrit	≥60		50–59.9	46–49.9	30–45.9		20–29.9		<20
WCC	≥40		20–39.9	15–19.9	3–14.9		1–2.9		<1
15-GCS					Score = 15 – actual GCS				

[a]FiO$_2$>0.5 record A-aDO$_2$; FiO$_2$<0.5 record only PaO$_2$.

variables to fit into a single-sheet paper. An increasing score (range from 0 to 71) indicates a higher risk of subsequent in-hospital death. It is worth mentioning that APACHE II score is not recalculated and updated through the period of ICU stay. If a patient is discharged from the ICU and readmitted, a new APACHE II score will be calculated. In the clinical practice, it was found that few patients have an APACHE II score greater than 55 [6]. Furthermore, the probability of in-hospital mortality is derived using a multivariate logistic regression model as $\ln\left(\frac{risk}{1\text{-}risk}\right) = a + \sum_i b_i x_i$, where risk is the risk of death, $\left(\frac{risk}{1\text{-}risk}\right)$ is the odds ratio, a is the intercept, b_i is the coefficient, and $x_i's$ are independent variables such as APACHE II score, age group, severe chronic health impairment, and 56 disease groups. However, the performance of APACHE II model deteriorates for mortality prediction because case-mix adjustment is not specifically considered and parameter estimation is based on 1979–1981 data.

Furthermore, APACHE III was developed in 1991 [11] to improve the scoring system by changing the number and weights of physiological variables. Also, APACHE III consists of predictive models for not only the in-hospital mortality but also hospital length of stay. Such predictions provide benchmarks for the assessment and comparison of ICU efficiency and resource use. Predictor variables are revised and updated to include 78 disease groups, acute physiological score, age, preexisting functional limitations, chronic health status measured with seven comorbidities, and admission type and source. Compared with previous APACHE versions, the APACHE III score has a five-point increase and ranges from 0 to 299 points. The points are mainly calculated from three components. The first component, also the largest one of APACHE III score, attributes to acute physiological scores (APS) and ranges from 0 to 252. The second component is chronic health index that measures the impact of comorbidities on a patient's immunologic condition and ranges from 0 to 23. The third component is a patient's age that accounts for 0–24 points. The summation of three components gives the APACHE III score, which stratifies the risk of mortality for critically ill patients within independently defined patient subgroups. Notably, APACHE III scores were re-evaluated for the initial 1 h after admission and the following 23 and 24 h. Statistical tests showed no significant differences in predictive scores for three readings. After the course of initial 24 h, the APACHE III system periodically updates the models and re-estimates weights of APS score, chronic health, and age components using the newly available physiologic data.

In 2006, a full review and update of APACHE III equations lead to the new APACHE IV models that incorporate new developments in ICU protocols and practices [12]. Note that APACHE III score provides risk stratification for ICU patients, while APACHE IV provides a set of predictive equations for a specific database. The APACHE III score is a major component in APACHE IV predictive equations. Specifically, predictor variables in the APACHE IV system include APS variables, chronic health variables, ICU admission diagnosis (116 disease groups), ICU admission source, length of stay before ICU admission, emergency surgery, thrombolytic therapy, GCS, and mechanical ventilation. A cubic spline transformation is used to expand predictors to additional spline terms to allow the estimation of nonlinear relationship in the predictive models. The APACHE IV predictive equations were developed and validated with a nationally representative database of over 131,618 patients admitted to 104 ICUs in 45 hospitals in the United States in 2002/2003 [12]. Three analytic methods were used to evaluate the prediction performance of APACHE IV models over the entire range of risk, namely graphical plotting of observed and predicted mortalities, goodness-of-fit test (i.e., Hosmer–Lemeshow C statistic), and Cox chi-square test. However, the APACHE IV system has several limitations: (i) It is developed and tested in the ICUs of the United States and may not be applicable to other countries due to the significant differences in protocols and practices. (ii) The training and validation data are only from hospitals that purchased the APACHE system, representing a selection bias. (iii) The logistic regression model is not generalized and robust to the selection of training data set. (iv) The prediction of mortality risk contains variance for an individual. (v) The APACHE IV accuracy will deteriorate in the future due to new knowledge, new therapies, and protocol changes in postsurgical care. There is a need to periodically retest the models, re-estimate model parameters, and reselect the variables with statistically significant prognostic values.

16.2.2 Simplified Acute Physiology Score (SAPS)

In 1984, a SAPS was developed for ICU comparative studies and management evaluation [13]. SAPS is a simpler and less time-consuming scoring system that uses 14 clinical variables (namely, GCS, HR, systolic blood pressure, temperature, RR, urine output, blood urea nitrogen, hematocrit, TLC, serum glucose, sodium, potassium, bicarbonate, and age) for predicting the risk of death of ICU patients. Similar to the APACHE I, SAPS calculation was based on the worst values of clinical variables during the first 24 h after ICU admission. However, clinical variables in SAPS were subjectively selected by a panel of human experts. In addition, the SAPS system was only validated with 679 patients from eight ICUs in France, which do not have a good case-mix. The SAPS system lacks the generality for applications to heterogeneous ICU patients worldwide.

In 1993, SAPS II was developed and validated using data from 13,152 patients in 137 medical/surgical ICUs in the European/North America study [14]. The SAPS II score is calculated from 17 variables: 12 physiological variables, age, admission types (scheduled surgical, unscheduled surgical, or medical), and 3 disease variables (immunodeficiency syndrome, metastatic cancer, and hematologic malignancy). Note that logistic regression is used in the SAPS II system to help (i) select important variables, (ii) perform optimal parameter (or weight) estimation, and (iii) predict the probability of in-hospital mortality. As the SAPS II score is highly skewed, log transformation is adopted. Hence, prediction equations for the mortality risks include two predictor variables (i.e., SAPS II score and ln(SAPS II score+1)):

$$Pr(risk) = \frac{\exp(X\beta)}{1 + \exp(X\beta)}$$

$$= \frac{\exp(\beta_0 + \beta_1(SAPS\,II\,Score) + \beta_2[\ln(SAPS\,II\,Score + 1)])}{1 + \exp(\beta_0 + \beta_1(SAPS\,II\,Score) + \beta_2[\ln(SAPS\,II\,Score + 1)])}$$

where β_0 is estimated to be -7.7631, β_1 is 0.0737, and β_2 is 0.9971. However, the SAPS II score only considered the first 24 h after ICU admission. The progression of risk of death is not investigated through the continuous monitoring of SAPS II scores using data collected on a daily basis.

In order to address the heterogeneity of ICU case-mix and typology, SAPS III was proposed in 2005 and evaluated using a database of 19,577 patients from 307 ICUs worldwide [15, 16]. In addition to the first 24 h after admission, the SAPS III system collects data continuously on days 1, 2, 3, and the last day of the ICU stay. It is worth mentioning that SAPS III designed a set of detailed definitions and protocols for data collection to avoid user-dependent problems. Also, SAPS III study aims to address patient-dependent problems by establishing a multinational database that are more representative of clinical variables and outcomes. As a result, this improves the generalization of SAPS III models. The SAPS III score is ranged from 0 to 217, which is the arithmetic sum of three subscores derived from 20 variables as follows:

- Subscore I (5 variables): patient characteristics before ICU admission, including age, previous health status, comorbidities, location before ICU admission, length of stay in the hospital before ICU admission, and use of major therapeutic options before ICU admission.
- Subscore II (5 variables): reason(s) for ICU admission, anatomic site of surgery (if applicable), planned or unplanned ICU admission, surgical status, and infection at ICU admission.
- Subscore III (10 variables): acute physiological variables (within 1 h before or after admission).

Furthermore, logistic regression is used to predict the probability of death during a certain period of time. The main model is to predict the probability of death at hospital discharge. Note that stepwise logistic regression is employed for important variable selection, and then a log transformation of SAPS III score is applied to reduce the impact of highly skewed distribution on the modeling. Both SAPS III score and $\log(\text{SAPS III} + g)$ score are used to predict hospital mortality in the logistic regression model, where g is a model parameter to be estimated. Fivefold cross-validation was performed on patients, as well as ICUs in the multinational databases to evaluate the SAPS III system. The model performances on the database were shown to have big variations across the world.

16.2.3 Mortality Probability Model (MPM)

The MPM was first proposed in 1985 to predict the survival and mortality of ICU patients at the time points of ICU admission and 24-h mark in the ICU [17]. Multiple logistic regression models were derived on the basis of data from 755 patients in a single hospital, and model parameters for predictor variables were objectively determined. The MPM system contained relatively few and easily obtained variables, including seven admission variables that are independent of ICU treatments, and seven 24-h variables that describe medical treatments and patients' conditions in the ICU. Notably, the admission model MPM_0 is independent of ICU treatments and can be used for patient stratification and ICU comparisons, while MPM_{24} is designed for more complex patients staying in the ICU for more than 24 h.

As the ICU environment is changing over time, a major revision of MPM_0 and MPM_{24} was conducted in 1993. The new MPM II system [18] was developed and validated with the data of 19,124 patients collected from 143 ICUs in 139 hospitals in 12 countries (i.e., 6 ICUs in the northeastern United States, as well as the European\North American Study of Severity Systems in 137 ICUs in 12 countries). The participating ICUs include diverse types, with 16% being medical, 24% surgical, and 60% mixed medical and surgical. Notably, the MPM II study excluded burn, coronary care, cardiac surgery patients, as well as those patients under the age of 18. The training data set includes 12,610 patients, and the testing data set consists of 6514 subjects. The admission model, MPM_0, considered only main effects of 15 variables that are readily obtainable at ICU admission. The MPM_0 probability of in-hospital mortality is calculated as follows:

1. Compute the logit value as logit $= b_0 + b_1x_1 + \ldots + b_kx_k$, where b_0 is the constant, $b_i, i = 1, \ldots, k$ is the coefficient for variable $x_i, i = 1, \ldots, k$. In contrast with APACHE and SAPS systems, the MPM II system dichotomized each variable x_i, with an exception of age. In other words, the variables take the values of 1 or 0 to describe the presence or absence.

2. Transform the logit into risk probability through the equation:

$$Pr(risk) = e^{logit}/(1 + e^{logit})$$

In addition, the 24-h model, MPM_{24}, was designed for patients who stayed in the ICU for more than 24 h. Those patients who were discharged alive or died in the first 24 h after ICU admission were excluded. As a result, 10,357 patients with ICU stays longer than 24 h were left for the development of MPM_{24}. Similar to the MPM_0 modeling, MPM_{24} used multiple logistic regression models that considered the main effects for eight variables during the 24-h ICU stay and five variables from the MPM_0 (see the detailed table of variables in [18]). It is worth mentioning that the MPM II system includes dichotomous variables, but APACHE and SAPS systems used the worst values in the 24-h period of ICU stays. The number of variables is relatively small in the MPM II system. This greatly simplified the scoring but may omit useful information in the clinical variables. Also, the MPM_0 included a radiological variable and the MPM_{24} consists of four variables from laboratory testing. However, a major limitation of MPM II is the general applicability for the population of ICUs and their patients. Because of fewer variables and dichotomous inputs, it is difficult to fully utilize the dynamic information of ICU patients and then develop a generalized scoring system to estimate the probability of in-hospital mortality.

However, the 1993 model of MPM_0 II was found to overpredict in-hospital mortality. Therefore, MPM_0 III was proposed in 2007 to update the MPM_0 II model using data from 124,855 patients collected between 2001 and 2004 in 135 ICUs at 98 hospitals [19]. In addition to MPM_0 II risk factors, MPM_0 III added two new variables (i.e., "full code" – resuscitation status at ICU admission and "zero factors" – absence of all MPM_0 II risk factors except age) and seven interaction terms (i.e., between age and systolic blood pressure, metastatic neoplasm, cirrhosis, cardiac dysrhythmia, intracranial mass, cardiopulmonary resuscitation, and coma/deep stupor). Notably, all independent variables take the binary values except the age and thus greatly decrease the burden of data collection. The MPM_0 III retained the "on admission" feature of MPM_0 II and estimated the mortality probability using 16 variables obtained within 1 h of ICU admission. There were 74,578 patients (59.7%) used in model development and 50,307 (40.3%) in model validation. First, univariate analysis was performed to select the important variables on mortality using statistical t-test and chi-square tests with the significance level $\alpha = 0.05$. Second, multivariate logistic regression models included those significant variables and interaction terms for predicting the probability of mortality. Because APACHE and SAPS cover the first 24 h after ICU admissions, MPM_{24} is not updated. MPM_0 characterization extracts the "quality of care" metric before ICU care begins and thus facilitates the evaluation of the appropriateness of ICU admissions, resource utilization, and patient flow. However, there are several limitations in the MPM_0 III system. For example, MPM_0 III excludes some patients whose conditions are rapidly varying at admission. APACHE IV and SAPS III were shown to yield better discrimination power than MPM models. Also, the main purpose of MPM_0 III is for patient stratification at ICU admission and is not expected to precisely predict acuity or outcome for individual patients [19].

16.2.4   Sequential Organ Failure Assessment (SOFA)

Organ failures were shown to be highly pertinent to ICU morbidity and mortality. The SOFA scoring system was developed to quantify the level of organ dysfunction and then take repeated measurements of SOFA scores (i.e., alternations over time) for predicting ICU mortality [20]. As shown in Table 16.2, SOFA assigns a subscore of 0–4 for each of six organs, namely respiratory, coagulation, liver, cardiovascular, neurological, and renal. The SOFA score is the sum of all six subscores and is ranged from 0 to 24. A higher score indicates more severe failure. In order to effectively represent the dynamics of illness, the SOFA score can be computed on admission and every 48 h until discharge. Prior research studied predictor variables such as initial, highest, mean SOFA scores, and δ-SOFA. The initial SOFA score measures the level of organ dysfunction on admission. The δ-SOFA score is the difference between two subsequent scores and describes the variability of dysfunction in the period of ICU stay. The mean SOFA score is calculated as the ratio of total SOFA score to the length of ICU stay, which characterizes the average degree of organ dysfunction over time. The highest SOFA score indicates the biggest variation of organ failure during the period of ICU stay. Univariate logistic regression model was used to calculate the odds ratio and 95% confidence interval for each predictor variable. The analysis results showed that mean and highest SOFA scores are strongly correlated with ICU mortality, followed by δ-SOFA and initial SOFA scores. SOFA throughout the ICU stay is shown to have great potentials for prognostic modeling of ICU outcomes. Notably, the SOFA system differs from traditional scoring systems such as APACHE,

TABLE 16.2 The SOFA Scoring System

	0	1	2	3	4
Respiratory FiO$_2$/PaO$_2$	>400	<400	<300	<200	<100
Coagulation Platelets	>150	<150	<100	<50	<50
Liver Bilirubin	<1.2	1.2–1.9	2–5.9	6–11.9	>12
Cardiovascular Hypotension	No hypotension	MAP<70	Dop≤5 or dob (any)	Dop>5 or norepi≤0.1	Dop>15 or norepi>0.1
Central nervous system GCS	15	13–14	10–12	6–9	<6
Renal Creatinine or Urine Output	<1.2	1.2–1.9	2–3.4	3.5–4.9 or <500	>5 or <200

Dop: dopamine; dob: dobutamine; norepi: norepinephrine.

SAPS, and MPM as follows: (i) SOFA is mainly targeted at the information of organ dysfunction/failure to evaluate morbidity rather than evaluating mortality. (ii) SOFA is designed to make description of ICU stay as opposed to making predictions. (iii) SOFA is based on simple and easily repeatable variables pertinent to specific organs. (iv) Serial SOFA scores provide a representation of the dynamics in the conditions of critically ill patients, thereby taking the time factor into accounts in the prediction of ICU outcomes.

Existing ICU scoring systems can be categorized into four groups, that is, general scoring systems for the severity of illness, disease-specific risk-scoring systems, organ dysfunction scoring systems, and trauma risk-scoring systems. However, most previous ICU scoring systems either focus on the worst values in the monitoring period or depend on human subjective decisions and visual inspection. Multiple logistic regression is commonly used to build the predictive model. It is important to note that temporal correlations among variables are not specifically considered. In addition, missing data pose significant challenges on the construction of predictive models. Although laboratory tests and patient monitoring provide rich information sources for monitoring critical conditions of postsurgical patients, the meaningful information extracted from the order-3 tensor form of ICU data sets (see Fig. 16.1b) is limited. As such, physicians need to make inferences about patient conditions based on most recent test results, ignoring important factors such as historical test results and the relationships among different types of tests.

In the general practice of medicine, physicians lack decision-support tools that can help them delineate hidden interactions among different lab tests, identify temporal variations of patient conditions, and predict mortality risks. There is a dire need to go beyond current medical practices and develop data-driven methods and tools that will enable and help (i) the handling of big data, (ii) the extraction of data-driven knowledge, and (iii) the exploitation of acquired knowledge for optimizing clinical decisions. In order to address the challenges of variable heterogeneity, patient heterogeneity, and time asynchronization, this chapter presents a postsurgical decision-support system that consists of a suite of analytical tools, including data categorization, data preprocessing, feature extraction, feature selection, and predictive modeling.

16.3   RESEARCH METHODOLOGY

Figure 16.2 shows the overall flowchart of the proposed data-driven postsurgical ICU decision-support system. Notably, healthcare technology in the 21st century has given rise to the big data in the ICU that involves a greater level of complexity and challenge, including variable heterogeneity, patient heterogeneity, and time asynchronization [22]. The proposed decision-support system is embodied by five core components

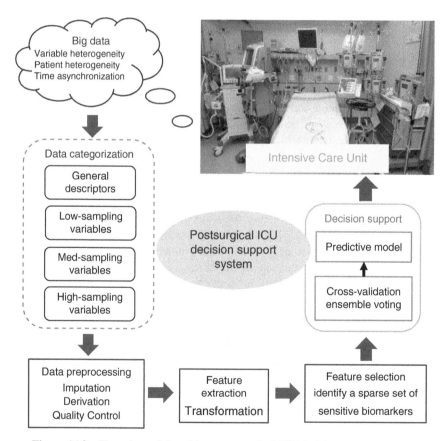

Figure 16.2   Flow chart of data-driven postsurgical ICU decision-support system.

(i.e., data categorization, data preprocessing, feature extraction, feature selection, and predictive modeling) that are effectively integrated to improve patient-specific prediction of in-hospital mortality.

First, we categorize various types of variables into four groups (namely, general descriptors, low-sampling variables, med-sampling variables, and high-sampling variables) based on the missing percentage in databases and the average number of observations per variable. Second, these four categories of variables will be preprocessed to ensure the data quality with various imputation and derivation methods (see details in Table 16.3). Third, we transform variables into features that contain critical clinical information and then use feature selection techniques to reduce high-dimensional features into a sparse set of sensitive biomarkers. Finally, we construct the predictive models with sensitive biomarkers that predict the clinical outcomes for ICU patients. These five components are detailed in the following sections.

16.3.1 Data Categorization

The common measurements in ICU consist of 44 variables (see details of variable names in Table 16.3). Over the course of 48 h, certain variables were measured at different time points with physicians' discretion due to different conditions of patients. It is very often that not all the 44 variables are recorded for each patient. Each patient may be monitored with a subset of variables at nonuniformly sampled time points. Variables may be recorded once, more than once, or not at all within 48 h of ICU stay.

For example, Figure 16.3 shows the percentage of missing data for common variables in one ICU database. Here, six general descriptors are excluded because they are recorded once in the beginning of ICU stay. It can be seen that none of variables is completely recorded for all patients. Also, some variables have more than 50% missing in the database. Based on the percentage of missing data and the average number of observations per variable, we categorize these 44 variables into four groups as shown in Table 16.3.

- *General Descriptors*: This group of variables includes general properties of a patient that are collected when the patient is first admitted into the ICU, for example, RecordID, Age, Gender, Height, ICUType, MechVent.
- *Low-Sampling Variables*: More than 50% patients do not record these variables in the database.
- *Med-Sampling Variables*: The average number of observations is less than 15 per patient per variable.
- *High-Sampling Variables*: Variables that do not meet with the above criteria.

16.3.2 Data Preprocessing and Missing Data Imputation

16.3.2.1 Data Preprocessing The step of data preprocessing is to ensure the data quality with various imputation and derivation methods that are detailed in Table 16.3.

TABLE 16.3 Postsurgical ICU Data Characteristics, Categorization, and Preprocessing

Data Category	Variables	Normal Range	Missing Percentage (%)	No. of Observations (Median ± SD)	Data Processing	Imputation Method
General Descriptor	RecordID		All available	Recorded once at the beginning		Remain unchanged
	Age					
	Gender					
	Height				Processing method 1[a]	
	ICUType					
	MechVent		35.87	7 ± 7.56	1: patient required mechanical ventilation; 0 otherwise	
Low-Sampling Variables	TroponinI	0–10	94.87	0 ± 0.55	Processing method 2[b]	SOM imputation
	TroponinT	0–0.1	78.42	0 ± 1.19		
	Cholesterol	200–1000	92.37	0 ± 0.27		
	RespRate	10–20	72.47	0 ± 23.55		
	Albumin	3.5–5.4	59.62	0 ± 0.9		
	ALP	44–147	57.75	0 ± 1.26		
	Bilirubin	0.2–1.9	57.05	0 ± 1.28		
	ALT	F: 10–50; M: 5–38	56.97	0 ± 1.28		
	AST	F: 8–40; M: 6–34	56.87	0 ± 1.28		
	SaO2	94–100	55.2	0 ± 3.46		

	Variable	Range		Mean ± SD	Processing	Sampling	Imputation
Med-sampling Variables	Lactate	3.7–5.2	45.42	1 ± 3.15		Sample every 4 h	Gaussian process and SOM imputation
	BUN	6–20	1.6	3 ± 1.68	Change to Creatinine Clearance[c]		
	Creatinine	F: 0.6–1.1; M: 0.7–1.3	1.6	3 ± 1.7			
	Glucose	70–100	2.82	3 ± 1.8			
	HCO$_3$	23–29	1.9	3 ± 1.7			
	K	0.5–2.2	2.4	3 ± 1.92			
	Mg	1.7–2.2	2.57	3 ± 1.77			
	Na	135–145	1.87	3 ± 1.86			
	Platelets	150–450	1.7	3 ± 1.91			
	WBC	4.5–10	1.82	3 ± 1.57			
	HCT	F: 35–48; M: 40–53	1.6	4 ± 2.58			
	PaCO2	35–45	24.42	5 ± 5.72			
	PaO2	75–100	24.42	5 ± 5.71			
	pH	7.38–7.42	24	5 ± 5.91			
High-sampling Variables	FiO$_2$	0.21~.5	32.07	8 ± 7.34		Sample every 1 h	
	GCS	0–3	1.6	13 ± 7.88			
	Temp	36~40	1.6	14 ± 17.45			
	Urine	1500	2.92	37 ± 12.49	Change to Urine.Sum[d] Processing method 1[a]		
	Weight		All available	37 ± 26.43			
	HR	60–100	1.57	55 ± 16.05			

(continued)

TABLE 16.3 (*Continued*)

Data Category	Variables	Normal Range	Missing Percentage (%)	No. of Observations (Median ± SD)	Data Processing	Imputation Method
	MAP	70–100	30.2	42 ± 30.14	Processing method 3[e]	
	NIMAP	70–100	12.97	21 ± 20.48		
	DiasABP	60–90	30.02	43 ± 29.57	Processing method 3[e]	
	NIDiasABP	60~90	12.92	21 ± 20.7		
	SysABP	100–140	30.02	43 ± 29.59	Processing method 3[e]	
	NISysABP	100–140	12.67	21 ± 20.7		

[a]Erroneous values were removed, and missing values were replaced using linear regression based on typical values by gender.
[b]Combine TroponinI and 100 * TroponinT as a new variable – Troponin.
[c]CreatinineClearance = (140 − Age) × Weight × (0.85 + 0.15 × Gender)/(72 × Creatinine).
[d]Urine.Sum is the cumulative sum of Urine.
[e]Combine two variables together.

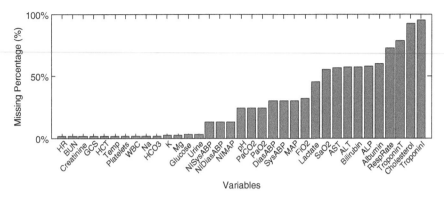

Figure 16.3 The percentage of missing data for variables.

First, erroneous weight and height values are removed, and missing height/weight values are replaced using a simple linear regression based on the most common height/weight values by gender. Second, TroponinT is multiplied by 100 and then combined with TroponinI as a new variable, Troponin. If one is missing, then the new variable Troponin takes the value of the other. Otherwise, it will take the average value. Third, Creatinine is replaced by CreatinineClearance, which is calculated based using the Cockcroft Gault equation:

$$CreatinineClearance = (140\text{-}Age)$$
$$\times Weight \times (0.85 + 0.15 \times Gender) / (72 \times Creatinine)$$

Fourth, Urine is replaced by a new variable Urine.Sum, which is the cumulative sum of the Urine measurements. Fifth, three pairs of variables, that is, DiasABP and NIDiasABP, MAP and NIMAP, SysABP and NISysABP, are combined, respectively, as three new time series and add a binary variable that will be assigned 1 if the majority observations were from the invasive procedure, 0 otherwise. Finally, missing values for med-sampling and high-sampling variables are firstly imputed at every 4 h and 1 h, respectively, via Gaussian process. The remaining missing data of all variables are then imputed by SOM imputation method. The detailed imputation methods are expressed in the following section.

16.3.2.2 Missing Data Imputation In this investigation, self-organizing map (SOM) is utilized for the imputation of low-sampling variables (see Table 16.3). SOM automatically organizes data with similar structures close to each other in the output layer of network [23, 24]. As shown in Figure 16.4, SOM neurons are usually represented on a low-dimensional map (e.g., two-dimensional map). Here, neurons will self-organize in the data space to recognize and characterize similar structures. Suppose the map contains M neurons, each neuron *i* is a vector

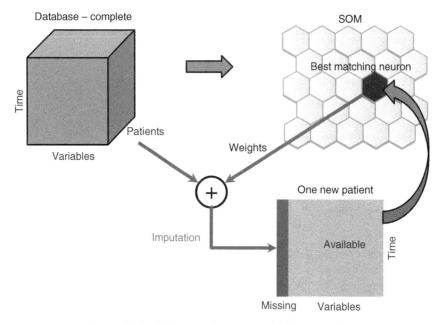

Figure 16.4   Self-organizing map model for imputation.

$w_i = [w_{i1}, w_{i2}, \ldots, w_{id}]$, $i = 1, 2, \ldots, M$, where d is the dimension that is the same as the vector of input features (or ICU variables) $x = [x_1, x_2, \cdots, x_d]$. In each training step, an input feature vector x is presented to SOM neurons. The index c of the best-matching neuron (BMN) is determined by

$$c = \arg \min_i \|x\text{-}w_i\|$$

The vector of BMN and its neighbors on the hexagonal map are updated by moving toward the input feature vector with the rule of Kohonen update as

$$w_i(t + 1) = w_i(t) + h_{ci}(t) \cdot [x(t) - w_i(t)], \quad i = 1, 2, \ldots, M$$

where $t = 0, 1, 2, \ldots$ is the iteration step of neurons. The neurons in an N-dimensional SOM are initialized so that the initial weights w_i are distributed across the space spanned by the most significant N principal components of the input features. Here, $h_{ci}(t)$ is the neighborhood function, which is usually formed as $h_{ci}(t) = h(\|r_c - r_i\|, t)$, where $r_c, r_i \in \mathfrak{R}^2$ are the locations of neuron c and i. This neighborhood function $h_{ci}(t) \to 0$ when $t \to \infty$, and $h_{ci}(t) \to 0$ when $\|r_c - r_i\|$ increases. Gaussian function is used for $h_{ci}(t)$ in this present investigation as

$$h_{ci}(t) = \alpha(t) \cdot \exp\left(-\frac{\|r_c - r_i\|^2}{2[\sigma(t)]^2}\right)$$

where $\alpha(t)$ is the learning-rate factor, and $\sigma(t)$ is the width of the neighborhood kernel function. Both $\alpha(t)$ and $\sigma(t)$ are monotonically decreasing functions of time.

Training the SOM can either use the complete database that does not contain missing variables or involve available variables from patients with some missing variables. Another advantage is that SOM training can be implemented in batches or in a sequential way. As shown in Figure 16.4, when a new patient with missing variables is presented to the SOM map, we can ignore the missing variables and compute the distances between this new patient and neurons using available variables. Then, distance measures will help select the neighboring neurons. The imputed values of missing variables in this new patient will be calculated based on the weights of neighboring neurons in the missing dimensions. Note that the complete database may be relatively small in terms of sample size, and thereby decrease the training performance of SOM. In order to fully utilize incomplete samples, SOM weight updating is flexible to incorporate the available variables from patients with missing variables. The SOM imputation approach is similar to traditional hot-deck and multilayer perceptron (MLP) imputation methods, but has an attractive feature of online sequential update of weights as well as the utilization of incomplete samples in the training.

For med-sampling and high-sampling variables, there are significant temporal variations involved in the data set. Therefore, missing values along the temporal dimension will be imputed at every 4 and 1 h, respectively, via the Gaussian process [25]. Let $(t_1, x_1), \ldots, (t_n, x_n)$ be time-varying ICU variables, where t_i is the time index and x_i is the value of an ICU variable. The temporal function $x = f(t) + \varepsilon$, where $\varepsilon \sim^{iid} N(0, \sigma_n^2)$ and $f(t)$ is modeled as a Gaussian process that is specified by the mean function $m(t)$ and covariance function $k(t, t')$, that is,

$$f(t) \sim \mathcal{GP}(m(t), k(t, t'))$$

$$m(t) = \mathbb{E}[f(t)]$$

$$k(t, t') = \mathbb{E}[(f(t) - m(t))(f(t') - m(t'))]$$

The GP is defined as a collection of random variables, any finite set of which follows a joint Gaussian distribution. The GP is treated as a functional prior on the time-varying ICU variables. In this investigation, we used the following covariance function to specify the covariance between pairs of random variables:

$$k(t, t') = \sigma_f^2 \exp\left(-\frac{1}{2}(t - t')^T M(t - t')\right)$$

where σ_f^2 is the signal variance and $M = \text{diag}(l)^{-2}$ with the length scale vector l. Note that $f(t)$ and $f(t')$ should be similar if t and t' are sufficiently close in the temporal dimension. Therefore, the length scale l defines the separation between different dimensions of input variables. For a missing data x_* at the time t_*, the training outputs $X = f(T)$ from $T = (t_1, \ldots, t_n)$, and the predicted $x_* = f_*(t_*)$ have a joint prior distribution with zero mean:

$$\begin{bmatrix} X \\ x_* \end{bmatrix} \sim N(0, \begin{bmatrix} K(T, T) + \sigma_n^2 I & K(T, t_*) \\ K(t_*, T) & K(t_*, t_*) \end{bmatrix}$$

In order to obtain the posterior distribution, this joint prior distribution is restricted to include only those functions that agree with the computed observations from the space-filling design. Hence, the posterior distribution of $f_*(t_*)$ is

$$p(x_*|T, X, t_*) \sim \mathcal{N}(\overline{x}_*, \text{cov}(x_*))$$

$$\overline{x}_* = \mathbb{E}(x_*|T, X, t_*) = K(t_*, T)[K(T, T) + \sigma_n^2 I]^{-1} X$$

$$\text{cov}(x_*) = K(t_*, t_*) - K(t_*, T)[K(T, T) + \sigma_n^2 I]^{-1} K(T, t_*)$$

However, the hyperparameters $\theta = \{M, \sigma_f, \sigma_n\}$ need to be optimally chosen in order to yield the best GP model for predicting the imputed values. These hyperparameters can be learned by maximizing the log-marginal likelihood,

$$\theta_{\text{optimal}} = \text{argmax}_\theta \{\log p(X|T, \theta)\}$$

$$\log p(XT, \theta) = -\frac{1}{2} \log|K + \sigma_n^2 I| - \frac{1}{2} X^T [K + \sigma_n^2 I]^{-1} X - \frac{n}{2} \log 2\pi$$

As such, the GP is optimally trained with the available data in the med-sampling and high-sampling ICU variables. Notably, the GP model provides both mean and variance for the imputed values of missing ICU variables in the temporal dimension.

16.3.3 Feature Extraction

After the data preprocessing, ICU data set is in the form of order-3 tensor. The next step is to characterize the structure and correlation in the high-dimensional tensor data and extract a sparse set of joint biomarkers sensitive to morbidity and mortality in the postoperative process. Dimensionality reduction is a subspace representation approach that not only transforms high-dimensional data into the low-dimensional feature space but also retains the underlying structures. Traditionally, principal component analysis (PCA) is a common approach for dimensionality reduction, but is not applicable here for high-order tensors. Naive application of PCA needs to reshape the tensor data into the form of 2D matrix. However, reshaping breaks the natural structure and correlation in the original tensor data. Hence, we propose a new approach of constrained tensor decomposition to extract a low-dimensional set of uncorrelated features from tensor data. This idea is originated from the recent literature on multilinear subspace learning in image and video processing [26, 27]. A significant difference between image/video processing and postoperative applications lies in data heterogeneity. Image/video data are homogeneous and synchronized in time, but postoperative sensing involves heterogeneous variables that are asynchronized and incomplete. Therefore, data preprocessing and missing data imputation (see Section 16.3.2) are specifically designed to tackle these challenges and facilitate the extraction of biomarkers using multilinear subspace learning in Section 16.3.3.

Multilinear subspace learning utilizes the tensor-to-vector projection (TVP) to extract uncorrelated features from tensor data [39]. These low-dimensional features are not only orthogonal to each other but also maximize the projection variances. The

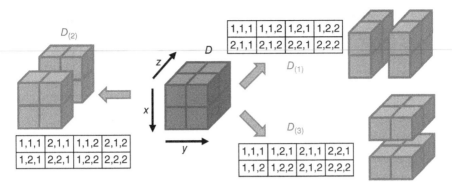

Figure 16.5   Illustration of reshaping order-3 tensor to matrix.

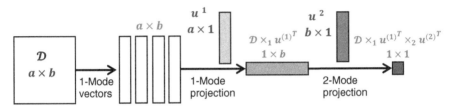

Figure 16.6   An illustration of elementary multilinear projection (EMP) of the order-2 tensor data.

TVP consists of multiple elementary multilinear projections (EMP), which project a tensor $D \in \mathbb{R}^{I_1 \times \cdots \times I_N}$ to a scalar x through the N projection vectors as

$$x = D \times_1 u^{(1)^T} \times_2 u^{(2)^T} \times_{N-1} \cdots \times_N u^{(N)^T}$$

where $u^{(n)}$ is the nth projection vector and $\times_n$ is the nth-mode multiplication. In order to calculate the nth-mode multiplication, we first need to reshape an order-N tensor into matrices. The nth-mode multiplication $\times_n$ of tensor D and matrix M is defined as $D \times_n M = M D_{(n)}$, where $D_{(n)}$ is the "flatting" of tensor data along the nth dimension. Figure 16.5 illustrates that an order-3 tensor is flatted over the dimension $n, n = 1, 2, 3$.

Figure 16.6 illustrates the EMP of an order-2 tensor to a scalar $x = D \times_1 u^{(1)^T} \times_2 u^{(2)^T}$. First, the order-2 tensor data $D \in \mathbb{R}^{a \times b}$ is flatted along the first dimension and then multiplied by the first projection vector $u^{(1)}$, resulting a vector $D \times_1 u^{(1)^T} = u^{(1)^T} D_{(1)}$. Second, this vector of size $1 \times b$ is multiplied by the second projection vector $u^{(2)}$ to get the scalar $x = D \times_1 u^{(1)^T} \times_2 u^{(2)^T}$.

The use of P EMPs will project the tensor data D to a vector $\mathbf{x} \in \mathbb{R}^P$ as

$$\mathbf{x} = D \times_{n=1}^{N} \left\{ \mathbf{u}_p^{(n)^T}, n = 1, 2, \dots, N \right\}_{p=1}^{P}$$

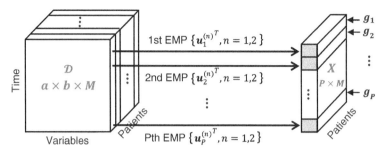

Figure 16.7   An illustration of uncorrelated multilinear subspace learning for order-3 data.

where p denotes the index of EMP. Figure 16.7 shows the projection of order-3 tensor $\mathcal{X}$ to a 2D matrix $\mathbf{Y}$. The $\mathbf{x}_m(p)$ is the projection of the mth patient $\mathcal{X}_m$ by EMPs: $\mathbf{x}_m(p) = \mathcal{X}_m \times_{n=1}^{N} \left\{ \mathbf{u}_p^{(n)^T}, n = 1, 2, \dots, N \right\}$. As shown in Figure 16.7, $\mathbf{g}_P$ denotes the pth coordinate vector and $\mathbf{g}_P(m) = \mathbf{x}_m(p)$. In order to maximize the variance of projections and extract uncorrelated features, a constraint function will be imposed on the pth EMP:

$$\left\{ \mathbf{u}_p^{(n)^T}, n = 1, 2, \dots, N \right\} = \operatorname{argmax}_{\mathbf{u}_p^{(n)^T}} \operatorname{Var}(\mathbf{g}_p)$$

$$\text{s.t.} \, \mathbf{u}_p^{(n)^T} \mathbf{u}_p^{(n)} = 1, \, p = 1, \dots, P \text{ and } \mathbf{g}_p^T \mathbf{g}_q = 0, \text{ for all } p, q, p \neq q.$$

It should be noted that multilinear subspace learning produces a low-dimensional set of uncorrelated features. In order to solve the constrained objective function, a sequential variance maximization algorithm is utilized (see details in Figure 16.8). The P EMPs $\left\{ \mathbf{u}_p^{(n)^T}, n = 1, 2, \dots, N \right\}_{p=1}^{P}$ are sequentially estimated in P steps subject to the orthogonal and normalization constraints.

16.3.4   Feature Selection

Multilinear subspace learning transforms the tensor data of size $a \times b \times M$ into the matrix of uncorrelated features of size $p \times M$. An advantage is that these features are now in the conventional table form of data (see Fig. 16.1a) for predictive modeling. However, there are still a large amount of features in the postdecomposition matrix, which may bring the "curse of dimensionality" issues for classification models, for example, increased number of model parameters and overfitting problems [28, 29]. There is an urgent need to select a sparse subset of features that are sensitive to ICU morbidity and mortality, as opposed to extraneous noises. Feature selection not only improves the robustness of predictive models but also increases the interpretability of features to further investigate the cause of ICU mortality.

Initialization:
$\mathcal{D}_m \in \mathbb{R}^{I_1 \times \cdots \times I_N}, m = 1,2,\ldots,M$ // A set of tensor samples
P// desired feature vector length
For $p = 1 : P$
$\boldsymbol{g}_p(m) = \mathcal{D}_m \times_{n=1}^{N} \left\{ \mathbf{u}_p^{(n)^T}, n = 1,2,\ldots,N \right\}$ // calculate the coordinate vector
If $p = 1$
          Maximizing $Var(\boldsymbol{g}_1)$ // maximizing variance
Else
          Maximizing $Var(\boldsymbol{g}_p)$ // maximizing variance
          Subject to $\boldsymbol{g}_p^T \boldsymbol{g}_q = 0, q = 1,2 \ldots, p - 1$ // subject to the constraints
End
End

Figure 16.8   The sequential variance maximization algorithm for tensor decomposition.

A common approach of feature selection is to maximize the feature relevance (Max-Relevance) to response variables (or outcomes). In other words, it is highly desirable to select feature variables that have the highest relevance to the response variables. Traditionally, such interrelationship between variables is estimated with correlation methods. Yet, correlation is a second-order quantity evaluating merely linear dependency among data. Notably, mutual information quantifies both linear and nonlinear dependency between variables, which is defined as

$$I(x,y) = \sum_{i,j} p(x_i, y_j) \log \frac{p(x_i, y_j)}{p(x_i)p(y_j)}$$

where $p(x,y)$ is the joint probabilistic distribution and $p(x)$ and $p(y)$ are marginal probabilities. Figure 16.9 shows the practical implementation to compute the mutual information. In the scatterplot of two variables x and y, the histogram is shown for each variable. Marginal probabilities $p(x_i)$ and $p(y_j)$ are computed as the number of points in x_i and y_j divided by the total number of points in the 2D space. The joint probability $p(x_i, y_j)$ is computed as the number of points in box (x_i, y_j) divided by the total number of points in the space. In the step of feature selection, features x_i that have bigger values of mutual information $I(x_i; c)$ with the response variable c reflect the strongest interdependency.

However, it was shown that high correlations among features (or predictor variables) often lead to sensitive predictive models that do not necessarily yield good classification performance. Thus, feature selection also needs to minimize the redundancy (Min-Redundancy) among features. In this chapter, we used a filtering method, namely minimum redundancy and maximum relevance (mRMR) [30], to reduce high-dimensional features into a sparse set of sensitive biomarkers. The mRMR method selects features that are maximally relevant to the response

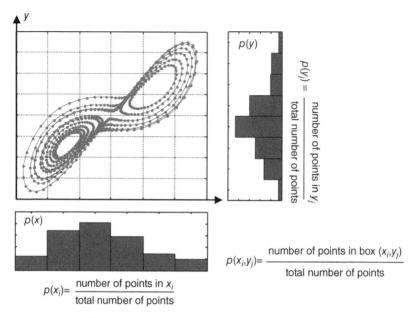

Figure 16.9 An illustration for the computation of mutual information.

variable while minimizing redundancy between selected features. Redundancy R_I and relevancy D_I are defined, respectively, according to the following equations:

$$R_I = \frac{1}{|S|^2} \sum_{x_i, x_j \in S} I(x_i, x_j); \; D_I = \frac{1}{|S|} \sum_{x_i \in S} I(x_i; c)$$

where $|S|$ represents the cardinality of the feature set S, x_i and x_j denote the ith and jth features, and c is the response variable. The mRMR aims to yield minimal redundancy among predictor variables and maximal relevancy between predictor and response variables. Here, a greedy search algorithm is utilized to achieve the mRMR objective and identify near-optimal features. Suppose there is an optimally selected feature set S_{k-1} with $k - 1$ features, the next best feature (i.e., the kth one) is selected by maximizing Mutual Information Difference (MID) in the remaining feature set $X \backslash S_{k-1}$, that is, MID = max($D_I - R_I$). The higher the MID score, the more significant the feature is. The objective function is defined as follows:

$$\underset{x_j \in X \backslash S_{k-1}}{\mathrm{argmax}} \left(I(x_j; c) - \frac{1}{k-1} \sum_{x_i \in S_{k-1}} I(x_j; x_i) \right)$$

It is worth mentioning that the greedy search algorithm is very efficient in terms of computational complexity, which is $o(|S| \cdot K)$ for K selected features. The mRMR methodology provides the most significant features by ranked scores from computationally efficient heuristic algorithms.

16.3.5 Predictive Model

Furthermore, we construct the predictive models that associate the input feature pattern $\jmath$ to one of the $\mathcal{K}$ classes of outcomes $C_1, \ldots, C_{\mathcal{K}}$. In this present study, clinical outcomes are binary ($\mathcal{K} = 2$), that is, survival or in-hospital death. The whole data set D is partitioned into the training data set $D_1 = \{\langle c(i), \jmath(i)\rangle | i = 1, \ldots, N_1\}$ and testing data set $D_2 = \{\langle c(i), \jmath(i)\rangle | i = N_1 + 1, \ldots, N_1 + N_2\}$, where N_1 and N_2 are the size of training and testing data sets, $c(i)$ takes values in the output sets $C_1, \ldots, C_{\mathcal{K}}$, and $\jmath(i) = \{x_{i1}, x_{i2}, \ldots, x_{i\ell}\}$ is the set of ℓ selected features for the ith patient recording in the database D.

Figure 16.10 shows the structure diagram of MLP network [31, 32] that is used to predict the ICU mortality. In this two-layered network, hyperbolic tangent sigmoid transfer function (tansig) is used in the hidden layer and log-sigmoid transfer function (logsig) in the output layer. The hidden layer includes $S = 40$ neurons and the output layer contains $O = 2$ neurons. Network parameters (e.g., weights IW and bias b^1) were optimized to learn and model the input–output mapping function with an efficient algorithm, namely backpropagation. In this literature, backpropagation algorithm is commonly used to train the multilayer feedforward network models. This section provides a brief introduction of backpropagation as follows:

1. *Forward Propagation.* As shown in Figure 16.10, the output of one layer in the multilayer network becomes the input to the next layer. The operation for the mth layer is defined as

$$a^m = f^m(W^m \cdot a^{m-1} + b^m), \ m = 0, 1, \ldots, M$$

   where M is number of layers in the network, W^m is the weights, b^m is the bias term, and f^m is the transfer function for the mth layer. If features are presented to the network as external inputs, then network outputs are derived with the forward propagation as follows:

$$a^0 = x$$
$$a^m = f^m(W^m \cdot a^{m-1} + b^m), \ m = 0, 1, \ldots, M$$
$$y = a^M$$

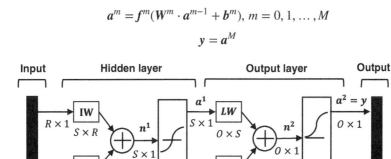

Figure 16.10   The structure diagram of multilayer neural network.

However, network parameters such as weights and biases need to be fine-tuned to achieve the optimal predictive performance. First, the multilayer network is initialized by randomly assigning values to network weights $W^m(0)$ and biases $b^m(0)$ for $m = 1, 2, \ldots, M$ at the iteration $k = 0$. Second, the discrepancy between network output and the ICU outcomes c will be used to sequentially update the weights $W^m(k + 1)$ and biases $W^m(k + 1)$ in each layer for the next iteration $k + 1$.

2. *Performance Index.* The training data set $\mathcal{D}_1 = \{\langle c(i), \jmath(i) \rangle | i = 1, \ldots, N_1\}$ is provided to learn network models and fine-tune network parameters. When input features $\jmath(i)$ are given to the network, the network outputs a^M are compared to the target $c(i)$. The discrepancy of network models is measured by the performance index, namely the mean squared error (MSE) as

$$F(\theta | \langle c, \jmath \rangle) = E(e^T e) = E((c - a)^T (c - a))$$

where θ is the parameter vector of network weights and biases. Therefore, the approximated performance index at iteration k is

$$\hat{F}(\theta) = e(k)^T e(k) = (t(k) - a(k))^T (t(k) - a(k))$$

where the expected errors are replaced by the squared error at iteration k.

3. *Backward Propagation.* Now, the next step is to calculate the gradient descent of squared errors with respect to model parameters. The error is an explicit function of parameters in the output layer. Hence, the gradient (or sensitivity) for the output layer is

$$s^M = \frac{\partial \hat{F}}{\partial n^M} = -2\dot{F}^M(n^M)(t - a)$$

$$\dot{F}^m(n^m) = \begin{bmatrix} \dot{f}^m(n_1^m) & \cdots & 0 \\ \vdots & \ddots & \vdots \\ 0 & \cdots & \dot{f}^m(n_{s^m}^m) \end{bmatrix} \text{ and } \dot{f}^m(n_j^m) = \frac{\partial f^m(n_j^m)}{\partial n_j^m}$$

where $\dot{F}^M(n^M)$ is the derivative matrix of transfer function with respect to the input n^M. However, the performance index is not a direct function of model parameters in the hidden layers. Hence, the chain rule in calculus is used to compute the derivatives for each layer as

$$s^m = \frac{\partial \hat{F}}{\partial n^m} = \left(\frac{\partial n^{m+1}}{\partial n^m} \right)^T \frac{\partial \hat{F}}{\partial n^{m+1}} = \dot{F}^m(n^m)(W^{m+1})^T \frac{\partial \hat{F}}{\partial n^{m+1}}$$

$$= \dot{F}^m(n^m)(W^{m+1})^T s^{m+1}$$

$$m = M - 1, \ldots, 2, 1$$

With the use of chain rule, the backpropagation algorithm calculates the sensitivities backward through the network from the last layer to the first layer.

As such, model parameters (i.e., weights and biases) are iteratively optimized using the steepest descent algorithm as

$$W^m(k+1) = W^m(k) - \alpha s^m(a^{m-1})^T$$

$$b^m(k+1) = b^m(k) - \alpha s^m$$

The backpropagation algorithm continues to fine-tune parameters by choosing input–output data from the training data set D_1. This process will iterate until the MSE between network outputs and the targets is minimized and converged to an acceptable level.

16.3.6 Cross-Validation and Ensemble Voting Processes

In this chapter, both K-fold cross-validation and bootstrapping were utilized to reduce the bias and overfitting of predictive models. K-fold cross-validation partitions the total data set D into K folds, in which $K - 1$ folds are used for the training purpose and the rest onefold for testing. After completion of all K folds, performance statistics are computed from the testing data sets. However, it may be noted that the class sizes are often not equal, that is, 3446 survivals and 554 in-hospital deaths. Conventional classification models assume that each class has enough representative cases in the training data set. The objective of classification algorithms is to maximize the overall prediction accuracy. When it comes to a highly imbalanced data sets, classification models tend to favor the majority class and relatively overlook the minority class [29, 33, 34]. Therefore, bootstrapping methods were utilized to reconstruct the balanced data sets. Bootstrapping is a statistical approach that does random sampling with replacement from a data set. It resamples the training data set to create a large number of "bootstrapping samples." It is generally agreed that the bootstrapping provides better approximations of the underlying distribution.

As shown in Figure 16.11, our ICU data set consists of m survival and n in-hospital death recordings ($m > n$). In the first place, the data set A is randomly partitioned into two subsets, that is, the training subset T and the out-of-bag testing subset $T^{(l)}$. The K-fold cross-validation uses $(K - 1)$ folds for the training purpose and the rest 1 fold for testing. It may be noted that the partition ratio, that is, $(K - 1)$ training folds versus 1 validation fold, is the same for survival and in-hospital death groups. Furthermore, a balanced training set T is reconstructed with the use of bootstrapping methods. The in-hospital death group is enlarged to yield the same size as the survival group in the new training set T'. In other words, in-hospital death recordings in training set T are resampled with replacement to increase the size from $(K - 1) \cdot n/K$ to $(K - 1) \cdot m/K$. In addition, the bootstrapping procedure is randomly replicated for R times to avoid biases. For each replicate of the training data sets T', a predictive model will be constructed and trained. A total of R predictive models are yielded for R replicated training data sets. A majority voting mechanism is designed to assign the majority class label to each recording in the validation subset $T^{(l)}$. In other words, a label that appears more than half $(R/2)$ the votes for R predictive models will be assigned to this recording. The final prediction results are based on the majority voting from n classifiers trained. As such, this ensemble voting approach provides more balanced estimates of performance metrics.

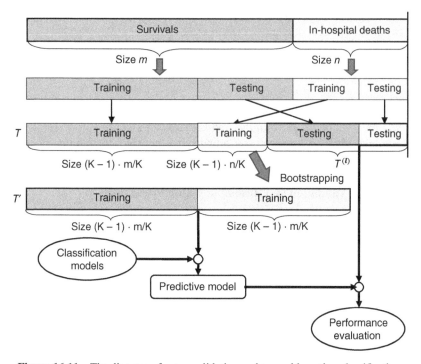

Figure 16.11   The diagram of cross-validation and ensemble voting classification.

Performance metrics used to evaluate predictive models are sensitivity (SEN), specificity (SPE), positive predictive value (PPV), negative predictive value (NPV), and accuracy (ACC). It may be noted that all metrics are computed from testing data set D_2. Sensitivity measures the proportion of actual positives, that is, in-hospital death conditions are correctly identified as such. While specificity measures the proportion of actual negatives, that is, in-hospital survival conditions are correctly identified as such. PPV measures the proportion of positives in the diagnostic test that are true positives, and NPV measures the proportion of negatives in the diagnostic test that are true negatives. Moreover, the accuracy is the ratio of subjects (i.e., either survival or death) that are correctly identified in the testing data sets. The performance metrics, that is, SEN, SPE, PPV, NPV, and ACC, are defined as

$$SEN = \frac{TP}{TP + FN}, SPE = \frac{TN}{FP + TN}, PPV = \frac{TP}{TP + FP},$$
$$NPV = \frac{TN}{TN + FN}, ACC = \frac{TP + TN}{TP + TN + FP + FN}$$

where TP, TN, FN, and FP mean "true positive," "true negative," "false negative," and "false positive," respectively. The final score of mortality prediction is the minimum of sensitivity and PPV.

16.4   MATERIALS AND EXPERIMENTAL DESIGN

Real-world ICU data set was used to evaluate and validate the proposed methodology in this present study. This data set is extracted from Multiparameter Intelligent Monitoring in Intensive Care (MIMIC) II Clinical Database [35–37], which was developed to advance intelligent patient monitoring research in the critical care environment. This data set is divided into two groups, that is, Set A and Set B, and each of them consists of 4,000 patient records from 48 h of ICU stays (including coronary care unit, cardiac surgery recovery unit, medical ICU, and surgical ICU). Clinical outcomes (i.e., in-hospital death or survival) are made available for Set A, but not for Set B. The training of predictive models is only based on 4000 subjects in Set A. As shown in Section 16.3, the proposed decision-support system consists of a suite of analytical tools, including data categorization, data preprocessing, feature extraction, feature selection, and predictive modeling. We conducted experiments on both Sets A and B to validate and evaluate the developed analytical tools for improving patient-specific prediction of in-hospital mortality.

First, we categorize ICU variables into four groups (namely general descriptors, low-sampling variables, med-sampling variables, and high-sampling variables) based on the missing percentage and the average number of observations per variable in Set A. *Second*, these four categories of variables will be preprocessed to ensure the data quality (see details in Table 16.3). Missing data are imputed with the use of SOM and Gaussian process models. In particular, med-sampling and high-sampling variables are imputed at every 4 and 1 h, respectively. Therefore, we obtain a $14 \times 12 \times 8000$ tensor for med-sampling variables, where 14 is the number of med-sampling variables, 12 is the number of temporal samples (1 sample per 4 for 48 h), and 8000 is the total number of patients for Sets A and B. In addition, we generate a $9 \times 48 \times 8000$ tensor for high-sampling variables, where 9 is the number of high-sampling variables, 48 is the number of temporal samples (1 sample/h for 48 h), and 8000 is the total number of patients for Sets A and B. Note that data categorization and data preprocessing are consistent for Sets A and B. *Third*, we transform the order-3 tensor form of ICU variables into the traditional table form of features (i.e., uncorrelated and orthogonal) with multilinear subspace learning. The feature extraction fully considers the inherent structure of tensor data, as opposed to the worst values during 48 h in traditional scoring systems. Then, mRMR technique is used to further reduce high-dimensional features (i.e., two feature matrices from med-sampling and high-sampling tensors, general descriptors, and low-sampling variables) into a sparse set of sensitive biomarkers. Finally, we construct the predictive models with sensitive biomarkers that predict the clinical outcomes for ICU patients.

16.5   EXPERIMENTAL RESULTS

Figure 16.12 shows an example of raw and imputed data for med-sampling and high-sampling variables of patient ID 133581. As mentioned in Section 16.3.1, we categorize 44 ICU variables into four groups (namely, general descriptor,

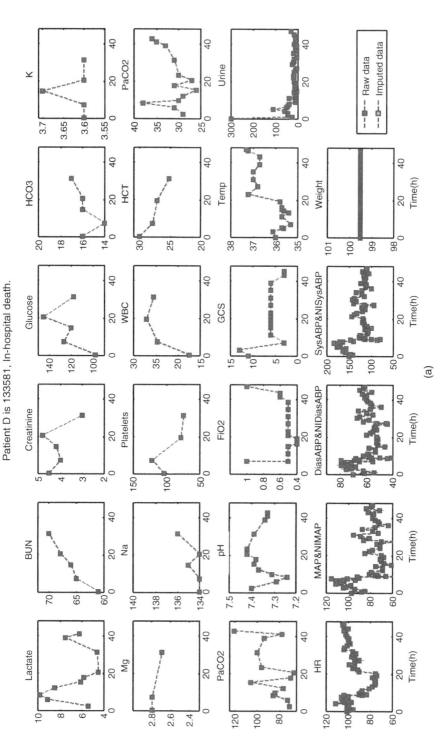

Figure 16.12 An example of missing data imputation for patient ID 133581: (a) raw data; (b) imputed data for med-sampling (from "Lactate" to "pH") and high-sampling variables (from "FiO2" to "Weight").

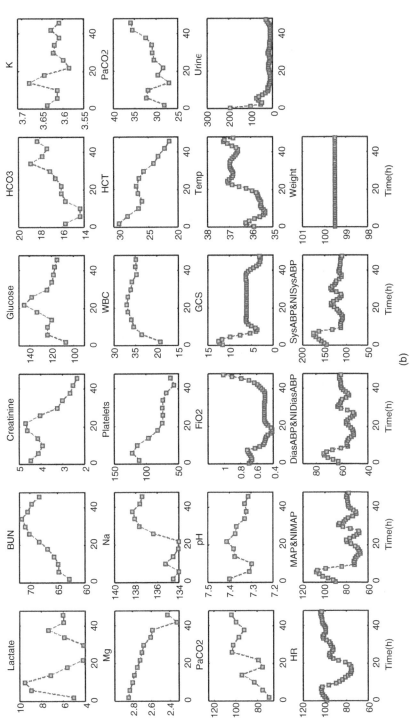

Figure 16.12 (*Continued*)

(b)

low-sampling, med-sampling, high-sampling) based on the percentage of missing data and the average number of observations per variable. Figure 16.12 shows the imputation results for med-sampling variables from "Lactate" to "pH" and high-sampling variables from "FiO2" to "Weight." As the protocol is not standardized for data collection in ICU, missing data and time asynchronization pose significant challenges for predictive modeling. In order to tackle these issues, we performed missing data imputation for med-sampling variables at the synchronized frequency of one sample per 4 h, as well as for high-sampling variables at the pace of one sample per 1 h. As shown in Figure 16.12a, missing values are common in the raw data. Also, the raw data are not synchronized for all variables. In most cases, data collection is subject to the physician's discretion. One way is to standardize the protocol of ICU data collection and then perform the data analysis. However, this cannot be practically implemented in a short time frame. The other way is to perform missing data imputation and take full advantage of available data. In this present study, we made an attempt to develop a hybrid method that integrates SOM with Gaussian process for imputing missing values and synchronizing variables in the tensor-form ICU data.

As illustrated in Figure 16.13, if two variables are collected arbitrarily, our objective is to impute the missing values as well as synchronize the data. Traditional methods for missing data imputation mainly focus on missing values in the table form data (see Fig. 16.1a) and have little considerations on the data synchronization. Therefore, we propose the hybrid method for ICU missing data imputation as follows:

```
Step 1 - Gaussian process kriging
Initialization
Check the number of data points N for patient m
If N > MinTol
```
$$\boldsymbol{X^i}(m) = \{x_{t_1}^i(m), x_{t_1}^i(m), ..., x_{t_N}^i(m)\} \quad \text{// the ith variable for patient } m$$
$$\boldsymbol{T} = \{t_1, t_2, ..., t_N\} \quad \text{// time of recorded data}$$
```
Construct a new time index Tk, k = 1 : K
// K = 12 for med-sampling variable; K = 48 for high-sampling
                                                      variable
      If t1 ≤ Tk ≤ tN  // Tk is the time index of imputed data
```
$$\begin{bmatrix} \boldsymbol{X^i}(m) \\ x_{T_k}^i(m) \end{bmatrix} \sim \mathcal{N}\left(0, \begin{bmatrix} K(\boldsymbol{T}, \boldsymbol{T}) + \sigma_n^2 \boldsymbol{I} & K(\boldsymbol{T}, T_k) \\ K(T_k, \boldsymbol{t}) & K(T_k, T_k) \end{bmatrix}\right)$$
```
        // xᵢTk(m) is imputed data at time Tk, K(·,·) is covariance
                                                            matrix
```
$$\tilde{x}_{T_k}^i(m) \triangleq \mathbb{E}(x_{T_k}^i | \boldsymbol{T}, \boldsymbol{X}, T_k) = K(T_k, \boldsymbol{T})[K(\boldsymbol{T}, \boldsymbol{T}) + \sigma_n^2 \boldsymbol{I}]^{-1} \boldsymbol{X}$$
```
      End
Else
   This variable is sparse or completely missing.
   goto step 2 - SOM imputation
End


Step 2 - SOM imputation
Initialization
   Flat the array of ICU data into a vector X⁽ⁱ,ᵀ⁾(m) for patient m
```
$$\boldsymbol{X}^{(i,T)}(m) = \{x_{T_1}^1(m), ..., x_{T_K}^1(m), ..., x_{T_1}^I(m), ..., x_{T_K}^I(m)\}$$
```
   // 1 ≤ i ≤ I, where I is the total number of variables
```

```
// synchronized time index T_k, k = 1 : K
// K = 12 for med-sampling variable; K = 48 for high-sampling
                                            variable
Find the best matching neuron for patient m
c = arg min{X^(i,T)(m) − w^(i,T)(j)_(i,T)∈A_m} // where A_m is the set of
       j
                                      synchronized index
    // Missing variables are not included in the computation
Missing data imputation for x^i_{T_k}(m)
    If X^i(m) is not completely missing
       // some data points {x^i_{T_1}(m), ..., x^i_{T_K}(m)} are available for the
                                            ith variable
       x^i_{T_k}(m) = ½(x^i_{T_{k'}}(m) + w^i_{T_k}(c)) // where k' = arg min k − k_1
                                                                    l
    Else
       x^i_{T_k}(m) = w^i_{T_k}(c) // replace the missing values with the weight of the
                                            best matching neuron
    End
```

As shown in Figure 16.12b, the proposed hybrid method handles both missing data imputation and data synchronization and generates uniformly sampled data for med-sampling and high-sampling variables. This greatly facilitates the following steps of feature extraction and predictive modeling. In particular, SOM map characterizes the population distribution of variables among patients, while Gaussian process kriging captures the temporal correlation among variables. An attractive feature of our proposed hybrid method is that both population distribution and temporal correlation are utilized in the missing data imputation. However, most of previous imputation methods considered either of these two but not both.

Figure 16.14a shows the U-matrix that characterizes the distances between neurons in the SOM (10-by-10 neuron map) for Set A. The dark gray hexagons represent neurons, and light gray lines are connections between two adjacent neurons. The distances between neurons are shown as colored hexagons that embrace red lines. The darker color indicates a larger distance between neurons, and the lighter color is for a smaller distance between neurons. The pattern of U-matrix describes the complex distribution of ICU variables. SOM automatically organizes neurons in the space of ICU data. Each neuron represents a cluster of patients that share similar data patterns

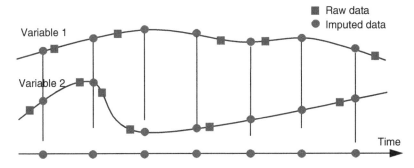

Figure 16.13 An illustration of missing data imputation to achieve data synchronization.

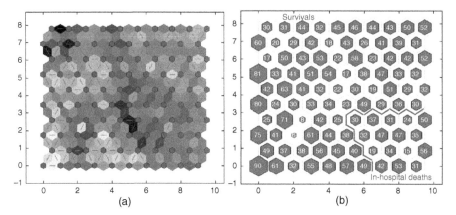

Figure 16.14 Optimized SOM structures for training Set A: (a) U-matrix of SOM neurons; (b) SOM sample hits.

in ICU variables. Figure 16.14b shows the hits of patients onto each neuron. In other words, each patient is associated with its BMN. Each hexagon in Figure 16.14b represents a neuron, and the number on hexagons is the number of patients hitting on this neuron. Because the recordings in Set A are highly imbalanced, that is, 3446 survivals and 554 in-hospital deaths, our experimental results show that most of the in-hospital deaths hit in the lower-right region. Based on the label information of patients in Set A, it is interesting to find that neurons in the lower-right region captures the data patterns of in-hospital deaths, while the upper-left region captures the data patterns for the survivals.

After the step of missing data imputation, we generated a $14 \times 12 \times 8000$ tensor for med-sampling variables, where 14 is the number of med-sampling variables, 12 is the number of temporal samples (1 sample per 4 h for 48 h), and 8000 is the total number of patients for Sets A and B. In addition, we generate a $9 \times 48 \times 8000$ tensor for high-sampling variables. Note that data categorization and data preprocessing are consistent for Sets A and B. Furthermore, we transform the order-3 tensor form of ICU variables into the traditional table form of features (i.e., uncorrelated and orthogonal) with multilinear subspace learning. The feature extraction takes full consideration of inherent structures of tensor data. As a result, 20 features are extracted from med-sampling variables and 9 features from high-sampling variables. Both feature sets retain 95% variances in the original data. Therefore, there is a total of 43 features (2 feature matrices from med-sampling and high-sampling tensors, 5 general descriptors, and 9 low-sampling variables). Figure 16.15 shows the sorted mRMR scores of all features extracted. It is worth mentioning that the first few principal components of med- and high-sampling variables are shown to be more significant than other features and contain sensitive information for the prediction of mortality risks. To this end, we selected 26 features with the mRMR score above 0 to build the classification model.

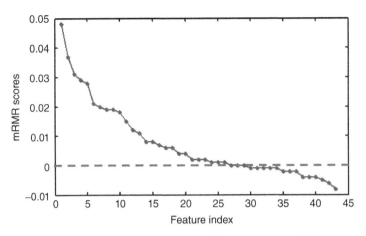

Figure 16.15 The sorted mRMR scores for all the extracted features.

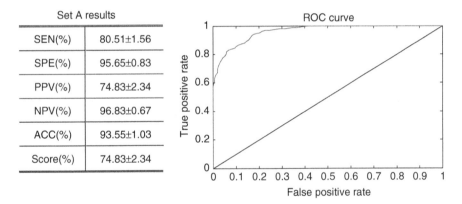

Figure 16.16 Performance measures of the ensemble NN model.

Figure 16.16 shows the average performance metrics of ensemble NN models (i.e., sensitivity, specificity, PPV, NPV, and accuracy) that are computed from 100 random replications of fourfold cross-validation of Set A. Note that the final score is the minimum of sensitivity and PPV. Figure 16.16 also shows the receive operating characteristic (ROC) curve, and the area under the curve (AUC) reaches 90.24% for the NN model. Table 16.4 shows the comparison of the proposed method with various methods in the state of the art [37]. The proposed method achieves the score of 74.83%, indicating that data-driven models can not only effectively extract the sensitive biomarkers but also provide accurate prediction of ICU mortality risks. In addition, it may be noted that the final score for Set B with undisclosed outcomes is 0.50, which was evaluated with the help of Dr Ikaro Silva at the Harvard-MIT Division of Health Sciences and Technology.

TABLE 16.4   Performance Comparisons of Predictive Models

Methods	Random Classifier	SOFA	SAPS-I	Fuzzy Rule	Cascaded AdaBoost
Scores (%)	15	28	32	36	38
Methods	Time Series Motifs	LR & HMM	Neural Network	Bayesian Ensemble	**Proposed Method**
Scores (%)	50	50	51	53	**74.83**

The score of proposed method is the minimum of sensitivity and PPV, according to Figure 16.16, the score of proposed method is 74.83%.

16.6   DISCUSSION AND CONCLUSIONS

The rapid advancement of sensing and information technology has resulted in data-rich environment in ICUs. After surgical operations, clinicians and nurses closely monitor clinical statuses of critically ill patients. ICU monitoring involves a large number of clinical variables such as heart rate, pulse oximetry, blood pressure, gas exchange, and blood test results (e.g., metabolic panel, complete blood count). Although clinicians have access to a great deal of ICU data, it is not uncommon that they make inferences about patient conditions based on most recent test results, ignoring important factors such as historical test results and the relationships among different types of tests. Notably, ICU monitoring leads to a new order-3 tensor form of data sets with unique properties (i.e., variable heterogeneity, patient heterogeneity, and time asynchronization), as opposed to the table form of data commonly used in predictive modeling. These data are not processed to be easily interpretable and then be useful for medical decision making. The tensor data and heterogeneous properties pose significant challenges to extract useful and meaningful knowledge from postsurgical data sets for the optimization of clinical decision making.

In the general practice of medicine, physicians lack decision-support tools that can help them delineate hidden interactions among clinical variables, identify temporal variations of patient conditions, and predict mortality risks. Over the past few decades, many efforts have been made to develop ICU scoring systems, for example, SAPS I-III, APACHE I-IV, MPM I-III, and SOFA. However, previous investigations either focus on the worst values in the monitoring period or depend on human subjective decisions and visual inspection. Multiple logistic regression is commonly used to build the predictive model. It is worth mentioning that temporal correlations among variables are not specifically considered. In addition, missing data pose significant challenges on the construction of predictive models. Although laboratory tests and patient monitoring provide rich information sources for monitoring critical conditions of postsurgical patients, the meaningful information extracted from the order-3 tensor form of ICU data sets is rather limited. As such, physicians need to make inferences about patient conditions based on most recent test results, ignoring important factors such as historical test results and the relationships among different types of tests.

This chapter reviews the state of the art of ICU scoring systems and discusses their advantages and limitations in the clinical practice. Furthermore, this chapter presents our preliminary studies on the development of data-driven ICU decision-support system with a series of analytical tools, including data categorization, data preprocessing, feature extraction, feature selection, and predictive modeling. As opposed to traditional ICU scoring systems, this investigation specifically considered the underlying structure and correlation in the order-3 tensor form of ICU data sets. In addition, we have made attempts to address the challenges of ICU data, including variable heterogeneity, patient heterogeneity, and time asynchronization. Real-world ICU data set from Multiparameter Intelligent Monitoring in Intensive Care (MIMIC) II Clinical Database was used to evaluate and validate the proposed methodology in this present study. Experimental results on real-world data show great potentials of data-driven analytics for improving the prediction of ICU mortality risks. Advances in postsurgical monitoring practices for patients who undergo surgical procedures will significantly decrease the mortality rates in ICU, improve the quality of healthcare services, and lead to broader social impacts.

ACKNOWLEDGMENTS

The authors thank the National Science Foundation (CMMI-1266331, IIP-1447289, and IOS-1146882) for support the research presented in this book chapter. In addition, the authors would like to thank Dr Ikaro Silva, Harvard-MIT Division of Health Sciences and Technology, for his kind help on the evaluation and scoring of the proposed methodology presented in this paper.

REFERENCES

[1] Keehan S, Sisko A, Truffer C, Smith S, Cowan C, Poisal J, Clemens MK, National Health Expenditure Accounts Projections Team. Health spending projections through 2017: The baby-boom generation is coming to Medicare. Health Aff 2008;27:w145–w155.

[2] Alemdar H, Ersoy C. Wireless sensor networks for healthcare: A survey. Comput Netw 2010;54:2688–2710.

[3] López G, Custodio V, Moreno JI. LOBIN: E-textile and wireless-sensor-network-based platform for healthcare monitoring in future hospital environments. Inf Technol Biomed 2010;14:1446–1458.

[4] Strand K, Flaatten H. Severity scoring in the ICU: A review. Acta Anaesthesiol Scand 2008;52:467–478.

[5] Pronovost PJ, Needham DM, Waters H, Birkmeyer CM, Calinawan JR, Birkmeyer JD, Dorman T. Intensive care unit physician staffing: financial modeling of the Leapfrog standard. Crit Care Med 2004;32:1247–1253.

[6] Knaus WA, Draper EA, Wagner DP, Zimmerman JE. APACHE II: A severity of disease classification system. Crit Care Med 1985;13:818–829.

[7] Vincent JL, Moreno R, Takala J, Willatts S, De Mendonça A, Bruining H, Reinhart CK, Suter PM, Thijs LG. The SOFA (Sepsis-related Organ Failure Assessment) score to describe organ dysfunction/failure. On behalf of the working group on sepsis-related problems of the European Society of Intensive Care Medicine. Intensive Care Med 1996;22:707–710.

[8] Apgar V. A proposal for a new method of evaluation of the newborn infant. Curr Res Anesth Analg 1953;32:260–267.

[9] Teasdale G, Jennett B. Assessment of coma and impaired consciousness. A practical scale. Lancet 1974;13:81–84.

[10] Knaus WA, Zimmerman JE, Wagner DP, Draper EA, Lawrence DE. APACHE – acute physiology and chronic health evaluation: a physiologically based classification system. Crit Care Med 1981;9:591–597.

[11] Knaus WA, Wagner DP, Draper EA, Zimmerman JE, Berqner M, Bastos PG, Sirio CA, Murphy DJ, Lotrinq T, Damiano A. The APACHE III prognostic system. Risk prediction of hospital mortality for critically ill hospitalized adults. Chest 1991;100:1619–1636.

[12] Zimmerman JE, Kramer AA, McNair DS, Malila FM. Acute physiology and chronic health evaluation (APACHE) IV: Hospital mortality assessment for today's critically ill patients. Crit Care Med 2006;34:1297–1310.

[13] Le Gall J, Loirat P, Alperovitch A, Glaser P, Granthil C, Mathiesu D, Mercier P, Thomas R, Villers D. A simplified acute physiology score for ICU patients. Crit Care Med 1984;12:975–977.

[14] Le Gall J, Lemeshow S, Saulnier F. A new simplified acute physiology score (SAPS II) based on a European/North American multicenter study. JAMA 1992;270:2957–2963.

[15] Metnitz PGH, Moreno RP, Almeida E, Jordan B, Bauer P, Abizanda CR, Lapichino G, Edbrooke D, Capuzzo M, Le Gall J. SAPS 3 – From evaluation of the patient to evaluation of the intensive care unit. Part 1: Objectives, methods and cohort description. Intensive Care Med 2005;31:1336–1344.

[16] Metnitz PGH, Moreno RP, Almeida E, Jordan B, Bauer P, Abizanda CR, Lapichino G, Edbrooke D, Capuzzo M, Le Gall J. SAPS 3 – From evaluation of the patient to evaluation of the intensive care unit. Part 2: Development of a prognostic model for hospital mortality at ICU admission. Intensive Care Med 2005;31:1345–1355.

[17] Lemeshow S, Teres D, Pastides H, Avrunin JS, Steinqrub JS. A method for predicting survival and mortality of ICU patients using objectively derived weights. Crit Care Med 1985;13:519–525.

[18] Lemeshow S, Teres D, Klar J, Avrunin JS, Gehlbach SH, Rapoport J. Mortality probability models (MPM II) based on an international cohort of intensive care unit patients. JAMA 1993;270:2478–2486.

[19] Higgins TL, Teres D, Copes WS, Nathanson BH, Stark M, Kramer AA. Assessing contemporary intensive care unit outcome: an updated mortality probability admission model (MPM0-III). Crit Care Med 2007;35:827–835.

[20] Ferreira FL, Bota DP, Bross A, Melot C, Vincent J. Serial evaluation of the SOFA score to predict outcome in critically ill patients. JAMA 2001;286:1754–1758.

[21] Ranson JH, Rifkind KM, Roses DF, Fink SD, Enq K, Spencer FC. Prognostic signs and the role of operative management in acute pancreatitis. Surg Gynecol Obstet 1974;139:69–81.

[22] Chen Y and Yang H. Heterogeneous postsurgical data analytics for predictive modeling of mortality risks in intensive care units. In: Proceedings of 2014 IEEE Engineering in Medicine and Biology Society Conference (EMBC); 2014 Aug 26–30; Chicago, IL; 2014.

[23] Kohonen T. *Self-Organizing Maps*. New York: Springer; 1997.

[24] Chen Y, Yang H. Self-organized neural network for the quality control of 12-lead ECG signals. Physiol Meas 2012;33:1399.

[25] Ba S, Joseph VR. Composite Gaussian process models for emulating expensive functions. Ann Appl Stat 2012;6:1838–1860.

[26] Ye J. Generalized low rank approximations of matric. Mach Learn 2005;61:167–191.

[27] Nolker C, Ritter H. Visual recognition of continuous hand postures. IEEE Trans Neural Netw 2002;13:983–994.

[28] Daly K, Beale R, Chang RW. Reduction in mortality after inappropriate early discharge from intensive care unit: Logistic regression triage model. BMJ 2001;322:1274–1276.

[29] Chen Y, Yang H. Multiscale recurrence analysis of long-term nonlinear and nonstationary time series. Chaos, Solitons Fractals 2012;45:978–987.

[30] Byon E, Shrivastava AK, Ding Y. A classification procedure for highly imbalanced class sizes. IIE Trans 2010;42:288.

[31] Hagan MT, Menhaj MB. Training feedforward networks with the Marquardt algorithm. IEEE Trans Neural Netw 1994;5:989–993.

[32] Hagan MT, Demuth HB, Beale MH, editors. *Neural Network Design*. University of Colorado Bookstore, Campus Pub. Service; 2002.

[33] Yang H. Multiscale recurrence quantification analysis of spatial cardiac vectorcardiogram (VCG) signals. IEEE Trans Biomed Eng February, 2011;58:339–347.

[34] Chen JJ, Tsai CA, Young JF, Kodell RL. Classification ensembles for unbalanced class sizes in predictive toxicology. SAR QSAR Environ Res 2005;16:517–529.

[35] Saeed M, Villarroel M, Reisner AT, Clifford G, Lehman L, Moody G, Heldt T, Kyaw TH, Moody B, Mark RG. Multiparameter intelligent monitoring in intensive care II (MIMIC-II): A public-access intensive care unit database. Crit Care Med 2011;39:952–960.

[36] Goldberger AL, Amaral L, Glass L, Haussdorff J, Ivanov PC, Mark R, Mietus J, Moody G, Peng C-K, Stanley HE. PhysioBank, physiotoolkit, and physionet: Components of a new research resource for complex physiologic signals. Circulation 2000;23:e215–e220.

[37] Silva I, Moody G, Scott J, Celi LA, Mark RG. Predicting in-hospital mortality of ICU patients: The PhysioNet/computing in cardiology challenge 2012. Comput Cardiol 2012;39:245–248.

[38] Hall MJ, DeFrances CJ, Williams SN, Golosinskiy A, Schwartzman A. National Hospital Discharge Survey: 2007 Summary. National Health Statistics Reports 2010;29:1–24.

[39] Lu H, Plataniotis KN, Venetsanopoulos AN. Uncorrelated multilinear principal component analysis for unsupervised multilinear subspace learning. IEEE Trans Neural Netw 2009;20:1820–1836.

17

ANALYZING PATIENT–PHYSICIAN INTERACTION IN CONSULTATION FOR SHARED DECISION MAKING

THEMBI MDLULI, JOYATEE SARKER, CAROLINA VIVAS-VALENCIA, AND NAN KONG

Weldon School of Biomedical Engineering, Purdue University, West Lafayette, IN, USA

CLEVELAND G. SHIELDS

Department of Human Development and Family Studies, Purdue University, West Lafayette, IN, USA

17.1 INTRODUCTION

Healthcare systems now strive to provide patient-centered care, which takes into account patient's needs, values, and perspectives [1]. A 2001 Institute of Medicine report identified patient-centeredness as one of six interrelated factors constituting high-quality health care, together with efficiency, effectiveness, safety, equity, and timeliness [1]. "Patient-centeredness" means considering patients' cultural traditions, personal preferences and values, family situations, social circumstances, and lifestyles [2]. Patient-centered care is expected to provide care guidance to patients in the context of full and unbiased information about options, benefits, and risks through most common patient–physician interactions as well as alternative means. Physicians practicing patient-centered care improve their patients' clinical outcomes and satisfaction rates by improving the quality of the patient–physician relationship, while at the same time decreasing the utilization of diagnostic testing, prescriptions, hospitalizations, and referrals. Although the principle behind the

Healthcare Analytics: From Data to Knowledge to Healthcare Improvement, First Edition.
Edited by Hui Yang and Eva K. Lee.
© 2016 John Wiley & Sons, Inc. Published 2016 by John Wiley & Sons, Inc.

growing movement toward patient-centered care is well established now, it remains unclear how to effectively implement patient-centered care in various settings, to different patient populations, and by practitioners from distinct medical specialties.

Effective care is typically defined by shared decision making in consultation with patients rather than by physician-dependent tools or standards. As an example, orthopedic surgeons employ the Harris Hip Score to judge the success of total hip replacements. It was designed solely by physicians and does not even ask patients to rate their satisfaction with the procedure, and it answers questions important to the physicians and only thought to be important to patients. However, it is unknown whether these tools, such as the Harris Hip Score, accurately reflect patient experience with a hip replacement or other aspects of their medical care. In this chapter, we focus on improving patient–physician interaction during outpatient oncology visits. It is well established that improved interaction helps ensure effective medical decision making and improved patient–physician relationship [3]. Patient-centered practitioners have thus been recommended to focus on employing measurable communication skills and behaviors to improve different aspects of the interaction. However, key questions remain, including what communication skills and behaviors would lead to improved outcomes and how they would be employed.

Traditionally, studies conducted by health psychologists and communication researchers are hypothesis driven, for which the key to success is designing measurement instruments of patient-centered interactions and controlling the human subject experimentation such that the hypothesis testing can be performed in a less variable condition. These studies verified certain associations of communication behaviors with interaction effectiveness for certain discussion topics. By identifying important markers on patient–physician communication effectiveness, these studies are expected to help develop promising strategies to educate physicians on how to improve their ability to collect critical information and attend to patient concerns. At present, as more surveys and conversational audio recordings become available, an increasing number of prediction models are developed that include more features than any hypothesis testing research has dealt with. Additionally, these models focus on the overall patient satisfaction of the interaction. In the future, it is anticipated that more sophisticated data mining techniques will be applied to develop models based on a much larger set of potential features from the interaction.

The remainder of this chapter is organized as follows. In Section 17.2, we survey the literature on patient-centered communication with emphasis on prognosis discussion and pain assessment with end-stage cancer patients. Our objective is to introduce this exciting applied decision theory research area to data analytics researchers with anticipation that soon the area of quantitative shared medical decision making will emerge. In Section 17.3, we describe our recent work on exploring the use of rating information and conversation topical data in predicting patient satisfaction in patient–physician communication. We clearly see the path lay ahead of us on making data-informed recommendations to physicians' communication skills and behaviors. In Section 17.4, we outline potential directions of applying data analytics tools to predict patient–physician interaction effectiveness and shared decision outcomes, and, more generally, to investigate smart medical encounter management. We conclude the chapter by providing final remarks in Section 17.5.

17.2 LITERATURE REVIEW

In the past 20 years, researchers from different areas (e.g., psychology, medicine, economics, sociology) have published a large number of papers, studying different aspects of shared decision making in various forms of medical encounters. The interest in shared decision making is so great in the various research communities that it has propelled a "paradigm shift" in medical practice in which the concept of shared decision making is said to be replacing the old notion of "doctor knows best" [4]. In 1998, a new international journal *Health Expectations* was launched. The aim of the journal is to disseminate research findings in the area of patient and public involvement in healthcare decision making [5]. In addition, a special issue on patient partnership was published in the *British Medical Journal* acknowledging the need of future study on the "paradigm shift." While seemingly, this new approach to medical decision making is promoted, the term shared decision making is used without a clear definition or, in fact, even without an agreement on what it is. The literature seems to suggest many other terms are used as synonyms for shared decision making, including informed decision making, informed shared decision making, partnership, patient involvement, patient-centered care, and evidence-based patient choice. Moumjid et al. [6] searched articles that were published in English and French between 1997 and 2014 and were available from Medline, HealthStar, Cancerlit, Cinahl, Sociological Abstracts, and Econlit. The authors highlighted several issues for those involved in shared decision-making research and those whose aim is to translate innovative research ideas into medical practice. They concluded that many researchers decided to provide their own definition when realizing the existing definitions were inadequate. However, it was problematic when no definition was given or cited in an article or the use of the definition was not being consistent. The authors called for a clear definition and typology of the terms used, which reflects the complexity of the study and consequently demands sophisticated data analytics tools to decipher the correlations among the terms. In addition to the ambiguity on the studied outcomes, it may be challenging to design reliable and valid measurement instruments. For example, to measure patient-centered communication, instruments may include eliciting and validating patient concerns and attentiveness voice tone. Furthermore, the study design is likely to be challenging due to the fact that knowing the purpose of the study may alter both patients' and physicians' behaviors. Hence, it is common to use trained actors to portray patients seeking new consultations and prompt physicians to assess pain, prognosis, and progression. This methodology, known as standardized patient (SP) methodology, implies that it is challenging to record a large number of interactions.

In previous studies, eliciting and validating patient concerns has been intensively studied and proven to be the most reliable and valid component of the measure [7]. However, there could be a large number of items related to measuring the carefulness of the physician in gathering relevant information about the patient. There can also be significant variation in quantifying the actual measurements. At present, we focus on analyzing various easily attainable features to predict communication effectiveness outcomes. Given the inaccuracy of data collection inherent in postinteraction surveys, text and audio recordings of patient–physician interactions in consultation have increasingly been used in the analysis. With the availability of text and audio information, one could potentially synthesize enormous amount of predictive features for the communication effectiveness. As a result, analyzing patient–physician interaction tends to face the large p small n paradigm, that is, there are few data points and many features. There are some fundamental challenges in the near future on enabling big data analytics techniques in the analysis. First, for reliability consideration, multiple coders are needed to code for the presence of physician behaviors. This, however, can lead to remarked variations between different coders. Second, since human interaction tends to present significant temporal causality, the variations on the final communication effectiveness may be aggregated over multiple time points during the interaction. In the remainder of the section, we provide details on two studies conducted by Shields et al. [8, 9]. These studies showcase some of the aforementioned challenges and motivate our recent studies that apply advanced data analytic tools to improve the predictions.

17.2.1 Patient–Physician Interaction on Prognosis Discussion

Shields et al. [8] examined patient–physician interaction on cancer prognosis discussion, which tends to be emotionally difficult. Prognosis discussions are hampered by the different focuses of patients and physicians [10]. Patients are focused on the impact of cancer on their lives and their discomfort and pain. Physicians, by contrast, are focused on the illness, particularly on its progression and treatment. While guidelines exist for discussing prognosis [11], there is no firm evidence supporting any one approach [12]. A large number of factors affect prognosis discussion in medical encounters [13]. Such factors include physician's style when discussing the prognosis [14] and patient's preference of knowing her prognosis [15]. The literature has also attributed culture to a main factor on the preference [16, 17].

Shields et al. [8] hypothesized that eliciting and validating patient concerns is a marker of physician willingness to discuss emotionally difficult topics. Eliciting and validating is a multifaceted construct that includes physicians' eliciting and understanding patients' perspective, understanding the patients' psychosocial context, developing a shared understanding of the problem, and sharing decision-making power if patients desire [18]. Eliciting and validating has been found to be associated with greater satisfaction with visits [7], reduced healthcare costs [17], and more appropriate prescription of antidepressants [19]. Eliciting and validating is also hypothesized to be an outcome of mindful practice [20]; thus, the authors hypothesized that an attentive posture in consultation would also be associated with greater eliciting and validating patient's concerns during prognosis communication.

To test these hypotheses, Shields et al. [8] recruited both family physicians and oncologists for a pilot study on prognosis discussion. The authors controlled patient characteristics by using SPs to present a consistent message about their desire for prognostic information. The SP methodology has been extensively used in primary care research [7, 21], but not in examination of oncology visits. The authors developed a model transcript complete with biological data for training the SPs to portray patients with end-stage cancer. They also sent a complete medical record to the recruited physician prior to each visit. The purpose of the medical record was to make the SP's diagnosis and stage of cancer believable. While making the visit, each SP carried two digital recorders that fit into his pocket in order to record the visit surreptitiously. The SP turned on the recorders in his car before entering the physician's office.

To test the above hypotheses, Shields et al. [8] designed measurement instruments for eliciting and validating patient concerns, using Component I in the Measure of Patient-Centered Communication [22] (see Table 17.1). Items for the measure were used to assess whether physicians conducted preliminary information elicitation, further exploration, and validation of discussion topics such as medication, mood/depression, family support, cancer's impact on life, and previous physicians. Table 17.2 shows the response categories for coding elicitation and validating. Two graduate students and two undergraduate students listened to the audio recordings and coded the physician behaviors during preliminary exploration, further exploration, validation, or cut-off in response to each issue discussed by the SP and the physician. Twenty recordings were coded by two different coders for reliability purposes.

TABLE 17.1 Eliciting and Validating Items [8]

Item Retained in Scale	Mean	SD	Range
1. Inquiries/discussion about mood/depression	0.8	1.5	0.0–5.0
2. Inquiries/discussion about cancer's impact on life	0.7	1.2	0.0–4.0
3. Inquiries/discussion about sleep	0.7	1.1	0.0–3.0
4. Inquiries/discussion about weight loss	1.7	1.4	0.0–5.0
5. Inquiries/discussion about appetite	0.7	1.1	0.0–3.0
6. Inquiries/discussion about previous physicians	2.1	1.4	0.0–5.0
7. Inquiries/discussion about current medications	2.3	1.2	0.0–3.0
8. Inquiries/discussion about alcohol use	1.3	1.5	0.0–5.0
9. Discusses working status	1.9	1.4	0.0–4.0
10. Discusses marital status	1.8	1.6	0.0–5.0
11. Treatment plan: discuss medication for treatment	1.9	1.3	0.0–3.0
12. Ask about ADLs and IADLs	0.5	1.1	0.0–3.0
Items Dropped from Scale			
13. Inquiries/discussion about medical problems unrelated to cancer	2.7	0.8	0.0–5.0
14. Conducts a physician exam	2.7	0.9	0.0–3.0
15. Inquiries/discussion about smoking	2.4	1.2	0.0–5.0
16. Discuss any at-risk exposure to carcinogens	0.1	0.5	0.0–3.0
17. Recommended change in pain medications	0.3	0.9	0.0–3.0
18. Cancer: scans done since treatment	1.4	1.3	0.0–3.0
19. Cancer: radiation done to back	2.6	1.2	0.0–5.0
20. Treatment plan: PET scan or some other scan	2.5	1.1	0.0–3.0
21. Treatment plan: discuss referral for radiation oncologist	1.4	1.5	0.0–5.0
22. Treatment plan: other blood tests	1.4	1.4	0.0–3.0

These items are dropped because (1) the behaviors happened too infrequently to be coded reliably, or (2) they did not correlate with the total score and their removal is conducive to improve Cronbach's alpha.

TABLE 17.2   Response Categories for Coding Eliciting and Validating Concerns and Prognosis Discussion [8]

	Preliminary Exploration (PE)	Further Exploration (FE)	Validation (VAL)	Cut-off (CO)	Score
Scoring protocol each item was scored on scale	0 = none 1 = occurred	0 = none 1 = occurred	0 = none 1 = occurred	0 = none 1 = occurred	1 = PE, FE, and CO 2 = PE or FE 3 = PE and FE or PE, FE, VAL, and CO 4 = PE and VAL 5 = PE, FE, and VAL

Preliminary exploration (PE) is scored when the physician acknowledges the patient concerns by saying "uh huh" or any other simple statement.

Further exploration (FE) is scored when the physician encourages the patient to tell him or her more about the concern.

Validation (VAL) is scored when the physician underscores or supports the patients about his or her concerns by using phrases as "I am glad you came to see me about this" or "I can see why you are worried about this."

Cut-off (CO) is scored when the patient talks about an issue but the physician responds by changing the topic rather than exploring the patient's concerns.

Each item was quantified with a 1–5 scale and the average score was reported. An item analysis was then conducted to eliminate several items. The final scale had a satisfactory level of coding reliability, that is, Cronbach's alpha of 0.78 and the intraclass correlation coefficient was 0.88, indicating that the coding differentiated the cases, not the coders. For details on internal consistency, we refer to [23].

The authors measured attentive voice tone by rating four separate factors, warmth, concern, worry, and openness, for each physician on a 1–7 scale. The authors also assessed prognosis communication by creating 10 items based on the components of the SPIKES protocol for delivering bad news [24]. The coding for these items was similar to coding elicitation and validating in that they both used the same physician response code. Nevertheless, they remain separate constructs because they coded very different communication behaviors.

From the above coding and rating, Shields et al. [8] collected a number of study variables related to prognosis communication. Additional variables included those related to a survey to the physicians on their suspicion on some patients visiting in the past being SPs and on adherence of SPs to their roles. The authors reported descriptive statistics of these study variables and examined the variables for their adherence to assumption of normality and for the presence of outliers. They also conducted correlation and regression analyses to examine which variables explained variance in prognosis communication.

17.2.2 Physician–Patient Interaction on Pain Assessment

Shields et al. [9] examined whether patient–physician interaction (particularly language indicating physician certainty) was associated with incomplete (i.e., premature closure) pain assessment among patients with serious illness. To conduct the examination, the authors again applied the SP method and used the same set of physicians. They also followed the same procedures for coding and reliability checking as those in [8]. In addition to measures already included in [8], the authors in [9] coded extent of pain management, additional aspects of physician voice tone, and physician use of certainty in their language. First, the authors developed a measure for premature closure of physician pain assessment by coding the presence and rating the degree of physician pain assessment behavior (see Table 17.3). Items for the measure were generated from self-report pain questionnaires [25, 26] and medical interviewing texts [27, 28]. Second, the authors assessed anxious/concerned voice tone using a 1–7 scale in a manner similar to the Roter Interaction Analysis System (RIAS) [29]. Lastly, the authors used Linguistic Inquiry and Word Count, a text program [30], to tally the amount and percentage of certainty words said by the physicians in consultation with the SPs. These certainty words include *absolute, certain, clear, complete, confident, definite,* and *sure*. Physicians who use more certainty-conveying words seek causal understandings [30], an important task for physicians making assessment. However, because physicians who have a need for certainty tend to be less tolerant of ambiguity, they may curtail data gathering and engage them in premature closure [31]. With the above coding and rating, Shields et al. [9] collected a set of study variables related to pain assessment. The authors again reported descriptive statistics of the study variables and conducted correlation and regression analyses to examine which variables explained variance in pain assessment.

TABLE 17.3 Measure of Physician Pain Assessment Items [9]

Item Retained in Scale	Mean	SD
1. Onset (when, duration, time course)	1.4	1.3
2. Location	2.5	0.9
3. Intensity/severity	0.9	1.1
4. Aggravating/alleviating factors	1.1	1.2
5. Associated symptoms	1.9	1.4
6. Previous/current methods of treatment	2.8	0.9
7. Other med/surge procedures	2.4	1.1
Items Dropped from Scale		
8. Temporal pattern	0.7	1.0
9. Substance use (tobacco, alcohol, illegal)	2.6	1.3
10. Evaluate pain on the 0–10 scale	0.1	0.6
11. Was medication offered	1.4	1.4
12. Did physician insist patient take new medication	0.3	0.9
13. Did physician deny patient new or more medication	0.2	0.8

Shields et al. [8, 9] implied that (i) there could be many markers that help explain the variations in patient–physician interaction; (ii) many of these markers are highly correlated; (iii) coding and rating consistency may be an issue. In [8, 9], the authors conducted mostly hypothesis-driven research, which mainly studied the effect of individual markers. Recently, we apply advanced data analytics tools to conduct more systematic investigations in the interdisciplinary area of quantitative health communication.

17.3   OUR RECENT DATA MINING STUDIES

Our recent studies examine satisfaction of end-stage cancer patients from interaction with physicians. We combined almost all independent variables investigated in [8, 9] to improve the model interpretability. To address the potential overfitting, we explored variable subset selection techniques in regression modeling.

17.3.1   Predicting Patient Satisfaction with Survey Data

In Fang et al. [32], we used sample interaction data of 39 physicians (20 family physicians and 19 oncologists). We used patient satisfaction as the outcome measure, which was acquired from a postvisit questionnaire given the SPs. The questionnaire contains five sections. They are (i) SP's perception on the physician's prognosis communication (HCCQ section with five questions); (ii) SP's believe on how well the physician knows his/her (KNOW section with four questions); (iii) how satisfied the SP is with the physician (sp_satisfied); (iv) SP's trust on the physician (TRUST section with seven questions); and (v) SP's overall trust on the physician (sp_overall_trust). All items in the HCCQ, KNOW, and TRUST sections were rated on a 1–5 scale and the sum scores were calculated. Variables sp_satisfied and sp_overall_trust were rated using a 1–6 scale with 1 being *completely satisfied couldn't be better* and 6 being the complete opposite, and a 0–10 scale with 0 being *not trusting at all* and 10 being *complete trusting*, respectively. Table 17.4 lists all five variables from the five sections. Given the fact that these variables were defined on different scales, we rescaled them to standard scores. We averaged the standard scores to get the final patient satisfaction outcome measure.

Based on several hypotheses in the existing literature [8, 9, 21], we selected 13 predictive variables (or features). The majority of them fall into four categories on eliciting/validating patient concerns, voice tone, physician use of certainty language, and assessment of prognosis communication. Other variables include total interaction time, patient's word count, as well as physician's gender, age, and occupation. Table 17.5 lists the descriptive statistics about these predictive variables.

To summarize, we have one predictive variable from the category of eliciting/ validating patient concerns, three variables related to voice tone (i.e., the additional one is associated with hostile voice tone), two variables related to physician use of certainty in the language (i.e., an indicator was recorded on whether the physician used phrases to strongly imply the mortality possibility to the SP), and two variables

TABLE 17.4 Predictive Variables and Descriptive Statistics about Them [32]

Category	Variable Name	Characteristic	Oncologist			Family Physician		
			Mean	SD	Range	Mean	SD	Range
Eliciting/validating patient concerns	Elicit_val	Average score of 19 items of 1–5 scale	1.05	0.66	0.17–2.33	1.42	0.65	0.42–2.67
Voice tone	attentive	Average scores among four raters using 1–7 scale	3.92	0.90	2.5–5.5	3.75	0.88	1.75–5
	anxious		2.94	1.06	2–5	3	0.78	1–4
	hostile		2.22	0.88	1–5	2	0.77	1–4
Physician use of certainty in the lang.	P_WC	Integer word count	1394	984	410–4249	1673	659	555–2961
	youdying	Binary indictor	0.61	0.50	{0,1}	0	0.44	{0,1}
Assessing prognosis communication	prog_sum	Aggregate score of items of 1–5 scale	11.72	7.30	0–27	7	6.18	0–23
	prog_freq	Integer	4.47	2.15	1–9	3	2.14	1–8
Miscellaneous	D_WC	Integer word count	1957	1150	486–5290	1928	1213	728–5394
	totaltime	Integer (in mins)	28.19	13.33	9.5–56	30	12.99	15–72.5
	Age	Integer	46.56	7.64	35–68	50	10.29	31–72
	Male	Binary indicator	0.72	0.46	{0,1}	1	0	{0,1}

TABLE 17.5   Measures Pertaining to Patient Satisfaction and Descriptive Statistics about Them [32]

Variable Name	Oncologist			Family Physician		
	Mean	SD	Range	Mean	SD	Range
hccq	10.78	3.21	6–18	10	3.73	6–17
know	9.83	2.81	5–16	10	3.13	5–16
sp_satisfied	2.61	1.14	1–5	3	1.20	1–5
trust	19.56	1.98	16–22	20	2.00	18–27
sp_overall_trust	7.44	1.38	5–9	6	2.02	3–10

related to assessing prognosis communication. In addition, we included one variable measuring the total patient–physician interaction time (in minutes), one variable measuring patient engagement by counting the words he/she spoke during the interaction, three variables indicating the physician's age (integer), gender (1 being Male and 0 being Female), and occupation (1 being an oncologist and 0 being a family physician). A preliminary correlation analysis indicated that most of the variables are significantly correlated. This motivated us to explore the use of variable selection techniques to systematically conduct regression analysis. We applied principal component analysis (PCA) to feature selection and applied linear regression to the selected principal components. We also applied standard linear regression assisted by model selection for comparison.

PCA [33] is a valuable and commonly used multivariate statistical analysis technique for finding patterns and reducing correlations in data of high dimensions. PCA uses orthogonal transformation to convert a set of observations of possibly correlated variables into a set of values of linearly uncorrelated variables called *principal components*. The transform is defined in such a way that the first principal component has the largest possible variance, accounting for as much of the variability in the data as possible. Each succeeding component, in turn, has the largest variance possible under the constraint that it is orthogonal to (i.e., uncorrelated with) the preceding components. Once we selected the first few principal components, we identified their associations with the predictive variables. Through preliminary experiment, we concluded that it would be reasonable to select four to eight principal components. With such selection, about 70–90% of the variability in the data could be explained. Table 17.6 shows the association pattern between the features and the principal components. For example, features *Elicit_val, attentive, P_WC, prog_sum, prog_freq, D_WC* should be grouped and they contribute significantly in explaining the variance in the data. We developed a regression model based on the selected principal components.

For comparison purpose, we performed correlation analysis and model selection on all 13 predictive variables. We then applied generalized linear regression with the selected variables. For model selection, we used the following criteria progressively: (i) higher adjusted R-square value; (ii) smaller difference between Mallow's Cp statistic [34] and the number of model coefficients plus 1; (iii) smaller Akaike information criterion (AIC) measure [35]; and (iv) Bayesian information

TABLE 17.6 Principal Component (PC) Pattern Table [32]

Var.\PC	PC1	PC2	PC3	PC4	PC5
Elicit_val	**0.635**	−0.324	0.272	0.153	−0.388
attentive	**0.720**	−0.152	−0.089	−0.373	0.216
anxious	−0.296	**0.759**	0.110	0.019	−0.115
hostile	−0.568	**0.587**	0.247	0.005	−0.128
P_WC	**0.641**	0.059	0.321	−0.303	−0.128
youdying	0.267	**0.800**	−0.177	−0.031	−0.004
prog_sum	**0.814**	0.198	−0.349	0.198	−0.200
prog_freq	**0.762**	0.146	−0.436	0.236	−0.217
D_WC	**0.583**	0.294	0.459	0.077	0.426
Totaltime	0.478	0.323	**0.575**	0.291	0.283
Age	−0.146	−0.022	0.216	**0.748**	−0.267
Male	−0.058	0.224	−0.388	**0.567**	0.504
Oncologist	0.018	0.460	**−0.654**	−0.062	0.092

TABLE 17.7 Prediction Model Comparison [32]

Predictive Modeling Method		SSE from Cross-Validation	Variance Explained
PCA in standard linear regression	4 PCs selected	17.40	68.9%
	5 PCs selected	16.96	76.0%
	6 PCs selected	17.32	81.8%
	7 PCs selected	16.01	86.9%
	8 PCs selected	18.90	90.6%
GLM with model selection[a]		26.88	n/a
GLM w/o model selection[a]		35.51	n/a

[a]The best SSE was reported over various assumptions on the residual distribution.

criterion (BIC) measure [36]. To compare the two models as earlier, we conducted leave-one-out cross-validation that used 38 samples to build a regression model and tested it with the remaining sample. We used the sum of square errors over all samples as the comparison criterion. Table 17.7 shows the comparison results. From the table, we observed that applying PCA in the framework of standard linear regression with normal distribution on the residual outperformed applying correlation analysis and model selection in the framework of generalized linear regression.

17.3.2 Predicting Patient Satisfaction with Conservation Data

In a more recent work, we further extended the studied data set to include conversational sequence data. We explored the use of several standard analytics methods for data processing, feature selection, and outlier detection. In Table 17.8, we display a portion of the conversational sequence data from the interaction between an SP and a physician, labeled no. 1 in the data set.

Usually, unstructured data as those in our study have to be preprocessed for efficient analysis. Thus, the first step in our analysis was to format the sequence data in a meaningful and amenable way for analysis. Formatting the data is a challenging task. In one approach, we considered each instance of a conversation sequence (each row in Table 17.8) as a time point. Then we assigned each time point with a numerical value based on whether the patient or doctor was speaking. A sequence was developed for each patient and topic/core, based on who was speaking (medical practitioners were assigned a "−1", patients was assigned a "+1"). When neither the patient nor the doctor was speaking for a particular topic (e.g., pain medication) at a given time point, another symbol (i.e., "NaN") was assigned. Each topic had a matrix associated with it. The dimensions of such matrix were $m \times n$ and where m is the number of patients and n is the length of the longest sequence, as shown in Table 17.9.

TABLE 17.8   Portion of Data Received from One Conversation Sequence

Case	Coder	Topic	Who	Code
1	LM	Oncologist visit	M	Init
1	LM	Oncologist visit	M	Rec
1	LM	Oncologist visit	P	Go Along
1	LM	Oncologist visit	M	Init
1	LM	Oncologist visit	M	Rec
1	LM	Oncologist visit	P	AG Plan
1	LM	Oncologist visit	M	Init
1	LM	Oncologist visit	M	Ask FB
1	LM	Oncologist visit	P	AG Plan
1	LM	Pain Meds	M	Init
1	LM	Pain Meds	M	Ask FB
1	LM	Pain Meds	P	Give Info

TABLE 17.9   Portion of Coded Sequence Data Matrix for "Init"

	1	2	3	4	5	6	7	8	9	10
1	−1	NaN	NaN	−1	NaN	NaN	−1	NaN	NaN	−1
2	+1	NaN	NaN	NaN	NaN	−1	NaN	NaN	NaN	−1
3	+1	NaN	NaN	NaN	−1	NaN	NaN	NaN	NaN	NaN
4	−1	NaN	NaN	−1	NaN	NaN	NaN	NaN	−1	NaN
5	−1	NaN	NaN	NaN	NaN	NaN	−1	NaN	NaN	NaN
6	−1	NaN	NaN	NaN	NaN	NaN	NaN	−1	NaN	NaN
7	NaN	NaN	NaN	NaN	NaN	−1	NaN	NaN	NaN	NaN
8	+1	NaN	NaN	NaN	NaN	NaN	NaN	−1	NaN	NaN
9	NaN	NaN	NaN	NaN	NaN	NaN	NaN	NaN	NaN	NaN
10	−1	NaN	NaN	NaN	NaN	NaN	−1	NaN	NaN	NaN
11	−1	NaN	NaN	NaN	NaN	NaN	NaN	NaN	NaN	−1
12	−1	NaN	NaN	NaN	NaN	NaN	−1	NaN	NaN	NaN

After enumerating all the interactions, there was a large list of topics. In order to extract useful information, we consolidated the topics to a smaller topic set.

With the formatted data, dimensionality became a big challenge in our problem. Hence, we next applied feature selection techniques to determine features that could be influential to patient's satisfaction. In this work, we intuitively extracted the following features either directly from the information provided or with appropriate summation queries. We used K-mean clustering to compare the different features in terms of patient satisfaction and applied stepwise forward model selection to determine which features were more influential. Finally, with suspicion that physician outliers may have caused the unsatisfied results in the regression, we used the local weighted scatterplot smoothing (LOWESS) method [37] to detect outliers and applied regression on the reduced sets of data points.

We concluded from this work that it is difficult to make inferences with a lot of confidence from the analyses. The major challenge is that there were many features compared to the number of data points. In addition, to many features, there is a large amount of NaN data. Other challenges are more fundamental that lie in data formatting and feature selection. We outline the potential future directions in the next section.

17.4   FUTURE DIRECTIONS

In this section, we review the literature of (i) regression shrinkage and selection and (ii) conversational characterization for medical encounters. The former area has the potential to directly address the issue of large amount of features in a regression framework. The latter one shows the potentials of some current studies and general directions for empowering more personalized patient–physician communication.

17.4.1   Regression Shrinkage and Selection

The method of least square is a standard approach in data fitting and regression. The best fit in the least square sense minimizes the sum of squared residuals. The problem statement is as follows. Let us consider a data set consisting of n points (data pairs) (x_i, y_i), $i = 1, \ldots, N$, where x_i is a feature (predictor) and y_i is an outcome (or label, category) whose value is found by observation. The model function has the form $f(x, \beta)$, where the p parameters associated with the features can be adjusted with the goal of finding a set of parameter values (a p-dimensional parameter vector β) to best fit the data set. The least square method is intended to find the "best fit" when the sum S of squared residuals, defined as $S = \sum_{i=}^{n} r_i^2$, is a minimum. A residual r is defined as the difference between the actual values of the features and the value predicted by the model, that is, $r_i = y_i - f(x_i, \beta)$.

In some contexts, a regularized version of the least squares solution may be preferable. An important regularized version of least square is lasso (least absolute and selection operator) proposed by Tibshirani [38]. Lasso inserts into the least square problem the constraint that $\|\beta\|_1$, the L_1-norm of the parameter vector, is no greater than a given value. For notational convenience, we assume the underlying model is linear. As in the usual regression setup, we assume either that the observations are independent or that the y_i's are conditionally independent given the x_{ij}'s. The lasso estimate $\widehat{\beta}$ is defined by

$$\widehat{\beta} = \arg\min\left\{\sum_{i=1}^{N}\left(y_i - \sum_j \beta_j x_{ij}\right)^2\right\}, \quad \text{subject to } \sum_{j=1}^{p}|\beta_j| \le t.$$

The parameter $t \ge 0$ is a tuning parameter. This parameter controls the amount of shrinkage that is applied to the estimates. The above problem is a quadratic programming problem with linear inequity constraints (in this case, a lasso constraint). It can be solved using quadratic programming or more general convex optimization methods, as well as by specific algorithms such as the least angle regression algorithm [39]. For example, Lawson and Hansen [40] provided the ingredients for a procedure that solves the least squares problem subject to a general inequality constraint $H\beta \le h$. Here H is a $m \times p$ matrix, corresponding to m linear inequality constraints on the p-dimensional vector β. For this problem, however, $m = 2^p$ may be very large so that direct application of this procedure is not practical. To alleviate the computational difficulty, one can solve the problem by introducing the inequality constraints sequentially, seeking a feasible solution satisfying the so-called Kuhn–Tucker conditions [40].

The lasso constraint $\sum_{j=1}^{p}|\beta_j| \le t$ is equivalent to the addition of a penalty term $\alpha \sum_{j=1}^{p}|\beta_j|$ to the residual sum of squares [41, Chapter 5]. Knowing $|\beta_j|$ is proportional to the (minus) log density of the double-exponential distribution, one can derive the lasso estimate as the Bayes posterior mode under independent double-exponential priors for the β_j's, $f(\beta_j) = \frac{\lambda}{2}\exp(-\lambda|\beta_j|)$. In other words, in the Bayesian context, the problem is equivalent to placing a zero-mean Laplace prior distribution on the parameter vector. Consequently, the above-mentioned optimization problem is equivalent to unconstrained minimization of the least squares penalty with $\alpha\|\beta\|_1$ added, where α is a constant. This minimization problem is the essentially Lagrangian form of the constrained problem.

Let $\widehat{\beta}_j^0$ be the full least square estimates and $t_0 = \sum_j |\widehat{\beta}_j^0|$. Values of $t < t_0$ will cause shrinkage of the solutions toward 0, and some coefficients may be exactly equal to 0. For example, if $t = t_0/2$, the effect will be roughly similar to finding the best subset of size $p/2$. Estimating t can be done with cross-validation, generalized cross-validation, and an analytical unbiased estimate of risk. The third method proposed in Stein [42] enjoys a significant computational advantage over the other two methods.

The idea of the lasso method was motivated from *non-negative garrote* in Breiman [43]. The garotte starts with the ordinary least square (OLS) estimates and shrinks them by nonnegative factors whose sum is constrained. To compute the garrote, the optimization problem is presented as

$$\arg\min\left\{\sum_{i=}^{N}(y_i-f(x_i,\beta))^2\right\},\quad\text{subject to }c_j\geq 0,\ \sum_{j}c_j\leq t.$$

In extensive simulation studies, Breiman [43] showed that the garotte has consistently lower prediction error than subset selection and is competitive with ridge regression except when the true model has many small nonzero coefficients. We briefly describe ridge regression here. Ridge regression, also known as Tikhonov regularization in the context of statistics, is an alternative version of regularization for least square problems. It adds a constraint that $\|\beta\|^2$, the L_2-norm of the parameter vector, is no greater than the given value t. It is equivalent to an unconstrained minimization of the least squares penalty with $\alpha\|\beta\|^2$ added, where α is a constant. One of the prime differences between lasso and ridge regression is that in ridge regression, as the penalty is increased, all parameters are reduced while still remaining nonzero, while in lasso, increasing the penalty will cause more and more of the parameters to be driven to zero. This, in fact, is due to the difference on the assumption of residual sum of squares between double-exponential density, used by the lasso, and normal density, used by ridge regression.

A drawback of the garotte is that its solution depends on both sign and magnitude of the OLS estimates. In overfit or highly correlated settings where the OLS estimates behave poorly, the garotte may suffer as a result. In contrast, the lasso avoids the explicit use of the OLS estimates. Frank and Friedman [44] proposed using a bound on the L^q-norm of the parameters, where $q\geq 0$; the lasso corresponds to $q=1$ and ridge regression corresponds to $q=2$.

In summary, the L_1-regularized formulation, in many contexts, enjoy the fact that it has the tendency to result in solutions with fewer nonzero parameter values. Consequently, one can efficiently reduce the number of variables that are effective to the given solution. For this reason, lasso and its variants are fundamental to the field of compressed sensing. An extension of the lasso method is the elastic net regularization, which linearly combines the L_1 and L_2 penalties of the lasso and ridge methods.

17.4.2   Conversational Characterization

Data analysis for conversational sequence data in shared medical decision has so far been mostly focused on verbal communication, for example, the two studies presented in this chapter [8, 9]. Verbal communication-based data analysis biases the results to the notion of "doctor knows best" because physicians tend to be the frequent speakers in the conversation. Advanced data mining tools have been used in the area of automated speech characterization. Among various aspects in automated speech characterization, intonation pattern categorization could be of great potential to move forward the area of shared medical decision making. Intonation patterns, which are evident to determine feelings across phrases and sentences, have been of great interest to linguists. For example, fundamental frequency on speech segments can be governed by stress and syntax [45]. Taylor [46] designed the tilt intonation model to facilitate automatic intonation processing for speech technology applications. In the model, intonation is represented as a linear sequence of events, which can be pitch accents or boundary tones. Each event is characterized by continuous parameters representing amplitude, duration, and tilt (a measure of the shape of the event). The tilt model is used to detect linguistically meaningful information while speaking. The most recognized applications are in the area of synthesis and recognition of speech processing. Recently, Taylor et al. [47] showed a way of using intonation to improve the performance of automatic speech recognition system by implementing a word error rate on spontaneous dialog.

Verbal communication is not isolated in conversation; nonverbal communication could also be essential to human interaction and conversation [48, 49]. Previous studies have shown that nonverbal cues in communication are critical to the quality of patient care [50, 51]. Riess and Kraft-Todd [52] introduce the concept of assessing nonverbal behavior in physician–patient communication with a tool called E.M.P.A.T.H.Y. This tool is a first attempt to help guide the detection of nonverbal cues in physician–patient communication. Although nonverbal cues have been assessed qualitatively in healthcare, data analysis tools have barely been applied in this area. Moving toward data mining in nonverbal communication, there is a need for advance methods in data collection, such as video recordings to capture nonverbal cues in physician–patient conversations. Data analysis tools could be used to map and associate the verbal and nonverbal cues [53] in speech categorization of physician–patient conversations in order to improve the shared medical decision process. Weighting schemes might also be considered to investigate the relative importance of different forms of communication.

It is widely understood that a conversation is a sequential process. Therefore, conversation analysis (CA) needs to take advantage of the correlation of prior utterances and responses to quantify mutual understanding and knowledge evolution in the conversation. Toyoaki [54] termed the interaction that brings mutual understanding between the participants of the conversation *dynamical knowledge interaction*. This will be particularly important in shared medical decisions because it allows physicians to determine how much patients follow a conversation in the way the interaction is expected to evolve in terms of responses, suggestions, nonverbal cues, and so on. Models that quantify the degree of mutual understanding of prior communication need to be developed, which can help physicians to determine the next action of conversation: to continue with conversation, ask more questions, or to further explain previous points. These models could outline the sequential logic of a conversation to improve its quality in terms of understanding and encouragement of all participating individuals. It is possible that the patient may not ask the physician questions about things they do not understand; therefore, deducting their understanding from the dynamics of the conversation could help guide the course of the conversation. In a shared decision process, it is important that the patient understands every step of the conversation for effective cooperation. Models that allow detecting whether the patient follows a conversation and informing the next action will enhance the effectiveness of shared medical decision by increasing the participation of the patient in the process.

Adaptive models are expected to allow physicians to adapt themselves to the level of understanding of patients and thus select appropriate conversational features to facilitate maximum patient participation in the decision-making process. Speech recognition systems have used Bayesian approaches to design adaptive online learning algorithms via hidden Markov models and construct decision rules for speech recognition [55]. Similar strategies could be effective in constructing adaptive conversation models that can learn the speech, knowledge, and behavior of a patient in order to predict how to engage them in the medical decision process. Furthermore, combining adaptive models and predictive models is another area that needs to be explored with data mining tools in the shared medical decision process. With a move toward adaptive and predictive models, data need to be collected and implemented into the models online and faster. This would direct the field of shared medical decision toward automated systems similar to Interactive Voice Response (IVS) systems used in marketing and customer service telephone responses for businesses. The use of IVS in health care has been proposed by Kedar et al. [56] to act as automated answering machines for hospital and schedule appointments for patients. The authors also proposed the potential use of the IVS systems as simple diagnosis machines to assist physicians in guided medical decision making. The use of IVS systems may also be extended to speedily collect conversation data, adapt conversation models, and guide the physician toward the next effective course of conversation.

17.5 CONCLUDING REMARKS

In this chapter, we survey existing research of physician–patient communication studies, describe our ongoing data mining research on analyzing coded communication sequence data, and outline future directions in the general areas of text and speech characterization to truly facilitate patient-centered medical decision making. In terms of data mining methodology research, we conclude that analyzing communication sequence data for decision-making effectiveness characterization face challenges in aspects of data formatting, feature selection, and regression modeling. We point out the potential of using methods such as lasso to alleviate the difficulties.

As the paradigm of medical practice is moving toward personalized medicine, it becomes increasingly crucial to develop research on personalized conversation analysis for improving shared medical decision processes. This development will propel the use of integrated predictive-adaptive models, which have the ability to track conversation dynamics and adapt the conversation in real time to allow for effective communication. Meanwhile, these models are designed to have the ability to accommodate personalized communication for patients who have different knowledge about their medical conditions and different levels of comfort about communicating with their physicians. Finally, this line of research will benefit various forms of patient–physician communication moving toward patient-centeredness in the new era of medical practice, which include more and more heterogeneous and decentralized healthcare delivery, for example, home care, telemedicine, and online medical consultation.

REFERENCES

[1] Committee on Quality of Health Care in America, Institute of Medicine. *Crossing the Quality Chasm: A New System for the 21st Century.* Washington, DC: The National Academies Press; 2001.

[2] Institute for Healthcare Improvement. Person- and Family-Centered Care. Available at http://www.ihi.org/Topics/PFCC/Pages/default.aspx. Accessed 2014 May 20. 2014.

[3] Brock DW. The ideal of shared decision making between physicians and patients. Kennedy Inst Ethics J 1991;1(1):28–47.

[4] Coulter A. Partnerships with patients: The pros and cons of shared clinical decision-making. J Health Serv Res Policy 1997;2(2):112–121.

[5] Coulter A. Editorial. Welcome to the inaugural issue. Health Expect 1998;1(1):1–2.

[6] Moumjid N, Gafni A, Brémond A. Shared decision making in the medical encounter: Are we all talking about the same thing? Med Decis Making 2007;27(5):539–546.

[7] Fiscella KM, Meldrum SM, Franks PM, Shields CG, Duberstein PP, McDaniel SH, Epstein RM. Patient trust: Is it related to patient-centered behavior of primary care physicians? Med Care 2004;42(11):1049–55.

[8] Shields CG, Coker CJ, Poulsen SS, Doyle JM, Fiscella K, Epstein RM, Griggs JJ. Patient-centered communication and prognosis discussions with cancer patients. Patient Educ Couns 2009;77(3):437–442.

[9] Shields CG, Finley MA, Elias CM, Coker CJ, Griggs JJ, Fiscella K, Epstein RM. Pain assessment: The roles of physician certainty and curiosity. Health Commun 2013;28(7):740–746.

[10] Donabedian A. *Aspects of Medical Care Administration: Specifying Requirements for Health Care.* Cambridge, MA: Harvard University Press; 1973.

[11] Clayton JM, Hancock KM, Butow P, Tattersall M, Currow DC, et al. Clinical practice guidelines for communicating prognosis and end-of-life issues with adults in the advanced stages of a life-limiting illness, and their caregivers. Med J Aust 2007;186(12 Suppl):S79, S83–S108.

[12] Hagerty RG, Butow PN, Ellis PM, Lobb EA, Pendlebury SC, Leighl N, MacLeod C, Tattersal MH. Communicating with realism and hope: Incurable cancer patients' views on the disclosure of prognosis. J Clin Oncol 2005;23(6):1278–88.

[13] Steinmetz D, Walsh M, Gabel LL, Williams PT. Family physicians' involvement with dying patients and their families. Attitudes, difficulties, and strategies. Arch Fam Med 1993;2(7):753–60.

[14] Hagerty RG, Butow PN, Ellis PM, Dimitry S, Tattersall MH. Communicating prognosis in cancer care: A systematic review of the literature. Ann Oncol 2005;16(7):1005–1053.

[15] Helft PR. Necessary collusion: Prognostic communication with advanced cancer patients. J Clin Oncol 2005;23(13):3146–50.

[16] Cassileth BR, Zupkis RV, Sutton-Smith K, March V. Information and participation preferences among cancer patients. Ann Intern Med 1980;92(6):832–836.

[17] Jenkins V, Fallowfield L, Saul J. Information needs of patients with cancer: results from a large study in UK cancer centres. Br J Cancer 2001;84(1):48–51.

[18] Epstein R, Franks P, Fiscella K, Shields C, Meldrum S, Kravitz R, Duberstein P. Measuring patient-centered communication in patient-physician consultations: Theory and practical issues. Soc Sci Med 2005;61(7):1516–1528.

[19] Epstein RM, Shields CG, Franks P, Meldrum SC, Feldman M, Kravitz RL. Exploring and validating patient concerns: Relation to prescribing for depression. Ann Fam Med 2007;5:21–8.

[20] Epstein RM. Mindful practice in action (I): Technical competence, evidence based medicine and relationship-centered care. Fam Syst Health 2003;21(1):1–9.

[21] Epstein RM, Franks P, Shields CG, Meldrum SC, Miller KN, Campbell TL, Fiscella K. Patient-centered communication and diagnostic testing. Ann Fam Med 2005;3(5):415–21.

[22] Brown JB, Stewart MA, Ryan BL. Assessing communication between patients and physicians: the measure of patient-centered communication (MPCC). Working Paper Series, Paper # 95-2, Second edition. London, Ontario, Canada: Thames Valley Family Practice Research Unit and Centre for Studies in Family Medicine; 2001.

[23] Cronbach LJ. Coefficient alpha and the internal structure of tests. Psychometrika 1951;16(3):297–334.

[24] Baile WR, Buckman R, Lenzi R, Glober G, Beale EA, Kudelka AP. SPIKES – A six step protocol for delivering bad news: Application to the patients with cancer. Oncologist 2000;5(4):302–11.

[25] Fishman B, Pasternak S, Wallenstein SL, Houde RW, Holland JC, Foley KM. The memorial pain assessment card: A valid instrument for the evaluation of cancer pain. Cancer 1987;60(5):1151–1158.

[26] Melzack R. The McGill pain questionnaire: From description to measurement. Anesthesiology 2005;103(1):199–202.

[27] Aldrich CK. *The Medical Interview: Gateway to the Doctor–Patient Relationship*. 2nd ed. New York, NY: Taylor & Francis; 1999.

[28] Lipkin M, Putnam SM, Lazare A. *The Medical Interview: Clinical Care, Education, and Research*. New York, NY: Springer-Verlag; 1995.

[29] Roter D, Larson S. The Roter interaction analysis system (RIAS): Utility and flexibility for analysis of medical interactions. Patient Educ Couns 2002;46(4):243–251.

[30] Pennebaker JW, Chung CK, Ireland M, Gonzales A, Booth RJ. 2007. Operator's manual: Linguistic inquiry and word count: LIWC 2007. Available at homepage.psy.utexas.edu/homepage/faculty/pennebaker/reprints/. Accessed 2015 Dec 18.

[31] Furnham A, Ribchester T. Tolerance of ambiguity: A review of the concept, its measurement and applications. Curr Psychol 1995;14(3):179–199.

[32] Fang S, Shi W, Kong N, Shields CG. A preliminary variable selection based regression analysis for predicting patient satisfaction on physician-patient cancer prognosis communication. In: Zheng, X. et al. (eds.) International Conference on Smart Health 2014, Beijing, China, July 10–11, 2014. Springer Lecture Notes in Computer Science (LNCS) 8549. p 173–182; 2014.

[33] Jolliffe IT. *Principal Component Analysis*. 2nd ed. Springer Series in Statistics; 2002. XXIX, 487, p 28.

[34] Mallows CL. Some comments on C_p. Technometrics 1973;15(4):661–675.

[35] Darlington RB. Multiple regression in psychological research and practice. Psychological 1968;69(3):161–182.

[36] Schwarz G. Estimating the dimension of a model. Ann Stat 1978;6:461–464.

[37] Cleveland WS. Robust locally weighted regression and smoothing scatterplots. J Am Stat Assoc 1979;74(368):829–836.

[38] Tibshirani R. Regression shrinkage and selection via the lasso. J R Stat Soc B 1996;58(1):267–288.

[39] Efron B, Hastie T, Johnstone L, Tibshirani R. Least angle regression. Ann Stat 2004;32(2):407–499.

[40] Lawson C, Hansen R. *Solving Least Squares Problems*. Englewood Cliffs, NJ: Prentice Hall; 1974.

[41] Murray W, Gill P, Wright M. *Practical Optimization*. New York: Academic Press; 1981.

[42] Stein C. Estimation of the mean of a multivariate normal distribution. Ann Stat 1981;9(6):1135–1151.

[43] Breiman L. Better subset selection using the non-negative garotte. Technical Report. University of California, Berkeley; 1993.

[44] Frank I, Friedman J. A statistical view of some chemometrics regression tools (with discussion). Technometrics 1993;35(2):109–135.

[45] Pierrehumbert J. Synthesizing intonation. J Acoust Soc Am 1981;70(4):985–995.

[46] Taylor P. Analysis and synthesis of intonation using the Tilt model. J Acoust Soc Am 2000;107(3):1697–1714.

[47] Taylor P, King S, Isard S, Wright H. Intonation and dialog context as constraints for speech recognition. Lang Speech 1998;41(Pt 3–4):493–512.

[48] Mehrabian A. *Nonverbal Communication*. Chicago, IL: Aldine-Atherton; 1972.

[49] Knapp ML, Hall JA, Horgan TG. *Nonverbal Communication in Human Interaction*. 8th ed. Boston, MA: Wadsworth, Cengage Learning; 2014.

[50] Roter DL, Frankel RM, Hall JA, Sluyter D. The expression of emotion through nonverbal behavior in medical visits. Mechanisms and outcomes. J Gen Intern Med 2006;14(Suppl 1):S28–S34.

[51] Marcinowicz L, Konstantynowicz J, Godlewski C. Patients' perceptions of GP non-verbal communication: A qualitative study. Br J Gen Pract 2010;60(571):83–87.

[52] Riess H, Kraft-Todd G. E.M.P.A.T.H.Y.: A tool to enhance nonverbal communication between clinicians and their patients. Acad Med 2014;89:1108–1112.

[53] Montague E, Chen P, Xu J, Chewning B, Barrett B. Nonverbal interpersonal interactions in clinical encounters and patient perceptions of empathy. J Particip Med 2013;5.

[54] Toyoaki N. A traveling conversation model for dynamic knowledge interaction. J Knowl Manage 2002;6(2):124–134.

[55] Qiang H, Lee C-H. Robust speech recognition based on adaptive classification and decision strategies. Speech Commun 2001;34(1–2):175–194.

[56] Kedar SV, Ganla NH, Khalate VK, Aher DD. Automation of hospital with decision making ability. Int J Adv Res Comput Sci Softw Eng 2012;2(4):417–422.

18

THE HISTORY AND MODERN APPLICATIONS OF INSURANCE CLAIMS DATA IN HEALTHCARE RESEARCH

MARGRÉT V. BJARNDÓTTIR

Robert. H. Smith School of Business, Decision, Operations & Information Technologies, University of Maryland, College Park, MD, USA

DAVID CZERWINSKI

Department of Marketing and Decision Sciences, San Jose State University, San Jose, CA, USA

YIHAN GUAN

Oracle Corporation, Redwood Shores, CA, USA

18.1 INTRODUCTION

Nearly every encounter that a patient has with a healthcare provider produces a health insurance claim. Health claims data, also called administrative data, consists of billing codes that hospitals, physicians, pharmacies, and other healthcare providers submit to third-party payers to receive payment for their services. A medical claim typically contains a Provider ID, Procedure Code, Diagnosis Code, Service Date, and billing data. Diagnosis coding uses the International Classification of Disease, Ninth Revision, Clinical Modification (ICD-9 CM) codes, soon to be updated to the 10th revision. A pharmacy claim usually contains data to identify the medication

Healthcare Analytics: From Data to Knowledge to Healthcare Improvement, First Edition.
Edited by Hui Yang and Eva K. Lee.

and its form, for example, National Drug Code (NDC), Quantity, Service Date, and billing data.

To the best of the authors' knowledge, the earliest claims-based research in health care was published by Roos et al. in 1979 in *Evaluation Review* [1]. This study explored methods of organizing and checking administrative data banks to increase their usefulness for research and evaluation. The claims data used in the study came from the Manitoba Health Services Commission data bank in Manitoba, Canada, which was a provincial health insurance database characterized by universal coverage.

Beginning in the 1980s and into the early 1990s, researchers started to explore claims data as a new data source on patient care, provider services, and resource utilization [2–6]. Most of the claims-based studies used data from government health plans such as Medicare and Medicaid [3, 7, 8]. In the mid-1990s, claims data from commercial (or private) insurance plans gradually started to be used for research [9]. Since the 2000s, claims data-based research has become increasingly popular in the healthcare domain [10, 11]. Figure 18.1 summarizes some of the highlights in the use of claims data in healthcare research.

In the 1980s, the value of health insurance claims databases for healthcare research was questioned due to the fact that these databases are not designed for medical research; hence, the comprehensiveness and quality of the data were a concern [12]. In the early 1990s, there was a heated debate on the usefulness of claims data for healthcare research. Some researchers found that claims data lack important diagnostic and prognostic information compared to clinical data [13], and the accuracy of diagnosis and procedure coding varies substantially across conditions [7]. Others saw the potential of claims data as a cost-effective alternative to traditional clinical data. Quam et al. concluded that *more thoroughly investigated, claims data should become a more widely accepted resource for epidemiologic research* since claims data provides high level of agreement with alternative and more costly data [14]. Lewis et al. further pointed out that improvements to claims databases would enhance the benefit of such databases [2]. Since the early 2000s, claims-based medical studies have become increasingly common and claims data have been shown to be valuable in a wide array of health applications [10].

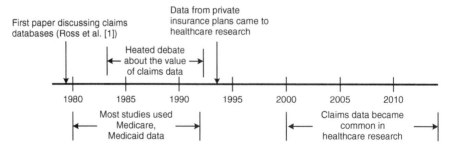

Figure 18.1   Timeline of healthcare research using claims data.

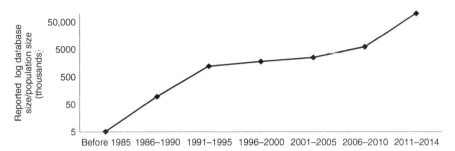

Figure 18.2 Maximum database or population log(size*1000) reported in top 10 cited claims-based studies.

The last three decades witnessed the emergence of claims databases in healthcare research and the rapid growth in the size of such databases. To reflect the trend in the scale of the claims databases used in healthcare research, we reviewed the 10 most cited research articles published in every 5-year period over the last 30 years (provided by Google Scholar when searching for "health" AND "claims data OR administrative data") and plotted the maximum database size or population/cohort size reported in the 10 articles, as shown in Figure 18.2. The vertical axis is in logarithmic scale.

18.1.1 Advantages and Limitations of Claims Data

Claims data have several strengths that explain their increasing popularity in healthcare research. They are population-based patient-level data and are often representative and complete for large populations [11]. Claims data have the breadth to allow long patient follow-up time, hence are extremely useful in longitudinal studies on chronic diseases. Their large scale enables the study of uncommon diseases and specific patient subgroups (based, e.g., on age, gender, or medical condition), which could be difficult to collect in other types of data [10]. Claims data are usually quickly available (a delay of 3 months can be expected due to processing and data cleaning); hence, large-scale real-time studies can be more efficient using claims data than clinical data. Their availability in electronic format makes claims data inexpensive and easy to access for researchers. In addition, claims data have billing information that is crucial to economic evaluations of health service utilization [2]. Another advantage of claims data is that patient bias, such as nonresponse or recall bias, does not exist in claims data because claims data are independent of a patient's memory [11], whereas patient bias usually exists in survey or interview data [10].

The limitations of claims data stem from the fact that the data are generated for insurance reimbursement; therefore, information irrelevant to reimbursement may be incomplete or excluded. Major complaints are coding inaccuracy, undercoding of comorbidities, overcoding of complications, typos and inconsistencies, and the inherent variability in the data recording process [2, 11]. Although diagnosis and procedure coding for medical claims start with a clinician, claims are often completed and submitted by a separate dedicated billing operator, which could result in discrepancies. In contrast to clinical data or electronic medical records (EMR), claims data do not contain the same level of medical details. For example, claims data do not include procedure outcomes, such as blood test results, although the results of tests can sometimes be inferred by subsequent procedures and/or diagnoses. Acknowledging the strengths and limitations of claims data, choosing appropriate data source(s) and utilizing methodologies driven by the data source(s) are crucial in research using claims data.

18.1.2 Application Areas

The applications of claims data studies have evolved over time. Early applications of claims data include drug utilization pattern research, disease burden estimation, quality-of-care assessment, and health policy evaluation. In the past 10 years, adverse drug event detection and outcome prediction emerged as new applications. In this section, we describe each of these application areas and provide references to several well-known studies in the area to demonstrate the range of applications.

In drug utilization pattern research, claims data have been used to investigate drug use both at a population level and within defined patient groups. Research studies have revealed information about prescription patterns, efficacy, and safety. As an example, Kotzan et al. used Medicaid data from 17,128 patients to study the influence of age, gender, and race on prescription drug use. They found that among all race–gender–age groups, white female patients of age greater than 65 had the most prescriptions per patient while nonwhite male patients of age between 6 and 23 had the fewest [15]. A second example is a study by Melander et al. that used prescription drug claims data from Sweden to investigate the relationships between anxiolytic–hypnotic drug[1] (AHD) prescribing, abuse, and suicide rates and found that AHD abuse and suicide can be greatly reduced by restricted prescribing of AHD [16]. Another example of drug utilization study is a research conducted by Glauber and Brown who used data from the northwest region of Kaiser Permanente, a health maintenance organization (HMO), to evaluate the use of medications by patients with diabetes. They found that the prescription data in the HMO database provided useful information on the cost impact and that patients with diabetes received a greater number of most types of medications with a greater overall cost than nondiabetic patients [17].

Early on, claims data became popular for estimating population disease burden for diseases such as hypertension, diabetes, stroke, and different heart conditions [8, 14, 18]. Subsequently claims data were used to develop a comorbidity index (a measure of coexisting medical conditions that are distinct from the primary diagnosis) to predict patient mortality, length of hospital stay, and hospital charges [19–21]. Pharmacy

---

[1] Anxiolytic–hypnotic drug is commonly prescribed by nonpsychiatrists for outpatient care in Sweden. In 1978, it was found that a large Swedish city (Malmo), which had the highest suicide frequency in Sweden, had a high rate of prescription of AHD [16].

claims data have also been used to develop a chronic disease score that measures chronic disease status [22]. These chronic disease scores are widely used in medical research and for reimbursement adjustment and pricing. More recently, diagnosis and procedure codes in claims data have been used to develop a computerized method, the Complications Screening Program, to identify potentially preventable complications of hospital care [23].

In Section 18.3, we discuss the development of quality measures from claims data in detail, both at population level and at patient level, as this is an important application area. Two examples that can provide insights into how claims data have been used to measure quality of care are as follows: Weiner et al. used claims data to identify categories of care that could be used to develop quality indicators such as preventive care, diagnostic services, and treatment and management [24]; Krumholz et al. developed a hierarchical regression model using Medicare claims data that produced hospital risk-standardized 30-day mortality rates, which were used to profile hospital performance among patients with heart failure. They concluded that the estimates of the risk-standardized state mortality produced by the claims-based model were very good surrogates for estimates derived from a medical record model [25].

Another active area of claims-based research is health policy evaluation. Because the data are generated for reimbursement purpose, they are extremely useful for evaluating the clinical and economic consequences of reimbursement policy changes. In 1991, Soumerai et al. analyzed 36 months of Medicaid data to determine if limiting the number of reimbursable medications in Medicaid would lead to an increased risk of admission to hospitals and nursing homes. They concluded that such a reimbursement policy change increased the risk of admission to nursing homes for frail, low-income, elderly patients [26]. A few years later, Grootendorst estimated the effect of enhanced insurance coverage in British Columbia, Canada, on the drug use among its residents aged 65 and older and found that the extension of insurance did not permanently increase drug use for most individuals and made only a minor contribution to growth in seniors' drug use [27]. In 2001, Tamblyn et al. used claims data from the Canadian province of Quebec to evaluate the impact of introducing prescription drug cost-sharing on drug use among elderly persons and welfare recipients, and concluded that increased cost-sharing was followed by reductions in use of essential drugs (defined as medications that would not likely be prescribed without a definitive diagnosis), which was associated with higher rates of serious adverse events and emergency department visits [28]. Around the same time, Schneeweiss et al. studied provincial health insurance claims data from British Columbia, Canada, to analyze the outcome of reference pricing (in which insurance covers the cost up to the reference price for drugs within a specific class) for angiotensin-converting enzyme (ACE) inhibitors for patients aged 65 or older. They found no evidence that patients would stop treatment for hypertension and no healthcare utilization and cost increases [29]. The above examples demonstrate that claims data can help evaluate, inform, and influence healthcare policy.

An emerging application of claims data is adverse drug event detection. A Google Scholar search on "adverse drug event" AND "claims data OR administrative data" returned 23 articles published between 1990 and 2000, 388 articles published between 2000 and 2010, and 312 articles published since 2010. Recent studies have shown claims data a promising data source for postmarketing drug surveillance and a cost-effective alternative to postmarketing clinical trial data [30–34]. Graham et al. used claims data from Kaiser Permanente in California to find an increased risk of serious coronary heart disease associated with the use of Rofecoxib (marketed under the name Vioxx) [35], which is one of the most well-known claim-based studies. Researchers have also used claims data to develop active surveillance systems for postmarketing drug and vaccine safety, aiming at early safety-signal detection [32, 34, 36]. In active surveillance designs, claims data have the advantage of large population size, which helps in the detection of rare events. At the same time, special adjustments and data modeling are needed to account for the limitations of claims data. As a sign of the importance of claims data in this area, the Food and Drug Administration is including claims data as one of the cornerstones of the Sentinel Project [37], a redesign of the US drug surveillance system aimed at monitoring adverse drug events using data of over 100 million lives.

Another more recent and active area of claims-based research is outcome prediction. A Google Scholar search on "outcome prediction" AND "claims data OR administrative data" returned 44 articles published between 1990 and 2000, 148 articles published between 2000 and 2010, and 148 articles published since 2010. An example of claim-based outcome prediction is the prediction of longevity and lifetime Medicare costs [38], where Cai et al. found that chronic obesity in middle age increased lifetime Medicare costs relative to those who remained normal weight. In Section 18.2, we elaborate on the use of claims data in cost prediction.

18.1.3   Statistical Methodologies Used in Claims-Based Studies

Various statistical methodologies have been used in mining claims data in the last three decades. When claims data first came to healthcare research, survival analysis was a widely used approach in measuring rates of outcomes [9, 26]. Classical hypothesis tests, such as t-tests and chi-square tests, were commonly used to test statistical significance of comparisons [3, 9, 17]. Regression models (e.g., logistic regression and linear regression) were used generally to identify significant predictors of the outcomes under study and to predict future outcomes [3, 9, 21, 24, 39]. We discuss the modeling of regression, clustering, and association rules in more detail later using three claim-based studies.

The following example demonstrates how regression is used to predict future healthcare costs. Fishman et al. [40] developed a pharmacy-based risk assessment model that first establishes an empirical relationship between prescription drugs and chronic conditions (e.g., prescriptions of insulins are linked to diabetes) and then uses a single-equation least squares regression model to estimate the risk weights (regression coefficients) associated with each of the demographic (age, gender, insurance benefit status) and chronic disease characteristics (described as a summarizing variable *RxRisk*). In this study, since the authors chose total healthcare costs as a proxy for medical risk, the risk weights were used to predict future healthcare cost. Specifically, medical risk (or total costs) in year t is modeled as a function of each individual's age, gender, health insurance (commercial, Medicare, or Medicaid) and *RxRisk* during year $t - 1$.

That is, for each individual i, total healthcare costs in year t, noted as $\text{Risk}_{i,t}$, are predicted by the following weighted least squares regression model:

$$\text{Risk}_{i,t} = X_{i,t-1}\beta_i + U_i$$

where $X_{i,t-1}$ is the set of independent variables for individual i in year $t - 1$, and β_i are the regression coefficients associated with each of the variables and U_i is a disturbance (error) term.

More recently, modern data-mining techniques have been utilized in claims-based studies. Clustering algorithms have been used to select comparison groups of eligible enrollees [41] and to predict healthcare costs [42]. Clustering algorithms have also been proposed as a method for discovering behavioral patterns in large-scale claim data [43]. Tsoi et al. [43] developed a two-step approach to apply recursively to Australian national claims database to reveal individual behavioral patterns. First, k-means clustering is used to segment the data into clusters based on the total benefit received within a rolling time-window. Second, hidden Markov models (HMM) are used to conduct pattern recognition within each of the clusters to further group those with similar temporal behavior patterns together into subclusters. Recursively applying the two steps yields a hierarchical tree model with multiple layers, where each layer describes the cluster of individuals of similar behavior patterns in increasing details. The key modeling steps in this approach are as follows.

The authors define an individual's profile as the total benefits paid (the amount paid by insurance policy) within a rolling 14-day time-window over 365 days, namely, individual i's profile is represented by a $352(=365 - 14 + 1)$ – dimensional vector, denoted as y_i, $i = 1,2, \ldots, n$ ($n =$ total population size). The goal of clustering is to group similar data points into a cluster. The k-means clustering algorithm is initiated by randomly selecting K points in the data set as cluster centroids. Individual data points are then assigned to clusters based on a distance metric, and the cluster centroids are recalculated. The algorithm terminates when there is no more update. In [43], the n data points are grouped together based on the total Euclidean norm from the centroids of the K clusters, as defined by

$$\sum_{k=1}^{K} \sum_{y_i \in D_k} \|y_i - m_k\|^2$$

where $D = \bigcup_{k=1}^{K} D_k$ is a possible partition of the n data points into K clusters and D_k denotes the kth cluster. m_k is the vector denoting the centroid of the kth cluster. The authors apply the k-means clustering algorithm with $k = 10$, which results in six coarse clusters of profiles (four clusters containing very small number of profiles are excluded). For each cluster, an HMM is then applied to detect sequences of events embedded in the profiles, and therefore to find finer grouping of the data based on temporal patterns. The HMM model in [43] assumes that the observed profiles are generated by a mixture of M Gaussian probability density function. After training an HMM on a training set in each cluster, the trained HMM is evaluated on all data within the cluster (e.g., cluster A) to label these data as cluster A, B, C, D, E, and F. As a result, the HMM misclassifies a number of profiles from one cluster as patterns from other clusters. To minimize the number of misclassifications, the authors apply k-means and HMM recursively to find more finely separated subclasses. The recursion can continue until either the k-means or the HMM is unable to find more clusters and classes.

The fine subclasses produced by the above-mentioned recursive two-step approach provide detailed representations to patient's behavior in claims data. For instance, one subclass represents patients who had frequent visits to doctors within 12 months with most benefit paid under $300, while another subclass represents patients who had a sudden change in their medical behavior, which incurred benefit paid of $800 in 12 months. These representations allow identification of common sequences of events as well as rare behavior patterns.

In addition to clustering, neural networks and association rule mining have been identified as two effective knowledge discovery approaches that can be applied to claims data to evaluate the relations between prespecified factors [44, 45]. An association rule takes the form $X \Rightarrow Y$, where X is called the "antecedent" and Y is called the "consequent" are two disjoint frequent item sets in a given database, that is, $X \cap Y = \emptyset$. Association rules are defined to have several properties based on the prevalence of the antecedent and consequent item sets. The support of the rule $X \Rightarrow Y$ is the percentage of observations that contain both X and Y, that is, $P(X \cup Y)$. The confidence of the rule $X \Rightarrow Y$ is its support divided by the support of X, which can be viewed as an estimate of $P(Y|X)$ [46]. Association rule algorithms are used to find all the association rules among item sets in a given database, where the support and confidence of these rules satisfy the user-specified minimum support and minimum confidence.

Kuo et al. [45] proposed a two-stage knowledge discovery approach that mines National Health Insurance databases in Taiwan using association rules following a preclustering of the data. The first stage uses clustering algorithms to cluster the data in order to dramatically decrease the association rule mining time due to the large-scale nature of the data (12 million individuals). The second stage involves the ant colony system-based (ACS-based) association rules mining algorithm to discover useful hidden relations between diseases within each cluster, for instance, "Essential hypertension => Hyperlipidemia," "Headache => Dizziness and giddiness," and "Conjunctival xerosis => Chronic conjunctivitis, unspecified." Fast discovering this type of useful rules from claims data allows researchers to pay attention to important groups (clusters) and to expose hidden relationships in the groups. Readers can find the details of the ACS-based association rules mining in [45]. In Section 18.2.7, we discuss the use of association rule mining in finding important variable interactions in regression modeling.

In summary, early on the focus of healthcare research using claims data was often on population-wide effects, using counting and traditional statistical techniques.

As computing power and database sizes have increased and modern data-mining techniques have been developed, healthcare analytics based on claims data have become more sophisticated. Prediction and risk adjustments, quality measurement, and drug surveillance have become increasingly common applications. Recent research efforts range from using advanced machine learning methods for knowledge discovery and pattern recognition, to discovering new correlations, as well as for early warning signals of patient's health [47] and increasingly sophisticated methodologies for the early detection of disease [48].

18.2 HEALTHCARE COST PREDICTIONS

The results of accurate cost prediction models have numerous applications such as group and individual insurance pricing, identification of members for disease and case management, fair reimbursement design, organizational planning, and benefit design. The predictive power of claims data became a topic of research in the 1980s [49], and numerous studies have since established the predictive power of administrative data for healthcare costs [49–52]. A number of health analytics companies have developed their own (proprietary) algorithms, for example, VeRisk Health and MEDai, and academic researchers have worked on the problem of cost prediction as well. In the following, we discuss some of the key aspects behind successful cost prediction based on claims data and discuss some of the models reported in the literature. For consistency, let the observation period be the time period for which data are observable and let the result period be the time period for which a prediction is made. In the following, we first discuss some of the high-level modeling considerations and performance measurement before discussing the applicable algorithms.

18.2.1 Modeling of Healthcare Costs

The distribution of healthcare costs is left-skewed, that is, a large part of the population has low healthcare costs, while a small fraction has healthcare costs in the hundreds of thousands of USD each year. The cumulative healthcare cost distribution, therefore, reflects the fact that a large proportion of population healthcare costs are the result of a small fraction of the population. This is displayed in Figure 18.3. The exact shape of the distribution will differ based on the population, and an older population with a heavier disease burden will display a "flatter" curve while a younger, healthier population will display a steeper curve.

Associated with this type of cost distribution are a few very high-cost members, who can be thought of as outliers. If these high-cost members are not addressed during the modeling stage depending on the selected method, they can overly influence the prediction model. There are a number of different ways to address high-cost members, including transforming the dependent variable, the cost. A common transformation is to use log (healthcare cost) as the dependent variable rather than the healthcare cost directly. Another approach taken in the literature [53] is to round down high-cost members to some user-defined upper limit. A third approach taken in the literature

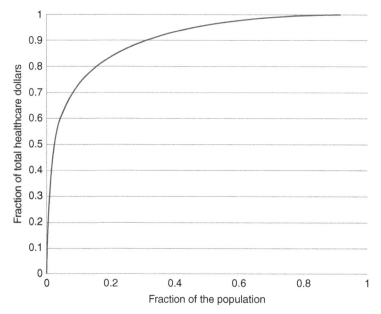

Figure 18.3 The fraction of population healthcare dollars as a function of the fraction of the population when the population is ordered in a descending order based on their healthcare spending.

is to divide up the range of healthcare costs into "cost buckets" [42], in which first predict the cost range of each member and then in a second step translate the cost range predictions into dollar amounts.

Healthcare costs are a very good surrogate for overall health conditions. In fact, the single most powerful predictor of future healthcare costs is a member's current healthcare costs [42]. However, it is not only the magnitude of costs that matter but also the temporal pattern. As a concrete example, consider the three members labeled A, B, and C in Figure 18.4. Member A has an acute spending pattern – a period of consistently low healthcare spending, then a high spike followed by a decline, returning to low healthcare spending for the remainder of the observation period. Such spending patterns are often the result of pregnancy complications or accidents and have limited risk of high costs in the result period. Member B has relatively low but rising healthcare costs, and member C has constant above average healthcare costs. The pattern of member C can be described as a chronic spending pattern and has a high probability of continuing. Perhaps surprisingly, increasing costs toward the end of the observation period are not universally an indicator of rising healthcare costs in the result period. Rather, only for specific subgroups are these costs an indicator. For example, members with such a spending pattern and their first cancer diagnosis of toward the end of the observation period have a high risk of high future healthcare costs.

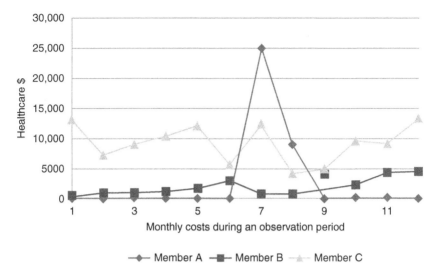

Figure 18.4   The cost trajectories of three members with different spending characteristics.

18.2.2   Modeling of Disease Burden and Interactions

One of the key considerations when modeling an individual's health condition is the compounding effect of multiple diseases. The cost effects of two (or more) conditions, for example, obesity and diabetes may be larger than the contributions of the two individual conditions in isolation. Other examples of such interactions include cardiac disease and being an older male, depression and a number of chronic conditions [54], and the combination of coronary artery disease (CAD) and hypertension. Given the large number of possible diagnosis codes, directly adding all possible two-way (and higher order) interactions to a prediction model may lead to overfitting, and as a result the modeler needs to either employ regularization, careful variable selection, or variable reduction. Of these approaches, variable selection has seen the widest use.

Variable selection for interactions can be done in several ways. One approach is to rely on the medical literature and expert knowledge and directly build (and test) variables based on this information, in essence to build in expert business rules. A second data-driven approach is to use association rule algorithms to identify high-impact rules that can be used in a secondary stage in the cost prediction model. To use association rules for cost prediction, one would mine for rules of the form {group of medical codes in the observation period} ⇒ {high costs in the result period}. An example of such groups of codes include {thyroid agents/hormones, insulin, antihyperlipidemic drugs} and another example is {renal failure, diabetes mellitus, and insulin} [55].

In addition to including specific interactions in prediction models, the use of comorbidity indices such as the Charlson index [56] is common practice. Other summarizing variables include a member's number of diagnoses, number of different classes of drugs taken, and other utilization measures such as the number of doctors and/or emergency department visits. All of these measures are correlated with higher costs in the result period.

18.2.3 Performance Measures and Baselines

Early on, R^2 was the error measure of choice in cost prediction, as much of the earlier research focused on the utilization of regression models, which maximize R^2. But R^2 is very sensitive to outliers and is dominated by the small high-cost group. As such, it does not reflect the overall quality of the predictions. Alternative error measures have been suggested, such as the mean absolute deviation (MAD).

Due to the skewed distribution of healthcare costs, the errors are not randomly distributed; rather they tend to be a function of the current health conditions and costs. This applies both to traditional R^2 as well as MAD and similarly defined measures. As a result, it may be advisable to analyze the error of the prediction model as a function of risk groups (low risk through high risk). The errors of current low-cost members will be very different in distribution than the errors of current higher cost members. The chosen error measure should reflect the *cost* of the errors to the user of the model. As an example, if the goal of the model is to identify impactable high-risk members for case management, penalizing missing those members (and, therefore, cost-saving opportunities) should carry a higher weight than inaccuracies in cost predictions for low-cost, low-risk members.

Baseline comparisons can also be used to assess prediction models. As previously mentioned, costs are a strong summary signal of overall health. Therefore, a naive prediction model that simply predicts the same cost in the observation period to be repeated in the result period will be fairly accurate. Any prediction algorithm should be able to significantly outperform this baseline model in order to add value, independent of the error measure.

18.2.4 Prediction Algorithms

Depending on the model's purpose, a balance needs to be struck between interpretability and predictive performance, as in most cases there is a trade-off between the two. Early researchers concentrated on using classical regression models [50–53, 57] for overall cost predictions. Regression models have the benefit of easy interpretability, but they are sensitive to outliers and as a result care needs to be taken when fitting them. This is less of a concern if the population size is in the millions, but for smaller sample approaches such as rounding down the costs of the highest cost members, regularization, or combining rare codes can help the fit and robustness of the model. Commonly regression models are combined with heuristic classification rules, that is, the regression models are built separately for different parts of the population. Commercial health analytics companies often use risk categories based on business rules, known as risk groups, and each member is assigned to a group based on his/her (chronic) disease burden measured by either diagnosis codes, pharmaceutical information, or both. Often, additional prediction modeling of cost is provided for each risk group. The Society of Actuaries has conducted comparison studies of many of the commercially available predictors and reported R^2 in the range of 0.16–0.31 depending on the application [53, 58]. The commercial models compared used both diagnosis and prescription data, sometimes augmented with cost information, which in all cases improved predictive performance.

More advanced machine learning algorithms applied to cost predictions include neural networks [59], classification trees, and clustering [42]. Classification trees have the advantage of being robust to the number of (correlated) variables, as well as outliers, and have a high accuracy, especially on a healthier population. Classification trees have the added benefit of being very interpretable and easily embedded into software, as the trees can be straightforwardly translated into if–then–else statements. For the most expensive members of a population, where the members' data are denser, methods that take advantage of the more complicated data structure such as clustering have been shown to outperform the simpler classification trees. The increased performance comes at the cost of more difficult interpretation, and the models are not as easily embedded in decision support software.

In addition to the observed improvement in commercial forecasting software when cost data are added, Bertsimas et al. [42] further showed the power of using cost data. The accuracy of trees using only cost information was the same as for trees using additional diagnostic, procedural, and drug information and indicator variables for risk factors identified in the medical literature. For clustering, the overall performance metrics were no more than 12% worse when using only cost information than when using the full set of information. Therefore, careful use of the cost information in claims data can be the key to increased prediction accuracy. However, if the use of the model is reimbursement, it has been argued that using prior costs may create the wrong incentives. In particular, there is a risk of indirectly awarding unnecessary care during the observation period as it would lead to higher expected payments during the reimbursement (result) period [60].

In summary, a number of supervised and unsupervised learning methods have been applied to cost prediction, ranging from simple linear regression with a small number of variables to advanced neural networks. Recent developments include using unsupervised learning methods such as clustering as the basis for prediction. In the following two sections, we discuss regression trees and clustering in more detail covering some technical considerations and providing insight into appropriately applying these methods to healthcare costs predictions.

18.2.5 Applying Regression Trees to Cost Predictions

Traditional linear regression models are global models, that is, a single prespecified model describes the effects of independent variables X_i (medical and cost characteristics in the observation period) on a dependent variable Y, in our case the healthcare costs in the result period. In contrast, Regression Trees recursively partition the independent variable space into a set of subspaces and assign a separate prediction rule to each subspace.

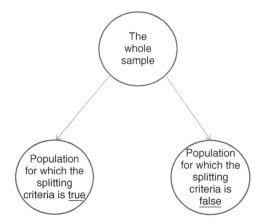

Figure 18.5   A demonstration of a first split in a regression tree.

The algorithm starts with the whole sample at a root node and then partitions the subspace, first into two subsets according to a splitting rule that minimizes a user-selected node impurity measure. The splitting rule commonly consists of an independent variable and a split value, that is, the population is split up into two groups, those with the value of the independent variable below the split value and those with the value above the split value. An example of the first split is shown in Figure 18.5. The split can be represented by a tree with the initial node containing the whole population and two terminal nodes containing the two subpopulations. The algorithm proceeds to continue to divide up the subspaces (represented by nodes in a tree) in a greedy manner until a defined stopping criterion is satisfied. Examples of stopping criteria include a minimum number of records in any node, a maximum level of the tree is reached or further splits give less than some minimal amount of improvement in predictive performance or reduction in node impurity. In practice, applying stopping rules has often proven unsuccessful, and therefore, especially in data-rich situations, using a validation sample to prune back the tree is preferred and avoids overfitting the training data.

Independent of whether a stopping rule or pruning is used to avoid overfitting, an impurity measure needs to be chosen to measure the goodness of possible splits and improvement in performance. Commonly used is the sum of the squared deviations from the mean. Let $\bar{y}_j$ be the healthcare costs in the result period of members in node j. Let S be the sum of squared errors for that node, that is, let

$$S = \Sigma_{i \in j}(Y_i - \bar{y}_j)^2.$$

When considering a split, S is calculated for a given node, and when evaluating a split into subnodes 1 and 2, the sum of S_1 and S_2 is compared to S. A split is only considered if the sum is smaller than S.

Tree algorithms can be split up into two types depending on the variable-split selection. Exhaustive search algorithms [61] are based on exhaustive search for the best split over all possible combinations of variable and split values. These exhaustive search algorithms have been shown to be biased toward numerical variables over categorical variables [62], as there are more possible splits for a numerical variable compared to a categorical variable. For example, consider two independent variables, the first one the overall healthcare cost in the observation periods and the second one an indicator variable for diabetes. When an exhaustive search algorithm searches for the best variable-value split, it will try a split between any two values of members' healthcare costs in the sample while there is only one possible split for the indicator variable, whether or not a member is diabetic. Since oftentimes the set of independent variables is a mix of binary, low-count categorical variables, and continuous variables, the second approach, a hypothesis-based algorithm, that first chooses the splitting variable based on a statistical hypothesis test before selecting the split may prove beneficial [63].

Once the tree is finalized, the mean (most commonly) of each node is assigned as a prediction rule for the members in each terminal node. An alternative is to assign the median if the goal is to minimize the MAD. In addition, fitting small one-variable regression models in the terminal nodes has been found to improve prediction for some data, but makes the interpretation of the tree more complex.

18.2.6 Applying Clustering Algorithms to Cost Predictions

Originally, clustering was developed as an exploratory methodology in contrast to a prediction algorithm. But based on the hypothesis that similar patients may have similar futures, a prediction algorithm can be built based on a clustering methodology. Multiple clustering algorithms exist ranging from simple hierarchical clustering to the more advanced, as many clever heuristics have been developed for different applications. A clustering approach that has proven successful in a range of applications is that of spectral clustering, which is based on dividing up a matrix of records based on the top singular vectors (for more details, see [64]). Independent of the clustering algorithm used, a similarity (or distance) function needs to be defined to measure how similar the members of the population are. Two key observations need to be accounted for when applying clustering to healthcare cost predictions. First, not all medical codes are equally important. For example, kidney disease is less serious than renal failure. Second, if a medical code is very common, it is not very distinctive, for example, some ENT coding is very common as it can include everything from the common cold to more serious ear, nose, and throat infections. Therefore, one should both weight more serious conditions more heavily in the similarity function and discount very common codes (ENT, labs indicators, etc.). Let k be an indicator for the distinct medical variables in the data and i and j be two members, Let their similarity s_{ij} be defined as

$$s_{ij} = \sum_k w_k \frac{x_{ik} x_{jk}}{\log(N_k)},$$

where N_k is the number of members with independent variable k greater than zero. The weights w_k can be derived from medical severity of conditions as ranked by experts, or alternatively be found via optimization or regression, for example, by fitting a regularized linear regression with the medical variables as the independent variables and the result period healthcare costs as the dependent variable.

An additional challenge of applying clustering to healthcare cost prediction results from the high dimensionality of the problem that leads to very few "similar" members. One approach to overcome this challenge is to implement a two-step approach based on the insight that costs in the observation period are strong predictors of costs in the result period. As a result, in the first step, members are clustered together using only their cost information. For example, using members' monthly cost and weighting the later months of the observation period more heavily than the early months. Then, once a clustering of cost-similar members is achieved, a clustering algorithm is applied again to each cost cluster separately using members' medical variables to form cost-similar and medical-similar clusters as shown schematically in Figure 18.6. In numerical experiments [42], it was found that cost information can distinguish members with different costs in the result period at a coarse level, which is difficult to achieve using only medical variables. On the other hand, medical information improves prediction accuracy at a finer level. Clustering algorithms have not traditionally been applied to healthcare costs prediction using claims data, but have been shown to perform well, especially for higher costs members.

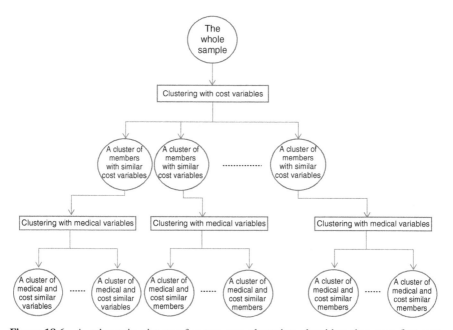

Figure 18.6 A schematic picture of a two-step clustering algorithm that uses first cost information to create cost-homogeneous subgroups before applying clustering with medical information.

18.2.7 Identifying High-Cost Members

Identifying members at high risk of high healthcare cost has been of interest to researchers and practitioners due to the potential of early intervention programs, such as case management, to curb healthcare costs. In their 2003 study, Meenan et al. [65] compare the ability of commercial healthcare cost prediction software in identifying the top 0.5% and top 1% of the population and compared the performance of the commercial applications to a baseline model of prior cost rankings (i.e., the top 0.5% or 1% in the observation period is predicted to be the top spenders in the result period). The researchers found that in some cases the commercial software outperformed the baseline model, but in other cases their performance was very similar. Additional work has focused on the use of more advanced algorithms. For example, Crawford et al. [66] use neural networks to identify disease-specific at-risk members and report performance, as measured by the area under the ROC curve, on par with Meenan et al.

In contrast to predicting high healthcare costs, a different approach to identifying members at risk of bad outcomes is to model the outcomes directly. Using logistic regression and careful variable modeling (indicator variables of undesirable utilization patterns such as visits to three or more different primary care physicians or poor treatment patterns such as risky drug combinations), researchers were able to identify members at increased risk of hospital readmission [67]. An additional study [68] looked at how well risk groups and a prior utilization model predict members with the highest utilization, which is defined as the number of days in the result period in which a member receives either inpatient or outpatient services. Using logistic regression the authors show that if the goal is to identify 90% of the top 2.2% of utilization members (sensitivity set to 0.9), the false positive rate is too high to be useful. However, when identifying the top 1% of healthcare users, one can do so almost perfectly with the prior utilization model. That is, the current top 1% will almost all be the next year's 1% (the sample used in the study only included members that survived the duration of the result period).

Independent of whether the dependent variable is next year's healthcare costs or an undesirable outcome, if the goal is cost reduction the key is the potential for impact. That is, the key to cost reduction is to distinguish preventable high-risk cases from nonpreventable cases. For example, looking forward a diabetic with end-stage renal failure is at high risk of high healthcare costs, but not much can be done to prevent these high costs. In contrast, a member with irregular utilization patterns and an underlying chronic condition without appropriate medication may be an example of a high-risk member for whom case management can have an impact. With this goal in mind, researchers have started to build models using association rule infused regression models [55] to identify current low-cost members at high risk of large costs in the result period.

18.2.8 Discussion

When applying cost prediction models in practice there are additional considerations. Many times there is a lag in the claims processing, and therefore case managers and planners may not have up-to-date information. Models therefore need to be trained and measured on lagged data to provide realistic picture of the models' performance. In addition, many times, insurance pricing and renewal decisions have to be made months in advance, which combined with the data-lag may result in an "information gap" of up to half a year, an important considerations when basing decision making on these models.

Earlier we have summarized some of the methods and modeling considerations used for cost prediction and high-risk member identification. One of the more recent developments in the data-mining community is the extensive use of ensemble methods, which combine a number of (independent) models into a single prediction model. The application of ensemble methods to healthcare cost predictions has, to the authors' best knowledge, not been attempted, at least not published, and may be a promising avenue to pursue to improve predictive performance. A good prediction model needs to be tailored to the application, whether it is pricing, planning, or prevention, and for those different purposes, different models and different performance measures may be appropriate.

18.3 MEASURING QUALITY OF CARE

The quality of care delivered in the United States varies considerably and in many cases is substandard [69, 70]. The measurement of quality is of vital interest to a number of stakeholders. For government agencies, measures of quality at the national, state, or local level are important for guiding and assessing healthcare policy. Quality measures of providers – such as hospitals, medical groups, or individual physicians – can be used by the providers to identify deficiencies in the care they are delivering. Consumers can also benefit from information about the quality of providers, for example, to choose a physician or to select a hospital at which to have a procedure performed. Measuring quality is also of interest to healthcare payers, such as Medicare and private insurers, who want to make sure they are getting their money's worth and pre-empt expenses that could result from poor care. Payers are experimenting with incentivizing quality care through "pay-for-performance" policies that tie reimbursements to quality measures [71]. Finally, measuring the quality of care received by individual patients can help identify those patients who are receiving poor care and who might benefit from interventions designed to improve their care.

18.3.1 Structure, Process, and Outcomes

There are three dimensions of healthcare quality: structure, process, and outcomes [72]. Structural aspects of care pertain to the setting in which healthcare takes place. This includes such aspects of care as physical facilities, the supply of doctors, access to medical technology, and government policies. The process of care refers to the steps taken by a patient's physician or team of providers in caring for them. For example, the process of care for a sore throat might involve taking the patient's temperature, ordering a strep test, and/or prescribing a medicine. The quality of the process of care indicates whether the care provided adhered with best practices or the relevant clinical guidelines. The quality of outcomes refers to the results of the patient's care. At its simplest level: did the patient get better or not? Different outcome measures are appropriate for different situations. For example, 5-year survival rates are a commonly used measure of the quality of cancer treatment. Blood glucose level would be a relevant outcome for measuring the quality of care for a diabetic.

Claims data are perhaps best suited to measuring the quality of the process of care. Many specialty medical societies have developed clinical guidelines that outline optimal care for a disease. The degree to which actual care coincides with the guidelines can be employed as a measure of quality. In this manner, claims data has played a role in measuring quality of care for a wide range of diseases including asthma [73], cancer [74], chronic obstructive pulmonary disease (COPD) [73], depression [75], and diabetes [73, 76–80].

Claims data can be used indirectly to study how structural aspects affect quality of care by comparing process of care in different structural settings. Differences revealed via the claims data in the quality of care delivered in the different settings could be attributed to differences in the settings. Two such studies measured how the quality of process of care for Medicare patients has changed over time [77, 81]. Kuo et al. [77] found that over the period 1992–2001, the rate of preventative care for diabetics in the Medicare program improved. The rate of short-term complications also improved although changes in the rates of long-term complications were mixed. Jencks et al. [81] analyzed the change in 22 quality indicators using a mix of claims data, medical records, and surveys for Medicare patients between the periods 1998–1999 and 2000–2001. They found improvements in 20 of the 22 indicators. Changes in quality over time are presumably the result of changes at the structural level for example, government policy, organizational changes geared toward quality, improved technology, or improved education.

Structural aspects of care have also been studied using claims data collected at the same time in different settings. Hollander et al. [76] compared the care received by diabetics in a fee-for-service setting to a managed care setting (HMO) and to the Veterans Administration (VA) using a mix of claims data and medical records. Contrary to what they expected to find, the care provided in the fee-for-service system was of high quality comparable to HMOs and the VA. Weiner et al. [80] found variations in the care provided to diabetics along a number of structural dimensions, including the type of primary care provider the patient saw and whether care was provided in an urban or rural setting. Piecoro et al. [82], in a study of the prescribing of inappropriate drugs to the elderly, found that nursing home residents were prescribed inappropriate drugs more frequently than non-nursing home residents. The authors posit a number of reasons why this might be.

In some situations, claims data are also useful for measuring outcomes [83], although in many cases they lack the necessary clinical details. For example, for a patient with hypertension, a successful outcome would be a lowering of their blood pressure. Since lab results and readings such as blood pressure are not recorded in claims data, claims data would not be useful in this case. On the other hand, for patients treated for heart attacks, a relevant outcome measure is whether they are re-admitted to the hospital within the next 30 days (re-admittance would be considered a negative outcome). Since claims data provide a record of hospitalizations, they would be useful in this case.

18.3.2   The Quality of Quality Data

While claims data have been shown to have high enough accuracy for many research purposes, their use for measuring quality of care continues to be scrutinized. The reason for this is likely tied to the fact that quality measures derived from claims data have been proposed for such high-stakes applications as facility ratings and pay-for-performance. If the quality of a provider's care is being assessed, it would be reasonable for the provider to insist that the data being used is an accurate reflection of the care actually provided. This can be contrasted with cost predictions, which attempt to forecast the future and so are inherently uncertain. In light of the large statistical uncertainty involved in predictions, the uncertainty introduced by any inaccuracies in the claims data is less significant. With pay-for-performance assessment, on the other hand, the care being assessed has already occurred so any uncertainty is strictly the result of the data or the method of measurement.

A number of limitations of claims data as a tool for quality measurement have been reported in the literature. Farmer et al. [84] discuss how the use of claims data for pay-for-performance and ranking of hospitals could lead to a change in behavior of what is recorded in claims. Ryoo et al. [85] demonstrated that some patients' care is inaccurately scored of lower quality because they did not receive care dictated by clinical guidelines when in fact the care was not appropriate due to contraindications recorded in their medical records (which may not be present in claims data). Keating et al. [86] found that a patient's race and age, and the type of clinic in which they received care, affected the accuracy of their claims data when compared to their medical record. The authors hypothesized that differences in the sophistication of the billing systems used by different clinics may account for some of this difference in accuracy. The limited ability to determine timing of events, particularly during hospitalizations, based on claims data limits their usefulness for identifying complications resulting from poor quality care [23, 87, 88]. Researchers must keep these challenges and limitation in mind while using claims data to assess quality of care. In what follows, we discuss some of the mathematical (Section 18.3.3) and practical (Section 18.3.4) considerations involved in constructing quality measures, a recent statistical approach (Section 18.3.5), and the application of quality measures to case management (Section 18.3.6).

18.3.3   Composite Quality Measures

Often, a quality score for a patient or provider is constructed from several individual quality indicators. For example, suppose a diabetic's quality of care was measured on four dimensions and he was found to have had his HbA1c measured and dilated eye exam, both performed at the appropriate frequency, but did not have his urine albumin level checked or have a foot exam. A simple numeric summary of his quality of care would be that he had two out of the four recommended procedures performed, or 50%. Similarly, if a physician treated 100 diabetics and performed foot exams on 75 of them, the physician's quality of care on this dimension could be summarized as 75%. Although both of these examples use simple averaging, quality indicators can be combined into a single composite measure in a number of ways. The choice of an appropriate composite measure can play a crucial role in the acceptance of the measurement by those being assessed.

There are two levels at which aggregation of quality indicators can take place: at the patient level or the provider level. At the individual patient level, the quality measures consist of a binary n-vector x where n is the number of quality indicators and $x_i = 1$ if the patient's care was in compliance with the ith quality measure and $x_i = 0$ otherwise. At the provider level, the quality measures consist of a real-valued vector y where y_i represents the percent of patients whose care was in compliance with the ith quality measure. If the size of the population served by the provider is p, then the relationship between x and y is

$$y_i = \frac{1}{p}\sum_{j=1}^{p} x_{ij} \tag{18.1}$$

where x_{ij} is the ith quality indicator on the jth patient.

The most straightforward approach to combining the patient-level quality measures is to take their average, as in the diabetes example above. For an individual patient, the composite quality metric would be

$$\frac{1}{n}\sum_{i=1}^{n} x_i \tag{18.2}$$

That is, the fraction of the indicators with which the patient's care was in compliance. At the provider level, the computation would be

$$\frac{1}{n}\sum_{i=1}^{n} y_i \tag{18.3}$$

which would be the average rate of compliance across all indicators. However, not all quality indicators may be of equal importance. Therefore, the indicators can be weighted by their importance before averaging, and a number of approaches to weighting have been suggested [89].

- *Judgment Weights.* The weights come from the judgment of medical experts.
- *Cost-based Weights.* The difference in average (or median) cost of care for patients in and out of compliance with a particular indicator can be used as weights. Indicators that are tied to larger differences in costs would have larger weights. To reduce noise, median cost rather than average cost can be used.

- *Opportunity-based Weights.* Not all quality indicators are applicable to all members of the patient population, since some patients may have contraindications to certain tests or procedures. Opportunity-based weights place more weight on broadly applicable processes [89]. Let p_i be the number of patients who the ith quality indicator applies to and let $p*$ be the number of patients for whom at least one of the quality indicators applies. Then the opportunity-based weighted composite score is

$$\frac{1}{p*} \sum_{i=1}^{n} p_i y_i. \tag{18.4}$$

- *Benefit-of-the-doubt Weights.* The rate at which each indicator is complied with may implicitly reveal the importance that the provider places on that particular indicator [89]. For example, if a provider is in compliance with Hba1c testing for a high percentage of patients, it may reflect the fact that the provider feels Hba1c testing is very important. By using the compliance rates themselves to determine the weights, weightings can be constructed to give the provider "the benefit of the doubt," that is, the provider is emphasizing those measures that they deem most important. Note the relationship to judgment weights, for which an external medical expert assigns weights based on importance; here the providers themselves act as the experts.

  Shwartz et al. [89] show that benefit-of-the-doubt weights w_i can be determined using a linear optimization model of the form

$$\text{Maximize } w_i y_i \text{ subject to } \sum_{i=1}^{n} w_i = 1, w_i \geq 0 \forall i, \tag{18.5}$$

along with side constraints that bound the deviation of the weights from the weights based on one of the other methods. Shwartz et al. show that under a broad range of bounds on the weights, the same providers tend to rise to the top.

- *Statistical Weights.* In this case, weights are derived from a statistical model of quality [90] where a single binary quality indicator for a patient's care is assigned by a medical expert after review of the patient's claims history. Next, a logistic regression model is fit that determines weights for individual components of care. Note the relationship with judgment weights, which also rely on a medical expert, but here the judgment is done at the level of the patient's overall care, not for each individual component of care. This approach is discussed further in Section 18.3.5.

18.3.4 Practical Considerations for Constructing Quality Scores

Comparing actual care to clinical guidelines is the most common approach to measuring quality of care. The approach can be applied at virtually any level of the healthcare system – physicians, medical groups, hospitals, or geographic regions such as states or nations. Each can be analyzed by aggregating care across the relevant patients and calculating the percent who received care that was in accordance with each item from the guidelines. But, the approach does have practical and theoretical limitations.

In practice, the analysis can be complicated when a patient sees multiple providers or has multiple payers for their care (such as a combination of Medicare and private insurance). In such a case, the entirety of the patient's care may not be contained within a single claims database. The researcher, as a result, may have an incomplete picture of the care that the patient received. To compound this problem, it is generally not readily apparent from the data recorded in a claims database whether another payer exists. Similarly, if one is assessing providers and the providers accept payment from different sources, then the entirety of their patients may not be contained within a single claims database. In this case, the researcher may only have access to a nonrandom sample of a provider's patients. This problem is obviated if the researcher has access to the provider's own billing database or if there is only a single payer, as is the case in many countries.

Quality can also be more complex to assess when a patient has multiple chronic diseases (although, for diabetes care at least, Halanych et al. [91] did not find a relationship between the number of diseases a patient had and the diabetes care they received). Treatment guidelines for one disease may come into conflict with the treatment guidelines for another. That is, it may not be possible (or appropriate) to give care that is "optimal" according to each guideline individually [92]. Or, when the disease burden is particularly high, it may become infeasible to perform all of the recommended tests and procedures because the time it would take would detract from the patient's quality of life.

Accurately assessing quality of care for complex patients with multiple chronic diseases is important for several reasons. From the payer's perspective, the most complex cases are the most costly and ensuring quality care is delivered can help contain costs. From a patient's perspective, the more complex their case, the more crucial quality care becomes. (It is easy to survive suboptimal care for a sore throat. A suboptimal open-heart surgery is another matter.)

18.3.5 A Statistical Approach to Measuring Quality

An alternative to the "checklist" approach of using clinical guidelines is to develop a statistical model of quality of care. Bertsimas et al. [90] used a logistic regression model to identify diabetes patients receiving poor quality care. Logistic regression models a binary response variable, in this case an indicator of poor quality of care, as a nonlinear function of a set of independent variables. Let Y be a vector of binary response outcomes for the data set and X be the corresponding matrix of independent variables. The logistic regression model is given by

$$Y = \frac{1}{1 + e^{-(\beta_0 + \beta X)}}$$

In contrast to ordinary linear regression that has a closed-form solution, the logistic regression model is fit via maximum-likelihood method. Logistic regression is widely used for modeling binary responses, in social and life sciences alike. Its popularity in part stems from the interpretability of the model; $\exp(\beta_k)$ is the increase in the odds of the quality of care being poor, when the kth independent variable is increased by one, everything else being equal. The modeling process in [90] relied on an experienced physician who reviewed the claims data of 101 diabetics, rating the quality of care they received. The logistic regression model was fit to the quality ratings, using variables derived from the patients' claims data.

The resulting model was able to classify 80% of cases accurately in an out-of-sample test (compared to a baseline accuracy of 63% for a naïve model classifying all care as good). The model used only three variables: the number of HbA1c tests a patient had during the study period, an indicator for polypharmacy (initiating treatment with two or more drugs simultaneously), and a measure of the frequency of use of acute pharmaceuticals (such as antibiotics).

The advantages of a statistical approach to measuring quality are several. Because it does not need to hew to clinical guidelines, a statistical model can capture aspects of care that are beyond the guidelines' purview. In fact, a statistical model of quality does not even require an explicit definition of quality [90]. Another benefit is that a statistical model is not reliant on *a priori* weights for different components of care – rather, it determines weights that best fit the data. Finally, because a statistical model need not be based on the guidelines for a specific disease, such an approach could be used for developing a model of quality that could be applied to a general patient population.

The statistical approach described in [90] is a "top-down" approach to measuring quality – the physician provides a rating of the patient's overall quality of care, which is then used to identify, through the statistical modeling process, particular aspects of care that correlate with the physician's ratings. The checklist approach to measuring quality, on the other hand, is "bottom-up" in that it begins with particular aspects of care – the individual quality indicators – which are then aggregated to yield an overall measure of quality. A limitation of the statistical modeling approach is that it is reliant on human medical experts, which limits the sample size that is practical for model building or makes the data collection expensive. One approach to overcoming this limitation is discussed in Section 18.3.6.

18.3.6 Quality as a Case Management Tool

Ongoing quality-of-care monitoring can be of benefit to case management organizations. In a typical case management setting, case workers (often nurses) interact with patients by phone or in person. As it is practiced today, case management is reactive – after a patient begins incurring high costs, a case manager intervenes. The case manager may educate the patient about their disease, help the patient navigate the healthcare system, encourage the patient to comply with their treatment, and so on.

Using cost predictions and measures of quality of care, a more proactive approach to case management can be taken. Rather than reacting to patients who have already incurred high costs, case managers can intervene ahead of time with patients who are predicted to have high costs in the future. Furthermore, intervention can be focused on those patients who have high predicted cost and are currently receiving poor quality care. This combination of high predicted costs and poor care may provide the most opportunity for the case manager to have an impact, improving the patients' care and containing costs before they balloon.

The use of quality measures based on claims data are less controversial for identifying candidates for case management, since the measures are not being used to judge any of the care providers nor tied to compensation. Even if the quality measure is not perfect, it can still help the case management team focus on patients who are more likely to be receiving poor care than the general population [90]. For these reasons, a statistical model of quality may be more suitable for use in this context than it would be, for example, for ranking hospitals.

The case management context also provides an opportunity to increase the sample size on which the statistical model is based. As case managers review cases, they can record their own quality rating in the database. Although the case managers are not highly trained physicians, they are often registered nurses. Furthermore, based on their experience, they may have a better sense of the types of patients who would benefit from case management. So perhaps they would identify different types of poor quality care than a physician would, but for the purposes of case management this is fine. As the quality ratings of the case managers accrue in the database, the model can then be refit and refined. The additional work load for the case managers would be small, since they would be reviewing the case anyway prior to their contact with the patients.

18.3.7 Discussion

An improved ability to measure quality of care has the potential to help target healthcare resources where they are needed. Quality measures based on insurance claims data have been developed for a broad array of chronic diseases, although the measurement is mainly done in a checklist manner. This is problematic because often the clinical guidelines that the measures are derived from are not applicable to all patients due to comorbidities, incompatibilities between treatments, and other extenuating circumstances. More recent studies have been careful to exclude such patients from the study population. This leads to more accurate assessment of the quality of care being delivered to the study population, uncontaminated by patients to whom the clinical guidelines do not apply. But at the same time, the quality of care received by patients excluded from studies due to complicating factors is no less important than the quality of care received by those patients who fit cleanly in study guidelines. So while more carefully applying exclusion criteria may lead to a more accurate picture of compliance with treatment guidelines, it leaves more and more patients out of the picture, their quality of care not as thoroughly measured. This is where more holistic measures of quality of care hold promise.

Quality of care has not seen the same innovative application of advanced analytics that cost prediction has. There is an opportunity for more sophisticated statistical approaches to overcome some of the limitations of the checklist approach, particularly by measuring the quality of care of patients with multiple chronic diseases and other complex cases to whom narrow clinical guidelines do not apply.

18.4 CONCLUSIONS

Ever larger claims databases provide the opportunity for improving the healthcare system and the health of individuals. Claims data provide a unique bird's-eye view of individual member's healthcare state, and as such offer not only opportunities for population-based research, but individual analysis as well. Currently, no other source of healthcare data comes close to the sheer volume of claims data. They offer a promising vista for the quantitative researcher with the statistical and data-mining tools needed to subdue their inherent noise. The health implications of the knowledge that can potentially be extracted from claims data make them intrinsically worthy of further research. In the field of claims data research, there is opportunity to develop new analytical techniques and to extract interesting medical knowledge using existing techniques. As the fields of computing and machine learning continue to evolve, pattern recognition and knowledge discovery have the potential to improve medical knowledge and healthcare practices, as these methods take advantage of the large size of the data that enables detection of patterns that would otherwise lie undiscovered. It is clear that claims data will continue to serve as a source for policy evaluation, population analysis, and inspiration of new knowledge discovery and data-mining algorithms.

REFERENCES

[1] Roos LL, Nicol JP, Johnson CF, Roos NP. Using administrative data banks for research and evaluation: A case study. Eval Rev 1979;3(2):236–255.

[2] Lewis NJ, Patwell JT, Briesacher BA. The role of insurance claims databases in drug therapy outcomes research. Pharmacoeconomics 1993;4(5):323–330.

[3] Wennberg JE, Roos N, Sola L, Schori A, Jaffe R. Use of claims data systems to evaluate health care outcomes: mortality and reoperation following prostatectomy. JAMA 1987;257(7):933–936.

[4] Roos LL Jr, Nicol JP, Cageorge SM. Using administrative data for longitudinal research: comparisons with primary data collection. J Chronic Dis 1987;40(1):41–49.

[5] Feldstein PJ, Wickizer TM, Wheeler JR. Private cost containment. The effects of utilization review programs on health care use and expenditures. N Engl J Med 1988;318(20):1310–1314.

[6] Anderson G, Steinberg EP, Whittle J, Powe NR, Antebi S, Herbert R. Development of clinical and economic prognoses from Medicare claims data. JAMA 1990;263(7):967–972.

[7] Fisher ES, Whaley FS, Krushat WM, Malenka DJ, Fleming C, Baron JA, Hsia DC. The accuracy of Medicare's hospital claims data: Progress has been made, but problems remain. Am J Public Health 1992;82(2):243–248.

[8] Hebert PL, Geiss LS, Tierney EF, Engelgau MM, Yawn BP, McBean AM. Identifying persons with diabetes using Medicare claims data. Am J Med Qual 1999;14(6):270–277.

[9] Topol EJ, Ellis SG, Cosgrove DM, Bates ER, Muller DW, Schork NJ, Schork MA, Loop FD. Analysis of coronary angioplasty practice in the United States with an insurance-claims data base. Circulation 1993;87(5):1489–1497.

[10] Ferver K, Burton B, Jesilow P. The use of claims data in healthcare research. Open Public Health J 2009;2:11–24.

[11] Schneeweiss S, Avorn J. A review of uses of health care utilization databases for epidemiologic research on therapeutics. J Clin Epidemiol 2005;58(4):323–337.

[12] Roos LL Jr, Roos NP, Cageorge SM, Nicol JP. How good are the data?: Reliability of one health care data bank. Med Care 1982;20(3):266–276.

[13] Jollis JG, Ancukiewicz M, DeLong ER, Pryor DB, Muhlbaier LH, Mark DB. Discordance of databases designed for claims payment versus clinical information systems: Implications for outcomes research. Ann Intern Med 1993;119(8):844–850.

[14] Quam L, Ellis LB, Venus P, Clouse J, Taylor CG, Leatherman S. Using claims data for epidemiologic research: The concordance of claims-based criteria with the medical record and patient survey for identifying a hypertensive population. Med Care 1993;498–507.

[15] Kotzan L, Carroll NV, Kotzan JA. Influence of age, sex, and race on prescription drug use among Georgia Medicaid recipients. Am J Health Syst Pharm 1989;46(2):287–290.

[16] Melander A, Henricson K, Stenberg P, Löwenhielm P, Malmvik J, Sternebring B, Bergdahl U. Anxiolytic-hypnotic drugs: Relationships between prescribing, abuse and suicide. Eur J Clin Pharmacol 1991;41(6):525–529.

[17] Glauber HS, Brown JB. Use of health maintenance organization data bases to study pharmacy resource usage in diabetes mellitus. Diabetes Care 1992;15(7):870–876.

[18] Robinson JR, Young TK, Roos LL, Gelskey DE. Estimating the burden of disease: Comparing administrative data and self-reports. Med Care 1997;35(9):932–947.

[19] Klabunde CN, Potosky AL, Legler JM, Warren JL. Development of a comorbidity index using physician claims data. J Clin Epidemiol 2000;53(12):1258–1267.

[20] Klabunde CN, Warren JL, Legler JM. Assessing comorbidity using claims data: An overview. Med Care 2002;40(8):IV-26.

[21] Elixhauser A, Steiner C, Harris DR, Coffey RM. Comorbidity measures for use with administrative data. Med Care 1998;36(1):8–27.

[22] Von Korff M, Wagner EH, Saunders K. A chronic disease score from automated pharmacy data. J Clin Epidemiol 1992;45(2):197–203.

[23] Lawthers AG, McCarthy EP, Davis RB, Peterson LE, Palmer RH, Iezzoni LI. Identification of in-hospital complications from claims data: is it valid? Med Care 2000;38(8):785–795.

[24] Weiner JP, Powe NR, Steinwachs DM, Dent G. Applying insurance claims data to assess quality of care: A compilation of potential indicators. Qual Rev Bull 1990;16(12):424–438.

[25] Krumholz HM, Wang Y, Mattera JA, Wang Y, Han LF, Ingber MJ, Roman S, Normand SLT. An administrative claims model suitable for profiling hospital performance based on 30-day mortality rates among patients with an acute myocardial infarction. Circulation 2006;113(13):1683–1692.

[26] Soumerai SB, Ross-Degnan D, Avorn J, McLaughlin TJ, Choodnovskiy I. Effects of Medicaid drug-payment limits on admission to hospitals and nursing homes. N Engl J Med 1991;325(15):1072–1077.

[27] Grootendorst PV. Health care policy evaluation using longitudinal insurance claims data: An application of the panel Tobit estimator. Health Econ 1997;6(4):365–382.

[28] Tamblyn R, Laprise R, Hanley JA, Abrahamowicz M, Scott S, Mayo N, Mallet L. Adverse events associated with prescription drug cost-sharing among poor and elderly persons. JAMA 2001;285(4):421–429.

[29] Schneeweiss S, Walker AM, Glynn RJ, Maclure M, Dormuth C, Soumerai SB. Outcomes of reference pricing for angiotensin-converting–enzyme inhibitors. N Engl J Med 2002;346(11):822–829.

[30] Rodriguez EM, Staffa JA, Graham DJ. The role of databases in drug postmarketing surveillance. Pharmacoepidemiol Drug Saf 2001;10(5):407–410.

[31] Gianfrancesco FD, Grogg AL, Mahmoud RA, Wang RH, Nasrallah HA. Differential effects of risperidone, olanzapine, clozapine, and conventional antipsychotics on type 2 diabetes: Findings from a large health plan database. J Clin Psychiatry 2002;63(10):920–930.

[32] Brown JS, Kulldorff M, Chan KA, Davis RL, Graham D, Pettus PT, Andrade SE, Raebel MA, Herrinton L, Roblin D, Boudreau D, Smith D, Gurwitz JH, Gunter MJ, Platt R. Early detection of adverse drug events within population-based health networks: Application of sequential testing methods. Pharmacoepidemiol Drug Saf 2007;16(12):1275–1284.

[33] Berlin JA, Glasser SC, Ellenberg SS. Adverse event detection in drug development: Recommendations and obligations beyond phase 3. Am J Public Health 2008;98(8):1366–1371.

[34] Bjarnadóttir, MV. Data-driven approach to health care: Applications using claims data, Doctoral dissertation, Massachusetts Institute of Technology; 2008.

[35] Graham DJ, Campen D, Hui R, Spence M, Cheetham C, Levy G, Shoor S, Ray WA. Risk of acute myocardial infarction and sudden cardiac death in patients treated with cyclo-oxygenase 2 selective and non-selective non-steroidal anti-inflammatory drugs: Nested case–control study. Lancet 2005;365(9458):475–481.

[36] Lieu TA, Kulldorff M, Davis RL, Lewis EM, Weintraub E, Yih K, Yin R, Brown JS, Platt R, Vaccine Safety Datalink Rapid Cycle Analysis Team. Real-time vaccine safety surveillance for the early detection of adverse events. Med Care 2007;45(10):S89–S95.

[37] Platt R, Carnahan R. The US food and drug administration's mini-sentinel program. Pharmacoepidemiol Drug Saf 2012;21(S1):1–303.

[38] Cai L, Lubitz J, Flegal KM, Pamuk ER. The predicted effects of chronic obesity in middle age on Medicare costs and mortality. Med Care 2010;48(6):510–517.

[39] Kerr EA, McGlynn EA, Van Vorst KA, Wickstrom SL. Measuring antidepressant prescribing practice in a health care system using administrative data: Implications for quality measurement and improvement. Jt Comm J Qual Patient Saf 2000;26(4):203–216.

[40] Fishman PA, Goodman MJ, Hornbrook MC, Meenan RT, Bachman DJ, Rosetti MCK. Risk adjustment using automated ambulatory pharmacy data: The RxRisk model. Med Care 2003;41(1):84–99.

[41] Huskamp HA, Deverka PA, Epstein AM, Epstein RS, McGuigan KA, Frank RG. The effect of incentive-based formularies on prescription-drug utilization and spending. N Engl J Med 2003;349(23):2224–2232.

[42] Bertsimas D, Bjarnadóttir MV, Kane MA, Kryder JC, Pandey R, Vempala S, Wang G. Algorithmic prediction of health-care costs. Oper Res 2008;56(6):1382–1392.

[43] Tsoi AC, Zhang S, Hagenbuchner M. Pattern discovery on Australian medical claim data-a systematic approach. Knowl Data Eng IEEE Trans 2005;17(10):1420–1435.

[44] Walker AM. Pattern recognition in health insurance claims databases. Pharmacoepidemiol Drug Saf 2001;10(5):393–397.

[45] Kuo RJ, Lin SY, Shih CW. Mining association rules through integration of clustering analysis and ant colony system for health insurance database in Taiwan. Exp Syst Appl 2007;33(3):794–808.

[46] Hastie T, Tibshirani R, Friedman J. *The elements of statistical learning (Vol. 2, No. 1)*. New York: Springer; 2009.

[47] Shenk KN. Patterns of heart attacks, MS thesis. Massachusetts Institute of Technology; 2010.

[48] Ghalwash MF, Radosavljevic V, Obradovic Z. Extraction of interpretable multivariate patterns for early diagnostics, In Data Mining (ICDM), 2013 IEEE 13th International Conference on (pp. 201–210). IEEE; 2013.

[49] Zhao Y, Ash AS, Ellis RP, Ayanian JZ, Pope GC, Bowen B, Weyuker L. Predicting pharmacy costs and other medical costs using diagnoses and drug claims. Med Care 2005;43(1):34–43.

[50] Ash AS, Ellis RP, Pope GC, Ayanian JZ, Bates DW, Burstin H, Iezzoni LI, MacKay E, Yu W. Using diagnoses to describe populations and predict costs. Health Care Financ Rev 2000;21(3):7–28.

[51] Zhao Y, Ellis RP, Ash AS, Calabrese D, Ayanian JZ, Slaughter JP, Weyuker L, Bowen B. Measuring population health risks using inpatient diagnoses and outpatient pharmacy data. Health Serv Res 2001;36(6 Pt 2):180.

[52] Farley JF, Harley CR, Devine JW. A comparison of comorbidity measurements to predict healthcare expenditures. Am J Manag Care 2006;12(2):110–119.

[53] Cumming R, Knutson D, Cameron B, Derrick B. A comparative analysis of claims-based methods of health risk assessment for commercial populations. Final report to the Society of Actuaries; 2002.

[54] Welch CA, Czerwinski D, Ghimire B, Bertsimas D. Depression and costs of health care. Psychosomatics 2009;50(4):392–401.

[55] Anderson D, Bjarnadottir M. Making the case for case management. Working paper; 2014.

[56] Charlson ME, Pompei P, Ales KL, MacKenzie CR. A new method of classifying prognostic comorbidity in longitudinal studies: Development and validation. J Chronic Dis 1987;40(5):373–383.

[57] Powers CA, Meyer CM, Roebuck MC, Vaziri B. Predictive modeling of total health-care costs using pharmacy claims data: A comparison of alternative econometric cost modeling techniques. Med Care 2005;43(11):1065–1072.

[58] Winkelman, R, Mehmud, S. A comparative analysis of claims-based tools for health risk assessment. Society of Actuaries, 1–70; 2007.

[59] Morrison JR, Johnson JD, Barnes JH, Summers K, Szeinbach SL. Predicting total health care costs of Medicaid recipients: An artificial neural systems approach. J Bus Res 1997;40(3):191–197.

[60] de Ven V, Wynand PMM, Ellis RP. Risk adjustment in competitive health plan markets. In: Culyer AJ, Newhouse JP, editors. *Handbook in Health Economics*. Amsterdam: Elsevier; 2000. p 756–845.

[61] Breiman L, Friedman JH, Olshen RA, Stone CI. *Classification and Regression Trees*. Belmont, California: Wadsworth; 1984.

[62] Loh WY, Shih YS. Split selection methods for classification trees. Stat Sin 1997;7:815–840.

[63] Classification and Regression Trees and Forests (GUIDE). 1997. Software. Available at http://www.stat.wisc.edu/~loh/guide.html. Accessed 2015 May 24.

[64] Kannan R, Vempala S, Vetta A. On clusterings: Good, bad and spectral. J ACM 2004;51(3):497–515.

[65] Meenan RT, Goodman MJ, Fishman PA, Hornbrook MC, O'Keeffe-Rosetti MC, Bachman DJ. Using risk-adjustment models to identify high-cost risks. Med Care 2003;41(11):1301–1312.

[66] Crawford AG, Fuhr JP Jr, Clarke J, Hubbs B. Comparative effectiveness of total population versus disease-specific neural network models in predicting medical costs. Dis Manag 2005;8(5):277–287.

[67] Roblin DW, Juhn PI, Preston BJ, Penna RD, Feitelberg SP, Khoury A, Scott JC. A low-cost approach to prospective identification of impending high cost outcomes. Med Care 1999;37:1155–1163.

[68] Rosen AK, Wang F, Montez ME, Rakovski CC, Berlowitz DR, Lucove JC. Identifying future high-healthcare users. Dis Manage Health Outcomes 2005;13(2):117–127.

[69] Schuster MA, McGlynn EA, Brook RH. How good is the quality of health care in the United States? Milbank Q 1998;76(4):517–563.

[70] Corrigan JM, Donaldson MS, Kohn LT, Maguire SK, Pike KC. *Crossing the Quality Chasm: A New Health System for the 21st Century*. Washington, DC: The Institute of Medicine; 2001.

[71] Rosenthal MB, Frank RG, Li Z, Epstein AM. Early experience with pay-for-performance: From concept to practice. JAMA 2005;294(14):1788–1793.

[72] Donabedian A. Evaluating the quality of medical care. Milbank Mem Fund Q 1966;166–206.

[73] Priest JL, Cantrell CR, Fincham J, Cook CL, Burch SP. Quality of care associated with common chronic diseases in a 9-state Medicaid population utilizing claims data: An evaluation of medication and health care use and costs. Popul Health Manag 2011;14(1):43–54.

[74] Earle CC, Park ER, Lai B, Weeks JC, Ayanian JZ, Block S. Identifying potential indicators of the quality of end-of-life cancer care from administrative data. J Clin Oncol 2003;21(6):1133–1138.

[75] Charbonneau A, Rosen AK, Ash AS, Owen RR, Kader B, Spiro A III, Berlowitz DR. Measuring the quality of depression care in a large integrated health system. Med Care 2003;41(5):669–680.

[76] Hollander P, Nicewander D, Couch C, Winter D, Herrin J, Haydar Z, Ballard DJ. Quality of care of Medicare patients with diabetes in a metropolitan fee-for-service primary care integrated delivery system. Am J Med Qual 2005;20(6):344–352.

[77] Kuo S, Fleming BB, Gittings NS, Han LF, Geiss LS, Engelgau MM, Roman SH. Trends in care practices and outcomes among Medicare beneficiaries with diabetes. Am J Prevent Med 2005;29(5):396–403.

[78] Tahrani AA, McCarthy M, Godson J, Taylor S, Slater H, Capps N, Macleod AF. Diabetes care and the new GMS contract: The evidence for a whole county. Br J Gen Pract 2007;57(539):483–485.

[79] Tomio J, Toyokawa S, Tanihara S, Inoue K, Kobayashi Y. Quality of care for diabetes patients using National Health Insurance claims data in Japan. J Eval Clin Pract 2010;16(6):1164–1169.

[80] Weiner JP, Parente ST, Garnick DW, Fowles J, Lawthers AG, Palmer RH. Variation in office-based quality: A claims-based profile of care provided to Medicare patients with diabetes. JAMA 1995;273(19):1503–1508.

[81] Jencks SF, Huff ED, Cuerdon T. Change in the quality of care delivered to Medicare beneficiaries, 1998–1999 to 2000–2001. JAMA 2003;289(3):305–312.

[82] Piecoro LT, Browning SR, Prince TS, Ranz TT, Scutchfield FD. A database analysis of potentially inappropriate drug use in an elderly Medicaid population. Pharmacotherapy 2000;20(2):221–228.

[83] Sinha S, Peach G, Poloniecki JD, Thompson MM, Holt PJ. Studies using English administrative data (Hospital Episode Statistics) to assess health-care outcomes – systematic review and recommendations for reporting. Eur J Public Health 2013;23(1):86–92.

[84] Farmer SA, Black B, Bonow RO. Tension between quality measurement, public quality reporting, and pay for performance. JAMA 2013;309(4):349–350.

[85] Ryoo JJ, Ordin DL, Antonio ALM, Oishi SM, Gould MK, Asch SM, Malin JL. Patient preference and contraindications in measuring quality of care: What do administrative data miss? J Clin Oncol 2013;31(21):2716–2723.

[86] Keating NL, Landrum MB, Landon BE, Ayanian JZ, Borbas C, Guadagnoli E. Measuring the quality of diabetes care using administrative data: Is there bias? Health Serv Res 2003;38(6p1):1529–1546.

[87] Glance LG, Osler TM, Mukamel DB, Dick AW. Impact of the present-on-admission indicator on hospital quality measurement: Experience with the Agency for Healthcare Research and Quality (AHRQ) Inpatient Quality Indicators. Med Care 2008;46(2):112–119.

[88] Weingart SN, Iezzoni LI, Davis RB, Palmer RH, Cahalane M, Hamel MB, Mukamal K, Phillips RS, Davies DT Jr, Banks NJ. Use of administrative data to find substandard care: validation of the complications screening program. Med Care 2000;38(8):796–806.

[89] Shwartz M, Burgess JF, Berlowitz D. Benefit-of-the-doubt approaches for calculating a composite measure of quality. Health Serv Outcomes Res Methodol 2009;9(4):234–251.

[90] Bertsimas D, Czerwinski D, Kane M. Measuring quality in diabetes care: An expert-based statistical approach. Springerplus 2013;2(1):1–10.

[91] Halanych JH, Safford MM, Keys WC, Person SD, Shikany JM, Kim YI, Centor RM, Allison JJ. Burden of comorbid medical conditions and quality of diabetes care. Diabetes Care 2007;30(12):2999–3004.

[92] Kerr EA, Krein SL, Vijan S, Hofer TP, Hayward RA. Avoiding pitfalls in chronic disease quality measurement: A case for the next generation of technical quality measures. Am J Manag Care 2001;7(11):1033–1043.

19

UNDERSTANDING THE ROLE OF SOCIAL MEDIA IN HEALTHCARE VIA ANALYTICS: A HEALTH PLAN PERSPECTIVE

SINJINI MITRA

Information Systems and Decision Sciences Department, California State University, Fullerton, CA, USA

REMA PADMAN

School of Information Systems and Management, School of Public Policy and Management, The H. John Heinz III College, Carnegie Mellon University, Pittsburgh, PA, USA

19.1 INTRODUCTION

The convergence of health reform regulation, consumer demand, market realities, and technology developments are driving healthcare organizations to explore new models of care and payment across the delivery spectrum [1, 2]. The *Affordable Health Care (AHC) Act* has emerged as a catalyst for changes in how insurance is obtained and how care is provided [3]. The focus has shifted toward consumers and there is an increasing demand for customer service as the concept of outcome-based health management grows [4]. Employers are increasingly turning to their health insurance providers to assist them to actively manage the health of their employees in an effort to sustain high levels of productivity [5, 6]. Layered onto this is the explosion of social media, creating an opportunity for insurers to not only market themselves using innovative tools but also engage their customers in highly accessible and customized

Healthcare Analytics: From Data to Knowledge to Healthcare Improvement, First Edition.
Edited by Hui Yang and Eva K. Lee.
© 2016 John Wiley & Sons, Inc. Published 2016 by John Wiley & Sons, Inc.

ways [7, 8]. Recent reports by the Pew Research Center indicate that 45% of the US adult population is living with one or more chronic conditions, are likely to be older, and also "seriously social" about seeking information from their healthcare providers, family members, and friends [9].

Health insurance plans are thus exploring new and creative methods to reach out to members to offer health information, provide support, encourage healthy behaviors, and leverage the emerging trend among consumers to play a more active and engaging role in self-health management. In general, more people turn to the Internet than any other source for health-related information and support. A reason for this trend can be attributed to the increasing healthcare costs and resulting changes in consumer behavior [10]. The explosion of Internet technologies has opened up new platforms to connect stakeholders such as patients, providers, and insurers. These relationships are vital to the long-term success of healthcare organizations.

Consumption of online media is widespread among the adult population who are active online users and is correlated with the growing penetration of broadband Internet access in the United States [11]. According to a survey that measured *patient activation*, less than half of the adults in the United States, at 41.4%, have the highest (fourth) level of activation [12]. At this level, people have the skills and confidence to manage their health; moreover, they are more likely to obtain preventive care, such as yearly health screenings, immunizations, and seek information about healthy eating habits and physical activity. At the third level, 37.2% individuals may lack confidence and skills to take action. Individuals in the first and the second levels are passive and more likely to be incapable of managing their own health effectively. The ability to move up and down rankings is possible with the accumulation of health information in conjunction with willingness to be active in personal health management. This is where the use of social media can provide value, namely, to offer health information and self-health management tools and services in a quick, credible, and convenient manner. The popularity of social media can be a transforming landscape for health management and healthcare delivery [13].

The rest of the chapter is organized as follows. Section 19.2 contains a comprehensive review of the existing literature on the use of social media for healthcare purposes along with the application of analytics tools in this field, Section 19.3 provides details about our particular case study based on a large health plan in Pennsylvania, and Section 19.4 introduces the analytical tools we employed. In Section 19.5, we include all our results along with discussions. We conclude in Section 19.6.

19.2 LITERATURE REVIEW

Whether it is Facebook, LinkedIn, or Twitter, social media is a big part of people's lives today. Social media uses the Internet and web technologies to facilitate social interactions by allowing for the exchange of user-generated content to share information, communicate, and collaborate [13]. The explosive growth of social networking sites – Facebook (1.2 billion active users as of March 2014), Twitter (200 million active users as of 2013), to name a few – has given users the ability to easily share information online by connecting individuals and groups [14–16]. These users are able to communicate their moods, opinions, thoughts, ideas, and actions through multimedia platforms such as networking sites, blogs, social forums, and wikis, allowing conversations to spread across these platforms reaching users with similar interests for particular topics, creating communities for knowledge sharing and interaction. User-generated content promotes a sense of belonging, creating a loyalty to the social media product itself [17].

Social media impacts us personally and professionally on a daily basis. Most of us could not have envisioned the effect that social media has had upon us within the healthcare sector. Recent studies have shown that consumers are increasingly turning to different forms of social media communities for healthcare-related information [18, 19]. A PwC consumer survey [6] showed that more people now turn to the Internet (48%) to make decisions about their healthcare than to doctors (43%). In a poll conducted in February 2012, 45% of consumers indicated that information found via social media affects their decision to seek a second opinion from another doctor, 42% use social media to cope with chronic conditions, diet, exercise or stress management, and 41% to help them choose a specific physician or a hospital. A similar survey by Accenture found that more than three-quarters of consumers used online sources to seek information about insurers [4]. Pew Research Center's Internet & American Life Project study, focusing on the impact of the Internet on health and health care, states that there is a shifting landscape where people are increasingly more reliant upon health information online compared to personalized physician visit [20, 21]. Today, about 75% of all American adults are connected to the Internet and 61% of them search online for health information [17]. A recent Frost and Sullivan survey of provider organizations indicated very high use of social media for both personal and professional purposes, particularly for marketing and brand awareness, and business development [22].

Leveraging existing social networks and peer groups within the workplace creates an environment of peer support and a culture of health-seeking behavior [23]. People get the opportunity to interact with peers with similar health goals leading to greater adoption of health-improving activities ranging from becoming more active and eating healthy foods to seeking preventive care and better management of chronic conditions. This is thus a very cost-effective way for consumers to maintain a healthy life, since such practices can potentially reduce their out-of-pocket medical expenses [24, 25]. On the other hand, this provides a great opportunity to healthcare companies of all types and sizes to improve their interactions with their customers. They can use these social media platforms to connect, engage, and educate customers in new ways by sharing news about new treatments or drugs for certain ailments via video streams, podcasts, webcasts or webinars, and online live chat groups, and in the process they gain insights into their needs and desires for reacting accordingly in a timely manner. Not only that, social media also provide healthcare companies a unique avenue for combating the negativity that often surrounds the industry and enhance their brands, thus equipping them with a new marketing strategy that is cost-efficient as well, since it has the capability of reaching millions of people at the same time with negligible amount of additional investment in terms of time and money [4].

For both government and commercial payers, when it comes to social media, it is critical to know and understand the audience, focusing not only on content but also on how it will be used. Companies with strong wellness programs, for example, have been able to extend the value of their existing programs by creating new, socially enhanced versions of their programs. Humana's *HumanaVille* [26] is one such endeavor, taking advantage of the increasing number of seniors who are actively engaging online. Humanaville is a dynamic social world filled with information, tools, games, and forums for seniors to get educated on health and wellness issues and concerns. Independence Blue Cross is building on its customers' desire for healthier lifestyles with its *Health Steps* campaign, which includes not only a Facebook page, Twitter handle, and blog but also the IBX Healthy Steps Pedometer app downloadable from iTunes and Android marketplaces [9]. Another health industry segment leader who is successfully engaging in social health is Aetna, offering *Life Game*, an online social game that engages people in setting and working toward personal wellness goals [27]. Kaiser Permanente, the country's largest nonprofit healthcare provider, also uses social media tools such as Facebook and Twitter to improve customer service and outreach. A recent report indicates that this has helped it grow its positive mentions close to 500% in the last 5 years [28].

Recent research has found that use of social media platforms by healthcare organizations continues to increase [29]. Analysis of a data set surveying 600 major healthcare organizations indicates that 470 healthcare organizations (of the 600 total surveyed) have at least one Twitter account with active updates; 280 also utilize YouTube as a means of communication; 82 use blogs actively; and, most significantly, 382 have an active Facebook profile for interaction with patients and other consumers.

Figure 19.1 depicts this breakdown. Of the 18 hospitals surveyed in Pennsylvania alone, 10 have YouTube profiles, 15 are on Facebook, and 12 use Twitter. Although

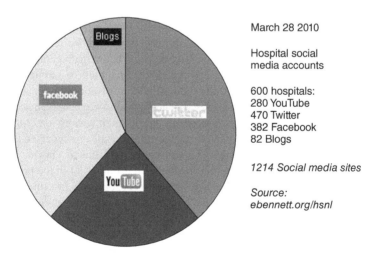

Figure 19.1   Social media use by healthcare organizations [29].

none are using blogs, one-third of these facilities are using all three major social media platforms (YouTube, Facebook, and Twitter). These studies motivated the health plan in this case study to investigate the potential of social media for reaching out to its member population with new services and tools for health and wellness management.

Additionally, with the advancement of mobile technology and the growing popularity of smartphones (iPhones, Android), many users are constantly connected to the Internet. People want to find health information fast, on-the-go, and in the cheapest possible way, with 69% of US adults tracking a health indicator such as weight and diet [21]. As of August to September 2012, 85% of Americans owned a cell phone or a smartphone and 55% of all adult phone users use it to access the Internet [7]. As of April 2012, there were 13,600 health, medical, and fitness applications within the Apple App Store, the official source for downloadable applications for iPhones, with the majority intended for use by patients [30]. Some popular examples of mobile applications include Text4baby [31], a free mobile information service that was designed to promote maternal and child health, and California's cellular texting to maximize the spread of knowledge about the 2009–2010 pandemic flu crisis [32].

19.2.1 Privacy and Security Concerns in Social Media and Healthcare

The main challenges for any organization, and more so for health plans, are in the area of *risk considerations* in the domains of security, privacy, and reliability. The implementation of a social media initiative for any health plan is not without risk. As an insurance company clearly in the business of risk assessment, health plans must carefully consider the different types of risks associated with each media platform before implementation. These risks primarily pertain to privacy, accuracy, financial, and legal issues.

The healthcare industry's concerns about the privacy, security, and confidentiality of patient information are not unique. The financial services industries, including banks and credit card companies, have been at the forefront of developing protections for personally identifiable financial information. Yet many consumers consider their health information to be more "private" than a bank account statement, which is routinely accessed by mortgage lenders, landlords, and other third parties. Patients with chronic health problems or more serious conditions, such as cancer or HIV/AIDS, may be vulnerable to involuntary disclosure that could affect their job status or relationships with peers. Therefore, it is reasonable to expect that a critical issue when accessing or using a social media site when communicating with and about patients is the degree of privacy and security available within that medium. As is common knowledge, patients are entitled to confidentiality and whichever form of social media outlet you use, it remains of the utmost importance.

Each medium has the opportunity to pose issues for the organization itself and the users of each of the platforms. The dynamic nature of social media makes their use particularly challenging to maintain reputable information and conversation. As such, social media users and the content they provide are often steered greatly by mood, current news, and personal biases. Many learn from others, although many are also interested in their own participation primarily. Excellent social media, with the purpose of enhancing the lives of those participating, that is, those pointed toward health promotion and wellness initiatives, will best involve users interested in learning and sharing, rather than simply broadcasting their lives and opinions.

As the degree of free response within a medium increases, the risk of privacy violations also increases. Forums, blogs, and WIKI-style media run the risk of potentially malicious users gaining a great deal of information about other users. Some individuals may be willing to share information ranging from demographics to medical history, but others may find reassurance in simply revealing under an alias username with little or no medical information [33]. These two bias extremes make it challenging to design an effective social media-enabled technology solution where all users will feel satisfied with the required level of input, with the varying levels of risk aversion related to privacy concerns potentially leading to incomplete or inaccurate information.

Social media, such as Facebook, inspire daily disputes about privacy controls and availability of particular types of information to third-party users, friends within social networks, and the site's administrators. Users do not seem reluctant to provide and post this type of information in the first place, but are particularly protective of their privacy rights once they have done so. Most major social networking sites are committed to ensuring that use of their services is as safe as possible. Users of personal health records (PHR) sites such as *Microsoft HealthVault* [34] place confidence in user agreements that guarantee the privacy of their information, although these sites are only loosely constrained by privacy legislation such as the Health Insurance Portability and Accountability Act (*HIPAA* for short) passed by the US Congress in 1996 to address the need for a national patient record privacy standard [35].

The risk of potentially inaccurate information is also significant. The social media strategies of the health plan, in order to be effective, would need to dedicate resources to protect the reliability and accountability of users and moderators of each medium. Users would expect accurate and reliable information to be provided from accountable and intelligent sources. Accuracy of facts, respectfulness of opinions, and sustainability of service should be the founding principles upon which the social media solutions that the health plan chooses to deploy will become reputable. Some sites proactively preview and approve content before it is publicly posted so that the information is accurate and reliable.

Additionally, the health plans may also be concerned about slanderous comments made about the company or particular individuals associated with it (e.g., specific physicians) and the resultant liability issues raised. Lastly, variations in population demographics, degree of technical knowledge of particular segments, and related factors clearly indicate that the notion of "one-size-fits-all" is certainly not appropriate in the social media arena, hence software services and tools need to be designed to be accessible to a disparate demographic population with respect to varying age, gender, education, technical knowledge, and Internet access. Thus, this study can potentially assist health plans to conduct a comprehensive assessment of benefits and risks by providing insights into stated member needs and usage preferences.

19.2.2   Analytics in Healthcare and Social Media

The use of analytics in the healthcare industry as well as in social media is becoming increasingly popular with the advancement of technology and computing resources, and availability of a large amount of data. With increasing demands from consumers for enhanced healthcare quality and increased value, healthcare providers and payers are under pressure to deliver better outcomes. Primary care physician and nursing shortages require overworked professionals to be even more productive and efficient. The cost dynamics of healthcare are changing, driven by people living longer, the pervasiveness of chronic illnesses and infectious diseases, and defensive medicine practices [36]. New market entrants and new approaches to healthcare delivery are increasing complexity and competition. Analytics can provide the mechanism to sort through this torrent of complexity and data and help healthcare organizations deliver on these demands. But it takes big plans, discrete actions, and some very specific management approaches to gain the benefits of analytics.

The types of analytics used can be categorized into the following: (i) *descriptive analytics*, which provides insights based on exploratory methods including visualization tools and summary statistics; (ii) *predictive analytics*, which uses statistical modeling and data mining techniques, and (iii) *prescriptive analytics*, which uses decision models based on simulation and optimization methods to make recommendations. Descriptive analytics are primarily used in analyzing survey data where simple frequency distributions and graphical techniques are employed to represent the underlying patterns in the data. Analysis of variance (ANOVA) or simple statistical hypothesis tests are also sometimes performed to determine whether different segments of the surveyed population are significantly different with respect to certain characteristics of interest included in the study. Unsupervised learning methods, such as clustering, and also association rules (also called "Market basket analysis") are employed to determine significant clusters in the population as well as study associations among variables. Predictive analytics includes rigorous statistical models such as linear regression, logistic regression, generalized linear models, and hierarchical regression; however, data mining or machine learning algorithms are used for performing classification such as decision trees, k-nearest neighbors, naïve Bayes, neural networks, and linear discriminant analysis (LDA). Dimensionality reduction is another major component of any data analytic task since most real data sets contain several variables (often hundreds of them in some applications), most of which are irrelevant or uncorrelated with the outcome variable of interest. Principal component analysis (PCA) is a well-known tool for this purpose; another commonly used method is subset selection in the case of regression models. Sarasohn-Kahn [37] includes details about the various statistical and data mining techniques that are popularly used to analyze data arising in different industries.

Analytics is widely being used in different areas of the healthcare industry today, from tracking and monitoring revenues and operational performance to monitoring quality initiatives and care programs to predicting outcomes relating to disease outbreaks and making decisions regarding treatment plans. Several healthcare companies have social media sites that help connect patients with providers and care givers and also offer communities for people suffering from chronic diseases via which they can communicate and share experiences and also provide support. Social media produces unstructured and complex data in massive volumes at a very rapid pace. Due to the overwhelming diversity of platforms and participants, it is challenging to discover relevant content, standardize extraction, and generate meaningful analytics that help in making decisions. An optimum blend of automated listening and human analysis is indispensable when it comes to contextualizing and interpreting patient-generated content. Text-based analytics are used often to perform "sentiment analysis" to discover patients' opinions and reactions to certain drugs or initiatives and programs conducted by a healthcare company (such as fitness programs, weight loss programs, to name a few). Moreover, time series and forecasting methods can be applied to detect trends in consumer opinions about certain products, how they vary over time, and predict outcomes at future time points. Clustering is also used in applications where the goal is to determine targeted population segments. For instance, a healthcare provider might be interested in knowing which people particularly express negative opinions about a certain product or how people in different geographic locations react to a certain new drug. This is useful not only for marketing purposes but also for identifying areas of improvements to better serve the consumer population.

The challenges associated with the huge amounts of data amassed by the healthcare organizations lie not only in processing and analysis but also in reporting the results in a consolidated way that can provide meaningful insights easily for efficient decision making. A number of industry solutions have emerged in this field in the recent years from companies such as SAS and IBM that help in communicating the outcomes through metrics-based scorecards and dashboards that are widely being adopted in the healthcare industry. Visualization analytics software such as Tableau, Spotfire, and QlikView are also being deployed widely to represent a wide variety of data using user-friendly and interactive interfaces. Moreover, several platforms are available now to handle the massive volumes of complex data (such as HADOOP).

19.3   CASE STUDY DESCRIPTION

This case study is associated with a large health plan in western Pennsylvania. The health plan offers five basic medical plan designs, which are distinguished mainly by varying levels of provider-coordinated versus self-directed care and the use of network versus out-of-network providers. Apart from consumer-specific plans, the health plan also offers a full range of commercial and government health management products and services, including commercial group health insurance, Medicare Assistance, Special Needs (SNP), Children's Health Insurance (CHIP), and customized benefit options for smaller employer groups. It also offers disease and behavioral health management programs, including programs to help employers promote health, prevention, and wellness in the workplace.

Recognizing that social media-based platforms for consumer engagement is building momentum, the health plan initiated a project to identify and develop strategies and solutions for the integration of these platforms to increase awareness of health-risk factors, promote healthy lifestyle behaviors, and deliver health coaching. In this chapter, we present results of a survey conducted among members of the health plan to assess the extent to which they are interested in adopting social media-enabled practices, tools, and services for their health and wellness needs. Recent studies have reported descriptive statistics using bar charts, proportions, and pie charts [29]. Our methods, on the contrary, include rigorous statistical analyses, from inference to predictive modeling, that enable us to draw statistically valid conclusions.

19.3.1 Survey Design

Collaborating with an academic institution, the health plan developed and executed a health and wellness survey among members to understand their propensity for social media usage and the potential to connect technology with members' health and wellness needs. The survey tool was created in a multistep process that included an extensive literature review; interviews with experts in nutrition, health coaching, and wellness promotion; and health plan administrators and executives; and several iterations for review and redesign based on a pilot survey in the academic institution [38]. Thus, the main goal of the overall study was to examine behaviors and stated preferences of a sample of health plan members to understand and identify technology and social media-enabled healthcare services to offer for effective self-health management. The platforms that were chosen for this study included social networking sites such as Facebook, MySpace, and LinkedIn; media sharing sites such as YouTube, online forums, blogs, and wikis; and microblogging sites such as Twitter.

The analysis in this case study examines the opportunities for social media for health and wellness promotion in the context of the particular demographics, needs, and current usage habits of health plan members. The main hypothesis of interest was to test whether there is general interest among members of the health plan to adopt different social media solutions for obtaining distinct types of health-related information and services, and to understand the factors that drive this interest. In order to test this hypothesis, we analyzed member responses with respect to adoption of social media for health-related information based on key demographic, clinical, and technology factors, the primary ones being (i) gender, (ii) age, (iii) general health condition, (iv) presence of a chronic condition, (v) level and frequency of computer use, (vi) level of social media usage, and (vi) types of online activities engaged in.

The survey was categorized into five main sections: (i) baseline technology usage, (ii) social media usage, (iii) health and wellness objectives, (iv) current behavior and interest associated with health-related information via the Internet, and (v) health status and demographic information. There were 28 questions on the survey, which was expected to take approximately 15 min to complete. It was completely voluntary and anonymous in order to protect the privacy of respondents.

The survey was administered using *Survey Monkey* to a subset of the health plan members who were current employees of the larger health system that included a provider organization. As an incentive to successfully complete the survey, participants were automatically entered into a raffle to win one of 10 $100 gift cards.

The survey was initially distributed through a company-wide email newsletter before being posted as a fixed link to the health system's intranet. The survey was available for approximately 2 weeks during which 4212 members participated and 4058 completed the survey (determined by the total number of responses to the last mandatory question), resulting in a yield of 96.3%.

19.4 RESEARCH METHODS AND ANALYTICS TOOLS

Descriptive analytics provides basic initial insights into the distribution of participants across the different categories and the relationship of key variables with social and mobile media usage for health-related information. We thus begin by presenting a descriptive summary of the different background variables in the study via tabular and visualization techniques. Next, we perform clustering of the member population based on the demographic, clinical, and technology factors via *chi-square* tests [39] since our variables are nominal or categorical in nature. *p*-Values obtained from these tests enable us to determine statistically significant associations that are not attributed to chance alone, and thus define the clusters.

We then develop a predictive model to assess the chances of members adopting different types of social media for health-related purposes based on *logistic regression* [40]. Logistic regression extends the idea of linear regression to the case when the outcome or the dependent variable (typically denoted by *Y*) is categorical in nature [25]. It can thus be used for predicting the class or category of a new observation (where the class is unknown) based on the values of the independent or predictor variables (typically denoted by $X_1, X_2, \ldots$). We use binary logistic regression as our model instance in which the observed outcome can have only two possible types.

19.4.1 The Logistic Regression Model

Let Y be a binary random variable that takes the values 0 and 1. By convention, the value of 1 is used to indicate "success" and the value of 0 is used to signify "failure." Let $X_1, X_2, \ldots, X_k$ be k predictors or independent variables that have an effect on *Y*, so that we can define $p = P(Y = 1 | X_1, X_2, \ldots, X_k)$. Hence, *p* can take any value in the interval [0,1]. Instead of using *Y* as the outcome or the dependent variable as in linear regression, logistic regression uses a function of *Y*, called *logit*, as the dependent variable. Logit is defined as the logarithm of odds, log(odds), where

$$\text{odds} = \frac{p}{1 - p}$$

with $p = P(Y = 1)$ as defined earlier. It is thus a type of *generalized linear model* with logit as the link function. So the logistic regression model with *k* predictors or independent variables $X_1, X_2, \ldots, X_k$ can be written as

$$\log(\text{odds}) = \beta_0 + \beta_1 x_1 + \beta_2 x_2 + \cdots + \beta_k x_k$$

where β_0, β_1, … are the regression coefficients or parameters associated with the predictor variables that describe the relationship between the predictors and the odds of the outcome variable belonging to class 1. For example, β_j can be interpreted as follows: a unit increase in the value of the predictor x_j is associated with an average increase of $\beta_j \times 100\%$ in the odds of Y belonging to class 1, holding all the other predictors constant.

The $k + 1$ regression coefficients (β's) are usually unknown and estimated from a given data set using the method of *maximum-likelihood estimation*. Unlike linear regression with normally distributed residuals, it is not possible to find a closed-form expression for the coefficient values that maximizes the likelihood function, so an iterative process must be used instead, for example, *Newton's method*. This process begins with a tentative solution, revises it slightly to see if it can be improved, and repeats this revision until improvement is negligible, at which point the process is said to have converged. In the following, the details of the estimation process are outlined.

19.4.1.1 Maximum-Likelihood Estimation
The maximum-likelihood estimation procedure entails finding the set of parameters for which the probability of the observed data is greatest. The maximum-likelihood equation is derived from the probability distribution of the dependent variable that has a binomial distribution with $n = 1$ (also called the *Bernoulli* distribution). The probability distribution of the random variable Y is thus given by

$$f(y) = p(1 - p)$$

where p is as defined earlier. Now since we estimate the parameters using the training set, let us assume that there are n records in the training set that are denoted by Y_1, Y_2, …, Y_n. Each Y_i then has a Bernoulli distribution with parameter p_i, and all the Y_i's are independent of each other. Each p_i in turn depends on the k independent variables X_1, X_2, …, X_k and on the unknown parameters β_0, β_1, …. Thus, in essence, p is a function of the unknown parameters β's as the X_i's are known. Let X_{i1}, X_{i2}, …, X_{ik} denote the predictor values corresponding to Y_i. So the likelihood function for the entire training sample is given by

$$L(y) = \prod_{i=1}^{n} f(y_i) = \prod_{i=1}^{n} p_i^{y_i}(1 - p_i)^{1-y_i}.$$

Here, $L(.)$ denotes the likelihood function when written in terms of the p_i's, which are functions of β_0, β_1, …. Taking logarithm on both sides, we can write down the log-likelihood function (denoted by $l(y)$) of the training sample as

$$l(y) = \sum_{i=1}^{n} \left[y_i \log(p_i) + (1 - y_i) \log(1 - p_i) \right]$$

$$= \sum_{i=1}^{n} \log\left(1 - p_i\right) + \sum_{i=1}^{n} y_i \log \frac{p_i}{1 - p_i}$$

Now recall that each p_i is a function of the independent variables and the regression coefficients via the relationship (we write out the formulas and expressions using general "p" for the sake of convenience; for each p_i, we have to replace x_1 by x_{1i}, x_2 by x_{2i}, etc.):

$$\log \frac{p}{1-p} = \beta_0 + \beta_1 x_1 + \beta_2 x_2 + \dots + \beta_k x_k, \text{ so that}$$

$$\frac{p}{1-p} = e^{\beta_0 + \beta_1 x_1 + \beta_2 x_2 + \dots + \beta_k x_k}$$

After some algebraic calculations, we get the expression for p as

$$p = \frac{e^{\beta_0 + \beta_1 x_1 + \beta_2 x_2 + \dots + \beta_k x_k}}{1 + e^{\beta_0 + \beta_1 x_1 + \beta_2 x_2 + \dots + \beta_k x_k}} = \frac{1}{1 + e^{-(\beta_0 + \beta_1 x_1 + \beta_2 x_2 + \dots + \beta_k x_k)}}, \text{ and so on}$$

$$1 - p = \frac{1}{1 + e^{\beta_0 + \beta_1 x_1 + \beta_2 x_2 + \dots + \beta_k x_k}}$$

Substituting the value of p in the expression for the log-likelihood above, we get

$$l(y) = \sum_{i=1}^{n} - \log \left[1 + e^{\beta_0 + \beta_1 x_{1i} + \beta_2 x_{2i} + \dots + \beta_k x_{ki}} \right]$$

$$+ \sum_{i=1}^{n} y_i \left[\beta_0 + \beta_1 x_{1i} + \beta_2 x_{2i} + \dots + \beta_k x_{ki} \right]$$

Note that the log-likelihood is a function of y_i's, x_i's, and the β's. Of these, the β's are the only unknown quantities. The maximum-likelihood method works by finding those estimates for the β's that will maximize the log-likelihood function. This is done by differentiating the latter with respect to each β coefficient and solving by setting the derivatives to zero. To demonstrate the process, let us take the derivative with one component of β, say β_j, the expression being shown as follows:

$$\frac{\partial l}{\partial \beta_j} = - \sum_{i=1}^{n} \frac{1}{1 + e^{\beta_0 + \beta_1 x_{1i} + \beta_2 x_{2i} + \dots + \beta_k x_{ki}}} e^{\beta_0 + \beta_1 x_{1i} + \beta_2 x_{2i} + \dots + \beta_k} x_{ji} + \sum_{i=1}^{n} y_i x_{ji}$$

$$= \sum_{i=1}^{n} (y_i - p_i) x_{ji}$$

by substituting the expression for p_i. As is clear, it is not possible to obtain a closed-form expression for β_j by solving this equation; hence, numerical optimization techniques need to be applied in order to get an approximate solution.

19.4.1.2 Newton's Method for Numerical Optimization   There are a large number of numerical optimization methods available to solve the above-mentioned derivative equation. However, we illustrate the use of one of the oldest, yet popular, numerical methods called the *Newton–Raphson method* (or Newton's method, for short). In this section, we briefly describe the application of this method to the simplest case of minimizing a function of one scalar variable, say $f(w)$.

We wish to find the location of the global minimum w^* and begin with the assumption that f is a smooth function. This will ensure that the derivative of f at w^* will be zero; hence, applying a Taylor expansion near the minimum, we get

$$f(w) = f(w^*) + \frac{1}{2}(w - w^*)\frac{d^2 f}{dw^2}\big|_{w=w^*},$$

since $\frac{df}{dw} = 0$ at $w = w^*$. Newton's method works by starting with an initial value of w, say w_0 so that the Taylor expansion at w_0 will be as follows:

$$f(w) \approx f(w_0) + (w - w_0)\frac{df}{dw}\big|_{w=w_0} + \frac{1}{2}(w - w_0)\frac{d^2 f}{dw^2}\big|_{w=w_0}$$

Now if w_0 is close to w^*, the above expression will be fairly accurate. Let us denote the first and second derivatives at $w = w_0$ by $f'(w_0)$ and $f''(w_0)$ for the sake of convenience. Then taking the derivative of the right-hand side of the last equation and setting it equal to zero at a point w_1, we have

$$0 = f'(w_0) + \frac{1}{2}f''(w_0)\, 2(w_1 - w_0)$$

$$\Rightarrow w_1 = w_0 - \frac{f'(w_0)}{f''(w_0)}$$

The value w_1 should provide a better approximation to the minimum value w^* than the initial guess w_0. Iterating this procedure several times, we arrive at the $(n + 1)$th step:

$$w_{n+1} = w_n - \frac{f'(w_n)}{f''(w_n)}$$

The procedure stops when w_{n+1} and w_n are very close. It can actually be proved that if w_0 is close enough to w^*, then w_n is converged to w^*, in fact $|w_n - w^*| = O(n^{-2})$, a very rapid rate of convergence. w_n is then the estimate of w^*, the value that minimizes the function $f(w)$.

In case of a high-dimensional coefficient vector $w = (w_1, w_2, \ldots, w_k)$, we replace $f'(w_0)$ by ∇f, which is the *gradient* of $\mathbf{f}$, its vector of partial derivatives $[\partial f/\partial w_1, \partial f/\partial w_2, \ldots, \partial f/\partial w_k]$, and $f''(w_0)$ by H, which is the *Hessian* of f, its matrix of second derivatives $H_{ij} = \partial^2 f/\partial w_i \partial w_j$.

19.4.1.3 Model Implementation

Software packages are available to compute the estimates of the coefficients of the logistic regression model. After estimation, the classification is performed using two steps: the first step yields an estimate of the probability of belonging to each class for each observation in the test set. In the binary case, we get an estimate of $P(Y = 1)$, the probability of belonging to class 1 (which implies

$P(Y=0) = 1 - P(Y=1))$. In the next step, we use a cut-off value on these probabilities in order to classify each new observation or case into one of these two classes. The typical cut-off value used is 0.5, which means that if $P(Y=1) > 0.5$ for a new case, it is classified as belonging to class 1, whereas a case for which $P(Y=1) < 0.5$, it is classified as belonging to class 0. However, this cut-off value is not fixed and can be changed based on a particular problem scenario although 0.5 is known to provide the optimal accuracies.

In our analysis, we use this model to determine the factors that can significantly affect people's interest in adopting various social media platforms for health information offered by the health plan, as well as predict the chances or odds of adopting the proposed platforms based on these factors.

19.5   RESULTS AND DISCUSSIONS

This section includes all our results from the data-driven analytics.

19.5.1   Descriptive Statistics

Tables 19.1 and 19.2 and Figures 19.2 and 19.3 depict breakdown of survey participants by key demographic and clinical variables via descriptive analytics. We see a substantially higher percentage of women responding to the survey (Table 19.1), which is consistent with prior research that women generally use the Internet more for getting health-related information [10]. A majority of respondents are aged between 31 and 65 (63%), with about 1% being under the age of 18 or over the age of 65 (Table 19.2).

TABLE 19.1   Breakdown of Participants by Gender ($n = 3994$, missing $= 218$)

Gender	Frequency (%)
Male	555 (13%)
Female	3439 (82%)

TABLE 19.2   Breakdown of Participants by Age Group ($n = 3432$, missing $= 780$)

Age Group	Frequency (%)
<18	1 ($\approx$0%)
19–30	744 (18%)
31–50	1635 (39%)
51–65	1025 (24%)
>65	27 (1%)

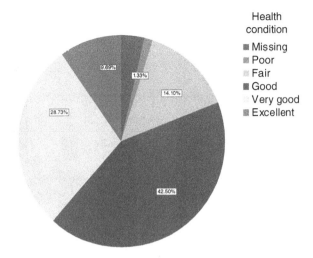

Figure 19.2 Perceived health conditions of health plan members.

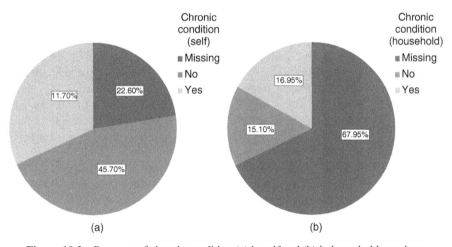

Figure 19.3 Presence of chronic condition (a) in self and (b) in household members.

As far as the perceived health condition of participants is concerned, Figure 19.2 shows that majority consider themselves to be in good or very good shape compared to others (72%), whereas only 1% believe that their condition is poor. Only one-third of the members mentioned that they are suffering from a chronic condition (Fig. 19.4). Given the high prevalence of multiple chronic conditions in the general population, particularly in the 51–65 age group [25], wide perception of health condition being excellent and lack of knowledge/willingness to share this information (missing values in Figs 19.2 and 19.3) may have a detrimental impact on self-health management initiatives.

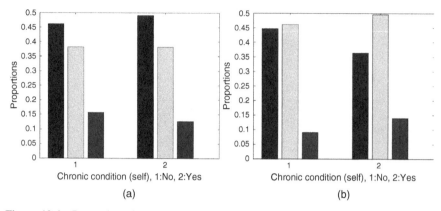

Figure 19.4   Proportion of members by the presence of a chronic condition (Yes/No) versus level of interest in listening to health-related podcasts. Interest-level categories: Not interested, might be interested, and very interested. (a) Cell phones (mobile apps) and (b) computer.

19.5.2   Baseline of Technology Usage

The technology section comprised of the first set of questions on the survey. These questions were intended to gauge technology integration in respondents' lives as well as measure the level of their knowledge about and frequency of use of current technology to assess the likelihood of adoption of these online and social media-based platforms for different segments of the population.

Table 19.3 shows the frequency distribution for the use of cell phones and computers (both desktop and laptop) at home as well as at work. According to this, cell phone usage is most popular with less than 1% of respondents, mentioning that they own neither a cell phone nor a computer.

However, cell phones also have other functions that should not be overlooked. The possibility of connecting to the Internet, downloading applications, and performing daily tasks has great potential when it comes to implementing new features for the health plan. Although we observed that majority of the users owned smartphones (33.9%: Blackberry, 25.5%: iPhone, 14.9%: Android) that possessed advanced capabilities, most of them do not access the Internet on their mobile phones measured at

TABLE 19.3   Breakdown of Participants by the Type of Technology They Own or Have Access

Devices Owned/Used	Frequency
Cell phone	4019 (95.4%)
Computer w/ Internet access at workplace	3491 (82.9%)
Computer w/ Internet access in the evenings	3786 (89.9%)
None of the above	28 (0.7%)

Note here that members were allowed to check as many options here as applicable

68%. Similarly, 77% stated that they do not download mobile applications on their cell phones. On the other hand, more people were inclined to use text messaging on their cell phones – more than 55% of people send or receive at least one text message daily whereas about 24% reported never or rarely using this service. Similarly, people tend to use their cell phones significantly more for emailing and chatting than for recreational activities such as watching videos, reading news, shopping, as well as for online banking.

In order for the health plan to cater to its members' needs through Internet-based technology, it is imperative to recognize the level of the respondents' computer usage and their ability to access features of the health plan through the Web. The data revealed that 45% reported spending their entire workdays in front of a computer with Internet access while another 15% reported spending more than half of their workday in front of a computer with Internet access. Furthermore, we found a significant portion (60%) of the health plan members have access to the Internet during most of the working day. This demonstrates the degree of penetration of the Internet within the daily routine of health plan members and suggests a strong potential to reach the members via that medium. In addition, about 80% of individuals access the Internet on a computer during their free time in the evenings with 50% spending less than an hour and 30% spending between 1 and 3 h. It can thus be concluded that a significant portion of the population spends at least some time on the computer during off-work hours.

The level of usage of different activities on computers such as sending and receiving emails, reading news online, followed by banking revealed similar trends as in case of cell phones. It is also interesting to observe that a significant portion of individuals (52.7%) do not use their computers to chat online. It is not only important to recognize the popular activities but also the unpopular activities as well to enable the health plan to offer appropriate online products.

19.5.3 Mobile and Social Media Usage

By understanding what forms of social media are accessed through the computers and cell phones by its members, the health plan can gain an insight into what members are currently engaged with online and use this channel to introduce health and wellness programs. The use of social media activities on cell phones, such as posting comments to an online blog and visiting sites such as Facebook, Twitter, LinkedIn, and so on appears to be quite limited among the health plan members. Nearly 90% of members never or rarely accessed Twitter, LinkedIn, and MySpace on their phones. Around 20–25% of the respondents had posted comments on online blogs and forums and visited Wikipedia on their cell phones at least couple of times a week and nearly 40% mentioned using Facebook at least once a day.

Social media usage on computers also appears to be quite low among the member population. The results show that most of the members have never used social networking sites such as Twitter, measured at 91.2%, MySpace at 86.4%, and LinkedIn at 87.0%. Facebook was the only platform that was claimed to have been utilized fairly frequently at 42.0%. Additionally, individuals show low levels of engagement regarding posting comments on online news groups, websites, blogs, and photo sites.

19.5.4   Clustering of Member Population by Technology, Social, and Mobile Media Usage

We now cluster the health plan member population based on technological, mobile, and social media usage by the demographic and clinical factors included in the study. For instance, we can determine if members' usage frequency of Facebook is significantly different across age groups. Some of the highlights of our findings are summarized in the following for cell phones:

- Use of text messaging differs significantly across age groups (p-value: <0.0001). Younger people (age group 18–30) tend to use text messaging more than older people.
- Use of Internet on the cell phone is significantly different across gender, age groups, and people with a chronic condition (p-values: <0.0001). Younger people tend to use the Internet and download mobile apps on their cell phones significantly more often, as do people without a chronic condition. Moreover, a higher percentage of male health plan members use Internet on their cell phones more than female members as well as download mobile apps.
- Gender seems to be the main segmenting factor with respect to the frequency of online activities performed on cell phones (p-values: <0.05) – men are found to engage in each of these activities significantly more frequently than women. The effect of age is also widespread, except for chatting (p-value: 0.0691), and in all of these cases, younger people are found to engage more than older people. Health status of members and the presence of chronic conditions do not have a significant effect on usage of online activities on cell phones.
- As far as social media usage on cell phones is concerned, there is very little variation across the various segments of the health plan member population with respect to demographic factors. The only predominant factor seems to be age, and we find significant differences in the usage between younger and older people for all the social media platforms except LinkedIn and Wikipedia (p-values: 0.0540 and 0.2786, respectively). Men seem to use Wikipedia and LinkedIn significantly more than women (p-values: <0.0001 and 0.0239, respectively); however, there is no significant usage difference between the two genders as far as using Facebook, Twitter, My Space, and blogs are concerned. No significant effect of health conditions was observed.

Some highlights of the effects of the different factors on computer activities are included as follows:

- The use of computer during the day seems to vary significantly across age groups but remain consistent across gender. Older people tend to spend significantly more time on a computer during the workday than younger people.

On the other hand, the length of time spent on the computer during the evenings varies significantly across gender and age. Men tend to spend significantly more time on the computer during the evenings than women, and older people spend more time than younger ones, but presence of a chronic condition (either self or in a household member) does not seem to have any statistically significant effects.

- There is a significant relationship between how often people engage in different online activities and demographic factors. Specifically, we see that age has very strong relationship with all the six activities and gender with emails and online banking. Men were observed to participate in such activities more than women, and younger people tend to participate more often than older people. Health condition or the presence of a chronic condition does not seem to be an important factor.

- Participants report different levels of usage of social media across demographic and clinical factors. Age and gender have the maximum effect, followed by perceived health status while presence of chronic condition has no significant relationship with social media usage habits. LinkedIn usage is the least variable across demographic factors (only effect is for gender: males using significantly more frequently than females), whereas Twitter shows the strongest statistical evidence of variation across demographic factors. Older people are seen to use twitter.com much less than younger people, and a similar behavior is observed for the other platforms also. For perceived health status, a higher proportion of people with poor to good health are found to be using MySpace.

19.5.5 Interest in Adopting Online Tools for Healthcare Purposes

Various Web and social media platforms that the health plan can offer to its members were explored through their potential to be incorporated into the members' health management programs. Seven different activities were investigated to assess the level of interest among the survey participants as follows:

- Activity 1: Connecting with others with similar health goals via an online forum
- Activity 2: Reading health-related blogs
- Activity 3: Adding comments to a health-related blog
- Activity 4: Watching health-related instructional videos
- Activity 5: Watching health-related webcasts and webinars
- Activity 6: Listening to health-related podcasts
- Activity 7: Interactive group chats with health experts

Three categories representing the level of member interest in these activities were as follows: "Not interested at all," "Might be interested," and Very interested." Looking at descriptive statistics, we find that the health plan members' interest in commenting on and consulting health-related blogs is the highest (17.7%). Watching health-related webcasts/webinars ranked low at 11%. The general trend shows that members are interested in collaborating with one another, whether it is interacting through blogs or receiving advice from experts. A summary of the clusters based on interest in the various health-related platforms with respect to demographic, clinical, and technology factors is listed as follows [41]:

- *Demographic and Clinical Factors.* Male clients of the health plan have a significantly higher interest in watching health-related instructional videos than women, but no gender differences were observed in case of the other seven activities. A greater proportion of members who are older than 65 years are very interested in watching videos and webcasts and listening to podcasts that deliver health-related information than the younger population.

  There is overwhelming evidence of significant differences in the level of interest among members with varying health conditions for Activities 1 and 7. Slightly less, yet significant, evidence of difference is also noted for Activities 3 and 4. In all of these cases, the pattern observed is consistent – a higher proportion of people with poor to good health condition have higher interest in these activities than people whose health is in very good or excellent condition. People suffering from chronic illness have significantly higher level on interest in all the online activities except for Activities 2 and 7. Similarly, people who have a household member with a chronic condition have more interest in all activities, except Activity 6.

- *Computer Usage.* People who use computers more during their leisure time in the evenings have significantly higher propensity to adopt online platforms for health-related purposes. On the other hand, computer usage during the work-day has a significant relationship with the level of interest in three out of the seven activities, namely, connecting with others with similar health goals via an online forum, reading health-related blogs, and watching health-related web-casts. Thus, there is stronger statistical evidence of clusters based on the length of time members spend in front of a computer during the evenings, while the case for daytime is much weaker.

- *Online Activities and Social Media Usage.* Analysis also indicates strong statistical evidence that the level of interest in online health-related activities (that the health plan may consider) differs significantly across people who engage in different (nonhealth-related) activities online with different fre-quencies. Those members who engage in online chatting and watching videos online more expressed a significantly higher level of interest in using these online platforms for receiving health-related information (*p*-values: <0.0001). Similarly, people using social media more expressed significantly higher interest in various online activities for health-related information, the least interest being among Facebook and MySpace users.

19.5.6 Interest in Adopting Mobile Apps for Healthcare Purposes

The health plan members were asked to express their level of interest in downloading seven different types of health-related mobile apps on their cell phones that the health plan was considering to offer to them, which are as follows (abbreviated names in brackets for ease of future reference):

- [Card app] App to display information included on their health insurance cards
- [Search app] App to search for doctors, hospitals, and pharmacies
- [PHR app] A mobile version of their PHR
- [Game app] App for health-related games
- [Claim app] App to display the status of their insurance claims
- [Video app] App with streaming health-related videos
- [Pod app] App with health-related podcasts

Table 19.4 provides the frequency distribution of the member responses that indicate maximum interest in obtaining a mobile version of PHR and least interest in obtaining mobile apps for health-related games, videos, and podcasts. Thus overall members seem to be more willing to obtain information about their own health via mobile apps than general health information.

Next, we present a summary of our conclusions regarding how the different demographic, clinical, and technological factors influence the level of interest in adopting these various mobile media for health-related purposes, thus leading to distinct clusters of the member population.

- *Demographic and Clinical Factors.* The level of interest among health plan members in downloading health-related apps on their cell phones does not vary significantly across people with varying health conditions and across different age groups. The only significant factor is gender. Men were found to have a significantly higher interest in using all these seven apps from the health plan than women.
- *Online Activity Usage on Cell Phones.* The effects observed here are far more widespread than in the case of the demographic factors. Of the six online activities, chatting has the least significant association with the level of interest in obtaining health-related information on cell phones, whereas the strongest associations are observed for watching videos, reading news, online

TABLE 19.4   Frequency Distribution of Members' Interest in the Different Health-Related Apps on Their Cell Phones

	Not Interested (%)	Might Be Interested (%)	Very Interested (%)
Card app	4.01	8.76	9.07
Search app	3.49	8.88	9.43
PHR app	4.23	7.24	10.26
Game app	10.80	7.19	3.63
Claim app	6.46	8.76	6.48
Video app	11.28	7.55	2.85
Pod app	10.30	8.17	3.09

banking, and shopping (*p*-values: <0.0001). In all of these cases, people who participated in online activities more frequently (say, at least a couple of times a month) were found to have an increased interest in adopting the mobile apps. Finally, people who used their cell phones to send or receive emails frequently had a greater interest in adopting health-related mobile apps.

- Social Media Usage on Cell Phones. As expected, our analysis revealed that people who engage in social media activities on their cell phones are more likely to express an interest in adopting social and mobile media for health-related information. The most widespread effect is found in case of commenting on blogs and using Wikipedia. People who participate in both of these cell phone activities at least a couple of times per month have a greater interest in adopting all the seven health-related mobile apps if offered by the health plan. On the other hand, we find that the frequency of MySpace usage on cell phones does not generally have a significant association with the level of interest in receiving health-related information via mobile apps. Finally, the frequency of using Facebook, Twitter, and LinkedIn had a significant association with the level of interest in using four out of the six mobile apps. The most popular mobile apps that people had interest in using were those for receiving PHRs and status of their insurance claims.

- Seeking Health-related Information Online. Our analyses revealed that people who visit the health plan's website quite frequently are significantly more likely to adopt a mobile version of their own PHR (*p*-value: 0.0212), but there is no significant effect on the other six mobile apps.

19.5.6.1 *Comparison of Clusters Based on Interest in Adopting Social Media on Computers and on Cell Phones*

Some major differences in the clusters obtained with respect to interest in adopting online and social media platforms for health-related purposes between computers and cell phones are enumerated as follows:

- Although more people own cell phones than computers, people use the Internet significantly more on their computers than on their cell phones.
- We observed significantly lower interest in downloading health-related mobile apps on cell phones than receiving online health information on their computers.
- We detected that members in poorer health and suffering from a chronic condition had a significantly elevated level of interest in receiving health information from various online and social media sources but not via mobile apps. Members with no chronic condition were seen to use cell phones, especially for text messaging, more than those with one. The multiple bar charts in Figure 19.4 highlight this distinctive difference in case of one social media platform – health-related podcasts. Similar patterns are observed for the remaining six applications too.
- Younger people (age group: 18–30) were found to use cell phones more, as expected, although the interest level for health-related mobile apps was not

found to be significantly different between older and younger people. However, in the case of computer use, older people (over 50 years of age) were found to have a significantly higher interest than the younger population in some of the social media platforms – watching health-related videos and listening to podcasts.

- With respect to the effect of usage frequency of online activities and social media on interest in adopting health-related social media was similar for cell phones and computers.

We thus conclude that people are more willing to utilize social media platforms for obtaining information pertaining to their health and wellness on the computer than on cell phones. Although the use of mobile apps and smartphones has increased considerably today, that is, mostly among the younger people, Zulman et al. [42] showed that older adults still distrust the Internet for health-related purposes based on a nationally representative survey of 1450 adults 50 years of age or older in the United States. Since our study included a higher proportion of respondents over 30 years of age, we expect our results to be relevant with the current trends. Furthermore, current literature shows that the use of health-related social and mobile media is still not as widespread as people would expect given the technological advancement with respect to cell phones. For instance, a recent study based on a national survey of 3104 adults living in the United States reports that 31% of people have looked at health information on their cell phone as opposed to 17% that was revealed by a national survey conducted 2 years ago [20]. Moreover, only 9% of cell phone owners say that they receive text updates or alerts about health or medical issues (although a whopping 80% of them said that they use text messaging) and only 19% of smartphone owners have a health app on their mobile phone.

19.5.7 Health and Wellness Objectives

This section of the survey aims at understanding the participants' perception of their current health status and their personal responsibilities for their wellness and health maintenance. A total of 25.3% of the individuals regularly look for health-related information online (at least once a week). Additionally, 97.2% of all members have used the Internet to search for health information at some point of time. Table 19.5 shows the relative frequency distribution for member visits to the health plan's website, wherein it is evident that more than 80% of the members had accessed that at least once in the last 10 months. Moreover, about 60% of the respondents use PHR offered by their health plan.

TABLE 19.5 Frequency of Visiting the Health Plan's Website by the Survey Respondents

Never	Not Sure	More Than a Year Ago	Within the Past 2–10 Months	Within the Past Month	Within the Past Week
4.6%	10.1%	2.7%	25%	29.4%	28.2%

The specific reasons for members' visits to the health plan's website are summarized as follows: (i) finding a provider: 31.5%, (ii) billing: 18.7%, (iii) benefits research: 24.8%, (iv) health information: 22.9%, (v) health and wellness management: 33.2%, (vi) participate in their "healthy step" program: 56.1%, (vii) customer service: 6.5%, and (ix) chat online with a representative: 1.2%.

Analyzing by demographic factors, we find that women are significantly more likely to obtain health information online as well as visit the health plan's website more frequently than men (p-values <0.0001). Moreover, people in the age group of 31–50 are significantly more likely to visit the website more frequently than people who are under 30 years of age and those who are more than 50 years of age (p-value: 0.019). A significantly higher number of women visit the website for health and wellness management and participate in healthy step program than men (p-value: 0.01). For the other seven activities, no statistically significant differences are observed between two genders as indicated by p-values >0.05. As far as age is concerned, members in the age group 31–50 are significantly more likely to participate in health and wellness management as well as find a provider online and look for general health information than people in other age categories (p-values: <0.0001, 0.023 and 0.033, respectively). Members' health condition did not have any significant effect on the frequency of accessing the health plan's website as well as on conducting any of the activities. However, people suffering from a chronic disease were found to have a significantly higher likelihood of visiting the health plan's website (p-value: 0.0105) as well as accessing health information, billing information, and conducting benefits research than people who do not (p-values: <0.0001 in all cases). All of these observations can lead the health plan to gain an understanding of what purposes customers are using different online services and which segments of the population are availing of which services more regularly than others.

19.5.7.1 Health Goals and Maintaining Them

In order to facilitate the health plan's program development to improve its members' health and lifestyles, it is important to understand the current goals that they are pursuing and the level of success achieved with these goals. A total of 11.7% of the members reported that they did not actively pursue any health goals in the past year. Of the rest who pursued some health goals, the responses can be summarized as follows: (i) chronic condition management, 4.6%; (ii) healthy eating, 18.3%; (iii) increased physical activity, 18.4%; (iv) stress management, 6.8%; (v) tobacco cessation, 2.7%; and (vi) weight loss, 36%.

Thus, majority of members are willing to improve their health by pursuing some goals, the most popular one being weight loss. When asked about their ability to achieve their personal goals, 53.9% mentioned working currently on that, whereas about 31% stated that they have already achieved and maintained their goals. About 16% of the members either did not achieve their goals or were not pursuing them anymore. For the latter group of people, majority mentioned lack of motivation as the main reason for their failure to achieve the goal (57%), followed by stress (48%) and work constraints (30%).

As to the media platform that members reported to prefer to assist them in achieving and/or maintaining their health goals, majority expressed an interest in online tools to track progress (52.3%) and to access online educational health information (53.6%). A total of 26.6% preferred tools to schedule appointments, 13.4% wished to join an online social support group, and 34.3% wished to receive online health coaching and health mentoring. Thus, although there seems to be a need for supervision and assistance with health information, there does not seem to be a high level of interest regarding the use of social groups.

Clustering revealed again that women are significantly more likely to pursue most of the health goals than men, particularly those involving weight loss, healthy eating, and increased physical activity (p-values <0.0001 for all cases). A significantly higher proportion of women expressed an interest in accessing online educational health information (p-value: 0.0178). With respect to age, a significantly greater number of people in age group 31–50 had weight loss as their goal (p-value: 0.041) although no significant age effect was observed for the other categories. As to the achievement of their goals, no significant differences were observed among the different age groups and between the two genders. Health conditions and the presence of chronic disease had no effect on people's choices of healthy lifestyle goals.

19.5.7.2 Association with Computer Usage The p-values in Table 19.6 clearly demonstrate that there is significantly strong dependence of the frequency with which people seek health-related online as well as visit their health plan's website on the amount of time they spend on the computer during the entire day, the statistical evidence being stronger in the former case. While computer usage during the evenings is more strongly related to how often people access health information online, the duration of computer use during the day has a stronger relationship with how frequently people seek information from their health plan's website.

Moreover, chi-square tests indicate overwhelming evidence in support of a significant relationship between time spent on six different social media sites and the time spent on seeking health-related information online and from the health plan's website, both on the computers and using cell phones (p-values: <0.0001). The general trend depicted increasing engagement with social media platforms, from Facebook and Twitter to Wikipedia, with higher access to health-related information online. Similar results were obtained in case of online activities as well, such as emailing, chatting, banking, and so on.

TABLE 19.6   Chi-Square Tests for Studying the Dependence of Frequency of Obtaining Health-Related Information Online and Visiting the Health Plan Website on Computer Usage

Computer Usage	Health Info Online	Visit Health Plan Website
During workday	<0.0001	<0.0001
During evenings	<0.0001	0.0082

TABLE 19.7 Frequency Statistics for the Level of Concern Expressed in Different Areas about the Use of Online Technologies for Health Purposes

	Not Concerned	Somewhat Concerned	Very Concerned	Missing
Too many messages	542 (13%)	1737 (41%)	1783 (42%)	150 (4%)
Privacy, confidentiality	702 (17%)	1416 (34%)	1939 (46%)	155 (3%)
Credibility and reliability	962 (23%)	1758 (42%)	1316 (31%)	176 (4%)
Relevance	807 (19%)	2130 (50%)	1083 (26%)	192 (5%)
Anonymity	887 (21%)	1598 (38%)	1526 (36%)	201 (5%)

19.5.8 Privacy and Security Concerns

The survey respondents were asked to report their level of concern, either "not concerned" or "somewhat concerned" or "very concerned" (three categories) in each of five different areas related to the use of online technology for health-related information, namely: (i) receiving too many unwanted messages, (ii) privacy and confidentiality of their own information, (iii) credibility and reliability of the information received, (iv) relevance of information, and (v) ability to remain anonymous, if so desired. Table 19.7 displays the frequency statistics for these.

These results clearly demonstrate that majority of the health plan members who took part in the survey had significant concerns about different aspects of privacy and security in relation to obtaining health-related information from online sources. The maximum concern was seen in case of privacy and confidentiality of their information, in keeping with expectations, followed by receiving too many messages and the ability to remain anonymous on the website. The least concern exists in cases of relevance, reliability, and credibility of the information received. So to sum it all up, people are mostly worried about the security of their own information and privacy intrusions, which is justified.

The effects of the different factors – demographical, clinical, and technological – are also investigated and the different clusters obtained are summarized as follows [43]:

- *Demographic and Clinical Factors*. Surprisingly, not much significant association was observed with people's perceived notions of security concerns for most of the demographic and clinical factors included in the study, the only noticeable one being concerns about privacy and confidentiality versus health status (p-value: 0.0351). People who were in good to very good health were found to be significantly less concerned about these issues than people in poorer health. We thus conclude that there is remarkable uniformity among the various segments in the general population (as defined by age, gender) regarding privacy and security concerns about the use of online and social media-based platforms for health-related information.
- *Online Technology and Social Media Usage*. Just as in the case of the demographic factors, there is overall uniformity in the level of different types of

privacy and security concerns based on the frequency of use of several online activities on the computer. Differences were mostly noted in case of emailing and chatting – people who engage in these two activities more frequently have significantly less concerns about privacy and security. The minimum overall association was seen in case of watching videos followed by banking, news, and shopping online. Similarly, the frequency and level of use of social media activities have not much significant effect on the level of privacy and security-related concerns that people may have about obtaining health-related information from different online platforms. The only significant outcome was that people who commented on online blogs more frequently had relatively lesser concerns about privacy and confidentiality in using online media for health and wellness purposes. The minimum effects were in cases of the use of Wikipedia.

- *Interest in Adopting Online Health-related Activities if Offered by the Health Plan.* People's propensity to use various social media sites had no significant association with their level of concerns about adopting online platforms for health purposes. We observed only significant differences in the levels of security concerns in terms of relevance of information obtained among users of a couple of activities (podcasts and group chats with health experts). In both cases, we found that people who were more interested in receiving health information via these two online sources had greater concerns about the relevance of information obtained from these sources.

19.5.9 Predictive Models

For each of the seven technology platforms that the health plan was contemplating offering to its member population, we build a separate logistic regression model to predict the chances and odds of adopting each of them. Note that we have only developed models for the social media platforms on computers so far and plan to pursue this for the mobile apps in the near future as well.

The binary outcome variable in each case is so defined as to have the two classes: *Interested* ("1") and *Not interested* ("0"). The responses in the "might be interested" class were few in number and hence were not considered. Each model is built using 60% of the data records (which constitute our "training set") and the rest 40% is treated as a "validation set" for generating predictions and measuring model accuracy.

First of all, we fitted several smaller models for each group of factors, where the goal was to determine which subset of a particular type of factor helps determine the chances of adopting social media-based channels for health-related information. These are as follows:

1. Model 1: Demographic and clinical factors
2. Model 2: Technical factors (include level of usage of computers during the whole day, frequency of use of online banking, shopping, watching news, etc.)
3. Model 3: Social media usage-related factors
4. Model 4: Privacy and security-related factors

The final modeling experiment consisted of using all the sets of factors together in a single model. Toward this end, we consolidated some factors to create new variables that are representative of those factors, and at the same time are able to reduce the model dimensionality to a considerable extent. It is always desirable to build statistical models that are "parsimonious," that is, simple with not too many variables and at the same time optimal in terms of performance. We have a total of 19 variables, which necessitated this step.

In order to achieve this, the factors representing online and social media activities are combined together to create two new variables representing two general categorical variables: *frequency of online activities on computer* and *frequency of social media usage on computer* (without considering the individual activities in each category). Each variable has four categories defined in the following manner:

1. *Heavy Users*. Use at least one out of the six activities one or more times a day.
2. *Medium Users*. Use at least three out of the six activities couple of times per month or at least one activity couple of times a week.
3. Light *Users*. Rarely use all six activities or use at most two out of six activities couple of times per month or never/rarely use all six activities (with at least one "rarely" – not "never" on all six).
4. *Nonusers*. Never use any of the six activities.

Another advantage of creating these generalized variables is that with the rapid evolution of Internet-based technology in recent times, new social media sites and online activities are being introduced regularly, so the specific ones included in this study (such as Facebook, Twitter, online blogs) may not accurately reflect the online and social media landscape after a decade or so. If this happens, the models using the isolated factors described earlier will fail to provide a valid representation and will be useless for predicting future consumer behavior. The generalized model, on the other hand, can still be useful in such a scenario provided consumer usage pattern of online and social media in general does not change drastically.

The number of independent variables is now reduced from 19 to 9 which are as follows: (i) X_1: gender, (ii) X_2: age, (iii) X_3: general health condition, (iv) X_4: presence of a chronic condition (self), (v) X_5: presence of a chronic condition (household member), (vi) X_6: computer usage (workday), (vii) X_7: computer usage (evenings), (viii) X_8: online activity usage, and (ix) X_9: social media usage. As before, the dependent variable in each case is the odds of being interested in adopting a particular social media platform for health-related purposes if offered by the health plan. Privacy and security-related factors are omitted due to their nonsignificance observed earlier with the statistical tests as well as with the smaller models.

We report here the results from the combined models only since they are very similar to those from the smaller models fitted in the first stage. Table 19.8 shows the significant predictors identified for these models using a 5% significance level. Social media usage is seen to be statistically significant in case of five out of the seven activities. Computer use during evenings is also significant for five out of the

TABLE 19.8 Significant Predictors for the Seven Online Social Media-Based Activities Chosen by the Health Plan

Activities	Significant Factors
(1) Connect with others via online forum	Social media usage
(2) Reading health-related blogs	Age, social media usage
(3) Commenting on health blogs	Computer use (eve), social media usage
(4) Watching health-related videos	Computer use (eve), social media usage
(5) Watching health-related webinars/webcasts	Age, computer use (eve)
(6) Listening to health-related podcasts	Computer use (eve)
(7) Group chats with health experts	Computer use (day), computer use (eve), social media usage

seven activities, a fact that is consistent with our findings via the smaller models. Age is a significant factor only in case of reading health-related blogs and watching health-related webcasts and webinars. Gender and health conditions are not relevant in any of these models.

The estimated coefficients β's help determine quantitatively how much the odds of adopting health-related online platforms will change for changes in the values of the predictor variables. For example, for Activity 1, the coefficient for X_4 is -0.18, which tells us that the members' odds of connecting with people with similar health goals via online forums is less (due to the negative sign) by a factor of $e^{-0.18} = 0.84$ for those with a chronic condition than those without, provided the other factors are held constant. Thus, people suffering from a chronic condition are less likely to be interested in this specific online activity related to their health and wellness management.

19.5.9.1 *Predictive Model Results*

The goal of the predictive models is to estimate or predict health plan members' interest in adopting the social media platforms to be offered by their health plan for obtaining health-related information.

As briefly mentioned earlier, the coefficients are estimated using the training data set and predictions are generated for the validation set. Each record in the latter set is classified as belonging to the class "1" (interested) or "0" (not interested) based on the predicted odds and probability from the fitted models. The proportion of incorrect predictions for each training/test set combination constitutes the "error rate" and is typically expressed in a percentage form. In order to remove selection bias underlying training and test set combinations, we repeat the random splitting 40 times and the final prediction errors and model accuracies are calculated by averaging over the set of 40 iterations.

Table 19.9 shows the accuracies (100 – error rates) expressed as percentages for the seven models along with standard deviations computed over the 40 repetitions. Overall, the average accuracies are around 60%. The maximum accuracy is obtained in case of participating group chats with health experts and highest in case of connecting with others with similar health goals via online forums. All these accuracy rates

TABLE 19.9   Prediction Error Rates and Accuracies from the Logistic Regression Models

Activities	Accuracy Rates (%)
(1) Connect with others via online forum	54 (±4)
(2) Reading health-related blogs	59 (±3)
(3) Commenting on health blogs	61 (±4)
(4) Watching health-related videos	60 (±3)
(5) Watching health-related webinars/webcasts	56 (±2)
(6) Listening to health-related podcasts	58 (±4)
(7) Group chats with health experts	64 (±2)

are considerably better than random chance without any background information on them (50% error for predicting randomly whether a person is or is not interested in a certain activity offered by the health plan) so that we can conclude that it is possible to predict a consumer's level of interest more accurately, given the knowledge about his demographic profile as well as behavior with respect to general computer usage and usage of online and social media-based activities. Based on these results, the health plan can make informed decisions about which of its members to target these activities toward maximum possible adoption chances. Furthermore, we note that the standard errors are considerably low, thus indicating the stability of our models and robustness to the selection of the training and the test sets for prediction.

As is clear, these prediction results have considerable room for improvement, thus calling for a refinement of our fitted logistic models. Extensions include (i) multinomial logistic model with three categories for the response variable, thus incorporating a separate class for "might be interested" and (ii) incorporating interactions among the variables.

19.6   CONCLUSIONS

All sectors of the healthcare industry are exploring the use of social media for making health information more accessible to consumers. This study examines how health plan members might respond to these new tools and identify segments of member population based on demographic and health condition related factors. Our overall primary findings include the following: (i) younger people and men are more interested in adopting social media-based platforms from the health plan via computers; (ii) people who engage in online activities and social media activities and use computers and mobile phone more regularly are more likely to adopt these technologies offered by the health plan via similar channels; (iii) people use their cell phones for Internet-based activities considerably less than computers, and a smaller number of significant clusters were detected with respect to most of the factors included in this study; (iv) members in poorer health and suffering from a chronic condition had a significantly elevated level of interest in receiving health information from various online and social media sources but not via mobile apps. Specifically, although the use of cell phones and mobile apps were found to be widespread among the younger segment of the population, no significant difference with respect to interest in adopting the proposed platforms of health-related information from their health plan was observed among the different age groups included in this study. Privacy and security-related concerns seemed to be fairly uniform across all segments of the populations and were not found to predict people's willingness to adopt technology-based platforms for their health and wellness management. Moreover, the predictive models helped us identify significant predictors of people's likelihood of adopting health-related online platforms on their computers as planned by their health plan provider, among a host of several factors initially believed to be of relevance in this context. The model-generated predictions also help characterize particular subpopulations of the health plan members that are most likely to adopt these technologies.

Our findings are expected to be greatly beneficial to this health plan as well as to other health plans exploring similar opportunities in designing effective social and mobile media-based tools for imparting valuable health and wellness-related information to their members. Particularly, the findings of this study enable them to tailor their products to specific population segments for the maximum outreach. For instance, the health plan should target members who already use their mobile phones for several online activities and accessing social media sites to deploy health-related information via these platforms. They may also devise health-related mobile apps specifically designed by gender, particularly for male members to begin with. Since age was surprisingly not found to have a significant association with interest in adopting mobile apps for health purposes, the health plan may not need to focus on age-specific, health-related, mobile apps for their members currently.

Future work includes integrating healthy lifestyle goals into the predictive models as well as building similar models for predicting people's interest in adopting health-related mobile apps. Moreover, career type and work-related activities are two important factors that play a large role in determining how, when, and what type of mobile applications fit into people's lifestyles. The current survey did not collect data on these factors but we plan to incorporate them in our future studies.

REFERENCES

[1] IOM (Institute of Medicine). *Patients Charting the Course: Citizen Engagement and the Learning Health System. Workshop Summary*. Washington, DC: The National Academies Press; 2011.

[2] IOM (Institute of Medicine). *Engineering a Learning Healthcare System: A Look at the Future: Workshop Summary*. Washington, DC: The National Academies Press; 2011.

[3] Healthcare.gov. Affordable health care act. Available at http://www.healthcare.gov/law/features/index.html. Accessed 2015 Dec 24.

[4] DeNicola C. *The Right Way for Payers to do Social Media*. Health Data Management and SourceMedia Inc.; 2012.

[5] Grensing-Pophal L. *Insurers Slow to Adopt Social Media Practices: Health plans weigh whether giving up control of the conversation with patients is worth all the possible benefits*. USA: MANAGED CARE, ©MediMedia; 2009.

[6] PwC Health Research Institute Report. *Social Media "likes" Healthcare: From Marketing to Social Business*. PwC Health Research Institute Report; 2012.

[7] CSC (Computer Sciences Corporation). Should healthcare organizations use social media: A global update; 2012. Available at http://assets1.csc.com/health_services/downloads/CSC_Should_Healthcare_Organizations_Use_Social_Media_A_Global_Update.pdf. Accessed 2014 Jan 15.

[8] Sarasohn-Kahn J. *Participatory Health: Online and Mobile Tools Help Chronically Ill Manage their Care*. California Health Care Foundation Report; 2009.

[9] Fox, S., Duggan, M., (2013). The Diagnisis Difference, Pew Internet and American Life Project, Pew Research Center.

[10] Cohen RA, Adams P. Use of the internet for health information: United States, 2009, NCHS Data Brief, No. 66; 2011.

[11] Estabrook L, Witt E, Rainie L. *Information Searches That Solve Problems*. Pew Internet & American Life Project; 2007.

[12] Hibbard JH, Cunningham PJ. *How Engaged Are Consumers in Their Health and Health Care, and Why Does It Matter?* Center for Studying Health System Change Research; 2008. brief No. 8.

[13] Elkin N. *How America Searches: Health And Wellness*. iCrossing, Inc; 2008.

[14] Munnariz RA. *7 Startling Numbers that We Now Know About Facebook*. Daily Finance; 2012. Website: http://www.dailyfinance.com/2012/02/02/7-startling-numbers-we-now-know-about-facebook/.

[15] Wikipedia page on Facebook. Available at http://en.wikipedia.org/wiki/Facebook. Accessed 2015 Dec 24.

[16] Wikipedia page on Twitter. Available at http://en.wikipedia.org/wiki/Twitter. Accessed 2015 Dec 24.

[17] Mayfield A. *What is Social Media?* iCrossing; 2008.

[18] Chou WS, Hunt YM, Beckjord EB, Moser RP, Hesse BW. Social media use in the United States: Implications for health communication. J Med Internet Res 2009;11(4):e48.

[19] Hawn C. Take two aspirin and tweet me in the morning: How twitter, facebook, and other social media are reshaping health care. Health Aff 2009;28(2):361–368.

[20] Fox S, Duggan M. Mobile Health 2012: Half of smartphone owners use their devices to get health information and one-fifth of smartphone owners have health apps. Pew Internet and American Life Project Report; 2012.

[21] Fox S, Duggan M. 2013. Tracking for Health, Pew Internet and American Life Project Report/California Healthcare Foundation. Accessed 2013 Feb 1.

[22] Frost & Sullivan. Social media use among U.S. healthcare provider institutions. N967-48; 2011.

[23] Divol R, Edelman D, Sarrazin H. *Demystifying Social Media*. McKinsey Quarterly; 2012.

[24] IOM (Institute of Medicine). *Living Well with Chronic Illness: A Call for Public Health Action*. Washington, DC: The National Academies Press; 2012.

[25] Shmueli G, Patel NR, Bruce PC. *Data Mining for Business Intelligence: Concepts, Techniques, and Applications in Microsoft Office Excel with XLMiner*. Wiley; 2010.

[26] Ivey S. 2011. Humana launches Humanaville online community for seniors. Business First. Available at http://www.bizjournals.com/louisville/news/2011/07/14/humana-launches-humanaville-online.html. Accessed 2015 Dec 24.

[27] Aetna News Release. 2011. Aetna and Mindbloom team up to encourage healthier, more balanced living through social gaming. Available at http://www.aetna.com/news/newsReleases/2011/0503_Mindbloom_SocialGaming.html. Accessed 2015 Dec 24.

[28] Kiron D. *Social Business at Kaiser Permanente: Using Social Tools to Improve Customer Service, Research and Internal Collaboration*. MIT Sloan Management Review; 2012. Website: http://sloanreview.mit.edu/feature/kaiser-permanente-using-social-tools-to-improve-customer-service-research-and-internal-collaboration/.

[29] Bennett Ed. Hospital Social Network List: US hospitals that use Social Networking Tools. Social media resources for health care professionals from Ed Bennett. [Online: March 28]; 2010.

[30] National eHealth Collaborative Survey. An analysis of Consumer health Apps for Apple's iPhone 2012: A definitive quantitative report on the 13,000+ available apps. 2012.

[31] Home Page: Text4baby. 2010. Text4baby. Available at www.text4baby.org. Accessed 2015 Dec 24.

[32] Calvan BC. Sacramento Bee News Page. Sacramento Bee Website; 2010.

[33] John LK, Acquisti A, Loewenstein GF. 2009. The best of strangers: Context dependent willingness to divulge personal information. Available at SSRN: http://papers.ssrn.com/sol3/papers.cfm?abstract_id=1430482 or, http://dx.doi.org/10.2139/ssrn.1430482. Accessed 2015 Dec 24.

[34] Microsoft HealthVault. Available at http://www.microsoft.com/en-us/healthvault/. Accessed 2015 Dec 24.

[35] US Department of Health and Human Services (HHS). Health Information Privacy. Available at http://www.hhs.gov/ocr/privacy/hipaa/understanding/index.html. Accessed 2015 Dec 24.

[36] Thorpe KE, Ogden LL, Galactionova K. Chronic conditions account for rise in medicare spending from 1987 to 2006. Health Aff 2010;29(4):718–724.

[37] Sarasohn-Kahn J. *The Wisdom of Patients: Health Care Meets Online Social Media*. California Health Care Foundation Report; 2009.

[38] Padman R, Adeyemi D, Halder P, Lee M, Li Y, Maram A, O' Halloran R, Wu V. *Exploring Mobile & Social Media for Health & Wellness, Technical Report*. Pittsburgh, USA: The Heinz College, Carnegie Mellon University; 2010.

[39] Keller G. *Statistics for Management and Economics*. 9th ed. Cengage-Learning; 2011.

[40] Hosmer DW, Lemeshow S. *Applied Logistic Regression*. Wiley Series in Statistics and Probability; 2000.

[41] Mitra S, Padman R. Exploring Social Media for Health and Wellness: A health plan case study. J Cases Inf Technol 2012;14(2):42–64.

[42] Zulman DM, Kirch M, Zheng K, An LC. Trust in the internet as a health resource among older adults: Analysis of data from a nationally representative survey. J Med Intern Res 2011;13(1):e19. DOI: 10.2196/jmir.1552.

[43] Mitra S, Padman R. Privacy and security concerns in adopting social media for personal health management: A Health plan case study. J Cases Inf Technol 2012;14(4):12–26.

INDEX

Healthcare Analytics: From Data to Knowledge to Healthcare Improvement, First Edition.
Edited by Hui Yang and Eva K. Lee.
© 2016 John Wiley & Sons, Inc. Published 2016 by John Wiley & Sons, Inc.

Wiley Series in
Operations Research and Management Science

Operations Research and Management Science (ORMS) is a broad, interdisciplinary branch of applied mathematics concerned with improving the quality of decisions and processes and is a major component of the global modern movement towards the use of advanced analytics in industry and scientific research. The *Wiley Series in Operations Research and Management Science* features a broad collection of books that meet the varied needs of researchers, practitioners, policy makers, and students who use or need to improve their use of analytics. Reflecting the wide range of current research within the ORMS community, the Series encompasses application, methodology, and theory and provides coverage of both classical and cutting edge ORMS concepts and developments. Written by recognized international experts in the field, this collection is appropriate for students as well as professionals from private and public sectors including industry, government, and nonprofit organization who are interested in ORMS at a technical level. The Series is comprised of four sections: Analytics; Decision and Risk Analysis; Optimization Models; and Stochastic Models.

Advisory Editors • Analytics
Jennifer Bachner, Johns Hopkins University
Khim Yong Goh, National University of Singapore

Founding Series Editor
James J. Cochran, University of Alabama

Analytics
Yang and Lee • *Healthcare Analytics: From Data to Knowledge to Healthcare Improvement*

Forthcoming Titles
Attoh-Okine • *Big Data and Differential Privacy: Analysis Strategies for Railway Track Engineering*
Kong and Zhang • *Decision Analytics and Optimization in Disease Prevention and Treatment*

Decision and Risk Analysis
Barron • *Game Theory: An Introduction,* Second Edition
Brailsford, Churilov, and Dangerfield • *Discrete-Event Simulation and System Dynamics for Management Decision Making*
Johnson, Keisler, Solak, Turcotte, Bayram, and Drew • *Decision Science for Housing and Community Development: Localized and Evidence-Based Responses to Distressed Housing and Blighted Communities*
Mislick and Nussbaum • *Cost Estimation: Methods and Tools*